# Communication Skills Training Series

*7 Books in 1*

*Read People Like a Book, Make People Laugh, Talk to Anyone, Increase Charisma and Persuasion, and Improve Your Listening Skills*

*Communication Skills Training Series*

**PUBLISHED BY: James W. Williams**

**© Copyright 2021 - All rights reserved.**

The content contained within this book may not be reproduced, duplicated or transmitted without direct written permission from the author or the publisher.

Under no circumstances will any blame or legal responsibility be held against the publisher, or author, for any damages, reparation, or monetary loss due to the information contained within this book. Either directly or indirectly.

Legal Notice:

This book is copyright protected. This book is only for personal use. You cannot amend, distribute, sell, use, quote or paraphrase any part, or the content within this book, without the consent of the author or publisher.

Disclaimer Notice:

Please note the information contained within this document is for educational and entertainment purposes only. All effort has been executed to present accurate, up to date, and reliable, complete information. No warranties of any kind are declared or implied. Readers acknowledge that the author is not engaging in the rendering of legal, financial, medical or professional advice. The content within this book has been derived from various sources. Please consult a licensed professional before attempting any techniques outlined in this book.

By reading this document, the reader agrees that under no circumstances is the author responsible for any losses, direct or indirect, which are incurred as a result of the use of information contained within this document, including, but not limited to, — errors, omissions, or inaccuracies.

# Table of Contents

2 FREE Gifts ............................................................................................... 1

**Book #1: Communication Skills Training** ............................................. 5

Introduction ............................................................................................... 7

Chapter 1: Some Basic Considerations ................................................... 9

Chapter 2: Why We Don't Communicate Right ..................................... 16

Chapter 3: The Art of Active Listening ................................................... 25

Chapter 4: The Basics of Interpersonal Communication ...................... 34

Chapter 5: Dealing with "Noise" Part I: Communicating When Angry ... 43

Chapter 6: Dealing with "Noise" Part 2: In Case of Miscommunication ... 48

Chapter 7: Dealing with "Noise" Part 3: Interactions in the Toxic Realm ... 54

Chapter 8: Having a Great Public Presentation ..................................... 59

Chapter 9: Feedback: How to Give and Respond to It .......................... 67

Chapter 10: Conclusion ........................................................................... 72

**Book# 2: How to Read People Like a Book** ....................................... 74

Introduction ............................................................................................. 76

Chapter 1: Explanation, Quotes, Facts .................................................. 78

Chapter 2: Problems and Benefits .......................................................... 84

Chapter 3: Introverts – Identify, Communicate, and Personality Type Motivations ... 89

Chapter 4: Extroverts – Identify, Communicate, and Personality Type Motivations ... 98

Chapter 5: Communication Styles ......................................................... 107

Chapter 6: Reading Lies in People ......................................................... 113

Chapter 7: Understanding People's Motivations .................................. 118

Chapter 8: Reading the Face and Body–Cues and What They Mean ... 125

Chapter 9: Verbal Cues – Reading Between the Lines ......................... 133

Chapter 10: The Art of Thin-Slicing ...................................................... 136

Chapter 11: What About Me? ................................................................. 140

Chapter 12: Further Body Language Tips ............................................. 145

Conclusion .............................................................................................. 147

## Book #3: How to Make People Laugh .................................................................. 151

Introduction ............................................................................................................. 153

Part One – A Dash of Charisma ............................................................................. 155

Chapter 1 – What Is Charisma? .............................................................................. 156

Chapter 2 – Creating a Presence ............................................................................ 159

Chapter 3 – Grace Under Fire ................................................................................ 160

Chapter 4 – Body Language .................................................................................. 164

Part Two – Buckets Full of Self-Discovery ............................................................ 166

Chapter 5. Making Jokes Based on Your Story and Personality ............................ 167

Chapter 6. Effects of Personality on Jokes ............................................................ 177

Chapter 7. Delivery/Joke Styles ............................................................................ 180

Part Three – Smattering of Acceptance ................................................................. 182

Part Four – Heated in Learning ............................................................................. 183

Part Five - Garnished with Stories and Experience ............................................... 192

Part Six – Keeping it Clean .................................................................................... 198

Part Seven – Improv Comedy ................................................................................ 201

Part Eight – Going Back Inwards .......................................................................... 219

Part Nine - More Jokes .......................................................................................... 223

Conclusion ............................................................................................................. 225

## Book #4: How to Make People Do What You Want ........................................ 227

Introduction & Foreword ....................................................................................... 229

Chapter One – Understanding the Art of Persuasion ............................................. 232

Chapter Two – Developing Your Own Mindset .................................................... 235

Chapter Three – Nurturing a Relationship ............................................................. 238

(Making Friends and Winning Them Over) .......................................................... 238

Chapter Four – Being Able to Talk to Anyone ...................................................... 243

Chapter Five - Deep-Diving into Control of the Mind .......................................... 248

Chapter Six – Mastering the Art of Body Language ............................................. 254

Chapter Seven – The Power of Social Pressure .................................................... 263

Chapter Eight – How Repetition Changes Everything .......................................... 269

Chapter Nine – Incentivise! Rewarding for Results ................................................. 273

Chapter Ten – The Power of Positivity ................................................. 277

Chapter Eleven – Getting Better with Practice (Tips & Tricks) ................................................. 281

Chapter Twelve – Final Thoughts ................................................. 284

# Book #5: How to Make People Like You ................................................. **285**

Introduction ................................................. 287

Part One – The Start of Something New ................................................. 290

Method 1 – It's About the Smile ................................................. 291

Method 2 – Always Make the First Move ................................................. 294

Method 3 – Excuse Me. Can You Help Me? ................................................. 297

Part Two – Sowing the Seeds for Something Beautiful ................................................. 299

Method 4 – Mastering the Art of Listening ................................................. 300

Method 5 – Improving the Flow of Conversion ................................................. 303

Method 6 – Discovering the Reflection of Yourself ................................................. 307

Method 7 – Choosing the Right Friends ................................................. 310

Method 8 – Share Experiences. Make Memories ................................................. 314

Part Three – The Advanced Teachings of Nurturing Stronger Relationships ................................................. 317

Method 9 – How to Open Up and Become Vulnerable ................................................. 318

Method 10 – Opening Your Door to the World ................................................. 321

Method 11 – Unconditionally Giving and Not Taking ................................................. 323

Method 12 – Words: The Power of Light and Dark Magic ................................................. 327

Part Four – It's Time to Work on You ................................................. 330

Method 13 – Becoming More Charismatic ................................................. 331

Method 14 – Everything You Need to Know about Confidence ................................................. 334

Method 15 – Your Outside Reflects Your Inside ................................................. 336

Method 16 – Trust is Everything ................................................. 339

Part Five – Maintaining Your Relationships & Looking to the Future ................................................. 342

Method 17 – Time: Quality Over Quantity ................................................. 343

Method 18 – Developing Patience for the Journey ................................................. 345

Method 19 – The Power of Forgiveness ................................................. 346

Final Thoughts ................................................. 348

## Book #6: How to Talk to Anyone About Anything .................................................. **349**

Introduction ........................................................................................................... 351

Chapter One – Everything Starts with You ...................................................... 354

Chapter Two – It All Begins with Listening ..................................................... 359

Chapter Three – Further Listening Skills ......................................................... 363

Chapter Four - It's All About Questions .......................................................... 365

Chapter Five - How to Have a Conversation with Anyone ............................ 371

Chapter Six – Mastering the Art of Small Talk ............................................... 379

Chapter Seven – Intricate Ways to Be More Charismatic .............................. 390

Chapter Eight – How to Be More Confident ................................................... 394

Chapter Nine – How to Tell Stories That Land ............................................... 399

Chapter Ten - Becoming an Interesting Person .............................................. 407

Chapter Eleven – Developing Meaningful Relationships .............................. 411

Final Thoughts ..................................................................................................... 414

## Book #7: Listening Skills Training ....................................................................... **415**

Introduction ......................................................................................................... 417

Chapter One - Never Has the World Been Louder, Yet No One Is Listening ............ 421

Chapter Two - The Psychology of Listening .................................................. 425

Chapter Three - How to Be a Better Active Listener 101 .............................. 431

Chapter Four - Validation: The Key to Extraordinary Listening .................. 444

Chapter Five - The Art of Mindreading Through Awareness ...................... 455

Chapter Six - Addressing the Obstacles of Listening .................................... 471

Chapter Seven - Continuing the Conversation .............................................. 474

Final Thoughts ..................................................................................................... 479

Thank you! ............................................................................................................ 481

## 2 FREE Gifts

To help you along your personal growth journey, I've created 2 FREE bonus books that will help you master your mind, become more confident, and eliminate intrusive thoughts.

You can get instant access by signing up to my email newsletter below.

On top of the 2 free books, you will also receive weekly tips along with free book giveaways, discounts, and more.

All of these bonuses are 100% free with no strings attached. You don't need to provide any personal information except your email address.

To get your bonus, go to:

https://theartofmastery.com/confidence/

*Communication Skills Training Series*

Free Bonus Book #1: *Master Your Mind: 11 Mental Hacks to Eliminate Negative Thoughts, Improve Your Emotional Intelligence, and End Procrastination*

Discover the techniques and strategies backed by scientific and psychological studies that dive into why your mind is preventing you from achieving success in life and how to fix them.

You will learn how to:

- Deal with stress, fear, and anxiety
- Become more emotionally intelligent
- Communicate better in your relationships
- Overcome any and all limiting beliefs you have
- Avoid procrastinating
- Actually enjoy doing difficult tasks
- And so much more!

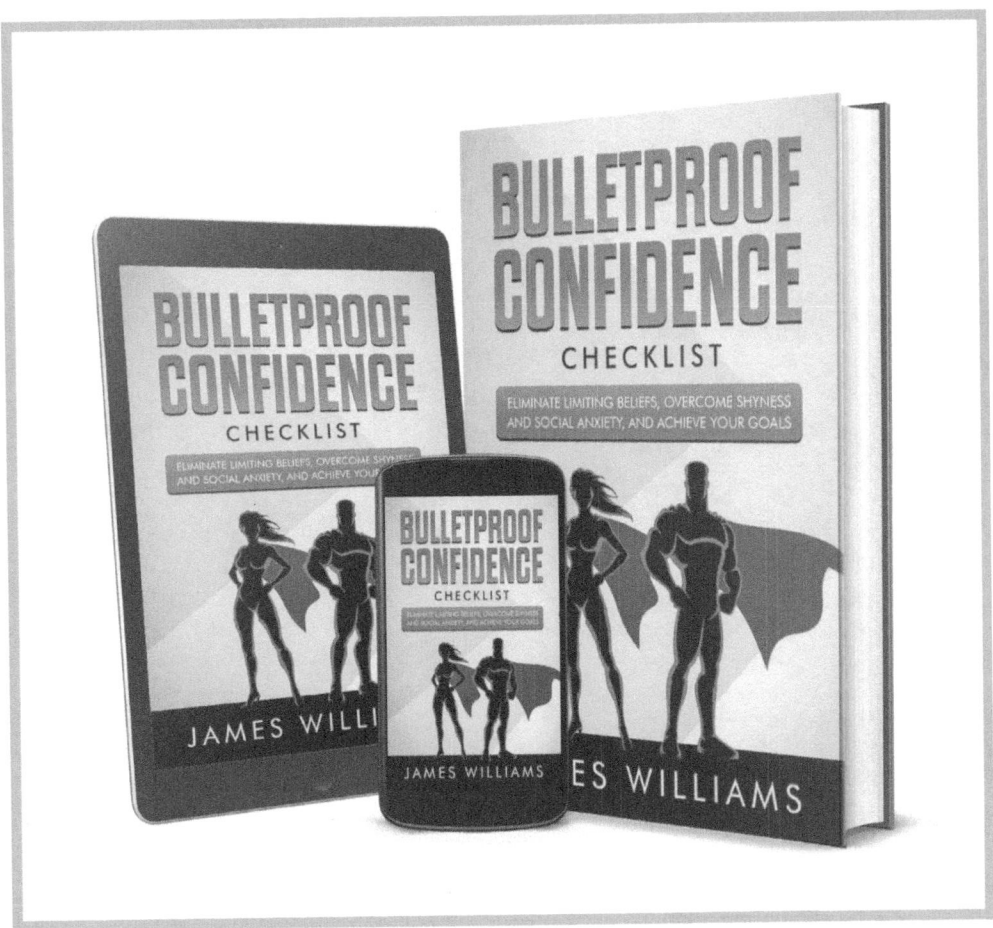

<u>Free Bonus Book #2</u>: *Bulletproof Confidence Checklist: Eliminate Limiting Beliefs, Overcome Shyness and Social Anxiety, and Achieve Your Goals*

In this book you will discover how to overcome the limiting beliefs that results in lack of confidence and social anxiety.

You will learn practical tips to rewire your negative thought patterns, break free from shyness, and become the best version of yourself.

*Communication Skills Training Series*

*James W. Williams*

# Book #1
# Communication Skills Training

*How to Talk to Anyone, Connect Effortlessly, Develop Charisma, and Become a People Person*

# Introduction

Thank you for purchasing this book, *Communication Skills Training: How to Talk to Anyone, Connect Effortlessly, Develop Charisma, and Become a People Person.*

By purchasing this book, you understand how much of an impact communication has on your daily life. From the transactions you complete to the more intimate moments, the way you convey your thoughts and feelings will determine how much people will interpret it.

Having been working in various industries for years and meeting people from all walks of life, I have found out that communicating your thoughts, feelings, and ideas is highly important for a lot of reasons. Whether you only want to close important deals or build long-lasting relationships, the ability to communicate is something that must be developed.

For some people, good communication skills are seemingly second nature. They have no problems telling people what is on their mind and have the same generally be positively accepted by anyone listening to it.

As a result, you could see notable examples of people easily building connections and generally succeeding in their endeavors. One simply needs to speak their thoughts, and others seemingly listen. You might have even heard of people so charismatic that they can even make huge social movements or be generally well-liked by everyone in a building.

For most people, the skill has to be learned and honed. And most likely than not, you belong in the latter group. If you are the type of person who has always been misinterpreted or have difficulties even expressing themselves, then this book is the cure to your predicament.

Everything you will learn here is based on a combination of years of research and personal experiences and is supported by factual and empirical data. You might encounter an abstract concept or two, but rest assured that all of the information you will get here can be applied in actual day-to-day scenarios.

What you have to understand is that communication skills, like any other ability in the world, has to be honed. Nobody becomes a charismatic person who can speak to a lot of people in a matter of hours.

More often than not, they started where you are right now: not quite sure how to do things, but having a clear goal of what needs to be done in order to improve.

And since it needs training, you need to take a look at different aspects that revolve around it. You see, communication is not just about talking. It involves picking the right words to say, combined with the right temper to convey the right message.

Communication is also not just about the things that come out of your mouth. The way you carry yourself in public and give off non-verbal cues can also lend a hand in making people understand what you are trying (or not trying) to say better.

Part of the process would also include identifying the basics of communication. With this, you will also identify the mistakes commonly made by people in communicating thoughts and ideas. You might even have committed these yourself, which negatively affected several interactions.

And, of course, communication is not a one-way thing. In as much as you are trying to convey a message, you must also learn how to interpret the verbal and non-verbal messages given to you by the people that you encounter daily.

Listening is also one skill that you must learn. You might be surprised to find out that the ability to process information being directed at you is just as important as clearly conveying your thoughts and ideas. But listening is not enough. You also have to do it in an empathetic and attentive manner to carry a conversation.

And speaking of conversations, it is also important for you to understand that you must adapt your communication style to different people. Remember that everybody has their way of perceiving things and their own set of priorities in communicating. As such, you have to find out how you can make yourself be heard to different personality types in a way that is conducive to effective communication.

One other thing you will also learn is how you can effectively communicate your thoughts and ideas in different formats and scenarios. There are challenges presented in each, and it is necessary for you to overcome these challenges and effectively convey what you are thinking and feeling with the tools at your disposal.

However, you will also realize that not every conversation is going to go as smoothly as possible. There is always that chance that you will fail in conveying your thoughts and ideas effectively, or even process information the way that a speaker wants you to do so.

You will learn how to deal with a breakdown in communication and try your best to veer back on course. Aside from this, you will also learn why communication can fail, which may be due to the inherent barriers set up by people or other external factors.

One other aspect you will also learn is how to deal with your emotions, anger especially, and still be an effective communicator. More often than not, we let our emotions run over us, which can be potentially damaging to our relationships. However, there is a way to manage such passionate feelings and still be as polite and diplomatic as ever.

In conjunction with that, you will also learn how to deal with different "difficult" conversations and people as well as build rapport with total strangers. After all, one of the goals of communication is to establish a connection with those around you.

So, is there a point in improving the way you communicate? The answer is yes. You will also learn throughout the book of some great examples of communication and form your own actionable strategies to improve the way you speak.

These are just some of the things that you will learn about communicating in this book. If you have no further questions or hesitation, now is the time to jump into the world of communication.

Let's get started!

# Chapter 1: Some Basic Considerations

*"Half the world is composed of people who have something to say and can't, and the other half who have nothing to say and keep on saying it."*

*-Robert Frost-*

Before we go into the more exciting stuff, we should cover the basics first. Considered as one of the most valuable interpersonal skills right now, communication helps you share information from one person to another and multiple people at once.

There are many ways and styles to communicate, and what you may be using right now is perfectly valid (albeit with some necessary tweaks here and there). But it would be best that you try to discover how crucial it is to properly communicate your thoughts and feelings to others as well as interpret those being directed at you.

## The Importance of Communication

So what is the point of trying to improve the way you communicate and interpret things? What you may not have realized is that communication is involved in almost every aspect of your life.

Have you ever had those moments when people were able to get what you were saying without technically saying anything at all? A mere nod of your head or how you grip another hand in a handshake can give lots of messages, depending on the context of the situation.

Or how about when you talk to three different people at the same time, and they end up reacting differently to what you just said? You told them the same thing, and yet one was happy, another became confused, and another was potentially offended. Why is this so? It goes back to the receiving part of communications, and people often react differently to the same stimulus.

The point is that communication helps you share ideas, build relationships, close potentially rewarding transactions, manage a group, and delegate tasks. If anything has to do with interacting with another living, breathing being, you can be certain that such a situation will rely heavily on your existing communication skills.

## The Types of Communication

Regardless of your approach to speaking your mind, all forms of communication will fall under four distinct categories:

### 1. Verbal

This is perhaps the one that is easiest to understand as it is the one that you are going to use a lot regularly. Verbal communication involves your mouth and your brain. Nothing else.

However, its sheer simplicity is also what makes verbal communication one of the trickier aspects of communicating your thoughts and feelings. Without the proper tone, body language, and mood, you could easily end up being misunderstood by what you just said a few seconds ago.

This aspect of communication also has the widest range of styles. Some people are so verbose that you'd think you are talking next to a humanoid thesaurus. Others are curt and blunt, getting straight to the point, damn all the consequences. And then some can take too long to get to their main message because they digress.

Learning how to make your style compatible with others will help you a lot in becoming an expert in verbal communication.

## 2. Non-Verbal

This is where all physical gestures and cues will fall under. Also, the facial expressions that you use to convey what you are verbally communicating will be included here as well. For example, smiling while telling a story gives the impression that the information you are about to offer is good to listen to.

What makes non-verbal communication so crucial is that your ability to pick them up and understand them will help you adjust your behavior in any situation. For instance, a potential client of yours is crossing his arms, and this could tell you that they are not sold on what you are saying and need further convincing.

Alternatively, the tapping of feet is a telltale sign that the person is in a hurry to cut the conversation and go somewhere else. A relaxed position, on the other hand, could tell you that the person might be agreeable to anything that you might propose. For now, at least.

## 3. Written

Technically speaking, written communication is also non-verbal, but it has some qualities that warrant it being its own class. Written communication involves every act to include writing, typing, or printing text and symbols onto something physical and digital.

Out of all the forms of communication, this is the one that is most tangible as it is seen through books, pamphlets, blogs, emails, memos, letters, and other printed mediums. Consequently, this is the type of communication that has a sense of permanency as the things that you wrote can be, figuratively speaking, set in stone.

For instance, Sun Tzu has been dead for over a millennium now, and yet, *The Art of War* is still being printed and read in different languages. The same goes for Shakespeare, Plato, Newton, King David, and even the Founding Fathers of America.

Because written words tend to last longer than you and might even represent your legacy to younger generations, you must be as accurate with it as possible.

## 4. Visual

Out of all the forms of communication, this is perhaps the most artistic. The phrase "a picture paints a thousand words" is highly applicable here as one image can tell very different messages for every person looking at it, depending on their mood in that instance.

The visual medium is often used to support your words by providing context. Let us say that you are telling your superiors that sales figures for the past few months have been subpar. Wouldn't it help your case if you had something like a pie chart that would give your listeners a visual anchor point to better understand your words?

But, even on its own, visuals can convey messages that could help someone make a connection with what they have seen and what they are feeling. As such, careful use of images is key to a lot of fields, especially advertising.

## What Good Communication Skills Can Bring to You

If communication is a major part of your day-to-day living, then improving your skills will yield you several benefits, which will accompany you through all the different facets of your life.

### 1. Trust Building

Learning how to properly convey your thoughts and feelings can be a good foundation where you can build trust with others. An ability to listen intently to whatever one person is telling you and seeing things from their perspective gives the impression that you are making decisions not only for yourself but for everyone else.

By being an active listener, you also make the people around you comfortable enough to be open with their thoughts and feelings. This fosters an atmosphere of trust, especially in relationships that require the performance of obligations and duties or collaborative effort.

Here is a classic scenario: If you are the team leader and your team is about to make a decision, the most sensible thing that you can do is to let others air out their concerns and provide alternatives. Then, once all concerns, issues, and alternative routes are presented, the team votes on which decision the entire group is going to take.

Sure, the final decision will not satisfy everyone, but, at the very least, you provide people on your team with a forum where they are free to speak their minds and be listened to. This is a far better option than a "It's my way or the highway!" approach to decision making where nobody else can dictate the actions of the team but you.

### 2. Solving Problems (and Preventing Them)

It is often said that problems exist because of pure miscommunication. There is no shortage of examples out there of a falling-out between groups or destruction of public images just because one person conveyed their thoughts and feelings poorly.

Here is a scenario: Let us say that one of your friends just got a makeover for a special event. When you see her, what would be the most sensible thing to say? Would it be "Why, you look lovelier today!" or "Hey, I never knew you could be this pretty!"? If your answer would sound something like the latter, then you tend to inadvertently generate conflict where you go.

Meaning well, yet being misunderstood, is a problem that most face. But learning how to be tactful with your words does help iron out issues that you have with others and prevent them from occurring again in the future.

### 3. Clarity and Direction

A good communicator knows how to provide clearly-defined expectations, objectives, and ideas to the people they are talking to. This is quite helpful in group efforts, where a clear line of communication between members is necessary.

Suppose that a member is not performing up to standard. A good communicator will know how to tell them that they need to get back on track without offending them. It is all too easy for a person to get angry and bite at the people they think are lagging. With good communication skills, on the other hand, you can help people understand what they need to do in the most diplomatic way possible.

Of course, fostering an open line of communication between group members helps in eliminating conflicts and misunderstanding. Perhaps one team member is about to get into a fight with another member. With good communication skills, you can intervene and give them a place where they can talk things out (with you as the mediator). This way, you can address issues that your team faces and get back on track to finish the task as quickly as possible.

And clarity does not only work with group efforts. Being clear requires you to be at your simplest and most direct when it comes to talking. This means you can tell people what you are trying to say in a few words or less with no digressions at all.

Doing so helps people get the message behind what you are trying to say without wasting time deciphering your monologue. After all, nobody likes to start a conversation with someone who takes five sentences to answer a simple categorical question.

### 4. Better Relationships

Perhaps the most direct benefit of improving your communication skills is that you can easily build or maintain interpersonal relationships. After all, you can now speak effectively, tactfully, and openly, which gives the impression to people that you are a person that has nothing to hide. Transparency, after all, is a quality that is hard to manifest unless you know how to say the right thing at the right time and using the right words.

Not only can you speak well, but you also learn how to listen to others. This gives the impression that you are also considerate with how other people think and feel and, in turn, respect differences in opinions. This would foster a relationship built on mutual trust and respect.

### 5. Reading and Responding to "Cues"

You might be surprised by this, but not everything that is ever conveyed to you will be 100%. This is quite true in tense and stressful situations where the things not said can dictate how things would happen as much as the things that were said in public.

And it also does not help that some personality types are difficult to handle by default. A pushy salesman, an angry boss, a detail-heavy mechanic, a mother who is stuck in traffic and is driving her kids to soccer practice. All of these require you to pick up on non-verbal cues in order to respond with the right words.

A bit of awareness of the body language of others can give you a great advantage when closing deals and finding solutions for problems. Also, it helps you adjust the tone of your verbal message so that it fits the overall mood of the place and the mentality of the people listening to you.

Here is a good example. Suppose you are delivering a lecture and notice that most of the class is tuning you out because your class is boring. You can inject humor or draw from your life experiences to get the attention of everybody as jokes and personal stories can make people connect to what you are saying. With good communication skills, you can pay attention to how people are reacting to your message and adjust your delivery accordingly.

### 6. Improving Productivity

Once the hindrances towards proper communication are done with (more of them on a later chapter), everybody around you knows what you can do and will find you a more reliable person. This is effective in group efforts as, now, members can get the idea that they don't have to do everything just to complete a task.

With good communication, workloads can be distributed quickly, conflicts settled before they get out of hand, and you can deal with your stress in the most direct yet diplomatic manner possible. In essence, by communicating better, you get things done as soon as possible, which makes you a more productive person overall.

### 7. Making a Good Impression

Presenting yourself can be a rather nerve-wracking experience. Even if you have well-prepared material for your presentation, the execution of your plan can be derailed if your nerves get the better of you.

One good skill you will learn in improving your communication is how to deal with what is effectively called "stage fright." Learning how to manage your nervousness before going in front of people and conveying your thoughts assertively and authoritatively can make you a far more convincing speaker.

Presentation also involves how you can recover from any mistake without losing stride in front of everyone. This will include learning how to turn your mistakes into something humorous to endear yourself to the public and also cut off dead air in your presentation.

All in all, good communication skills can allow you to present your message in a way that is attractive and yet easy to understand.

## The Qualities of Good Communicators

As was stated, communication is a skill that must be developed over time. Practice is what eventually elevates you from a less than efficient communicator to a good one.

The end goal of becoming a good communicator is to make everyone who is involved in a conversation feel like their contribution to it will matter. And in order for that to happen, a communicator must possess a certain set of skills.

### 1. Active Listening

Knowing how to form your message is one good skill, but a more important one is to receive those messages being directed to you. Instead of interrupting other people or taking away the focus from that person to them, a good communicator focuses on what is being told to them.

Listening intently and letting the other person finish is also not enough. A good communicator also understands the value of letting the person talking confirm that their message is being received and processed. Through nods and other short non-verbal messages, a communicator tells the speaker that they are tuned in to the conversation.

This would help in preventing conversations from becoming monologues while also helping a person with a problem find the most effective solution for it.

## 2. Empathy

There is this misconception that communication needs to be mired with protocol and politically-correct term usage in order to be effective. This only makes conversations stiffer for the participants and, in some cases, artificial.

Instead, a good communicator will seek opportunities wherein meaningful dialogue can take place, and collaboration is assured. These can only be made possible if they truly understand where the other person is coming from and how they view certain issues.

Rather than force their own opinions into a certain matter, a good communicator will understand how people feel in a certain situation and adjust their approach accordingly. This is quite essential in negotiations or even in building cordial relationships with others. If you are not the person that can see things from perspectives other than your own, or learn how to adjust in situations, then you need to acquire these skills to be an effective communicator.

## 3. An Open Mind

To assume is a human tendency, but this can often lead to conflicts. For instance, you might think that a person is dominating the conversation when it is just his natural way of speaking. Or what if you assume a person to be shy or timid just because he does not talk a lot?

Either way, assuming too quickly can be detrimental in conversations as it leaves space open for future conflict. A good communicator will clarify things first and seek to get the most basic information right. This way, the message that they are about to deliver gets perceived in a manner that they intended for it to be perceived as.

## 4. A Positive Mindset

Enthusiasm can be a rather hard emotion to maintain, especially if one is already used to being cynical. However, it can also be an effective tool in engaging with people as it naturally makes them excited for what is to transpire in the conversation.

Offsetting negativity is a key quality good communicators have since a few negative comments are all it takes to derail an entire conversation. By rallying people to their cause and making them excited for what is about to happen next, a good communicator can teach people to be motivated and even resilient when the tougher times come.

## To Summarize

The truth is that communication is a rather simple concept to follow. You do not need to even have a higher level of learning to be a good communicator. All it takes is for you to have the right mindset and approach to get the best benefits of being a good communicator.

Now, in a perfect world, the conveying of thoughts and ideas follows a rather simple path and would lead to a beneficial conclusion. But we aren't living in a perfect world, are we?

So why do our day-to-day communications seem, for lack of a better word, flawed?

# Chapter 2: Why We Don't Communicate Right

*"The single biggest problem in communication is the illusion that it has taken place."*

*-George Bernard Shaw*

In as much as it can be easy to get communication right, it is also equally easy to get things wrong with it. Sadly, the latter is more likely to happen in one's day-to-day.

There are quite a lot of reasons why a lot of our conversations can get derailed in a matter of a few seconds and several poorly-worded statements. And surprisingly, there are quite a lot of them that you have encountered for yourself on a regular basis.

## The Barriers towards Effective Communication

Man, whether he is conscious of it or not, has several barriers erected around him that would prevent messages from being interpreted the way they should be.

By identifying what these barriers are, you are one step closer to improving your communication skills. After all, what is there left to do with a barrier that you identified than to, well, smash it?

### 1. Physical Barriers

This is the one easiest to spot because it depends on actual physical conditions in the environment. For instance, you are trying to talk to a person, but they are several meters away from you. Or what if you are trying to talk to somebody in a crowded, noisy room?

Even the layout of an office can serve as a barrier to effective communication. Cubicle walls, for example, can absorb a lot of noise, which prevents workers from talking to each other unless they stand up and talk with each other over the wall.

And, of course, faulty equipment is a physical barrier, especially in remote communication. A broken microphone or a sudden weakening of the Internet connection can cause messages to be distorted, preventing listeners from interpreting a message properly.

Fortunately, being easy to spot means that physical communication barriers are the easiest to solve. If one can't hear you because you're too far away, you get closer to the listener. If the walls in your office are preventing communications, you talk over them. And if your communication equipment is faulty, then you invest in newer and more reliable ones. And so on and so forth.

### 2. Language Barriers

A barrier of the linguistic one is something that you will also encounter often but is a bit trickier to deal with. The fact that each region of the world has their own preferred set of languages can be a barrier to effective communication because two people may not know how to talk to each other in one language that both know.

"But isn't English the universal language now?" you might ask. That is true. Ever since the world has become globalized, many countries have adopted English as the standard for international communications.

But here is the thing: English is not the same in one country over another. For instance, the kind of English used in America is completely different from the one used in Britain or Canada. The same goes for other continents that have their own colloquial terms used in conjunction with English words.

On a more local scale, there are the dialects that change from one region to another or, more accurately, once every few thousand kilometers. Of course, some nationalities speak English with a rather thick accent.

Included here are the different linguistic styles. Some people speak in a simple and yet direct manner while others are very verbose and use highfalutin words. And then there are those professions who encourage people to talk at an advanced level of English like law, academics, and science.

As a result, in one modern neighborhood, you can find more than three dialects, accents, and linguistic levels being used in daily communication.

### 3. Psychological Barriers

This is one of the more insidious barriers as you will not know that they exist until they manifest themselves. The most common psychological barrier is stage fright, where you experience massive nervousness before speaking in front of several people. If overwhelmed by their nerves, the person may even experience difficulty delivering a single sentence clearly.

But there are far more potent psychological barriers being erected around people out there. These include depression, speech disorders, phobias, and other deep psychological problems that limit one's ability to speak clearly.

In most cases, some psychological issues collaterally affect your speech only. This means that fixing them must be done not only to improve your communication skills but to improve your mental health as well.

### 4. Emotional Barriers

Although closely related to psychological barriers, emotional barriers have a shorter lifespan. In other words, they are barriers only because your emotional state at that moment made them so.

A strong emotional quotient allows a person to communicate effectively and perceive messages the way their speaker intends for them to be received. However, high emotional states can affect your way of receiving messages.

For example, anger and sadness can make a person interpret a message negatively. On the opposite side of the spectrum are happiness and contentment, which makes a person even more receptive to messages.

### 5. Cultural Barriers

A more recent barrier faced by people is the exposure to different cultures coming from different nations. It cannot be helped that one culture is different from yours, and such differences can be manifested by the way you communicate with them.

People coming from reserved, isolationist cultures tend to speak only when spoken to while those coming from more open and highly social cultures tend to be easy conversationalists.

There are also other cultural factors to consider like a religious practice or lack of one, sexual identity, diet, preferred pets, and overall general behavior. And this might even surprise you, but cultural factors will also dictate the type of topics you can expect to talk about when it comes to certain cultures.

As such, it is a must to take into consideration the differences in cultures when communicating with other people. You cannot assume that they will perceive things the same way as you do due to these differences. This is the very essence of being culturally appropriate.

### 6. Attitude Barriers

The way that a person is predisposed towards interpersonal interactions will also determine how well they communicate with others. Introverts like to be left alone and thus shy away from most verbal communications and physical contact. However, they might excel in remote communications like online chatting.

And then there are those personality types that are social or clingy. Of course, there are personality types that could be perceived as blunt and inconsiderate or egotistical and domineering. All of these could play into how you can communicate with people. Under the right conditions, they could even serve as an impediment to you getting your message across properly.

### 7. Organizational Barriers

This barrier is commonly seen in places where there is an organizational structure. Here is a scenario: have you ever wanted to talk to a person but feel hesitant because they are one rank or several ranks higher than you in the company's organizational chart? That's an organizational barrier.

Or what if you wanted to tell a person something but can't because company protocol demands that you do not disclose sensitive information to people that are lower in the chart? That is an organizational barrier right there.

Admittedly, a lot of companies are doing away with the rigidity of the organizational charts and employ a more transparent line of communication between people regardless of their position. This means that how much the organization's structure can impede communications depends greatly on the culture of that group.

**One Important Reminder:** Although these barriers are prevalent, it does not mean that you will have to face all seven of them even in your lifetime. If you are the person who has never traveled to another country, you may have never had a linguistic barrier problem. And if you do know how to circumvent them, physical barriers might not even be a problem for you.

Also, the magnitude of the problems that one faces is different from another person. Your psychological barriers might be minor compared to another person, but you might have more problems dealing with organizational barriers than those around you.

The point is that knowing what barriers you have to face in your communication skills is the key to finding a way to discover a creative workaround for problems they might pose.

## Busting Some Misconceptions

As with any other skill out there, it is easy to build your communication skills on the wrong foundations. Such foundations are based on some misconceptions regarding the art of conveying your thoughts and feelings to others or perceiving the same. As such, we must correct such wrong information in order to proceed properly.

## Myth 1: Listening Skills are not Needed

This myth is based on the notion that communication is simply the relaying of your thoughts and ideas to another person and nothing else. As such, you only need to learn how to craft your message to be a good communicator.

But the truth is that it only makes you a good talker, not a communicator. Listening is an essential skill to learn, as it helps you form your words in response to how people are feeling or most likely will receive your message. In essence, good listening skills help you refine your message and make it resonate with whoever you are conversing with.

## Myth 2: Sharing of Information is the Same as Communicating

The truth is that communication is always a dialogue, not a monologue. This means that more than one person is involved, and a back and forth of responses are to be expected if an interaction is to be labeled as a conversation.

As such, communication focuses on the two sides between participants, which means that a considerable focus is put on how you can maintain a healthy conversation with people. In other words, your ability to read non-verbal cues, process responses, and adjust your way of talking accordingly are crucial skills in become a better communicator.

## Myth 3: You Must Only Share the Message in One Way for Optimum Effect

Here is the thing about humans: they won't get what you are trying to say at once. This is dependent on whatever barriers they have inadvertently erected for themselves that prevent such a message from being processed properly.

As such, you need to find ways to make your message reach out to a lot of people. This can be done by finding the right platforms where you should air out your message as well as the type of form it will take. For instance, if you have a good speech, you can convert into text form for easy reading or make it a supplement to a lecture.

It's up to you to find out how you can keep your message "evergreen" for as long as possible. And, fortunately for you, there are ways to convert your message from one format to another (which will be discussed later on).

## Myth 4: Constant Communication is Always Good

Sure, talking regularly is one way to improve your skills. After all, practice makes perfect.

However, as with all things, the best signifier that you have improved as a communicator is not quantity, but quality. There are a lot of people out there that talk a lot without saying anything meaningful. And then there are those who say important things but keep repeating them.

Frequency is also a matter that you need to figure out in delivering your message. Say it too many times and it might become annoying; say it sparingly and it won't have an impact. The right amount of repetition for your message, while also keeping its form diverse enough, should help in making whatever you are trying to say last in the minds of listeners for as long as possible.

## Communication Mistakes (and How to Avoid Committing Them)

Communication is labeled as a competency. This only means that the skill is best gauged not through conceptual, abstract means, but through actual application.

And there lies the problem. With application comes the tendency to make mistakes, and humans are particularly known for their tendency to commit mistakes. For communication, these mistakes can either be substantial or formal, but they will most likely affect your interactions negatively. As such, identifying them is crucial if you want to improve your skills.

### 1. Not Exactly Listening

The most common mistake people make in communicating is giving it the bare minimum of effort while giving the appearance of paying attention. When somebody is talking, you might be busy going through your phone or writing something or watching the television. Worse, your mind is wandering off to somewhere else, so everything being relayed to you does not even register in your brain.

This is problematic on two fronts. First, it makes the person talking feel invalidated as you are unintentionally shutting off whatever they are trying to convey to you. Second, it makes you miss out on important non-verbal cues being displayed, which makes you run the risk of misreading the entire situation and giving an improper reply.

The only remedy here is to give your full attention to the speaker, which is one of the crucial skills you will learn later on.

### 2. Interrupting the Speaker

We have all done this. How often have you cut off a person mid-sentence since you think you know what they are going to say next? For instance, a person might be telling you what just happened to them, but you just butt in and say, "get to the point already!" That's a rather rude thing to do, and it stops any momentum that the speaker is building on.

An even worse thing that you could do is interrupt the speaker and then interject your own story. Not only did you cut the momentum of the story off, you just took the attention away from the speaker to you.

Interrupting a person mid-sentence is often seen as a power move, but it's a rather discourteous one at that. The end result is that you are invalidating the person as if telling them subtly that whatever they are trying to say does not matter.

This can be remedied with a bit of courtesy. You have to learn when a person has stopped talking, which tells you that it is now time to respond.

### 3. Assuming the Message

This often happens between friends since this mistake is dependent on how well you know that other person to act and think. When a person is trying to speak, our minds are already formulating assumptions as to what they are trying to convey to you or, at the very least, their intentions behind such.

More often than not, the assumption is wrong. This only becomes a problem, however, if you make the assumption manifest by performing mistake number two or giving the wrong response.

When one assumes what a person is trying to say, they miss out on the person's true message. Maintaining an open and curious mindset in regards to the speaker and his message should solve this problem.

### 4. Emphasizing the "Incorrect" Nouns

You might be surprised by this, but the nouns that you use in your message can be determined by the tone of that message. Let us say that you are trying to address a problem in front of your team.

So, more often than not, you would use the nouns "you" so everything you are going to say next falls along the lines of "You didn't do this," "You should have done that," or "You did this."

The "you" statements are often uncomfortable to listen to as they feel like personal attacks. This makes the listeners form negative connotations about what you are trying to say to them, resulting in miscommunication.

A more cautious usage of your words is necessary here. Instead of using "you" statements, you should use "I" and "we." The latter two are more inclusive and lean towards personal accountability. With these, you can soften the blow for any message that you would try to convey, especially serious ones.

### 5. Being an Emotional Responder

Emotions are good for making sure that you adjust your responses in accordance with the situation. But what happens if you let your emotions run over you? More often than not, you are going to say things that you don't mean and would regret later on.

There have been far too many instances of people saying stuff that bring with them serious interpersonal consequences just because they were sad, angry, or emotionally distraught. One crucial skill you will have to develop, then, is to let your emotions run through you while still picking the right words to say in response to any person talking to you.

The key here is to not say anything when your emotions are at a high. For instance, if you are extremely angry, it is best to let the anger burn through you before you do anything. You may even vocalize your frustrations, but just make sure that you don't vent it out on somebody you'd rather not want to hear you rant and rave.

And, of course, a little bit of restraint can go a long way here. Even if you have a social media account, do not use it as a diary where you channel your anger. Things often said online have a tendency of coming back and doing some serious damage to your credibility.

### 6. Plain Misinterpretation

More often than not, human beings fail to properly interpret messages. Perhaps it is because of the barriers listed above, perhaps it is because of our emotional state upon receiving the message, perhaps it is because of our lack of skill in perceiving the different nuances of a message.

Whatever the case, we perceive the message in a manner that is not intended by the speaker. This is even more prevalent with modern-day technology when other elements like voice, tone, and non-verbal cues are done away with. Even the ability to detect sarcasm and condescension is harder with the Internet nowadays.

This problem is often avoided if you pay full attention to what is being directed at you. This involves more than mere listening as you have to analyze what is being said, how it is said, and what other non-verbal messages were accompanying it.

There is no assurance that you will perceive the message 100% correctly, depending on the situation. However, you can be certain that your response will be a better-informed one if you take the time to listen and analyze.

### 7. Being Vague

This might be in response to the need to not accidentally offend other people nowadays, but becoming too vague or subtle in your communication is a rather ineffective style. The reason for this is that vagueness always leaves wide room for interpretation.

An all-too-common example of this is when we feel upset and post something rather vague on Facebook. When pressed for more details, we talk in the vaguest of terms possible. In some cases, we use a passive-aggressive tone just to mask the fact that whatever happened has gotten to us on an emotional level.

If you are not careful, you may end up having wildly different interpretations of something that could have been otherwise simply understood. Worse, you may be perceived to be talking without actually saying anything.

The only remedy here is to not beat around the bush. Be as direct as possible while maintaining a level of courtesy with the way you convey your thoughts and feelings. You cannot expect people to read your mind, so do not make that a requirement in conversing with you.

### 8. Not Accounting for Cultural Differences

Even if both parties speak at the same level of English, there are minute differences in the way that they convey thoughts and feelings. Cross-cultural conversations are often hard because not everyone gives the same verbal cues. They don't even mean the same thing for one word, depending on the region.

One great example of this is between American and British English. For starters, both have different sets of idioms and colloquial terms. Next, they have different tones and approaches, with the British being perceived as more formal and verbose while Americans are seen as curt and simple.

Either way, failing to account for key differences in term usage, sentence structure, and non-verbal cues can lead to miscommunication between parties.

Again, the solution here is to make things as plain as possible. Use a level of language used by all and try not to impress others with advanced words or idioms that are not used by the general public. The point with communication, after all, is to express and not to impress.

## 9. The Ad Hominem

When you do not like what a person is saying, the most common thing that humans do is to attack the messenger. This often happens in informal debates when the person starts looking for defects that are observable in the person instead of any logical flaw in their argument.

The reason for this is rather simple: character flaws are easy to spot and can derail an otherwise well-structured conversation with minimal effort. On the other hand, it is a telltale sign that you no longer have anything valuable to offer to the dialogue.

As such, we often hear things like "You're just an (insert politician's name here) supporter!" or "Why should I listen to a (insert political party/race/social status here)?" easily thrown by people nowadays. It's a way of ending a difficult conversation, but it is one that does nothing in improving your credibility as a conversationalist.

The only way to prevent yourself from committing a mistake of this kind is to stick to the facts contained within the message. Make sure that your arguments are responsive to what was being directed at you and not merely hostile by default. You have to realize that you may not agree with the person on principle but, at the very least, you can respect their views while also presenting your own in a manner that is not offensive to all.

And speaking of difficult conversations….

## 10. Deflecting or Delaying

When faced with the prospect of conveying difficult subject matters, we often make the mistake of prolonging the conversation for as long as possible. Perhaps you'd rather not be scrutinized over something you have done or know of. Or perhaps you can't find the words to tell everybody else of something they would not like to hear.

As such, you resort to veering off the issue so that you won't be placed in a position where you will become the bearer of bad news. The problem with this, however, is that it only makes matters worse in the long run.

Careful management of tension is key to telling people what they must hear without creating conflicts or damaging relationships. A bit of tact and proper selection of words would also help you in this matter.

Timing is also necessary for delivering your message. You must not wait too long when delivering the news, but you must not rush things through until you have all the information confirmed. This way, you can craft a message that is going to be received by all in the best manner possible.

Either way, you must not withhold information to protect the feelings of others at the expense of telling the truth. In the most mindful and diplomatic manner, of course.

## In a Nutshell

There is no denying that the path of the message from its source to its listener is fraught with many obstacles. These obstacles might not exactly impede the message from being received, but it does affect how the person receiving it responds.

Fortunately, most of these obstacles, mistakes, and other barriers towards effective communication can be addressed and corrected. This means that, with training, you can slowly correct the flaws in the way you communicate and prevent yourself from committing the mistakes listed above. That is, of course, if you commit to constantly improving your communication skills.

# Chapter 3: The Art of Active Listening

*"I remind myself every morning: Nothing I say this day will teach me anything. So if I'm going to learn, I must do it by listening."*

**-Larry King**

Surprisingly, one of the most important tools that you need to develop in your communication skills is not your mouth. It is those two things that lie on either side of your head.

The concept of listening sounds rather simple and straightforward. All you have to do is receive the sound waves coming from a person's mouth and have your brain interpret what those waves are carrying. And so as long as you have a perfectly healthy (and clean) set of ears, you are bound to be a rather decent listener.

But to truly be listening in the sense that you get the essence of what the other person is saying to you is often hard to pull off. Conversations are tricky, after all, as they fraught with nuances, innuendos, non-verbal cues, and other hidden messages. And there are topics out there that are hard to interpret if you do not give it your undivided attention.

It is at these moments that you have to learn how to understand a person, even if they are not sure of what they are trying to say to you. This is where you will apply what is called active listening.

## What Exactly is Active Listening?

The most basic explanation of active listening is that it is the kind of listening that involves the use of one's full concentration. The goal of this type of listening is to understand the person delivering the message.

By understanding, it means to delve deeper into their message and find out what exactly they are trying to say. This does not only include the words that they use but the emotions and the body language that accompanies such.

Using this type of listening, you are expected to form the most appropriate response to what had just been said to you. At the same time, you have a better chance of recalling fully what you just listened to.

The premise of active listening is that it paves the way for a clear exchange of thoughts and feelings. This, in turn, would increase the chances of you coming to an understanding of every person involved in a single conversation.

One key element necessary to make active listening possible is empathy. This is the ability to see things from the perspective of other people, even if you do not agree with them in principle.

With this quality, active listening is made possible, especially in three critical areas.

### 1. Empathetic Understanding

The most basic aspect of active understanding, this simply involves listening while also trying to perceive things similarly to how the other person perceives them. In essence, you are subtly telling the person that you understand what they are saying and also understand what they mean and are feeling right now.

## 2. Listening Without Agreeing

If you understand where that person comes from, does it mean that you have to agree with them? No. It simply means that you now understand their perspective and can formulate a response that counters that without disrespecting the person on a personal level.

In essence, you can now tactfully share your viewpoints while respecting the differences that other viewpoints have with it.

## 3. Willingness to Listen

This aspect covers your readiness to listen to what a person is saying with **no distractions at all**. This is the more challenging part as there are quite a lot of distractions that could prevent you from listening to that person fully. This includes your busy schedule and the devices that you surround yourself with.

This also includes fighting all urges to pretend to listen. This is not only rude but runs contrary to the basic concept of actively listening to another person. If done all too frequently, you run the risk of damaging relationships, personal or otherwise.

## The Steps towards Active Listening

Active listening is a skill which means that you have to develop it over time. To do this, here are some steps to help you make yourself an active and effective listener.

### 1. Eye Contact

When you talk to a person and you try your best to avoid meeting their eyes, this is a telltale sign that you are not giving the conversation your full attention. This includes constantly checking your watch or phone, scanning the room, or looking out the window.

Most Western countries value eye contact as a basic foundation for active communication. This is quite important as certain conversations can take a while to get finished. If you are not comfortable locking eyes with the other person, you invite all urges to get up and move.

As such, when a person is speaking to you, put everything unnecessary down. If you are typing something at your computer, stop it. If you are writing something down, stop it. If you are eating, for the sake of the conversation and to prevent yourself from choking on your food, stop it.

"But what if the person does not want to make eye contact?" There are some cultures out there where eye contact is either discouraged or subtly not recommended. This includes some parts in Asia and the Middle East.

If the other person finds it hard to make eye contact, let them be. Stay focused on your gaze to lock in your attention to the conversation at hand.

### 2. Relax

There is a difference between making eye contact and staring fixedly at the person. You can always look away and maintain a mindful awareness of your surroundings since this is a basic human instinct.

Being "attentive" can mean a lot of things. This includes being present at the moment and giving most, if not all, of your attention to the object in front of you.

The goal here is to actively maintain focus while tuning out all distractions, like noise and activity, in the background. Lastly, do not let yourself be distracted by your feelings, biases, and other inner trains of thought. Your mind must be open enough to let information come through from the conversation so that you can respond appropriately.

And speaking of your mental state...

### 3. An Open Mind

It is often part of human nature to make a mental note of the person's distinct features and mannerisms when they are talking to you. For instance, if they say something incredulous, your mind immediately makes a mental note along the lines of *well, that was a stupid thing to say,* followed by an instinctive raising of the eyebrows.

Or what if the person has a visible distraction on their face like a mole on their cheek or a piece of lettuce in their teeth? Your eyes would immediately travel there, and your focus is now on the "fault" and not on the messenger.

Either way, indulging in mental criticisms in the middle of a conversation will impede your ability to effectively listen to the other person. As such, you must listen without making any hasty conclusions.

Always remember that the person, despite their mistakes, is doing their best to relay what they are thinking and feeling. If you don't listen, you will never get to what they truly want to say to you.

Also, it is at this point that you must correct your tendency to hasten the person in finishing their narration. You may be the type of person who wants to speed conversations up or are just bothered with people beating around the bush. Whatever the case, do not cut a person off so they can get to the point at their own pace.

### 4. Visualize

The best way to retain and process information in your brain is to convert that information into a "mental image" of sorts. This could be a sequence of abstract things forming a narrative or even an actual mental picture, but the image helps you keep focus on what the person is saying.

This is rather important, especially if the person is relaying to you a narrative of events leading to an incident. That narration could go on for several sentences and paragraphs, which takes a while to get condensed in your brain without some mental aid.

Your mental picture can be a sequence of mental images, or abstract things, or even keywords. The point is that it will help you formulate what to say next.

But here is the kicker: while you are listening, you must not spend even a fraction of your time planning what to say next. The mind is not designed to listen while also rehearsing your response internally at the same time. While listening, your one and only focus should be the things the other person is saying even if they happen to be rather boring.

## 5. Avoid Interjections

When we were young, we were most likely taught that it's a rather rude thing to interrupt people who are talking. Despite what modern media is telling you (i.e., that in-your-face, confrontational behavior is good), being rude and obnoxious during conversations will always lead to an aggressive put-down, verbal or otherwise.

When you interrupt a person, you can convey a lot of messages, which include "My story is more important than yours" or "I do not have time for you." What you have to understand is that people think and feel at very different paces.

This means that the burden of adjusting to the speaker's pace is, well, on you.

And even if you do not wish ill, you can be an interrupter if you tend to provide a solution when it is not solicited. Think of it this way: if that person is seeking your advice, they would gladly ask for it once their narration is over.

If not, then refrain from giving unsolicited advice. More often than not, people just want a person to listen, and not a solution. But if you do have a brilliant idea, always ask the speaker if they want to hear it. But only do this once that person has said their piece.

## 6. Wait for the Stop

How would you know that a person has stopped their narration? It is easy to say that this is the moment when their jaws stopped flapping, but there is an actual "pause" that you have to look for, the intangible "stop" that signifies you that a sentence or paragraph has ended.

The stop happens when a person does not add anything else after a second or so of not talking. You could even tell in certain people that they are not about to add anything else because they do not visibly catch their breath as if winding up for another paragraph of narration.

Once the stop has occurred, you can then present your response. Or, better yet, you can ask the person to go back on some details, especially the ones that you were the most confused with.

This makes for a perfect segue with the next step, which is…

## 7. Maintain Course

Picture this scenario: Your friend has just been talking to you in the last few minutes about a wonderful experience he had at the last Superbowl season. You, in all of your meticulousness, zeroed in on the part of the story where he was sitting next to an acquaintance of yours that you hadn't heard from since 2010.

Then you asked, "Oh, you were sitting next to Bobby from way back in high school? How is he? I heard he's going through a rough divorce. It must suck for the kids."

Question: Was what you just said relevant to his Superbowl experience, or did you just unconsciously veer the conversation into somebody else's personal life?

If you answered the latter, then you at least know that you unconsciously committed one of the biggest mistakes in communication: changing the topic. The things that we say right after a person is done talking have, more often than not, nothing to do with what they just said. It takes a while to get back on topic, but it is easy to derail an entire conversation this way.

If you know that you have an annoying tendency to do this, you have to learn how to veer back to the primary topic. After the person is done answering what you just asked, say something like, "Oh, that's hard to hear coming from Bobby. But tell me more about your Superbowl experience. It was great, right?"

In just a few sentences, you just shifted the focus back to the speaker's topic with them none the wiser for it.

## 8. Step in their Shoes

As the person speaks, you might notice that their emotions would start to surface. This is good as emotions are rarely hidden, especially if the person is talking about something personal.

What you have to do here is synchronize your emotions with that of the speaker's. If they are joyful, show joy. If they are fearful as they describe what is troubling them, show concern.

A key element here is to make your reactions visible through the words you say and the expressions you show. And this is where empathy can help you as it allows you to see things from that person's point of view. It takes concentration and time to master, but it will eventually help you become an effective listener and communicator.

## 9. Give Feedback

It is not enough that you see things from that person's perspective or understand what they are feeling. You also have to visibly confirm to the speaker that you are listening.

There are multiple ways to do this. The easiest one is to vocalize your reactions with phrases like "Wow, that's wonderful!" or "I'm sad to hear about that," or "That sucks. I can see why you're frustrated!"

But what if the person's message or feelings are unclear or you don't know how to react out of fear of being misunderstood as indifferent? You can easily confirm that you are paying attention by nodding or using filler words like "mm-hmm" or "uh-huh."

The goal here is to assure the speaker that they have your undivided attention and that you are following their narrative. This is important in situations where the person is not only telling a story but giving you instructions for performing certain things.

## 10. Pay Attention to What *Isn't Said*

Email notwithstanding, most of the direct forms of communication you will regularly encounter is non-verbal. There are a lot of things that a person can tell you without opening their mouth. It is up to you, then, to know how to pick up on these non-verbal cues.

Here's a good example: When somebody talks to you over the phone, you might wonder how to tell if they are happy or not. Listen for the tone they use whenever they start the conversation. If it is a happy one, you can be 75% sure that the rest of the conversation will be a lighthearted one. If you detect a sense of seriousness in their tone, you could be certain that what they are about to tell you is urgent. And so on.

These non-verbal cues are even more pronounced in face-to-face conversations. If you are that astute, you can even detect things like boredom, irritation, and even sarcasm coming from the other person as well as obvious facial expressions. These are things that any person could not ignore, which is why you should consider them when responding to what the person has just said.

## Some Exercises to Improve on Your Listening Skills

Active listening is something that you would not develop overnight. It takes time and practice to master in order to be an effective listener. To do that, here are some exercises that you could implement in your daily interactions.

### 1. Paraphrasing

Most of the time, it is hard to process a lot of information in one passing. Chances are that you won't get everything that the person has said, which means that your response is going to be far from good.

So, how could you make them repeat what you just said without giving the impression that you were not paying attention? You paraphrase.

How this is done is easy: you only have to repeat what they just said or what you understood about the situation and ask for a clarification at the end.

A paraphrase should sound like this: "So, you (the speaker) just had (insert situation here), and you would like to (insert their question or proposition here). Is that right?"

More often than not, the speaker would indulge you by clarifying certain details of their story without going through everything again.

Paraphrasing is also good for summarizing all their key points, which keeps the conversation going. If a person is angry at something you did, you can zero in on that point of their narrative and say something like, "Would you like to hear the reasons why I did that?"

Or what if a person made an observation? You could follow it with a question like, "Are you referring to (information A) or is it (information B)?"

Paraphrasing works not only to clarify any detail in the speaker's story, it also helps the person collect themselves and reorganize their thoughts. In either case, you and the other person have a better chance of reaching an understanding.

### 2. Words to Avoid

Reacting to what has just been said is important. However, we often make mistakes when responding to the message. All of this can be traced back to our instinct to have the problem solved instead of actually listening to the person.

Here are some of the responses that you should try your best to avoid saying when a person is speaking:

- Telling a story: "That happened to you, too? That reminds of that time when..."
- Pitying the person: "You poor thing..."
- Correcting them: "Uh, I don't think that's how it went..."
- Comforting them: "I know it's hard, and none of this is your fault...."
- One-upping the person: "You think that's bad? What happened to me was worse!"
- Cutting them short: "Uh, I'd love to listen more. Can we do it later?"

What you normally say when in a conversation might be different from the ones above. Either way, you should identify your response gaffes so you would know which ones to avoid when talking with other people.

### 3. Your Own Non-Verbal Cues

Listening to what isn't said works just as much on yourself as it does on the speaker. What are your usual ticks when listening to a person while he's talking? List them down and find out whether or not they help the conversation or harm it.

For instance, crossing your arms while a person is talking can be perceived as you being uncomfortable with either the message or the speaker. The same is true when you constantly tap or shuffle your feet or make a loud clicking noise when a person is talking. It signifies that you would rather be somewhere else.

As such, you have to identify which of your non-verbal messages are hostile, or could be potentially perceived as hostile, and find ways to minimize doing them when in front of people. Doing so could make the conversation that follows easier for you and the other person.

## What Makes Active Listening Hard?

The truth is that active listening is not the easiest thing to perform at all times. If it were, then a lot of miscommunication would be avoided, which, as far as your personal experiences can be gleaned upon, is far from the truth.

As such, you have to identify where you could also make a mistake in trying to be an active listener. Here are three areas to consider:

### 1. The "No Solution" Stance

The biggest issue with active listening is that people, by default, are problem solvers. Some fields and disciplines have this mentality so hardwired that it becomes hard for people in those areas to become effective listeners.

How hard is it, you ask? Here's a classic example: Let us say that a friend of yours is telling you that one of their family is sick with something serious like cancer. As they are narrating their story, you are already coming up with suggestions like where to get treatment, dealing with the complications, and managing the stress.

What you are not doing, on the other hand, is listening to the narrative. You fail to get the context of the story or even understand the intention of the person relaying this information to you. In your haste to provide them with solutions, you fail to reach an understanding with the person.

Arguably, it is your eagerness to solve problems that should be dealt with the most in learning how to actively listen. That is not to say that providing advice is not good (it is), but you should get the context of the story first before you start doling out advice.

### 2. Dealing with Tough Emotions

If the subject is rather personal, emotions are expected to run high. Like the example above, you can expect the person telling you their story to start tearing or choking up. This is a sign that their emotion for the story is still raw, and they are visibly hurting from even relaying it to you.

The first impulse with people, however, is to find a way to make the person stop crying. Perhaps you might say something like, "It's okay. Don't cry!" or try to change the topic. The reason for this is rather simple: it is rather uncomfortable to see a person display strong emotions. In some cultures, being emotionally expressive is even seen as a sign of weakness. Either way, a lot of people are not designed to cope with the emotions of others, let alone their own.

The biggest challenge that you would face here is to embrace the emotions being directed at you, no matter how hard it is. It is essential to let those feelings be seen and heard for you to respond appropriately.

### 3. Dealing with the Silence

Being silent is often uncomfortable in a conversation. While you are refining your skills, you might even allow entire seconds of silence to go by before the conversation resumes. In most cases, those periods of silence can be awkward for you.

However, dealing with those periods of silence is but part of the process of becoming an active listener. What matters more is that you visually confirm what has been relayed to you by your own emotions and the expressions you make.

You can cut through the silence with the clarification or paraphrase to help the other person relax. This could also give the impression that you are trying to understand them and were paying attention to their story, thus validating themselves before your eyes.

The key here is timing. You have to hone the ability to detect pauses and stops in the person's narration of events. Once you identify when these occur, you can then add to the conversation without coming off as rude or impatient.

### To Conclude

If we were to summarize the active listening process, it would look something like this:

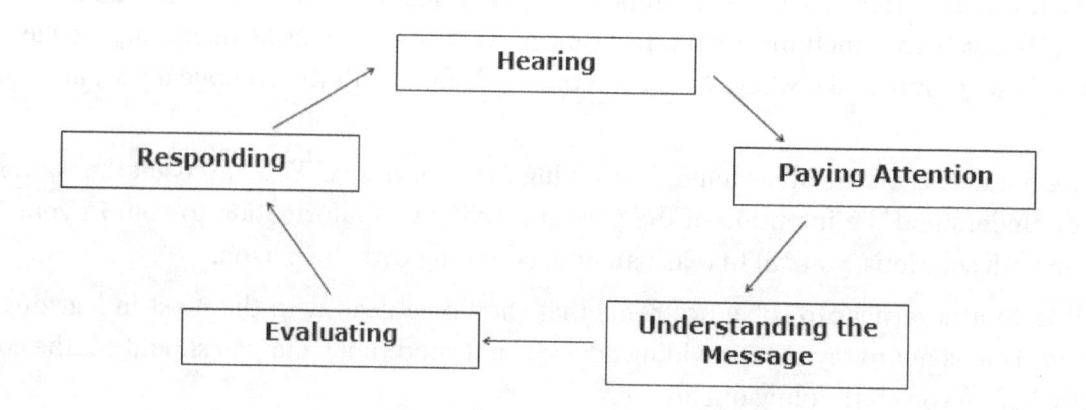

Hearing → Paying Attention → Understanding the Message → Evaluating → Responding → Hearing

Sounds simple and straightforward, right? That's because it is.

The only thing that you have to remember in order to be an active listener is to fully invest yourself in the conversation. Allow nothing else to distract you from receiving the message and its context so that you can mold the best possible response.

Of course, it takes time to develop this skill, which means you must constantly engage in conversation to improve as an active listener. Sure, you will make mistakes down the road, but you will eventually learn how to listen first before acting or responding.

# Chapter 4: The Basics of Interpersonal Communication

*"Communicating to a relationship is like oxygen to life. Without it....it dies."*

-*Tony Gaskins*-

Connecting with others is a valuable skill. If you look at the history of humankind, you will find little examples of people who managed to live on their own. Sure, you might know of a few examples, but they are mostly under dire circumstances.

And unless you're stuck in a rock or lost in a miles-long tundra, you are bound to meet other humans in your day-to-day living. And with this high probability of near-constant human encounters comes the need for constant interaction.

Mingling with other people should not be a difficult concept. But you might be surprised at how a lot of people screw up on the basics of interpersonal communications. As such, here is a refresher of sorts to help you enhance the way you can communicate with other people. And this is regardless of how they think and feel from you.

## The Different Personality Types

The biggest hurdle that you will face with communicating your thoughts and ideas are the very walls that people have set up themselves from all outside elements. The biggest of these so-called "walls" is their own personality.

To keep things simple, how a person communicates and processes information is different depending on their personality type. Your ability to find a creative workaround through each personality type can help you effectively communicate with that person without necessarily changing how they think, feel, and perceive things.

To do this, you must first get acquainted with the DiSC system for personalities. Just keep in mind that understanding the DiSC personality profiles is not a surefire success in improving your interpersonal relationships and communication. It is just there to give you a baseline understanding of how one person could be different from another.

### 1. D for Dominant

Personality styles under this profile are hardwired for one thing only: results. They are fast-paced individuals who aim to achieve at all costs.

As a consequence, they tend to be strong-willed and forceful. On more negative terms, they could be pushy and domineering. A D-type personality tends to act fast and is eager to see changes resulting from their actions.

Due to this, D-types are also highly opinionated and expect everybody else to follow along with their pace. At worst, they could come off as blunt and uncaring and can border on recklessness.

However, their results-driven personality means that they don't waste too much time feeling sorry for themselves, especially if they make a mistake (which is highly likely given their "act first, think later" style). They can also be visionaries, focusing on the bigger picture while also motivating others to do their best.

## 2. I for Interactive

These set of personality types are perhaps the most outgoing and interactive among the four personality profiles. They are primarily designed to be as social as possible.

Because of this, I-types are not as detail-oriented as other profiles, nor are they too keen about working on their own. However, like the D-type, I-types are as fast-paced and oriented towards getting things done. They only want to make sure that everybody is in the same car before starting their trip.

I-types thrive on being liked and, as such, don't take too nicely towards being rejected. As such, they would rather not deal with people who tend to be as abrasive or confrontational when it comes to dealing with others. And this fear of being the pariah tends to make I-types make sure that everybody has had their say before making any decision.

When under stress, the I-type becomes too talkative or emotionally disorganized. They also have a tendency to promise something but fail to follow through it.

However, their greatest strength is maintaining high spirits, which can be motivational for others. They also are rather great in starting discussions with people, which easily makes them catalysts for great ideas. And, more often than not, I-types are considered as the proverbial "glue" that keeps everyone within a group connected.

## 3. S for Stable

This is perhaps the most laid back of all the personality types. They are mostly described as even-tempered and supportive as they also value collaborative effort, equality, and a bit of justice.

Stability is the main goal of S-types, which makes them the least accepting of personality types towards changes in the status quo. S-types are also constantly needing reassurances from their peers, especially when approaching new challenges and situations.

This overly-cautious approach towards change makes S-types one of the "slower-paced" personality profiles out there. They are the ones that take the longest to decide on something and might take a while in elaborating any information to listeners. However, this has an upside: if an S-type decides to do something, nothing save for divine intervention will stop them from completing their task.

Under pressure, an S-type becomes supportive, but that can easily become too enabling or, worse, smothering. As a matter of fact, S-types tend to sacrifice personal creature comforts just to diffuse conflicts and help everybody settle.

## 4. C for Cautious

The most detail-oriented personality profile out there, C-types are known for their intense passion for getting things right on the first attempt. C-types are the ones that tend to have the highest possible personal standards and work ethic in any group, although it is not uncommon for them to lower their expectations and deal with how things are right now, not how they are supposed to be.

C-types are meticulous to a fault. When relaying their ideas, they would rather make sure that whatever they are saying leaves no room for interpretation. Every possible argument has to be preeminently shot down, and any contradiction corrected or, at least, explained.

As such, it is common for C-types to go into these long, complex, and tangent-heavy explanations, which will require a lot of time to process and respond accordingly. They are not the ones that do well with being criticized or even corrected, which they often see as a personal attack.

Outwardly, C-types can be too critical and can offer unsolicited advice. As such, people tend to only talk to a C-type or involve them in discussions only when it is truly necessary.

However, you must understand that C-types are aiming not to improve a person but, rather, a system. Their attention to detail and commitment to excellent performance would make any C-type the designated expert of a group.

## Talking with the Personality Types

Right at the get-go, you would already have an idea as to how you would approach the different DiSC profiles just by looking at their general description. Either way, your goal should be about synchronizing with how they think and perceive in order to have your message be received by them the way you want it to be received.

D-types want things fast and with little to no fluff. As such, you are better off being direct when talking with them. Get to the point within the first few sentences and minimize filler words like "um," "like," and "sort of." And if you do want to correct them, be as direct as possible as these profiles can take that feedback. The less you waste their time, the more you get in their good graces.

For I-types, you would want to come off not as intense but still high-spirited. The trick here is to let them make a move first. If they are happy, you must respond in kind with a happy remark. If they propose something, do not hesitate to affirm or build on it by contributing your own ideas.

For S-types, you should take your time to communicate with them. If you are proposing something new and radical, your best approach to these people is helping them see things from a logical standpoint. Explain to them all possible consequences coming from such a decision to make them see things from your perspective. You have to assure them that whatever new challenge they are about to take is within their ability to complete.

As for the C-type, it is best that you be as careful with them as possible. You must develop an ability to diplomatically relay information that prevents the C-type from seeing it as a personal attack. You also need to be as detail-oriented as them, dealing with facts and figures over abstract concepts.

In all four personality profiles, your strategy is the same: empathize with how they think and feel, and see things from their point of view. You cannot browbeat them or force them to adopt new ways of thinking. What you can do, instead, is mold your message to fit their personal biases.

If done right, you should be able to build a strong—or at least functional—relationship with different personalities.

## Establishing Rapport

Maintaining good relationships is a worthy goal. But what about building them in the first place? You might find that it is easier to maintain a connection with the people that you already know as opposed to welcoming new people to your personal or professional life.

However, that can be hard as changes in your life will force you to meet new people and establish contacts. As such, you have to know how to build rapport with the people around you. And here's how:

### 1. Managing Self-Worth

The first hurdle you have to clear here is how you view yourself. And the problem can go in two ways. It is either you think too highly of yourself or too lowly.

If your problem is the former, you have to always consider the fact that you are not infallible. Any idea you can contribute or opinion you air out can be corrected or enhanced further by the people around you. In essence, you must not put yourself at a level above others to shield yourself from criticism.

If your problem is the latter, then you must train to believe that you are worthy of being communicated with. You should remember that you are worthy enough to share your ideas and even challenge ideas that run against what you believe in.

Why is managing your self-worth crucial in building rapport? The answer is that how people treat you will be directly or inversely proportional to the way you view yourself. If you think too highly of yourself, people will automatically try to put you in your place. If you think too lowly of yourself, well, you are just giving people the consent to run you over in every interaction.

But viewing yourself as an equal to everybody around you allows for a clean slate of sorts where you can start building on relationships. An even-keeled view of yourself tends to make the act of building rapport easier.

### 2. Be Genuine

The best first thing that you can do in building rapport is to present yourself as you are. You don't have to adopt a new persona or even sound like a salesman when presenting yourself.

So what does it mean to be genuine, then? It only means that you present yourself the way you are. Of course, you'd have to be presentable and behave yourself in public, but you have to make sure that all your interactions are founded on the most genuine version of yourself.

If you are the one to burst out laughing at jokes, do so. If you are the one that loves to be loud and jovial, do so. Just relax, smile, and go with the flow in any social gathering. Just make sure that you address the more abrasive aspects of your personality before you meet other people, however.

### 3. "Tell Me About Yourself"

It cannot be avoided that people can get defensive when being asked something personal. This is a common thing to happen when you are talking with a stranger.

However, you can diffuse tension right from the start if you ask a person to tell you more about themselves. This technique has a twofold effect. First, it helps ease the person by signifying that you are there to make a connection with them. The more at ease they are, the less defensive they will get when you prod more.

Second, it helps you learn what is important to them by their own words. The request is a rather broad one, after all. When a person talks more about themselves, they subconsciously reveal tidbits of information that can help you smooth out the conversation as it progresses. This also goes well with the next tip, which is...

## 4. Finding Shared Humanity

As you learn more about that person, you will find out that you and they might share the same interest in certain things. Perhaps they like golf and reading like you do. Perhaps they are into deep-dish pizzas like you. Or perhaps they think that the Golden State Warriors are the best NBA team now like you do. And so on.

The point is that there are some commonalities you share with that other person, which allows you to connect with them. This is rather important as you would have to remember that everyone within one room is totally different from one another. Perhaps others have bigger savings on the bank, others have multiple degrees, and others have an intimate knowledge of car engines, and so on.

But, at the very least, everyone can relate to each other by what they like or don't like. Use these shared interests and viewpoints as a foundation of sorts for any potential relationship you will build.

## 5. Mind Your Body Language

Your non-verbal messages also play a role in you establishing rapport. For starters, your hand gestures—from the firmness of your handshake to the things that you do with your hands while a person is talking—can tell them whether or not you genuinely want to be left alone in their presence.

The way people react with hand gestures is hardwired to our evolution as our caveman ancestors often gauge how threatening another human is by what is in their hands.

To be seen as non-threatening, keep your hands at a comfortable distance from your body but make them as relaxed as possible. This means that you should not conceal your hands inside your pockets or fold your arms.

One foolproof way to make yourself less intimidating is to simply mirror what the other person is doing. If they are relaxed in their chair, be relaxed in yours. If they are eating while conversing, do so as well.

This is a rather helpful trick for you as your focus shifts from trying to make an impression to blending in with the general mood of the room. You will be surprised to see how many non-verbal cues you can pick up if you are not too overly cautious with your body language.

## 6. Tone Matters

The way you say things can also lend a hand to your impression of other people. A loud and booming tone is often seen as either boisterous or confident, while a quiet and softer tone is seen as shy and reserved.

This is also important, especially when you are responding to other people. If you tend to shout out your words, you are perceived as a person who lacks control. But if you are too soft-spoken, then you are perceived as someone who generally lacks confidence.

As such, your only solution here is to be aware of your tone and voice. If you are not sure what tone to use in a situation, use something calm and collected. This is vital in business meetings and important deals.

The FBI has been using the calm and collected voice to diffuse high-tension situations like a hostage-taking. By lowering their voice to something calm and non-threatening, they tend to help in calming the hostage-taker, so they don't do something drastic. Use this voice when approaching potential contacts to give the impression that you are in control without being domineering about it.

### 7. Always Project Confidence

It is human nature to gravitate towards people who are passionate, positive, and confident. It is the first thing that people often look for when searching for friends or, better yet, suitable life partners.

In the first few seconds of meeting, you will be judged as either an equal, an inferior, or a superior depending on your confidence. So, how do you project confidence? It is all in how you carry yourself. A confident person has an upright statute with shoulders down, chest forward, and chin up. The hands are also visible as if welcoming a person.

As for eye contact, it should be straight and can lock gazes with another person within two to three seconds after meeting them. And then there is the assertiveness of how you say things. In essence, you must speak your mind in a manner that is clear and forceful without being too intimidating.

One good example here is when then-presidential candidate John F. Kennedy appeared in a series of live debates again then-incumbent President Richard Nixon. JFK exuded confidence and was rather smart and articulate in all of his responses. His charisma was to the point that he was the more presidential-looking candidate out of the two. Nixon, for some reason, looked pallid and fumbled through his lines. Eventually, JFK's impressive performance in his public appearance won him the Presidency.

**Something to Remember:** Like everything else in this book, building rapport takes practice. For your projection, you can practice in front of your mirror. Rehearse some lines and responses in advance and address any flaws you might spot as you speak. If done right, you should easily endear yourself with people in a room minutes after meeting them.

### Humor and Why it Works

You have seen countless examples of people gravitating towards an individual who can tell jokes. All they need is one punchline and boom, they have endeared themselves to ten or twenty people.

So why is humor a rather effective tool in any human social interaction? Surprisingly, the answer lies in biology.

When the brain detects something stimulating like humor, it sends signals to the body to release endorphins all throughout the body. Endorphins are pheromones that do a lot of things, but the one that is most relevant to conversations is that it helps the body relax and feel good. And when the person feels good and is relaxed, they are more open to any suggestion or proposition.

In practice, here's how it works: imagine that the person you are talking to just had one of the worst days of their life. Their car got towed, the neighbor's dachshund just dug another hole in the backyard, and to top it all, they overcooked their sausages, so now they have to settle for stale cereal for breakfast.

And here comes you, with another thing that might add to their burden. Perhaps it's just you telling them that their mail was sent to your address or that you want to borrow some money. Chances are that you will be rejected way before you can even say something.

However, if you come to them in a manner that makes them lighten up for just a bit, then your overall presence around them would be more welcomed. The same goes for interpersonal relations. With humor, you can diffuse tense situations while also making your presence a valuable one within any group.

And this does beg the question: How do you become a natural jokester? Here are a few tips to help you with that.

### 1. Know When and What to Joke About

When it comes to jokes, there is acceptable humor, and then there is offensive humor. When diffusing situations, you might opt for the kind of humor that offends the very least.

Take the time to analyze what kind of humor works in that situation. You need to determine whether or not you should be cracking jokes in that situation.

Of course, this does not mean that vulgar jokes do not have their place in any group interaction. Doctors and lawyers, for example, are down with some nasty jokes given the nature of their work, but the same could not be said for younger folk.

You only have to make sure that whatever you are going to say next is going to be received positively in any situation that you are in, especially statements that were supposed to lighten up the mood.

### 2. Be Subtle About it

You will have to understand that there is intelligent humor, and then there is low-brow humor. In any given situation, you'd rather stick with the one that is impactful and relevant, which is why you'd pick the former over the latter.

Intelligent humor does not mean that you must start quoting smart shows like *Rick and Morty* or *Monty Python* to be funny. It is all about finding a way to inject your jokes into conversations as if they were a natural part of it. It also helps if you could come up with an observational, on-the-spot quip there to help the other person feel at ease (if they need to, of course).

### 3. Curb that Inhibition

Surprisingly enough, one key trick that helps you become an effective communicator will also help you in becoming a bit more humorous: get rid of that shyness. This is where your confidence as a person will come into play as you have to deliver the punchline in one single stroke.

The best kind of jokesters out there are those that can deliver one good line and can recover from a bad one without fumbling over their lines or stammering.

Of course, you have to practice on your line delivery in order to get good at it. But just remember that funny people are rarely shy, and those that are often use their shyness as a punchline. Whatever your style, you should have enough confidence to say what you want to say and maintain a straight face while doing it.

**4. Get Some Inspiration**

Here's a secret comedians wouldn't want you to know: Most of them were inspired by previous generations of comedians. The *Monty Python* crew inspired the writers of *South Park* and Eric Andre while Red Foxx and George Carlin can be considered as the predecessors of the likes of Dave Chappelle and Bill Burr.

The point is that humor does not have to be original to be funny. Chances are that your audience has yet to hear about that joke, so it's okay to use some lines. After all, people will remember you more for the connections you made and less from the jokes you cracked. Just make some changes here and there to be relevant to the topic at hand.

## Networking Tips

The natural consequence of learning how to interact with people is that you end up making important connections in every aspect of your life. A network, if you will, that will help you get the resources and information you need to achieve more out of a single day.

Maintaining one is rather easy as long as you are agreeable and know how to convey your thoughts and feelings politely. It's in building one where the challenges are usually located. To build your network, there are a few tips that you have to keep in mind.

**1. Make a Good First Impression**

The impression that you leave on introducing yourself to people can determine how successful you can be in starting a relationship with them.

For starters, you have to look the part. Look like someone that people would love to communicate with at first glance. Second, you have to freshen up on your social skills. Just don't do anything that will give people the idea that you are sloppy and messy by default.

**2. Practice Your "Elevator Pitch"**

The elevator pitch is a technique that salespeople use to promote themselves and their products within seconds after meeting a person. It doesn't have to be something elaborate, but what is necessary is for you to lay out the essential information about yourself within a minute or so.

It could look something like this:

"Hi, I'm (state your name). I'm a (state your credentials). I've noticed that you are (state something that you noticed about the person). I have been (state your experience). Maybe we could talk about this matter more. Here's my number (give your business card if you have one). I look forward to hearing from you."

Within a minute or so, you would have told that person who you are why they should start a relationship with you. This one takes practice, but you are bound to engage in conversations without leaving your would-be contacts confused or annoyed.

### 3. Avoid Small Talk

Small talk is something that should be reserved only among friends and colleagues. It is something that should not be the core topic of your conversation with a would-be contact.

More often than not, you will encounter networking opportunities in meetings, conferences, and other events. As such, you should be doing plenty of research before heading to these events. And if you do meet that contact on a chance encounter, just pay attention to what they are saying. Your conversation with them is bound to yield a lot of information that could be helpful to you.

### 4. Pull Out

You just had a rather productive conversation with a potential new friend. Now what? Your ability to excuse yourself out of any conversation would matter here because nobody is ever going to tell you that this conversation is over at all times.

You can make up any excuse like you having to go to the bathroom or moving to another group to see another friend. All of these are valid, so long as they give the people you meet the subtle hint that your dialogue with them is over.

And avoid "dead air" where you and that person you were talking to stare at each other, saying nothing for entire seconds. Once you excuse yourself, go in the general direction of where you said you were going.

### The Bottom Line

Creating those bonds is easy if you break everything down to their most basic components. Different people have different ways to perceive things and relay such information to you. This means that any conversation could go anywhere, depending on what you are and the kind of people that you are talking to.

Conversations involving the same topic can go differently, and that depends on the overall mood of the room. You can use this to your advantage by learning how to defuse tensions or just give off a confident and welcoming vibe.

Remember that just because you have an inkling of how people think and feel, it does not mean that your conversations with them would go 100% smoothly. There is always that chance of failure and misunderstanding, depending on how you carry yourself and come into the conversation.

Either way, your primary strategy towards interpersonal communications is always the same: Adjust to the things around you and not the other way around. You must be flexible enough to change some elements in your approach while still being confident enough to carry yourself out of any situation in the most direct manner possible.

If done right, you should come out of any conversation successfully. And by successfully, that means getting what you want out of the conversation while also building relationships that could last for as long as humanly possible.

# Chapter 5: Dealing with "Noise" Part I: Communicating When Angry

*"Between what is said and not meant, and what is meant and not said, most of love is lost."*
*-Khalil Gibran-*

In a perfect world, we only have to say what we are thinking, and everybody understands us. Better yet, everybody is in the right mood to receive messages and respond in a way that is healthy and conducive to a healthy conversation.

But we don't live in a perfect world now, do we?

More often than not, you will encounter situations where the chance of miscommunication is quite high. All it takes is one poorly-worded response or a blazing temper to derail a conversation, preventing you and the other person from reaching an understanding.

Why is this so? To answer that question, let us break down the concept of communication into its basic elements.

Let us say that communication is a network of nodes comprised of several connections, namely:

- Source
- Sender
- Medium
- Receiver
- Outcome

In practice, the source gives a message to the sender who then relays it to the receiver via their chosen medium, like verbal, written, or electronic. The receiver then interprets the message, which results in the conversation generating an outcome.

However, here is the problem: In the nodes of the sender, medium, and receiver lies a certain element called "noise." How great this noise's influence is in each node will determine the outcome. If the noise is too great, then the outcome is miscommunication or misunderstanding. If not, then it results in an understanding.

The process can be further simplified in the following table.

```
   Source                           Outcome
     │                                 ▲
     ▼                                 │
   Sender  →   Medium    →   Receiver
                 ▲
                 │
               Noise
```

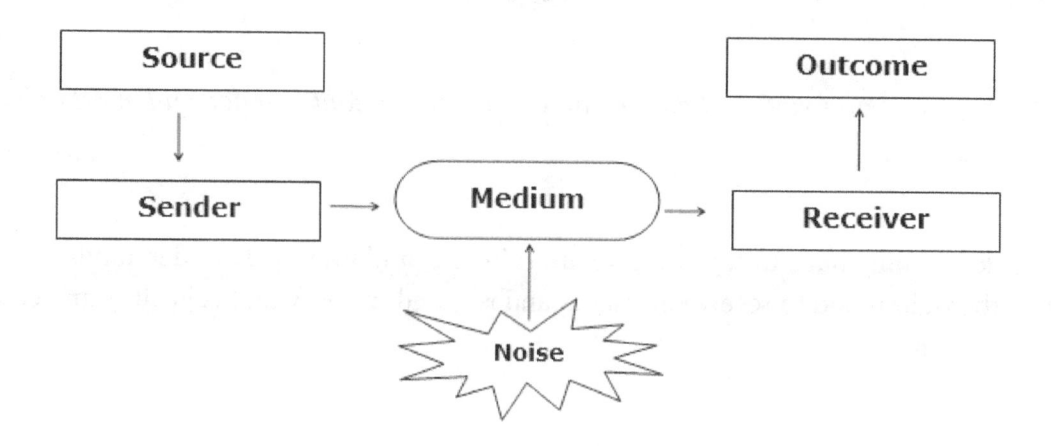

So what's the noise in the medium that ruins your chances of a successful communication opportunity with people? It can take on many forms, and this chapter will be dedicated to identifying the most egregious ones you will regularly encounter.

## Dealing with Stress and Anger

First things first—when we talk about noise, we are not talking about that physical auditory barrage of sounds that hinders your ears from hearing anything important. At least, not technically.

Noise is something that can effectively disrupt the transmission of information between the sender, the medium, and the receiver.

In that regard, it is best to start with the noise that is within your sphere of absolute control (i.e., the ones that exist within you.) Internal noise is simply the distractions inside your body and mind that prevent you from properly processing external information.

Internal noise can include something as simple as being tired or having an upset stomach or becoming drunk. Any change in your body is undoubtedly going to impede the way you communicate, think, and feel.

But, in this regard, it is best to deal with the most common and intense internal noises: stress and anger.

Being under pressure is a universal feeling among humans. However, it does change the way we communicate and, for most of the time, it is for the worst.

On the flip side, no good has ever come out of suppressing your anger and frustrations. Instead, you should learn how to act on feelings of anger and stress in more positive ways. Here are a few tips to remember.

### 1. Change Your Perceptions

The thing with anger and stress is that everything is so raw that it only takes one small push for you to blow up. Under stress and intense anger, people tend to become overreactive.

Here's an example: Imagine that you just came home from a bad day at work. Then, you notice that a few things were misplaced, your partner has not yet made dinner, and there is unwashed laundry on the sofa.

So, to no surprise to anyone, you blow up. You might start with the typical "Am I the only who notices things here?!" and then proceed on a long tirade with increasing intensity, cadence, and profanity. To put it colorfully, you overreacted.

The best way to deal with your stress first is to control how you react to stressors. As you are about to blow your lid off, try replacing your increasingly negative thoughts with more rational ones. You might start rationalizing that maybe your housemates were busy or that the laundry had been there for a few minutes before your arrival. Any excuse would work so as long as your brain starts thinking that maybe, just maybe, you don't need to start yelling.

## 2. Always Plan for the "Difficult" Scenarios

One good practice you must maintain is identifying what scenarios tend to rustle your jimmies the most. Perhaps it's an angry customer. Or perhaps it's people misplacing stuff at home. Or being stuck in traffic next to a loud, obnoxious motorist.

Whatever sets you up, you have to identify it. This is so that you can prepare a script of sorts of what to do when you find yourself in that situation again. This way, you can let the raw emotions go over you while you maintain composure. Rehearse this script as often as you can, and you might find yourself becoming more refined with your angry outbursts.

## 3. Express Yourself (Positively)

This might be the most challenging aspect of your exercise but, whatever you do, refrain from performing any act or saying any statement that you will regret later on.

As you are about to go off, try to anchor yourself to that script you have made. Depending on your script, you might remove yourself from the room or start counting to ten. The goal here is to let that surge of high emotion go through you long enough for your more rational side to take control again.

In this aspect, it is also a good idea to address your aggressive tendencies. You might have a knack towards clutching something until it snaps, punching a wall, or dropping some F-bombs when you are angry. These are natural expressions of anger and stress, but they will leave a nasty impression on anyone who witnesses your outburst.

If possible, replace your aggressive actions with subtler and more positive actions to channel your rage through.

## 4. Deal with Resentment

Resentment can be best described as any lingering negative emotion you have over a situation or a person. If not addressed, it could progressively change the way you communicate around a certain person, group, or situation.

To deal with resentment, you have to accept the fact that everyone is different. What they do and how they choose to interact with you is beyond your control. As such, you should not be holding any negative feelings for things that you are not mostly responsible for. By addressing any lingering resentment, you can quickly move on to more pressing tasks and interactions in your schedule.

### 5. Maintain an "Anger Diary"

Writing things down can help you deal with your anger in two fronts. First, it's cathartic as you are pouring all your anger into something that is not destructive. And think about it, the only person who is going to get potentially hurt by what you just wrote is someone who would accidentally peruse your notes.

Second, writing taps into the more rational part of your brain. This means that you allow yourself to organize your thoughts and rationalize why things happened in that particular sequence. Thus, you can make a better judgment call and determine whether or not your anger was founded on something reasonable.

### 6. Use "I Feel" Statements

It is easy to get accusatory when you are angry. As such, you tend to start your statements with a "you," which can be perceived as a personal attack. Depending on the other person's personality, this could be the start of a conversation with an ever-escalating level of aggression.

Yes, there is no denying that you are angry, but you can be less abrasive about it with your choice of words. Start with something like "I feel" because this still validates your anger but does not attack the other person whatsoever. This way, they will be more open to what you have to say.

### 7. Always, Always Stick to the Subject

When angry, it is easy to go on a tirade where you list everything that has ticked you off to that point. However, this does not help with any conversation you have as anyone listening to you will now struggle in finding the context of what you are trying to say.

A lot of self-restraint is necessary here as you would want your listeners to exactly know what made you feel this way. Stick with the issue that is most relevant to the situation and refrain from digressing. The less you rant and rage, the quicker it is for people to understand what you are trying to communicate.

## For Adversarial Relations

Let us say that you have a long-running confrontational relationship with someone. As such, both of you cannot properly hear each other and resort to being defensive, dismissive, and argumentative with each other.

In essence, dealing with your internal noise is no longer enough. Building trust with that long-standing thorn in your side must be done over a series of conversations.

To facilitate a healthy line of communication with special cases, you have to consider the following.

### 1. Write a Special Script

First, you have to identify which people you tend to have the most disagreements with in a room. Identify what they do or say that could set you off and what you, in turn, do and say that could set them off.

At the same time, try to anticipate what they feel and need in every conversation that you have with them and prepare some responses. However, it is best that you do not assume what they want from that encounter. Your script should be something that, at the very least, accommodates what that person could possibly want out of you whenever they have to talk with you.

## 2. Explain

The best way to make a person trust you gradually is to be as transparent as possible. When you are the one approaching them, wave a proverbial white flag by stating why you want to talk with them. This, at the very least, gives them the signal that you come in peace.

As for your conversation, it is best that you stick to the facts and carefully lay out your proposal. And if you do find yourself getting incensed by their response, stick to your reasons without becoming too aggressive. And if things do fail, just say something like, "I respect your views, and I think it's best that we stop here," and ask them if they want to do this again later on. Perhaps cooler heads will prevail next time.

## 3. Take Turns

One good strategy in talking with a person you are predisposed to get angry at is to treat the entire conversation as a game of chess. No, this is not about the mind games (not outwardly, at least) but is all about letting each party finish a turn before the other makes a move.

This means that nobody is to interject while the other person is talking. Cutting a person off mid-sentence tends to be perceived negatively, which can escalate aggression. If possible, have another person facilitate the conversation, warning both parties to respect the other person's turn and signifying when they can say something in response.

It is a bit tedious and more demanding of a conversation, mind you. But it does help in ensuring that any anger does not surface and derail the entire dialogue for everyone.

## To Summarize

There is no doubt that being under stress and getting angry is a lousy experience. However, it is not the sensation itself that sucks. Rather, it is the potential you have to create interpersonal conflict while in such a frenzied state. Then again, there are times when you have to talk to someone even when you are mad.

The primary strategy here is to do a bit of self-censoring. Get to the point immediately and say things in the most direct and passive of statements possible. Do it right, and you will not say anything regretful by the time your anger has finished its course through your system.

# Chapter 6: Dealing with "Noise" Part 2: In Case of Miscommunication

*"Well, it's really no use our talking in the way we have been doing if the words we use mean something different to each of us...and nothing."*

-Malcolm Bradbury

Once you have dealt with your own "noise," the next part involves dealing with the noise coming from the transition of your ideas to the receiver. And this is where things get crucial as an improper delivery could lead to an entirely different (and mostly negative) outcome.

Miscommunication is rife in places where a constant need to convey information is necessary, like a workplace. The problem with miscommunicating, however, is not limited to the fact that the information was not received properly. It could also be the source of interpersonal conflicts which, in turn, prevents future healthy interactions.

As such, the remedy here is to avoid miscommunication. But how should you do it?

## Why Does Miscommunication Occur?

The first thing that we have to address in this part is why we tend to miscommunicate. To do that, let us go back to your previous table.

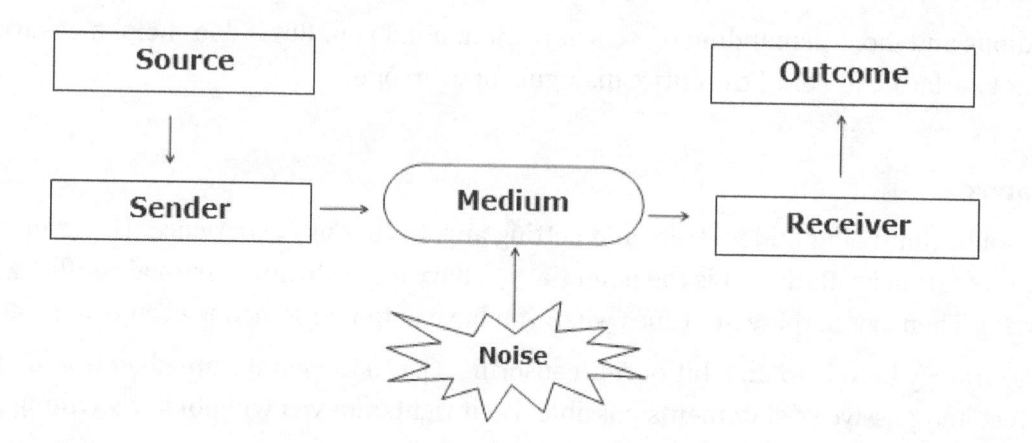

```
Source                              Outcome
  ↓                                    ↑
Sender  →  Medium  →  Receiver
              ↑
            Noise
```

You might notice that the noise element is pointed directly at the medium, but make no mistake—that noise can appear in different nodes across the process.

To elaborate, here are some possible scenarios where miscommunication can occur.

## 1. The Wrong Source and Destination

For example, you tell someone in your workplace that he has to do something. But what if you have no authority to tell that person to do anything? The end result is that the person does nothing in response to the message.

Here is another scenario: what if you tell someone to do something but that something is not in that person's jurisdiction? Perhaps you are asking them to look at a report from production, but that person is in marketing. The end result is that the person would find someone else to do what you asked.

## 2. An Unspecified Message

In this aspect, the most common mistake is not specifying exactly what you want. For example, you told a subordinate to finish a report on something but failed to specify to whom it should be sent to (i.e., you). The result is that person would do the report and then submit it to the channels he usually sends his reports to but not directly to your office.

Or, more specifically, what if you never specified the period that the data to be processed should come from? Chances are that person will prepare an extensive report filled with data that you have no need for right now.

## 3. The Wrong Signal

What if you asked someone to buy you a book on Arizona's penal code but forgot to specify that it has to be the most recent edition of the author? That person would just grab a copy of whatever book fits your description, but you would not be happy because it is the wrong edition or the wrong book overall.

Or how about if you asked for a report but did not specify the format? The people you asked for that report would use the format they are most comfortable with or send you multiple formats of the same report.

## 4. The Wrong Medium

Here, you try to reach out to someone in a medium that they either don't use frequently or is inappropriate to the message. For example, you want to address a private matter to someone, but you sent it through the company mail.

Or, more commonly these days, you want to settle an issue with someone over social media but, instead of privately messaging them, you accidentally tagged their profile in a public post. In either case, the receiver would respond negatively to the message, no matter how good your intentions were.

## 5. Messaged Alter by Noise

This is all too common in electronic media. For example, you ask someone over a video call to prepare you a report, but a change in internet speeds caused that part of your message to get garbled.

Or, even more commonly, what if you meant for a person to do one thing, but you inadvertently typed out a command to do the other? Another common example here is if you intended to send a message to person A but tagged or sent it to person B or C instead.

In these scenarios, the message is either given a poor response or not responded to at all.

### 6. Wrong Reception

In this instance, the receiver successfully got the message. However, they failed to properly interpret it, resulting in the improper response.

For example, you are dating someone, and you proposed to them. They said "not now," much to your dismay. However, in your mind, they said "no." Technically, they insinuated for you do this again some time later, but your mind perceived the denial as one that involves the relationship, not the proposal itself. So, you misinterpreted the "not now" and got angry about it.

This is also common in the workplace when employees, too eager to please their superiors, might do something without going into the assignment details further. As such, they might do something with the wrong parameters. Either way, what they did is not something that you exactly asked for.

## Preventing Miscommunications

The most sensible thing that you could do is to make sure that you are properly understood to prevent any miscommunication. Here's how.

### 1. Be Clear and Concise

Differences in interpretation occur when parties fail to grasp the actual directives, provided that there were any given. It is important that you say what you want to say in the most direct manner possible and using the most common of terms.

Avoid speaking randomly or in circles so as not to baffle your audience. Also, digressing from the issue or giving away too many tiny details tends to confuse people as well.

If possible, set up a clear narrative of what you are saying. You can use a step-by-step module so people can easily connect the dots and do exactly what you are asking of them. The goal here is to make your message follow a simple, short, and clear line so that everyone is on the same page when trying to understand you.

### 2. Never, Ever, Assume

There is no bigger culprit to miscommunication than assuming. For instance, if you asked a person why he didn't do exactly what you asked, 90% of the time, his answer will be because he assumed that it was supposed to be done this way. Or you might assume that a person has understood your message in the way that you intended for it to be understood.

Assumption in communication occurs when all participants interpret things according to their own understanding and perspective. And since both parties failed to relay and interpret signals, conflict tends to arise from assuming.

Before ending a conversation, always ask if that person has fully grasped what you are asking of them. This way, if ever failure arises, the blame is not on you but on the person listening to you.

On the flip side, if you are the one listening, remember to do the active listening technique and take time to comprehend the core issue of the conversation along with the set of instructions given to you.

## 3. Adjust your Communication Style

As was stated, people have different ways of absorbing and processing information. Some people need to be instructed to the letter and do well working under specific guidelines. Others want to communicate via email and others through the phone or directly.

Others are best when they can receive instructions in writing while others can do with being told once. The point is that people eventually come to an understanding with you at their own pace and style.

Be mindful of the preferred style or medium that your audience has with receiving messages. From that point on, all you have to do is to re-mold your message so that it fits what they are used to the most.

## 4. Know that Text Media has its Limits

Text, emails, and other forms of electronic media are the most popular forms of communication now. However, they also tend to be the most problematic right now. You might be surprised at how entire relationships can be ruined just because of one poorly worded tweet or status update. Even entire careers and reputations went down in flames because of the things those people said online.

What you have to remember is that text has two disadvantages. First, it cannot carry the subtler elements of communications like nuance, context, and even sarcasm. Second, it has an element of perpetuity to it, so anything poorly-worded you say now will come back to haunt you in a few weeks or years.

The strategy here, then, is to think before you click. Make sure that your choice of words have been thoroughly thought out and your overall message leaves no room for interpretation, especially negative ones. If you check your message one to three times, then and only then can you send it to your intended audience.

## 5. Check and Follow Up

If the conversation is rather long, it might be a bit too pointless to ask them for clarification once and only at the ending. This is quite true in situations where you have to talk to multiple people over a long period of time, like in a class or a large symposium.

At every point of your talk, stop the conversation and ask whether or not they understood that part of your discussion. Also, ask them if there are any terms or directives that they do not understand properly. This will give them the chance to raise any questions that they have in mind and have the same answered, reaching an understanding with you.

One nifty trick you can do here is to do a summary. This allows you to go through every major point of the discussion without having to spend another hour or two explaining what has already been covered.

For situations when you are giving directives to people, make sure to do a follow-up. Check on them regularly to see how they are progressing and address any issue that they might have with the task as it progresses. A follow-up is your way of showing that you are willing to go above and beyond the call of duty to make sure that you and the person can reach an understanding.

## A Miscommunication Recovery Plan

What happens, then, if there is a misunderstanding? Is that conversation a lost cause? Not really.

There is still a way to prevent a total breakdown of communication and clear up the misunderstanding. What it requires from you is the ability to act and adjust quickly.

Just remember that there is no hard and fast rule for recovering from misunderstandings. That being said, there are a few tips that you could easily apply in your interactions. Here are some of them:

### 1. Acknowledge the Breakdown

First and foremost, you have to quickly realize that things are not going the way you wanted them to happen. Nobody's getting what they wanted, and the entire dialogue is about to devolve into a shouting match.

You have to know at which point things are about to go awry so that you can immediately adopt a de-escalation stance. If you are fast enough, you can quickly pull the communication back to a more productive direction.

### 2. Set the Goalpost

In order to help the dialogue go back to something more conducive to an understanding, you have to have a guide. This is where a goal will come into play as it helps you direct your efforts in the communication, so everything remains productive.

In most cases, your goal in any communication is an understanding. Being vindicated, proven right, or even "winning" is not something that you ought to aim for unless, of course, you are in a debate or a trial. In every interaction you have, the goal is to always make that other person see your perspective and you of theirs.

Keep this goal in mind and you could guide every word that you say to make that relationship functional.

### 3. Find the Point of Failure

You have to also identify where exactly in the dialogue did things get out of hand. Was it something you said, or was it a gesture you made? Was it some throwaway quip you uttered that set the other person off?

Alternatively, what did that person say or do that started this problem? You have to find this exact point where the communication broke down so you can start fixing it. Perhaps you might want to apologize and say you did not mean what you said or did.

Once that point has been cleared up, your dialogue should go back to its original course as planned.

### 4. Behave Assertively

One other useful thing that you can do to prevent things from breaking down is to be mindful of your reactions towards anything offensive that the person might say. For example, if that person is criticizing your views or correcting you on your mistakes, the best that you could do is to remain objective and acknowledge their input.

What you should never do, on the other hand, is flare up and meet the aggression with your own aggression. This results in an escalation, which leads to conflict.

Undoubtedly, the ability to remain composed even as your opinions and character are being deconstructed in your face is a hard skill to learn. But it is eventually learned, and you can maintain at least a decent level of surface-level civility to keep your interpersonal relationships from breaking down further.

### 5. Do Not Let Others Join in on the Fight

When clearing up a misunderstanding, you should limit the involvement to you and the people that were directly tied to the incident. Do not let other people join in as they also have their own opinions, which could fan the flames of conflict even further.

Talk to the involved persons directly and, if possible, in a discreet place. More prying eyes lead to more miscommunication. And miscommunication does have a nasty habit of feeding on itself.

### 6. Be the Bigger Person

This is perhaps the most crucial lesson you will have to learn with conflict management; you are not infallible. Your opinions are not always right. Your advice is not always solicited. And your comments are not always tactful. You are human, after all, which means there is always a part of you that makes mistakes.

So, what you have to do is to own up to anything that you might have done to contribute to the misunderstanding instead of looking for something to blame. With your ego out of the way, the path towards a peaceful resolution is now clear.

### To Conclude

The one element that will give you the most worry about miscommunication is its prevalence. It is surprisingly easy for people to misunderstand each other due to the high potential of failure at every point of the communication pathway. If one element is wrong or tampered by noise, then the outcome is not going to be to anyone's liking.

As such, you have to be mindful of every element in the communication process. Find out where a potential breakdown could occur and be quick enough to patch it up. If everything is done right, you could avoid a misunderstanding at best or prevent things from escalating further, at least.

# Chapter 7: Dealing with "Noise" Part 3: Interactions in the Toxic Realm

*"Sadly, whenever I make my opinions more important than the difficult people God made, I turn the wine back into water."*

*-Bob Goff*

More often than not, the biggest problem you have to deal with is not the noise coming from the medium or yourself. It's the noise coming from the receiver. Perhaps they did not understand you fully, or they misinterpreted what you just said. Either way, a breakdown of communication is sure to happen.

The best part of dealing with noise coming from the receiver is that it is easy to handle so as long as you maintain a confident stance and stick to reason and logic. In time, you would win these people over and reach an understanding with them in every conversation.

But what if the receiver itself is not hindered by noise, but IS the noise? What if their personality is rather abrasive to the point of toxicity? Can you still get through a conversation with them without being run over? The answer is yes, and there are a few things that you have to keep in mind.

Wading through a toxic interaction can be difficult if you do not know who you are dealing with. Toxic people can come in any shape or size, but they often fall into six distinct categories.

What will follow is a series of descriptions of what forms a toxic person can take, what they can do to any conversation, and what you can do to deal with them.

## The Naysayer

The most favorite word of this person is "No!" To them, that short, one-syllable utterance has so much power in the sense that it can cut off any dialogue short. And aside from any interaction, their statements could even dissuade you from doing anything you have planned for yourself.

You have a good idea? Too bad, it's not going to work. You're going to college? Tough luck, you'll quit in a semester or two. How's that new job of yours? I heard it's not paying much. And so on and so forth.

Whether they are aware of it or not, the naysayer's primary export is negativity of varying scale and intensity. That does not mean, however, they are ill-willed towards you. They are just inclined to look at life through highly cynical glasses, leading to a rather dour world view.

## How to Deal with Them

More often than not, naysayers have something to contribute and are generally concerned about how you are going to pull things off. So, it is best to let this inner desire shine through their abrasive negativity.

Start by acknowledging their concerns. Say something like, "thank you for your perspective. I do appreciate your concern for me/this project." Now, their negativity is disarmed as the focus now shifts from their comments to their intentions.

Next, you will have to make their intentions actionable. Say something like, "What do you have in mind?" Now, the spotlight is on them to add something to enhance your proposition.

## The Complainer

The difference between a naysayer and a complainer is similar to the difference between a word and a sentence. Where the naysayer says one or a few comments of negativity, the complainer makes a litany of them.

Propose something, and the complainer will tell you five to ten instances why it is wrong and where everything could go wrong. Is there enough budget for this? What about working schedules? All of you are busy enough, so why did management give you this extra burden? Now, they'll have to cancel their schedules for this! And the list goes on.

Another notable element with the complainer is their ability to build momentum. If left to their own devices, their list of worries can increase in intensity. Some of their fears are even so prospective that they could border on the irrational.

## How to Deal with Them

What you will have to understand about complainers is that they are merely venting their frustrations. They are not there to sour the mood for everybody else, at least, not intentionally. This means that it is best to let everything out of their system.

The trick here is where you should let them vent their feelings. If possible, let them do it with you in private. This allows you to discuss such issues with them extensively without putting the group's discussion on hold.

Once they have cooled down and the rational part of their brain kicks in, they can start focusing on addressing actual problems with actual solutions.

## The Shifter

If there was any person in a group that could quickly make a conversation veer off course, it is the shifter. The game plan of the shifter is rather ingenious. All they have to do is to participate and then contribute to the discussion. Shifters are one of the more active communicators out there.

This is where things get tricky; they might add some comments here and there and raise some questions, but whatever they contribute is not relevant to the discussion at all. Soon enough, you will find that your discussion has drifted far away from the core topic. At their worst, the shifter can generate a lot of discussions, but ones that tend to not answer the primary issue you raised.

## How to Deal with Them

Make no mistake. A lot of shifters mean well. The only problem they have is that whatever they have to bring serves no actual purpose to the conversation at hand.

The best way to deal with a shifter is to always ask for a point of order. If the shifter starts raising an issue while another is still active, say something like, "Thank you for the comment. To help in the discussion, please elaborate on how it ties to what we are trying to cover here?"

If that sounds a bit patronizing, then you might need some creativity on your part. Let us say that what the person raised is an issue that will be covered later on, partly or exactly. You could say something like, "That's a great observation. You've figured out something we are going to cover later!"

In both cases, you are trying to give the shifter the help they need to reorganize their thoughts without humiliating them in public.

## The Nitpicker

There is no doubt that getting the details right is important, but the nitpicker obsesses over the minutiae to the point of aggravation. Unlike the naysayer who shoots your ideas wholesale, the nitpicker will be the one to strike at every minute point or detail you raised in the hopes of disarming your argument.

Let us say, for example, that you are arguing with a nitpicker. Suddenly, they criticize you for what you just said because it's the wrong noun or because your grammar is atrocious. Soon enough, you'll be defending your entire argument in depth.

The nitpicker is common in group interactions. They'd be the first to pick up any flaw in your idea and wave it around like a prospector finding gold. If left to their devices, a nitpicker can derail any conversation more than what a shifter could ever hope to achieve.

### How to Deal with Them

The goal of the nitpicker is rather simple: Triumph over their opponents by exposing the flaws in their ideas. It can be petty, but it can also be used on more productive channels.

To do this, you have to make the nitpicker see the bigger picture. When they start scrutinizing the smallest of details, it is your responsibility to snap them back to their senses. Say something like, "Point taken. But first, let us do things step by step."

Or, if you are in an argument with them, say something like, "Noted. Now, let's get back on point." The goal here is to stop the nitpicker from obsessing over the details so that you can quickly go through the entire proposition first.

But do extend an olive branch to these people by assuring them that their observations will be taken into consideration later on. You could even make them a resource person to help you in future projects.

## The "Yes" Man

Eager to please but always failing to deliver, the yes man is someone who wants to fit in in any group or organization. They want to make a good impression, so they agree to any proposition or request you give despite their limitations.

For instance, you request a yes man to do something, and they agree to it. While doing what you asked for, another person asks the yes man to do something, and they agree to it. Then, another person asks the yes man to do something, and they agree to it. And the pattern continues.

There is no doubt that their intentions are noble but, more often than not, they run the risk of overwhelming themselves. At collaborative efforts, this results in something called bottlenecking, where work has to be stopped because one part (or person, in this regard) has gotten clogged up.

### How to Deal with Them

The yes man means well, which is why you'd rather be compassionate with them instead of being argumentative. What you should do to a yes man is encourage them to be as honest and transparent as possible.

Naturally, they'd not do this on their own, which is why you should prod them with some hints here and there. When you ask them to do something, clarify first if their schedule allows for your task. If they say yes, follow up with a question like, "How much time will this need to be finished?" or "Do you have any other task that needs to be done?" or the ever-potent "What do you need to get this task done quickly?"

The goal here is to make the yes man determine for himself whether or not what you are proposing is something that they are amenable with. With all options laid out, the yes man can chart a better course for themselves while still feeling that they are already accepted in the group.

### The Tank

The tank is the epitome of pushy and aggressive behavior. When this person comes through, they'll push their ideas and commands at anyone without any consideration as to what that person feels and thinks. For the tank, it's their way or the highway.

But the tank's bossiness and domineering bravado is not them at their most lethal. The tank loves a fight and will absolutely demolish the opposition through sheer force and a louder, shriller voice. They might even goad others to oppose them for the thrill of it. Once they are done with you, you will feel defeated and confused as to what the hell just happened.

One other element that makes the tank deadly is their relationship with you, professional or otherwise. Perhaps they are your boss or your close friend. They might even be your partner, much to your dismay.

Tanks often occupy the topmost positions in any group due to their personality or were made into tanks because of their position. Either way, you can't just do away with the tank without experiencing some serious consequences in your career and personal life.

### How to Deal with Them

The only way you are going to survive the tank's onslaught is to be methodical and calm as much as you can. First is that you have to brace yourself. Look at them in the eye as they are about to deliver a verbal beatdown. Manage your breathing and temper here as you want to be as calm as possible when the tank is delivering their verbal payload.

As the tank starts belting out their opinions, you must interrupt their attack. You can do this by slowly saying their name over and over again until you get their attention. The goal here is to slowly increase the tone of your voice so the tank can get the idea that you mean business.

After you have stopped the tank dead in their tracks, now is the time to aim and fire. The goal here is to reinforce your bottom line with the right words. Use phrases like "From my viewpoint" or "The way I see it." Do not use "I feel" or "I think" statements because that gives the tank new ammunition to fire at you, restarting their attack.

Once you delivered your line (as calmly and assertively as possible), let the tank have the last word. They might berate you more but, now, they'd look foolish being the only one yelling throughout the exchange.

However, do not close the door on them just yet. Give the tank the opportunity to discuss this matter with you later on.

**To Conclude**

What makes these people difficult to communicate with is not their personality. At least, not technically speaking.

If you think about it, these personalities do bring something of value to the conversation and the relationship. Naysayers, complainers, and nitpickers do help us ground our ambitions and aim for something more realistic and achievable.

Shifters help you explore other avenues to your ideas, giving you access to an even bigger picture than what you originally envisioned. Lastly, tanks and yes men do aim for results that help in motivating people to get things done.

What makes any relationship or interaction with them potentially toxic is in the application of such personalities. In general, they are seen as difficult people because their egos, methodologies, and overall behavior comes at the expense of a good conversation and a chance to build better relationships.

Your goal in communicating with them, then, is not to change how they think or act, but channel all that toxicity into more productive methods. You will find that, with the right re-calibration, these individuals can offer something valuable to you and you to them in return.

# Chapter 8: Having a Great Public Presentation

*"Public Speaking is the art of diluting a two-minute idea with a two-hour vocabulary."*
**-John F. Kennedy**

More often than not, it is speaking in front of an audience where your skills as a communicator will be tested. In fact, you absolutely dread or loathe the idea of having to go up in front of many people, say your piece, and deal with the consequences from that act later.

But knowing how to speak in public is not only easy if you get the basics. It can be even beneficial for you in improving your own skills and make money off it in the end. It could even be a platform where you could sell your ideas and increase your network of contacts.

All of this can be yours if you master the basics of giving a good public presentation. And here's how:

## Preparing your Speech

Every good performance out there starts with a script which is, in this regard, your speech. Writing a speech is basic enough in concept. All you have to do is prepare a monologue where your major points are contained and written in a linear, narrative fashion.

It is in the methodology where things get tricky. If you're not careful, you will end up with something boring. If you try too hard, you end up with something pointless.

As such, you must remember a few tips when writing your speech.

### 1. Know Your Audience

Before anything else, you have to know who you are presenting yourself to. Each audience member has their own needs and expectations, and you must meet those to the best of your abilities.

When preparing your speech, ask the following questions:
- Who is going to listen to my speech?
- What problems do they have that I can solve?
- Are there any considerations about my listeners that I also need to address as well?

For example, if you are speaking in front of a group of doctors, professionals, and academic experts, your presentation is going to be a bit more formal. But if you are talking to regular folks, teenagers, and college students, perhaps a bit more excitement and formality in your message's content will help you.

### 2. Choose a Topic

The subject matter of your presentation should be relevant to the questions you have answered in the previous section. If, for example, your audience expects to learn more about how they are going to close deals, then your topic may revolve around advanced negotiating or sales techniques.

But choosing a topic is the easy part. Now, you will have to give your presentation structure. Depending on the topic, a presentation can last for half an hour to no more than three. Regardless of the allotted time, your presentation should follow a structured narrative.

For solution-centric presentations (ones like "How to..." or something similar), they should follow a sequence like this.

1. **State the Problem**
2. **Support with Facts**
3. **Present the Solution**
4. **Support with Strategies**
5. **Integrate**
6. **Conclude**

You could even use the basic storytelling sequence for your presentation, which is as follows:

1. **Setup**
2. **Conflict**
3. **Middle Point**
4. **Climax**
5. **Resolution**

Also, do not overwhelm your audience with too much information. Just cover the basics of your chosen topic so that your audience can remember a point or two once your presentation is over.

### 3. Research

It is important that you sound as authoritative as possible when presenting your ideas. This means that you sound like you have mastered the topic well and are more than able to take on any question in the latter portion of your presentation.

This means that you have to research intently on every piece of information relevant to your topic. If possible, you have to cover every angle regarding the subject matter so you would not be blindsided with a question you have no prepared answer for.

### 4. Write it Down

Once you have the subject matter, the structure, and information, you have to write things down. Here are some tips to remember when creating your speech:

- **Start with an outline:** The outline serves as an introduction of sorts to your audience as to what they can expect to learn from your presentation. On your part, it helps you make the structure of your speech even more tangible so you could easily follow it.
- **Be conversational:** You should write your speech in the same style that you talk. You can even add some small talk here and there and some jokes if it helps in easing the tension between you and your audience.
- **Set up some speaker notes:** These are mini "cue cards" that help you deliver important parts of your presentation. Have them placed anywhere that you can see but beyond the sight of the audience.
- **KISS (Keep it Short and Simple)**: Use short sentences and be specific as possible in your speech. It's not as if you have to recite that material word for word, anyway.

### 5. Bring Some Aids with You

Now, your presentation is not going to be as memorable if you don't use some visuals to get the attention of your audience. While preparing your speech, you should also set up a PowerPoint presentation using the major points in your discussion. Be as visual as possible here, using graphs, images, and other visual media to drive your point across to the audience.

It would also be a good idea to spend a bit on printing handouts. These will summarize your discussion and guide the listener through your presentation and after it.

## Delivery

Now that you have everything needed for your presentation, all that is left to do is to deliver it. This is rather crucial as you will only have one chance to do this presentation. This only means that you have to make a good impression.

To do that, there are a few tips that you must remember:

### 1. Do Not Read

If you can, memorize your presentation. And if you can't, you can always use your speaker notes or your prepared speech.

What is to be avoided here is to show that you are reading from something while conveying your ideas. Audiences will know if you are reading because your head is lowered and your eyes are fixed on something.

Just memorize your speech as much as you can and refer only to your material if you get stuck. And if you do find yourself getting stuck, there is always the option to improve (more on this later). The audience wouldn't know that you are fumbling if you know how to recover quickly from a blunder.

## 2. Practice

So how do you memorize your speech and prevent yourself from going off-script? The answer is to practice your material.

Spend the few days before the presentation going through your material. It helps you feel calm, get comfortable with your presentation, and find out how you can refine your script to fit with the time allotted to you.

## 3. Dress for the Occasion

It goes without saying that you have to look your best but do not overdress to the point of being uncomfortable. A suit and tie combo are enough, but some speakers nowadays opt for more "casual" attire in the vein of Steve Jobs or Mark Zuckerberg.

Either way, if you are not sure, ask the event organizer what the expected attire will be of the audience. This way, you can match what you are wearing with their overall getup to be as comfortable when delivering your speech.

## 4. Mind Your Posture

Try to act as naturally as you can but maintain control over your body's movements. Stand straight and keep your head up so as to control your nerves and breathe regularly.

And even if you do make some mistakes, keep on going. Nobody but you would know that you've made a mistake so as long as you don't show it.

## 5. Have Some Enthusiasm

The one thing that you will have to remember is that excitement is contagious. With the right amount of enthusiasm, a speaker can build hype for any subject matter, even boring and complicated ones.

One great example of this is Carlos Matos, who presented BitConnect to an audience in the late 2010s. The offer itself can be dubious in hindsight now and the premise boring, but the way Matos draws up hype as he sings, yells, and builds on his energy in front of hundreds of people is effective, if not memorable.

Here's the video if you want to watch how he drums up interest for a premise that would have otherwise bored people out of their minds: https://www.youtube.com/watch?v=vabXXkZjKiw.

The point is that if you are excited about the topic, your audience will be as well.

## Common Public Speaking Pitfalls

Even with the right preparation and the right setup for good delivery, there is still that chance that you are going to muck up the execution of your presentation.

There is the off-chance that factors beyond your control were not to your favor for that instance. But, for most of the time, it is because you tend to commit some of the most common public presentation mistakes. They include, but are not limited to, the following.

## 1. Being Too Intelligent-Sounding

It is your goal to be as authoritative as possible when presenting your topic. However, you also run the risk of becoming too "intellectually oriented."

A lot of smart people often commit this mistake and sometimes unintentionally. Their choice of words are too advanced for common folk, their content lacks that emotional involvement, and the tone of their message is too stern or with no passion at all.

Your presentation should have a balance between factual information and emotional investment. Do not forget to add some personal tangents here and there so people can get a glimpse of the person behind the presentation. A joke or two is also good to ease the tension, especially if you have mastered the art of being funny.

And, most important of all, you have to establish that correlation that whatever idea or solution you're presenting will affect the audience on a personal level.

## 2. Getting Stiff

Think of it this way: why are you so comfortable talking with five to ten friends, but you immediately freeze in front of strangers of the same quantity? The source of your problem, then, is not the number of people but your overall level of comfort in them.

It is easy to spot a nervous presenter because their body language is stiff as if somebody glued their elbows and knees shut. However, you can easily remedy this by constantly rehearsing your piece and preparing for every possible query or response.

Use a camera or a mirror so you could see what you are doing as you are delivering that message in your rehearsals. Correct any physical and verbal tic you make and find a way to release all that tension in your upper body. If you are comfortable with your message now, the chances of you successfully delivering your presentation has increased.

And speaking of verbal tics...

## 3. Filler

When we talk about filler, we are referring to those seemingly inconsequential phrases we utter before, during, and after every sentence we say. Here are some of the most popular fillers in the English language.

| Sounds | Phrases | Words |
|--------|---------|-------|
|        |         |       |

| | | |
|---|---|---|
| Um | I think.... | Okay |
| Hmm | You know? | So |
| Uh | What I am trying to say is... | Like |
| Er | You see... | Basically |
| Mm-hmm | I mean... | Actually |
| Uh-huh | At the end of the day... | Literally |
| | Believe me... | Seriously |
| | I suppose | Essentially |
| | Kind of/Kinda | Quite |
| | It is what it is... | Reasonably |
| | Or something | Well |
| | Stuff like that | Honestly |

Fillers tend to happen because your brain is trying to catch up with the speed of your mouth. They are essentially non-silent pauses so your brain can reorganize itself and continue with the presentation.

They only become problematic if their frequency increases. Some unprepared speakers even have three to four filler words and phrases for a single sentence, which breaks immersion.

Again, your remedy here is to practice your material. Internalizing the points of your presentation and mastering the cues you have set up can help you prevent your presentation from being filled with too many unnecessary pauses.

### 4. A Lame Opening

How you start your presentation can make or break the entire endeavor. A common bad habit among public speakers is to meander in their first parts. They might tell a joke, or ramble for several seconds, or apologize profusely for some bad attempt at self-deprecation. All of these tend to fail at getting the attention of the audience.

To avoid this, open your presentation with a bang. You don't have to do something bombastic, mind you. What you need is a good pitch.

Start with some engaging story or tell a startling statistic. Better yet, open your presentation with a thought-provoking question. These tend to get your audience's attention right from the start and should give you a foundation where you can keep them hooked for the duration of your presentation.

### 5. "Any Questions?"

Most speakers think that this is a good end to their presentation but, in truth, it is not. There are two reasons for this. First, it invites you to a lot of backtracking and deviation, especially if an audience member asks a far-off question.

Second, your audience is still processing everything that you have said. So, more often than not, they don't have any questions that you need to answer. And if you do a Q&A while they are still processing information, you are bound to end your presentation with a dud.

Instead of a Q&A, end your presentation with a call to action and then a closing statement. You can do an open mic period right before ending things. This way, you end your presentation with high energy.

## Storytelling Tips

Storytelling is one of the better strategies you could use to get your audience emotionally invested in what you are trying to say. The reason for this is that a story has everything that a person could want from a narration. It has information, it has that emotional appeal, and it has a sequence that helps people correlate one different idea to another.

The opportunity to tell a story can happen at any moment. As such, you should learn how to tell one effectively, and the tips below will help you.

### 1. Hit the Curiosity Gap

A lot of salespeople get the attention of their audience by opening their pitch with a question. Let us say that you are invited to talk about passive income to college students.

You could say something like, "What If I told you that you could earn money while you are still getting your degree? And what if you could earn this money without doing anything else extra?"

And right at that instance, you have gotten the attention of your audience. To hit that curiosity gap, you have to know the needs of the audience and present them with a situation that they are familiar with.

### 2. VAK

VAK simply means Visual, Audio, and Kinesthetic modalities in your line delivery and is a strategy used by psychologists and therapists to make listeners do what they are saying.

This technique works by helping your listeners put up a "mental picture" of what you are trying to say. If you are just saying stuff without any passion, your listeners could not make that mental picture and thus cannot connect with your presentation.

This is where changes in your tone and the delivery of your line could help you. Visual aids like pictures and videos can also help you here. Even if you are talking about something bland, changes in your VAK modalities can help your audience get emotionally invested in your story.

### 3. Introduce Conflict and Resolution

The two traditional storytelling elements that you have to get right are conflict and resolution. This is because every person out there is familiar with adversity and knows that solutions are the best workaround to anything adverse that they counter.

To do this, always identify a problem and one that your audience can relate to. One mistake that presenters often make is just looking at their presentation from their own perspective or that of their team's. As such, the entire thing could be self-serving or highly intellectual.

You could prevent this by re-framing the way you present your idea to the audience. Bring to their attention a problem that they know and have your ideas provide the solution to that problem.

### 4. Appeal to their Ego

You have to understand that everyone in that audience is there for personal reasons. So why not leverage that self-focused motivation in crafting your story? The one thing about stories like the ones Aesop makes is that they are too "preachy." They tell good lessons, there's no doubt about that, but they always talk to the audience from a certain moral high ground.

Do not do this and, instead, use your stories as a bridge between a person and the solution to their problem. Think of it this way; your stories are going to be more relatable if the endpoint involves your audience learning how to triple their earnings, master the basics of photography, or any other thing that you were proposing at the start of your presentation.

### To Summarize

There is no doubt that public presentation or speaking engagements are nerve-wracking experiences. The fact that you only have one chance to pull it off successfully and that there is a wide margin of error only puts more pressure on your part to get things right.

Before accepting any speaking engagement, you should have set up a system where you can prepare, research, and rehearse your material. At the same time, you must plan for every deviation to your script and set up different fallbacks in the event that they pop up in your discussion.

Then, you have to make yourself comfortable with the prospect of presenting your ideas, feelings, and thoughts to a lot of people. And, in some cases, you must even come to terms with the fact that your presentation will generate a lot of pushback and scrutiny from the public.

And, most important, you have to keep telling yourself that whatever happens from your public presentation will not harm you; at least not directly. And with that, you might start getting comfortable with the concept of presenting yourself before the masses on a regular basis.

# Chapter 9: Feedback: How to Give and Respond to It

*"Criticism, like rain, should be gentle enough to nourish a Man's growth without destroying his roots."*
-Frank A. Clark

Whether we like it or not, feedback is part of our day-to-day communication. It cannot be helped that a major part of our interactions with people revolve around responding to what they said, how they look, and what they are proposing.

As such, the ability to give feedback is an essential skill to master. But an even more important skill is in receiving it and acting on it in the healthiest manner possible.

## Feedback and Your Brain

What exactly happens inside your head when we receive feedback? Chances are that you already feel bad for something that you did, but it is even harder to hear the same thoughts being voiced by others.

And why is this so? Neuroscience tells us that the brain is designed to be a rather protective organ in the sense that it will prioritize its own welfare over others, whether you are aware of it or not.

In essence, it goes out of its way to protect you from negativity and make you feel that you are in the right, even if clearly you are not.

How it works is quite simple: Almost all types of feedback are viewed by the brain as criticism, and criticism, in itself, is perceived as an external threat.

To help you understand this concept better, here's Abraham Maslow's Hierarchy of Needs.

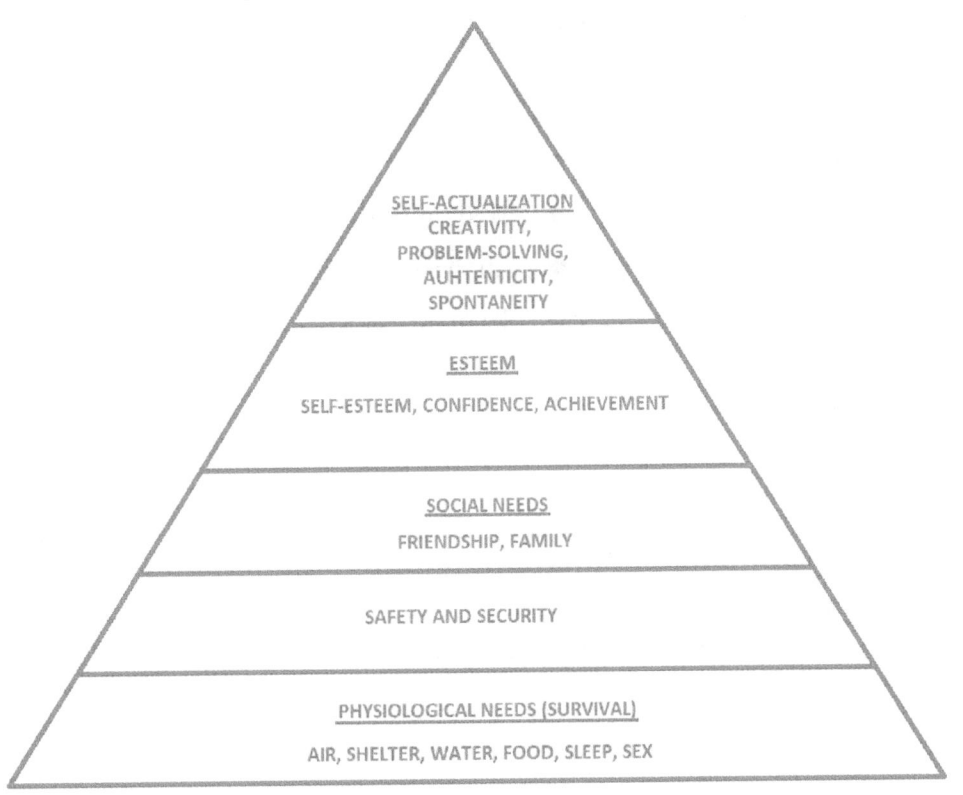

SELF-ACTUALIZATION
CREATIVITY, PROBLEM-SOLVING, AUHTENTICITY, SPONTANEITY

ESTEEM
SELF-ESTEEM, CONFIDENCE, ACHIEVEMENT

SOCIAL NEEDS
FRIENDSHIP, FAMILY

SAFETY AND SECURITY

PHYSIOLOGICAL NEEDS (SURVIVAL)
AIR, SHELTER, WATER, FOOD, SLEEP, SEX

Generally speaking, criticism attacks the upper tiers of the hierarchy, namely self-actualization and esteem. But, for the brain, it feels like it is attacking the lower tiers (i.e., the ones primarily focused on basic survival).

Here's an example: Let us say that you had presented a report and one of your audience members says something like, "Hey, your report had a lot of errors. I couldn't agree with what you were saying because of those."

To them, they were just saying that you need to do more research on your report before presenting it. To you, more often than not, they just attacked your very being and seemingly made your contributions to the group worthless.

One other thing about negativity is that it is retained easier on the brain but often done so inaccurately. An off-hand comment can be remembered as a serious insult or a request to do better as a personal attack depending on your mind frame in that instant.

This is what is called a negativity bias. Our brains tend to process negative feedback more than the positive but in a way that hinders proper development and communication.

Finding a workaround for this bias, then, is important in learning how to give and receive feedback.

## Offering Feedback

### A. Mind Your Purpose

For what particular reason are you giving that feedback? What is your primary goal in telling something to a person who needs to hear it? Here is a list of some of the negative and positive motivations behind giving people feedback that they need to hear.

| **Positive** | **Negative** |
|---|---|
| • Concern for another | • To lash out |
| • A sense of responsibility for that person | • To defend or deflect your behavior |
| • Guidance | • To demoralize |
| • Support | • Appeasement for another party |
| • Encouragement | • To make the person inferior |
| • Discipline | |

It goes without saying that the more positive motivations can result in better-worded feedback. However, just make sure that whatever feedback you give reflects that actual reason as to why you are giving it in the first place.

## 2. Focus on the Act, not the Actor

A crucial step to learn here is to always separate the person from his actions. In essence, try to focus on correcting the action and not the character of the person when giving criticism.

This will separate the person from the situation that they put themselves in. It's not that they are stupid or idiotic or evil, it's just that they did something not exactly good in that instance. This way, they can focus on what you are trying to say without being personally insulted.

## 3. Give a Criticism Sandwich

A method popularized by Cosmetics mogul Mary Kay Ash, the criticism sandwich is feedback that gives a more comprehensive "review" of a person's actions and the situations that they are in. In essence, you give them a detailed appraisal of what just happened so that your feedback will not be seen as entirely negative.

The criticism sandwich follows this sequence:

A. Start with a positive comment

B. Focus on the strong points of the person

C. Support with complements

D. Give the criticism

E. Remind the person of their strong points

F. End on a positive note.

Let us say, for this example, that an employee of yours named Bobby went out and sealed a deal with a client without notifying you first. Perhaps you wanted to talk with that client yourself and had prepared a presentation, but one of your own just did it but without your consent.

Giving a criticism sandwich should sound like this:

"Bobby, thank you for what you did (**positive comment**). Had you not acted this way (**strong point**), we would not have sealed such a deal with that client. Thank you very much (**compliment**).

But next time, please notify me or your team of any interaction you will initiate with our clients. We work as a team and we should communicate as one (**criticism**). But, despite that, you did good and your initiative really helped the team! (**strong point**)

Rest assured that our bosses and we appreciated what you did. You might even have saved your team a lot of time and money in convincing the client to close the deal. Drinks are on me tonight! (**end on a positive note**)."

You could even make the criticism even less stinging if you phrase it positively. Say something like "I would really love if you…" or "You could really do a great job if you…" or "The one thing that will make this even greater than it is is if you…" If done right, you could prevent a lot of toxicity from leaking into your dialogue with that person.

# Receiving Feedback

### 1. Build up an Immunity

What stings the most with feedback is the fact that it almost always catches us off-guard. You could prevent this by asking for feedback as often as possible, especially with the people that you trust.

How you could do this is rather easy. Before you do anything, ask some open-ended questions like the following:

- If you can make two or three suggestions on how I could have done things better, what would they be?
- Is there a better way for me to handle that situation?
- Do you know of a way to make my job easier?
- If you were in my position now, would you have done things differently?

Asking these questions frequently puts you on a direct path towards receiving feedback. As such, you tend to get less offended if people voice their concerns about you.

On the other hand, these questions immediately put the other person in a position where they can add value to the conversation. They can now comment on what you did without fear of repercussions from your side.

### 2. Take time to Reflect

The one thing that you shouldn't do is respond immediately to feedback. The reason for this is that humans tend to "explain away" what they did, which is seen as a rather defensive move.

Let the person finish their feedback and listen intently. Once they have said their piece, reflect on what was said. You could even do multiple reflections for the same feedback before you respond to it.

The goal here is to get the essence of what they are saying and what they want out of that feedback. If you understand this, your response will be more effective.

### 3. Embrace Your Mistakes and Grow

It is hard to admit to our mistakes, which is why receiving feedback is often next to impossible. More often than not, we blame our mistakes on external factors like the weather, the setup of the system, and even other people.

The idea of embracing your failures, however, has become a more prevalent concept these days. There is something so liberating and endearing with admitting that you are capable of mucking it up. And, if you do embrace your faults and mistakes, feedback that was intended to demoralize hurts less for you now.

But knowing that you make mistakes is not enough. You also have to give the assurance that you are working on ironing out the kinks in your personality, methodology, and any other aspect in your life that invites criticism. Once that assurance is given, all that is left to do is to show that such changes are taking place.

## The Bottom Line

More often than not, it is the way we provide and receive feedback that is problematic, not the content itself. Your biggest problem here will always be your perceptions. It is either you don't think too much of what the other person feels when you provide feedback or overthink the feedback you received.

This is why your personal barriers are the biggest hurdles you will have to clear in order to communicate properly. Take the time to plan what you have to say before saying them so the person receives it in a manner that is healthy.

On the flip side, you also must curb your tendencies towards perceiving feedback negatively. Unless it is out in the open that that person hates the fact that you exist, do not assume negative intent for everything that they throw against you. With your negativity bias dealt with, you can easily go through life without accidentally offending people by the way you interact with them or getting needlessly offended yourself.

# Chapter 10: Conclusion

*Effective communication is 20% what you know and 80% how you feel about what you know."*

*-Jim Rohn*

After everything you have learned from here, the one question that you may want to ask is this:

*How should I know if I've become a better communicator?*

The first thing that you have to look for is an ability to balance between talking and listening. More often than not, we tend to focus on getting the former right and disregard the latter. And then there are those that prefer to stay by the sidelines and not actively contribute to the conversation. Striking a balance between your ability to express and receive information can help you engage more with people.

The second ability is to not pay attention to your biases and presumptions too much. A lot of miscommunication occurs because we assume one thing over the other when it comes to people and how they think and feel. Being self-aware of how your actions can negatively affect others can help foster a clearer line of communication at home or work and prevent any sort of toxicity from coming out in your relationships.

Lastly, you become aware of how every move you make can be perceived by others. Every comment you utter, the body language and verbal tics that you make, and the way you present your ideas all play a role in how people perceive you. Thus, you become more mindful of the words that you say and the non-verbal cues that you give out when interacting with people.

With these elements, you are bound to develop one of the most important abilities that all sapient beings tend have: the ability to create connections with others wherever they go.

And how would you know that you already have these abilities? You don't. Or, technically speaking, you won't unless you actively apply all that you have learned here in your day-to-day interactions.

Thank you for taking the time to go through the entire book. I hope that you have learned all that you can about communicating your thoughts and ideas to other people. All that is left to do now is to start working on improving your communication skills following the strategies laid out in this book. Over time, you will be able to improve your relationships with the people that surround you.

*James W. Williams*

# Book# 2
# How to Read People Like a Book

*A Guide to Speed-Reading People, Understand Body Language and Emotions, Decode Intentions, and Connect Effortlessly*

*James W. Williams*

# Introduction

First things first, I'd like to start by saying thank you for purchasing this book. As the title confesses, this book is all about learning how to read people like, well, a book, in order to communicate effectively, nurture meaningful relationships, and ultimately connect with others effortlessly. I can't stress this latter part enough—I want this book to help you CONNECT with people, forge relationships, and for the most part strengthen your existing ties with others around you.

But we'll get to how to develop these aspects of your life in time. Let's start at the beginning. My name is James and I've been studying body language and verbal communication for a very long time. Amazing how quickly the years go! I got my start from my interest in TV shows that seemed to glamorize body language and profiling. This started with your traditional crime and thriller TV shows that would profile in the very literal sense, but this evolved over time. When I began to look into commercials and advertisers and the way people are presenting themselves, the over-sexualization of some reality TV shows, and more recently, social media influencing and other forms of online content, I found it all fascinating. However, and perhaps most importantly, I was interested in learning about verbal communication and effective communication in general because I wasn't happy with the way I was living life.

I used to live life suffering from severe shyness and social anxiety, which crippled me in almost any social interaction. Upon learning how to compose myself and connect with others, I naturally learned how to see what I was learning in others, aka, reading them. I then dedicated my time to learning this art of how to *read people* and how it would help me connect with them easier. As I learned, there is really nothing glamorous about it. The process is instead grounded on cold-hard science and research. I'm grateful for this opportunity to share what I know with you—especially since it helped me so much in life and can do the same in yours! Learning to read between the lines allowed me to advance in work, marry the woman of my dreams, nurture a good relationship with my kids, and be fulfilled in many of my social circles.

Knowing how to communicate properly with people is the hallmark of good relationships. These methods that you're about to learn have given me the kind of deep relationships that I could only dream about before. But first, the question is: How did we get to this point in our lives?

Why do we find it so hard to connect and communicate with people? A good reason is that what people say isn't always what they mean or even what they want to say. This leads to mixed signals, confusion, and everyone ends up getting something out of an interaction that they really didn't want to get.

Let's look at a real-world view. Have you ever given a presentation and noticed people dozing off or not paying attention? Have you ever had problems with your boss for reasons that you just can't grasp? Perhaps your boss quickly latches on to suggestions made by a coworker when you suggested the exact same thing before?

Or let's look at your dating life. Do you always strike out with your dates? Do you find yourself unsure of what to do or what to say when spending time with someone? Do you have a hard time figuring out whether the other person is also into you?

These are all problems that can be solved with just the right amount of insight when it comes to body language. Body language will tell you at what point your boss has lost interest or which part of the presentation is perceived as boring by your office mates. It can also tell you when a date is interested even before you walk towards them in a bar. It will also show you how to be more confident in both situations or, at least, cause others to perceive you in this way.

Knowing how to master this art gives you the chance to assess and change direction through any interaction as needed. This knowledge can help you formulate your techniques depending on what the audience needs and what you want to achieve. Simply put, it can help you fulfill goals through subtle but effective means.

This isn't a pseudo-science either. Studies have shown that body language has a huge impact on day-to-day conversations. A large part of human communication is done through body language.

The good news is that you don't have to spend thousands of dollars on classes to learn these techniques. This book can help you with those and so much more! Throughout the following chapters, I intend to help you learn how to figure out the different personality types you'll come across in your day-to-day life and the unique traits each one has, communicate with these different personality types, how to read body language in any situation, how to understand verbal cues, and of course—how to train yourself to become a better reader of the people around you.

I want you to be able to achieve bigger and better things through this book, so don't wait around—flip over to the next page and let's begin!

# Chapter 1: Explanation, Quotes, Facts

People are an endless source of interest. Why people think, what they think about, or why they do what they do has created an entire branch of science called *Personality Psychology*. It's basically a branch of psychology that studies personality, no surprises there, and how they differ from one person to the next. The study deals with the construction of a coherent picture of an individual, their psychological process, psychological differences, psychological similarities, and human nature. Simply, it tries to answer these five questions:

- What traits make up a person?
- How does a person think?
- What makes one personality different from another?
- What makes one personality similar to another?
- What personality traits are already present from the moment a person is born?

It seems like such a simple five-question study at first, but it's actually such a big field that I doubt any book will be able to discuss everything about people without being incredibly long-winded. However, we will try to focus our discussion on the important stuff, mainly communication. More importantly, we're going to talk about how you can forge a connection with different personalities through both verbal and non-verbal communication.

## What Is Personality?

Personality has many definitions, but for this book, we're going to define it as a set of characteristics possessed by an individual. This set of characteristics influences a person's cognition, emotion, motivation, behavior, and environment. Hence, the way you behave often changes depending on who you are, where you are, and who you're with. In fact, the word *personality* originated from the Latin word *persona*, which means *mask*. This is why people often say they wear different masks depending on different situations.

Studies targeted towards defining, describing, and categorizing personality have been in existence for many years. In case you didn't know, the ever-popular Zodiac signs are actually a way to categorize personality based on a birthdate. Of course, since this way of categorizing personality isn't backed by science, we won't be talking about it, but it does go to show that this is nothing new. Instead, we shall be focusing on the meanings backed with lots of juicy studies.

## Introvert and Extrovert

This is perhaps the most common personality classification known today. The common belief is that introverts are quiet, and extroverts are loud. However, that's actually just a manifestation of what makes each personality unique. The main difference between an extrovert and an introvert is how their brains operate. That's right—this goes all the way to the brain, and scientific studies prove it.

Studies show that an extrovert's dopamine trigger is typically shorter than that of an introvert. Dopamine is the body's happy hormone, and accordingly, stimulation for extroverts runs the path of taste, touch, visual, and auditory sensory processing. It's quick and very much felt by all five senses. This is why when extroverts gamble, the rush they get is stronger and faster. Introverts, on the other hand, run a more complicated course. The dopamine pathway runs through planning, remembering, and solving problems.

What does this all mean? Extroverts have a brain makeup that encourages them to seek fast-rewards, while the same does not hold true for introverts. In other words, an extrovert gets their high from hard and fast sources of stimulation. An introvert likes slow and steady.

Of course, this feels like such a vague explanation, so how else can we make a distinction? Perhaps a better way of explaining the difference is in terms of energy. How do introverts and extroverts gain energy, and how do they recharge?

You see, introverts recharge best alone. Being with people saps their energy quickly, and in order to bring that energy back up, they need to be alone.

Extroverts are the complete opposite. If they're alone for long periods of time, it feels as though their energy is being drained. Hence, extroverts need to socialize with other people in order to recharge their energy.

It's really that simple. This is why even if a person is an introvert, they still enjoy socializing with others, participating in parties, and going to different occasions. In the same way, some extroverts can become overcharged and may need some quiet alone time. I don't want you to think that extroverts never want quiet moments or that introverts never want to be with other people. Both personalities are capable of jumping to the other side, but their default setting means they will go back to their default when they need to.

This difference between the two types will tell you how you want to communicate or enable a connection with another person. For example, if you're planning a birthday party for an introvert, a small quiet event would be closer to their style. And with that, you've just read someone and acting accordingly! Nice. I suppose you can read people now, so we'll just end here. I joke, of course.

Once you've highlighted an introverted person, you can use this information to your advantage. For example, this person is perhaps more likely to appreciate gifts that they can enjoy alone, and when setting up a meeting with an introvert, you would want to pick a quiet spot with little music and enough privacy for a personal conversation. On the flip side, an extrovert would appreciate a gift that encourages socialization or activities that involve great adrenaline rushes. Forging a connection with an extrovert can mean a trip to the local bar or a local festival.

Later in this book, we'll talk more about how introverts and extroverts appreciate human connection and what makes them tick.

## Myers Briggs Type Indicator

An online search for a term like *personalities* or *how to identify someone's personality* will bring up dozens or even hundreds of pages dedicated to the Myers Briggs Type Indicator, also known as the MBTI Personality Test. This test was popularized by Carl Jung and was even commonly once used by companies for hiring purposes. Carl Jung was the main proponent of this personality typing and was the psychoanalyst and psychiatrist who founded analytical psychology.

Under the MBTI personality characterization, the introvert and extrovert classifications have been expanded. Instead of the traditional introvert versus extrovert, personalities are now typed depending on eight different categories.

Under the MBTI school of thought, you can either be:
- Introverted or Extroverted
- Sensing or INtuitive
- Thinking or Feeling
- Perceiving or Judging

The IN in intuitive is intentional. I'll explain in a second, although you may already be familiar with it yourself if you've completed a test like this. The chances are you did one online, and the most common and most comprehensive of which is the *16 Personalities* test. Complete this test, and it will tell you your personality type and describe what kind of person you are, how you think, how you perceive the world, and so on. In total, there are 16 Personality Types under the MBTI principle. Most people find the results are shockingly accurate and may make you feel a little taken aback. So, how does this work?

Let's say the test concludes you're an Introvert, an INtuitive, a Thinker, and Judging, so your personality type is: INTJ.

On the flip side, you may also be an Extrovert, an Intuitive, a Sensor, and a Perceiver—making you an ENSP. Do you see where this is going? All possible combinations of these characteristics churn out 16 different personalities, and each one has its own unique charm and, of course, its own unique vice. What I want you to understand, however, is that ESFP is not the automatic opposite of INTJ just because all the letters are flipped. It's far more complicated than that, which is why it can be tough to fully explain, but I'll definitely try.

The question here is: why are there so many personality types? Carl Jung once said, "There's no such thing as a pure extrovert or introvert. Such a person should be in a lunatic asylum."

This is perhaps why there has been an expansion of the classic introvert and extrovert scenario.

## What do the letters mean?

Since we already talked about the Introvert versus Extrovert situation, I won't be describing that one in the listing. Here are what the other letters mean when it comes to MBTI:

- Sensing: If you're this type, this means that you become aware of specific facts first, or you prefer to focus on the precise details before making a decision about something. This also means that you rely primarily on your five senses and use them to move forward, perceive your surroundings, and come up with decisions.
- INtuitive: Denoted by the letter "N," this means that you prefer to focus on the big picture first. Intuitive people also rely heavily on hunches or intuition when perceiving their surroundings.

- Thinkers: This category describes the process by which you arrive at a decision. Sensing or Intuition is the way you *receive* the message. Thinking or Feeling is how you *process* that message. Thinkers use logical analysis to process the message they receive.
- Feeling: On the other end of the spectrum are the Feelers, who primarily use emotions. They consider the values of everyone involved and try to hit a harmony with them. The chances are this kind of person will make spontaneous decisions based on how they feel in the moment.
- Judging: Judging people are those who want their life planned out. You want to create a Plan A, Plan B, Plan C, or any other backup plan that might be necessary to achieve your goal. Lists and checklists are common with this type of person.
- Perceivers: These people are the ones who prefer to go with the flow. You want to keep your options open and change them accordingly.

Later on, we'll talk about this some more. But from the general look of things, you can already tell how this personality classification can help guide you in connecting with others.

## Enneagram Personality Typing

In addition to the Myers Briggs personality test, you may like to try the Enneagram of Personality school of thought, where you'll find there are a total of nine different personality types. All of these are interconnected and were principally derived from the teachings of a Chilean psychiatrist, Claudio Naranjo. Like the MBTI, the Enneagram was also used in business management to help business owners gain insight into their employees and their fitness for specific roles. Nowadays, it's not considered a huge determining factor for hiring, but some companies may still use it to guide their hiring process.

Here's a rough look at the different personality types as defined under the Enneagram System.

1. The Reformer: rational, principled, purposeful, perfectionist, self-controlled, and idealistic
2. The Helper: caring, demonstrative, generous, possessive, people-pleasing, and interpersonal
3. The Achiever: success-oriented, adaptive, excelling, image-conscious, driven, and pragmatic
4. The Individualist: sensitive, expressive, dramatic, temperamental, self-absorbed, and withdrawn
5. The Investigator: the cerebral type, perceptive, secretive, isolated, innovative, and intense
6. The Loyalist: committed, engaging, anxious, suspicious, responsible, and security-oriented
7. The Enthusiast: busy, fun-loving, versatile, scattered, distractible, and spontaneous
8. The Challenger: dominating, decisive, confrontational, self-confident, willful, and powerful
9. The Peacemaker: easygoing, receptive, reassuring, complacent, agreeable, and self-effacing

Of course, this is just a basic outline, but it's a fantastic foundation to think about. While you're probably not going to conduct this test on someone you've just met, it can be a lot of fun with people you're already close to, and it's a great idea to bear in mind these personality types.

Reread them and submit them to memory. When you meet someone, or you're interacting with someone, bear these traits in mind. Let's say you speak to your boss all the time, but you've never really taken the time to define them using a category system such as this.

You think about what kind of person they are. For example, you might say they're The Challenger role or an ETJP. You now know that they prefer to talk about the details of a project and get straight to planning and organizing everything. They never really just go with the flow or hope things will turn out okay.

With this information by your side, you can now start communicating effectively with your boss far more precisely than you have before, and in a way that they'll really connect with. The more they resonate with you, the better the results of your interactions will be, and the ceiling for which your relationship can grow becomes limitless.

These are the two main personality types you'll want to think about and the categories that many scientists believe are the most effective. Take the test yourself or have a read through the personality types and you'll be able to start applying them to people in your life.

Just for clarity, and to see if it suits you, here's another popular personality classification system you could use.

## Keirsey Temperament Sorter

Known as the KTS, this personality typing system is slightly related to the MBTI. It had a big impact on the hiring practices of some of the biggest businesses in the world. For example, at some point, corporations like Coca-Cola, 7-Eleven, IBM, Bank of America, and even the US Air Force used this personality assessment technique.

Under this principle, there are basically four temperaments divided into two categories and with two types each. Hence, just like the MBTI, there's a total of 16 types under the Keirsey system. Beautifully, these 16 personalities correlate with the 16 personalities found in the MBTI personality classification, albeit with different names, but you might find it easier to remember these rather than a code of letters.

Here's a rough outlook of these personality types:

- Artisans: Artisans want to make an impact with an adaptable personality that makes them excellent in troubleshooting. They're known for their agile abilities and excellence in using instruments, tools, and equipment needed for whatever goal they may have in mind. They often seek virtuosity and stimulation, with their greatest asset being the ability to develop tactics to meet their needs. Artisans fall into two different roles:
    - The Entertainers: These are the informative or reactive Artisans. This basically means that their intelligence is catered towards improvising, allowing them to adapt to a situation as it comes. Entertainers are further classified into Composers and Performers.
    - The Operators: These are the proactive or directive Artisans. What makes them distinctive is the unique talent to expedite a process or basically make activities go quicker without losing much of the goal. They are further divided into Crafters and Promoters.
- Guardians: These are the ones who like things scheduled and organized. They want security and value responsibility in themselves and other people. They're excellent at logistics and make good supporters and facilitators. They branch out into two different roles:
    - The Administrators: They're the ones who are proactive with an intelligence developed towards regulation. They're further classified into Inspectors and Supervisors.

- o   The Conservators: Known as the reactive Guardians, they are best when put in roles of support. Classifications of this type include Protectors and Providers.
- Idealists: They are both compassionate and abstract. Their motivations center towards personal growth and meaning. Because of their unique connection with themselves, they are excellent when put into roles requiring diplomacy. They have two different roles, which are:
    - o   The Mentors: These are the ones that are best in developing roles. As the name suggests, they're perfect for guiding people and helping them to develop into their full potential. Role variants are Counselors and Teachers.
    - o   The Advocates: As the name suggests, this role of the Idealist is centered towards mediation. They're advocates that are excellent in bridging the gap between people. Role variants include Healers and Champions.
- Rational: They're the ones who are both objective and abstract. Their main goal includes self-control and mastery of whatever they need to achieve. People who fall under this personality type value knowledge and competence above all else. Their greatest strength is their strategy and the ability to approach problems from a logical standpoint. They fall into two roles:
    - o   Coordinators: Their intelligence is primarily developed towards arranging. Role variants include Masterminds and Field Marshals.
    - o   Engineers: Excellent at constructing the Engineers have the following role variants—Architects and Inventors.

## The Spectrum of All Personality Types

I can't stress this enough—personality is a spectrum meaning there's no set or permanent personality type. A person isn't 100% introvert or extrovert. This designation is merely a *preference*. To make matters more complex, people can even change throughout their lives, but usually not too much.

You can use this information to try to identify the kinds of people in your life and alter your interactions accordingly. We're going to talk about how to do all this in a later chapter, but for now, let's continue our journey into the art of reading people.

# Chapter 2: Problems and Benefits

In this chapter, we're going to talk about the advantages and pitfalls of reading body language. The fact is that body language is an inexact science, and as much as it can be useful, it can also be detrimental to your social life.

We'll explore some things you need to watch out for and how you'll need to adapt your reading skills, depending on the situations in life you find yourself in. Let's start with the biggest point.

## The Impact of Culture

One thing I want you to consider is the impact of culture on body language. When trying to communicate with people, whether verbally or non-verbally, you will find that there are certain actions unique to their culture or the environment where they grew up. For example, in Asian countries, bowing is a sign of respect, while in American countries, the typical *bow* has been shortened to a simple nod of the head to someone. Also note that in Asian countries, the depth of the bow indicates the depth of respect one might have for the other person.

Why is this problematic? Well, if you're trying to communicate with someone of a different background, you will have to do your research on their culture. What gestures are considered proper, and which ones are a show of respect? While the other person may understand that you're from a different background and don't know about their gestures, you will find that making that extra effort can make you stand out from the crowd.

This is an incredibly interesting point and can vary with severity. If you're going on vacation to a country with a different culture, people will see you and probably expect that you won't know the traditions. However, taking the time to learn and practice, and ultimately applying them when you're in the country, will garner so much respect, and it may open new opportunities that you wouldn't have had access to before.

The art of reading people does come down to putting in time and effort. Whether you're reading people for work, preparing for a meeting with a client who lives on the other side of the world, or just practicing by talking to people outside your social circles, experience is your best friend. And you can only get experience if you're willing to put the work in.

## How Do I Know Their Personality Type?

Now you know the different personality types as detailed in the previous chapter, but there's a very clear problem. How do you make the distinction? Unfortunately, you can't just go up to people and ask them about their personality type hoping they've done a test, nor can you really jump in and try to guess. You have a one in sixteen chance of getting it right.

In fact, the average person you'll come across is unlikely to know anything about the MBTI, the Enneagram, or other personality indicator types. Unless you're good friends with them, it's also unlikely that you can have them answer a questionnaire to determine their personality type.

So, what do you do then?

Simply put, you look at cues, behaviors, speech patterns, and the like in order to determine an individual's personality type. This can be difficult and, in all likelihood, you may not be 100% correct all the time, but again, it's all about putting in the time and effort to learning what the cues and behaviors are. The more familiar with the knowledge and science you are, the more you should have an idea on how to proceed further when communicating with another person.

Here's some good news: you already have a clue on how body language works. Even as babies, it was observed that humans naturally react depending on the current mood or expression of their nannies, moms, dads, or any person who happens to be handling them. Chances are you can pretty much tell when someone close to you is sad, angry, frustrated, or experiencing any other emotion. As a general rule, the closer you are to a person, the easier it is for you to read their inner thoughts and emotions.

We'll come back to this later when we take a look at specific strategies for reading people, but for now, be mindful of the fact you need to start trying to read people if you want to get any good at it. Failure to practice, and you'll end up reading people incorrectly.

## Relying Too Much on Body Language

While body language is such a key part of communication, I also want you to note that body language is supplemental to actually listening and won't give you the full story. Body language will give you an insight into what a person thinks or feels inside, but you also shouldn't ignore what they're saying. Listen to what they're telling you first and if you're confused or unsure, look at their body language. This should more or less tell you about the lay of the land. Remember, there are instances when listening is better than simply watching a person's body language. The fact is that in many cases, body language is simply used to emphasize what they're already saying, so it's best if you listen AND look.

## The Power of Groups

Being part of a group is another obstacle when trying to read people's thoughts, ideas, expressions, and body language. Groups tend to affect how a person approaches a particular situation, especially when put under pressure. I'm sure that at some point in your life you changed your mind because of a group. They might be all in agreement over a particular course of action, and you feel forced to agree with that decision. Or perhaps you've made a decision in order to look good in that particular group. Conformity is the magic word when it comes to groups. Every person wants to be accepted by the community, and in order to do so, they have to *conform* to what the community thinks must be done.

This is why it can be tough to spot an introvert during a party because some introverts conform to extrovert characteristics when thrown into the company of extroverts. In fact, a study was conducted to measure just how badly a group can affect a person's decision.

When made to choose between what they believe to be the *right* answer and what the group thinks, 75% of people chose the group answer, despite the fact that it was the wrong one.

One of my favorite examples of this was on the UK television show featuring psychological illusionist Derren Brown. He set up a room where he was auditioning people for a role. There was a line of ten chairs for those who were auditioning to fill out forms while waiting to be called. The first two seats were filled with actors.

Members of the public came in and sat next to the actors. In the room, a bell sound was played, and the actors stood up, doing nothing else but continuing to write on their form as though standing up to a bell was completely normal. The members of the public were not told to do this.

As the set went on and the actors stood up and sat back down with each bell played, some members of the public would join in with the standing and sitting, despite never being told to do anything. They were simply conforming because they didn't want to be left out of the group, despite there being no obligation to do anything.

In some cases, groups can be so powerful that they can *normalize* a wrong behavior. This simply means that an action that is generally seen as *bad* becomes normal when allowed or repeatedly done by a group. Prime examples of this include bullying, drinking in excess, drugs, or trying cigarettes. Groups also impose penalties when a person doesn't conform to their decisions, by throwing them out of the group or turning a person into a social pariah.

How else does a group affect a person's thoughts, ideas, and emotions?

- Groups can magnify an idea or make an opinion more powerful. People feel confident when they join groups that validate their own opinions or thoughts. This is how labor unions, civic unions, or charities become so powerful and widespread. Think of it as little voices joining together to become a powerful one that can be heard all over by others.
- Leaders also have a huge impact on how a person thinks when that person forms a group. Leaders can steer groups in the direction they want to go or convince people to agree to certain ideas. There's no better example of this than politics.

## The Problem of Face-ism

Face-ism is a problem that occurs often in society, although you may not realize it. It's basically when people make judgments towards a person based on their appearance but goes beyond prejudice. This rests primarily on the face of a person—specifically the shape of the face. Face-ism states that simply based on the shape of a person's face, impressions are made about their personality. For example, studies show that features with a feminine appearance are often seen as extroverted. They're also seen as happier and more trustworthy. Does that mean that feminine features predict extroversion? No. It simply means when you see someone with very feminine features, you instantly label them an extrovert. But this doesn't have to be true and is just a predetermined way of thinking many of are conditioned to believe.

I want you to distinguish between impressions on facial features and reading a person's body language. Impressions you make via facial features are stagnant or non-moving. Basically, this means that a person is not doing anything—their face is neutral. The impressions you get from their face are based purely on their blank features.

When reading faces and body language, however, we're looking at movement. People are reacting, doing, or thinking about something, and therefore causing their facial expressions and body to change in relation to what they're thinking or feeling. This movement is what we want to read here, not the blank expressions.

## Physical Attractiveness

I hate to throw this out there, but beauty is a very strong motivator when it comes to reading body language. More than just the shape of the face or skin color, having a face that matches societal standards of beauty can really screw up a person's reading of body language. As science shows, when you see someone you're attracted to, you get that rush of dopamine that makes you want to spend more time with someone, which can impair your logical decision-making ability. The same applies if you're talking to someone who finds you attractive.

Physical attractiveness can instill positive characteristics in a person that they haven't really lived up to. At the same time, being beautiful can also make it easier for an individual to distract you from their actual motives, depending on the nature of the person. On the flip side, being attracted to someone can make you read deeper into their superficial actions so that your interpretation would match your personal goals. For example, you might like someone and perceive a kind act as a flirtatious one when, in fact, they are acting perfectly normal in the given situation.

## Your Mood Affects Your Reading

Another problem here is that your interpretation is affected by what you think or feel at that particular moment. If you're sad, then chances are you'll interpret the same thing in people. This isn't surprising since *reading people* effectively is basically you reacting to a situation, and reactions are hindered by overall mental and emotional health. This is why when reading people, it's important to maintain an unbiased view of things. If you're forced to make a decision, consider both sides of the story, take a good look at the different people involved, read them, and then make your decision. It's only smart to make readings when you're in a calm and collected frame of mind.

Like most of the strategies we're talking about throughout this book, this will come with practice. Sometimes you're going to get it right, and sometimes you won't, but the more you practice, the better at it you'll become.

## Still, There Are Benefits

So, you're probably thinking, *with all these problems associated with reading body language, why should I even bother?* Well, there might be drawbacks, but I promise you that the benefits are just as many—perhaps even more in number. Here are some of the benefits of being able to read a person's expression and body language:

- *You can connect better with people.* This is the most important benefit listed here because this is really the result you want to get when reading this book. To be able to look at a person and instantly find out what they feel or think can help you adjust your own response in order to help them. This can be very useful in any social situation and will help you navigate through interactions with ease. Having an idea about what people think also lets you temper your conversation to make sure that no one is offended by what you said and cause you to communicate your own messages effectively. In essence, you'll be able to get what you want in life!
- *Helps with business or employment.* The workplace is packed with subtle, non-verbal manners of communication, and it can be very useful to know what's happening under the surface. Is the client interested in your presentation, or does he look completely distracted? You can take note of what

pitches have a positive or negative reaction from your boss or client. With coworkers, having a good grasp on silent communication between people makes it easier to adjust to the demands of the office. At the very least, being able to read these subtle cues will tell you if you've made an impression in the office.

- *Help prevent conflict.* Another incredibly useful benefit of reading body language is conflict resolution. You can tell the silent signs of aggression before they actually occur, therefore allowing you to stop any negative action at just the right stage. This is useful in many situations from work, to parties, to disagreements with your partner. Knowing exactly when to defuse a situation before you reach that point of no return all starts with awareness.

- *Improve people's impression of you.* First impressions are always important, no matter what setting you're in. Knowing how to read body language doesn't just tell you how other people think, it also tells you how you're supposed to act in their presence. This means that you will be able to adjust people's impressions of you depending on a given situation. This is important if you want to create a strong presence in the office or if you want to keep things on the down-low during family gatherings. Knowing the time to spread out your arms or make yourself blend in with the background can definitely help in achieving the effects you want to have in a situation.

- *Become a better communicator.* Of course, if you're in the position to receive and interpret verbal and non-verbal communication, this puts you in the perfect place to respond to these same messages. Don't forget—communication is a two-way street, and in order to send a message in the right context, you have to be able to receive a message in the right context. Doing both correctly guarantees that the flow of information is stable, quick, and accurate.

As you can see, there are pros and cons to reading body language, but through awareness of this information, you can act accordingly. Bear in mind the weaknesses you may have when it comes to reading body language in your own life.

For me, during the peak of my social anxiety, I would find myself getting very emotional in situations. If someone at work made a passing comment, even with no harm meant, I would take it extremely personally. This almost always resulted in my being unable to read a situation properly because I was clouded by whatever emotions I was feeling.

Through research and experience, I learned that things didn't need to be this way, but I instead had control over how I could respond in any given situation. When I felt an emotion rise up, I could take a breather and choose to act accordingly rather than getting carried away with the emotions themselves. This is what it means to be an effective communicator. This applies to all points in both lists.

With this in mind, it's time to move to the next chapter where we're going to start learning some core strategies you can use in your day-to-day life when it comes to reading people of varying personalities, starting with the introvert.

# Chapter 3: Introverts – Identify, Communicate, and Personality Type Motivations

This chapter will delve deeper into personality types and how to make connections with people depending on their perceived personality types. I want to stress the use of the word *perceive* here because unless you've made them take a test to figure out their personality type, chances are you're going to be guessing what category they fall into. Again, the more experience you have in reading people, and the more familiar you are with these personality types, the more accurate you'll find yourself. Practice makes perfect, people! This is why this chapter also helps you with that particular problem.

We're going to deal with varying personality types in three ways.

The first one answers the question: What are the characteristics of a specific personality type?

The second one answers the question: How do you communicate and connect with a specific personality type once you've identified it? This will help you tailor your communication style to connect with this particular person. Remember, the whole goal of this book is to help you forge better relations with people.

And finally, the third one answers the question: What is the typical motivation of this personality type? This is crucial because every person has a different motivation. Different personality types often have endgames or purposes when interacting with people. You will find that these different motivations can help you better figure out what they ultimately want in a given situation.

In this chapter and the next one, we're going to answer the question: How do you identify an introvert or extrovert? As mentioned before, people can be very good at hiding their actual personality preferences. Hence, an introvert may not always be sitting in the corner of the room but may be in the center of action doing their best-extroverted act, vibing off the energy of others in the room.

Here are some signs that can help you identify these personality preferences and how to interact with them.

Just a little preface before talking about spotting and communicating. I want you to take a good look at the classifications we've made in the previous chapter. This time, we won't stop at just the introvert and extrovert. Instead, we're going to go a little bit further and talk about the different MBTI personalities and how you're supposed to communicate with them after you've made an identification. I want you to understand that it's not always easy to make a classification, especially if you're doing it for the first time. Some characteristics are completely internal, which means that you won't be able to quickly see it in the person's words and actions.

Here I'm going to give you the best chance of connecting with introverted people.

## Signs of an Introvert

- Zoning out: In social situations, introverts are likely to zone out during conversations or in the middle of all the parties. They can easily become quiet during conversations as if they've mentally left the place. Don't worry, they'll come back sooner or later, often asking questions to help them catch up to the conversation.

A Finnish study back in 2016 found that extroverted people are far more likely to get a high from socializing in a similar way to introverted people, although their fatigue level hits around three hours after an introverted person's does. In other words, introverted people get tired around people quicker and need some time to catch up!

- They're the ones who leave early. This doesn't happen just once but all the time during parties or social situations. This goes hand in hand with the study above. Introverted people are all about having their alone time to recharge!

- Introverts are also the ones who tend to *disappear* during parties. They're the ones who gravitate towards the quieter part of the house, often grouping up with other introverts and just talking quietly in a private space. Often, introverts stick close to the people they already know.

- They're the ones who have an intense interest in books, the arts, or even the animals in the room. This kind of interest often allows them to be alone while still appearing as if they're enjoying themselves at the party.

There are many studies that back this up, perhaps the most popular being featured in a book titled 'The Secret Lives of Introverts' by Jenn Granneman. Throughout her book, she talks about how introverts require less social stimulation than extroverts and are more content with simple highs, like brief interactions and alone time activities, like reading and writing.

- They can be quite irritable if you're together for long periods of time. This is because introverts often need *downtime* after socializing for quite some time. Since introverts require time to recharge, it's like having an introverted or social hangover if they spend too long with other people.

- They're also the ones who are happy to lend a helping hand when it comes to activities that let them be alone. Hence, they can volunteer to serve the DJ, clean up the house, take food to someone, or even take photographs. This lets them stay clear from all the activities while still being part of the actual party.

## Introvert Types According to the MBTI

### *INFJ – Introvert, Intuitive, Feeling, Judging*

INFJs are big users of metaphors and symbols during conversations. They like to talk about insights, visions, and predictions, all while being emphatic and warm in their conversations. Being introverts, their conversational skills are best displayed in small circles or one-on-one interactions.

Here are the typical characteristics of the INFJ:

- They talk using symbols and metaphors to really convey what they're trying to say. Their preferred topics of conversation revolve around visions of the future, predictions, and possibilities. They're probably the sort of people who would end up using the term 'INFJ' in a conversation.

- They like to show solidarity with others by saying words like *I understand* when in conversations. Well-mannered, INFJ's are tactful and very adaptable. In fact, they can switch back and forth in social events, managing to establish rapport all the while.

- INFJs are introverted intuitive, which means that their process is mostly internal. This is why they like metaphors and symbols in conversations. They're simply conveying what they're thinking in the way they're thinking it. When it comes to topics they're passionate about, they can be tough to understand because they just open the floodgates. In fact, when it comes to certain topics, it appears as though they're only rambling. When in truth, they're trying to process an idea.
- When confronted by a debate or an argument, the INFJs are the ones who prefer to take on the role of peacemakers.
- These personality types tend to flock to the following careers: missionary work, clergy, counseling, medical doctors, chiropractic, psychiatry, writing, photography, dentistry, social work, librarians, and education consultant.

## *INTJ – Introvert, Intuitive, Thinking, Judging*

INTJs are considered to be one of the rarest types in the MBTI scheme. This is why when you do finally meet one, there's a good chance that you will have a hard time understanding their personality. Here are the typical characteristics of an INTJ:

- INTJs are quiet and prefer to spend the day by themselves. When they do start talking, however, they prefer to focus on future events and enjoy discussing the many implications or meanings of events, topics, or situations.
- They tend to speak using lots of symbols or metaphors to describe things. They're the ones who often say phrases like: "If this happened, then that means that…" as they like to establish connections between events in a logical but futuristic manner.
- They love to strategize and often focus on creating long-term solutions to problems. Because they're intuitive instead of being sensors, it can be difficult for them to explain their thoughts and ideas to people, so be patient.
- Don't be surprised if you get lost when talking to an INTJ. They tend to go straight from point A to point D, skipping several letters along the way. Combined with their love for metaphors, it can be very confusing, especially if you're talking to one for the first time.
- They stick to logical and analytical modes of thinking. They can also be very direct to the point of being rude. Like other NTs, they like to process information quietly so that when they finally say something they sound very sure of their conclusion.
- Common careers include professorships, teaching, medical doctor, corporate strategizing, engineering, computer programming, photography, managing, military, and research department managing.

## *ISTJ – Introvert, Sensing, Thinking, Judging*

They like to think before they speak, which seems true for all introvert types to an extent. You will notice how their body language shows they're mulling over a question or comment before they even respond. These are the kind of people who will take a long time composing a comment through Facebook and will review their message before eventually hitting send. Here are some of the characteristics of this type:

- They're the types who like to keep things as linear as possible. This means that during speeches or meetings, they're the types who recap conversations. They will repeat what another person said and then tack their comment at the end, just to make sure everyone is on the same page.
- They also like to connect current situations with past ones in order to make a correlation or to keep it factual. They'd say words like "it looks like" or "it's the same as" or "remember when" to keep the conversation grounded and make sure everyone can see the similarity or difference to a current situation. Typically, this is done to add some authority to their conclusions or ideas.
- When talking, they tend to focus on facts and rarely exaggerate what they're trying to say. This also means that their movements tend to be limited as they focus on the context of what they're trying to say. Note that these types are not big on facial expressions or body language so you might have a harder time reading them.
- They don't like being the center of attention when in fact, they actually have an air of mystery on them that draws in people.
- Feelings and emotions are kept close and private by the ISTJ so don't expect great shows of affection from them. They're not good with surprises, especially if they're socially accepted to respond with lots of emotions. These feelings are often reserved for really close people in their lives.
- These personality types are typically found in professions of business, administration, dentistry, programming, law, judging, accountants, detectives, math teaching, engineering, and technicians.

### *ISTP – Introvert, Sensing, Thinking, Perceiving*

ISTPs prefer to process their thoughts internally. You're not going to hear them reciting their analysis out loud but instead keeping it secret and intact before talking. As a result, their words would be factual, direct, and concise because they choose only to speak them out loud when they're already fully formed. Here's how to spot one out in the wild:

- They're the types who are likely to pause in the middle of a sentence in order to find the perfect word for what they're trying to say. Their vocabulary and phrasing are very precise as they want to keep things quick and simple.
- They're the ones who seem like they're very opinionated. This is because of their factual approach to any problem as well as the precision of their logic. Everything has been cross-checked before entering into any kind of debate or discussion. They're not afraid to raise issues if they see any, especially since their detailed sensory data managed to go through the logical pros and cons of a specific pathway.
- Because of their love for the logical and the concise, they're not very good with feelings or emotions. ISTPs will feel very out of place and ill-at-ease if asked to talk about their feelings. If pushed or in a very stressful situation, however, you might find that ISTPs suddenly become overly emotional even if it is out of their character.
- ISTP personality types tend to gravitate to careers like forensic pathology, system analysis, computer programming, firefighting, paramedics, electrical engineering, piloting, and transportation operation.

## Communicating with INFJs, INTJs, ISTJs, and ISTPs

When communicating with any person in this particular group, you want to remember that they're strong introverts. This means that their ability to maintain social communication is shorter—they often prefer their interactions to be quick and straight to the point.

Here are some of the things you have to remember when communicating with any of these types:

- Don't ramble, they hate that. If you want to communicate specific information, tell it to them straight.
- Do not use small talk if you want to get information from them. Ask about it straight out and you will get a straight answer from them.
- They may enjoy bantering, but if they're working on a particular project, it's important to stay away and just allow them to focus.
- Learn to listen because these types put a lot of stock into listening. Remember that their main goal is information so if someone is talking, they will make every effort to listen. Hence, they expect the same courtesy from others and hate it when people interrupt them in the middle of a sentence.
- Give them time to think about their answer before voicing it out loud.
- Greet them with a smile, but don't expect to stand there and exchange pleasantries. They're not really fond of that. Instead, greet them but give them their personal space. No hugs or any kind of air kisses unless you're very close or are a family member.
- Eye contact every now and then is okay simply to affirm connection. Don't overdo it, however. This can create a feeling of pressure.
- Do not rush them. Introverts like to enjoy their time working on a project. They're careful and particular about their goals and believe that distractions can lower the precision of their executions.
- When working with this type, it helps to always update them on what's going on. They want to find out at what stage you are in your job and not only when it's finished. This helps them assess the situation and adjust accordingly.
- Note that these types can go quickly from friendly to distant. They have a short social fuse which means that after some time socializing with others, they're going to need some alone time to recharge. True introverts, their social fuse tends to be shorter than most, unless they've managed to train themselves into it.
- During tense situations or when stressed, introverted types draw into themselves. They become quiet and stoic, unlike other types, which tend to burst out or let everyone know what they're feeling.

And with that, let's move onto the next batch of introverted personality types. Just a quick note, I understand this is a lot of information to process and there's pretty much no way you're going to remember it all. I write in detail in case there's a certain person in your life you really want to connect with and be able to read.

Whether you're nurturing a relationship with your partner, your children, your boss, or even your best friend, looking into their personality type in detail using this information and information you find online can be incredibly beneficial to your relationship.

However, you're probably not going to have the opportunity to go into this much detail with someone you've just met (which is why we'll be cover body language and strategies on this later). Yet for now, just keep in the mind the general idea of what personality traits introverts are like and how to communicate with them since most of the strategies will remain fairly similar throughout.

### *INFP – Introverted, Intuitive, Feeling, Perceiving*

Having a strong sense of personal values, INFPs are emphatic and imaginative. Their creative streak makes them very adept at discussing theoretical possibilities. Their favorite topics usually include how to help animals, how to help people, or even how to help the world overall. Think therapist or counselor types of people. Here are typical characteristics of this personality type:

- They have strong values but they're not the preachy type. They will keep their thoughts and beliefs close to heart unless specifically asked about them. They're the kind of people who let others live their lives and don't interfere unless they think they're in the position to make changes. Usually, this privilege is extended only to friends and relatives.
- Because of their belief in allowing people to express their individuality, INFPs are not very good in conversations when people try to impose their thoughts and ideas on others. They will have an internal cringe or at worst, they might even confront someone about it.
- Gentle and modest, they're often shy and prefer one-to-one conversations. At parties, they're going to be the ones who gravitate to the people they already know and spend most of the time in a quieter area of the house.
- You will often find them thriving in their careers as writers, counselors, childcare workers, missionaries, psychiatrists, scientists, psychologists, education consultants, journalists, and social scientists.

### *INTP – Introvert, Intuitive, Thinking, Perceiving*

INTPs are pretty rare among the ranges of personality types and have a very quiet personality. All their thought processes are done internally, which means that they'll only speak out their opinions after having had an internal monologue in their head. This makes them very likely to blend into the background of most situations. Here are some signs of an INTP:

- They're very precise with words. They don't just think about the implications but also how to word their thoughts in a way that keeps them brief and concise. This means that they take a long time to respond because they're looking for the perfect words to convey their meaning.
- They keep things logical and rarely venture towards emotions and feelings. In fact, they like to keep things on the topic at hand and don't like veering off into tangents.

- They're the kind of people who categorize information into smaller pieces. This means that they will group information based on specific characteristics. This allows them to better remember information and create connections between different subjects.
- Because of their preference for categorization and connecting information together, it takes a fairly long time for INTPs to arrive at a conclusion. Once the planning is over, however, they will execute their plan to perfection and will not veer away from it.
- Give INTPs sufficient time to think about answers to questions. They don't like being pressured, especially when coming to a conclusion.
- They're outside-the-box thinkers so don't be surprised if they sometimes put forward an idea that's out of this world. Be assured, however, that they thought about it first before voicing it.
- INTPs are not very good when it comes to expressing feelings and emotions so unless you absolutely have to, try not to dwell too much about it during conversations.
- Common careers include chemistry, photography, biology, mathematics, computer programming, university professorships, forensic research, psychology, art, and social science.

## *ISFJ – Introvert, Sensing, Feeling, Judging*

ISFJs are a lot like ISTJs in the sense that they think long and hard before talking. Do not rush them as they want to delve into every possibility before deciding on a course of action. Here are some of the typical characteristics of the ISFJ:

- ISFJs like to keep a timeline in their head, which reflects when they speak. When trying to prove a point or convey information, they will make use of past experiences to make their argument more believable.
- When talking, they often use words such as *like*, or *reminds me of*, or *remember when*.
- Unlike other introverts, ISFJs are actually very good at relaying empathy. This is their way of connecting with people or showing solidarity.
- They have a constantly professional and polite demeanor. They're actually quite responsive but prefer one-on-one interactions over groups. Hence, these are the people who will be looking for familiar faces in a party and spending most of their time in a quiet corner of the room.
- They're not very good with criticism and will often feel uncomfortable if made the subject of any conversation. They can take these criticisms personally and will not do well in arguments or debates, even a friendly one, like a thought experiment. Hence, they are also the type to think about past blunders over and over in their head. This can sometimes portray them as being anxious.
- Note that long-range forecasting is not their forte. Unlike NT types who have no problem predicting possibilities, ISFJs like to keep their future predictions within safe short-term levels. However, as a result, their predictions are often good and well thought of by others.
- Common careers for this type include childcare, administrating, career counseling, clerical supervising, law enforcement, church work, and medical.

## *ISFP - Introverted, Sensing, Feeling, and Perceiving*

The open-minded introverts who can be emphatic and easygoing if they feel like it, ISFPs can blend in with the extroverts if the need arises for it—but not too much. They have strong values but don't really want to show it on the surface unless they're in the company of someone they really trust and have emotional connections with.

These are the kinds of people who respect the differences between people and will therefore not tell other people what they should or should not do. Sure, ISFPs may have a fairly good idea of what your next move should be, but they're not the types to give unsolicited advice. If you try to challenge their values, however, the ISFP will definitely fight with you in a tone of voice that is far from their usual character.

Some characteristics of the ISFP include:

- They're quiet and honest with everyone they meet. During conversations, they're the ones who like to listen and seldom draw attention to themselves. In fact, if they suddenly find themselves the center of attention, an ISFP will grow quiet.
- Believe it or not, ISFPs love adventure. They're the ones who enjoy going to concerts or vacations and will happily talk about them if given the chance. They also delve deeply into projects and can be quite impulsive as they always want to add to their collection of memorable experiences.
- They're not really happy being in conflict-packed environments. They will actively put effort into avoiding these situations or making sure that they're not part of the conflict.
- ISFPs tend to be attracted to careers in music, art, childcare, social work, teaching, animal care, medicine, bookkeeping, and physical therapy.

### *Communicating with INFPs, INTPs, ISFJs, and ISFPs*

Communicating with these four types are more or less the same. Here are some tips when approaching or connecting with any of these types:

- Keep your greetings quiet and friendly. Try not to overload them with affection or be very public with your greetings. Make sure you're patient with the other person, giving them time to think and process the interaction.

  A Harvard study from back in 2012, conducted by Randy Buckner, found that the grey matter of the prefrontal cortex of an introvert is thicker and larger than that of an extrovert. This grey matter is linked with the decision-making processes. Since there's more matter, there are more processes happening, which could prove why they take longer to make decisions and process information.

- Don't rush things with them. Never interrupt; allow these types to fully say what they want to say before responding. Perhaps one of their biggest pet-peeves is being interrupted while in the middle of a sentence. Give nods every now and then to let them know you're following the conversation. This goes hand in hand with the information above!
- When push comes to shove, these personality types can become quite critical. That's okay, and not something you should take personally. Just relax and take on board what is being said from a neutral standpoint. Chances are they're just processing what is happening.
- Quality is more important than speed so be prepared to revise and rework your output several times before you'll get their approval. The same applies to conversations. Don't beat around the bush and carry on with small talk. Introverts like quality conversations, not quantity.

This is backed by a study carried out by Inna Fishman in the Salk Institute for Biological Sciences in California. The study found that extroverted people are more sensitive to social stimuli than neutral stimuli, such as the weather or surrounding events. This means extroverts (surprise surprise) like socializing.

On the other hand, introverts respond well to both social stimuli and neutral stimuli, basically stating that introverts don't need social interaction to feel good. The surrounding environment is just as stimulating, so make the conversations worth their while!

- Public recognition and compliments can be quite embarrassing and very uncomfortable for these types of people. While congratulations and celebrating accomplishments are good for anybody, keeping things small scale will deliver the best results.

As before, you're not expected to remember all this information, nor are you going to, but reading through some of the descriptions, you've probably thought to yourself *ah, that sounds like this person or that person*, so already you're starting to use the information.

With the communication strategies accompanying each section, try to tailor your communication accordingly.

# Chapter 4: Extroverts – Identify, Communicate, and Personality Type Motivations

Just like we did in the previous chapter, we're now going to take a look at the other end of the personality spectrum and dive into what makes an extrovert an extrovert, and the eight personality types that make up this group of people.

Now, remember, you don't need to remember them all, but reading through these traits and descriptions are probably going to help you identify some of the people who are closest to you in your life and will equip you with the general knowledge you need to address and read other people.

Let's dive into the signs of an extrovert and highlight what you need to be on the lookout for.

## Signs of an Extrovert

One thing I want to remember is that extroversion is not a *bad* thing. There seems to be a current trend nowadays where introverts are viewed as the nice, sweet, unassuming people while extroverts are the gregarious ones who are flighty and talk too much. Note though that this isn't always the case. There is no *better* type and both introverts and extroverts have their own strengths and weaknesses.

Here are some of the typical distinguishing marks of an extrovert:

- They have broad and numerous interests, usually the types that encourage socializing and being with other people. Surfing, biking, and team games are some of the activities they usually enjoy.
- They communicate best through conversations, rarely with writing. In fact, they're very enthusiastic when talking, often adding punch to their argument through hand gestures. They're also comfortable showing affection in public. Hence, they're the types who will air kiss with friends, give people a slap on the back, and give shoulder hugs when they're happy.
- They have no problem being the center of attention. In fact, they can quickly lighten up when the attention is pulled towards them and such energy can make them feel more themselves, perpetuating them further.
- They're happy with group work and can seamlessly blend with any group, regardless of the task.
- They like going out on a routine basis. They're the ones who may have a routine when it comes to nights out or drinks after dinner or work.
- Of course, they also like to talk about their thoughts and feelings out loud. They will have no problem seeking out inspiration and advice from people they believe are capable of providing help.

## Extrovert Types According to the MBTI

Just like introverts, extrovert personality types can be broken down into eight main types. Let's jump in.

### ENFP – Extrovert, Intuitive, Feeling, Perceiving

ENFPs are very lively and jump into conversations with an unmistakable zest for connecting with people. Their liveliness is very contagious and can draw in people, especially during brainstorming sessions. Here are the typical characteristics of an ENFP:

- They love to focus on personal growth and self-help related conversations and will happily jump into conversations that involve this kind of topic. Their values are focused on improvement for themselves, other people, and the world.
- This need for growth and improvement actually makes many ENFPs rebels. This means that instead of going through the tried and tested road, they prefer to forge their own paths. They have no problem questioning the typical societal rules and if it doesn't work for them, then they'll choose to do something else.
- These creative types gravitate towards careers that allow them to be writers, painters, musicians, journalists, psychologists, teachers, politicians, television reports, and social workers.

## ENTP – Extrovert, Intuitive, Thinking, Perceiving

Creative and energetic, these personality types like to make good use of logic when they communicate with others. They like to brainstorm and thrown ideas out in the open to get everyone in on the thinking game. Discussions invigorate them and help them move on to further possibilities.

Note though that when conversing with ENTPs, they often focus on the general side of things and leave the nitty-gritty details to others. Here are some of the characteristics of an ENTP:

- They have the ability to form connections in their mind instantly and are not afraid to voice it. The problem here is that most people don't instantly see the connection so there's a chance that they'll be looked at strangely by others at first.
- Quite logical when it comes to making decisions or arriving at assessments, these personality types love to analyze things and keep subjects categorized according to their personal preferences. They essentially want to put everything in its place in the grand scheme of things.
- They love tracing connections between different parts of life, from the theoretical to the realistic. They're the ones who will tell you about cool facts and about how seemingly small inconsequential things have a big impact in the world. They're big fans of what is known as the butterfly effect.
- They have no problem participating in debates but tend to pause during conversations in order to contemplate specific topics.
- These types are great in conversations as they are willing to change their opinion if given sufficient information to make an impact. They're not afraid to burst out with their doubts, but keep in mind that any arguments they may have are just their way of figuring out the truth.
- These personality types aren't really fans of small talk and nitty-gritty details. They like to maintain their focus on the big picture and their thoughts on bigger goals.
- You will often find these people in careers like law, photography, psychology, consultancy, acting, engineering, marketing, computer programming, writing, the arts, and psychiatry.

## ESFJ – Extrovert, Sensing, Feeling, Judging

Despite the similarities in many of the letters, the ESTJ and the ESFJ are wildly different. They're both extroverts so they have no problem being part of parties or showing up at events. Here's what you need to know about the ESFJ:

- They like to use the words *we* and *us* a lot because this helps them establish a connection with people. Basically, they always want to create a sense of inclusion and make sure that everyone is in perfect harmony with each other. It's not surprising to find them as the ones who prefer to be politically correct in everything they do.

- They want people to feel comfortable to the point where they would even make fun of themselves just to put someone at ease. This self-deprecating humor makes them likable in large groups. Matched with their conscious efforts to not offend anyone, and you should be able to get a generally likable person.

- They want to relate to other people, so these are the kinds of people who will share similar experiences with you. They'd tell you they can relate or understand experiences you might have and make you feel included. They don't like conflict and will try to stop debates or arguments.

- They're very good at picking up emotional tension and will try their best to diffuse the situation. The problem here is that even friendly debates are viewed as conflicts by these types, which is why even these lively conversations are actively stopped by them if possible.

- They're very conscious about socializing within boundaries. Sure, they have no problem being at parties, but they're likely to leave at a time they deem appropriate. They don't want to overstay their welcome and are therefore deeply conscious of the right amount of time to stay during social events.

- They're sensors, which means that they are fully aware of the concrete needs of people. They're the ones who will notice if someone needs water or if someone hasn't eaten yet. They like to give solid solutions to solid problems, so don't expect too many feelings from them.

- These personality types typically have the following careers: nursing, childcare, physicians, office managing, social work, bookkeeping, clergy, home economics, reception, pathology, and religious educating.

So how do you connect with an ESFJ? Here are some things to remember:

- Be focused on the task – An ESFJ will respect you for that. You need to be encouraging without losing sight of the ultimate goal. Greet people, be warm, encouraging, and open—but when it's time to work, focus on the work.

- Offer concrete evidence when making presentations. They want cold, hard facts instead of presumptions or predictions that have no basis. Always use hard data and don't be afraid to cite your resources for that data. Make sure it's accurate and precise, as vague information is something ESFJs hate.

- They also want practical applications to problems. Simply put, your input should be actionable or something that can be done, measured, and observed. It doesn't matter if its long term or short term; ESFJs have no problem with waiting for the results they want. As long as the actions leading to those results are something they have practical control over.

- Be transparent when talking to an ESFJ about objectives and the plan on how to get to them. If you have an ESFJ working under you, it's important to explain to them not just the end goal but also the steps you want to take in order to arrive at that end goal. They need to see how these actions have a practical link to the end result.

- They like the status quo, especially if it's an office policy that has been proven to work before. Hence, if you're pushing new things to them, it's important to explain exactly why the shift is happening. They're not unreasonable. ESFJs have no problem welcoming something different as long as they can see the logical link between the new thing and the ultimate goal.

## *ESFP – Extrovert, Sensing, Feeling, Perceiving*

Warm, caring, and very enthusiastic, ESFPs are packed with energy and have the charisma to match. They often bring that unidentifiable *buzz* into a room that makes it very difficult to resist them when they're set to make an impression. Here are some of the typical characteristics of the ESFP:

- They love making lots of physical gestures so keep your eye out for the person who is expressive with their hands. They have a very upbeat tone that engages everyone to be part of the conversation.
- They're the kind of people who like to focus on the present because the future is prone to change. They make excellent storytellers and love dwelling in reality. They're very literal and if you engage them in theoretical discussions, they're bound to get bored quickly.
- They don't like being rushed, especially when it comes to making decisions.
- ESFPs are also very good at identifying the different mannerisms of people. They can quickly tell if a person is getting bored and can therefore make their company more interesting for that person.
- ESFPs typically gravitate to creative careers and work as painters, actors, comedians, teachers, counselors, childcare, interior design, fashion, managers, human resources, photography, coaches, and clerical supervisors. Their amazing enthusiasm makes them great motivators in any activity they choose to invest in.

## *Communicating with the ENFPs, ENTPs, ESFJs, and ESFPs*

Since they're all extroverts, communicating with these personality types are more or less the same. Here are basic tips on how to forge connections with people in this category:

- Always smile and make eye contact when you greet them in the morning, or during whatever time you might see them. They're extroverts—they're happy to make that initial connection with you.
- Keep the energetic vibe up with gestures that are open and encompassing. Use your hands and arms, allowing for vibrant and obvious movements that encourage participation.
- Be responsive to questions asked and if you're the one asking the questions, keep them open-ended. Allow these personality types to expand on their answers or give them the chance to elaborate on the topic.
- They're the types who think out loud so let them rant out their thoughts before pitching in. This isn't them saying nothing out of thin air, it's actually their thought process.
- If you want to communicate information to them, then the best way to do that is to give personal examples or use stories. This will get their attention and make a better impact instead of just stating possibilities in a detached manner.

- Allow them to explore different options before arriving at a decision. Try not to pressure them into arriving at a conclusion, as this will only irritate them and lower the quality of their answer. Since they like to think out loud, allow them to rant it out before asking what their *final* thoughts on the matter would be. Do not assume the first thing they said is their answer because chances are they're just going through the instances in their head.

- If you want them to do something or are trying to convince them to be part of something, try pointing out something that you think would be fun or entertaining for them to do.

- There will be some debate and arguments when you're interacting with these personality types. Don't take it personally as this is their way of having fun.

- When trying to explain something to them, allow for more time when it comes to questions and conversations. Present the main points and let them ponder the information for as long as possible.

- Note that people with this kind of personality type tend to use humor during tense moments. This is their way of breaking the tense atmosphere.

Take note that when angry or stressed, these personality types tend to become louder, more expressive, and heavily animated. It may seem completely out of context, but this is how they handle typical stressful situations.

### ESTJ – Extrovert, Sensing, Thinking, Judging

An ESTJ is an out-loud thinker, which makes sense because they're extroverted thinkers. They're the ones who speak out facts and make out-loud judgments, making it seem as though they're stating the obvious, but really, they're just saying these ideas out loud to make them more concrete. Hence, if you want to connect with an ESTJ, don't throw out "duh" or "obviously" reactions to them because this is exactly how their thought process works. In fact, you'll find that even when alone, an ESTJ will talk to themselves in order to properly process their thoughts before arriving at a conclusion.

Here are other typical characteristics of the ESTJ:

- They're confident when speaking and like to stick to factual and realistic topics. They're the ones who can easily remember facts and are more likely to compare past and present situations before moving forward with anything.

- In some instances, the ESTJ can appear quite tactless as they don't like to sugarcoat things for the sake of peace. They will try to tone down their words, but it would still be slightly edged compared to those who are used to social situations.

- They're the ones who enjoy debates and can still keep things friendly. They love the argumentative discourse and like it when their thoughts are said out loud and examined for a mutual give and take.

- They're also the ones who have a hard time maintaining an emotional situation. If the conversation needs them to be in touch with another person's feelings, then an ESTJ would be out the door or be very uncomfortable when participating.

- Most ESTJs are attracted to the following careers: managing, administrating, judging, finances, teaching, insurance, underwriting, and nurse administrating.

So how do you connect with an ESTJ or make an impression with this personality type? Here are some tips to get you started:

- They receive information best via charts, graphs, or diagrams. ESTJs will definitely appreciate visual presentations of an idea, a thought, or a problem.
- They're the ones who like to talk about problems. They're likely to discuss the issues by going over the information with other people before concluding with possible answers. Hence, they're the personality types who like to brainstorm in groups.

## *ENFJ – Extrovert, Intuitive, Feeling, Judging*

They can be quite warm and engaging when in the presence of others. ENFJs always make you feel included since they use a lot of *we* and *us* in their language. These extroverts are all about unity and helping each other achieve a common goal. Here's what to look for when with a suspected ENFJ:

- They like in-depth conversations that are all about theories and possibilities. Remember, they're intuitive so they tend to look towards the future.
- They're the ones who can anticipate the moods, emotions, and feelings of other people. They're good conversationalists and can impact talks in a way that everyone gets exactly what they need out of the conversation. The goal for them is to make sure everyone becomes engaged, and no one feels bored or left out.
- They can be very persuasive when it comes to things they value, especially if they think it will help others. This can be both a good thing and a bad thing because their enthusiasm can sometimes be too much, irritating others around them. If you're the receptive kind, however, their enthusiasm can be very inspiring.
- Take careful note of how they talk. As communicators, ENFJs like to use abstract ideas and metaphors to make their point. When talking about something they're passionate about, they can quickly tune out others and go off on a tangent.
- They're not very good in impersonal situations. ENFJs need to feel constantly connected to people, which is why they avoid technical situations and focus instead on topics that have a positive impact on their surroundings.
- Typical careers for this type include teaching, psychiatry, counseling, the clergy, sales representing, human resources, event coordinating, writing, music, and religious work.

## *ENTJ – Extrovert, Intuitive, Thinking, Judging*

ENTJs are confident and businesslike. They make incredible speeches that would make you think they're visionaries. Like most extroverts, they like to vocalize their thoughts in order to facilitate processing them. Hence, they're far more likely to talk during meetings or activities; this is simply how they handle tasks at hand, as talking creates a more concrete situation for them. Here are some of the characteristics to look at when you're trying to identify an ENTJ:

- They love talking out their thoughts although, during these conversations, they may seem like they're laying out hard and fast judgment. This doesn't mean they arrive at conclusions quickly; it's simply how they process new information best.

- They love to argue and debate over different theories. Their strengths usually lie on theoretical issues, however, rather than technical matters of debate.

- Don't look at them weirdly if they talk to themselves. In many cases, this is also how ENTJs process their ideas. They also like to take notes, create charts, or make diagrams of situations in order to solve them.

- They're quick thinkers and tend to jump from one idea to the next when it comes to discussions. At first, the things they say can be confusing as they tend to make future predictions that are hard to follow. Some decisions seem nonsensical, but all of these actually contribute towards a long-term plan.

- They're bad when discussing feelings and emotions. In fact, they prefer to keep things private, often seeing emotions as irrelevant or unimportant in their lives.

- These types tend to gravitate to careers that have them working as CEOs, founders of organizations, entrepreneurs, lawyers, judges, university professors, bankers, scientists, and analysts.

### *ESTP – Extrovert, Sensing, Thinking, Perceiving*

They're extroverts so they are going to love friendly and lively conversations and all the physical gestures that go with it. They will hook you in with engaging expressions and their quick wit makes them very enjoyable in social gatherings.

Here are some characterizes of the ESTP personality:

- They're excellent storytellers with a vocabulary that keeps them well-grounded and literal. They have the panache in the way they talk that people remain interested in what they have to say.

- In fact, ESTPs are fairly good with body language and can easily detect the mannerisms of people around them. This simply means that they know exactly what to do and say to make a person smile, laugh, or feel better. Of course, this also means that they know what to say if they want to make someone feel bad.

- Despite being extroverts, ESTPs like to keep their thoughts tucked inside until they're ready to voice them. Their decisions are internally analyzed, and conclusions are reached before they speak out.

- They're also very uncomfortable when asked to talk about feelings. However, they are perfectly happy to swap stories or share experiences with other people.

- Although this isn't 100 percent accurate, ESTPs are usually employed as sales representatives, paramedics, computer technicians, farmers, laborers, service workers, detectives, military, auditors, comedians, craft workers, and transportation operatives.

So how do you talk to one? Here are some tips on how to communicate with an ESTP:

- Keep it friendly and straightforward. Simplicity is the key here. You don't want to give them unnecessary detail as this will only make an ESTP lose interest. Instead, lay down the facts as you know them and offer evidence to support your claim.
- Here is an important thing though—when presenting to an ESTP, suggest several options that can help the ESTP make his decision. He is still going to go through the raw facts, but he will appreciate the options you've laid out as this will speed up the decision process for him.
- Never underestimate their logical manner of thinking. This doesn't mean you can't question their analysis; you simply have to ask them how they arrived at a specific conclusion. The ESTP will actually enjoy telling you how they got from point A to point B.
- Never rush an ESTP if you want to stay on their good side. Do not impose a timetable or a chore chart and just expect them to follow through, especially if you don't offer logical explanations for it.

## Communicating with the ENFJs, ENTJs, ESTJs, and ESTPs

These personality types like to be in charge and have no problem interacting with people. They're the kind of people who can walk into a room and instantly gain the attention of others because they have such a commanding presence. Here are some tips on how to best communicate with these personality types:

- When greeting them, keep things friendly but allow them to talk. As you've probably gathered from the points above, extroverts like to talk, so give them the opportunity to do so. This includes not cutting them off or interrupting and allow them to get to the end of their thoughts.
- Make direct eye contact when talking to them. Speak what you want to say quickly after thinking it through. Let them know what you want and why. They will appreciate this kind of discourse instead of running around the issue.
- Provide dopamine hits! Remember, extroverts can get mentally stimulated easily, so providing them with a challenge or activity can be a great way to excite them. Whether you're turning work into a game, asking a thoughtful question, or posing either a mental or physical challenge can be a great way to get them to engage.

  One study by Michael X. Cohen that concluded back in 2005 found that extroverts receive far more dopamine far quicker than other people, usually instantly after a behavior has taken place (such as completing an action, getting a question right, and so on), or comes after a 7.5 second anticipation period.

  An example of this in action would be saying something like, "I bet you can't print off your report in less than a minute." Then the intensity of the action takes place, and then not letting them know they won for about five seconds afterward the challenge is over is going to give them so much satisfaction. Psychology is weird, right?

- Positivity is everything! Extroverts who fall into this category love positivity because it gives them a wave to ride on. A simple 2010 study carried out at the Annual Convention of the American Psychological Association found that extroverts were far more mentally stimulated by pictures and images of people than introverts were, concluding that they place a far higher amount of importance on social connection.

This then translates into the fact that if the said interaction that they were so excited about didn't go well, was awkward, or left a bitter taste in someone's mouth, this is going to crush the extrovert. Instead, keeping things positive is key!

- Be honest if you don't know the answer to a question. Tell them instead that you'll find out the answer as soon as possible.
- Don't be vague and interpret their words as is. If you already know exactly what they're telling you, then don't try to extrapolate on possible other meanings. If something is unclear, ask them outright. You should not be afraid about clarifying things with this type, as they prefer this to someone who just *guesses* on what needs to be done.

Okay, phew. That's a lot to handle. I know that's a ton of information there, and don't worry, for the last time, you're not expected to remember it all, and nor do you need to. I include it because you can use this information as a reference to look back on if you ever want more information on someone specific in your life.

However, you should have a great idea now on all the different personality types out there, and what category people fall into. Think about certain people in your own life: your partner, your boss, your best friend, or your teenager.

For me, I struggled with my relationship with my boss. I didn't know how to present myself properly or get results. I had ideas, and I had all the drive to succeed on projects and with clients, but I could never seem to bring myself to take action.

Then, when I started learning about all this, I concluded that my boss was an ETNJ, which meant he was decisive and confident and thrived on exploring new ideas and debating. For the first time in my life, I had read the personality of someone else.

I was then able to change up and have purpose in my conversational approaches. I would bring up new ideas and challenge his existing ones, finally coming to a quality conclusion that got results. Over time, the respect from my boss grew because I was pushing all the right buttons, and eventually this way of thinking spread into plenty of other areas of my life. The results speak for themselves. Be your own proof.

But, alas, we must continue our journey. If you haven't already, I highly recommend doing a personality test yourself to see which one you are and how people can relate to you ([www.16personalities.com](www.16personalities.com)) and trying to match people in your own life. Bookmark these chapters as well so you can come back any time!

Of course, the main point we're talking about all this for is so you can communicate effectively with people in your life, so let's zero in on this in more detail as we dive deep into different communication types in this next chapter.

# Chapter 5: Communication Styles

I, and many people, define *communication style* as the way you exchange information with other people. There are basically four styles known today: passive, aggressive, passive-aggressive, and assertive. It's important to make a distinction between these four because the way information is communicated to you will affect how you respond to it.

The chances are you come across all these types of communication in everyone you meet, day in, day out, in one form or another, so becoming familiar with them is a powerful key that's going to unlock many doors when it comes to effective and meaningful communication.

One thing you have to understand though is that you can't box people into single communication styles. People also change the way they communicate based on the results they want to get and will change depending on their life situation and environment. In other words, someone who is usually quite passive can be aggressive if they're having a bad day. Hence, it's often best to classify the communication style as it comes. Let's explore the different types of communication styles.

## Passive

Passive communication is pretty self-explanatory as it's literally the definition of the word. This means there's a lack of assertiveness in what someone is saying. In many cases, a passive person may even avoid saying what they think or what they want because of the anxious thoughts telling them of the effect it may have.

For example, someone may hold a strong political opinion and be too afraid to share it. Or they may love another person but will be unwilling to share how they feel in case it's taken the wrong way. If conversations revolve around risk and reward, passive people are unable to take the risk.

However, by being passive, this in itself is a style of communication, which means it can be read. The trick is to zero in on the person to figure out what hints they're giving away. Are you ready? Here's where we start really diving into reading strategies.

When you're a passive communicator, you don't directly say something; you *hint* at it and expect the other person to get the hint. This can lead to all kinds of problems, such as miscommunication and situations that don't need to evolve.

Let's say you respond passively when you are on a date because you're shy and you don't want to scare the other person away. Remember, anyone can be a passive person at any time, and we all switch roles throughout our lifetime, depending on the situations we find ourselves in. You're feeling passive and your date is asking where you want to go for dinner.

They suggest Thai food and being passive you don't object, nor really say anything. You just agree and go along with it. You get to the Thai place, and, in reality, you hate Thai food and don't really eat much. Your body language gives off all the messages that you're not having a good time and not enjoying yourself, thus the date goes badly, and you never see each other again. Ouch.

Now, people can be passive for all kinds of reasons. They might be having a bad day, they may feel intimated or scared of someone in the surrounding area (think a child unable to speak their mind because they're scared of what their parents might think), or just don't have a strong opinion and feel it's worthless. The point is, how can you still read someone and what they're trying to say?

How do you know when someone is trying to tell you something different from what they're actually saying? Fortunately, there are signs you can think about. Passive communication usually has the following body language tells:

- Lack of eye contact or in some cases, extreme, excessive eye contact
- Dropped shoulders and hunched back
- Keeping their head down
- A low or quiet voice
- Emphasizing certain words
- May repeat basic sentences in an effort to communicate what they're trying to say
- May say phrases like: "It really doesn't matter" or "As long as everyone is happy"
- They tend to go with the flow

### *How to Communicate with Passive Communicators*

The problem with communicating with passive people is the fact that they don't want to come out of their shells. They either lack confidence or don't have a degree of self-worth where they end up believing that their opinions, thoughts, and perspectives aren't valid, and nobody wants to hear them.

As an effective communicator yourself, the trick here is to boost the self-worth of a passive individual and help to coax them into opening up. The simplest way to do this is simply to ask them what their thoughts are on a subject. You could say something like "Hey, what do you think?"

If someone has a hard stuck habit of being passive, they may respond with something like "Oh. Me? Nothing." This is where you'll respond with something like "No, tell me. I'm genuinely interested in what you have to say."

It can take time and energy over an extended period of time to get someone to open up, but it's not impossible. It's important to remember there are endless reasons as to why someone is passive in the first place.

They may be scared of being judged (think about a child afraid of sharing their opinion because they feel their parents may judge them negatively for it), or even intimated by other people in the interaction. Even in situations like this, boosting someone's confidence by acknowledging them and then validating what they're saying is the best way to helping them to open up and communicate. It's all about the balance of respect, compassion, and empathy.

On that note, it's important to remember not to try to force someone to open up if they really don't want to, thus becoming an aggressive communicator yourself. This isn't going to benefit anyone and is only going to push the person into becoming more passive. If someone doesn't want to open up, accept this and move on. You can always try again another time. The more consistent you are, the more likely they'll be to increase their confidence in themselves and you thus open up, eventually.

The final consideration is that you actually need to listen to what the passive person is saying. And take note that listening is different than hearing. It can take a lot for a passive person to open up, so to not be listened to or heard is only going to validate their fears and push them away further.

This means when you're talking to a passive person, you need to validate what they're saying, make them feel heard, repeat keywords back to them to prove it, and acknowledge them and what they're saying. Body language, such as keeping eye contact and nodding for them to continue what they're saying, is key in situations like this.

## Aggressive

Aggressive communication isn't something you can just ignore, usually because you're being forced to hear what they have to say. If someone communicates information in an aggressive manner, you will be able to tell.

Aggressive communication is usually the result of an emotional person and doesn't have to mean a violent or tempered interaction (although it certainly does include this), it can also revolve around someone who is stubborn, unwilling to change their opinion, or is forceful with their perspective.

Additionally, aggressive communication usually comes with a lack of compassion and empathy because the person is more focused on trying to force their point of view, rather than respecting and listening to others. It can be hard to deal with someone who's aggressively communicating, and relationships commonly tend to suffer because of it.

This style has the following signs:

- A loud and demanding voice
- There are threats, criticisms, blaming, intimidation, or any other tactic to compel you into doing what they want
- Aggressive posture and forceful body language
- Intense eye contact

Aggressive communication isn't so much about conveying information but rather, telling a person what they should do. It can also signal a lack of patience or show signs of stress. Remember, someone could be acting aggressive because they are being defensive, and they're trying to protect themselves from a perceived threat.

However, aggressive communication isn't always a negative thing as aggression can be interpreted as a great sign of leadership if used in a productive way. It can extend to confrontations or telling people exactly what they think without regard to circumstances, reactions, or feelings.

### *How to Communicate with Aggressive Communicators*

It's very difficult dealing with aggressive communicators because when someone is acting this way, they are only thinking of themselves and their own points of view. Rarely are they thinking about you, your perspective, or how they feel. It's all about gaining power and control of the situation, whatever the cost.

Now, remember, there are many reasons why someone would be aggressive. If you're unlucky, this is just the nature of the person, perhaps from previous trauma in life, but whether someone is suffering or just having a bad day and taking it out on everyone else, the main reason someone will be aggressive is that they're being defensive.

Dealing with aggression like this is hard work, and you only have a few options. The first and perhaps most important thing to remember is that you can leave the situation.

Let's say you're arguing with your partner about something trivial and things get heated. It happens. Emotions are heightened and stressful feelings cloud judgments. Your partner is aggressively communicating because they don't feel heard or acknowledged. Usually, the best way to deal with this is to give the conversation room to breathe.

Whether you're going to physically leave the room to allow everyone to calm down, go for a walk, or even go to bed and sleep on the situation, allowing time for a bit of space can do wonders for allowing the dust to settle. When you come back to the conversation, everyone can be refreshed in a more balanced state of mind.

Of course, this works in some situations, but what if you're dealing with an aggressive person and you can't leave? Well, you have two choices. Firstly, you can just let the person tire themselves out. Since aggressive people aren't thinking of you and just want to be heard, let them get on with it. You can try being quiet yourself and only validating what they're saying. The sooner it's over with, the better.

Alternatively, you can remain assertive, a communication style we'll explore in the next sections. This means sharing your point of view and striving for a balanced and fair conversation by doing the best you can. Unfortunately, this is pretty much all you're limited to because the capacity of the aggressive person is also limited.

Now, the final point you absolutely must remember when dealing with aggressive people, no matter what strategy you use to deal with it, is to remain levelheaded and balanced, keep your composure, and never let the aggressive person get under your skin.

As soon as that person is under your skin and you're taking what they're saying personally, you'll become clouded by feelings and emotions just like they are, and any hope of a productive conversation will have gone out of the window. Remain balanced and do the best you can. Nobody can ask for anything more.

**Passive-Aggressive**

The passive-aggressive manner of communication is perhaps the most frustrating for both the sender and the receiver. It's a subtle combination of the two previous communication styles, allowing a person to appear passive on the surface but with a hint of aggressiveness under the layer of passivity.

We all know someone at some point in our lives who have been passive-aggressive, perhaps coming across as being sarcastic with what they're saying. Recently in my own life, I saw a coworker who was passive aggressive towards another coworker who won a contract that they wanted to have.

The jealous coworker was saying things like "Yes, oh my god, the project was amazing, and they did such a wonderful job." On paper, this looks like a nice thing to say. But, couple their actual tone of voice while saying it, with what they said, and it was clearly aggressive while trying to keep a straight face.

What are the typical signs of this communication style? Watch out for these:

- Muttering under their breath instead of confronting a person
- Verbally agreeing but doing something else entirely
- Denying the existence of a problem despite body language showing opposition or reluctance
- Silent treatment or sarcasm
- Spreading rumors or talking behind someone's back
- Saying things like, "I'm okay with it, but someone else may not like it."

The problem is that passive-aggressive people are on the defense. These are people who often feel powerless and stuck in their situation. In the case of my coworker, she really didn't like that she didn't get the project, but there was nothing she could do about it. Thus, she resorts to passive-aggressive attitudes because she feels like she has no other option. Like aggressive communication styles, she's clouded by her emotions. Don't worry, I'm sure we've all been like this at some point, and perhaps will again. It's all about looking out for the signs and moving forward productively.

### *How to Communicate with Passive-Aggressive Communicators*

Just like the other negative communication styles, passive-aggressive communication can be hard to deal with, mainly because the person is defensive and mourning a lack of control in a given situation. The best thing you can do here is to remain assertive (see below).

This means you need to stick to being you. You voice your opinion and thoughts, and you remain respectful of the other people within the interaction. This means you remain honest and open and recognize the fact that fighting fire with fire is only going to spread the blaze further. Use these interactions as an opportunity to practice your patience and empathy.

The most important thing to remember, similar to how you deal with all these communication styles, is to remain calm, not to let their words get under your skin, and to not take things personally. As soon as you bite and allow emotion to take you over, it's game over and the situation is only going to get worse.

Of course, if someone is passive aggressive on a regular basis, then there comes a time where you'll need to set boundaries that limit the amount of time you're spending around this person, just to preserve your sanity!

## Assertive

Of all the communication styles, this is perhaps the best one as well as being the most effective. Assertiveness is a manner of communicating what you want to do without (hopefully) hurting anyone's feelings. You get to say what you want to say, sharing your views and opinions, but you also have the respect and empathy to listen to others and take on board what they're saying.

This is not very important if you have the same goal and mindset as other people. If that's the case, then all you have to do is agree with each other. Simple. Assertiveness comes to the surface when you want to have open communication with another person, allowing both of you to express your thoughts, ideas, feelings, desires, and needs—without causing unnecessary friction. The goal is to create a balance so that all parties come out of the conversation content.

How do you do this? An assertive communicator has the following characteristics:

The primary way to be more assertive in conversations is actually fairly easy. You simply need to use 'I' more in what you say. Contrary to what you may think, this does not translate as selfishness but simply validates what you feel without putting blame on other people. Words like "I feel frustrated" or "I feel helpless" are used (rather than a phrase like it's helpless) which allows other people into your thoughts, giving them room to adjust and empathize with your situation. It allows you to claim ownership over what you feel and the behaviors that go along with that feeling, as well as opening the door for someone else to share how they feel.

Some of the key signs to look out, or ways to become more assertive yourself, include;

- Maintaining contact. Contact can be in the form of eye contact or if you're comfortable with it, physical contact. The confidence you have with the other person helps you to carry what you're saying.
- Smile and assume a positive posture. Listen to what people have to say but make sure that you get your own time to speak. It's all about having a balance.
- If you want to be assertive, make sure to address any objections on a point-by-point basis. Repeat what they said and address each one individually until you've tackled all the issues raised. You can then present your own, provide the benefits for them, and bring forth a call to action to encourage people to join in.
- Keep your tone calm and low without any hint of smugness or superiority. In many cases, people resist new ideas simply because of the speaker or the way the new idea is introduced in a conversation. You want to make it as gentle and as friendly as possible to help people be more welcoming to the idea.

Now, with that list completed, we come to the end of this chapter. Hopefully, you're feeling very familiar with the communication styles that are out there and you know what to look for, how to identify the communication style of others, and how to choose what kind of communicator you want to be yourself.

It's time to move onto one of the areas of communication I find most interesting, and that's figuring out whether the messages that people are giving you are honest or not. In other words, we're going to explore how to tell when people are lying.

# Chapter 6: Reading Lies in People

One of the most valuable skills when reading people is being able to tell when they're lying. Admit it—you've always wanted to know when someone is lying to you, and what a skill it would be.

I worked in sales for many years, and we would frequently be up against other companies trying to score contracts and negotiate deals. While I must stress it's not as glamorous as it sounds, it was a fantastic opportunity to improve myself while adapting my people skills, like communication.

In the case of honesty, there were frequent situations where I would be talking to clients or competitors about contracts, and it would be evident that they were lying. *No, we're sticking with your company. We're not looking anywhere else. Yes, we can get the work done by such-and-such a date. No, this is all the budget we can afford for this project.* The list is literally limitless.

The trick to telling if someone is lying may seem like a superpower, but there's no mind-reading involved. In fact, the solution is really quite simple. Studies show that when someone is lying, people have specific *tells*, such as scratching their nose or brushing their hair with their fingers. People who play poker often use these *tells* to see if they should match the other person's bet and take a risk on their hand. If you head over to YouTube and search "example of poker tells", there are several videos that show you things to look out for that are specific to the game. For example, someone raising the stacks may instantly start playing with their chips, their mind trying to occupy itself naturally while attempting to convince someone of their lie. This psychological *tell* can be found everywhere in all aspects of life, and it's what we're going to be exploring throughout this chapter.

One thing I want to remind you of is that reading lies in a person is not an exact science. People's actions when lying can vary, which is why familiarity with the person is important. The longer you know a person, the more accurate your prediction will be about the truthfulness of what they're saying.

So, that being the case, here are the typical signs of lying according to experts.

## Understanding a Baseline

One thing I want you to remember is that when reading body language, there's usually a *baseline* that allows you to start somewhere. A baseline is simply the *normal* way in which an individual acts when around other people. Simply put, if a person is being truthful and confident in their usual surroundings, how exactly do they act? Knowing a person's baseline lets you know when they're acting out of character. Sure, you can walk into a room full of strangers and do a casual *read* of the room, but reading people close to you is often easier as you've known them for a longer period of time. You have a point of reference, to put it simply.

As mentioned, people have varied *lying* gestures. Some people just love to talk with their hands while other people just love to fidget with their hair, even on normal days. Just because someone is playing with their hair, that doesn't mean it's a tell if it's something they do regularly. Hence, seeing them do this doesn't automatically mean they are lying, it might simply be a part of their personality.

So, as you spend time with people in your life, be it friends, family, or coworkers, start to observe how they act normally and how they carry themselves. When they do someone out of the ordinary, you'll know something is up.

## Observe Hand Movements

People who are lying tend to use gestures, but they do it after speaking. Typically, you'd find people gesturing while talking because this is a natural part of the process. Their body is working with the mind in telling a story or conveying a message.

In contrast, a person lying is focusing too much on making up the story that the body fails to catch up. Hence, they make up the lie first and then perform the gestures to emphasize their point. Also, take note that gestures of people who are lying often involve both hands as opposed to truthful people who only use one hand.

Back in 2015, the University of Michigan broke down 120 video clips of important court cases to see how people behaved when they were lying versus when they were telling the truth. The study concluded that people use both hands to exaggerate their truth in 40% of cases, whereas only 25% of people use both hands while telling the truth.

Another unconscious body language done by dishonest people is keeping their palms away from you. This is a subliminal way of holding information away from other people that most people will do unconsciously during conversations, so keep an eye open for it. Hence, they may put their hands in their pocket or keep them close to their body, as if they're trying to keep something a secret inside their palms. So basically, people who lie can go two ways with their hands: they can either use them too much or not at all. Look for the extremes.

## Itching and Fidgeting

There's a popular belief that when a person lies, they tend to scratch their nose. It's only one of the most stereotypical poker tells out there. Of course, this isn't true 100% of the time for every single person since everyone is different—but it does bear noting in many cases, this could be a surefire tell.

The fact is that it's fairly normal for people to have an itching sensation or fidget in their seat when they're uncomfortable; the body naturally looks for a way to distract itself while trying to avoid getting caught. Research carried out by UCLA by Dr. Lillian Glass and professor R. Edward Geiselman has concluded similar results in this field of research. Also note that when lying, people are often nervous about what they're saying, which causes the autonomic nervous system to fluctuate thus creating that tingling sensation all over the body. It's a lot like the nerves you get when you sit close to someone you like during those younger days.

However, nose scratching isn't the only itching movement associated with lying. When people lie, they play with their hair, play with their fingers, scribble on a notebook, or perhaps the most go-to technique nowadays—they play with their phones. Whatever the tell, when someone is talking to you and they start acting restless, this could be a sign that they're not telling the truth. You see it all the time in children who are lying to their parents about not taking chocolate biscuits when they shouldn't have. They twiddle their fingers in their palms and can't make eye contact. These behaviors continue throughout our lifetime.

## Facial Expressions

Of course, let us not forget how the face itself can signify when someone is lying. The eyes in particular can tell you so much depending on when a person chooses to look at you and when they choose to look away. Looking too much or not looking at all can be indicative of lying. Some people prefer to meet your gaze when lying because they *think* this will impress upon you their sincerity.

Commonly, non-experienced liars tend to look away when uttering a lie. They feel as though they can't bear to look at you in case of getting caught and something will give them away, when in fact this refusal to act normal says it all. But the same does work in the reverse for staring.

The same 2015 Geiselman UCLA study I mentioned above researched this as well. In the court clips, over 70% of people who were lying would stare at the people they were lying to. Again, when trying to read someone, you're looking for the extremes. Too much staring or a complete lack of eye contact will be a dead giveaway. However, it's granted that this can be a little confusing when judging people simply through their eyes. This is why it's important to have a baseline when it comes to people, as I will explain later on.

One thing I want you to remember, though, is that a 2012 study published by *PLOS One* has already debunked the popular myth about where a person looks when lying. The myth goes that when a person is fabricating something they look left and when they're recalling something, they're looking right. This is not true as the direction people look is largely based on their mannerisms. That being the case, try not to focus too much on the direction but instead simply on the overall mannerisms of the individual you're communicating with.

## Change in Complexion

This one's pretty obvious, and you've probably heard of it before or have seen it for yourself. Look for skin color and complexion changes. People blush, people become red or become pale depending on the circumstances. People tend to become pale when they're nervous or afraid of something. When the skin turns a shade of red, however, that's indicative of anger or perhaps even excitement, like when a teenager typically blushes when sitting beside their crush. Basically, if you read a change in skin color, you know something's up.

## Sweat in the T Zone

This is something you definitely have to watch out for when wondering if a person is lying to you or not. The T Zone is an area of the face that spans up across the forehead, down the nose, and onwards towards the mouth. Sweating is fairly common in this area if a person is lying, especially if they're nervous about it.

## Tone of Voice

Obviously, we're trying to focus on non-verbal communication here, but the tone of voice is still a strong indicator, absent from the words themselves. High-pitched voices tend to come out of nervous people as the vocal cords tighten, making it hard to push out the particular words. There can also be a croak, a stutter, or some broken words coming out of a nervous individual. Some people clear their throats to help improve their speech, which is also indicative of nervousness. In contrast, a loud and booming voice can be a sign of confidence or anger, depending on the situation. A sudden change in the volume can also indicate defensiveness in people, especially when confronted with possible mistakes.

## The Mouth

Playing with the lips, such as rolling them back until they almost disappear, is another good indicator, as well as biting a lip. It's typically a sign of lying by omission as people physically try to hold back a word or a thought by pulling in their lips. If it goes the other way, however, it can be a sign of resistance or when a person doesn't want to talk about something.

## The Words Themselves

Again, we're trying to focus on the non-verbal way of communicating, but I still want to cover all bases. After all, experienced liars can easily control their body language to match the situation. Hence, you still have to listen to the words themselves as they can indicate when a person is trying too hard to convince you of their truthfulness. Some common phrases used by liars include:

- "Honestly…"
- "Let me tell you the truth…"
- "Uh…"
- "Like…"
- "Um…"

### *Understanding How a Lie Works*

One of the most interesting facts I ever read was that people who are lying spend way more energy on presenting themselves in a truthful way and trying to hide their tells that they spend energy on the actual story itself. Telling lies in such a way is incredibly taxing on a person's cognitive system because they're creating a story out of nothing, even if the story or lie is a simple one by nature.

One way to overcome this is simply to ask the person you think is lying to you to tell you the same story but in reverse chronological order. Since the person has spent so much energy trying to get away with the lie, the chances are they've skipped over the details and won't be able to remember them properly recalling them back.

This technique is backed by a scientific study conducted back in 2008 aptly named *Increasing cognitive load to facilitate lie detection: The benefit of recalling an event in reverse order*. Within the study, a false, staged situation was created in which 80 people either told the truth or told lies. Some people were told to retell the events in chronological order, and others in reverse. The liars telling the story in reverse found it much more difficult and were easier to spot than any other group.

### Your Gut Instinct Knows All

This final consideration is perhaps the most important. You ever just get that gut feeling that something isn't right, and the person you're speaking with is lying to you? Yeah, we all get that feeling from time to time. It's like standing at the end of a dark alley on your way home alone late at night and you get that strong feeling that, no, you're not going down there tonight. You're going to take the well-lit street down the road. This is your natural human instinct in full effect.

It's important to remember that your human instinct is incredibly powerful when it comes to things like this because it knows every human interaction you've ever had and will be able to pick up on tells and signs of dishonesty, even if you can't consciously place your finger on what is wrong.

A 2014 study in unconscious lie detection published in Psychological Science set up a situation where 72 people watched videos of fake crime suspects who were accused of taking a $100 bill off a bookshelf. Some people had taken it, whereas others had not. All the suspects had been told to state that they had not taken the money.

While the method proved to be inconsistent, with liars being identified 43% of the time, and truth-tellers identified 48% of the time, this was when people were given a time frame to think and observe the footage. In the time-restricted trials, where participants had to give quick-reaction answers based on what they saw, the participants would unconsciously use words like *dishonest* more frequently when the person was actually lying, and words like *honest* when people were telling the truth.

In other words, there's a very high chance your initial gut reaction going into a social interaction is right, so bear it in mind and be mindful of how you feel when identifying a liar.

Phew. That's a lot of information. I remember when I first learned some of these tactics after completing a body language and charisma course during my early twenties, and I was astounded with how well they worked. Like I said before, the more you know someone, the more of a baseline you have of them, the easier they'll be to read because you'll be able to spot the clear differences in their characters.

However, with this knowledge in your mind, and with some experience, you can even spot these signs in strangers you've only just met. While humans are so different, we are all fairly similar in so many ways, especially when it comes to basic psychology and how our brains work; aka tells and reacting in certain ways when certain things happen.

Keep an eye out for these signs in people you interact with, or perhaps even try lying to your friends (let them know this is the plan, you don't want to fall out with anyone.) One of my favorite games to play while walking in the city with my family is saying three statements, two are true and one is false, and everyone else has to guess which is false. It's a great way to practice and a lot of fun.

Now we're going to dive into something new, another of my favorite topics, which is understanding the motivations and drive behind people when they are communicating. What do they want and why are they saying what they are saying? Are their hidden, underlying messages something we should be aware of? Let's find out.

# Chapter 7: Understanding People's Motivations

In the previous chapter, we talked about lying and how to more or less tell when someone is lying to you. If you ever watched one of my favorite television series, *House*, you may remember a quote by the famous doctor himself that goes: "Everybody lies; the only variable is about what."

So basically, what House is trying to say is that you may be able to tell when someone is lying, but can you tell what they're lying about, what they're covering up, or basically what the motivation behind the lie is?

In this chapter, we're going to talk about the motivations of people. Everybody is motivated by something. The feeling of hunger is your body giving you the motivation to want to eat so it can survive. It's basic human motivation. There are, of course, more complex motivations that we're going to get into. The thing is, if you want to be able to read a person's body language correctly, you need to be able to understand the motivations that drive them towards that end goal which is done by figuring out why someone is communicating in the way that they're communicating.

Think of this as driving on a highway. Every person is driving towards a destination which is their main motivation. If you're driving right alongside them, you might not be 100% sure of where they're going. However, if you take a good look at the car's movements, the blinkers, the position on the lane, the speed they approach the exits at, and so on, you should be able to make a close-to-accurate prediction of what they're doing and therefore adjust your own driving accordingly. Even if a person is lying to you, knowing what motivates them or what their *end game* is can help you figure out what the lie is all about and why they're doing what they do.

This one is going to be a little more difficult as it can get quite complicated, so bear with me as we go through this. Don't worry, we'll move slow and steady. Just so we're on the same page moving forward, I'll be defining *motives* as the conscious or unconscious moving factors for people's behaviors. Motives are the reasons we do what we do. *Behaviors* are the performances themselves or the actions that are reflective of a person's motivation. In other words, you feel the motive to eat, and your behavior is to get food from the fridge. Okay, let's get into it.

## Maslow's Hierarchy of Needs

I remember first being introduced to motives and behaviors and this phrase came up and I thought to myself *Oh God, this is so complicated already. I'm in too deep!* Don't worry, it's not like that.

Maslow's Hierarchy of Needs is possibly one of the oldest rationales for understanding human motivation. It's not perfect, but what is? Maslow's Hierarchy of Needs is a lot like the Nutrition Pyramid. It explains that motives have a bottom-up approach. The bottom needs are the most basic and prevalent which must be met first before the other needs are addressed. There are five levels to basic human need, starting from the bottom, and these are:

- Physiological
- Safety
- Love/Belonging
- Esteem
- Self-Actualization

So, in the shape of a pyramid, physiological needs are on the bottom, aka, your basic human needs that need to be fulfilled, moving up to more spiritual needs. If it helps, you can easily find a visual diagram online. Here is a brief look at how these sections work and what they mean:

## *Physiological Needs*

These are the main components that are aimed towards survival. According to Maslow's theory, humans are compelled to fulfill these needs first before they can ascend to higher levels. So, what exactly are these physiological needs? These are things like:

- Homeostasis, or the balance of the body in order to preserve its living condition
- Health
- Food
- Water
- Sleep
- Clothes
- Shelter

Notice how safety comes next. If you're fighting for your life after your plane goes down in the middle of the woods with no one around for miles, your first thoughts are going to be on survival. If you're starving and dehydrated, the chances are you're going to take risks to get food and water. Of course, we don't have this problem so much these days.

## *Safety Needs*

After a person meets their basic physiological needs, the next step is their safety needs. Here are the typical considerations when it comes to safety needs:

- Personal security
- Emotional security
- Financial security
- Health and wellbeing
- Safety needs against accidents and illnesses

How do these things usually show themselves in an individual? You can see this by the way individuals purchase insurance policies, set up a retirement account, get jobs with security, open and maintain a savings account, and so on. Of course, you also have to consider people who are in war zones who are seeking out security in its most basic form: physical security. You will find that when in the midst of war, people seek security to maintain homeostasis or stay alive. The two stages are very much connected.

## *Social Belonging*

Once you have the most basic needs and security, the next step is to seek out social belonging. You're surviving and your basic needs are met. Now it's time to bring other people into the equation.

We are social beings after all. It's hard-wired into us to connect with other people because fulfilling our basic needs is much easier when you're working together with other people. This need to be accepted by our peers is one of the most common driving forces for people. The need for social belonging is typically met by the following:

- Friendships
- Intimacy and romantic relationships
- Family

The need to be accepted in social groups is true regardless of the size of the group itself. This is why even when a person forms part of a small club in school, they still need to be part of the social circle within that club. Small social connections include family, friends, and colleagues in the typical workforce. You will notice that most people will go to extra lengths in order to have this sense of acceptance and belongingness in their chosen social circle. Failure to meet these needs leads to problems like social anxiety, clinical depression, and loneliness.

### *Self-Esteem*

Fourth is self-esteem, which is somewhat connected to the third level. One thing you'll notice is that most people use the third level to jump to the fourth. Acceptance in their social circle tends to promote a person's self-esteem as they find themselves worthy because others find them worthy. What does this level cover? There are actually two versions of this: the lower and the higher version. The higher version speaks of self-esteem derived from others. There's a need for status, fame, prestige, recognition, and attention from others. This level is all about the ego.

The more difficult version is the higher one which speaks of self-esteem deriving from your own competency. This speaks of self-confidence, of knowing that you're capable of independence. This means being able to take care of yourself, knowing and fulfilling your own basic needs, and have the ability to meet those needs, perhaps even providing for the needs of others. This gives an individual a sense of value and prevents the possibility of having an inferiority complex.

### *Self-Actualization*

This is the toughest level of the motivation pyramid and is all about managing to reach a person's full potential. Maslow describes it as the ability of an individual to accomplish everything they can possibly achieve in life. It is a lifetime goal and for many people, it can be difficult to pinpoint what that lifetime goal actually is. Others, however, know what this goal is but have a hard time reaching the lower levels, therefore making them unable to reach this pinnacle.

Self-actualization can include:

- Parenting
- Partner acquisition
- Utilizing and developing abilities
- Utilizing and developing talents
- Pursuing other goals
- Fulfilling your dreams

These self-actualization motives are described by Maslow as the intrinsic drive that pushes people forward into completion. People who have a clear grasp of this goal need to understand how their four needs in the pyramid interact with each other to help them achieve their ultimate goal.

### *The Sixth Level - Transcendence*

Oddly enough, Maslow himself, creator of this hierarchy, has also talked about a sixth level. He called it Transcendence and according to him, it is a level of achievement where a person surrenders himself to something or someone more powerful than himself. You could call it God or surrendering yourself to the universe. While you may be thinking this is all about religion, but that's not all there is to it. Transcendence is also pursued through meditative exercises. According to Maslow, transcendence refers to the highest and most holistic level of human consciousness.

I could write a whole book on this topic of transcendence, and trust me, I might. It's very interesting to read about and explore but would be hard to conceptualize as we look into motives, so I'm going to leave it for now. If you are interested, I recommend reading about Buddhist philosophy. It might surprise you.

### Now I know what you're thinking. How does all this relate to reading people?

If you rely completely on Maslow's Hierarchy of Needs, you'll note that most people's actions are built towards reaching any of these five needs. It can be a tad difficult, but what you want to do is try to figure which of these five needs a person wants to achieve when confronted with a particular behavior. Is someone seeking social acceptance? Do they want to achieve the basic necessities of maintaining life? Do they want to have a sense of security? Are they trying to maintain a certain level of self-esteem? If you can figure out exactly what ultimate need one wants to fulfill, you can at least fill in the gaps and make a reading on what their body is saying.

### Experience Matters when it comes to Motives

Unfortunately, there is a lot more to motivation than just figuring out which of the five needs a person wants to meet. The fact is that experience is a big predictor when it comes to figuring out motivations. Plus, it's on a case-by-case basis, with YOU as a big factor in the equation. Simply put—what does this person want from me? What need is this person trying to fulfill through me? What need can I fill for this person?

Let's say you're ready to figure out people's motivations. You want to understand someone and help them fulfill their needs, to forge better connections. The question now is this: how do you start? The way you start varies from person to person, but there are certain *general rules* that can help you move forward with connections.

Here are some of the typical guidelines to make things easier for you:

### Hidden Social Behaviors

We've been talking about the different actions of people and what they mean, but it's also important to look at the opposite end of the scale. You should keep in mind that more often than not, people draw in instead of pushing out. Many actions or reactions are done in order to suppress rather than express. For example, people close their arms, suck in their lips, or look away from people when withdrawing from an interaction and trying to hide. It's a pull motion rather than a push. How does this apply when you're trying to connect with people?

Well, you have to pay extra attention. There's this precise moment between a push and a pull when a person starts to react about something and then quickly holds that back in because they realize that they're showing emotions and feelings they don't want people to see. That's the moment you have to watch out for looking at people.

While you might not always catch this deliberate inaction, knowing that it's there is half the battle. More importantly, this should tell you that a lot of things are beneath the surface. This is why you need to focus on empathy, delving deep into the surface instead of just interpreting what people say without applying empathy.

Put yourself in the person's shoes and you should be able to at least have an idea of what they're trying to do or what they're trying to achieve. Allow me to give you an example for clarity.

You're at work. A project is due to be completed by the end of the week and it's Friday. You and your team realize that a large section of the project has been forgotten about and is missing. Everyone is trying to find who is responsible. People are stressed out and arguing amongst each other, and you suddenly realize that someone is about to speak and then stops themselves.

Using all the techniques we've spoken about throughout this book, it's pretty clear that you've just experienced the person who was supposed to do the work realize that they're supposed to do the work and have potentially gotten everyone else in trouble.

Notice how this person was about to say something but understands that they messed up, and now want to blend into the background, thus they remain silent. Their motive is to remain accepted by the group (social acceptance motives) and they don't want everyone to turn on them.

This is motives and hidden social behaviors in full effect. What do you do now that you have this information? You have a lot of options, but having empathy and compassion, you would perhaps choose to say it doesn't matter who forgot, what matters is pulling together and moving forward. Instead of pointing fingers, it's time to brainstorm solutions and explore your options.

When exploring solutions, you could perhaps pull up the person who withdrew to see what ideas they have and can bring to the table. Perhaps some of the work has already been done and wasn't finished on time. Either way, you're providing opportunities for redemption, once again (I would assume in a positive way) fulfilling this person's need of being socially accepted, and the problem is alleviated.

Of course, this is a simple example, but you can see how the logic applies. You're looking for signs, reading everyone in the room, getting answers, identify motives, and using this information to get things done.

**Conceit trumps malice.**

Another thing to keep in mind is that the vast majority of people aren't naturally evil, even if they may seem like it from time to time. If you're going to guess a person's motivation, malice should NOT be your first choice. In law, accused people are often considered *innocent until proven guilty* because the default setting is that a person is *good* unless there's enough evidence to show that they've been bad. This is also important if you want to understand people better. More often than not, people don't want to watch the world burn, but instead are acting through clouded emotions, acting out through past traumas, or are in a rough position.

In any situation where people are doing something that is harmful to others, first assume that they're doing it because they're unaware or ignorant or believe that their way is more important. By having this mindset, you are more likely to react in a kinder, more empathetic manner, which can be incredibly defusing to an intense situation. The chances are you'd react by explaining to them exactly why their choice of action is not the best one. In contrast, walking into a situation believing a person is simply *evil* makes you react badly, perhaps even rudely or even violently, and that's not going to benefit anyone.

## Selfish altruism often dictates behavior

Selfishness is often viewed as a desire to please only yourself while altruism is its exact opposite. Altruistic people are said to be selfless or want only the best for others. Oddly enough, people are driven by these two factors at the same time. Perhaps the simplest way to explain this is: people are giving, but they are giving in a way that also helps themselves. For example, people have no problem lending money to a friend, knowing that this particular friend can help them fix their computer or fix their car without charge. You trade in a car from a dealer and the two of you benefit. In some cases, helping someone is a sign that you have more power than that person, therefore helping you establish a feeling of dominance over another person.

When I was growing up, I lived in the country next to a charity farm. It was the kind of place where people with special needs would learn skills and kids could spend weekends outside. On paper, it's a good place, except the people running it seemed to be very much for show.

I'm not going to get into the politics of it, but a prime example that stuck with me for whatever reason was litter picking around the small town. The owners would do an annual litter pick up where they would publicize what they were doing and ensured that everyone understood that they were going out of their way to make the town a better place.

On the other hand, my father would go out and walk the dog every single morning and evening and would always come back with a small bag of litter chucked out the windows of drivers on the highway. Sure, he didn't walk all over the town and do it everywhere, only around our area, but he used to do it without any recognition from anyone else. If everyone in town had the same attitude, there would be no need for an annual litter pick up where everyone is doing it to make themselves feel as though they're doing some good.

Now, I'm not saying that any kind of litter pick up is wrong, or that the group activity is doing more harm than it is good. I use this example because it highlights how people will do good things sometimes because it benefits themselves and fulfills their own self-altruistic needs. Bear this in mind during your own interactions.

## Memory is fickle

Another thing that might help you in understanding people for the better is that they don't have excellent memories. Memory is incredibly fickle for people and people are likely to forget certain things, ideas, or concepts. I love the exercise of imagining you are holding a pen in your hand right now and then imagine dropping it. If you imagine hard enough, you can really convince yourself that you just dropped your pen.

Weird, right? This is how bad human memories actually are. From experience, you'll think back to dropping your pen right now in a few weeks, and although you know it never happened, they'll still be a part of your memory that is trying to work out whether you did or not.

In the art of reading communication, if you're expecting someone to call or someone promised to do something for you, but they didn't, you can always assume it's because they simply forgot instead of deliberate malice. Hand in hand with the point above, do not go the route of assuming people are naturally evil as this will leave you feeling bitter and closed to the possibility of connecting and understanding others. Be loving and compassionate. This is how the best relationships are formed.

## People are more emotional than they let on

Have you ever looked at someone being given surprising news and they seem to have very little reaction to it, even though the news is fairly shocking? That's because they're in shock and can't quite believe what they're being told, and even though they're feeling a ton of emotion, there are very few signs of it on the surface (apart from the silence and stunned look). The truth is that people are more emotional than they let on. If there's something seething beneath the surface, it's important to recognize that emotion even if you don't see it bubble out. It's perfectly normal for people to hold their feelings in. After all, outbursts are usually frowned upon in society and flamboyant enthusiasm is discouraged as being hyper or childish. There is, of course, the taboo that men hold out and won't outwardly display their emotions as signs of being *weak*. These taboos are being challenged all the time, but they definitely still exist in many parts of the world. In other words, someone could be feeling really sad, but in an attempt to feel strong and in control, they are holding the feelings and emotions in, trying to bury them down as though they're not there whatsoever. In conversations and social interactions, you have to remember that people may not always be displaying their actual thoughts and emotions. Do not call people out on it unless you have to, but it's important to take it into consideration when interacting with them.

Unfortunately, the reverse of this holds true too. Unless you have made a full display of emotions or had a breakdown, people generally assume you're okay and act as if nothing has changed. It can be quite frustrating if you're the one who's suppressing your emotions, but it feels perfectly fine for those at the other end. If you're on the opposite side of the situation (which means you're the one holding in your emotions), then do not take it personally. Don't *assume* that they *should* know your thoughts because people can only see as much as you allow them to see.

To round it all off, whenever you're interacting with someone, think about what kind of motives they have and what needs they are trying to fulfill. Everybody, every single human on the planet, is driven by a motive and need of some kind, and being able to highlight and understand what that is can take you such a long way in the journey of reading other people and their intentions.

# Chapter 8: Reading the Face and Body–Cues and What They Mean

Body language is a wide field and contrary to what you may think, it's not just the *body* per se, but also covers facial expressions, posture, gesture, eye movements, body movement, and even the lack of body movement itself. Body language is not unique to humans though; in fact, it's very obvious if you watch animals during their mating seasons. The dances and postures are hardly subtle as they do their best to attract the opposite sex.

But what about us humans? Body language in humans is far more complicated, however, so you'll have to be doubly observant. Unlike animals, there are lots of possible motivations that affect our body language. Even worse, some people make it a point of controlling their body's natural reaction or make sure that nothing shows through their body and facial expressions. Sometimes, they even fake those postures to give others the wrong impression. It's a minefield of infinite possibilities out there, but with the right foundations of knowledge, it's easily traversed.

## The Science of Body Language

One thing you should note is that body language reading is not some difficult pseudoscience. It has actually been studied for years and has been solidified by legitimate studies. Today, the science of studying body language is called Kinesics and was founded by Ray Birdwhistell. It covers the following actions or conditions:

- Facial expressions
- Body posture
- Eye movement
- Use of space
- Touch
- Gestures

Throughout this chapter, we're going to explore each type of Kinesics, learning the foundations and basics of each so you know exactly what to look out for in your social interactions and what people mean through their non-verbal communications towards you.

## Facial Expressions

How good are you at reading facial expressions?

There are currently tests online that tells you whether you're good at reading facial expressions or not. In fact, some tests like Reading the Mind in the Eyes Test checks to see whether you can read a person's mind simply by looking at their eyes. If you're interested in taking the test yourself, check out the website: socialintelligence.labinthewild.org/mite. See how well you fare if you want. It's a lot of fun. I got 32 out of 36. Can you beat it? For purposes of improving communication, we're going to include all the elements that are included when it comes to reading facial expressions, which involves the eyes, eyebrows, lips, nose, and even the wrinkles around the eyes and mouth.

- Pupils – There is practically no way to fake the movement of the pupils when reading facial expressions. The pupils of the eye contract and expand without any sort of control on the part of a person. Typically, the pupils will expand when a person is interested and contract when they're not. Try this with a loved one. Say the name of a famous person they find attractive or a favorite food, and you can noticeably see the difference.
- Blinking Motion – The eyes typically blink six to ten times per minute. When a person looks at something they find interesting, however, that blinking rate slows down drastically. It's therefore a great indicator when someone finds something interesting or attractive. In fact, it's often used as a sign of flirting or interest in a romantic setting. In an office or social setting, unblinking eyes could be a signal that a person is very interested in what you have to say and listening and engaged to you throughout.
- Raising the head – Raising the head from a lowered position is a sign of captured interest. Think of a student who's looking down during an exam who suddenly raises their head when they hear something important. This is the kind of movement that we are trying to describe in this situation.
- Head tilt – A head tilt usually starts from a normal position of the head and then juts out at an angle. This is what makes it different from the motion of raising your head from a lowered position. A head tilt also indicates interest, usually towards the person or activity where it happens to be tilted towards. When combined with facial expressions like a narrowing of the eyebrows, it can be a sign of confusion, curiosity, questioning, or uncertainty. A head that's tilted backward may be a sign of suspicion.

Of course, let's not forget the typical head gestures that mean practically the same for everyone. These are:
- Nodding – usually signifies agreement
- Shaking the head – usually signifies disagreement

What's important about these gestures is that people are often conscious of doing this. Hence, gestures can be easily controlled by them depending on the situation. Some are able to stop the motion entirely while others turn it into very subtle gestures so that it would be very difficult to notice. However, more often than not, especially among most people going about their day-to-day lives, these are unconscious actions we all do.

## Hands, Arms, and Gestures

- Shrug – A shrug is composed alongside a multitude of gestures which include exposed palms, hunched shoulders, and raised brows. It's a universal sign that indicates a lack of knowledge or uncertainty over a particular activity. It can often be translated as a sign that the other person doesn't know what you're saying or doesn't understand what you're trying to convey.

- Clenched Hands – Clenched hands are a sign of repression. You're trying to prevent the burst of emotions like anger or frustration. It's a self-containment mechanism often used by people who don't want to do or say something out of order. In some cases, you can read this gesture as a sign that someone has a closed mind about what you're trying to say. In the alternative, open and relaxed hands are a sign of comfort and show a positive attitude with a mind welcome to new ideas.

- Hand Wringing – This is often interpreted as a sign of anxiety or nervousness. Playing with something in your hands also has the same interpretation.

- Handshake – You have to be careful with handshakes as this can say so much about a person and vice versa. I'm sure you've managed to have presumptions of people simply because of the way they shook your hand. The best handshake is often considered to be a firm, dry grip, that's quick but not too long. It shouldn't be too tight as to cause pain, but it should be strong enough to signify competence on the part of the person shaking their hand.

    My advice is you practice your handshake with another person to help you decide on the best pressure to use when greeting someone this way. Note though—not all cultures accept handshakes as a viable way of greeting others. For example, people in India or those who practice the Muslim faith do not approve of handshakes as a way of greeting between men and women.

- Covering the mouth – Doing this is often shown as a sign of repression like a person wanted to say something but decided against it at the last minute. Some people use this gesture as a way to show thinking or a thought process. A classic unconscious motion is pressing a thumb against a closed mouth, which indicates someone is actively holding back on what they want to say.

## How to Apply this Knowledge

Simply noticing any of these actions can give you a clear indication of how the other person you're interacting with is feeling and will allow you the foundation to make a decision on how you want to proceed.

For example, if you say something and the other person clenches their fists or tightens their mouth, you know you may have overstepped a line and made the other person defensive. You can then choose to lighten the situation with a joke or clarify that no disrespect or malicious intent was meant, but instead, you meant something else, in which you would try to share your point of view from another perspective.

By ebbing and flowing in conversation this way, you're adapting how you communicate your messages, so they are best received by the people you're speaking to, thus nurturing the best possible relationships with these people, and have more chance of successfully getting what you want out of life.

## Body Posture and Movement

You've probably noticed that reading body language involves paying attention to different parts of the body all at once. Some gestures are centered in just one area, like the face, and therefore are slightly easier than others. Some gestures, however, are scattered all over the body, which means that different parts are moving all at once. This makes it tougher to do a reading, but you'll find that with practice, the whole thing becomes easier.

Body posture and movement are big predictors of a person's thoughts and emotions. The general position of the chest, shoulders, legs, and so on will tell you if a person is aggressive, afraid, unsure, excited, and so on. Here are some of the typical changes in the body and what they indicate:

- A pumped-out chest is a sign of power, confidence, and dominance. Typically, when the chest is spread out, the shoulders are also stretched into a straight line, pushing the chest forward and making the person appear bigger. Combined with hands placed on the hips and this can be dubbed as the *Superman* pose which makes a person appear bigger and occupy more space. This is often seen as a sign of confidence and dominance. If you'll notice, many animals in the wild, when protecting their territory or trying to attract a mate, tend to make their bodies appear bigger so that they'll be easily noticed. Men and women do the same thing and often for the same reasons. What's more, the heart space is in the middle of the chest, making it a vulnerable area. To pump out your chest is to expose this space means that you're not afraid of anything in the given situation.

- Touching the chest can also be a sign of sincerity. You'll notice how people do this when they're trying to apologize or communicate how bad they feel or their condolences to another person. Again, this indicates the heart, meaning you're sharing this emotion you're feeling from the heart.

- Scratching or touching the chest can also be a sign of discomfort. Any kind of twitch along these lines can signify an uncomfortable feeling. Another point along these lines is when someone strokes their arms or shoulders. This is a self-soothing motion which also highlights a feeling of discomfort or uncertainty.

Just like the face gestures section, once you've identified a tell, it's important to make sure you're adapting your conversation style to follow suit, which is the best way to ensure you're being well received. Highlight cues in a person and keep the conversation moving forward.

## Breathing

Breathing can tell you a lot about what a person feels.

You've probably noticed this already, not just in other people, but also in yourself. For example, you might hold your breath when excited or take short and shallow breaths when scared. Ever find yourself in a situation where it feels like you've forgotten to breathe or haven't breathed in a long time? That's what we're talking about here. Typically, deep and even breaths are indicative of relaxation, such as when you're sleeping or when you're sitting down watching a relaxing movie.

Excessive or shallow breathing, or holding your breath entirely, on the other hand, can be a sign of emotional turmoil. According to experts, mirroring a person's breathing pattern can also help forge a connection of mutual understanding between the two of you. Being able to match someone's breathing pattern essentially allows you to create a sense of normalcy in the situation, thereby guiding them into a sense of relaxation. Of course, this takes some skill to do, especially if the situation is nerve-wracking or intense. This comes back to having the ability to stay calm, balanced, and focused, without allowing your emotions to take you over. At the very least, being able to identify nervous breathing patterns can help you adjust your stance to make the other person feels comfortable—all without a word said to each other.

# Proxemics

An excellent non-verbal way of communication is proxemics, which is the measurable distance between people. Basically, it characterizes relationships between people depending on their preferred distance in given situations. People often have personal space or a perceived territory that they're uncomfortable sharing with others. Think of this in a social setting. Would you feel comfortable if someone you met for the first time stands just mere inches away from you? Of course not! But if you're with your spouse or partner, you have no problem holding hands or putting your arms around each other. This is exactly what proxemics looks into and fortunately, the developer (Edward T. Hall) has done the research. He managed to write down the specifics of proximity and what they often indicate about relationships between people. Note that this proximity usually refers to men as women usually have a different idea of what the proper distance is in different situations:

### *Intimate Distance*

This covers situations of touching, embracing, or even whispering

- Close – less than 6 inches
- Far – 6 to 18 inches

This is the type of distance you'll have with people you are intimate with. In the sense of reading other people, people who are this close to each other will typically be people who are close and have a tight relationship with each other. However, you may find yourself in a position where someone is in this distance and the rest of the body language is telling you that one person is not comfortable with the situation, allowing you the opportunity to step in and provide help if required.

### *Personal Distance*

This typically involves interactions between family members or good friends

- Close – 1.5 to 2.5 feet
- Far – 2.5 to 4 feet

This is typically the distance you'll be when hanging out with people you know. If people are spending time this close to you, it means they trust you and feel comfortable with you.

### *Social Distance*

This is the typical distance between acquaintances, and we're not just talking about COVID-19 requirements. This is perhaps the distance you would typically stand when talking to someone you've just met.

- Close – 4 to 7 feet
- Far – 7 to 12 feet

### *Public Distance*

This is the distance used for public speaking purposes and would be used when addressing a crowd of people.

- Close – 12 to 25 feet
- Far – 25 feet or more

It's also important to note that distance can affect the posture or gestures of people. This is because there are instances when people don't have a say in the distance they have with others. For example, if you're in a cramped elevator or in a commercial airline, you do not exactly have the option of moving your body farther away from another person. In these instances, the rest of the body compensates by taking on some other form or angle relative to their position. This is why people in a cramped elevator tend to focus on their phones or look in any other direction aside from the person they're next to. It's a distraction from the uncomfortable feelings of being too close to someone they don't know. However, if someone's body language tells you that they're feeling confident and not uncomfortable by the presence of other people, even in traditionally awkward situations, it says a lot about this person.

An example of this would be in a job interview meeting. For example, a group of people is all riding an elevator up to a meeting, and you are one of three candidates for a job. One person is shy and in the corner, distracting themselves on their phone, you know they are nervous. If the other person is standing in the middle of the elevator and gives off the impression they're confident, you know they are perhaps well-prepared for the meeting and the person who will be the most competition to you for the job role.

In the alternative, people who are in an intimate relationship, or would like to be in an intimate relationship, tend to sit close to each other often.

Remember what we said about culture in a previous chapter, though? Acceptable proximity range varies from culture to culture. For example, touching cheeks with each other can be a typical greeting in some countries while in others it is reserved for close family and friends.

## Oculesics

This is actually known as a subcategory of body language. It focuses primarily on the movement of the eye, gazes, and other eye-centric movements that can help indicate what a person is thinking or feeling. Remember how people used to say the eyes are the windows to the soul? Well, there's a little bit of truth into it and with oculesics, you can have a bit more insight (pardon the pun!) on how the eyes can tell you what a person thinks or feels without a single word being said.

This body language technique is, again, limited by culture, however, as eye gestures can change from one country to the next. For example, Latinos view extended eye contact as a sign of aggression while in some cases, it can show an interest in an individual. Asians see eye contact as anger while with Anglo-Saxons, the gesture could mean that they are telling the truth. Couple this with everything we spoke about in the previous chapter!

## Haptics

Haptics is a non-verbal communication style that deals primarily with touching. Touching or skin-to-skin contact is perhaps the very first way people communicate. Parents communicate or connect with their babies through touch via different gestures. In fact, according to the Body Language Project, touching is the most developed sense at birth. In day-to-day life, touching includes handshakes, pats on the back, ruffles of the hair, brushes of the cheek, and so on. It signifies communication at different levels, managing to showcase all kinds of emotions from excitement, happiness, anger, devastation, and disappointment.

Haptics currently has five categories of communication by touch:

- *Functional or Professional.* This one is pretty self-explanatory. Basically, it refers to touch made in an office setting. One thing you have to remember in the office, however, is that touching is rarely encouraged. While at work, you're expected to maintain formal relationships, which means that skin-to-skin contact is not well-received. So, when is touching okay? Usually, touching gestures in the workplace are indicative of close friendship or sometimes *congratulations* for a job well done. It's a way of acknowledging that someone did well in their workplace, the gesture often encompassing a slap on the back, a handshake, or a simple squeezing motion of the shoulders. If you agree on the terms of a contract, you may shake hands that says: *yes, we're both happy and are in agreement*, so now we're allowing physical contact to prove this.

- *Friendship or Warmth.* This doesn't really necessitate explanation because friendly gestures may vary from one person to the next. Stereotypically, women will hug one another while men tend to have an energetic hug followed by a controlled slap on the back or an exaggerated handshake or fist bump. Some people do some air kisses; others do a complicated handshake routine, while others happily hug it out.

    Either way, any kind of friendly touch is a sign that the other person is trusted and allowed within someone's inner circle. You can use this in your own interactions by initiating handshakes if someone is feeling left out or isolated because you're telling them that everything is okay and you're allowing them into your inner circle.

- *Love or Intimacy.* This is all about emotional attachment and is usually displayed between romantic partners. They are public gestures that indicate that a person is *taken*. You've probably seen this through hand-holding, an arm around the shoulders, or placing hands on the hips.

- *Sexual or Arousal.* This one's a tad different from intimacy because this has sex for its motivation. During these touches, the intent is to have sexual relations, or perhaps they are right after one. It is often done in private, although the extent of a public display depends primarily on the culture of the people displaying it.

## Bringing it All Together

There are two ways you can use this information. Don't worry, you don't need to remember it all and imprint every detail of what you've just read; the key is to be aware of what kinds of touch and gestures exist and then make decisions accordingly.

Let's say you walk into a business meeting. You can tell, just by how people are standing around each other and how close they are, who in the room is surrounded by friends, and which people aren't very connected, just based on physical space alone.

If you meet a group of friends and there's a couple in your group and they are physically keeping their distance more than you would expect, you'll have read the situation that something might not be right, such as they may have had an argument or falling out. You can then choose to distract the rest of the group or provide support. It's your call to decide.

Say your partner comes home from work and is being physically close with you. This means they are wanting to spend time with you, be intimate with you, and be in your company.

The point is, it doesn't matter what situation you're in, what you're doing by reading people is gathering the information that gives you a better stance at communicating effectively. Instead of mindlessly going into a situation and hoping for the best, you're actively looking for ways to relate to people in ways that will resonate with them in that moment of time. This is what it means to communicative effectively.

# Chapter 9: Verbal Cues – Reading Between the Lines

Like it or not, most communication nowadays is done through words in a way that it has never been before—either written or oral. With the rise of the internet, written communication through email or chat messages is becoming the norm which means that your ability to read people shouldn't be limited to just face-to-face conversations.

In this chapter, we're going to do our best to decipher what people are really saying behind their words. Often dubbed as *reading between the lines* or *reading the room*, it's important to make a distinction between what people SAY and what they MEAN.

A word of caution before we go any further: you should know that there are people who mean exactly what they say. Take a good look at the MBTI we talked about in a previous chapter. The NT types are usually the ones who will tell you exactly what they want, and it would be in the most literal way possible—although, of course, this may vary depending on the situation and the unique style of the person. In these instances, I want you to follow a rule in law: when the words are clear you interpret them as straightforward and apply them accordingly. Only when words are ambiguous and vague should you consider the other cues in deciphering exactly what a person is trying to say.

Let's explore some of the best strategies when it comes to learning how to read between the lines.

## Being a Better Listener

The first step in learning how to read between the lines is first listening with as much attention as you can muster. Remember, there is a big difference between listening and hearing. When listening, your main goal should be to learn new information. Don't be one of those people who simply listen in order to be polite to the person talking. Many psychologists will state that there are two types of listening. There is listening to learn and listening to respond.

I'm sure you know people in your life who you feel never listen to you but are rather waiting for you to finish talking so they can share their thoughts and opinions, not actually conversing with you in a proper conversation. This is not a nice way to be and won't win you any friends.

Instead, aim to find out something or glean information from them. You need to be curious about what the other person is saying; otherwise, you won't really absorb anything. Here's a test: if you walked out of a conversation without learning anything new, then you weren't really listening.

How do you become a better listener? Here are some tips:

### *Ask More Questions*

Asking questions tells a person that you are interested and listening to the words they say. More importantly, questions allow you to clarify the situation, making it easier for you to forge connections between the information being given. This makes it possible for you to simplify the image in your head, arrive at accurate conclusions, and practice empathy or sympathy. Whatever the case may be, asking questions allows other people to elaborate and explain their position. More importantly, it encourages truthfulness in people because they feel compelled to tell you the unvarnished truth as recognition of the attention you are actually giving them.

### Practice Active Listening

This is a technique that's been used for years and can help you really understand and create a story in your head. According to the director of the Center for Leadership at Northwestern University, active listening can be as simple as repeating back key words of what the speaker just said. It's like a little verbal nod of acknowledgment that says you're on the same page. The fact is that there are lots of opportunities to misunderstand what someone is saying. Active listening or giving a recap of what the other person said tells them that you're on the same page. Or if you aren't, it lets them correct any misconceptions you might have about the situation.

### Wait Before Responding

Except for the instances when you need clarification, it's important to stay quiet until the speaker is finished. It's a typical rule in debates, meetings, and conversations, but you'll be surprised at how often people fail to follow this basic rule. The fact is that people can be so impatient that they don't even bother listening to a proposal completely before deciding to voice their thoughts, opinions, arguments, or even agreements. Remember what we said about listening to learn and listening to respond. This can be frustrating for the speaker and makes it impossible for you to fully absorb all the ideas at once. Also note that every interruption can distort the message the person is trying to convey, therefore making it more difficult for them to explain their standpoint.

### Take Note of the Tone

As previously mentioned, the tone of voice can convey so much about a person. A low voice adds a sense of authority, a high-pitched one conveys nervousness, stammering can indicate doubt, and fast-paced words can indicate anxiety. Also, paying attention to which words are given emphasis can change how the sentence is perceived. For example, they may be putting emphasis on the word *maybe* or perhaps they stuttered the word *yes* as a reply. This could be indicative that although they want to say *no*, they're put in the position where they feel as though they can't refuse.

### Taking Action: Aligning Body Language with Verbal Cues

Let's say you're in a conversation with someone and you're piecing together everything we've been learning about so far. You're reading their body language and picking up on physical cues, and you're listening to what they're saying properly and picking up on their verbal cues. How do you piece the two together to get an accurate image of what someone is saying, therefore providing you with the foundation of knowledge that allows you to communicate back most effectively?

First, start with the basics. Are the physical and verbal cues you're receiving in alignment? For a running example, we're going to say you're in a job interview for your dream job, and you're obviously hoping to make a good impression.

You're talking to the recruiter. Their body language is open and positive. You feel welcomed and things are going well. The verbal cues are also positive. The recruiter is saying positive things and saying you're doing well, and you'd make a great fit at the company. That's excellent. Keep doing what you're doing.

On the other hand, what if the cues aren't aligned? Let's say you're being told *this is good. That's excellent.* But what if the recruiter is closed off, there's a lack of eye contact, and you're not being paid much attention? You're reading the situation and you're reading that the recruiter is not on the same wavelength as you.

What do you do?

Well, you use what you've learned to turn the situation around. What body language do you read? If the recruiter is closed off and slumped, are they bored or having a bad day? If shoulders are raised and they are clearly experiencing stress, this could be the case. Now you can decide whether to carry on or connect with the recruiter. You could say something like;

"Just out of curiosity, do you think it's incredibly stressful to work here? Should I be prepared for the worst?"

To which they reply:

"Well, you know how it is. There are good days and bad days. I'm just due for a day off."

"You know, if I did end up here, I'd be more than happy to advocate with you for more days off during the week. We could set up a picket fence and everything."

Obviously, you're just joking, but what you've done is change the situation entirely. Instead of just being another candidate that sat in front of the recruiter who's having a bad day, you've made the situation personal. You've connected with the recruiter and lightened the situation. You're not just here for the job, but you're actually a people person who talks to other people like they are people, not just holding the image that you're dealing with a faceless business.

Guess who's going to stand out in the recruiter's mind now? I'm not saying you need to dive into the situation and give the recruiter a space to talk about all their problems. That's not professional. What you are doing, however, is reading the situation, identifying the problems, and taking action to communicate as effectively as possible.

It all starts with reading and being aware of the situation. Then choose to react. If you're in a group interview with another candidate, you'll want to use your knowledge of body language to make yourself come across as confident and as though you're supposed to be where you are.

If you get onto a topic of conversation where the other candidate shrinks away and becomes quiet, you know this is going to be a topic that might be their downfall and can run off of this. On the other hand, if the recruiter is energetic and placing special interest in a certain topic, then you know this is going to be an important area of business that the company is looking into, so you know the section you're heading into may require more care and attention with your approach.

Of course, we could go into situations and examples until the cows come home, but the main takeaway I want you to think about is how you can actionably use the information you're learning in your day-to-day interactions. Through trial, error, and experience, you'll see dramatic results.

# Chapter 10: The Art of Thin-Slicing

Time and again, I talked about the importance of practice and experience in this book. I placed emphasis on the fact that you need to know a person, or at the very least, be able to establish a baseline before making readings or arriving at conclusions about a specific individual. Making assumptions is probably going to leave you in a worse place than if you didn't try these techniques at all.

You're probably asking: but what if I don't know the person for a long time before trying these techniques? What if I never have the chance to actually know them? So far in this book, I still haven't discussed the possibility of *speed reading* people through non-verbal communication. There will be instances when you don't have the luxury of time. You will need to make a snap-second decision in a particular situation based only on non-verbal cues. What do you do then?

Let me introduce to you the concept of thin-slicing. This is a concept that's been talked about by various authors, including the best-selling writer, Malcolm Gladwell in his book: Blink.

## What Is Thin-Slicing?

Thin-slicing is a *reading* technique that needs only a short span of time for reading. It's a term used in psychology that describes a person's ability to find patterns and make conclusions based only on very small factors or narrow windows of exposure—hence the thin slices. The beauty here is that even with such thinly sliced information, you can still get accurate results as if you've observed this person for a long period of time.

## How Thin-Slicing Translates to Day-to-Day Life

In Gladwell's book *Blink*, he talks about how art connoisseurs often know when a particular work of art is the real thing or just the copy of an original. In that split second that they see something, even before all the scientific tests are done, they can say when a work does not deserve all the accolades given to it. A good example would be the Getty Kouros, which was sold for 10 million dollars and was verified by scientists to be from around 530 B.C. However, many art scholars look at it and see a modern forgery, which means that it's not worth the 10 million dollars that were used to buy it. How do they do it? What are the tells that give it away? What are the scholars looking for?

This split-second ability of art scholars to identify what's fake and what's not is the very context of thin slicing. Believe it or not, we also do this in day-to-day life, you just might not realize it yet. Here are some situations when thin-slicing has been proven to be effective.

### *First Impressions*

Have you ever listened to a lecture for five minutes and could instantly tell if the lecturer is a good one or not? Studies show that students listening to a five-minute lecture are capable of judging whether a professor is good or not, in the same way as a student who has had that same professor for the whole semester.

### Sexual Preferences

A study conducted in 1999 showed that people can perceive a person's sexual orientation accurately. Based only on silent videos spanning 10 seconds, people had an accuracy rate of 70% when perceiving a person's gender preference or sexual orientation. This goes back to using your gut instinct to read someone. While you can't be completely sure, using this information coupled with reading verbal and non-verbal cues is essential when accurately reading someone.

### Detecting Lies

Okay, so I dedicated a whole chapter to this, so it doesn't really bear repeating. Let's just say that most people have a gut feeling when they're being lied to. Perhaps one of the most powerful examples of thin-slicing lies is when it comes to relationships. People in relationships sometimes say they *feel* as though their partner is being dishonest, but perhaps can't seem to prove why they feel this way.

A study conducted by the University of Texas at El Paso once tested the theory of thin slicing by asking one group to provide a verbal rationale for why they did something.

It turns out that the group asked to rationalize their decisions performed more poorly than the group asked to just make their decisions instantaneously using gut instinct.

What does this tell us?

It says that when confronted with rationalized thinking, logic is not always the best approach and that our gut instinct can be more accurate. Again, if you get a feeling about someone while reading them, don't take it as 100% truth, but instead, be exact with using this information when trying to get an accurate image of what a person is communicating to you.

### Parent Interactions

One interesting aspect of thin-slicing where it becomes prominent is the interaction of parents with their children. According to research, a parent's tone of voice when addressing a normal child and one with a behavioral problem have a slight variation that's obvious enough to be noted by teachers.

This is crucial in educational settings as teachers meet parents on the first day of class usually. By simply watching parent-child interactions, teachers can already tell if they have to pay more attention to the child for behavioral issues, or if they can relax more knowing that the child will probably behave. Simply through teacher-student interaction, observers can tell which teachers are biased and which teachers have unrealistic expectations over their charges.

These are just a handful of ways that thin slicing can appear in your day-to-day life. You're basically reading situations quickly using your instincts and a bit of background knowledge that you've learned throughout this book. Now, let's start honing these abilities even further.

## The Basics of Thin-Slicing

Here's a question: what's the element we're looking at when it comes to thin-slicing?

When you're thin-slicing, you're looking at a small portion of information to judge a whole. But what information are we really looking at? What's the important information to look at to make an accurate reading, and what information is best left to the side?

Imagine you're speed dating. What particular factor do you look at in deciding whether you want to see someone else again? What is the heaviest element that decides the case?

As much as I want to answer this question, the fact is that it varies from one situation to the next, and it varies depending on the person you are. If you're speed dating because you want to hook up with someone for the night, you're going to be looking for different things than someone looking for a long-term relationship. My question is, how do you determine who is on the lookout for what, allowing you to spend your efforts in the right places? Of course, I'm talking about in all aspects of your life, not just in a speed dating concept! In an effort to answer this question, however, let me give you an example.

In Malcom Gladwell's book, he talks about thin-slicing marriages. Within seconds of seeing a couple, Gladwell claims it's possible to accurately tell if it will result in a divorce or not. How?

Accordingly, this one element is: contempt. Marriages that seem to be doomed to fail involve those where one partner seems to be contemptuous or resentful of another. This means that one person in a couple feels superior over the other and interacts with them in a way that makes the other person feel less of a person. Contempt can be seen through some of the interactions between these couples, which leads to a conclusion that they're not bound to last.

So, is this true for all thin-slices? Can you just focus on ONE element and already make an accurate prediction of a specific situation? Studies show that you can, but again, the accuracy is not as reliable as when you rely on big slices of information.

## How Do You Thin-Slice?

Okay, let's get to the core of it. How do you accurately thin slice? Remember, you're really only going to be thin-slicing people you don't have a baseline for, so let's say you've rolled up to a business and you're about to try to sell a product.

Let's go.

First, take note of the person's appearance. Are they dressed for the meeting? Do they look professional, like they pride themselves on their work, or do they look disinterested? If it's the latter, they might not be interested at all, so you can decide whether you're wasting your time or you want to take a different, more engaging approach.

This continues with how much attention they are paying you. Are they engaged? If someone says they're not interested in paying such a high price for your product, but they're engaged with what you're saying, then you know that the price isn't so much of a turn off because they still want or need what you have to offer. If the price was too high and they weren't engaged, they would simply tell you they're not interested.

Remember to go with your gut feelings. If you apply too much logic and overthink reading someone, you can provide yourself with false information. If you feel like the person is bored, then start engaging with them more, make your presentation more exciting, or get more personal. Draw the other person into what you're saying. Act on impulse. When you know what you're looking for, less is more.

Finally, go off the situation you're in. In a business setting, there are typically a few personal cues you'll be picking up on. However, on a date, you'll be looking for intimate cues, such as eye contact, touch, and physical proximity. The context of things you're looking for changes depending on the situation you're in. You should hopefully have more of an idea of what to look for here as you've made your way through this book.

# Chapter 11: What About Me?

So far in this book, we talked about other people. Specifically, about the different personality types, how to identify a personality type, how to read body language, and so on. Really, the only thing we haven't talked about is you. When it comes right down to it, YOU are the most important part of the equation.

Why is this? I'd like to remind you that this book's ultimate goal is to help you *connect* with people, and not all connections are equal. The way you connect with a work friend is very different from the way you connect with a school friend or a neighbor.

Would you tell a work friend in-depth information about yourself in the same way you'd tell a high school friend or your best friend? Of course not!

Of course, that's not the only factor at play here. The way you communicate is also dictated by the type of person you are. All the personality types and traits we discussed in a previous chapter apply to you too! Hence, you have to figure out if you're an introvert or extrovert, an intuitive or a sensor, a thinker or a feeler, and a perceiver or judger.

To effectively communicate with someone, you can't just read the other person and hope for the best, because they're unconsciously, or even consciously, going to be reading you too. This means you need to be in control of how you communicate and present yourself in the most effective way, depending on the situation you're in and who you're talking to.

### *Understanding the Importance of You*

Your ability to connect with people is limited by your own personality. For example, if you're an extrovert, how are you supposed to connect with someone who is an introvert? If you're a feeler, how do you make connections with someone who is a sensor? This is why I strongly encourage you to take the Myers Briggs test I wrote about earlier and learn as much about yourself as possible.

This is crucial because if you *really* want to make that connection, you might find yourself in situations that you're uncomfortable in.

## What is your personality type?

I want you to be aware of your own strengths and shortcomings when it comes to connecting and communicating with people, which is another reason why I recommend the Myers Briggs test. Once you learn about who you are, whether you're introverted and extroverted and so on, you can then play to your strengths and address your weaknesses.

You might be an introvert trying to connect with an extrovert which makes the job doubly hard for you. Perhaps the situation is vice versa. By realizing your personality type, you should be able to make headway and figure out what factors are holding you back from reaching your communication goals.

## What is my communication style?

Now that you're learning about yourself, we have to talk about the kind of communicator you happen to be. You might not realize it, but you have a specific way of communicating, just like everyone else does.

The goal is to adjust your communication style slightly so that you can easily connect with others through verbal and non-verbal means.

Here are the typical communication styles today. Keep in mind that these communication styles apply to others as well as to you.

### *Analytical Communicator*

The analytical communicator makes good use of data and real numbers. If this is you, then you like to use references when establishing your point. If this is you, then this is probably your biggest drawback as you are likely to become silent during emotional conversations, having problems putting what you think or feel into words.

If you prefer this type of communication, keep in mind that you may sound completely cold or unfeeling. People are going to feel unsure about making emotional gestures towards you because they think you're going to react badly to them. You have to learn how to be a bit softer or open up to others in order to encourage discourse.

### *Intuitive*

Intuitive communicators are the kinds who like to see the big picture. They like to start with the general rule and then whittle it down to the basics. They are really not fond of the details but prefer a big view or a bird's-eye view of what's going on.

What adjustment could you make as an intuitive? You could perhaps make an effort towards explaining your thought process. Give others the time to follow your idea, making sure that each point has been explained before arriving at the conclusion. Try to develop a bit more patience because not everyone prefers your quick method of communication.

### *Functional*

Functional communicators are the types who like to itemize steps from Point A to Point Z. Basically they are the opposite of an intuitive communicator. They like the step-by-step fashion, making sure that nothing gets missed.

An important thing to remember as a functional communicator is to improve your skills in grabbing and maintaining the attention of your audience. The small details leading towards a bigger end can be quite taxing for people and they will quickly lose interest during a representation. Hence, you can make use of body language techniques to encourage interest and guarantee that people are on the same page as you.

### *Personal Communicator*

Finally, we have the personal communicator who prefers to focus on the emotional aspect of things. You find it important to figure out not just what a person is thinking but also what they feel about a particular situation.

The downside of this is that personal communicators can be easily affected by the underlying emotional atmosphere. If overwhelmed, you might find yourself acting out instead of being the glue that keeps the group sane. Hence, as a personal communicator, your best adjustment would be to keep a rational and level head in order to keep everyone within acceptable ranges of communication.

One thing I want you to understand is that there is no *best* communication style. All these styles have a specific advantage, depending on the use. It's therefore important to be flexible with your communication style so that you'll be able to adjust to the situation. Remember, this is all about preferences so you might actually find yourself able to switch from one communication style to the next. The more you practice these techniques, the better you become in taking on any role that's needed in that particular situation.

## The Checklist of Body Language

When talking to someone, it's crucial that you're aware of how you're presenting yourself and the message that you're unconsciously sending out to others. Bear things in mind like:

### Signs of Negative Body Language

- Arms folded in front of the body
- Tense or minimal facial expression
- Body turned away from another person
- Downcast eyes
- A lack of eye contact

### Disengaged Body Language

- Bad sitting posture
- Writing or doodling
- Gazing or staring off into space
- Downcast head
- Fidgeting or fiddling with an item

Of course, you might want to act this way to send a certain message. If, however, you want to keep things positive, you'll need to switch things up.

### Positive Body Language

- Have an open posture
- Keep the muscles relaxed without slouching on the chair
- Keep your body upright and hands placed on the side or comfortably folded in front of you.
- Avoid touching your face when talking to another person.
- Maintain eye contact.
- Use a firm handshake.

## Practicing at Home

Before you head out into the world and start practicing some of these techniques yourself, try honing them in front of the mirror at home and see for yourself how much of a difference it can make in your confidence, and your ability to portray yourself to others.

Here are some tips on things to try.

### *Maintain a positive posture.*

Stand or sit upright with your shoulders and arms at your sides. You can fold your hands in front of you or keep them relaxed at your sides. You can also use hand gestures to emphasize what you're trying to say. Whatever you do, do NOT slouch or put those hands in your pockets, as this would make you look like you're not interested in the situation.

### *Make use of open hand gestures.*

Open hand gestures invite the audience to listen and give off positive vibes. If you can't keep your hands relaxed at your sides, then position them so that the upper arms are close to your body and the palms are facing up. This communicates a willingness to communicate on a deeper level.

### *Mastering Your Voice*

Have you ever tried hearing yourself speak in front of a mirror? Don't worry, it doesn't mean you're crazy to talk to yourself, especially in the context of practicing to become a more effective communicator.

Try talking as though you're having a conversation with someone and see how changing your tone of voice can make such a big difference to what you're saying. Again, practice makes perfect, so experiment and see what works for you.

## Don't Forget the Golden Rule!

Remember, the whole point of this book is to help you *connect* with people, so I need you to understand that the Golden Rule still applies here. What's that?

It simply states: Do unto others what you would have them do unto you.

Hence, if you want to connect with people and forge stronger relationships with them, you'll have to keep their wants and needs in mind. If you find yourself getting mixed signals or unsure about how to go forward, just ask yourself, *Would I want this for me?* If you don't want the same thing to be done to you, then it makes sense that others don't want it to be done to them either!

## Mastering Intermediate Body Language Techniques

Once you've mastered the basics of controlling how you communicate, you can start implementing more advanced strategies to help you achieve even better results. These can seem a little weird or maybe even forced at first, but they can make such a big difference in the way you're perceived and connect with others. However, you can start implementing these in your own time.

### *Use mirroring.*

You've probably heard about this often, which is only because it works so well. Mirroring is a technique where you subtly mirror or copy the body language of the person you're talking to. This has the effect of building rapport, as mirroring makes it look like the two of you are on the same page.

It is important to note though mirroring is a fairly well-known technique nowadays so there's a chance the other person also knows you're doing it. Therefore, it's important not to copy every single gesture they make, as this will have the opposite effect.

### *Put emphasis on the gestures that show interest.*

Do not overdo it, but make a point of nodding, smiling, and keeping your body relaxed during an interview. The technique of slightly leaning in towards the other person can also work, allowing you to create the image of rapport.

If you're ever asked a difficult question, don't be afraid to pause and think about what you're going to say first. Touch your cheek, gaze off a little, or bite your lips. This will show the other person that you're reflecting on your answer or putting the proper amount of thought into it.

# Chapter 12: Further Body Language Tips

Your ability to read the non-verbal communication of the people around you is one thing. Your ability to convey non-verbal messages on your own is another. Communication takes two things: the initial message and the reply. Simply put, I want you to be good with non-verbal communication as well, not just with the initial message but also with the reply. At the very least, I want you to be able to use body language to your advantage.

Here's a secret though: studies show that how you move or the body posture you assume also contributes to how you feel. It is not just a one-way street.

*What does this mean?*

For example, if you feel sad or down, you tend to slouch your body. When people see you doing this, they can instantly tell that you feel sad or are depressed. Your posture is a non-verbal sign of what you're feeling inside.

But the reverse actually holds true! This means that even if you feel bad but posture your body in a way that conveys confidence, you will slowly gain confidence. It's a mind over matter thing and it can help you through many problems in life, wiring your mind to deal with situations in different ways, and you actually have control over this as long as you're mindful!

How do you do this? Here are some body language tips to help you convey the exact message you want to make in any situation:

## If You Want to Feel Confident

Ever seen the pose Superman makes? This is the *confidence* pose that could make you feel like you're more confident than usual. This high-power pose stimulates testosterone levels and lowers the amount of cortisol in the body. As you probably know, cortisol is a stress hormone and the less of this in your body, the better it would be for you. What's the pose exactly? Hands on your hips, feet apart, and your shoulders stretched wide with the chest puffed out.

Try not to overdo it too much so people don't look at you weirdly because there is such a thing as taking it too far. But this should work perfectly and give you the confidence boost you need for any given situation.

Of course, there are other confidence poses out there, verified by Harvard no less. It's the high-power pose of leaning back in your chair, hands on your head, and feet up on the desk. You've probably seen this being done by businessmen in movies when they want to show how confident they are. As it turns out, it works perfectly in boosting morale and ego. Of course, you can't do this while in a meeting, but if you're tackling a hard problem at the office, assuming this pose for a few seconds should help.

## To Make People Participate, Look Like You Are Actually Listening

This might seem like a no-brainer, but a lot of people forget the value of listening when someone speaks. If you want to increase the participation in a meeting, verbal methods aren't enough. You have to *show* people that you're really listening to what they have to say. Look at people when they speak and nod along with them in order to create the sense of being listened to.

Don't doodle or tap on your phone or check the room to see what the others are doing. Instead, focus on the person speaking and establish eye contact. This will help encourage people into verbalizing their thoughts and create a more honest atmosphere for discourse.

## Smile to Promote Good Feelings

A genuine smile stimulates not only your sense of well-being, but it likewise tells those around that you're cooperative, approachable, and trustworthy. A genuine smile comes on slowly, lights up the face, crinkles the eyes, and fades slowly away. Most importantly, smiling has a direct influence on how people respond to you. When you smile at somebody, they almost always will smile in return. That's just basic human psychology. Since facial expressions elicit corresponding feelings, the smiles you get back actually change the person's emotional state positively.

## Look at People's Feet for Added Insight

The feet are also a big deal when it comes to body language. Feet are tapped, played with, or pointed in different directions, depending on a person's mood. Perhaps one of the biggest indicators is where the feet are pointed.

If the foot is directed away from you during a conversation, then chances are that person doesn't really want to talk. If it is pointed towards you, however, then they're fully engaged in the conversation.

## Keep Your Voice Low for an Authoritative Sound

Let your voice relax before making an important call or speech. It appears that a low and steady voice communicates authority and power as opposed to a high one. It's a very subtle way of affecting the senses, relaxing other people, and putting you in a position of power without trying too much.

## Be Naturally You

Perhaps the most important consideration here is to make sure you're being yourself. With everything you've learned, it could be so easy to fall into the trap of just being a body language reading robot, but that seems stiff and unnatural. If you're forcing how you are and it comes across as fake, this is simply counterproductive to your efforts.

Be relaxed. Don't take things too seriously, and just be yourself!

# Conclusion

So there we have it, we've arrived at the end of this book! I'm happy you have made it this far and I hope you found all the information stated here useful for day-to-day life. Practice makes perfect, so take everything you've learned and apply it. Even if it feels weird or unusual at first, experience will take you places and will help you build your confidence tenfold, allowing you to communicate most effectively during the times where it matters most.

You can nurture such beautiful, meaningful relationships with anybody in your life if you're able to communicate properly, which means both listening and speaking with purpose and accuracy.

I understand there's a lot to take in and a ton of information to learn, but don't worry. Even if things are a little bit confusing even at this stage—it's supposed to be. Humans aren't simple creatures, and our minds are infinitely complex. You're never going to understand everything, nor do you need to. The fact is that understanding people is a lifetime process so you will find the need to constantly evaluate your baselines as you move forward.

There's one thing I want you to remember when using this book: you only have control over your own values, actions, and reactions. It doesn't matter how badly you want to connect or forge ties with someone—you cannot *make* people like you if their values are intrinsically different from yours.

Keep in mind that connection is based on similarities and there's no point connecting with someone when nothing is similar between the two of you. Remember, you matter first. Your values are personal to you and you should NOT allow other people to choose your values.

So, what do you do now? Here's what I want you to do:

1. I want you to take a good look at yourself and assess your values, personality, communication style, goals, and everything else that pertains to you. I want you to get to know yourself deeply first before attempting to know others.
2. Your next step would be to observe yourself. What are your mannerisms, your behavior, and your tendencies when confronted with specific situations? I want you to know exactly what you're doing wrong and what you're doing right.
3. Next is cultivating a system of thinking, analyzing, and discovering your values and motivations before pursuing a behavior. Even before you do something, I want you to pause and think about why you're doing it. What's your ultimate goal and what's the motivation behind it? Feel free to use Maslow's Hierarchy of Needs for this to help you further narrow down your own motivations.
4. Once you've figured out your goals and motivations, I want you to take a good look at the actions you propose to take. Are those actions in line with your goals and motivations? Will they achieve the results you want? What other roads are there for you to take to get the same results, but with much less hindrance on your part?
5. I encourage you to practice these four steps consistently to get to know yourself better through personal analysis. Only after you're comfortable understanding yourself, can you feel comfortable in understanding others. One thing I want you to remember though: you don't have to understand yourself 100%! Face it, people are a mystery and sometimes, we can be a mystery to ourselves too. All I encourage you to do is to try as often and as hard as you can to trace your motivations before pursuing any sort of significant action.

Let's say you're comfortable understanding your own motivations at this point—what about other people? Here's what I want you to do:

a)  First, I discourage you against reading too much into people you don't know or barely know. While thin-slicing is highly effective, you should not use this as a way to figure out everything around you. People-watching can be fun and a good way to hone your skills, but don't take things too seriously.
b)  Start by focusing only on a small group of people. Make decisions based on conscious *reading* efforts but keep it simple or in situations where getting it wrong wouldn't have negative consequences in your life. Remember, you're testing the waters here and honing your skills.
c)  I want you to always keep in mind that this book was written to help you CONNECT with people through developed verbal and non-verbal skills. Hence, try not to use your new superpowers for evil and keep connections in mind when trying to decipher people. You're not trying to maliciously manipulate people into doing what you want. Of course, you have goals and needs to fulfill, but this is about communicating that effectively.
d)  Develop a pattern when observing people. Routine is everything when it comes to learning a new skill. This means having a fairly good idea of where to start when attempting to understand them. For example, you look at the feet first, then the hands, then the face, or any other sequence you may choose. Having this pre-set programming on where to look gives you a story-type reading experience that can help with any conclusions you might have about the situation. The beauty here is that as you practice this technique, it becomes second nature to the point where you don't even have to consciously guide yourself through the process. Your mind instantly goes to these body parts in order to interpret what they mean.
e)  Learn the art of listening and try not to be too self-absorbed. Even as an extrovert, you should be able to recognize the enjoyment of being able to sit back in one corner of the room and just take in the different movements and reactions of people as they interact with each other.
f)  If you find things too difficult, I suggest you watch a movie multiple times and pay attention not just to the words but also to the actions and movements of the actors. Actors are trained in the proper action and reaction processes in different situations to make them look realistic. Their facial expressions and even the slightest movement of the hands can convey so much and can help hone your skills in prediction. It's by far the safest way of approaching body language understanding while enjoying yourself in the process. Make sure to watch movies with very good actors known for their excellent skills in the art. Meryl Streep movies are perhaps one of the best to do this, focusing primarily on the movement of this amazing actress.
g)  The beauty of watching movies is that there's a way for you to confirm what you suspect about a certain situation. You can look at a person's expression in one scene and guess what they think or feel. In a later scene, these emotions are often expressed out loud or given further focus, therefore allowing you to figure out if what you initially thought was correct.
h)  When reading people in the real world, observe and keep your conclusions to yourself. Do not go around telling people that you've *read* how a particular coworker acts and make expressive predictions because of it. I want you to keep any conclusions or ideas you have close to your heart and only use them when needed.

i) Practice, practice, practice! The beauty of reading body language is that you never run out of people to observe or body language to read. There's always an endless supply of them, so feel free to practice as often as you want. Note though that acting on those observations isn't always advisable. Think about it multiple times before actually making a decision.

Yes, you are capable of reading people and making connections simply by honing your verbal and non-verbal skills! But it takes time, patience, and drive. It might seem like a big project at first, but don't let this stop you! Unless you live under a rock, forging connections and communicating with others is an integral part of your life. You will find that by mastering this talent, you too can achieve the kind of success that only a few can boast about.

# Book #3
# How to Make People Laugh

*Develop Confidence and Charisma, Master Improv Comedy, and Be More Witty with Anyone, Anytime, Anywhere*

# Introduction

*"You don't stop laughing because you grow older. You grow older because you stop laughing." - Maurice Chevalier*

This saying reveals the secret to youth. We do not stay young because of any serum that we buy from a beauty shop, or through any facial exercise. Of course, you may say slapstick comedy can involve facial exercises. Humor, however, changes something within you. It makes you quicker to accept your follies and see the world with a brighter set of eyes. It does not mean that you are stuck with a pair of rose-colored glasses. Some of the best comedians are often thought of as some of the smartest people. They have to read their audience and ensure that the timing is right. They know what humor applies to what situation. So, it means that they recognize the dark side of this world; they are not blind. However, they choose to use a lighthearted approach to life that they incorporate into their private thoughts and also into their interactions with other people. How would you like to inject some humor into our everyday lives? This book has the answers: There is no stage. There is no laugh track. It is about purely being able to make people laugh.

This book will take you and me—ordinary people—and find ways in which we can be a lot funnier. Hey, there is such a thing as charisma that people like to talk about. No doubt, some people are naturally charismatic. That is a given fact. However, anything that is worth trying can be learned. You don't have to fabricate a personality, either. There is always some humor that we can draw from ourselves.

This book will make use of the How to Make People Laugh recipe:
- A dash of charisma
- Buckets full of self-discovery
- Smattering of acceptance
- Heated in learning
- Garnished with stories and experience
- Keeping it clean and nice

All of these ingredients are within every person. None of us can say we cannot go through this journey. All of us should be able to make people laugh, beyond a stage or without the promise of financial returns. You will find out that laughter itself and life of humor are worth all this focus.

## *Why would you want people to laugh?*

1. It is a health booster—for both you and the other person.
   The release of serotonin and endorphins provide you with not just a happier attitude but also enhances pleasure while regulating pain. This is why it is a good idea to visit people who are sick and try to cheer them up with jokes. Laughing is also an excellent pastime for those who are at high risk of hypertension and cardiovascular diseases. It is great for everyone!

2. It burns calories.
   You burn about 40 calories when you laugh for about 10 to 15 minutes daily. If you are on the other side of the equation, the effort of making someone laugh while also laughing may increase this for a bit. However, you should not forget to do your daily exercise.

3. It lightens the mood.
   As a stress buster, joking around with a friend certainly works. Your chest no longer feels tight, and you just give in to the laughter.

4. It boosts your immune system.
   Because joking around helps get rid of stress, it helps strengthen your immune system.

5. It helps you bond with other people.
   A few jokes among friends, family members, and colleagues can create lifetime bonds. They make people more comfortable with each other.

6. It makes you look more attractive.
   Photographers have already tested this theory. When people are smiling or laughing, their whole faces light up. This makes people more attractive. In a way, the laughter also draws you to a person, beyond appearances. You want to spend more time with a person who can make you feel better.

7. It regulates breathing.
   Swimming and other cardio exercises strengthen your lungs and heart. However, laughter does have its share in improving the way you breathe. In simple terms, laughing makes you breathe deeper. It allows you to dig deep as your heart rate increases, and your lungs draw in more fresh air.

Even without knowing the science behind the benefits of laughter, people will be drawn to you because of your capability to make them laugh. Making people laugh helps people forget about their problems even for a little while. It makes them bond with you.

# Part One – A Dash of Charisma

This part of the book will deal with the mystery of charisma:
- What is it exactly?
- How do you create a likable presence?
- What are the different types of charisma?
- Which type applies to you?
- How do you retain the charisma even with pressure all around you?
- Do you get to express yourself better—through words and gestures—when you are charismatic?
- Would it be easier for you to make jokes when you are charismatic?
- In the end, how do you apply this charisma to your sense of humor?

Let us find out more in the succeeding chapters.

**Chapter 1: What is Charisma?**

**Chapter 2: Creating a Presence**

**Chapter 3: Grace Under Fire**

**Chapter 4: Body Language**

# Chapter 1 – What Is Charisma?

*"Charisma is a sparkle in people that money can't buy. It's an invisible energy with visible effects."*
— Marianne Williamson

You have probably met some people whose presence creates a commotion—a good kind of commotion. They are those who you just have to crane your neck to see and strain your ears to hear. Here is how a celebrity is born and made.

Even in simple scenarios, you will find people such as these. They are the popular kids, but nice ones. Here are those who are almost revered, but nobody cannot blame them for it because they are gracious and not at all unkind. It seems that they have been packaged perfectly as people. Who wouldn't want to be categorized as one of these golden ones?

But there are different types of charisma. Not all of them will make people laugh.

However, all of them can make people notice. You need to be able to make people notice you first.

1. Authority

    Some people exude charisma through their sense of authority. They just appear to know a lot. Their bodily movements show self-confidence. For you to be able to express your brand of comedy, you should also be able to convey a sense of authority. Note that not everyone who has a sense of authority can make others laugh. Some can convey arrogance instead. So, you need to be able to juggle being an authority of your topics with being likable. People do not laugh **with** someone they do not like. They may prefer to find an opportunity to laugh *at* the person instead.

    So, being a know-it-all isn't the best way to start your journey to making others laugh. You don't want people waiting for the next chance to laugh at your mistakes. While boosting your confidence is a plus, people laughing at you or avoiding you just may not be the reaction you want. That will doom your goal of making people laugh.

2. Focus

    When you make people laugh, it should be about them. You should genuinely care about what they feel. It is not about making you a star of some sort, although it does give you some feeling of triumph when you can do just that.

    Focus on the person if you have to. Establish some eye contact without making the other person uncomfortable. By making the connection, you will know just when to drive in the punchline. You should also be able to read if the other person is following your train of thought. Perhaps the type of joke that you are going for only clicks with a specific group of people with a particular set of interests.

3. Kindness

    A relaxed person who imbues positivity can project an easygoing type of charisma. Making people feel comfortable first is an act of kindness. Most kind people do not even have to practice being generous; they have the family structure and childhood development that may have encouraged such value. However, people who have not been able to showcase their kindness—perhaps because of shyness—can slowly incorporate it into their interactions with other people.

In kindness, you can also find the humor of the right kind. A kind person will not be quick to use mean-spiritedness as a means of making others laugh. Laughing at someone else's expense is just meanness. This may make fellow meanspirited people laugh, but it sure does not create a thriving environment for humor. While you want to make people laugh, you should always strive to do so for the right reason and without hurting others.

4. Visionary

Yes, very few people get to be crowned as a visionary in their lifetimes. However, this does not mean you cannot strive towards something akin to it. Think of humor that you like to convey, the kind of humor that you want people to associate with you. Your thoughts identify who you are because they are original. There may not be many original thoughts left in this world today, but your approach provides uniqueness. This is what makes people drawn to you.

Charisma can also be conveyed through some distinctive features. People with charisma have been shown to:

- Exude self-confidence
    - A charismatic person has a lot of self-confidence. He believes in what he is saying or doing, and this is what makes him compelling.
    - You should be able to exude the same self-confidence by focusing first on things that you believe in. It is easier to talk about them or to navigate them because you naturally gravitate toward them.
    - When making jokes, start with people who have the same interests as you. They will be better able to relate, and the banter becomes natural.
- Show an open body language
    - A charismatic person has an approachable stance. His body is open: arms unfolded, toes pointing towards you, and face animated with emotion instead of controlled and detached.
    - You should be able to open yourself up to people by revealing more about yourself. When you are self-confident, you can do this more.
    - When making jokes, gestures and facial expressions can drive them home. On the other hand, you may become well known for deadpan deliveries, if these are in keeping with your personality.
- Tell stories people want to listen to
    - A charismatic person can easily tell you stories that he is passionate about. You can tell from the sparkle in their eyes.
    - You should be able to share personal anecdotes with no fear. People can tell when you are genuine. So, your stories become more accepted. They want to hear more. People usually appreciate those who put themselves out there.
    - When making jokes using personal anecdotes, a healthy dose of self-deprecation is necessary. However, you have to balance it so that it does not show itself as insecurity. People would be uncomfortable listening to someone who appears not to believe in themselves.
- Listen well

- A charismatic person sees the value in turning the spotlight towards the other person. He knows that he cannot hog the conversation. The other person needs to be able to speak his mind. A steady banter between two humorous people is quite a pleasure to listen to, compared to one person delivering all the jokes.
- You should be able to find a person who can match wits with you, without any personal agenda or hidden displeasure. It is not matching wits to win over the other person, but just appreciating others whether they are humorous or not. The other person will better appreciate you when they feel noticed and listened to.
- When making jokes, listen to the other person. Listening may just be hearing their laughter or their feedback. It may also be about letting the other person express his character.

What are the biggest threats to charisma?
1. Self-doubt:
   When you don't believe in yourself, you may lose your chance at charisma. Charismatic people get a following. You don't get that following when you are not even sure you are worth listening to.
2. Detachment from others
   You cannot develop charisma when you cannot even connect with people. Charisma is all about that connection. Someone has to be able to like you or care about what you are doing. Charisma is not just about being good looking, talented, or smart.
3. Self-absorption
   Too much self-focus may just be the opposite of self-doubt. Take care that while you are on your journey towards developing your charisma and humor that you also see beyond yourself. Stay humble. Stay connected.

### *Can charisma start becoming a bad thing?*
Too much of a good thing always ends up becoming spoiled. So, yes, even charisma can deteriorate into something unpleasant.

When you become too aware of this charisma, it may go to your head. When that happens, you become the opposite of charismatic—arrogant and unlikeable.

## Chapter 2 – Creating a Presence

*"Charisma is the fancy name given to the knack of giving people your full attention."*

- Robert Brault

When you make use of charisma, you create a presence. You are not just any person, you are that funny person. You are that person who usually makes somebody's day.

Have you ever entered a room and have someone look at you with a look of pure happiness? Then, yes, you have a presence. It may be a presence that is acknowledged by only a few, but yes, it is a presence.

What does that mean? If you are a little shy, you may find yourself still having a great time with a select few. You may be more participative in conversations with family and friends, than with any other person. So, you take advantage of that. Practice more interactions within your comfort zone. See what makes people tick. See what makes you relax and let go.

When you are not in the room, do people seek you out? Have people missed your presence just because you are not there for a day or two? If this is the case, then they know that you cannot be replaced. Maybe they cannot put it exactly into words, but they can sense it.

Yes, working towards charisma can be hit or miss, just like comedy—however, the more that you put yourself out there, the more that your self-doubt wanes. The more you let go of your self-doubt, the easier it is for you to relax and have fun. It is at your most relaxed that you can pull off some of the best jokes.

When you pull off a presence, people will always notice you. You do need to gain the full attention of your intended audience if you want them to laugh.

Some people, on the other hand, may not be missed when they are not present. However, they have a certain presence when they do arrive. You know that they are there. They do not have to be loud, but people take notice. They make others want to come closer and check out what is up with them. The clamoring seems to show that they have been missed, after all, emphasized by their presence.

Comedy takes timing. The timing involved here does not only consider your part in the equation; it also depends on just how committed the other person is.

So, this is what happens:

Interact more/put yourself out there → less self-doubt → more confident → more relaxed → more fun → more effective jokes

# Chapter 3 – Grace Under Fire

*"I learned that courage was not the absence of fear, but the triumph over it. The brave man is not he who does not feel afraid, but he who conquers that fear."*

- *Nelson Mandela*

The best-loved people are not just charming when they are putting up a front. For politicians, the most trusted ones do not just pop up when they are expected to be campaigning. Instead, they have always been out there, mingling and doing things that people usually classify as good deeds. Those who have overcome difficulties or are breaking through the glass ceiling are regarded as better, as well.

If you have read *A Little Princess* as a child, there may be a quotation there from Sarah that you may find endearing. The little rich girl conveyed a lot of wisdom when she said that she was good because she had no reason to be mean. According to her, she had no trials to test her. So, she could not help but remain pleasant.

What Sarah did not see here was that she already had enough charm and wisdom to state or simply just know these things at a young age. She may not be a real princess, but she behaves like everyone's idea of one. When she does meet with some trials to test her (stripping of her place at the boarding school, her dad dying, her riches gone), Sarah has proven herself to be above those trials. She is grace under fire. Most charismatic people seem to be above mundane problems. They always seem to know what to do or how to behave.

Of course, it does not mean that these charmers have never had it hard. It is just that they know what to do during their worst trials and tribulations. They may be giving themselves pep talks, even as they see the reality of their problems.

### *How will this show up in humor?*

You may have noticed that standup comics know how to make fun of their troubles. Because they do it so easily without any hitch or sign of sadness, you can say that they have moved on. They not only move on, but they are brave enough to keep on revisiting the issue. They can take the issue and come up with something witty about it. Often, they will include what they have learned during the process of grief and recovery. Motivational instruction is delivered in a fun way. Your listener does not have to feel awkward about the situation. He may even learn something new from your experience.

### *How should sad events pop up in jokes?*

Trials or sad events are often swept under the table. This is understandable. They are not pleasant, perhaps not only for the person making the joke. You can be regarded as insensitive if you proceed without caution.

You can proceed if:

- You are over the event. You don't want to trigger your own emotions. If you attempt the joke while you are still deeply affected, you and your listener(s) may find yourselves in an awkward situation. Can you imagine what your listener will feel if you were to attempt a joke and then suddenly cry? Yes, it is probably just fine—especially if you are among friends or family who understand. This defeats the purpose of making people laugh, though.

- The listener is not affected by whatever problems you want to joke about. While you may be over it, the other person may still be secretly just trying to hold on. This is where your miscalculation may negatively affect someone else. So, hold on right there. You cannot just make people laugh when they are ready. If you want to cheer them up, pick a different topic.

No matter what you do, you should not joke about other people's tragedies. You should not joke about a large-scale event; you would not know if you were talking to someone who is affected by that event. Events that should never be joked about:

- A murder
- A rape
- Jokes with racist overtones
- Jokes with religious discrimination
- Cancer or any other serious diseases
- Terrorism
- People who have lost someone, e.g., a child, a parent, etc.
- People with autism
- People with mental health issues

If you dare try joking about any of the above, that will reflect on you badly. Yes, laughter is the best medicine. You, however, will not get a laugh from such jokes. If you ever do get some wholehearted laughter after making such jokes, be cautious; you may be running with the wrong crowd. There is nothing brave or admirable about jokes that deal with such tragedies and sensitive issues.

When the setup is right, humor is a lighthouse illuminating dark waters. Some say laughter is the best medicine, and they are correct. When you face your problems with good humor, you avoid some of the worst effects of stress: chest pains, developing heart problems, anxiety, depression, and more.

How can humor help you become the grace under pressure you want to become?

Remember, grace under pressure is a sign of charisma. You can overcome your personal troubles through humor.

Humor can help:

- Diffuse tension: Sometimes, you can cut the heavy feeling surrounding you with a knife. People are not sure how to handle the situation. So, you cut it with well-timed humor to ease the tension a bit, without ending up offending anyone. It is a tough job to do, but when it works, people will be grateful to you.
- Smooth over differences: When you can lead people into laughter, albeit in a gentle, thoughtful manner, you can enjoy camaraderie during that moment.

- Overcome your troubles: Having a sense of humor can help you get out of the rut of the moment. It may not solve your problems, but it will help you become strong enough to face them.
- Analyze your situation: Sometimes, taking on a lighthearted point of view can help you see your situation in a better light. This is when you realize that there is, after all, the cliched light beyond the tunnel.
- Bonding with people: When you find people with the same sense of humor or similar desire to get over their setbacks, you may have found your tribe. People do appreciate being in the presence of someone more optimistic or eager to get on with light. Similarly, two people who wallow in negativity can pull each other down into the mire.

Charisma during troubled times gets a direct lift from a sense of humor. Other people displaying grace under pressure may not always be funny. You can observe some who simply try to be more optimistic about their lives. Instead of simply waiting for others to give them advice, they give themselves advice. They know that the solution is inside them all along; they just need to tap into it. However, they are also aware that there is no more magic cure for grief. They must be able to go through the process slowly but surely.

However, there are some points you need to remember:

1. Never use humor to cover up your true emotions.
   Again, you need to be ready. You cannot just think: Oh, I need to joke around so that people will believe that I am fine. Well, are you fine? At least be honest about what exactly is going on inside of you. Are there still some issues that continue to require resolution? Perhaps you need to face your problems first.

   While laughter is the best medicine, it is also not healthy to suppress emotions. You have to deal with them first. You need to know whether you should face your issues first. See if you need to talk to someone who can help you manage your emotions.

2. Don't jest about people just because you feel bad about yourself.
   Sometimes, it is tempting to put other people down just because you feel terrible about yourself. Do not be tempted. Think about being on the other side of the equation. How would you feel about it? Would you want to get some laughs by putting others down? Being mean to others will make you feel worse about yourself in the long run.

3. Use inside jokes.
   The first few people that you joke about your past troubles with are those close to you. They know you enough to understand whether you have moved on or are simply trying to put up a front. Because you know each other well enough, a few inside jokes about that particular situation can bond you for life. The idea of laughing about this little inside joke while others look at the two of you as if you have gone crazy can make you laugh even more.

It is difficult to find humor in tragedy or any other sad situation. Imagine getting fired from your job. You go home, shoulders slumped, and spine bent. You go to your desk, rest your head on your hands. Your elbows seem to carry the whole world. Would you like to joke about what happened to you just then?

Of course not.

The experience is still fresh. You do not know how quite to tackle it. It is natural for you not to feel any semblance of positivity anywhere.

That is normal.

So, you think. How are you going to get out of that situation? Grieve a little, of course. Then, analyze. What happened? Why did I lose my job? Is it me or is it my boss? There are so many possible answers here. Different people will have different experiences.

For example, you may have been fired because of the pandemic. The firing is not due to anything that you have done wrong. So many people have become helpless victims. So, you think: *How can I solve this problem?* That will be your natural frame of mind. There will be no jokes from you for a time. You need to survive first. So, you do—try to survive—by trying to find a job to put food on the table. Later on, having fully survived and thrived, you may find some humor in the details. You may start joking about how you spent nights eating tubs of ice cream that you cannot afford in front of the television. For now, you cannot do that yet.

# Chapter 4 – Body Language

*"A shoulder clap is more appropriate in a business setting. But the underlying principle holds: touch more than the majority of people would in the same context. It demonstrates comfort, leadership, and conviction in your communication skills."*

— Charlie Houpert, Charisma on Command: Inspire, Impress, and Energize Everyone You Meet

Your body language says so much about you. A charismatic person will be more open to others. So, they do not hide behind folded arms and bowed heads.

Remember that part of your charisma has something about how you treat others. How do you look at them? Do you stare at them with animosity without you knowing it? They usually call that the "resting b*tch face." Some do have this face at rest. However, this will not happen if you are truly aware of the person right in front of you. Are you genuinely glad to hear about what they have to say? It will show on your facial expressions and how you talk to them.

The rest of your body will follow suit. When you are comfortable with somebody, your body language tends to be more open. Here are some signs that show you are willing to engage in the conversation:

- A smile or at least an open expression
- Open (unfolded) arms
- Straight back
- Toes pointed toward the person talking to you

The following, on the other hand, may suggest that you are not interested:

- Yawning (blatantly or furtively, but perhaps you just had a hard night)
- Folded arms
- Bored or distant expression
- Slumped back
- Body directed towards the exit, or anywhere else other than the person you are talking to

Sometimes, we don't even notice that we are revealing so much with the way that we move. We may think that we are hiding our feelings just because we are not saying anything, but we are wrong. So, all the while, we think we are sending our intended signals, our bodies are telling the whole truth.

But here is the thing. To be truly charismatic, you need to genuinely like people. Work your charm on people that you like and who like you. That should be easy, right? It could. It may be a little more challenging for those who are on the shy side. However, despite it all, it is more comfortable.

Of course, you have to eventually bridge out and expand. You have to go beyond your comfort zone, but with the right intentions. You cannot just go around, turning up the charm for everyone if you are starting from a very introverted place. Once you do get a feel for mingling with people beyond your usual cliques, you can incorporate some of the following tips:

- Stand and walk with your back straight. Do not let your shoulders slump. Instead, pull them back. Hold your head up, chin parallel to the horizon. You can already feel a little more confident when you do this.
- To further influence your mood and attitude, give a smile to the world. Notice that when you give in to the temptation of just pouting and slouching, your attitude also continues to deteriorate. Conversely, you boost your enthusiasm by starting your day with a smile. Yes, not everything can be perfect every day. However, it is up to you how you should face that day.
- During your interactions with people, make sure that your body language is sympathetic, empathetic, and supportive. People will more likely listen to you when they know that you can do likewise.
- Focus on the emotions of what you are trying to convey. When you do, you are more fully able to express yourself both in words and gestures.

A cliched expression is that "actions speak louder than words." This is true. You can control what you say. You can stop yourself from saying hurtful words, for example. However, it is more difficult to control your gestures. Perhaps you can keep your hands still, but there will be other parts of the body acting out your emotions. Your nose can flare due to disgust or alarm. Sometimes, you just cannot help it. Some also reveal too much by the way that they blush. If you are like this, people can easily see when you are embarrassed. Similarly, some people grow pale when scared or caught.

Charm is all about being as honest in your interactions as possible. Your "audience" would want the genuine article—a person they can look up to or at least relate with. To be truly charming, you need to see the best in people, as much as you can. Interact with them with the real desire to get to know them. Charm is not just about painting yourself well so that others will like you. You need to love being with people. That is how your charm develops.

*Communication Skills Training Series*

# Part Two – Buckets Full of Self-Discovery

*"When you love and laugh abundantly, you live a beautiful life."* – Unknown

*"A well-balanced person is one who finds both sides of an issue laughable."* — Herbert Procknow

You grabbed this book because there is something within you that wants to make people laugh. While you cannot claim that you will change the lives of others by making them laugh, you are attempting to give them a moment they can relish.

Making people laugh also changes you. It begins within you. That desire has sprouted from somewhere inside of you. So, the very first person that you will change during your journey is you.

Hey, nobody is expecting you to behave like a Mr. Bean. It is alright to be a serious person at work or school. You can wipe away that goofy grin from time to time. You don't have to be funny all the time.

However, you have that desire. This desire continues to make you want to make people laugh. You want them to share in your vision of a beautiful life—one that is full of laughter.

So, you begin with your self-discovery. Ask yourself the following questions:
 a. Why do I want to make people laugh? Is it a desire that stems from a secret ambition of becoming a comedian, or do I just feel good about hearing other people's laughter?
 b. If I make this joke, how will people react? Will somebody get hurt or offended? Will people laugh because they like me or laugh because the jokes are funny?
 c. Will I be willing to be the butt of jokes, too? How will I feel about it? If my friends, family, or colleagues realize that I like to make them laugh, will they also make jokes with me or about me?
 d. Am I a natural storyteller? Will I be able to pull off a punchline without laughing hysterically? Can I do deadpan or slapstick? Will I have enough range to make people laugh in various ways?
 e. Am I an extrovert or an introvert? Will my personality affect the way I deliver jokes?

This part of the book will deal with you, your personality, the types of jokes you like, and the means you plan on delivering your jokes. Specifically, it is divided into the following chapters:

**Chapter 5. Making Jokes Based on Your Story and Personality**

**Chapter 6. Effects of Personality on Jokes**

**Chapter 7. Delivery Styles**

# Chapter 5. Making Jokes Based on Your Story and Personality

*"Be who you are and say what you feel, because those who mind don't matter and those who matter don't mind."– Bernard Baruch*

Writers often fashion their first novels into barely veiled reimaginings of their own lives. This is what they know. So, the descriptions are rich, the events are vivid, and the emotions are raw. They have real-life events to draw these stories from.

After they are done publishing this first almost non-fiction novel, they read the reviews and the regular readers' feedback. Those who clamor for more have been drawn not only to the story but unknowingly to the writer himself. There was a connection somewhere. So, the writer's sophomore efforts may still slightly resemble his first novel. Someone wiser may only copy the style but steer the story away from the possibility of repeating a plot or subplot.

When making jokes, sometimes it is easier to start from yourself, as well. You can start zeroing in on yourself as the focus of the funny vignette. It is safer to do so after all. Sometimes, though, you have to let go of jokes that are too close to home if people start feeling as if you have nothing else to talk about. So, you delve deeper into jokes that your personality feels comfortable with.

### *Here are some ideas:*

- Find funny moments that have happened in your real life. It can be as cute as a Kid's Say joke involving your child or student. It can be a humorous look at an otherwise stressful situation that you have found yourself in.
- Recognize the folly of people around you. Examine why these actions seem funny to you. Is it something that you can freely joke about without being mean or offensive? Perhaps it is a joke shared by a friend who recognized silliness in his behavior.
- Watch comedy films or listen to standup comics. What type of humor do you easily react to? Are you a person who is difficult to please, or are you someone who laughs at both wry wit and slapstick?
- How about jokes that you have to read? Read the Sunday comic on your local newspaper and check if the humor works for you. Then, compare that humor to the type that you read from *Mad* magazine when it was still being published.
- Observe your life and its many aspects. Are there some particular moments that you normally chuckle to? For example, someone who has a better attitude in life will probably laugh at himself if he finds out that what he has been looking for has been in his hand the whole time. On the other hand, someone who is under a lot of stress will end up throwing a tantrum.

### *How about making your life abundant with laughter?*

- Have more pictures of yourself smiling taken. You want to see yourself at your best. Forget about how puffy your cheeks look when you smile widely. When you smile genuinely, it reaches your

eyes—and that is a glorious thing to see. People will more likely want to interact with you when they see such an open expression of happiness.
- Be around people who like funny stuff. They will appreciate a little banter now and then. This will act as your natural means to practice your humor. Be around naturally happy people. They are not perfect. They are not free from problems and responsibilities, but they know how to look at the lighter side of things.
- Watch a lot of comedy. Not only will you get a good laugh as lung exercise, but you also lower your cortisol this way. With the stress hormone down, you are less likely to crave too many calories. You may lose weight. If not, then at least you have lowered your stress even for about an hour or so. Comedy sitcoms may also provide you with ideas on how to make jokes work in the ordinary world setup. Yeah, they have a laugh track, but at least you will discover what makes you laugh and what makes you annoyed.

To test all that you have read above, you have a little assignment:

1. Watch your favorite standup comic. Take note of his/her best jokes.
2. Do those jokes reflect a moment in their lives?
3. Do those jokes reflect their point of view?
4. Do those jokes reveal a lot about who they are?

Standup comics have to write their comedy routines. They have to draw upon their experiences to write the most effective jokes. After all, these are jokes that they are invested in.

For you to do something similar, you can first BRAINSTORM. Fill the blanks below:

I love _____ so much that I _____!

I hate _____ because _____.

My pet peeve is _____. I just cannot stand it when _____.

The best moments in my life happen _____

I am scared of _____! When I see _____, I _____!

I am ashamed of the fact that _____.

I am addicted to _____. I just have to _____.

When answering the above questions, you are finding possibly humorous situations from your life. However, you don't have to attempt at making them funny right away. You can first fill in the blanks, read the answers aloud to try them for size, and then check your tone.

Are you too serious when you are answering the questions? Do you sound like someone answering an '80s slam book? Perhaps, the answers can be tweaked to make them sound like deadpan jokes.

Are you sarcastic? Do you think you can tweak that sarcasm to be funnier, and not hurtful? Sarcasm may just be your style, especially if this is grounded in your personality. People will know right away that you are just being you.

Are your answers naturally humorous upon close inspection? It seems that you are on your way.

*James W. Williams*

Give it a try. Then, compare what you have with what we have come up with.
1. I love chocolates so much that I have a secret stash in the house I keep away from my siblings.
2. I hate Facebook memes because they usually remind me of jokes that I was not able to tell myself. They speak so much about my life.
3. My pet peeve is a tall man with sweaty armpits. I just cannot stand when I have to commute with one on the subway. I am short.
4. The best moments in my life happen when I am asleep. Seriously! Everyone is like, "Oh, you should have been awake, but we felt bad waking you up!" I am a night shift nurse.
5. I am scared of little toddlers with big grins on their faces. I don't know if I should make sure they are okay, or if I should make a run for it.
6. I am ashamed of the fact that I fart whenever I am nervous.
7. I am addicted to grandma games—you know, not those cool games on PS4 but the ones that require you to buy gems to move along.

Some of the responses above are funnier than the others, but each can be material for your next joke. If the person you are going to tell the joke to knows you well enough, then it becomes an inside joke of sorts. You know when they make that connection when they start grinning widely even though you have not finished the joke. You may also observe the other person nodding in comprehension.

So, don't force it. Upon seeing the fill-in-the-blanks statements, do a few rounds:

First: Just answer. Do not think too much. It is much better to take a response from your reality. It is easier to build a story from something that you know well or believe in.

Second: Examine your answers. Are you a positive or a negative person based on them?

Third: Add details that can make the story vivid.

Fourth: See what happens when you swap the answers to "I love_" and "I hate_," and other opposites.

Another exercise that you can work on is a variation of either FREE ASSOCIATION or the Rorschach test.

You can either take a look at a random set of words or pictures (instead of the actual inkblot test referenced above) and say the first thing that pops in your head. Don't overthink. Don't try to be so cool at the first try. Just say or write the very first thing. You have nobody to fool, except yourself.

What you need:
- A pen
- A pad to write on/sheets of paper
- Random words (You can make someone give you the words OR you can use Charades or any word generator online)
- Random pictures (cut-outs that someone has prepared for you) OR even children's flashcards

You may need a little help because you should not know the random words and random pictures beforehand. Someone can flash you the words or just prepare them for you to work on alone.

Try some of these words on your own:

PET

*Communication Skills Training Series*

1. HOUSE
2. OVEN
3. FRIEND
4. LIST
5. WORK
6. COFFEE
7. CAKE
8. FIRE
9. SLEEP

How about the following pictures/inkblots? Numbers 1 to 3 are commonly used inkblots in psychoanalysis. Numbers 4 and 5 are non-copyrighted photos of a breakfast feast and a bag, respectively.

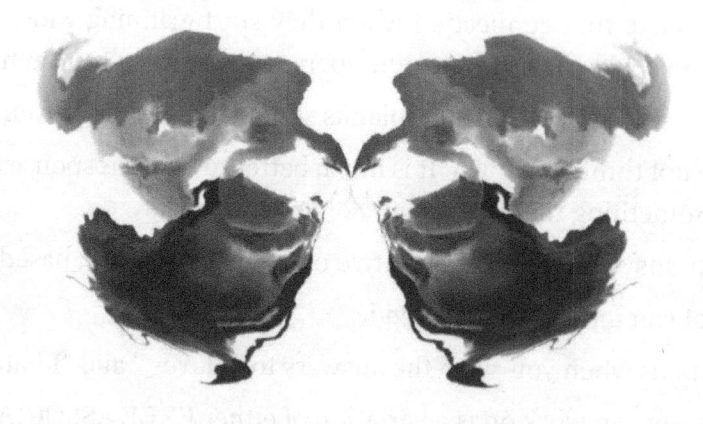

**1.**

**2.**

*James W. Williams*

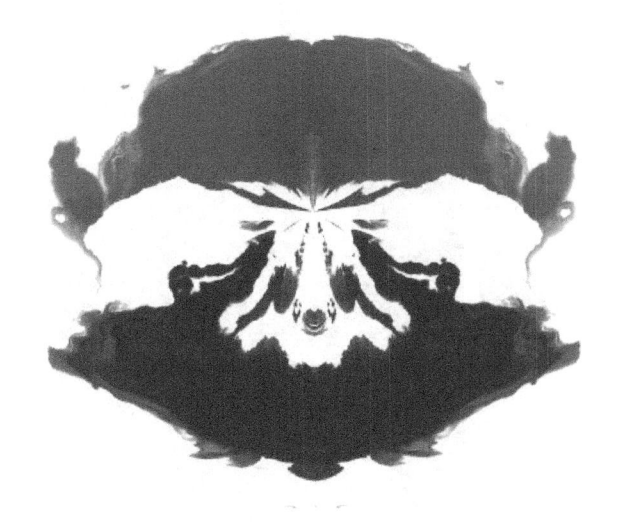

3.

4.

**5.**

Before you read our answers, try doing the FREE ASSOCIATION exercise on the above words, inkblots, and pictures. Again, remember: Be quick. Be honest. Use a timer so that you don't spend a lot of time on each. Finish the word association in 30 seconds. Finish the picture association in 15 seconds.

Possible results:

Each person will have a different set of answers because the answers reflect who he is deep inside.

1. PET – little beloved that does not stop bouncing around
2. HOUSE – not my own
3. OVEN – my stress baking friend
4. FRIEND – virtual
5. LIST – of things I need to do
6. WORK – 24/7
7. COFFEE – my source of life
8. CAKE – a slice for my thighs
9. FIRE - fear
10. SLEEP – barely get any

There is no right or wrong way of answering free association exercises. Sometimes, answers can even stray. This straying reveals a lot about your mindset. You may also not be familiar with everything that will be put in front of you—or you know what they are, but you just do not have much of a relationship with the object or person.

Not all of your answers will be funny, of course. However, all of them have the potential to be expanded.

The first answer above for PET may be expanded to write pet jokes.

Pet jokes can be general. In the joke below, Seinfeld was talking about all dogs:

*"Dogs have no money. Isn't that amazing? They're broke their entire lives. But they get through. You know why dogs have no money? No pockets."*
*Jerry Seinfeld*

It could be personal.

*"I took my dog for a walk, all the way from New York to Florida. I said to him, "There, now you're done."*
*Steven Wright*

While we find Seinfeld's joke funny, some of us who have dogs that like to walk way too much will appreciate Wright's joke. It feels personal. It becomes an inside joke among pet lovers.

The HOUSE joke may also be expanded. The answer "not my own" can be a little sad. It means the person who answered does not have his own home yet. He is renting or continuously paying a huge mortgage. Whatever the case may be, a joke stemming from this has to rely on the delivery.

*What is your attitude about not owning your home?*

Yes, ultimately, it can be sad. However, have you decided to see the light side of this situation? You will be surprised at the material that you can get from this one topic. Some people may choose to write a serious commentary about how it is difficult to buy a house in the 21st century. You can follow the same thoughts, but with a lighter tone. You are, after all, seeking to make people laugh. The first step is to make yourself feel good about life, see its positives, despite all the difficulties.

The OVEN response can be expanded. It can play with your obsession with baking. It may offer a little insight into how you go to the extremes when you like doing something. It does not have to be merely about baking.

The FRIEND response can go sad quickly, as the answer suggests that the Improv Partner does not have any nearby friends, just ones that he can contact via social media. It can also mean that he does not have any friends at all, just imaginary ones or ones that he interacts with from time to time online.

The LIST response can support the person's overworked, slightly antisocial stance. Together, the picture is becoming clearer. The funny person's personality is starting to emerge. This is why it is best to brainstorm with several words. You will find that some of them will start making connections.

Similarly, the COFFEE and SLEEP questions further drive the idea that you are a workaholic with coffee as fuel and a sleep deficit as your main problem. The more your materials are based on real life, the better that you can do them justice.

Even the CAKE question can still support a certain lifestyle. People are starting to see you as that workaholic who drinks too much coffee, cannot sleep well, stress bakes, and gains weight, but cannot stop working because the mortgage is up.

You are, in fact, a very relatable person. Others experience most of your struggles. Of course, the exact details may be different, but you can further highlight the similarities.

Because you are making people laugh in your daily life—not on stage—it is easier to know which jokes may be relatable to the person you are talking to. You may have heard the concerns of your work colleagues, friends, and family members. You also have an inkling of what could make them feel hurt or offended. Joking about how you finally earned enough money to buy that home you have been struggling to get may have to be put aside in front of a person who has just lost his job or home.

Now, let us move on to the INKBLOTS and PICTURES.

These are a lot more complicated, but may be effective in discovering who you are and what you are passionate about or scared of.

Try it on your own first. Then check the sample answers below:

1. The first inkblot is of two identical old men fighting.
2. The second inkblot is of two shrimps on a dish—about to get cooked—plotting their escape.
3. The third inkblot is of an enraged French soldier, squinting at you.
4. This reminds me of breakfasts in movies. They are abundant, but they never really get eaten. I volunteer to eat the rest.
5. This reminds me of how my bag carries a lot of what I value in life: wallet, IDs, chargers, devices, pocket change, pepper spray, extra underwear, a slice of a ham sandwich, etc.

The three inkblots can generate a whole range of answers. You may even use inkblots as the main focus of the joke. The joke can see you looking at a wide array of inkblots and saying:

a. Outrageous, detailed answers for each (possibly with backstories)
b. Saying the same thing for everything
c. Dismissing all as inkblots
d. Giving one-liner jokes as answers for all

What was your inkblot test like? Don't worry about sounding a little crazy. You are doing it for fun. However, you should also consider trying to stick to what the inkblots kind of look like. You want your "audience" to say, "Oh, it kinda looks like that. Doesn't it?"

The two pictures included in the exercise may also be used to reveal your attitude towards those objects. They may also paint a clearer picture of what your life is like.

Now, let us move on to creating mini-chunks of your life, otherwise known as TWEET format statements.

As with the FREE ASSOCIATION exercise, you will write without the intention of being funny. You can examine the thoughts afterward to see if there is anything funny there at all or the potential for development.

### Tweet Exercise

A tweet can only go up to 280 characters maximum. It is compact and precise. You may be able to write some of your thoughts based on the following:

1. Life in general
2. The state of the world

3. Taking care of babies
4. Teaching someone how to do something
5. Eating whatever you like

Now, try it. It is better to type it on your computer, or even on the Twitter app of your phone so that you can easily tell if it already reached 280 characters.

1. Life in general right now is just about getting up in the morning and letting the rest just happen to me. I have gotten tired of planning things that never happen, anyway. I am letting life grab me unawares now. Well, at least when I am not at work. I don't want to lose my job.

2. The world is still battling the pandemic. So much else is going on, though. This pandemic has revealed a lot more: corruption, mismanagement, poor health care systems, poverty in general, and a lack of trust in the government. We now see a lot of silly horror mistakes in real life.

3. Taking care of babies is much more different than taking care of eggs for a high school project. When you break the egg, you get a failing grade. When you do not take care of a baby, you can risk its life. Its effects are a whole lot more fatal. You won't get over it.

4. I would rather do everything than teach someone something. Well, if I were a teacher, I don't really have a choice. At home, though, it is easier to cook the whole meal on your own than teach someone to do it. It is not wise, though. That will be teaching someone to be lazy.

5. Eating what you like is only good for the moment. When the calories start making themselves known, you have to do something else that you hate doing—exercise. Exercise and diet experts, I really need your help! This waistline is exponentially expanding.

As you can tell, none of the above has been written to be funny. They are matter-of-fact thoughts of a person. It is not beyond the realm of possibility that some may get retweeted, but usually groundbreaking and hilarious tweets are the ones that get more traction.

How did you do? Did you fare better than us? Did you post them on your Twitter account and get any reactions or retweets?

Tweet #1 is serious. However, it has the possibility of becoming funny if you take a look at the lighter side of it.

This popular meme is a funny interpretation of it. You may have seen variations of this meme on social media.

In real life, people have joked around about their life with friends when they are at their most stressed. The punchline serves as a mood lifter. Though worried, the person making the joke will still go on to do whatever task it is that is causing him stress.

Tweet #2 is a lot more serious. It involves a pandemic that can cost hundreds of thousands of lives—or even more. Not only is it a health issue, but it brought forward some very dark themes. Making a joke about it is going to be complicated. Do not dare to make jokes about the pandemic to:

- People who have lost their jobs because of it
- People who have family or friends who lost their lives because of the virus
- Just about anyone who will keep on passing the joke (The Internet already has a name for the passing on of such jokes for the sake of how it makes them feel to react—emotional contagion.)

So, tweet #2 is best left as a serious tweet. People have to take the situation seriously.

Tweet #3 is serious, as well. It can be tweaked to be funny, but it can be dangerously close to being tacky and irresponsible. Parents may not fully appreciate your jokes unless you are a parent yourself and they know your brand of humor can sometimes go to the dark side.

There is a meme doing the rounds on social media that shows the Dos and Donts of baby care. A particular meme of a hand pulling a baby by the head can be offensive, but darkly funny. The Do parts shows the baby being carried the right way, with hands supporting the torso and the neck.

Some may find it hilarious, but there is a possibility that some may find this offensive.

Tweet #4 can be pretty serious, as well. However, teaching jokes seem to be safe enough to get into. You can find a way to tweak the tweet, which provides you with so much material: teaching, stress, spoiling others, being a good example, impatience, and more.

Tweet #5 has attempted to be funnier than the other tweets. It can still be reworded to emphasize what is going on. This is a joke that is better off done in a self-deprecatory way. Yes, it is better to joke about yourself gaining weight, than involving anyone else. If you joke about yourself gaining weight, you see the lighter side of things. On the other hand, joking about somebody else gaining weight is insensitive.

# Chapter 6. Effects of Personality on Jokes

*"Jokes proper thrive in the company of joke tellers." – Agnes Heller, Aesthetics and Modernity: Essays*

Now you know where to get some funny material from your personal life. Now, how does your personality affect the delivery of jokes?

It can make or break it.

Heller, in her book *Aesthetics and Modernity: Essays*, has commented that reading joke books are not the proper way to receive jokes. This means she does not believe in how social media memes are being delivered.

*What gets discarded when you read jokes instead of listening to them?*

- You lose the camaraderie that is formed when the joke-teller and the audience create a bond. As the audience laughs, it shows that it understands the joke as it is meant to be. The same happens between friends or colleagues making jokes at the office pantry.
- You lose the opportunity to witness a great storyteller create a performance, complete with acting, timing, and proper intonation. A great joke-teller knows when to pause, hush, and change his tone.

*So, how do you deliver your jokes to your family and friends?*

Much value is being given to how a joke-teller delivers his jokes. Your delivery, however, does not have to follow the requirements of a standup comic's own.

For stand-up comics, they have:

- To make the most of the stage that they are on: adding physical comedy and facial expressions that are appropriate to the joke
- To write original jokes: it would be in bad taste to recycle other people's jokes
- To connect to a big audience

You, on the other hand, can make use of existing jokes and give your twist to it. You don't need a stage, and your setup is more intimate.

What you need to do:

- Be confident about your joke—who will laugh if the joke-teller seems uncertain about what he is trying to say?
- Convey the appropriate emotion to carry the joke
- If you are going to say an existing joke, add your twist or attempt to make it sound better
- Make it feel like an inside joke
- Appeal to the particular person's interests

So, anyone can make other people laugh. Even the shyest among us have some concept of what we find humorous. With likeminded people, these jokes can work well.

## Myers-Briggs and their Effects on Sense of Humor

Personality can certainly color the way you make your jokes. So, it is no surprise that the Myers-Briggs can come up with not only 16 distinctive personalities but also with 16 distinctive types of humor.

Half of these personality groups are made up of introverts. Introverts are not exactly what you will think of when you are trying to find some worthy joke tellers. However, they do have their brand of humor. Steve Martin and James Belushi may be famous comedians, but they are also known to be introverts.

There should be more famous introverted comedians out there, but most would not have categorized themselves as such. You would know that there must be a whole group of them because of the advantages posed by being an introverted comedian:

They are more observant. So, they are likely to find material from their surroundings that people can relate to.

- They are empathetic. So, they know when to move on because the audience is not responding the way he intended them to.
- They are more reflective. This means that they can take any subject or situation and analyze each. They can make their conclusions about anything that interests them. They are not simply interested in the surface issues, but also the details. Yes, introverts can be more detail-oriented.
- They can work independently, as well. So, they have no problems with creating their jokes without a whole group of writers. Because of this, the content is even closer to their hearts.

With Myers-Briggs, you can find eight personalities that are considered introverted. They have their unique way of handling humor.

While not all of the eight have specific characteristics that truly identify them over the rest of the introverts, they all have the advantages mentioned above.

You can be sure, however, that the ISFJs will be more aware of other people's feelings. So, they are less likely to make jokes that can hurt other people's feelings. INFJ's sense of organization can produce some well-formed setups and punchlines, while the INTJ's can provide original, creative content. Most of the other introverts are well suited to making genuine connections with their audience.

### *Now, what about the extroverts?*

Most people may think that extroverts have the proper sensibilities to become great comics. They can be because of the way they desire interactions with people. However, you may argue that introverts also love interacting with the people closest to them. This book, after all, is not about becoming a professional comic or standup comedian; it is all about being able to make people laugh. Sensitive people care about how they can make their loved ones happy.

For extroverts, however, it is the norm for them to try to keep on making people laugh and be happy. Comedy or any other human-to-human interaction is their natural setting. You could say that extroverts have fewer inhibitions when it comes to being on a stage or chatting up a storm with a friend.

Extroverts such as ESFPs are friendly and outgoing. These are the friends that will not leave you with any awkward silence between the two of you. ENTPs have the quick thinking needed to make jokes that can adjust to different people. ENFPs have the enthusiasm needed for great physical comedy. ESTJs, meanwhile, will have the efficiency in formulating great jokes with meat. You may expect some blunt, straight jokes from an ENTJ. What they have in common is the ability to bounce with any other person.

### *An Insight into a Comic's Mind*

While the statistics of the ratio of introverts and extroverts in the comedy world are not clear, a lot of studies show that some comics are not as happy or outgoing as they seem on stage.

Some comics, such as Robin Williams, have been revealed to have depression. Jokes seem to be the most fun they have. Others may not have been depressed but were shy or very introverted that they content themselves in being wallflowers in get-togethers. They are usually quiet offstage.

### *Now, what does this have to do with you?*

With making people laugh offstage, it is less complicated. You have to deal with people who may already have a connection with you. So, extrovert or introvert, you already have a unique relationship with whoever it is that you are talking to. You don't have to have extra powers of observation; you will be communicating with someone that you already know.

Introverts will have their friends and family that they can already relate to. Extroverts have several people to choose from (acquaintances, colleagues, and more).

# Chapter 7. Delivery/Joke Styles

*"My vibe is like, hey you could probably pour some on my lap and I'll apologize to you."* – John Mulaney

There are various types of jokes out there. Some, however, can only work on the big screen with effects to support them. Others are better off the stage. How do you then find jokes and delivery styles that will work with your friends, family, and colleagues?

**Joke Styles/Types**

Anecdotal – What you have been working on in the earlier chapters will mostly fall under this type of joke. This is a comedy that you draw from your personal life. Director Judd Apatow says that comedy improves "as it becomes more personal." Your audience best appreciates your joke when they can see something similar to their own lives. Here is the camaraderie that can occur when jokes are exchanged either through performance or an exchange.

Deadpan – If you are known for being serious most of the time, some people may stop and think: is he joking with me? However, as they start listening more to what you have to say and recognize the pure humor in what you are saying, they will accept that this is the way you deliver your jokes. Seemingly both trivial and nonconsequential in tone, the deadpan delivery can make people laugh a little louder. The contrast of hilarious content and serious monotone can set some off.

Observational - Taking a closer look at everyday situations can provide you with some observational jokes. Anything can be transformed into a humorous observation. However, you must make sure that people can relate to you. If you are going to observe doctors, for example, it will work best among health professionals, their families, or some active patients.

One-liner - The setup and the punchline are delivered in one short, witty sentence. There is no room for hesitation here. You just deliver the whole thing and get the results. On the other hand, a punchline can take some time to simmer before it explodes—and you just may change your mind.

Rick Moranis's character in *Spaceballs* said: "I am your father's brother's nephew's cousin's former roommate." It is simple, possibly factual, but also undoubtedly funny. You don't have to be in a particular demographic to understand this.

Self-deprecating - Are you ready to make fun of yourself? Well, this is where you go with self-deprecating jokes. The joke-teller is, in reality, a lot more self-assured when he can submit himself to judgment and ridicule in a joke. You have to be comfortable with your flaws for you to be able to use them in such jokes. The delivery is also important. It must be clear to the person that you are talking to that you are, in fact, joking. You don't want the reaction to be, "Are you okay?" or "I am here for you." The only reaction you need when your self-deprecating joke is successful is loud laughter.

While self-deprecating jokes are still best delivered verbally, quite a number of tweets have been successful at conveying them.

Twitter has many self-deprecating jokes to offer, coming from celebrities and regular folks alike. The upside to these jokes is that this can boost the mood of people who can relate to the litany of negative traits the joke teller supposedly has. The self-deprecating joke can be in the form of a wordless picture, a one-liner, or a setup and punchline combo.

# Part Three – Smattering of Acceptance

*"If fate doesn't make you laugh, you just don't get the joke."*
— Gregory David Roberts

*"A sense of humor is the best indicator that you will recover; it is often the best indicator that people will love you. Sustain that, and you have hope."*
— Andrew Solomon, The Noonday Demon: An Atlas of Depression

It is in the acceptance of the imperfect lives that we have that we can find the humor in everything.

Part three is simply a transition. By the time that you have reached this page, you have already gathered enough material from your life, other people's lives, and your own worldviews to be able to make sense of them and find the humor in them.

# Part Four – Heated in Learning

*"All students can learn and succeed, but not on the same day and the same way."* – *William G. Spady*

Just like any other skill, making people laugh can be learned. You cannot just give and say the following:

- I cannot do it because I am too shy.
- I cannot do it because I am too hyper and will give up my punchline right away.
- I cannot do it because I don't know how to do it.

Here are some ideas on how you can start trying to be funny (yes, nobody is born funny):

1. Think of things that you find funny.
   Think of concepts and existing jokes that make you laugh. Do you smile a bit when you hear them? Do you giggle or do you guffaw? Think about what makes you laugh. Are they the types of jokes that you can share with people you like if they have the same interests?
   Then, think of people you are close to who find the same things funny. Perhaps you can deliver some of the jokes that you have come up with or even existing jokes that you have found. Bounce the jokes with these likeminded people. Check how they react to these jokes. Find out what makes them laugh. It would be great if you can find someone willing to assist you with this comedic journey. That person should be able to represent any audience.
   However, make sure that you don't make it a point to be funny all the time. Sometimes, when you are not a professional comic, it is better when your audience does not expect your jokes. Of course, you should not insert the joke when your audience is trying to be serious. However, you can use jokes to cheer someone up.

2. Act dumb. See how it works.
   Some comedians get away with making people laugh by simply acting dumb. This is a little tricky to pull off because you must show that it is just an act without destroying the joke. Don't do this all the time, though. People may start thinking that this is your true personality.

3. Exaggerate
   Some people naturally exaggerate. However, the results can be varied. Some can end up being funny, but some are just plain annoying.
   Think about it: a person who exaggerates to complain is not exactly very endearing. Such a person is labeled as entitled or harsh. Do not be that person.
   Have you heard those "Your mama" jokes?
   Sometimes, they go like this:
   Your mama is so <exaggerated descriptive word> that she <exaggerated comparison, explanation, etc.>
   You will find that some may still giggle. However, this is an old hyperbole. People will be amused by it, but will not exactly be filled with hilarity.

4. Tell a funny story

Sometimes, though, the solution to being funny is simple. Tell a funny story. You may ask, "But if I knew how to do that, why would I be reading this book?" Remember, there is always something funny that you see on your daily commute, hear from a young child, or experience in a new environment. If you find it funny, then chances are someone else will find it funny.

What you can do to make the joke work better, however, is to apply actions and facial expressions. Storytelling is always about being able to make the events more vivid to the person who is listening. Your audience should be able to transport themselves to the world that you are imagining.

The world is full of material. Bring a journal when you go out daily. Write what captures your interest. What is so funny about the experience?

5. Use puns

    Some people prefer clever jokes. They like playing with words. If you know your puns, then you should be able to come up with all kinds of twists and jumbles.

The stock image has a black background. The white text says, "Bad puns. That's how eye roll." When you use puns, you have to make sure that whoever is listening to you know all the words and phrases that are used to deliver the jokes.

For example, in the joke, "What do you call a cow with no legs? Ground beef," you need to know what:
- o  A cow is
- o  Not having legs entails
- o  Ground beef is

In a picture joke, "I tell dad jokes periodically," the word "jokes" is divided into three parts: JO-K-ES, which represents chemicals in the periodical table. The picture is a great way of delivering this pun joke. However, this does not mean that you can deliver it verbally.

The above are just some of the strategies on how you can jumpstart your making-people-laugh journey. What else do you need?

1. You need a partner that can tell you if you are being funny or not. Since you are not making a career out of it, you can simply try the joke on them. Check their reactions.
2. You need to build more of your confidence. Sometimes, making people laugh is less about the actual material and more about the confidence and hilarity that you are bringing in.
3. It's a good idea to have a book of jokes that you can read for some ideas. Try to practice some of them aloud so that you can hear how they sound. Read the jokes to someone and see how they work.
4. Get familiar with memes that are going around on social media. This way, you are updated with what people find humorous and what they find to be stale and overused.

What is the anatomy of a typical joke?

1. Setup
2. Details
3. Punchline
4. Closing

These parts do not affect how long the joke becomes. Some handle everything in a one-liner, for example. Most jokes only need the setup and the punchline. So, how come you need the above?

Setup – The setup provides you with an introduction. It plays with the audience's assumptions. Some setups are obviously jokes:

- A priest, a rabbi, and an atheist went into a bar... (or any of its variations)
- "Knock, knock..."

Setup is basically what propels the joke. The two examples above can sometimes make some people immediately laugh, and let the others anticipate the next few words.

Anything can be a setup, however. It can be a simple sentence. It is meant to raise an expectation in the audience. If your audience is not biting or has already gone bored from the very setup, then you must be doing something wrong. It is not just the punchline that makes the joke. The setup should already grab your audience's attention. It is what ultimately decides whether the punchline is funny or not.

Here is an example of a setup from a Steve Martin joke:

**"I gave my cat a bath the other day."**

This perks up the interest of the audience. Of course, this is Steve Martin talking. So, most people will anticipate a joke. If you were the one who started your joke this way, you would still inspire the curiosity of your audience. The other person may think, *Why is this person telling me about his cat?*

Details – Sometimes, a joke needs additional details for the audience to fully appreciate it. However, a good setup may do away with this. Details may be best included in story-type jokes, wherein the joke-teller takes the audience for a ride first before giving the punchline.

In some cases, the details already contain some of the jokes. The audience may have already had a good laugh before the punchline arrives to bring home the point.

The detail may sometimes sound like the punchline, but there is a huge pause plus a certain air that suggests the joke-teller is not yet done with his joke.

Detailed jokes are also delivered in situation comedy (sitcom) shows. The comedians (or rather, the joke writers) have enough time to fill with details. In your case, you can easily use this because you and your possible audience may have had enough knowledge about each other to make it work. Story-form jokes can fall under the four-part joke, as well.

To continue the Steve Martin joke, this is the detail that he added:

**"He sat there, he enjoyed it, and it was fun for me, too."**

At this point, the other person starts suspecting something, but he is not sure if he is getting a joke or something else.

Punchline – This should be the end of the joke. It should end strong. It must be delivered clearly to avoid the awkward "huh?" moment. This is your ace if you are going gambling. You keep it hidden, but you also give some clues as to what it is about. Then, you deliver it. When you do, people should not be too surprised because you set it up well. You don't want them bewildered. At the same time, they should not go, "I knew it all along."

Two-part joke structures cite this as the endpoint of a joke.

There may be cases when a different punchline can still end the joke well if the setup is rich in meaning and possibilities.

The possibilities are countless, depending on the joke-teller's wealth of knowledge of the topic. He also has to rely on the audience's interest and knowledge of the topic.

Whatever the setup may be, however, if the audience does not "get" the punchline, it is best to leave it that way. If you keep on trying, then you will just appear to be desperate for approval.

Steve Martin ends his joke with this punchline:

**"The fur would stick to my tongue, but other than that, it was great."**

By this time, everyone knows that Steve Martin's joke persona has ended up licking his cat. The joke can end right here on the punchline, as people absorb and react to it.

You may also dissect the punchline further. Notice that the first part can already hammer the joke in:

**"The fur would stick to my tongue…"**

The last part can be removed and added to the last part of the four-act structure. This maneuver can be done with a simple pause after the word "tongue."

However, some joke structures still include the fourth part.

Closing – In my humble opinion, a joke must end with the punchline. The audience should be left, still gasping in laughter. The punchline must be strong enough to carry the whole joke. However, some comedians still provide a closing.

Whatever you may plan to do, do not use an explanation as a closing. If your setup is strong and the punchline is driven home, then the two-part structure should have been enough.

However, not all jokes follow a structure. Just like with writing stories, the structure of a joke can also take on a unique form. Writing a joke is a creative enterprise. Nobody should be able to tell you how you should go about it.

The second part of Steve Martin's punchline can be considered the closing. People are already laughing by the time they hear, "The fur would stick to my tongue." Hearing the comedian say, "but other than that, it was great" may encourage a fresh bout of laughter.

Of course, if you do like to follow a structure to guide you for now, here are some possible "templates."

1. Broken Assumptions

The structure of a broken assumption looks somewhat like this:

Setup: We start with what we assume to be true.

Punchline: Boo! It is not the case. The Steve Martin joke in the four-act structure example is a broken assumption joke. The listeners were expecting that the character was bathing the cat with regular soap and water.

2. Contradiction Jokes

You can probably explain these away as ironic humor. In stories, irony provides a truth that is the opposite of what a character says, a character does, or what the audience knows. In contradiction jokes, this irony is simply made humorous.

    a. Words contradict Words
       Child A: I did not throw the pencil at you!
       Child B: Yes, you did! I saw you!
       Child A: No, I didn't. I missed!

    b. Words contradict Actions
       Alice (calls husband by phone urgently): Bob, you need to drive carefully. There is a madman driving by 43rd Street in the opposite direction.
       Bob: You got that right. It is not just one madman. There are several of them, and they have been honking a lot.

This may be best seen than read. Bob is enraged that there are madmen on the road, but he was the one driving in the wrong direction.

    c. Words contradict What Audience Already Knows
       Person A: Hello. Happy birthday! (with a box containing a mug, shown to the audience beforehand)
       Person B: Hi. Come on in!
       Person A: How are things?
       Person B: Been getting so many mugs for my birthday. I was pretty sure I said I don't need them. I am a teacher. So, I get them all the time!

Person A: Uh-oh. (throws box in the bin) I am much worse. I was so busy, I haven't bought you a gift yet. I will bring it to you tomorrow.

3. Puns/Double Entendres

Puns and double entendres do not necessarily have to be sexualized, but they are often utilized this way. Even with people that you know well, it is better to keep things clean. You don't want to end up with a reputation as someone who likes dirty jokes way too much.

Puns, however, can be a means for you to display your intellect and wit. They can also dangerously go into the corny territory. On the other hand, puns can be paired up with deadpan delivery.

Some puns or double entendres are, however, best delivered via images and will not be good material for you. Well, it won't be recommended unless you are an artist who likes to draw funny stuff to make your friends laugh.

Famous example:

**Light travels faster than sound. That's why some people appear bright until you hear them speak.**

4. Rule of Three

There is something magical about the number three. Even in fairy tales, we often see things that come in threes. In *The Firebird,* as with many other fairy tales, a king has three sons. The third one is the good prince. It is as if fate has made the king and queen fail twice before finally ending up with an honorable son. This is a very common setup in fairy tales. These are often more tragic than funny, though.

In the world of jokes, the rule of three is also very common. The first two serve as the setup while the third of the series breaks the rule. So, in a way, it is a type of broken assumption joke as well.

Here is a common joke:

Genie: I grant you three wishes.

Man: Great! For my first wish, I want a huge mansion.

Genie: Granted!

Man: For my second wish, I want tons of cash.

Genie: Here you go!

Man: For my third wish, I want you back inside the lamp!

This is so common that many people already expect the punchline. You may twist it a bit when joking around with friends. Perhaps, you can change the punchline to:

Man: For my third wish, I want you back inside the lamp!

Genie: You should read the fine print. (Goes in the lamp, with the house and the cash.)

5. Punchline First

Some joke-tellers like to begin from the punchline. What this means is that they already settled on a punchline that they want to end with. They have decided that it would be funny or even dramatic to end with the chosen punchline. So, they write the punchline first. Afterward, they add the details leading towards the end. It sometimes works if the punchline is strong enough. However, the punchline also cannot save poor storytelling in the setup.

A meta version of this joke is:

The punchline comes first.

What's the worse thing about time travel jokes?

6. Omitted Punchline

When the punchline is very obvious, the joke-teller does not have to say it. He can just make a certain face that suggests what he really means. A successfully omitted punchline joke can be very hilarious. The audience is also thrilled that they are able to get it without it being spelled out for them. This means that the setup must have been very good to make it work.

The punchline has become almost like a requirement to a joke that the image above is a visual representation of how that in itself can become a joke. This is a result of the fact that people still believe that punchlines should always be there somewhere, perhaps in an unexpected form.

Example:

Let's eat Grandma!

For those who are familiar with this joke will know that the punchline is in the punctuation. There is no need to add any other detail. However, some do include a punchline:

Punctuation saves lives.

7. Meta Jokes

Just as there are some meta moments on television and in books, there are meta moments in jokes, as well.

What does meta mean, anyway? It means that it is self-aware and even breaks the fourth wall by talking to the audience.

A joke can be self-referential. For example, it can talk about how terrible a joke it is. This is a joke that will be difficult to pull off on stage, but other forms of the meta-joke can be uttered vocally and still make an impact. An example of such a joke is one that jokes about a well-known joke or joke format. It is like the inception for jokes: a joke within a joke!

Example:

An Englishman, an Irishman, and a Scotsman walk into a bar. The barman looks at them and says: "Is this some kind of a joke?"

The above joke makes fun of a popular joke format, which has three people walking into a bar. The barman here, however, is fully aware of the connotation of having the three men enter the bar.

Even with templates, jokes can still be difficult to write. You have to keep on finding original material. Since you are not going to take it on stage, you are forgiven when you take on even the most obvious jokes—sometimes dubbed as dad jokes—and make them work for you if your personality is just right.

Of course, you may want to provide good material. It is worthwhile to see people laugh at your jokes, with a mix of surprise and appreciation.

### Short and Long formats

For some comics, the exact content and specific formats are not that important. They just categorize them as short and long formats.

### What is a short format joke?

A short format joke refers to a joke that is told like a knock-knock joke. It is a quick pairing of setup and punchline. You can deliver a whole series of this for a party. Some party clowns actually give several of these short-format jokes while also doing other fun stuff, such as juggling and magic tricks.

For extroverts, sharing short-format jokes with your colleagues should be easier. Sometimes, the joke pairing structure does not require a lot of details. You just get in. You may introduce it as, "Have you heard the joke about so and so?" Then, your colleague will say, "I am not sure. What is it? Tell me the joke." So, you deliver the joke. Usually, it is quick. Sometimes, it can be a little corny. Turning up the charm can help you successfully deliver it.

### What is a long-format joke?

A long-format joke relies on a story. You can talk about something funny that happened to you. Within the longer format, there may be a smattering of shorter jokes, which could provide a certain degree of satisfaction along the way to the big punchline.

Tall tales

While both types of personalities can take advantage of the long format, the way they use this format may vary. An extrovert may successfully deliver a tall tale, for example. This is a tale with several bombastic or unbelievable details that usually favor the joke-teller. The obviously fantastical details are often forgiven because they are usually told with a lot of charm involved.

Example:

Three men went hiking. It was their first hike together. It was early in the morning, and they will be going up a steep hill. They plan to eat lunch there. To make things easier, each guy takes turns telling stories, jokes, or whatever they decide to entertain the other two. The first man made everyone listen to his jokes for the first three kilometers. The second man sang many songs that made the other two sing along for the second three kilometers. Now, Leroy, the third man, had to tell stories for the next three kilometers, and they will rest for the last one kilometer. He says he was going to tell a sad story, instead, much to the surprise of the other two:

Leroy: One early morning, a man went hiking with his friends. Six kilometers in, he realized that he left everyone's sandwiches in his car.

You may also make up your own tall tales, based on your personal life. It would be easier to make people care for something that you can be animated about.

Shaggy dog story

Another type of long-format story that an extrovert can get away with, albeit with a few groans at the end, is the shaggy dog story. It is a longwinded story that may involve lots of irrelevant details. Because of its length and sense of adventure, the audience may be fooled to think that there is so much to it. However, it ends with an anticlimactic event, capped off with a shrug and mischievous smile from the comic.

Example:

This example is a variation of the tall tale, but done shaggy-dog style:

One morning, three men went off to hike up a hill. Billy brought five hotdogs, three pencils, and a bottle of coffee. Danny brought a camera, a broom, and a donut. Leroy brought a folding table, a folding tent, and a fork.

By the time they were almost at the top of the hill, they met a witch. They knew she was a witch because she was wearing a pink smock with spiders drawn on them. She also had warts on her otherwise polished toes. She grinned at Billy and asked for a hotdog. She said she could smell them from five kilometers away.

Billy whispered angrily, "Oh, she is really a witch! My mum cooked me these hotdogs!"

Danny: Don't worry Billy, just give her one. You still have four, I have a hotdog, and Leroy has a fork.

Billy begrudgingly did so. The witch was so happy that she gave Billy a folding chair.

Billy: This looks more like Leroy's type of thing.

Leroy: I will take it.

Leroy put the folding chair on his head. On his back, he still had the tent and the table. Sticking out in his pocket was the fork.

The three walked some more and met a fox. The fox welcomed them with a plate where they put the hotdogs and the fork. There were four more hotdogs and a donut left, and the fox was happy with the hotdog.

All four sat by the low table and ate happily. They had a good hike.

The story does not seem like it had a point. You can make it fun by making it seem so much more important than it is, then end it as if nothing was special about it.

Observational comedy

For introverts, reflection and observation are some of their stronger skills. This is why it is good for them to make use of the events and scenes that they have observed in their daily lives. The closer to the truth their stories are, the more likely they will be effective. Here, the story is intimate in the sense that the comic takes a real event or scenario and highlights the funny aspects of the story.

Example:

I love how my neighbors shout at each other every day, throw plates through the window, and then tell us to behave well.

Here is one from Jerry Seinfeld:

**"They show you how to use the seatbelt, in case you haven't been in a car since 1965. 'Oh, you lift up on the buckle! Oh! I was trying to break the metal apart. I thought that's how it works.'"**

*Communication Skills Training Series*

# Part Five - Garnished with Stories and Experience

*"Life is a shipwreck, but let us not forget tossing in the sailboats." – Voltaire*

Your life is rich with experience. Therefore, it is a well of material. All you need to do is to take a little journal and write down some of the most notable experiences for the day. Sometimes, you can immediately recognize the funny bits because it makes you giggle as you experience them. In some cases, though, you have to stop and think about it and then realize—aha! That is the perfect material. I can talk about it—be sarcastic or snarky about it, complain about, be giddy about it—and a whole lot more heightened reactions to experiences.

So, you may say, but what can I joke about when my life is full of tragedies and mishaps? Well, here is the thing. How you express your story depends on your attitude towards your situation. We have previously mentioned how some famous comedians are depressed introverts. They try to find some humor in their lives to make people laugh and to keep their own moods light.

All our experiences can be material for just about any genre that we can think about. We just need to know at what point of view or angle we should be looking at the details. When there are too many sad events in our lives, we can either capitalize on that and write sad stories that will make people cry. On the other hand, we can take those same events, find the humor in them, and make people laugh.

Let us take a look at this sad and funny retelling of the same story:

1. The sad truth:
   I woke up that morning feeling nauseated. I had drunk so much alcohol the night before. I should not have done that, but I still did. It was the fault of that lady calling herself Clara. She was drinking glass after glass, and my boyfriend Chris was looking at her in what appeared to be admiration. I just could not stand them. I will have to fix myself now, or else I may lose my job.

2. Still sad, but funnier:
   My head was spinning when I woke up this morning. I could still hear the chirping birds that made a halo around it. If only I could flick them dead so that they would feel what I was feeling and not bother me. I believe I must have cleared all the booze from that bar last night. Yeah, I am a big woman, and I knew that I was not supposed to do that. But guess what? Yes, I did. I downed the Bacardi, Johnny Walker, and even the non-descript gin that old man was nursing in his corner. It was all because of that Clara, who I could swear had sights on my boyfriend, Chris. She was drinking glass after glass as if she was a tube with a hole at the end. The alcohol just seemed to pass through her, seamlessly. Chris was gawking at her with admiration, at how she still looked like she could join a pageant and do a nice little half-wave at all the bar patrons. I could not stand them. They were making my eyes sting—or was that the alcohol? Well, I am forgetting about them for the moment and throwing myself in the shower, or else I may lose my job.
   The two scenarios are basically the same. Some may say that the only difference is the personality that each has injected into the narrative. The second one has added some exaggeration and vivid descriptions compared to the first, which is a more matter-of-fact version of the same tale.

Is one of the two narratives a lie? No, both of the stories are truths. However, the first one sparsely narrates the events, while the second one highlights the ridiculousness of the situation.

Now, what about this other scenario?

1. David has insomnia. Every night, he has to struggle with himself. Whenever he sees the sun is about to set, he starts becoming anxious. So, he goes through a whole ritual of taking that warm bath, drinking milk, and winding down. He stops watching television and checking his phone by 8 pm. Somehow, he still ends up wide awake in the middle of the night. He does not want to wake his wife, Emily, up because he knows that she juggles work and cares for the kids all day long. He does not want her to fly into a rage when disturbed.

2. David has insomnia. He has not been officially diagnosed, but he knows he has it. Every night is a battlefield. He practically trembles whenever he sees that the sun is about to set, like some sort of reverse vampire. So, he goes through all the typical ritual steps that are supposed to make him sleep: warm bath (check!), drinking warm milk (check!), and winding down (check!). He stops watching television and checking his phone by 8 pm. So, he ends up watching TV-14 shows and the news. He is like a kid trying to discipline himself into sleeping early. The sad thing about all this is that he still manages to be wide awake in the middle of the night, eyes so wide somebody must have supported them with matchsticks. He does not disturb his wife, Emily, because she juggles so much during the day already. He would instead stare at the ceiling the whole night rather than do so with Emily grumbling in his ears, too.

Again, the two are the same stories. David is still in a lot of distress in both. The storyteller and the reader are the ones getting some fun out of the telling. If David's story ends up becoming filmed, the first one will make it out to be a sort of existential drama while the second will showcase it as a comedy of manners or exaggerated misfortune kind of tale.

What the two tales that we have looked at so far have in common are the following:
1. The second tale is always more detailed. It stretches some parts to highlight them.
2. The second tale is exaggerated. It takes the little humor of mundane life from the first one and squeezes as much as it can from it.
3. The first tale is matter-of-fact, like the objective retelling of a series of events.

What have we learned from them so far?

To make something funny out of your life experiences, you just have to find the details that you can exaggerate, highlight, and pull a little more. Yes, most of these scenarios will not be a funny laugh out loud, haha kind of humor, but you can add in wit. If you can still see wit even in your saddest tales, then you are not down yet. There is a fight in you. You need that fight to make sure that you can make others laugh. Make yourself laugh first. Heck, maybe let out a small giggle or even a knowing smile.

Exercise:

Now, it is your turn. Below, you will see some moments that are typically sad or mundane. Write your first and second version of the following:

1. Waiting at the doctor's reception for your appointment
2. Queueing for milk at the supermarket when the line is extra long
3. Getting fired from a job you did not want, anyway
4. Finding out that the refrigerator has nothing left to eat inside
5. You discovered that your friend has been lying to you about something

You can try your storytelling prowess if you cannot relate to some of the instances above. If you have not experienced any of the above:

- Think of your most boring, redundant experiences (e.g., commute, going to the market) and write about those instead.
- Pick the most stressful event that you have experienced recently.
- Share about your more recent sad experience that you have moved on from

Give yourself time. You are not expected to write everything in two hours, for example. It may take time for inspiration to strike, especially for the second, funnier variation. Do not share bitter experiences that you have not gotten over. It will be counterproductive. You are trying to find material that can help you make people laugh.

Now, what if I write #1 for each of the situations in the first section? Would you be able to write a funnier version now?

1. Waiting at the doctor's reception for your appointment
   I arrived at the doctor's office at 9 am. I had an appointment for 9:30 am, but I liked being early. Not really expecting to get called right away, I decided to read some magazines first. At 9:25 am, I straightened my back a little, waiting for the secretary to holler within five minutes. Then, by 9:30 am, the secretary called a person who came after me. I was perplexed. The other patient headed straight into the inner room where the doctor was, and I was left outside, slightly bewildered. I approached the secretary to ask what has happened. She gave me a slight shrug and said, "That patient is in a lot of pain." I recalled how the patient sat on a chair across me, back straight and smiling a little. He did not look like he was in any kind of pain.

2. Queueing for milk at the supermarket when the line is extra long
   I did not like going to the supermarket. However, I needed some milk for my cereal. So, I decided to go. It was still early. I did not expect the line to be so long, but I needed my milk. I already made a lot of effort, walking three blocks just to get to the supermarket. To my dismay, I saw a lot of the people in the line have full carts of food and other stuff.

3. Getting fired from a job you did not want, anyway
   I received a memo from my boss. I already suspected what it could be. Because of the pandemic, we were already warned that this could happen. However, it was still a shock when it did happen. I hated my job. There was so much stress attached to it. My hair was prematurely growing grey,

and I could barely sleep at night because of everything that it had put me through. However, I also needed to put food on the table. Now, the break happened. It was just devastating.

4. Finding out that the refrigerator has nothing left to eat inside
   It was midnight when I heard and felt my stomach grumble. I went to check the refrigerator to get a snack. I usually had a glass of juice to tame my cravings. To be honest, though, I would rather put together a huge sandwich for ultimate satisfaction. That night, though, I could not do either. The refrigerator was empty for some reason. I could swear I bought some stuff just the other day.

5. You discovered that your friend has been lying to you about something.
   My friend could not look me in the eye when I asked him about whether he lied about being sick. I found out that he was at a party the night I asked if he had time to talk. I was very depressed at that time and needed a ready ear to listen. He immediately made excuses, but I was in no mood to listen. I just left him there, while he was still talking.

   For your guidance, we also prepared some #2 versions. You may read through them to see how they fare against yours. Of course, your work can be funnier than our versions. Some people are naturally inclined but just have not tried creating their material.

   1b. Waiting at the doctor's reception for your appointment

   I rushed to the doctor's office as usual because I hated being late. I was there at 9:00 am, 30 minutes early for my appointment. I cozied up for my wait with some magazines. By 9:25 am, my slumped back became straighter. I did not want the secretary to call me while I was drooling on a magazine, bored fast to sleep. But guess what? At 9:30 am (my appointment!) the secretary dared call somebody else's name. I was perplexed. This smug-looking man in a suit made a beeline for the doctor's office, chin high as if fully aware that he one-upped me. I was left outside, my mouth wide open and my shoulders trembling with anger. I approached the secretary to demand an explanation. She gave me a slight shrug that seemed to say, "Oh, you don't know how this works, do you?" She said in that bored monotone, "That patient is in a lot of pain." I stared at her as if to challenge that answer, but she was deep in her magazine. Here was somebody who would not care if I caught her drooling on her reading material. I remembered quite clearly that Mr. Suit and Pants was not in pain at all. He was just sitting across me, back ramrod straight as if he was trained with books on his head. He had a smile on his face as if he was thinking of something funny. I suspected that he was laughing at me all along.

   *The second version is longer and possibly exaggerated, just like a tall tale. More of what the narrator was feeling was added. Sometimes, our unedited versions are funnier.

   2b. Queueing for milk at the supermarket when the line is extra long

   I loathed going to the supermarket. However, milk for my cereal was an absolute requirement. I would not dare dive into my breakfast without it. Suffice it to say that my day would be bust without any milk. So, I decided to give the supermarket a go. It was still early, and the supermarket was not too far away. I would not drive my car to places too near. Also, I would not have to carry much. I just needed my milk.

Lo and behold! The line was so long I could swear it had all the people in my building, and I lived in a 12-story building with four apartments on each floor. What was worse: each buyer had as many random objects in their carts as my apartment!

*The exaggeration here stems from frustration, just like in the first one. People who are frustrated and in a lot of stress can describe an event in a way that they do not usually mean to be funny.

3b. Getting fired from a job you did not want, anyway

I hated my job. Everyone knew it. So, getting fired should not hurt as much, but it did. When I got the memo, I already had an idea of what it was. Our boss gave us a heads-up at the beginning of the pandemic. But it was still a shock to know it for sure—I was fired!

Now, what was my job like? It was horrible. It was stressful. My hair was turning prematurely grey that I wished it was at least Cruella de Ville fashionable, but it just spelled out old hag. I was thirty-four, you know, but my niece was suspicious every time I mentioned my age. She claimed that she could swear I had my thirty-fourth birthday ten years ago. I wanted to give her a discreet pinch. Anyway, the job not only made me look grey before my time, but it also put me through insomnia hell. After getting fired, I found myself more than willing to go through all nine circles just to get back the job that helped me put food on the table.

*Not all the details in the second version were in the original. Sometimes, a rewrite can inspire you to write more information about the events, especially those that you did not feel was appropriate to the more somber mood of the original.

4b. Finding out that the refrigerator has nothing left to eat inside

At midnight, I felt—and heard—my stomach grumble. I tiptoed to the refrigerator to get a snack. A glass of juice was usually enough to ease my cravings. If I were to be completely honest, though, a large sandwich would be preferable. That would be a ham and cheese, with lettuce bits, thank you! My mouth was watering, and my stomach was expectant, but I was in for a shock. There was nothing in the refrigerator—at all!

*This was not a lot different from the original. The scant material can benefit from being performed. This tall tale is something that you can narrate to your friend with eyes wide in shock and horror. You may further exaggerate if you prefer so.

5b. You discovered that your friend has been lying to you about something.

My friend looked guilty. If he could put his hands over his eyes, like a kid playing peekaboo, he would. He was that guilty. Of course, he knew he could not avoid me altogether. So, here was the thing: I found out he was at the party while I was crying my eyes out. I was bawling over some girl, and he was at a party with lots of girls. I called him that night, but he said he was too ill to come over. It seemed that the raspy voice with a slur was due to all the vodka he downed. Yeah, he was probably right. He was too sick to talk to me that night—he could barely control his tongue. My ex-friend started giving out excuses, but I was fed up and a little bit jealous that I was not invited to that party. I left him there, mouth hanging. I guess he was still sick because he was trying to get that tongue to work. I was not going to listen.

*The pettiness could be heightened up a notch to make the joke work better for some people.

So, how was your other exercise going? You have now come to realize that making jokes is just like writing stories. Here are some things that you need to remember:

- The more vivid the joke is, the better the impact.
- The more familiar the situation is to the audience, the more that they can relate.
- The setup should be well done. Do not just focus on the punchline.
- Stories that do not have a punchline can still be funny, but you will need to exaggerate, add details, and even act it out for your audience.

## Part Six – Keeping it Clean

*"We've begun to long for the pitter-patter of little feet, so we bought a dog. It's cheaper, and you get more feet."* - Rita Rudner

In this chapter, we will be looking at why we should keep jokes clean. Strangely enough, there aren't a lot of quotations that promote clean jokes. However, various jokes are labeled as clean.

The above quote remains wholesome, although it goes against expectations, as well. Families can be diverse, but jokes that should be directed to them should be the same in the sense that they should remain clean and suitable for all ages.

Whoa. Let us take a breather.

How do jokes flow?

- A regular pun or joke has rising action in the middle of the joke. Then, the action goes down smoothly.
- A self-deprecating joke rises early. Then, it goes down and it simmers down on a plateau.
- An offensive joke has a long starting plateau. Then, it peaks near the end and suddenly goes down.
- The passive-aggressive joke peaks, plateaus, peaks again, then goes down near the end.

It seems that the jokes that leave a lot of tension at the end are the offensive jokes and the passive-aggressive jokes. An inoffensive punchline helps you relax right after.

Remember that you are making material to make people laugh, not on the stage but in real life. You will be dealing with people like your family, friends, colleagues, and other people that you regularly mix with. So, doesn't it make perfect sense that you should keep things clean?

Yes, it does.

You don't want to earn a reputation for making off-color jokes. Some comedians get away with it. People who like those kinds of jokes can watch their movies or their stage shows. So, it is a matter of choice in that case. With everyday jokes, however, you need to keep it clean and safe for everyone else.

What is a clean joke, anyway?

A clean joke is one that does not make use of profanity and sex to make people laugh. Jokes that make use of profanity usually depend on the shock factor to make the story hilarious. Some are too dependent on the obscenity that it becomes part of the punchline.

Just think about it. Some people hear a little toddler cursing, and they start squealing with laughter. It can be funny, true. We don't have to be completely unaffected by these jokes. However, if you dissect the content of the joke, was there really a joke? It was just profanity for the sake of laughter at the ridiculousness of the situation.

Others rely too much on sex to make their joke sell. Innuendos are used to make people feel giddy about the setup. People may laugh nervously because they know that they are tiptoeing on a taboo and somehow getting away with it. On the other hand, some people let out guffaws because sex sells easily. It seems that the only way to discuss sex nowadays is through a joke or a blatant display of sexuality.

Here are some of the reasons for keeping your jokes clean:

1. It is more difficult to come up with material that does not cater to popular strategies, such as adding cursing and sexual content.
2. Clean jokes tend to have more substantial and well-thought material.
3. Clean jokes will not put you at risk of being sued for sexual harassment. You are now in the "me too" world, where the spotlight is shining on sexual harassment, whether you are male or female.
4. Clean jokes, even if they border on being corny, overused jokes, can bring a whole family together. You want a joke that even the kids can appreciate.
5. Clean jokes will not get you in trouble at work. You don't want people to think you are a pervert of some sort just because you mentioned a couple of off-color jokes.
6. Humor is meant to built camaraderie and trust. Dirty jokes are not supposed to be the means to bond.
7. Humor helps people relax. Adding material that can cause friction inside the office or home is not the way to help people relax enough to laugh.
8. An upbeat, happy atmosphere can improve productivity at work. It is best to keep the jokes tasteful, though.
9. Clean jokes help you gain more friends. They are safer and more comfortable to relate to.

Taking out the curse words and sexual content is not enough, though. You should also avoid jokes that may cause friction between you and the rest. These jokes can also reflect poorly on who you are as a person. After all, what makes you laugh says so much about you, as well.

- Do not joke about race and nationality. This topic is a very sensitive issue, no matter what era you are in. Such jokes can reflect poorly on you as a person, no matter how much you claim that these are just for fun. They show that you tend to differentiate by race or at least have the means to perpetuate stereotypes. In today's political climate, you may even lose your job if you go by this way. But that is not the real point, is it? You may have to do some soul-searching if you still find race jokes funny.

Not all jokes that mention nationalities are offensive. The Three Rule joke that involves an Englishman, a Scottsman, and an Irishman are just using the nationalities as markers. They could be anyone from anywhere, and the joke will remain as is.

- Do not joke about religion. Some people are indeed freer with these types of jokes. They may even tell you to lighten up. However, people who can make such jokes more likely have an agenda. Are you ready to be part of that agenda? If not, then stay away. Yes, you will not believe all the religions and sects that are out there, but you must show some respect. Even cults have to be taken seriously. They destroy lives, and should not be taken lightly at all.
Some jokes are best delivered by the people involved in the joke. What does this mean? It means that if a Catholic person jokes about the Catholic religion based on what he knows about it, then it is more acceptable. The material comes from his personal experiences, and it is not meant to put down Catholicism. The joke may just be a means to highlight some of the hilarity he encounters as a believer.

- Do not joke about politics, unless you are ready to lose a few friends. You can post your political beliefs online if you like, but they are not something that you should use to make people laugh. Some may, if they agree with you. Others will not because they are on the other side. Even people who may be on the same political side will still refuse to be part of such banter.
  As with religion, jokes that involve politics can only be made among people on the same side of the fence. However, sometimes it is best not to do so because politics can dim the happiness of a gathering.

- Do not stereotype. People do not like it when they are limited and generalized using a few characteristics. It does not matter if the group you are stereotyping is represented in your clique at work or elsewhere.

The point is when you are making people laugh, you should not end up in dangerous territory. Some topics are best left alone, especially if you are trying to have some fun.

As people become more focused on being politically correct, you will find that more topics are becoming off-limits. For example, sexuality and gender jokes will offend certain groups of people. Moreover, jokes about stress and death will hurt people who are suffering from mental illnesses. You may find yourself walking on eggshells wherever you go.

The best thing that you can do is:
- Deliver jokes to people that you know well enough.
- Know what makes your friends, family, and colleagues tick. What are their interests? What are their pet peeves?
- Err on the side of corny and overused than go by way of politically incorrect, sexualized, or full of swear words. If you come across as stale, your audience may still laugh, possibly at you. At least they won't think you are a pervert or any other dubious person they should stay away from.
- Remember that you will be joking to a particular person or group. There is something more personal about it. So, don't color that relationship with something you cannot take back.

When you avoid offensive and dirty jokes, you make your jokes inclusive. So what if your jokes are not considered funny by some groups? There will be others who will appreciate them. Maybe you are more adept at interacting with children, for example. Some primary school teachers find it easier to joke around with their pupils than with adults in their circles. Others may be great at joking with friends but are uncomfortable with taking the humor home.

It happens.

You cannot please everyone. However, do not try to please everyone by throwing your morality out the window.

You are a would-be real-life comic. You are supposed to make people feel happy and light, not offended, angry, defensive, or sad.

# Part Seven – Improv Comedy

*"In improv, there are no mistakes, only beautiful happy accidents. And many of the world's greatest discoveries have been by accident." – Tina Fey*

What we have been attempting to accomplish all along is to come up with improv comedy material to make people laugh. Standup comics use improv comedy to bounce around some content with other comedians or even with the audience. These are mostly unscripted jokes that are fresh but not obnoxious. You can tease, but you are not supposed to take it personally.

## *Why do you need to study improv comedy?*

So, yes, you have no ambition of becoming a professional comic. You just want people to think of you as funny. Heck, you just want people to be happy around you. You want to stop spilling out the same serious or awkward talk that has been plaguing your social life.

However, great conversations and awesome jokes do not just come out of nowhere. They have to be either planned or sought continuously and practiced.

1. You will be attempting to make a person laugh. This real person may be a family member, a friend, or a colleague for years. Still, you cannot claim to read their minds. Yes, you will have more success trying your jokes out with familiar people, but your chances are less than perfect.
2. Practice makes perfect. People practice making speeches so that the delivery comes out as seamless. The same goes for improv comedy.
3. You may not know all the reactions to your jokes. However, you know how you can frame your jokes. You are aware of the approach and the possible responses. Deep inside, you gear yourself up even for the most unexpected reactions.
4. One of the most important aspects of themselves that improv comics have to prepare is their emotional intelligence. The more they are capable of "reading" other people's facial expressions and gestures, the more that they can respond appropriately.
5. You have to be open and comfortable enough to make the banter flow between you and your audience. The more you tighten up to hide something, the more that you are not able to respond freely and continue the humorous conversation.
6. Make it fun. Think of it as a game. It is like a prolonged mental exercise that also makes you laugh a lot.

## *Why should you focus on the other person?*

When you are making someone laugh, you focus on them. Don't dwell too much on how you were not able to deliver your material as planned. That happens. Do not force something that is not happening at all. Instead, take cues from your audience.

Are they bored? Do they look like they just want to check on their phone? Think back. What was it that made your audience turn to you and smile or laugh? Pursue that line of thought. If nothing is happening, let it go graciously and gracefully. You don't want to gain a reputation for being a try-hard comic. Fix up your material for another day. Make the joke slither indiscreetly at first, incorporated in normal conversation.

Are they trying to tell you something? Listen to them. While you may have planned to say a joke from setup to punchline, your audience is key to making that successful. If your audience is more interested in pitching in an idea or two, let him do so. You never know: his ideas may fit right into your joke. This new turn may be the beginning of pure banter. If, however, he has changed paths a bit, you can try to follow him onto his road, then see if you have a way to connect what he said to the rest of your joke. If he is playing the polite audience, he has meant to make a connection somewhere himself.

Are they saying "yes" or "no" to your questions? If your improv comedy skit involves asking the audience, then you have to anticipate the possible answers. It is like creating a flowchart to see where the conversation leads each way.

Whatever the case may be, you should check on what direction your audience wants to go. You are the one who started the banter. You are the one who wants to make your audience laugh. So, it is your responsibility to prepare yourself for anything. You need to be able to gauge the direction in which your audience wants to go. Good improv comedy relies on having the same goal and direction.

### Why should you ask specific questions?

While your audience is the focus, the brunt of the comedy weight still rests on you. You are the one who initiates the interaction. So, you have to give detailed questions. This way, your audience knows where the conversation is going.

You can also start with a more general question to see where it will go for both of you. You especially need this if you are dealing with a person you are not particularly familiar with yet. Yes, you may work with the person five days a week, but have you gone into a conversation with him?

- You: What do you like to eat?
- Audience member: Well, just about anything.

You can get some material from that response unless it has completely gone another path from what you were trying to achieve.

While leading statements are not allowed in court, they are especially useful in improv comedy. With leading statements, you get more detailed responses that you can work with.

- You: I bet you like to eat pizza.
- Improv Partner 1: How did you know that? Yes! I love pizza!
- You: Do you like pineapples on them?
- Improv Partner 1: No way! I said I love pizza. When there are pineapples on them, that is just disrespect to real pizza. That is a mutant!

OR

- You: I bet you like to eat pizza.
- Improv Partner 2: No! Not me. What made you say that, though?
- You: I don't know. Everyone likes pizza.

- Improv Partner 2: Not this person, no way. It is fatty, full of calories, and just too greasy for me.
- You: What if I can get you a non-greasy pizza?
- Improv Partner 2: Oh, really? No. Still a no.
- You: But you are Italian.
- Improv Partner 2: Italian-American.

The conversations that ensue after the leading statement contain more information in a short period compared to asking a vague, general question.

## Why should you ask for/give a lot of details?

As with the previous question, asking for and giving a lot of details will provide you with the material. You don't want any dead air between you and your improv partner. Even when the content is not funny yet, the mere act of bombarding the other person with questions and getting quick but detailed answers will at least elicit a fascination from the rest of the audience. If it is just the two of you, you will find the humor in the fast exchange.

Let us compare Set A and Set B:

Set A:

You: What is your name?

Improv Partner: Stacey.

You: Where are you from?

Improv Partner: New York.

You: Who do you live with?

Improv Partner: My family.

The first Improv Partner seems bent on just sticking to one word or two-word answers. You get information, but not detailed ones.

Set B:

You: What is your name?

Improv Partner: Stacey Stevens from HR.

You: Stacey Stevens from HR, where are you from?

Improv Partner: New York City. Okay, not really. I just like saying that because I work here in New York, but I have to commute from New Jersey. I wake up very early!

You: Who do you live with?

Improv Partner: Oh, you don't want to know. It's the whole bunch: my mom, my dad, my brother, my sister, and my sister's friend who has managed to not go back to her own place in like three months now.

With Set B, you have gotten more information that you can work with. You can use the information that you got to fill in more blanks. Let us take a look at Set C.

Set C:

You: What is your name?

Improv Partner: Stacey Stevens from HR.

You: Aha, Stacey Stevens from HR. Now, I know who to go to when I want to complain about Bob (make sure Bob is your friend) who has been badgering me with his Tik-Tok videos.

Improv Partner: Yes, you can go to me, or Bob can just show me his Tik-Tok videos.

You: Where are you from?

Improv Partner: I like saying I am from New York, but I actually have to commute from New Jersey early in the morning.

You: Wow! I don't know if I would be able to do that. So, I am just lying down on the floor of Bob's apartment until I can afford my own place.

Improv Partner: I am pretty sure you are kidding!

You: I am not. Who do you live with, by the way? Is it someone who snores like Bob? (Make sure Bob can hear this; wiggle your eyebrows at him to show him you are kidding.)

Improv Partner: I bet I can beat you there. I live with my whole family: mom, dad, brother, sister, and sister's friend, who just would not leave the house. We are a rowdy bunch. I am pretty sure you have a much better time at Bob's.

Because this is improv, the conversation can go in several possible directions. It can also fail.

Here are some possible reasons it can fail:

- Bob is not in the mood to be the butt of jokes.
- Stacey is not as chatty as presented in Sets B and C.
- Stacey may be friendly, but she may not have a lot of material to work with. So, you have to help her along.

Here are some possible reasons it can succeed:

- Your friend Bob can add to the banter.
- Stacey may just be a funny girl herself.
- If Sets B and C are made possible, then you can make her laugh, or at least giggle.

Asking a lot of questions and providing several details together provide you with the opportunity to command most of the content creation. Yes, co-creation is vital to improv. However, remember, you are going to apply this to real life. You will be talking to people who are not primarily in with the joke. Perhaps they are not even comfortable with their sense of humor.

However, when you supply the world in which the conversation will exist, the person you decide to include in the improv will generally know what to say or do. What can destroy this is the other person's complete unwillingness to participate—which brings us to the next question.

### Why should you need to know a little background of your Improv Partner?

You must have some idea what your Improv Partner likes. Just like a salesperson, you should be able to read his cues and body language. Before you even attempt to engage in banter with this person, you must know a few things about his likes and dislikes. If the person responds with a sharp "No" or a "not really," then your prospects to continue the improv work are nearly dead on arrival.

The power of listening and observation can help you here. Instead of getting offended by some of the responses, listen. Perhaps, you are the one who missed the joke. Probably, you are talking to someone who has a slightly sarcastic, or even acerbic sense of humor.

### Why should you keep creating motion?

Before answering this question, let us clarify that motion in improv does not always mean physical movement. It can also refer to other types of motion. Let us explore every kind of motion:

- Movement from one topic to another
  Good improv will not survive if you stick to one topic throughout. No matter how funny the beginning is, it will get old. Imagine talking about the weather—or maybe a burger—for several minutes. Will humor survive?
  You: You look like you enjoy rainy weather. (Observing the improv partner's fashionable raincoat, boats, etc.)
  Improv partner: Why yes. Oh, you've noticed my attire today?
  You: Yes, it looks like you have been praying to the rain god to give you some showers.
  Improv partner: How else will I get to wear these?
  While there is a possibility that you can continue this line of banter, it may start getting old after the two responses that you got.

- Movement from one place to the next
  You can move from one place to the next. Sometimes, the talk is dynamic and physically active. So, you and the person you are talking to are moving from one location to the next.
  Because the location changes, the narrative can also change. You can use the environment to give you cues.

  You: Hi, do you always walk this fast?
  Improv partner: Yes, I do. I am always in a rush.
  You: So, it will be okay with me to talk to you as long as I walk fast?
  Improv partner: That's right.
  You: Oh, look. They opened a new shop. That looks something that you may like.
  Improv partner: Wow! A new gadgets store. How do you know?
  You: Well, you have the latest ear pods on and a charging backpack.
  Improv partner: You have sharp eyes.
  You: I adapt. I need something to quickly catch what you have.
  Improv partner: Well, here we are. This is where I work.
  You: Are you sure you are not the one who has the keys to open up?
  Improv partner: No. I may be fast, but Edgar right here practically lives in the office.

You: Hi Edgar!

- Movement in terms of gestures

    Without becoming a slapstick version of yourself, you can add animated gestures to make the conversation more vivid and fun. The younger your audience is, the better this will work. Improv work with kids may require you to act sillier than you are usually like.

    With kids, you may be able to make them laugh even without words. You can use some improv games with them, somewhat similar to "Simon Says."

    There are many variants out there, but you can start with either "Simon Says" or "Frozen." It may work best if you have a group of kids right in front of you, instead of just one, although it can also work with only one child.

    You: Simon Says jump. (Jump but do so in a very exaggerated manner.)
    Child(ren): jumps and tries to do the same exaggerated movements
    You: Simon Says close your eyes
    Child(ren): close their eyes
    You: Simon Says: open your left eye
    Child(ren): open their left eye (Some may struggle with this a bit, making the whole situation funnier for them.)

    Frozen is a sneakier version of Simon Says. The kids will be asked to roam around the room and do whatever they want. Approach one child and tell the child to freeze. Then, freeze, as well. Do so with an amusing expression or pose.

    The other children who see that someone has already frozen will stop moving. Some will attempt to follow your silly approach. Some will fail at this because they will already start laughing. Others will see that some have frozen and will try to stop moving, as well.

    The success of this game is relative. You may find it successful if everyone gets to stop moving—or you may find it successful if everyone fails at that and starts laughing. It is a win-win situation.

- Movement in terms of purpose

    Your purpose should also change. If you start the improv sketch with interrogation, it may get old if you continue with that train of thought even after several minutes. You may want to change the purpose or switch roles.

    After asking a few questions that establish the person's character and preferences, you can switch roles. This switch is easier to do if the other person is intent on asking you questions, as well.

    Another way to move from one purpose to another is to start commenting on what the two of you should do in your free time. You may also suggest a game. The decision will depend on whatever link the two of you have managed to establish during your earlier conversation. You do have to engage them in activities that they will be interested in and have time for. Being able to read your improv partner will make things a lot easier for you.

- Movement in terms of characters

Sometimes, while you engage in banter with one person, another one may be listening and may approach. You should not shoo the person away just because you have come up with a plan with the first person. The movement to include more people may work in your favor.

The conversation below may be familiar to you, but with a slight twist.

> You: What is your name?
>
> Improv Partner: Stacey Stevens from HR.
>
> You: Aha, Stacey Stevens from HR. Now, I know who to go to when I want to complain about Bob (make sure Bob is your friend) who has been badgering me with his Tik-Tok videos.
>
> Improv Partner: Yes, you can go to me, or Bob can just show me his Tik-Tok videos.
>
> Add in Bob (from a few feet away): My Tik-Tok videos are award-winning, Stacey!
>
> You: Where are you from?
>
> Improv Partner: I like saying I am from New York, but I actually have to commute from New Jersey early in the morning.
>
> You: Wow! I don't know if I would be able to do that. So, I am just lying down on the floor of Bob's apartment until I can afford my own place.
>
> Improv Partner: I am pretty sure you are kidding!
>
> Add in Bob (getting a little closer): I've offered to share my bed, but he refuses (slight innuendo; keep it mild).
>
> You: I am not. Who do you live with, by the way? Is it someone who snores like Bob? (Make sure Bob can hear this; wiggle your eyebrows at him to show him you are kidding.)
>
> Add in Bob (very close now, a few inches from your face), just watching you intently. However, he is kidding.
>
> Improv Partner: I bet I can beat you there. I live with my whole family: mom, dad, brother, sister, and sister's friend, who just would not leave the house. We are a rowdy bunch. I am pretty sure you have a much better time at Bob's.

Whatever movement you decide to use, it should keep on making you and your improv partner explore and discover various possible pathways for your conversation.

## How do you make sure you create quality entertainment?

Let us inspect that word again: entertainment.

You must remember that you are not simply making conversation with another guest at a party: you are supposed to be the life of the party! Okay, perhaps that is pushing it a little bit. That also sounds a little arrogant. But hey, remember that your goal is to make people laugh.

Since you want to make people laugh, you have to shine the spotlight on yourself somehow. It does not have to be in a party setting. You could be at the office during lunchtime, trying to cheer up some of your officemates. You have noticed how they seem drained of energy, and there are still hours before home time.

You have to make someone laugh or at least smile. Because you have chosen to read this book, you have committed to being the source of entertainment.

So, the improv world that you are trying to build must have the hallmarks of good entertainment.

1. Where is the setting of your story? You cannot just fill the void of an empty room with grey walls. Describe its appearance, from its purpose to the actual décor. It may be a spaceship about to take off or a crowded restaurant.
2. Who are you in this skit? Are you an everyman? If so, then you have to make the most of that. Help that character connect with everyone else. More likely, they can relate to you. However, perhaps you can better entertain as a bald guy who lives across the street—you know, the one who always wears a fedora hat that keeps on flying off?

### *What should you do if the conversation does not go the way it is planned?*

Well, this is improv, after all. Anything can happen. Just like life, your reaction to it is what makes or breaks the joke.

You are supposed to try to make people laugh. The emphasis is on the word "laugh." Of course, there is the possibility of failing in some sections of your joke. However, that does not mean to say that you just throw in the towel. You can continue pursuing the narrative if the only problem is getting the story to work as you envision it. When the material is the only issue, the other person can still be let in on the joke if you manage to meet him halfway.

Unfortunately, it is also possible that you have read a person wrong. Perhaps the other person is not interested in being part of your improv work. If a person wants out of the supposedly entertaining banter, let him go. You are not a standup comedian. The other person is not a fan who bought tickets to see a standup comedian. So, he may have other things to do, is too shy, or is just not interested in banter of any kind.

Do not take it seriously.

You are trying to entertain people. If it is stressing you out, it is just not worth it. You need your positivity and charm to stay strong.

It can be challenging to stay humorous if the subject itself is serious. Say, for example, you started talking to a colleague in the hopes of starting an improvised banter. Then, you are the one who got unpleasantly surprised because your intro has become a means for the other person to share what is wrong with him.

You: How was your weekend?

Other person: It was terrible. I slipped and fell right in front of my crush.

You: Oh, I am so sorry to hear that. Are you okay now?

Compare this to the following:

You: How was your weekend?

Other person: It was terrible. I slipped and fell right in front of my crush.

You: I always knew you were so smooth.

Other person: Yes, I slid right through the marble floor right next to his feet.

The first one shows how concerned you are for the other person. This reaction is, of course, socially acceptable. However, it does not make for a fun conversation. After you have raised your concern, the chance for improv laughs has already passed you by. You can only either keep quiet, move on to the next person, or just chat with this other person quietly. You may wait for a little bit more to take another chance at making her laugh.

The second instance allows you not to take the situation too seriously. Instead, you teased the other person by making a joke about her possibly embarrassing experience. This response lightens the mood for her, as well. So, you have made her laugh—or smile—and thus, you have helped her get over the situation.

Of course, not all situations are easy to joke about. You may want to get into a humorous banter about death, for example. Morbid jokes may only work if the case is not based on reality. For example, you may joke about the deaths or kills in a horror movie to make you feel less nervous about it.

### Why should you go for the road less traveled?

When you plan improvised conversations, you don't want to stick to generic topics. Just how far can you go when you are talking about the weather, about your current status, and the like?

You need to spark your audience's interest. Start talking about more controversial topics, while keeping the conversation clean.

That should be a challenge.

Some comedians will urge you to use the "big guns": taboo topics, such as sex, religion, politics, family, and more. Well, you can joke about your family, but make sure you don't offend the family member, especially if you are joking around at home.

Politics and religion can place you in the line of fire. If you do not know the other person well, you may not know what their beliefs are. Instead of making someone laugh that day, you may end up creating a new foe. So, tread carefully. Do you want to get stressed that day? Nobody is paying you to make people laugh. It is just a genuine desire coming from you that makes you want to do that. If that will be rewarded with conflict, then you know that it is not worth it.

### How do you think on your feet?

Improvisation comics must have enough wit and smarts to carry them through. Once you have put yourself on their feet, you will better appreciate the quick mental processes that whizz by in their heads to make the success of a joke possible.

It can be difficult, especially for a beginner.

But it is not impossible to learn.

How do you help yourself think on your feet better?

- You have to practice conversing with various people in your circles.
- Be genuinely concerned about how they are and what they can share with you.
- Be as knowledgeable as possible about topics that may interest your target.
- Practice on your own. Pick a random topic by flipping through the dictionary randomly or by preparing some strips of paper with subject matters and picking one of them. Then, just talk aloud about the topic like in an impromptu speech competition.

It is possible to get backed into a corner, especially when you are just starting. Here are a few things that you can do:

- Play word association games. When you hear a word but you don't exactly have a response to the particular context it was placed in, you can go another possible route. You can take that word in a more familiar direction.
- You can repeat the question that your target person asked you. This tactic will give you time to think of a witty answer. Reiterate it in such a way that you seem surprised that it was ever asked. Make a funny face as if you are bewildered that you have ever been asked that question. You have just made use of a pageant-style delaying tactic.
- You can express what you are feeling. Do so in an exaggerated manner. For example: "I am so sorry if I am not paying attention 100%. I am so tired!" Make a big show of yawning and stretching. This tactic may make it more slapstick material, but it can help you make the other person smile even when you may have run out of content for the time being.
- Ask a question. Maybe even turn the question to the person who asked it in the first place. It will surprise the other person. Make it playful and not rude.
    - Did you like the book that I wrote?
    - Did I like the book that you wrote? What kind of question is that? Of course, I did. I still sleep with that book under my pillow. That is how much I like it. I am close to marrying it.

Thinking on your feet is better said than done. Thinking of the best retorts is sometimes better during the training stage. When you are in the middle of the conversation, it is possible to go blank. However, if you have entered the discussion with an open attitude and without taking yourself seriously, you should find a way to respond to anything wittily. Keep on practicing with a close friend who does not mind being a drill partner.

## What is the importance of a callback in improv?

An improv can start simple enough. You plant the seeds carefully. You have to establish some "facts" in the world that you are about to build.

- A callback does not have to be laugh-out-loud funny. Sometimes, it is a groan-worthy moment. However, recalling it makes people laugh.
- A callback cannot be done right after the "facts" have been established. It is one of those moments wherein waiting is worth it.

An example of a callback in movies is a scene in *Airplane!* The cab driver leaves a passenger behind, saying he will just be back in a moment. However, the driver ends up boarding a plane and leaving. After a few minutes, the audience is assumed to have forgotten about the situation. The camera then goes back to the passenger. He is still in the cab. Seeing how ridiculous it is that this passenger decides to wait that long elicits laughter from the audience.

Using callback is very tricky, however. You can quickly alienate your audience members, especially if they were not paying attention. However, if you are sure that your audience was in it when you were establishing the scene, it might be worth exploring. Once you manage to pull off the callback and you get a knowing burst of laughter, then it is worth revisiting the same joke at a later date. The callback has become an inside joke.

## Why do you need to let people talk?

Improv comedy or banter only works when you let other people talk as well. You cannot be hogging everything. People will be less inclined to speak to you if they notice that you don't listen.

Let others talk. This improv setup is not an official comedy partnership, but it can spell out your relationship in the future. While you may want to make your friends or colleagues laugh, they may also want to showcase their humor. You never know: your sense of humor may be compatible with others to the point that your future conversations will be more seamless and relaxed.

Talking too much can also be a sign of selfishness and disrespect. It is selfish because you are not allowing the other person to share their thoughts. It is disrespectful because you are cutting off their side of the communication. Yes, you may be the funniest among the group. Yes, you may be the one with the most material. However, it does not mean that you can dominate each conversation that you become a part of.

Silence also wields some power. Sometimes, it helps you with your comedic timing. It also allows you to be more open to what the other person has to say. The most effective funny responses originate from being able to listen to the other person carefully, instead of constantly thinking of the next thing to say. Yes, you can prepare the general setup. The details and flow, however, may have to depend on how the conversation ends up flowing.

The key to great improv comedy (or any type of conversation) is collaboration.

How would you fix this?

George: You look tired.

Fred: Yes, I am. I had a long night last night.

George: Oh, you know what? I have a trick to show you.

While it is true that Fred responds in a way that George does not find funny, it should not mean that he should just discard Fred's answer. George probably did not find any suitable material from the response and chose to move on. Do you think Fred is in any mood to laugh at any trick or joke George has in store for him? It does not seem that way. George had a clue all along: Fred is tired and may not be completely receptive. Also, he could have responded to Fred's current state. Then maybe Fred would have been more thankful and, therefore, more responsive.

This conversation could have happened:

George: You look tired.

Fred: Yes, I am. I had a long night last night.

George: I am sorry to hear that. Did you paint the town red again last night? (Fred is a homebody.)

Fred: (laughs) No. It is the same old thing. Work.

George: If you are going to tire yourself all night anyway, leave some time for fun. You are starting to look like my dad. (They are the same age.)

Fred: I might need to lighten up.

George: Oh, you know what? I have a trick to show you.

Framed better, both Fred and George get to say what they need to say.

### *How does "history" have to do with improv comedy?*

No, we are not talking about textbook history here. We are referring to history in terms of what happened to you. Some characters call out history very well, like Sophia from the *Golden Girls*. When an event or topic reminds her of the past, she will start with:

"Sicily [insert year here],...."

When your friend and colleague talks about something that you cannot directly respond to, you can call out one of the topics or subtopics mentioned and relate it to an event that happened to you before.

Even in a non-comedic situation, it can work.

Friend: I lost my wallet in the worst place possible! I lost it right in the mall.

[You have several possible paths here: losing your wallet, doing something at the worst place possible, losing something at the mall, the last time you were at the mall, etc.]

You (response 1): Are you kidding? I just lost my wallet last week, but it was at the cafeteria. I was already picturing how it would unfold, but someone had found it and gave it to me. I was so thankful I did not ask about why there was a missing $20 bill from it."

You (response 2): It reminds me that I cursed in the worst place possible last Sunday—at church. Fr. Luke was right behind me. He was pretending he didn't hear. Was it a sin for priests to pretend anything?

You (response 3): I just lost something at the mall the other day—well, thankfully, it was only for a moment. It was my son.

You (response 4): I cannot remember when I was last at the mall. It is a dangerous place.

So, you can see that by simply digging up through your history, you can find some possibly serious answers and wisecracks, too.

### *How do you use exaggerated similes and metaphors to your advantage?*

Ever since you were a child, you have been taught what a metaphor is. You know that you are comparing two different things without using "like a" or "as _____ as a." In that way, it differs from a simile.

Some similes have been overused:

- As bright as the sun
- As cold as ice

Some metaphors have also been overused:

- Drinking the Kool-Aid
- Laughingstock
- Deadline
- In the same boat
- Green with envy

Then, some similes have their serious beginnings, but have been subjected to parody:
- "Life is like a box of chocolates; you never know what you're gonna get."
  - Life is like a box of chocolates; halfway through, you realize how much you hate yourself. (One of the clean parody versions you can find online.)

With improv jokes, however, sometimes you can go all the way crazy with your metaphors and similes.

Here are some possible zany descriptions:
- Going shopping with Zelma is like going to war because you have to weaponize yourself with either a credit card or a blind eye to all that she says is good for you.
- Whenever you visit Alfred, make sure your stomach is empty. You cannot say no to his wife's cooking, and she cooks up quite a storm when she knows Alfred's friends are coming over.
- I like how cupcakes taste like the end of my dreams of joining a beauty pageant in this lifetime. Then, I remember that I am also too short and too opinionated to be accepted or to go through all the grinning and waving.

The wordiness is part of the exaggerated response or statement. You may start with 0 and end up with a 100. I know. The term "from zero to hero" popped into your head, but I am trying to avoid it just like a child's gaze avoiding his mother's after she opened his report card and found all the red marks all over it.

Other descriptions that may not fall under similes and metaphors, but still create a particular "so vivid, it's so funny feel."

1. Oh, you are asking what type of mom I am? Sorry, I am not a soccer mom. That is too generic. I am a watch-like-a-hawk while working both full time and part time, tiger slash soccer mom.
2. At the office, I am the "eat fast while standing at the pantry and gulp my drink so that I can avoid other people" type of employee.

### *How do you use exaggerated reactions to your advantage?*

So, you have already done quite your share with exaggeration, using similes and metaphors. Now, you are going to try performing exaggeration expressions and reactions. George Peart's "You Can Be Funny & Make People Laugh" refers to this as the YouTuber's reaction. He is right. There is something in that.

Have you watched YouTube videos? More likely, you have. Some people are addicted to these videos and have even subscribed to some channels. Usually, the channels that rise to popularity are those that can lighten up and be funny if they cannot deliver the celebrity status.

When I am talking about YouTuber reactions, however, I am talking about those that do unboxing videos. These YouTubers would not normally open boxes like children, but for their videos, they seem to go back in time: eyes wide, mouth open, and voices full of wonder. You may either get amused or annoyed by such a display. However, if a friend of yours does this little stunt offline, you may burst out laughing. You cannot believe that your friend can be this amazed by, say, a new pen.

Yes, the humbler the object of your awe, the funnier it will be. There is some acting involved here in most cases. To make it work better, though, you can start with objects that you are genuinely in awe of that your friends just do not understand.

### What about making up a story as you go along?

Remember when you were a kid at school? Your teacher has suddenly decided it is time to patch a story together. She will start with one sentence. Then, the next child will add something to that story, and the rest of the class will add to it, and so forth.

If you were a bubbly kid, then this would have been your chance to shine. Bubbliness would not have been enough, though. You also needed to think on your feet, which is basically what most of improv is all about.

Conversely, if you were a shy kid with a quick mind, then all the magic would have been happening in your head. Yes, you may start giggling quietly, but you just made yourself laugh. Other people in your class had no idea what you were thinking about.

Today, the bubbly kid with fewer ideas would have to open himself to the process. If you were this kid, then you already have the personality to carry the conversation. Do not overthink. Stories can start as serious but can be buoyed by someone else in the group. Similarly, stories can become hilarious without you trying. Again, it is all in how much you practice.

On the other hand, the shy kid with ideas would just have to go with it. Do not let those ideas die down without anyone hearing about them. Share!

Coming up with a funny story should have been taught in school at some point. At that time, it falls under the generic category of writing a story, any story. So, you just have to be creative but in a fun way.

Stories begin with prompts such as:

- What if this happens?
- A character goes to this place because he wants to achieve his goal but encounters problems along the way.

You can begin with a simple "what if" question.

- What if I wake up tomorrow to discover that giant poodles have taken over the city?
- What if my boss decides to give us truckloads of pizza instead of our cash salary?
- What if my friend decides he cannot stand me because I wear blue shirts all the time?

These storytelling prompts may in themselves be funny or ridiculous, depending on what you can come up with.

Exercise:

Can you give at least three "What if" statements that you can use in real life?

Another variation of the above exercise is to create hypothetical scenarios such as the following:

- The family eating at the next table look intent in munching their lettuce. They all look like calorie counters.
- I don't think I should stay on this planet anymore. Look at how human beings treat me. Even dogs bark at me as if I look like a thief.

Exercise:

Use the prompts below to make up your own jokes:

1. You are trapped in a spaceship, with nothing else but the suit you have on and a violin.
   _____
   _____
   _____

2. It was still dark when you woke up. You did not hear your alarm, but you are wide awake.
   _____
   _____
   _____

3. Your grandma turns 103 tomorrow. She wants you to be there at 7 o'clock sharp.
   _____
   _____
   _____

4. A neighbor has been screaming wildly for a few minutes now. You cannot rush to her because
   _____
   _____
   _____

5. A dog approaches you, sniffing your shoes.
   _____
   _____
   _____

You can play scenarios like these at a party or get-together. It is like a recreation of the classroom game from when you were little. The more creative and outlandish the details become, the more hilarious it can be.

You know your team better. The personalities and preferences of your friends and colleagues will ultimately decide the details that can be added. Let it be clear that off-color, offensive, and highly sexualized jokes should not be added to the brew.

## *What about imagining the consequences of an event or action?*

Sometimes, people's assumptions can be hurtful, annoying, and offensive. We have dealt with such assumptions throughout our lives. Sadly, we also make the same types of assumptions about other people.

What if the consequences are pretty much a given among a group of friends or family members? Then, it becomes inside information. Inside information can be converted to inside jokes, depending on how you treat the information. It is in how you treat the facts given, rather than the facts themselves. We have mentioned this earlier in the book. Some people always find humor in even the most disastrous events. However, finding humor in cases such as death can be offensive any which way you look at it.

Read the following situations and observe how they make their predictions or assumptions humorous:

- Stacey: Eva is going to join a pageant.
  Lisa: Wow! She would win it if she did not end up tripping on her heels and falling on the judges.

  (Stacey and Lisa BOTH KNOW how pretty Eva is, but they also BOTH KNOW that Eva is clumsy and is probably not comfortable wearing heels. So, they ASSUME that there is a possibility that she may fall on heels.)

  Using someone as the object of a joke is a little cruel. The situation can only be mitigated if Eva is friends with the two, and she is also aware of her inherent awkwardness.

  An inoffensive, but slightly dull version of the above would be:

  Stacey: Eva is going to join a pageant.

  Lisa: Wow! She is pretty enough to win, but she needs to practice on heels. She can be quite clumsy.

- John: Let us go to Lulu's place.
  Tony: Oh, you want me to go with you? You just want someone who can guide you through that maze of a neighborhood.
  (John and Tony have been to Lulu's place. It seems that John has no sense of direction, and Lulu's house is in a neighborhood with lots of twists and turns. As the third wheel, Tony feels like he has only been asked because of one particular reason.)
  Tony could well just say "Yes" to the invitation, staying polite and loyal to his friend, John. He may also just say "No" because he knows what his role would have been like. However, Tony has decided to show John that he is fully aware of the situation, but he is still willing to help. It may sound like a rough answer, but Tony is still down for the ride.

### How do you add in crazy explanations?

Formal and factual responses are helpful. They are informative. But are they funny? Most of the time, they are not. There is a possibility that a fact can still be entertaining, but you may not always get that chance.

Here are some conversations with crazy explanations:

- Ted: Andy got 100% on the exam. There is no way he could have cheated with the way Mr. Phillip was watching all of us.
  Luis: His parents did not see him at dinner last night. He might have been abducted by aliens and returned with a full computer chip in his head before anybody noticed.
  This conversation could have gone entirely factual, like:
  Ted: Andy got 100% on the exam. There is no way he could have cheated with the way Mr. Phillip was watching all of us.
  Luis: His parents did not see him at dinner last night. He might have studied from the afternoon until night at the library.

Luis could have utilized the second response, but he would instead put in a highly creative, funny reply. There is an assumption here that both boys do not believe Andy would get high marks unless he had supernatural or extraordinary help.

- Farrah (the babysitter): Mr. and Mrs. Fielding, I am going home! Danny has been so well-behaved today. I got scared for a minute and thought he was sick.
  Mr. Fielding: Danny was well-behaved. Well, honey (turns to his wife), the Diazepam that we gave him worked out quite well!
  Of course, the above is merely a joke. However, it could have gone this way:
  Farrah (the babysitter): Mr. and Mrs. Fielding, I am going home! Danny has been so well-behaved today. I got scared for a minute and thought he was sick.
  Mr. Fielding: Danny was well-behaved. Well, honey (turns to his wife), I gave him the talk last night. Danny has been very receptive.

Again, factual responses are helpful but are rarely funny. You may want to switch to humorous answers from time to time, depending on the mood that you plan to create.

## *How do you let the other person fill in the blanks?*

How another person fills in the blanks for you can result in hilarious misunderstandings or funny but accurate conclusions.

Take a look at this conversation:

Amber: Are you going to join us at the concert tomorrow?

Taylor: My mom will visit me at my dorm.

Amber: Uh, oh.

Taylor does not directly respond to Amber's question. However, an understanding passes from one girl to the other. An observer may not know what is up. Here is possible missing information:

- Taylor's mom is very strict. She will not allow Taylor to attend the concert.
- Taylor's mom is too fun-loving. She might want to get invited to the concert, as well.
- Taylor's boyfriend is staying in the dorm. She would be in trouble with her mom, thus endangering her concert plans.

When some information is omitted, we can assume that both persons talking should have the extra information tucked in somewhere.

If you leave out information on purpose, make sure you do it with someone who knows you or your situation well. This tactic can be hilarious as an improv skit because you can make the other members of the audience raise their eyebrows in suspicion or recognition.

The above examples are a testament that improv conversations and jokes cannot be planned. However, you need to do the following:

- Be receptive. Listen to the other person well.

- Be in good humor. If you have a positive outlook, then you are more likely to engage in fun banter.
- Keep away from possibly offensive humor.
- Have a good knowledge of the other person's sense of humor or at least overall personality.

Not everyone will want to be part of your extended banter. Short quips may establish your desire to communicate in this fun manner. Someone will likely take the bait within your circle of friends or colleagues. According to the *Psychological Science* article, "The Science of Humor is no Laughing Matter," people are more likely to laugh at videos with canned laughter. Now, you are not in a video. You are also not a professional comedian. However, if you can find people who can respond to you—like some kind of clique—you may be able to recreate that effect in real life. Perhaps, you can do it as a duo kind of natural performance.

# Part Eight – Going Back Inwards

*"My life has been one great big joke, a dance that's walked a song that's spoke. I laugh so hard I almost choke when I think about myself." - Maya Angelou*

Whenever you feel like you are lost in your improv game or even just your witty, conversational skills, you have to go back to yourself.

One thing that you will never forget is yourself. As long as you remain honest with yourself and others, you have a self that you can go back to. You don't have to be dishonest to be funny. You can take the truth and look at it at a humorous angle.

No matter how truthful you are, however, you still have to follow some rules:

1. You cannot take everything seriously and literally.
2. You must be ready to laugh at yourself.
3. You need to put as much energy and enthusiasm as possible into the situation.

The above are just some of the unspoken rules.

Well, if you take things at face value all the time, you sound boring. You are one of those people in novels who "say" and "reply" and "speak" or whatever other non-enthusiastic verbs the author can attach to you.

You are just there, saying facts.

Facts are excellent; that is a given. However, you are trying to make people laugh. You are not a reporter narrating the news. You are also not a scientist explaining graphs and charts that other people could not understand.

You have to take something—a fact—and twirl it around in your head and spin it further with your words until everyone is heady with laughter.

So, your friend tells you that it was too cold outside. How do you respond?

Concerned, but very literal and boring: Oh, did you at least have your coat on?

Affirms the statement, but still very literal and boring: Yes, I was just outside. I had to clutch at my coat tighter.

Well, some of us indeed have a powerful motherly or fatherly inclination to care for others. So, this response comes from within you. It is genuine, as well, and should not be discarded; it is part of who you are.

However, you consulted this book for a reason. You want to make people laugh. Then, you have to find material within yourself that you will want to laugh about, as well.

Will the following responses fare better?

Flirty, but joking: At least you are here now. Just sit close to me. I have enough heat to warm you up. (Make sure that this is only done with close friends. You don't want to be sued for sexual harassment. You can even be self-deprecatory in the end, to show that the response usually is not the type you go for.)

Referencing a movie: But I thought the cold never bothered you, anyway. (This is safer but will have to rely on a callback. The other person should either have said that he/she did not mind the cold or have clearly stated that he/she is a fan of *Frozen*, the animated movie.)

Referring to the current situation: Are you complaining now? The office a/c usually freezes us over every day, anyway. That's why I made sure I have at least five different sweaters to settle in comfortably and fashionably.

Going for an inside joke or inside knowledge: Oh, you're feeling cold now? Wait until Mrs. Thomas comes. I heard she was raised in the wilds of Siberia. She sweats in this kind of temperature.

Exercise

Respond to the following questions and statements in two ways: formal and humorous:

1. What is the latest news about the storm?
2. Who will wash the dishes tonight?
3. Where do you think we should bring your dad for his birthday?
4. Why are you still sleeping at 10 am?
5. When is your anniversary?

We just used the five Ws to create some possible scenarios.

Formal responses :

1. The storm has strengthened further. The news reporter said we would start feeling it by tomorrow night.
2. I believe it is Caitlyn's turn. I washed the dishes last night.
3. Dad likes burgers. I know it is not good for him, but since it is his birthday, we can bring him to that new burger place across the pharmacy.
4. Sorry, I was so tired last night. I had to finish a report for work. Then, when I was done, I had problems sleeping.
5. My anniversary isn't until next week.

Formal responses have to stick to the facts. You cannot do much about it. You may try becoming more literary about it, but you cannot really change the details.

Possible humorous responses:

1. Do you know what the name of the storm is? Yeah, it has the same name as our delivery guy. So, while the weather station says it should be here at 11 pm tomorrow night, you may have to wait a few more hours later.
(This joke will work if the person you are talking to knows the guy you are talking about.)

2. For sure, it is not going to be me for a few more nights. I washed a gazillion dishes last night because of Caitlyn's party. She has a few more nights' duty to pay for it since she did not help at all last night.

(The delivery is crucial here. This can easily sound more petty than funny.)
It could be simpler, like:
Oh, I know it is not going to be my turn for a few more nights, right, Caitlyn?
(This can be done in a teasing way.)

3. Dad will gladly go anywhere with food, booze, and an agreeable version of mom.
   (While this may have a playful delivery, it can also reveal some truths about the marriage. Dad seems to be happy if he has his favorite things. He has simple wishes.)

4. Why was I still sleeping at 10 am? What were you doing sending me messages at 5 am? Are you the sun? Everyone else I know was snoring when you were texting me.
   (Notice that the response started by repeating the question asked. This is the person biding his time. He was able to ask the other person a question, as well. This response suggests that it was not him who was strange by sleeping in at 10 am, but his friend who was awake as early as 5 am.)
   The friend can rebut this, as well, to continue the banter:

   *Excuse me. Wasn't it you who said we were going jogging early this morning? You would rather work on your report late at night than wake up to make sure you can still work years from now.

5. If I don't get my wife something she likes, there may as well be no anniversary—again.
   (This response suggests that he does not get to celebrate his wedding anniversary the way he expects to do so whenever he cannot please his wife. There should be a short pause after "anniversary," wait for the reaction, then reveal that it has happened before.)

## *Comedic Persona*

Part of going back to yourself is analyzing whether you were able to create a comedic persona. You have reached this far, but perhaps you are still struggling with your implementation.

If you have failed in some way, remind yourself: you are not a comedian. You are a person who only wants to make other people laugh, and that is an admirable trait. Failing from time to time should be part of the agenda. With failures, you can learn more. You will realize, "Oh, that did not work out because I was so busy focusing on my script and not my audience." It may also be a case of the joke not really aligning with your personality.

According to the book, *How to Kill in Comedy,* a comedic persona is made up of four parts: Flaw, BlindSpot, Attitude, and Agenda.

Most of your favorite comedians filled in the four parts of a comedic persona, whether they know it or not. If you can create a structure for your comedic persona, your jokes may become more consistent, purposeful, and yet also authentic to who you are.

So, let us explore one of the comedic personas that were discussed in the same book referenced above—Jim Carrey. He is an identifiable comedian. So, we are going to look at his flaw, blindspot, attitude, and agenda.

According to *How to Kill in Comedy,* Jim Carry has Attention Deficit Disorder. Some of us may agree, and some of us may consider him as a childish, super hyper, almost lunatic type. His blind spot is that he is not aware of the vibe that he gives off. His attitude shows his real self. So, his agenda is to make people believe that he can behave normally and rationally.

If you have been watching his movies, you will notice that he usually follows these four parts. The movie version of *A Series of Unfortunate Events* was able to showcase his ability through a character that was close to his comedic persona. Count Olaf is always running around pretending to be a different, saner character, but he is ultimately a crazy, self-absorbed villain. Jim Carry has had other similar stints such as *Dumb and Dumber*, *Ace Ventura: Pet Detective*, *Liar, Liar*, and more.

Now, let us take a look at you.

Perhaps the reason some of your jokes work more than others is that your comedic persona is either non-existent or inconsistent. The jokes that may have worked may have been closer to who you are as a person. So, you were able to incorporate them into a conversation without a lot of issues.

Here is a possible comedic persona: the Tiger-Soccer Mom

Flaw: possessive, obsessive

Blindspot: her determination to raise her kids the ways she likes

Attitude: pretends to be relaxed and casual, but obviously gritting her teeth when trying to make small talk

Agenda: Raise A+ students who are good at sports and just about everything, without making it look like a struggle—which it is

You don't have to be a tiger-soccer mom in real life. However, you need to have some of the main ingredients: achievers for kids, a seemingly tough look, and a deadpan delivery. It will help if you are joking around with people who know the real you: a mom who is serious about her kids' achievements but not to the point of obsession. You just exaggerated your authentic self. So, it was not hard to get into character. This character can randomly pop up during discussions about related topics: children, achievements, sports, and anything else that you can associate with the comedic persona.


Another comedic persona: Kindhearted buddy who pretends to be tough

Flaw: Big guy, but really a fraidy cat

Blindspot: Thinks people do not know that he quickly gets scared

Attitude: Pretends to be tough and gruff, even going as far as making his voice deeper

Agenda: Appear to assist and save people when he is more scared than them


This comedic persona will work if you are a big guy, not necessarily a scaredy-cat but someone willing to play the role.

# Part Nine - More Jokes

*"Everyone has a sense of humor. If you don't laugh at jokes, you probably laugh at opinions."*
— *Criss Jami, Killosophy*

As we wind down to the end of this ebook, we will take a look at a few more joke styles that you can try to incorporate into your conversations. We have made use of several self-deprecating jokes and jokes that appeal to your sense of humor. Most professional comedians do the same thing, apparently. They look at their own lives and come up with a wealth of material. The way that they joke about these aspects of their lives shows that they don't really look down at themselves, as the words may suggest.

1. Exaggeration Formula
   The idea of using exaggeration to make anything funny has been mentioned before. However, a formula may help to drive this concept in using only one or two lines.

   Example:
   I drink **too** much **that** the bar had to close down hours before midnight.
   The keywords here are "too" and "that." Can you think of a sentence that will make use of this simple exaggeration formula?

2. Too Much Information
   Sometimes, TMI jokes still skirt closely to the self-deprecating jokes. However, sometimes, they are just there to make the other person either uncomfortable, laughing hard, or both. This is best delivered deadpan to counter the possibly shocking detail.

   Example:
   Setup: I love Saturdays.
   Ordinary related information about the setup:
   These are the days when you could probably lounge on the couch, don't shower until the afternoon...

   TMI: Or realize that you need to do extra work because your girlfriend asked you to pay for her credit card bills. Since she is so smart and pretty, all you could do is say "yes" to all the work and preparing her dinner for that same Saturday night.
   Back to normal: Yeah, Saturdays are heavenly.

3. Crazy Facts
   Sometimes, going back to your own crazy life may just be the trick to make your friends or colleagues laugh, scoff, or watch you with bewilderment. Your delivery will have to win the game for this one.

   Here are some possible crazy facts:

- When I was nine, I read *The Exorcist*. Nobody really minded me much because they were too focused on my constantly-high cousin throwing stones at the local clinic. It was also probably a time when people were still flexible about parental guidance and such.
- My music teacher had this habit of letting us sing in front of the blackboard so that we would not feel too shy. I felt even more ridiculous.
- My brother used to like catching lizards and moths. He would experiment with them with water in a pot.

For some people, crazy facts themselves can make them laugh or at least see in a new, albeit strange, light. For others, you may want to add fictional details to drive the humor home. The above can work with the follow-ups below:

- When I was ten, and everyone had relaxed, I could not even score a Stephen King paperback, and they started looking at my Nancy Drews suspiciously.
- Now, whenever I feel shy about something, I still have the tendency to turn around and look for a blackboard to talk to.
- I am just glad that he is now a surgeon, not a serial killer. Or should I be happy?

4. Knock-Knock Jokes

Oh, they do still work with some people. If you cannot get a laugh, then you can at least get a groan with a smile. Nobody can really blame you for trying to make people laugh unless you are making it obnoxious and in-your-face.

There is an extensive collection of jokes out there for you to use. You can get silly and corny sometimes, but do not forget to avoid tasteless jokes that rely on sexuality, putting others down, stereotyping, and offensiveness. It is better to take yourself as an example rather than pick on someone else. After all, your goal is to make people laugh. You want them to laugh hilariously, giggle, smile, or even groan from time to time. You are not out there to reduce them to tears, anger, or defensiveness. The joke styles that you have learned from this book are meant for fun and sharing great times together.

# Conclusion

Have you tried any of the strategies and joke types that are included in this book? How was it? Did it work right away, or did you have to warm up and wait for people to get connected with your joke style?

You will find that it is better to practice with family members and close friends. They are more likely to tell you if your jokes are funny or corny. They will be brutally honest with their feedback. After all, they will be the ones who will likely be at the receiving end of your efforts.

Of course, even if they find your jokes funny, there will still be a chance that others will not. Don't be hard on yourself. More likely, people who will not laugh at your jokes are not receptive in the first place. If you start taking it personally, then it will be challenging for you to take things lightly and attempt again. We don't know what problems the other person is going through.

In real life, you can plan to make a joke, but you still need to be more spontaneous. The spontaneous jokes are the ones that usually work best. They work best because you are more relaxed and open to how the scene will unfold.

So, lighten up! This way, you can help others lighten up. Go out there and make people laugh. It is a noble cause and a beautiful contribution to this world.

# Book #4
# How to Make People Do What You Want

*Methods of Subtle Psychology to Read People, Persuade, and Influence Human Behavior*

# Introduction & Foreword

*"At the end of reasons, comes persuasion."* – Ludwig Wittgenstein

Here's something to get your brain juices flowing.

The human race wouldn't be where it is today without communication.

The way we talk, act, and perceive ourselves, others, and the world around us is singlehandedly responsible for everything that has happened. And I mean absolutely everything. Through redemption and destruction. Through thick and thin. Both morally and immorally. The whole of society as we know it is what it is because of the effects of communication.

That's a bold statement, I know, but take a moment to think about it on a personal level. Consider every single experience that comes to mind. Every relationship you've been in. Every job you've ever loved and hated. Every chance encounter and every plan fulfilled. At every step of the way, there has been a degree of communication. Similarly, many of our professional and personal problems stem from a *lack* of communication.

In a roundabout sense, you could say communication is the key to being human, which would mean that through understanding the power that comes with mastering the art of communication, you can unlock a new way of living your life. New doors will open, and vibrant opportunities you couldn't even imagine will present themselves to you.

By mastering communication, you can achieve what only so many people dreamed of achieving.

Okay, allow me to kick it back a notch.

While this all sounds very exciting, you're probably wondering what it has to do with you and learning how to persuade people. We all persuade people in many different ways and many different forms. Many of us persuade others every day, or least are persuaded by someone else. Some people are better at it than others, just as some people are more persuadable than others.

You cannot get through life without persuading people. In your relationships, you persuade people to go on dates, get a pet, move in together, get married, and have kids. You make friends and take vacations, choose movies, and read books. Every single advertisement of any form is an attempt to persuade you to buy something.

In your professional life, you're selling to your customers, promoting and pitching your ideas to your bosses, and surviving employee evaluation meetings. Every single aspect of human life in the modern world is affected by persuasion, or similarly, the art of influence.

But let's break this down further. Yes, people persuade other people all the time. You do it to people, and people do it to you. Understanding this, you'll soon realize that to get what you want out of life, you're going to need to persuade people. But what does this mean?

At the core of communication, there is a single thing that drives motivation for speech. It's the centre of every society, every political campaign, every message you've ever read, and every lover's proposal asked under the stars.

**That single core factor is a message.**

Any time you talk, ask something, share an idea (from starting a business to choosing a vacation destination), or request a favor, you're sending a message. Discussing what takeout you're going to get is sending a message. You're saying that you want pizza when your partner sends their message detailing that they want pasta.

However, choosing what takeout you have and trying to persuade your partner to get pizza over pasta is small fish to what you'll be able to achieve once you've finished with this book. Ever wanted to have your ideas listened to at work? Ever wanted to start a social movement? Ever wanted to walk into a room and actually have people listen to what you have to say in a way that isn't arrogant and egotistical, but charismatic and genuinely appealing?

This is what it means to master the art of persuasion. These are just grains of sand on the beach of what is possible. To really break this down:

You have a message to send. Sending a message is easy. Anyone can do it. I can go and stand in the street and shout for ten minutes about how pizza is so much better than pasta. That's sending a message. So is whispering it. The difficulties come when trying to get others to listen to your message.

The real art of influencing others comes with sending your message in a way that other people hear what you have to say and then actually take it on board. Getting people to listen and hear what you're saying is the message and core focus of this book. Robert Cialdini, the author of *Influencer and Pre-Suasion: A Revolutionary Way to Influence and Persuade,* once wrote:

"It's not about your message, but the skill you put into crafting it, that matters."

Never a truer word written.

By mastering the fundamentals and then the complexities of persuasion, you're harnessing your inner ability to send your message in a way that can be clearly acknowledged, received, accepted, and understood. You're enabling people to hear you and open their minds to your thoughts, concepts, and perceptions.

Let's face it: human beings these days are pretty closed off. The vast majority of people walk around all day stuck in their own minds, thoughts of stuff they read on social media and the contents of ads ricocheting off the sides of their heads. There's no doubt we live in an age where people are more polarized than ever before politically, socially, and so on.

Having the skill set to strike through the constant thinking and closed-mindedness that most people have to be genuinely heard is a lifelong skill that brings so many benefits. Within the following pages, this is a skill set I'm going to nurture within you.

We're going to be touching base with a wide range of communication techniques, including understanding NLP, learning how to read and control your body language, and applying pressure in the right places and the right time to get people to perceive what you're saying to them in a more suggestive way. We'll also cover the basics and set a foundation of human psychology and how it works, and how to send your message using these techniques.

Using these methods, you'll become far more influential in all areas of your life, both with the people you know and love, and even strangers. These are techniques that work across the board whenever you want to use them.

The book is split into chapters in such a way that it will take you on a journey. I'm going to talk you through how persuasion can be used in your day-to-day life, and eventually onto bigger ventures, as well as detailing the kind of mindset you need to carry out these skills. This is all in what is essentially a step-by-step guide to persuading an individual or group of people.

In a world of constant, high-speed communication, mastering the ability to communicate and protecting yourself from unwanted influence has never been more important.

*Communication Skills Training Series*

# Chapter One – Understanding the Art of Persuasion

*"Think twice before you speak, because your words and influence will plant the seed of either success or failure in the mind of another."* – Napoleon Hill

My interest in the art of persuasion first came to me while I was in college. I was studying business marketing, and one day my professor split the class into groups and set us to work on a project. The project was to create a marketing campaign for a new pair of Nike trainers that had just been released.

The exercise was clearly to take into account everything we had learned during the year so far and to combine it all into a concept that could sell units. I love this kind of task because it's a chance to exercise my creative side; by far, my favorite aspect of marketing. It's what I love about the world of business. The exploration of new ideas. The telling of stories. A creative process.

I went back to my dorm and brainstormed some ideas. I did some market research, watching old trainer ads and researching brands. I checked out other brands to see what they were up to at the time, and, just as I was falling to sleep, the idea hit me. There's nothing like the tingle you get when inspiration hits, and I knew right away that my idea was a winner.

The idea was this. Picture a girl getting up in the morning and putting on her Nike trainers. She leaves her house and starts running through the city. As she runs, the film would cut to shots of distractions that are symbolic in her own life. Email notifications pinging on her computer. Bosses slamming piles of reports on her desk. Shots of the busy flow of traffic. That kind of thing.

As she ran, she slowly lost herself to the running. The city and all the distractions she had in her life would fade away, and she would begin running past trees and finally into a full-blown forest. She lost herself in her running. It was her escape. It was her *freedom*. She would eventually arrive at a clearing in the woods, rain pouring down onto her, music playing through her headphones. She would savor the freedom that her trainers had helped her achieve. That *Nike* had helped her achieve. Then, refreshed and revitalized, she would run back into the city and back to her life, ready to face whatever her day threw her way.

I don't know whether Nike would have loved that idea for an ad nor any clue how successful it would have been, but I loved that idea, and I truly believed in it. I got to college the next day and sat down with the group, and I couldn't wait to share my idea. *This is it*, I thought to myself. *We've nailed this.*

We met up, went to a café in the city, and the others started listing off their ideas. There were some okay ideas, and when it got to me, I shared my idea with as much enthusiasm as I thought I could muster. I was returned blank faces, a couple of people taking notes, and then the guy to my left shared his idea. And that was it.

Now, when I was in college, I was a pretty shy kid. I had such crippling social anxiety, which was probably a key reason why my idea didn't land as impactfully as I wanted it too, but I was still heartbroken. My message—the message I had so much love and passion for—was rejected. Practically ignored.

One guy opposite me, who was easily the most charismatic of the group, shared his idea of a sports day and followed the kid growing up into an athlete. His idea was chosen, and the group ran with it. We didn't do too badly with the final result and got average marks for the project, but I was left with something far more powerful.

The day after sharing our ideas, I was left wondering what I could have done better. How could I have communicated my message more effectively? Could I have been more passionate or personal? Should I have been more dramatic or over the top? How could I have presented my ideas differently?

It wasn't until after spending many years in a career in sales and marketing and having learned about the fundamentals of human psychology and the art of persuasion that I started to learn that communicating effectively is a mastery that is learned and practiced. It's a skill that's honed over the years, not something that we just have.

**Anyone can talk, but few speak value.**

It doesn't matter what you want to achieve in your life; persuasion is the way you're going to make it happen. When you meet someone for the first time, and you have a romantic interest in them, you'll persuade them to spend time with you. You'll act funny or kind. You'll compliment them, or you'll act in some other way. Whatever you do, you're sending the message that "This is who I am. I like you, and I hope you like me too." If you persuade well enough, you'll go on a few dates and eventually get together. You could date for a few years and will decide to get married.

Even within the proposal of marriage itself, you're hoping you've persuaded your partner enough that they're going to say yes and will want to spend the rest of their life with you. Of course, writing about the process of love in this way makes it feel a bit robotic and not very exciting at all, but the core of what I'm saying is that you're always sending a message to other people with everything you do. If you're not in control of the message you're sending, then you'll be lucky if you get the outcome you want.

This is the purpose of this book. Persuasion is not just about getting what you want and having things your way, although you could certainly look at it that way if you wish. Instead, it's more about being in control of the messages you're sending and showing up in the world the way you want to, not just showing your face to the world and hoping for the best.

I've been that way for most of my life, and it never got me anywhere. I was always working under the people I disliked, was always the second choice for everything, and was never listened to nor barely acknowledged. It wasn't until I took control of my actions and messages that life started to swing in my favor.

I've spoken a lot about using persuasion on the personal side of life, but I can't stress enough how it extends to every part, especially from a professional standpoint. I spent many years in sales and marketing, in which the very essence of the work is persuading people to buy a product or use a service. These techniques work here in the very same way.

I take a product, no matter what it is, and send a message to a customer that says, "Buy this product, and it will make your life better in x-amount of ways." Fast food chains claim their food tastes good. Car companies sell you freedom when you drive. Clothing companies say their products will make you feel good in your own body.

It's up to you whether or not you believe in the messages these companies are selling you, but since many of these businesses are multi-million, if not billion, dollar companies, there's no denying that it works. The messages of these companies are received loud and clear.

Bringing it back to you, let's say it's time for your employee evaluation time, and you're sitting down with your boss to see how well you're doing. You're going through your figures, and they're asking you how you see yourself within the company. How confident and in control are you of the message you're sending? Will your boss want to keep you on and see you as a valuable asset within the company, or are they doubting you and your abilities? You're persuading them either way with the words you say.

Let's say you want to work for yourself, and you have an idea for a business. Whether you're pitching your idea to friends, family, colleagues, or investors, you're controlling your message to say, "This is my idea, and I want you to be on board with it." However, as Cialdini wrote, it's not about the message you're sending, it's about how you craft it that matters.

In the real world, anyone can sell you anything or influence you into believing anything. It's all about how it's presented, all of which I'm going to describe in the following chapters.

# Chapter Two – Developing Your Own Mindset

*"Life isn't about finding yourself. Life is about creating yourself."* – George Bernard Shaw

Before you start influencing other people, it's so important to start thinking about yourself, particularly the mindset you have. When I was in college with my killer Nike trainers idea, my mindset was in the right place, but it wasn't developed enough to send a message. I suffered from crippling social anxiety and wasn't confident in myself in front of others. My message was good, but the way I crafted it and presented it wasn't.

This social anxiety created a shy, introverted "vibe" to my being. My body language screamed it, and my verbal communication confirmed it. Before I had even uttered a word, the people in my marketing group decided whether they would listen to me or not, whether they were conscious of that decision or not, and my mindset was the basis of where this decision came from.

When it comes to showing up how you want to show up in your life, taking control of the messages you're sending, and ultimately influencing others, what kind of mindset should you have to make these efforts successful? Here are some traits you need to be thinking about.

## Confidence and Belief in Yourself

This mindset trait you should have goes without saying, but it's crucial and has to be mentioned. If you don't believe in yourself, and I mean truly believe in yourself, others are not going to believe in you either. Building up confidence in yourself is a process and a journey you'll need to undertake if you want to persuade people and live a happy and fulfilling life. Since you, like everybody else, change who you are as you go through life, don't be surprised that there's no endpoint where you're confident in yourself always and forever.

Your circumstances are always changing, which means you'll constantly need to be adapting your mindset to keep believing in yourself. It's a lifelong journey that you always need to be thinking about. What's more, everybody is different, so what confidence practices work for someone else may not work for you. Most of this process is trial and error, but once you start making progress, you'll start seeing unbelievable results.

By adopting a self-confident mindset, you'll already see incredible changes in the way people see you, hear you, and perceive your ideas and your messages. Fortunately, there are a few things you can do to start working towards a more confident you.

Firstly, confidence starts with you. It doesn't come from an external source. You need to start considering what limiting beliefs you have that hold you back and start letting them go. For me, my social anxiety held me back, and it made me believe on an identity level that I was not a social person. It became who I was.

In truth, this was just a belief I *gave* myself. I was full of self-doubt and never believed I was good enough, and that I never would be. As soon as I acknowledged these thoughts I held about myself and realized they existed, I was able to bring this awareness into my interactions with the world. If I wanted to share an idea and the limiting belief crept in, I could notice it and let it go, rather than being reactive to it and letting it dictate the flow of conversation.

For example, if I were in a meeting and had to give a presentation, the time would draw closer to the slot I was presenting in, and I would sit around the table thinking to myself, *Nobody's going to listen or care what I have to say.* I would notice this thought and change it. I would think something along the lines of, *No, I do believe in myself, and this presentation is going to be a hit. Even if the idea isn't chosen, I'm still going to present it to the best of my ability.*

It took some time, but eventually, my limiting beliefs were not the first point of call for my mind. Instead, I had more confident beliefs in myself, and thus I started to believe in myself fully. This confidence radiated through my conversations, and people noticeably started to respect me and treat me with authority.

This confidence that you should be building in yourself needs to be accompanied by respecting yourself. You're a human being, and you're going to make mistakes throughout your life. Instead of beating yourself up because you did something wrong, treat every negative experience positively by viewing it as a lesson to be learned.

Life is all about learning lessons, and as long as you're open to learning them, you'll always have the ability to grow as an individual. This capability to grow is how respect, confidence, and self-belief for yourself are nurtured.

## Be Patient

When it comes to developing yourself within your persuasion journey, whether you're influencing someone using psychological techniques or learning to believe in yourself, patience is absolutely key.

Let's say you're trying to convince your boss to give you a promotion. You say your piece, and now the ball is in their court. This is where patience comes in. If you're constantly bothering your boss, nagging for an answer, or you're so distracted at work worrying about whether you've got the job or not, this is going to send out the message into the world that you're distracted, worried, and anxious. Well, guess what? This message won't get you the promotion!

Instead, if you're calm, collected, and patient, you're sending out the message that you're fully in control. You're relaxing to be around. You're confident that what you've said is enough (believing in yourself and your abilities), and you're giving the other people involved the opportunity to think things through and make their own decision. At least they think they're making their own decision, when actually you've persuaded them in such a way that they've already made their decision, they just don't know it yet. But more on that later.

The best way to instill patience into your life is to recognize that everything takes time. Simon Sinek once said, "You didn't fall in love with your wife the day you met her, nor five years down the line. You can't tell me the exact day you fell in love with her, but you know it was a process that happened over time."

Big things happen over time.

## Be a Relationship Person

I never used to be a "people person," and unless you're super confident in yourself already, then chances are you're not either, but it's vital to be interested in relationships with people if you want to succeed with your influencing efforts. However, I'm not talking about snapping your fingers and suddenly becoming the most charismatic and charming person in the room. You still need to be yourself. I'm talking about focusing on building valuable relationships with people, no matter who you're with or what the situation is.

About five years ago, I was busy trying to secure a new client for my work. The contract was worth around $50,000, and it was one my company was paying special attention to. We wanted to approach them in just the right way that they didn't want to go with any other company, thus confirming the contract as ours. The boss was anxious because if we approached them in the wrong way, we might scare them away forever.

We didn't end up securing the contract, and looking back on the situation in hindsight, I've realized one very important lesson. My company's bosses were not interested in working with the client on a personal or even professional level. They were much more interested in chasing the instant financial gain that would come with securing the $50,000 contract. They wanted money in the bank over a partnership with the client.

I spoke to a peer from the rival company several years later, who told me they were still working with that same client. The bosses played golf together every other weekend, and the sales team knew their contacts by name and had quarterly meetings where they went to dinner as a group; employees and all.

Instead of my company chasing the money, a different way to approach would have been to communicate with the client on a personal level while aiming to build a relationship with them. Sure, we may not have secured the $50,000 leading product contract, but if we had a nurtured relationship with them, we could have secured a $20,000 contract every year for the next three years on smaller product lines, which is ultimately more profitable. Instead, we severed ties altogether.

This logic applies to both personal and professional relationships. If you focus on the value of the relationship itself, instead of what value you can get out of the relationship, you can start to persuade far more effectively. Naturally, you'll be much more likely to get more from your relationship, all without actually looking for it.

Bearing all these points in mind, you should start to form the mindset of someone capable of persuading and influencing others. It's a timely process, but with attention and effort, you should start to see the effects of a growth mindset almost instantly. Once you've created a positive relationship with yourself, it's then time to start focusing on your relationship with other people.

# Chapter Three – Nurturing a Relationship
# (Making Friends and Winning Them Over)

*"You can make more friends in two months by becoming interested in other people than you can in two years by trying to get other people interested in you."* – Dale Carnegie

In that last paragraph, I wrote about forming a mindset where you focus on creating and nurturing valuable relationships with other people and the importance of doing so when it comes to persuasion. That's a very special point because if you don't have relationships with others, you can't persuade them. This is why it's important to focus on this as a chapter of its own since it's the first step you'll take when you're starting to influence someone.

So far, you've read about persuading people, why you'd want to, and the power it can bring into your life, so you should have a pretty clear grasp on the concept. That means for the remainder of this book, I'm going to take you on a journey into how you can begin to master this fine art.

Now it's time to start taking action by controlling the messages you're sending to the world.

First, unless you're in a position of power, nobody will be persuaded or influenced by you if they don't like you. When I was a teenager, I worked in a supermarket as a shelf stacker on the weekends. It was an okay job, but my team leader was one of the worst people I had ever met. Sure, I did the work he told me to do begrudgingly, but if he called up trying to get me to fill vacant overtime slots or work an extra shift when the store was behind, there was absolutely no way I was doing it. The idea of working with him was awful, and everyone felt the same.

On my shift, I would avoid him like the plague, and would always cringe, along with everyone else, as he ranted about whatever subject was hot that day in the staff cafeteria. In contrast, there was another team leader who was simply the polar opposite. She was kind and caring, always asked how my day was, and made me feel valued as an employee—and more importantly, as a person. I know stacking shelves is not the most fulfilling job in the world, but she always made me feel appreciated for doing it. I was happy to work with her.

Whenever she called to fill an overtime shift or needed help during the busy periods, I was happy to help. I wasn't alone in this way of thinking. All the staff felt the same and treated both team leaders in the same contrasting ways, all because one team leader was liked, and the other wasn't. If you want people to do what you want, you first need to get them to like you.

There are several ways you can get in people's good books, many of which we're going to explore throughout this chapter. Remember, these points can be applied in any situation. You can apply them with your partner or someone you're working with, like a co-worker or client. You can even apply them to a stranger you've just met.

I encourage you to try these points out in any situation you can, because the more you practice them, the better and more confident you'll be at presenting yourself, thus achieving better results.

## Put the Other Person First

The first step to making someone like you is to put them first in your conversations. People love to be listened to, heard, and acknowledged, and giving someone that feeling in a world where seemingly nobody is really listening is instantly going to make you stand out, and they'll remember you. This always means they'll want to speak with you again and will be much more susceptible to your persuasion attempts.

Imagine you're arguing with your partner, and you're both screaming at each other, trying to share your point of view on a particular topic. Yeah, we've all been there. After a lot of shouting, you realize the conversation isn't going to go anywhere, and you're both going to end up driving each other away. By stepping back from this approach and putting your points of view on the back burner, and instead by listening to your partner and giving them a platform to talk, you allow progress to be made.

This may sound counterproductive, because how are you going to persuade someone if they're doing all the talking? We'll get to that later. The first thing you want to focus on is building a relationship with the person you're speaking to, getting them to connect with you positively. If other people see you as a friend, then you're heading in the right direction.

In a nutshell, let the other person do all the talking.

## Listen More Than You Talk

This point goes along with everything I've already said, but the more you can listen to someone, the more connected they're going to feel to you. This doesn't just mean listening and nodding along with whatever they're talking about. It means *actively* listening and asking questions if you don't understand. It means progressing the conversation in line with what they're talking about, not just holding in what you want to say until they're finished.

Whenever I deal with a new client, I let them talk about their project in their own time. I won't say how I can help them, what my ideas are, or where I can take their product or service. I first hear their ideas and build up an image of what they're telling me.

A recent customer was trying to think of ways to market their bakery. I had some ideas, and some themes instantly come to mind, but I listened and homed in on what they were saying. When I wanted to know more, such as whether it was a family business, or what kind of market they were aiming to tap into, I wasn't afraid to ask. The act of asking questions to clarify what someone is saying is vital because it shows you're listening. It tells that person you care.

## Create Trust

Trust is a key part of any relationship, and whether you're talking with a loved one you've known for years or someone who's just appeared in front of you for the first time, you need to invoke a sense of trust. If people trust you, you'll be able to influence them naturally. Nobody wants to work with a leader they can't trust. The world is already full of enough of them as it is.

There are endless ways you can encourage and nurture trust in any relationship. Firstly, you can start as simply as using the person's name in your conversations with them. Yeah, it's really that simple. Being able to make your message personal and direct to an individual already shows that you're on board with them, recognizing them as a person, and speaking to them directly. This is especially important in professional relationships.

Next, be able to admit when you're wrong, own up to your mistakes, and share any baggage you're carrying when it's necessary to do so. Everyone knows that everybody messes up from time to time. It's an inescapable fact of life. However, when most people mess up and run into problems, their first response is to try and cover everything up as best as they can. This is where lying and deceit thrive.

If you do something wrong and have the ability to own it and take responsibility for it, everyone is going to trust you from the word *go*. Let's say you're working on a project with other people, and you fill out a budget form incorrectly. It's something small, but it causes a few problems that need to be resolved. Instead of trying to shift the blame or make it look like something outside of your control happened, you simply raise your hand and admit to your shortcoming.

Suddenly, what could be quite a big problem is now not so much of a big deal. Everybody involved understands what happened and thinks, *Yes, we know what happened, and they* (being you) *weren't afraid to admit it.* Suddenly, even though you did something wrong, massive positives came from the situation because everyone saw that you were willing to own up to your mistakes in a respectful way.

Suddenly, your words have power and truth.

## Work on your Body Language

We're going to discuss this topic in a lot more detail in a following chapter, but as a little introduction that ties in nicely with learning how to befriend people and get them to like you, you need to think about your body language and how people perceive you because of it. When I was a shy college student, my body was hunched over, and I would physically hide away from the main group, whether through crossing my arms or not making eye contact. Nobody paid any attention to me because my body language sent the message that I wanted to be left alone.

Of course, if you're pushing people away, nobody is going to want to approach you. Instead, you need to be inviting and welcoming with the way you act. This means smiling and acting relaxed. If you're tense, crossing your arms, or scowling at people, you're going to give off the message that you don't want to talk or connect with that person. Instead, try lowering your shoulders, smiling, and exposing your chest. But again, more on this later in the book.

## Leave People Better Than You Started

As a rule of thumb, one of the best blanket statements to remember when trying to get people to like you is to always leave them in a better, happier, more thoughtful way than before. Whether you're talking to your partner, your boss, a customer, or a stranger, always aim to leave them better off than when you started interacting with them.

If you bear this concept in mind, you're going to naturally listen more and put the other person first. You're going to make them feel heard and acknowledged with what they're saying, and they're going to feel a much deeper connection with you. With this deeper connection, they're going to keep thinking about you long after the conversation has taken place, and they'll be much more likely to want to interact with you again.

Once you reach this point, you're then ready to move on with the next stage of persuading and influencing them with your message.

## Be Natural

If you're focusing too much on everything you're saying and trying to implement everything you've read in this book, then your conversations are unlikely to seem natural, and this is going to put people off. Remember, when it comes to your journey into the world of persuasion, you need to start small. Master the basics first and then add to your skills over time once you feel comfortable with your foundations.

This is crucial. Imagine you're having a conversation with someone, and all you can think about is what you're doing with your body language and what message you're sending. You're probably going to end up missing what they say, and then they'll believe you're not listening to them, and it will all go down the drain. No matter what, remember to be human!

## Molding Their Perceptions

In some of your relationships, you may find that becoming friends in this way is enough to get them thinking the way you think. Through the conversations you have, you may be able to convince them of your ideas and send them your messages, and they'll take them on board, perhaps even incorporating them into their way of life.

Think of persuasion in this sense. Every human being on the planet sees their own life and the world through their perceptions. These perceptions are formed by a combination of experiences—childhood upbringing, social conditioning based on parents, their educational system, geographic demographics, and the direction their life has taken.

To persuade someone is to take control of this and input your thoughts and ideas in place of what already exists there. Once you begin to mold those perceptions and those realities, it becomes easier to persuade someone with your message.

The debate about whether veganism is an effective diet choice is a fantastic example of this. If you have a hippy-styled vegan hammering away at you for hours about the benefits of veganism and why meat-eaters are so bad (thus making a meat-eater feel defensive about their own lifestyle choices), that meat-eating individual is going to shut down and won't listen. The approach is too aggressive. They'll put up mental barriers to protect themselves and their ego, and won't listen to the information discussed.

However, if this information is being presented differently, the individual may begin to change their perception. For example, if you start listening to the individual and you realize they have an interest in the environment, or are passionate about global warming and like talking about science, then you could begin introducing the scientific benefits that adopting a vegan lifestyle can bring.

If that individual was passionate about animals, you could start introducing the facts you know about the wellbeing of farmed animals, and how veganism is helping to counter the industry in terms of wellbeing. In my own experiences, a friend I knew in school grew up on a farm and was quite familiar with slaughtering animals and the sight of the human food cycle. While he cared about animals, he knew never to grow attached to them. Therefore, the animal-loving approach wouldn't sit in the same way as it would your typical animal lover.

We'll talk more about introducing these points in a later chapter, but the important thing to remember here is that you're taking the perceptions that an individual already has, and then basing your attempts to influence them off of these perceptions.

# Chapter Four – Being Able to Talk to Anyone

*"If you have no confidence in self, you are twice defeated in the race of life."*
– Marcus Garvey

Hand in hand with the last chapter, I want to take the time to speak about the ability to talk to anyone. More specifically, this means taking the time to build up your confidence to really harness the ability to persuade and influence someone. If you're not confident with how you speak to people, the cues and techniques we talk about in the remainder of this book will not have the best possible outcome.

In line with the Robert Cialdini quote in the front of this book, it's not about the message you're sending, it's about how you craft it, which means portraying yourself confidently and with purpose. Imagine if marketing advertisements on the television "ummed" and "ahhed" with their messaging. You'd probably laugh with how silly it all seemed and definitely wouldn't take their message seriously. The same applies to you.

With all this in mind, it's worth noting that being able to speak confidently with anyone is no easy feat, especially if you're more of a shy or introverted person by nature. Fortunately, there are ways you can overcome your fears and anxieties, and things you can do to improve your confidence when speaking to others.

## Five Ways to Boost Your Self-Confidence Dramatically

While many of us admire the confidence some people have, the way they seem to control the flow of a conversation with ease and command the attention of people around them in any room they enter (be honest, we all have a friend like this), is actually something anybody can do. Most people aren't born this way, but it's picked up, learned, and practiced over time.

With that, I'm going to detail five ways you can boost your levels of confidence in yourself dramatically. Bear in mind it's not something that's going to happen overnight, but rather takes time and energy. But, if you're able to stay mindful and focused, you should start to see an improvement in your confidence fairly quickly.

1. **Be Prepared for Any Situation**

Being confident starts before you even enter the room. The more prepared you are for any given situation, the more confident you're going to be. Imagine two people both going into the same job interview. Person A knows everything about the company. They know the figures. They know what job they're applying for. They know what they're doing and what's expected of them. They know the targets and the industry. They know the company's objectives, mission, and values. They know the customer base, and they know what sort of person the company is looking for. Person A has done their research and knows what to expect.

On the other hand, Person B just applied for the job, forgot they had the interview until that morning, and turns up with nothing while planning to give their pitch off the cuff. It's very clear who's got the better chances of getting the job.

Even if your preparation for heading into a conversation is thinking about a few things you're going to ask and the things you're going to say, this is better than nothing. Having some idea of what direction you want a situation to go in is great for helping you take it there, and it will mean you have some kind of structure, rather than heading into the interaction mindlessly.

That's not to say that you should plan every detail meticulously and then rigidly stick to your plan. If you're having a conversation with someone, they may ask a question that completely changes the direction of the conversation, and that's okay. You just need to be prepared for that happening. Be free and go with the flow. With this kind of mindset, it's basically impossible not to be confident.

### 2. Work on the Voices in Your Head

While speaking to yourself may be a traditional sign of madness, the truth is we all have a voice in our head, which is constantly talking. Nag, nag, nag. Some of the time, you'll notice it, and at others, it will be muttering away in the background somewhere. Even if you're not conscious of it, it's still there, and if you're like the majority of people, the chances are it's a negative voice.

We all have a protective, anxious voice to some degree. It's that voice that imagines all the crazy unfathomable things that are going to happen when you head into an interview or meeting. It's the voice that beats you up when you say something wrong in a conversation, even if it isn't that bad. It's that voice that tells you you're going to mess things up when you try something new.

It's impossible to be confident when you have these voices in your head, especially when you're listening to them and letting them dictate how you feel about yourself. You'll find that the people with the lowest confidence and the lowest self-esteem will have the most negative voices. It's all about being mindful of how you talk about yourself.

If you say you're not smart, not good enough, or not beautiful enough, then you're limiting yourself based on what you believe about yourself and how others view you. It's almost like a self-fulfilling prophecy. The best thing you can do is to become mindful of the voices. Listen to what they're saying, but not by taking it on board. Instead, be an observer to your mind.

Whenever you hear negativity in your mind, say to yourself, "Oh, there's a negative thought" and replace it with a positive affirmation instead. Over time, you'll create a positive image in yourself, and thus will become more confident.

### 3. Don't Compare Yourself to Others

Comparison is the thief of joy, and when you compare yourself to others, you're putting yourself in a position where you're vulnerable to lowering your self-esteem and confidence. If you compare how you run to the running abilities of an Olympic runner, you're going to think you're awful at running when that probably isn't the case.

As Einstein reportedly once said, *"Everybody is a genius, but if you judge a fish by its ability to climb a tree, it will live its whole life believing it's stupid."*

When you're going about your day, be mindful of how often you're comparing yourself to others. Once you become conscious of doing this, then chances are you're going to notice you do it far more often than you originally thought. It could happen in small ways, like wishing you had a nice coat or lunch like someone else, or bigger things like having a partner like somebody else's, a house, or a job.

This is a surefire way to create dissatisfaction in your life, and you're going to be left miserable, wishing you were somebody else or living someone else's life. Of course, you're not going to be confident in yourself if this is the way you look at things.

Instead, just like being mindful of how you speak to yourself, be aware of how you compare yourself to others. If you catch yourself thinking these kinds of thoughts, then say, "Oh, I just noticed I compared myself to someone else," and then let that judgment go. Of course, there are times when comparing yourself to someone could be valuable, or even inspirational, but this will be defined on a circumstantial basis.

Ask yourself, "Does this comparison make me happy, and does it provide value in my life, or is it harming my self-esteem?" If the thought doesn't provide value, then it doesn't serve you. Instead, be accepting and grateful for who you are as an individual, and if you want to get better at something, then work at it. Don't put yourself down for not being there already.

### 4. Look After Yourself—Mentally and Physically

If you don't feel good about yourself, then you won't be confident in yourself. This applies to you both mentally and physically. If you have a bit of extra weight that you don't like, or you're not mentally in a good place (i.e., experiencing a sleep deficit, eating poorly, or not exercising and beating yourself up about it), then of course you're not going to be confident in who you are as an individual.

No matter who you are or what walk of life you're from, you need to make sure you're putting self-care at the top of your priority list. After all, what's the point in doing what you do if you're not looking after yourself in the best possible way? You could work yourself in the ground or eat takeout every day because it tastes good, but you know this is always going to do more harm than good in the long term.

If you look and feel good, you're going to feel confident, but how you go about this is completely up to you. Maybe you like meditating and journaling. Perhaps crystals work for you. Maybe you like unwinding in the gym, going for runs, and taking your nutrition seriously. It's completely up to you, so try out lots of things and see what works best for you.

Be compassionate with yourself, and always show yourself the love you would expect from others. Social anxiety and low self-esteem plagued me throughout my entire life, and it wasn't until I started looking after myself that these dark feelings began to lift.

### 5. Trust in Yourself

If you only take one of the points from this list, let it be this one. How often do you doubt your ability to do something and let the anxieties and worries play around in your mind? For me, the answer is often, or at least it used to be throughout the majority of my life until I learned to take control and to trust myself.

From when I was in school and college and then moving into the world of work, I used to always hesitate before I jumped. I remember once I had to give a presentation to a client on how we were going to market their new product line, and I was *so* nervous. I believed in my ideas, and I knew they were good, but still, something inside me made me doubt my ability to do my job.

So many times, I felt as though I would pass out due to nerves, which affected every aspect of my life. From my relationships and work to even asking someone in the store if they had a shoe in a different size, there was always a nagging voice in the back of my mind claiming I would mess it up or cause an embarrassing scene.

I was sick of feeling this way, and it shattered my confidence and self-esteem. I couldn't talk to anyone because I thought I was always going to mess it up, and people were going to look at me and judge me in a bad way. Little did I know that I was simply projecting how I felt about myself and imagining that everyone else felt the same. This just isn't true.

I can't say this enough: You **need** to start trusting yourself. Remember, you're a human being, and you're going to make mistakes. You're going to go through hard times, just like you're going to go through good times. There are plenty of lessons to be learned ahead of you, and your life will twist and turn in all directions, and that's all okay.

You're going to be doing the best you can at any given time, and as long as you're trying to do that, you've got nothing to worry about. And don't worry, your best will change from time to time. On the days you're healthy, your best will be a lot greater than the days where you're ill.

It all comes down to your mindset.

You can do a few things to actively increase trust in yourself, such as making a small commitment and then sticking to it—like saying you're going to drink water as the first thing you do every morning when you wake up. You stick to the commitment, and you start trusting yourself more and more, but there is a time element to it, so stick with it.

As with all the points above, it's all about working on yourself over time and developing an esteemed mindset towards yourself. It's an ongoing process that's going to have some amazing days and not-so-great others. As long as you're focused on walking the path you want to take, you're heading in the right direction.

## How to Talk to Anyone

Let's jump forward a few months, and you've been hard at work on your confidence. You can walk into a room and hold your own. You believe in yourself, and you believe you're capable of anything you put your mind to. This is a great place to be, but now it's time to bring it to the outside world. You need to start talking with people.

And I'm not just talking about people in your immediate circles. I mean anybody. It literally could be the next person who passes you on the street. How do you do this and remain confident in a world where everyone seems to be scared of everyone else?

Simple.

First, engage the person and find out where they stand. You could ask a question of where something is or whether they could help you with something. You could just make a passing comment on whatever is happening around you. Whatever it is, try to make it interesting, but more importantly, judge their response.

What kind of mood is this person in? Are they busy or preoccupied? Are they cheerful and happy? Are they shy? Are they angry? Are they crying? Try to figure out what mood that person is in and go from there.

If someone is angry, you may want to leave them alone, or you may want to find out what's bothering them. If you can get angry with them, then you're justifying that person's anger, which is a great way to build a relationship with someone.

Let's say you see someone, and they look angry. They look like they've been crying. Immediately, you know something is going on in their life, so be concerned. If they say they've broken up with their partner because they cheated on them, you can validate their feelings and say how horrible their partner was.

Once you've engaged and you've validated this person and how they feel, then you can start building a relationship with them. So, to recap:

- First, engage the person and assess how they're feeling
- Second, validate how they're feeling
- Third, focus on building a genuine connection and relationship

Remember how, in the previous chapter, I spoke about building that trust and leaving that person better off than when you started talking to them? This applies to strangers, co-workers, relatives, and everyone in between. Being able to talk to people in this way will come with practice, so again, look for opportunities to practice, and like every skill in life, you'll get better over time.

Now, if you bear these points in mind, you'll start developing the confident mindset that's essential for persuading and influencing others. It's all about the mindset, which leads us very nicely onto the next chapter, which is all about how the human mind works. This is the best place to start when learning how you can influence, persuade, and send your message out into the world.

# Chapter Five - Deep-Diving into Control of the Mind

*"The power of persuasion would be the greatest superpower of all time."* – Jenny Mollen

A person's mindset is the most powerful attribute to their character and who they are, as your mindset is to yours. It doesn't matter what the physical reality is for someone; their mindset will dictate everything. If they feel defeated, they are defeated, for example.

I was watching a documentary the other night that detailed the struggles of people living in Africa. Some people were so far below the poverty line that they had to dig for scraps, mainly grains of rice and corn, that had been left on the ground outside of rat holes by the rodents that lived in them. Some days, that was those people's main source of food. Yet, despite their despair, the people were hopeful that better days were coming. They worked hard to provide a brighter future for their children and their children's children.

In the same hour, I spoke to a friend who has been in a rut the past few months. He quit his full-time job to make money on the stock exchange as a day trader but had practically lost all his investment. He's not a bad investor and had only invested his budget, meaning he still had his house and his car and his savings to support his family. Yet, he felt utterly defeated and was struggling to find a way forward.

This is the power of mindsets.

When it comes to learning how to tap into other people's mindsets, granting you an understanding of how their mind works and how you can then begin to alter their perceptions, there are three main subjects you need to think about. Schemas. Priming. Spreading Activation. Allow me to explain.

## An Introduction to Schemas

Simply put, schemas are the associations that you have with the world and are, therefore, responsible for the majority of your perceptions. They were first coined by Jean Piaget, a developmental psychologist, back in 1923. There are plenty of examples to consider, most of which come in the form of stereotypes. A really basic example comes in the form of a child and their perception of a cat.

The child is living at home and frequently sees the four legs and the fur and thinks, *Yes, this is a cat.*

This perception of what a cat is is that child's *cat* schema. When the child then goes to a zoo and sees a lion, the associated cat schema is activated. Sure, both cats and lions have a lot in common, but a house cat doesn't roar, hunt wild food, and has a different body size. Once the differences have been made, the child will develop a *lion* schema to sit alongside the *cat* schema.

Schemas are created within us to hold our perceptions of the world—to give us an understanding of the world around us. These schemas can include anything from objects, social situations, and events to people, their perspectives of themselves, and their roles in life (such as within a family, a relationship, and a place of work). Others' roles and expectations are also considered, such as a schema that says waiters in a restaurant will be warm, friendly, and welcoming.

These schemas that are created based on how we view the world can be formed at any time, but—and this is the most important point—they can also be modified at any time, just as the child's cat schema was modified when they learned about the lion for the first time. With this in mind, there are two main ways a schema can be formed:

1. A schema can be created with the introduction of new information, thus being able to perceive something new with new clarity and understanding.
2. A new schema can be created by adjusting an old schema based on new information received, or by creating a brand new one because the new information doesn't fit an existing schema.

Let's say you're talking to a friend about political parties, and you want to vote left, and they want to vote right. You both have different experiences within your lives and varying political opinions. This means your political schemas are different. If you can change someone's schema, then you'll be able to change their mind, thus persuading them to be able to vote in a different way.

The real question is, how do you trigger this process of developing or adjusting a schema, whether altering one or creating a new one entirely? The answer lies in priming.

## An Introduction to Priming

Priming is a term that simply describes the process of activating a schema. When the child saw the lion, their cat schema was activated and brought from their subconsciousness into their consciousness for thought to take place. Take a moment to think about your bank account and your current financial status. You could be financially secure, or you may be in debt. You have schemas about both ways of living, and me asking you to think about it brought whichever schema is relevant to you to the front of your mind.

You may have also thought about being very wealthy or very in debt, both of which you also have a schema for. The statement of me asking you to think about your bank account is an example of priming. But what's the purpose of priming? Well, interestingly, it affects your behavior. Dramatically.

A popular study carried out by Bargh, Chen, and Burrows (1996) showed people relating various words to elderly people, such as "wise," "Bingo," "retired," etc. The study found that people who had been primed with elderly-related words then walked slower after they had been primed with said words, much in the way that elderly people do.

Simply putting the words in someone's mind was enough to change their behavior in a way that related to the words spoken. Spooky, right?

Another study published in *Aging and Mental Health* found that priming people with negatively orientated words and stereotypes negatively affected the individuals who were being primed with the words. This included effects such as increased attempts to seek help and increased loneliness.

This means that if you give someone the mental image of a lonely and fragile elderly person using the words you say, this can make people feel lonelier and more fragile. You're changing someone's behavior and mindset using only your words.

You've perhaps witnessed this in your own life. When someone mentions running water or food, you may feel the need to go to the toilet or feel hungry. The actions, words, and situations around you are priming you and your behavior. When you think about life in this way, you realize the human mind is quite simple in many ways. It's just looking for patterns in its immediate environment.

This is very common in people who have PTSD. American military vets can feel startled, their bodies physically going into shock when they hear loud bangs that resemble the sounds of gunshots and explosions from their tours in service.

When it comes to mastering the art of persuasion, you must learn about how effective priming is in the way you speak. For example, if you're persuading a client to buy into your web development package, you may talk about Facebook, Twitter, or other successful websites related to your client's niche that will prime their schemas into thinking about successful websites and then relating this thought pattern with you and your pitch.

However, we have one more stop to think about that brings this all together.

## An Introduction to Spreading Activation

Spreading activation is a much more scientifically in-depth way of looking at persuasion, so I'm going to break it down as easily as possible. You have your brain. Your brain is physically made as a semantic network. It's like a spiderweb with lots of different sections and nodes that contain all the knowledge that you know. Each concept or thought or idea you know has its own individual node. Think of it like a spider's web full of raindrops, each raindrop being a node.

If I say "pets," all the nodes related to common pets related to you and your life experiences will light up. You might start thinking about cats, dogs, and hamsters. If you had some unusual pets, you might think about parrots or guinea pigs. If you grew up on a farm, you might think of pigs and cows being your pets. The point is, the priming words of "pets" lights up a node in your brain, and what lights up per priming term will be different, depending on who you are and your own life experiences.

When you think of certain pets, this inevitably lights up other parts of your mind and other related nodes, and this process is known as spreading activation, as coined by Collins and Loftus in 1975. A simple example of this could be the term "color."

You start thinking about colors: blue, green, yellow, red, etc. With red, you may then think of fire, roses, flowers, fire engines, trucks, cars, city roads, and so on. Simply from the color red, this whole network of nodes has lit up. A stream of thought is created from just a single concept. But you're probably wondering, why is this important when it comes to persuasion?

If we'd been having a conversation, and we've been talking about sunsets and flowers and fires and roses, your mind could be very primed. If I asked you to pick a color, you're more than likely going to pick red because of the previous topics of conversation.

This is mind control at its core. It may seem limited for now, but with practice and experience, this can go a long way and create some powerful effects.

This approach also works as a popular children's game where they can guess what you're thinking.

Think of a type of juice. Think of a fruit. Think of a color. Now think of a vegetable. Were you thinking carrot? It's a really simple technique, but once you've mastered it on a basic level, you can start doing some incredible things with it. While this works for kids, it may take a little more to work on adults.

## A Strategy for Persuasion Using Mind Control

This kind of persuasive influence is very common among magicians. Performers will drop subtle words into a conversation that will then influence their audience to think in a certain way, usually towards a word that they wrote down as a prediction before the show even started. The audience member was always going to pick that word because the magician persuaded them through subtle clues to choose it.

When using this approach in your conversations and interactions with people, you have a lot of options to think about. Firstly, you need to think about priming the person. Let's say someone is having a bad day. They're in a bad mood, a family member or pet has passed away, or they feel like they're about to lose their job. Your goal is trying to sell them your idea for a business you have.

Trying to communicate with them about something so positive and inspiring during the negative time they're having is the worst idea because they're going to associate the meeting and conversation you have with the dark and depressing feelings they had that day. On the other hand, talking to them about such a positive idea when they're in a good mood will connect the dots in their mind of your idea being a good thing, thus making it far more likely they're going to get involved. And this is simply through choosing the right time to talk.

If you're taking into account everything we spoke about in the previous chapter about making friends and building relationships with people, then you're going to know when the best times for approaching a person is. I've spoken a lot about the art of persuading is all about sending a message, and you're always going to want to send that message in the best possible way and at the best possible time for the best possible reception.

When you've decided there's an appropriate time to talk, focus on which schema(s) you're going to bring up. Going back to the example that you have a business idea you want to share with someone, you could talk about new beginnings and getting involved in new projects. You could talk about how starting a new chapter in life can lead to great things. Perhaps drop in a story of how you or someone you know is starting a new chapter in their life.

Just using these terms is priming the person you're speaking to, to start thinking about new chapters and new beginnings. Thanks to spreading activation, this will activate other nodes. Keep listening closely to what the other person is talking about, because you'll be able to get a glimpse into what these other nodes are, ultimately providing you with more information about which direction you can prime in.

Let's say you've spoken about new beginnings and trying new things, and you know the person is in a good mood. You may start speaking about the concept of hard work and how rewarding it is to put your all into a project. It's such a good feeling, right?

In this part of the persuasion process, you should never lie to get what you want or push the conversation in a direction that isn't true, and unless you're pro at mastering communication, your body language and the way you're speaking is going to give you away, even if that's on an unconscious level. Always stick to the truth, be genuine, and focus on developing true and honest relationships.

After several conversations (depending on what you're trying to achieve), you can start introducing the idea you're trying to influence that person on; in this case, your business idea. They'll be so primed at this point, they'll be open to the idea that you won't have to do much else.

## The Mind Control Art of NLP

There's no way I could write a chapter on controlling the mind without mentioning a communication technique known as NLP. NLP, or Neuro-Linguistic Programming, is known as a psychological technique for controlling the minds of other people, although the reality is that the practice isn't that ominous. It is revered by many to have destructive potential in the wrong hands due to just how powerful it really is, but mainly it can be used to bring so much good into the world.

The majority of people who use it are therapists, counsellors, and psychologists who treat patients who suffer from traumas, PTSD, stress, low confidence, low self-esteem, etc. NLP has been used in various situations and environments, although the studies have been small in scale and produced varied results.

For example, paying attention to someone and their body language (more of which I'll speak about in the next chapter) can reveal a lot of what they're thinking about. If you ask someone to think of their house and they look up to the top right or left corner of their eye, this means they're thinking of their house visually. By noticing this kind of body language, you can then continue the conversation in a visual way that will make what you're saying more appealing.

Using techniques like this, you're able to form a connection with the person you're speaking to because you'll be highlighting what resonates in what you say and what doesn't, and then furthering the conversation in the same best possible way.

NLP is also not just about listening but always about focusing on how you craft your message. Can you see or feel about the following questions,

- Let's go and have another drink.
- Do you want another drink?

Of course, the latter is a question, which means you've enabled the person you're talking with to have a choice in the matter, unlike the first statement. Not only are you giving the illusion that the other person is in control because you're not going to ask if you don't want one, but you're using words like "want." The other person is now thinking, *Hmmm, I want a drink,* and the brain interprets this by saying, "Yes, I want a drink."

If you were with a client and wanted them to have a good time and think about an offer while you were drinking, this is how you could easily persuade them to have another drink. Another fantastic example of this is when a waiter comes over and asks, "What would you like to start with?" which instantly gets you to look over at the menu. It's all about the wording and the image this creates in the person's mind.

The waiter asks what you're starting with, your brain asks the same question and starts looking at the menu and looking for food options. It's simple mind control, but it's mind control nonetheless. Let's take it a step further.

Look at these two sentences:

- My son is very good at his job, but he's not great at turning up on time.
- My son is not great at turning up on time, but he's very good at his job.

How you create a sentence using the word "but" as the foundation massively changes how the sentence sounds and is received. Even changing your wording in such a way can make a huge difference in someone's perspective towards something. In this case, the father could be trying to get his son a job in which the second sentence would be the obvious choice for the most positive results.

In the same way, there are plenty of other ways you can use NLP techniques to bring yourself closer to the person you're speaking with, ultimately giving you the connection that can help you persuade and influence them just that little bit more.

## Control the Tempo of Your Voice

Mimicking the beat of the human heart with the tempo of your voice is a very common NLP technique that helps you connect. This is known as talking to the "suggestive frequency of the human mind." The average human heart tends to beat between 50 and 80 beats per minute, so aim for this. However, if you're in a particularly calm situation, you may want to be slower. Think soothing a child to help them sleep kind of slow.

On the other hand, if you're in a tense situation where heart rates are high, speaking quickly and powerfully could be the best way to communicate and deliver the best results.

## Use Hot Words

Using hot words, or buzzwords, refers to visual trigger words that NLP professionals will use to get their subjects into a more susceptible mindset. When you say phrases such as hear this, see this, feel free, now, because, and smell that, you're instantly tapping into a particular sense, thus putting your subject's mind into a state where that sense is going to be at the forefront.

This is a powerful way to help you send a message.

It's worth bearing in mind that NLP is a route you can take, and there is lots to learn. To master the profession will require a lot of training and practice, so it's well worth looking into a course of sorts if it's something that interests you. When it comes to the art of persuasion, however, there are other simpler methods and practices you can use, one of the most important of which we're going to be talking about in the next chapter.

Communication Skills Training Series

# Chapter Six – Mastering the Art of Body Language

*"If you want to find the truth, do not listen to the words coming to you. Rather see the body language of the speaker. It speaks the fact not audible."* – Bhavesh Chhatbar

We've already covered body language a lot in the previous chapters, and that's because it's such an important point. Phew, I can hear you thinking, *It's about time!* You've probably heard of the saying that 90% of all communication is non-verbal and body language, and while that urban myth is a little extreme, the actual number is around 58%. When you consider verbal communication around 38%, you still see how important body language is when communicating a message.

Okay, making that a bit more realistic, if you're trying to get a job at a new business and you've gone into the interview, how do you think you should present yourself? If you're slouched back in the chair with your arms folded while staring at the employer, it doesn't matter what answers you give or what experience you have, you're not going to get the job.

Body language is big business. It says so much. Whether you're reading books and articles on relationships, sales, marketing, or self-help, there will be sections and chapters dedicated to body language. The point is, your body language is sending out a message to everyone around you, and it works both ways. The body language of those around you is telling you messages about them if you know what to look for and how to read the signs.

Every facial expression, every movement of the body, and every position of your hands is telling people what's going on. If you're sitting closed up and reserved and biting your nails while avoiding eye contact, you're giving away the impression you're nervous and on edge. If you walk into a room big and broad, making eye contact and smiling at everyone you pass, you give the impression you're completely at ease.

This extends into the tone and volume of your voice, the way you're standing, the amount of eye contact you give each person, and your overall posture. When you control your body language and read the body language of others, this puts you in a prime position to influence others effectively.

When it comes to body language, there's a vast library of information out there to explore, but when specifically focusing on persuading and influencing people, there's one key aspect you'll want to be thinking about known as **embodied cognition**.

Embodied cognition is all about defining the link between the mind and the body, exploring how the two are connected, and how one influences the other. It is how your mind controls the body, in all the ways you would expect, but also how the body controls the mind in the opposite direction. Think about how leaning your elbow on a desk with your head in your hand acts as and signifies that you're bored. Even when you're not bored, doing this action can make you feel bored, thus triggering a mental, and ultimately physical, response.

This appears throughout our lives. Making a fist is associated with being violent, aggressive, and assertive. Writing down negative thoughts you have about yourself can solidify them in your mind if you write them down in your dominant hand, but can oppositely affect you less if you write them with your non-dominant hand. This is the power of embodied cognition.

So, how to use this to influence?

In 1988, Strack, Martin, and Stepper conducted a study where they asked two groups of people to hold pens in their mouths. One group was asked to hold the pen in their lips, while the other was asked to bite on it. Both groups then looked through cartoon sketches and rated how funny they were. The group who were asked to bite the pens, thus putting their mouths into a natural smiling position, found the cartoons most amusing.

This is an effect known as the Facial Feedback Hypothesis. Robert Zajonc researched this theory back in 1989 and found that the body language we make can physically trigger biological responses within our bodies. You know when you're feeling sad, and people say fake a smile because it will make you feel better—the fake it 'til you make it kind of an attitude? That's what he discovered.

Within his research, he asked German students to repeat vowel sounds (a, e, i, o, u) and found that when students said "e" and "ah," it made them make smiling expressions. Try it for yourself now. On a biological level, making these expressions cooled the blood in the students' arteries, therefore lowering the brain temperature and making the students' experience a more pleasant mood.

On the other hand, he found that making the "u" sound caused a frowning expression, which caused the opposite effects. The frown raised brain temperature and decreased blood flow, causing a more negative-slanting mood. This effect can work when you use body language on yourself and others.

## Applying Body Language as a Persuasive Strategy

Imagine you're talking to me about a hobby you enjoy. It could be sports, food, travel, lifestyle, or anything you want. You're telling me the details of your passion and describing above average detail. As you speak, I'm nodding my head. What do you feel? What is my body language communicating to you?

Since in the vast majority of cultures the act of "head-nodding" is a sign of agreement and open-mindedness if I nod my head at what you're saying indicates that I'm on the same page as you. I'm listening. I understand. I'm following. I want you to carry on. My act of head nodding is a non-verbal cue that tells you all of this subconsciously without me saying a word.

Take control of this act to send a message. When you're speaking to someone, and you're going to ask someone to do something, for a favor, or you're wanting to influence them with information, start bringing head nodding into your conversation. Since this has such a strong tie with the concept of agreement and understanding, you're encouraging a more agreeable statement of mind.

So, once you've made a request or shared information with someone, how can you make them agree? How can you bring the head-nodding action out of someone else? Simple. You use more body language.

When you're speaking to someone, there are naturally going to be points in any conversation where someone will acknowledge what the other person is saying. Verbally, this will sound like someone saying "uh-huh" or "yes," showing their agreement. That's the verbal parallel to a head nod. However, to trigger these acknowledgment cues, you need to create these natural pauses.

Using body language, you can do this by physically pausing what you're saying for a minute, but not too long because you don't want to disrupt the flow and momentum of what you're saying. Alternatively, you can raise your eyebrows, another non-verbal cue that you're looking for acknowledgment. This all happens within a second or so and happens so subconsciously that nobody is going to notice you doing it.

When you're in a conversation with someone, as you're building up to your request, start implementing these non-verbal cues into your body language to prime the person's mind into an agreement. Once they've agreed several times, you then share your request, and the person is far more likely to agree, which will be showcased as a visual head nod response.

## Other Body Language Cues

In truth, every aspect of body language is saying something, but being aware of the core body language attributes, you can start to control them, thus controlling the message you're sending out to the world and the people around you. Remember what we said earlier about someone being defeated? What do you imagine? Someone bent or hunched over, the weight of the world on their back. This is the physical representation of someone being defeated.

Hand in hand with the persuasive head nodding and pausing cues above, let's take a moment to explore other body language cues that send a message. With awareness of these cues, you can control them how you wish, ultimately sending the message you want to send.

## The Power of Posture

Posture is such a massive message sending form of body language. When someone walks into a room with their head held high, their body exposed, and their back straight, they ooze power and status wherever they go. People instantly respect people in this way because they are exposing themselves in a way that shows no fear. It shows confidence and authority. This person is meant to be here, and they feel comfortable doing it.

On the other hand, a slumped position, hunched over, or hiding certain parts of your body, such as your hands or chest, sends the impression you're anxious or nervous. Try it now, and you'll see the effect on yourself. Sit up straight, push your shoulders down, and hold your head high. Feels powerful, right?

Now slump your back, and hold your hands in your lap, hiding them between your legs. Look at the ground and never above the horizon. Feels weak and defeated, right? Even moving and positioning yourself in this way is having an effect on you and how you feel, and you're aware you're doing it, so now imagine what kind of subconscious messages you're sending out to those around you.

When applied to a conversation where you're trying to persuade someone, use your posture accordingly. If you're trying to convey authority to get somebody to listen to you, hold a high position that presents power and confidence. Likewise, when you strike this posture, you may see the other person physically backing down and slumping, which means they're feeling anxious and defeated in your presence.

When influencing someone, you don't want them to shut down completely, but instead respect what you're saying, so you don't want to go all the way. Just find the balance with each person you're speaking to on an individual level. On the other hand, you may want to empower and make someone feel good about themselves, in which case slumping back yourself may be the sign they need to feel powerful and believe in themselves.

It's all about finding what works in any given situation, depending on the outcome you want to achieve.

## The Message Sent With the Eyes

We all know that eye contact is an important part of communication, and if you're speaking to someone who's looking everywhere else but at you, this sends the message that they're not there with you. Of course, depending on the circumstances of the individual situation, this can mean different things.

It could indicate boredom or distraction, or they may be shy or nervous about speaking with you. Aligned with this, where you're looking with your eyes as you converse will say a lot about you, but always on an unconscious level. Watch any street magician on YouTube, David Blaine being a prime example.

Watch how he always maintains eye contact with the people he's performing too. He directs such a strong and powerful message and influences the people he's performing because he maintains such a strong connection with his eyes.

A long story short; eye contact is direct and connecting, and powerful for sending a message. Eye contact makes people listen, feel included, and feel a part of a conversation. A lack of eye contact creates the opposite effect. How can you apply this knowledge in your conversations? Well, think about the macro of your speech.

When you're thinking about what you're saying, chances are you tend to look away. Everybody does. When you're umming and ahhing, you'll look to the side or at your feet while trying to find the words to say. This breaking of eye contact detracts from your message, and it ultimately has much less impact and power.

If, however, you take a moment to think about what you're saying before you speak, and then share your message while making full eye contact, then your message will retain its full power and impact. As the saying goes, always think before you speak. Eye contact also increases the perception of trust, whereas speaking without contact can seem suspicious and deceitful, so bear these in mind.

## Exposure of Your Chest

This may seem like a strange point to consider, because I'm not talking about undoing the buttons of your shirt and exposing your chest in the literal sense, but more in the sense that your chest and how open it is is a clear body language sign that details how vulnerable someone is, and a whole lot more than that.

When I was a child, I used to play cops and robbers with my friends. I would always play the robber because my friend has a proper kids-play police outfit, and he would always run around the big tree in the back garden and shout, "Put your hands up!"

Of course, as anybody would and still do, even in real-time situations, people raise their hands and expose their chest, but what message is this sending? Well, think of it in the opposite manner. When you cross your hands in front of your chest or hold something up against it, what message are you sending now?

In most cultures and societies around the world, crossed arms and covering your chest is a sign of self-defense. If I stand up and give a speech in a meeting and sit back down and cross my arms, I'm negating any chance for people to ask questions. When someone is sat with their arms crossed, they're defensive and protecting themselves from external harm.

Use this information wisely. If you need a favor from someone, when's the best time to ask? When they are open and free to do something, or when they have something in their hands, and their arms are crossed? Clearly, the first option is best. If you can get your timing right, you'll see far more success with your persuasion efforts.

## Cutting Off Your Message Before It's Over

Have you ever watched an advertisement and it seems to glitch right at the end? Like it gets cut off abruptly, only by a second or so, but it feels blunt and unfinished? This is actually a psychological tactic to help people remember what you previously said, far more effectively than if you carried on.

If you head over to YouTube, hit the Music channel, and listen to any song for several seconds and then close the tab, you're going to remember that song for the rest of the day. Guaranteed. It's because you heard a snippet of information, and your brain is thinking, *Okay, well now I want to know more*. It feels unfinished, and the mind is eager to fill in the gaps, thus holding onto everything else that has been said before.

Oppositely, if someone is talking to you sentence after sentence, and they're just going on and on and repeating the same points, you're going to get bored, switch off, and forget everything.

Applying this tactic to your own conversation, if you're detailing points to someone, share your first point, and your second point, and then it looks like you're going to share a third point, but don't. See how it makes you...

Exactly. Stopping yourself in this way abruptly stops the flow, which engages the mind in such a way that it cements the information. Of course, I'm not saying be rude with what you're saying and just stop mid-sentence and walk off, but instead use body language cues, like opening your mouth, to fake continuing. This is a fantastic tactic when you want someone to remember what you're saying.

## Gestures and Hand Movements

Hand gestures are known for being able to communicate so much in such small actions. If I wave, I'm saying hello or goodbye. A more energetic version of this movement would be to try and grab your attention. If I raise my hands horizontally, palms facing down, and pat the air, I'm telling you to be quiet and settle down.

This is all basic stuff, but it's still a very important form of body language, so we have to cover it. Let's go through this rapidly. As you read through, try mimicking the gestures to see how they make you feel, what they look like to do, and then imprinting them so you can see them in other people.

- **Touch**

While I don't recommend touching everyone you meet, touching in some ways is a very powerful way to connect with other people. Even just a touch on someone's arm or shoulder can connect you to them, and it displays signs of comfort, warmth, and connection.

Be careful with how you touch people, though. If you touch with just your fingertips, this can make people very uncomfortable, and it shows you're nervous but trying to hide it. When you agree with someone, placing a firm hand on their shoulder can amplify your acknowledgments.

When touching or being touched by someone, you can also tell their state of mind and being by the temperature of their hands. Warm hands mean they are comfortable and positive, whereas cold hands may indicate tenseness and anxiety, but of course, the temperature of the room can play a big part in this.

- **Hand on Heart**

If you want to invoke feelings of trust in another person, placing your hand on your heart is a great way to do so. Hence the saying "hand on my heart," which means you can trust me or insinuates you are saying, "I promise." It means, "Believe what I'm saying or accept what I'm telling you."

- **Pointing**

Pointing can mean a lot of things. If I point at you during a conversation, it's a very imposing and authoritative gesture. Teachers and parents will point at their children when telling them off, almost as though it's directing the words of discipline they're saying directly at the children and their being.

This gesture amplifies your ability to talk down to someone and is often interpreted as angry, aggressive, and even violent. If you jab your finger, a more vigorous point, this is deemed very aggressive. As a whole, pointing is deemed impolite by most people and cultures.

However, depending on the situation, if you point with a wink or in a playful way, it can be a very empowering gesture to the person being pointed at. They can feel acknowledged and recognized, like saying, "You're the man!" when they've done a good job. It's all about the body language that accompanies the point and the context of the conversation.

- **Palms Up**

Just like exposing your chest, palms facing up is usually a very positive sign that means openness, readiness, and trustworthiness. Opening your entire arms up with upward-facing palms can be empowering and enlightening, but you can also say you don't know by shrugging your shoulders with your hands up.

However, this isn't a sign of weakness, but more a sign saying, "I don't know, but I'm comfortable enough, confident enough, and ready enough to admit that."

- **Palms Down**

With your palms facing down, you're saying you believe in what you're saying, and you're confident with your stand. This may be viewed with authority and trust, but it can also mean defiance, as though saying, "I'm not going to budge, and you can't change my mind."

- **Hands on Hips**

While there is a common idea that placing your hands on your hips can be a sign that you're unready to partake in something, or sometimes even frustration or irritated, it is much more commonly a sign that someone is ready to take action. That's why you'll see it all the time in athletes and work-lovers.

Sure, you will also see it in authority figures, such as police, military generals, and others in charge as a way of displaying assertiveness, but this still shows the individual is ready to take action.

- **Fists**

A very powerful gesture, a clenched fist is all about resolution and determination. It can be seen as violent, depending on the context of a situation, but mainly showcases an unwillingness to back down. Think about when a sports team scores and the fans will raise their fists in triumph, not unlike when a business secures a big contract after fighting for it for a long time.

If someone has made a fist with their thumb hidden in their hands, this can be a sign of anxiousness, as though the person is hardening themselves for what is to come.

- **Hand Chops**

When someone chops their hands through the air, it's a power move saying, "This is what I'm saying. I've made up my mind. Nobody can change that." It's a very definitive and authoritative move. You'll see politicians and CEOs using this gesture a lot.

- **Hands Rubbing Together**

This is a gesture that represents excitement for the future, reward, and happy times ahead. When someone places a large bet on odds that are massively stacked in their favor, this is the hand gesture that comes to mind. It's all about channeling the stress and excitement that comes from an upcoming positive situation, as well as preparing themselves for it.

- **Hands in Pockets**

Hands in pockets is usually a powerful sign that there is a reluctance to do something or an unwillingness to proceed. If you're talking to someone and they put their hands in their pockets, this shows you've lost their interest, or their mind is elsewhere.

This can also be a sign that someone is hiding the truth since hand signals can give away the truth, and they're hiding the ability to show this.

- **Hands Behind Back**

As we spoke about with regard to exposing your chest and keeping it open, placing your hands behind your back is a sign of confidence and comfort. Of course, it's always more trustworthy to show your hands in a situation, but if the level of trust is already there, perhaps if you're around colleagues, friends, and family members, then you may not need to do this.

Even if you're with strangers, having your hands behind your back can showcase signs of confidence and comfort. You're saying, "Here I am, and I am vulnerable," but in a controlled sense.

- **Steepling**

Steepling is the term given to an individual who places their fingertips together without their palms touching. This is a massive display of power, which is why you see it with evil villains in movies, chess players who are contemplating moves, or lawyers. This move is all about confidence, especially self-confidence and assurance in the future.

If you saw someone doing this in a board meeting, you can read that they truly believe they know what you're doing, and they've got some powerful information related to what's being said.

- **Squeezing or Clasping Hands Together**

When someone squeezes their hands together, either their entire hand or their fingers, this is a sign that someone is uncomfortable, nervous, or anxious about the situation they're in. This move is all about self-settling and trying to ground themselves. It's like a comfort gesture people give to themselves to try and make themselves feel better.

Sometimes people will rub their wrists, and this is the same sign. When you spot this in someone or yourself, you may need to comfort that person, empower them, or there's an opportunity to find out what's going on.

## Reading the Body Language of Others

While there is a whole range of benefits that come with controlling your own body language in any given situation, remember, it's not all about controlling your own language, but also reading the language of others. Let's take a trip back in time to the previous chapter, where we were talking about making friends with people. You're talking to a stranger and have just started a conversation, perhaps over the water cooler at the office.

The individual is talking and making a lot of eye contact, they're making wild hand gestures as they speak, and their chest is open, almost inviting you in. What is this body language communicating? It's saying, *I'm happy in this conversation. I'm engaged. I'm connected to you.* This is a conversation I'm enjoying being a part of.

This shows you that the person is probably in a positive mood, having a good day, and is more likely to be agreeable and open with what you're saying. If you needed to ask a favor, this is a good person to engage with.

On the other hand, if someone is leaning against the water cooler and not looking at anyone, is blunt with their responses, and has their arms crossed, this says the complete opposite to the example above. Use this information wisely when choosing how to approach a situation and deal with certain people, finally allowing you to determine the best approach to influencing someone.

## Mirroring Someone's Body Language

You may have already heard about mirroring the body language of others and the power that comes with that, but there's a fine line when it comes to using the art of mirroring properly. If you mirror someone exactly, movement to movement, this is just plainly obvious, and it's going to make the other person feel uncomfortable.

However, mirroring in the right way, with just the right amount of mirroring, you can connect far deeper than you normally would with even a complete stranger. This has been proven in endless studies, including Val Barren 2003, where waitresses made higher tips, and in Gueguen, Martin, and Meineri in 2011, where students convinced other students to write their essays for them.

Mirroring is a fantastic way to persuade someone and influence them to do something because it makes the other person feel way more at ease and connected. Because they're already doing the body movements and gestures and now, you're doing them on a subconscious level, they believe that everything is being acknowledged and accepted, providing complete comfort and a state of mind, which is much more agreeable.

There are four main steps you can follow if you want to mirror someone properly.

## Step One

Start by fronting the person you're speaking with, which means being with them and giving them your full attention. Put them in front of you and make them everything to you at that moment. Give them full eye contact and nod when they speak. Roughly, nod three times when agreeing to really drive home your acknowledgment.

You can boost this further with a bit of imagination. For a moment while they're speaking, pretend they are the most important person in the world, even just for a second or two, and then stop pretending and return to giving them your full attention. Even in these few seconds, you'll send all the non-verbal cues that make them feel like, to you, nothing else but them matters.

**Step Two**

Start mirroring their actions. If they sit back in their chair and slump, wait a few seconds and do the same. If the other person starts speaking faster or louder, slower and quieter, then do the same. The two main things to remember here is matching their pace and their volume.

**Step Three**

Find their punctuator. A punctuator is the non-verbal cue or tell which the person will do every time they make a point and display the tell to clarify that point. A common one is tipping their head forwards and perhaps raising an eyebrow. Another common one is using a hand gesture, like the chopping or pointing we spoke about above.

Find the punctuator and start mirroring it!

**Step Four**

Okay, at this point, you and the person you're speaking to should already feel a strong connection, and they should already be in an agreeable state of mind, which makes this step optional, but if you really want to see how strong the connection is, then test it for yourself.

The easiest way to do this is to take any action that is unrelated to the conversation so far and then see if they mirror it back. If you've gone out for a drink, you may take a sip, or even just move your glass randomly to another nearby point on the table. If they mirror and do the same, you know your connection is strong!

One final point to remember is to ensure you're only mirroring the positive actions and cues the person is giving you. If someone picks up their phone, or is distracted and looks away, or sits with their arms folded with their chest closed off, don't mirror these actions. Instead, remain patient, keep mirroring the positives, and you'll see the connection forming.

When it comes to body language aligned with the art of persuasion, changing the way you act and stand isn't going to be the be-all and end-all strategy that will influence people to do what you want while controlling their behavior.

However, when applied alongside the other strategies in this book, and when it comes to reading the situation and person and defining what approach you're going to take, the body language strategies you've learned here are invaluable. This applies in both individual and group settings, the latter of which we're going to explore in the following chapter.

# Chapter Seven – The Power of Social Pressure

*"As much as people refuse to believe it, the company you keep does have an impact and influence on your choices."*
– Unknown.

It doesn't matter what book, article, or video you watch on persuasion—social pressure is always going to be a part of it. It's nearly the most important form of persuasion, as well as being one of the most powerful. You'll be absolutely amazed at the ways that social pressure can affect and influence the behavior of an individual.

Think about how children are subject to social pressure, in particular, peer pressure, throughout their lives. If a teenager is hanging out with a group of teenagers who are all smoking, even if the teenager in question is against smoking, if offered a cigarette when everyone else is doing it, then they're more likely to do it.

This effect follows everyone throughout their entire lives, from the time they are children to the day they die. Social pressure is enormous, and it's vital for you to understand the power it has.

Within the sections of this chapter, we're going to explore the intricacies of social pressure, allowing you to understand the psychology of this theory, and then how to control this pressure and weave it such a way that you can begin to influence and persuade people on different levels and with varying intensities.

## Real-Life Examples of Social Pressure

You can see examples of social pressure in everyday life. From children in school, like the example we spoke about above, to football fans rioting together due to mob mentality, social pressure is everywhere. A really fantastic example of this was showcased in a television series by a hypnotist and psychological illusionist Derren Brown.

In his Apocalypse series, he was scouting for people who were susceptible enough to be hypnotized and placed through the challenges. During the vetting part of the series, he hired a room with ten chairs, in which people would come, sit down, and fill out their application form. The first two chairs had hired actors who were always there filling out the forms.

Members of the public started to walk in, sit down, and fill out their forms. Every few minutes, a bell would ding, and the two hired actors would stand until the next bell, in which they would sit back down. Members of the public were given no such instruction, but it was amazing to see that some people would stand up with the bell and the other people, but others wouldn't.

Remember, the members of the public were not given any instructions. They were simply standing up with the hired actors because social pressure told them to. They wanted to fit in and not feel as though they would be left out or were doing something wrong, perhaps because they were at fault and had missed the instructions given to them to stand.

This shows a radical change in behavior (i.e., people doing what they wouldn't normally do, simply because other people are doing it). This is reflected in all forms and cultures throughout the societies of the world, which is what makes it so powerful.

It is reflected in our societal norms, such as you need to be in a relationship to be happy. Money is a key to freedom. If you don't have lots of friends, you won't be happy. You need to be on social media. Makeup and fashion make you confident and feel good about yourself.

On a personal level, if you're in school and everyone in your class is going to college, the chances are you're going to sign up and enroll at college, too, even if it's something that you don't really want to do. To a degree, your music tastes, fashion sense, the drugs you do or don't take, and your attitude and perception you have on the world will all be dictated by the people you hang around with.

If you and your friends listen to hardcore techno music as teenagers, and you one day picked your friend up in your car while listening to Justin Bieber, you're probably going to get belittled and flamed because you're going against the social pressures set by your friend group.

There's a very fine line between doing the things you do in life because you want to do them and because it's part of the societal pressures you've been conditioned to follow, whether that's on a national basis or an individual level.

The question is, why is this social pressure so powerful?

## The Science Behind Social Pressure

Social pressure is a type of influence known as "normative" influence. This is the influence where people conform to the environment they're in. Even if you're not religious and you have never been in a mosque in your life, if you were to visit one, you would take your shoes off at the door because you see everyone else is doing so. This is normative social influence at play.

This form of influence works so well because it's ingrained into your instinct, your genetics, and your millions-of-years-old brain. It's a survival tool that is the basics of what makes us humans and is responsible for how the human race got to where it is today.

Rewind back to caveman times. You're wandering around the forests or the mountains on your own. How likely are you to survive? Back then, your chances are basically zero. You'd need to do everything yourself to survive, like finding water and building camp and hunting food. If you were sick or injured, or you simply didn't have enough time to get everything done, you would die.

On the other hand, if there was a group of ten humans working together, the workload was spread out, and even if you were injured, you could be looked after until you felt better and then your chances of survival, and not just for you but for everyone in that group, is dramatically higher.

Therefore, in order for the group dynamic to work, every person in the group conforms to unwritten social standards. Everybody then feels like part of the pack and part of the group, and to differ from that image or unwritten agreement, literally as your mind is telling you, would mean death.

Nowadays, it is possible to survive on your own with very few people around you. If you had money and didn't have to work, you could live on your own and never venture outside, and you would physically survive. I wouldn't recommend it because you'd be very lonely and would probably go crazy, but it's possible. Being a part of a group in the modern world isn't a matter of life or death, although our minds still believe it is.

Since this is the case, there's no doubt we are evolving in this new age, but these changes will take millions of years to settle in, and won't take place in our lifetime. Instead, we need to deal with the fact that conforming to social pressure is hardwired into each and every one of us.

This science of social pressure affects you in every aspect of your life. Obviously, it affects your family life and your personal relationships, but it also extends to your friend groups, offices, neighborhoods, towns, and communities. It's essential in a sense because without social pressures, the communities we live in would break down and crumble.

Social pressure has been scientifically proven over and over again, but it all started back in 1951 when social psychology researcher Solomon Asch tested this for himself. In his study, he showed people a 10 cm line labelled A on one side, and then three lines of varying sizes on the other. The three lines were 1 cm, 10 cm, and 4 cm, and labelled A, B, and C.

In the study, the lines were positioned in front of a line of ten chairs, where people sat down and were asked which line on the right-hand side was most similar to the line on the left. Of course, the answer was B. However, people were asked from left to right in the line of chairs what they thought the answer was.

Let's say you're sitting in chair seven, and you're thinking, *Of course the answer is B,* but when they start asking the people in the line, and they're answering C, you start doubting yourself. The first person answers C, and the second does, and so on, and you're left thinking, *Oh God, do they see something I don't? I don't want to be left out or the odd one out.* With this line of thinking, you cave, and despite knowing the real answer is B, you conform and state C as your answer, just like everyone else.

In this study, people were persuaded and influenced time and time again to say C, even though it's so painfully obvious the answer was B.

## Harnessing the Power of Social Pressure to Persuade and Influence

As you can see from how social pressure works and how deeply ingrained it is in our being, it's an incredibly powerful tool. As someone who wants to persuade and influence people, harnessing the power of social pressure is going to be the biggest tool in your arsenal. The trick here is to trigger the social pressure response when requesting something or influencing someone, thus achieving the result you want.

Before learning how to take control of this power and learning the triggers, you need to be aware that there are two main types of social pressure, known as informative and normative influence.

We've already explored normative influence, which is by far the most powerful type of influence out of the two. In Asch's experiment, this is normative influence because people don't want to be publicly seen as being different or abnormal. In a follow-up study, people were staggered upon entry to see the lines and were told to write their answers down privately.

Of course, everyone wrote down B because their answers were private and weren't discussed with others, but as we spoke about above, people will conform when they're afraid of being rejected by others. This is known as social rejection, which is the hardwiring our brains have to help keep human beings in groups.

In comparison, informative influence occurs in situations where there is no clear goal, answer, direction, or objective. In Derren Brown's bell interview, where you would normally believe that you go into a room, sit down, and fill out an application form, a new twist has been thrown into the mix, and you're left feeling like your original belief in the matter is now no longer relevant.

You distrust your own belief to sit still and simply fill out the form when others are standing up at the sound of the bell, and instead take on the beliefs and actions of others around you, taking their beliefs and opinions as truth and making them your own. Without a word being spoken and simply through the actions of a group, you've been persuaded to change your behavior and act in a different way.

## The Final Example (Darley & Latane 1968)

Okay, I've gone on and on about social pressure, so this is the last example I'm going to share. There are just so many examples of how social pressure is so powerful, and it even works in a way that can stop people from helping others, even when it's a matter of life or death. In the Darley & Latane 1968 study, they set up a simple experiment.

Participants would come into a room and talk about personal issues related to them. However, the conversations would take place over an intercom, so there was an anonymous feel to the experiment, and the participants would feel comfortable sharing information about their life. However, to help make the participants feel even more secure, the intercom would record the conversations, and the experimenters would listen to them back later.

You simply go into the room, speak into the intercom, one person at a time, and then when you're finished, you hand over the intercom to another person, and you move on, listening to the others and what they have to say from their own private room.

So, you're sitting there, and you start talking about personal issues, and one person admits that they had seizures in college, so it was a bit of a hard time for them. The conversation moves on, but suddenly out of nowhere, the person who told you they had seizures starts having one and starts pleading for help over the intercom.

What do you do?

Of course, like any sane human being, you would get up and leave the room, seeking out assistance to get medical help for the person on the other end of the intercom. In the study, when two people talked over the intercom, and the other started having a seizure, this is exactly what the participants did.

However, things changed dramatically when more people were added to the intercom discussions. When it was two people—one actor and one participant—when the actor had a seizure the participant went for help right away, but when there was more than one participant, the chances they would help dropped dramatically. The researchers actually only played the recordings of other participants, to make it seem like there were more people in the conversation, although there were still only ever two.

Turns out, when people believe there are just two people in a conversation, just them and their unknown actor, there was an 85% chance they would go for help when the actor was in danger. However, in a three-person conversation, this figure dropped to 62%, and in six people's conversations, just a measly 31%. The conclusion? People are more likely to sit and listen to someone die in group settings than get help than they would in one-to-one conversations.

How disturbing is that?

Okay, as disturbing as it may sound, there's perfectly logical explanations that again go back to how our minds work. It's all based on psychology, and by becoming aware of how it works, you can apply awareness to it in your own life, as well as taking advantage of how this psychology works.

The first psychological theory is known as diffusion of responsibility. When you're in a one-on-one situation, there are two people responsible—you and the other person. It's much easier to define who is in control and who is the authoritative person. In terms of the study, one person is healthy, and the other is having a seizure; therefore, it's common sense that the healthy individual is the one who gets help.

On the other hand, when you have a large group of people, responsibility for any given situation is diffused, and if there's no clear leader in charge, the responsibility gets lost on individuals. This is why when people collapse in the street, people will look on, but will very rarely help. It's not their responsibility. Therefore it's not on them to act. If you're a doctor or nurse, you'll probably act because you know you're the one who needs to take action.

There are cases where people have murdered in front of people in broad daylight in the middle of the street, yet the police were only called 45 minutes later, after the victim was already dead, because out of the dozens of bystanders who witnessed the event, they all assumed (falsely) that the emergency services had already been called.

The second force is known as the audience inhibition effect, and it refers to the fact that someone may not call the police because there's a momentary glimmer that the emergency may not be real, and they don't want to risk the embarrassment of calling the emergency services in case it was a mistake, and they look stupid in front of all the people around them.

Phew! That's a lot of data. With all this information to think about when it comes to social pressure, you should start understanding how powerful this psychological force is, and it should already be clear how you can start using social pressure to influence and affect the behaviours of others. It's all about being able to exert the right amount of pressure and just the right time.

## How to Apply Social Pressure When Influencing and Persuading Others

There are several ways you can apply social pressure to influence and persuade others, but you need to remember that social pressure will differ in a number of different circumstances. This includes the environment of where you are, how well everyone in the environment knows each other, how these people connect, and the social norms for the country or culture you're in.

Let's say you want to persuade someone in your office to come to the Christmas party. They don't really want to go, but you really want them to. What can you do?

One of the best ways to do this is by empathizing that attending the Christmas party is the "social norm" in your workplace. While you may not directly ask the person whether they want to come, you may talk about how exciting the idea of the party is with other people in your office who are going around them.

This will create the impression that everyone is going to the party, and everyone is looking forward to having a good time. In the mind of the person you're influencing, this is the image they'll see, thus making them feel more inclined to come. In this situation, there's also the psychological pressure of FOMO—Fear of Missing Out.

Human beings don't want to be left out of the best thing that's happened, because it makes them feel as though they've missed out on an amazing opportunity. I remember when I was in school, I had a root canal and took a week off. When I went back, I heard from all my friends that a big exciting fight happened (which is exciting when you're a kid, don't judge me) and a teacher retired, and they had a big party instead of normal lessons. This made me feel bad because I missed out, and nobody wants to feel that way.

By creating the impression that the norm in your environment is to do whatever you're trying to persuade someone to do, you're far more likely to convince that person. As I spoke about in the examples earlier in the chapter, when people are faced with group pressure, they're much more likely to conform simply because individuals don't want to be the odd one out.

Another example of a social norm you can play off is the tilt of reciprocity, or if I scratch your back, you'll scratch mine. When you do a favor for someone, this usually feels like the balance is tipped in your favor.

When you've done something for someone else, more often than not, when you want a favor, they're going to be the person you go to.

This is another form of social pressure that you can take advantage of. This works very well and is a very powerful method of persuasion because not following through on the favor dramatically increases the risk of social rejection, therefore being an outcast in the group.

For example, Bill and Andy are neighbors. Bill breaks his leg and is recovering at home, even though he has some jobs in the garden to do. He's talking with Andy over the fence one day, and Andy goes, "Don't worry, Bill. Your grass is growing long, but I'll cut it as a favor." Andy cuts the lawn, and Bill is happy with his garden.

Now, when Andy has something that he wants done, the chances that Bill is going to accept the favor are very high. If Bill says no to the favor, or any subsequent favors until the scales of reciprocity are balanced, how's that going to make Bill look in front of the neighborhood?

Andy will tell everyone how selfish Bill is, and when Bill really needed help, Andy was there to help, but when it was the other way around, Bill just made excuses and did his own thing. This is going to make Bill look very bad and will turn the neighborhood against him. He obviously doesn't want this, so conforms to Andy's favor, regardless of whether or not he wants to do it.

Now, it's worth noting that usually the scales will need to be balanced with equal parts. So if Andy cuts Bill's lawn, Andy is then owed a favor of an equal caliber, such as help in the garden that takes the same amount of time, a lift to the airport, or something along these lines. However, if you can build up favors with someone to a point where they owe you a lot, then you may be able to ask for even bigger favors.

People tend to be forgetful when it comes to things like this, so make it very clear, but remain friendly with what you've done for people. A gentle reminder can be enough for the other person to think. *Okay, yeah, you have helped me a lot. I can now help you.*

As you can see, playing off social norms plays a big part in adding pressure. I've spoken a little bit about mob mentality, and this is an extreme version of social pressure. Imagine you have a football stadium, and the home team loses. Everyone, angry and upset with the result, walks out onto the street after the game, and tensions are high.

One person reacts by kicking over a bin or throwing something at the fans of the other team, and suddenly the crowd erupts. Because one person has thrown something, suddenly, this justifies the actions of everyone doing it. If one person has done it and got away with it, then why can't everyone else?

Of course, specifically with mob mentality, there's a degree of anonymity, so people believe they won't be caught and penalized for their actions because they're unrecognizable in a crowd of people, but you can see what I mean when I say that even in an intense situation like a football stadium car park, when the norm of that environment changes, people are very quick to attach to these ideas and change their behaviors and what they deem acceptable and normal very quickly.

This leads us very nicely into our next chapter, where we're going to be talking about creating even more "normal" situations in which the traditional norms of environments can be changed to suit the outcome you're trying to achieve.

# Chapter Eight – How Repetition Changes Everything

*"It's the repetition of affirmations that leads to belief. And once that belief becomes a deep conviction, things begin to happen." – Muhammad Ali*

Playing off the last chapter, you should start to see how interesting social norms are. When you travel from the Western world to the Eastern world, you may see scenes that shock you. When I first traveled to India in my twenties, I saw naked women washing clothes in the streets, and children running around the road while men butchered and skinned cattle next to the dusty paths. At first, I was in shock with how all these things were happening so openly, but I soon realized that this is just the norm in other countries. Most countries, societies, and nations are unique in their own way.

This happens everywhere in the world, on both big and small scales. Some families are very strict, disciplined, and will sit down and have dinner with each member of the family present every single night. Some families don't eat together, but instead eat whenever they want, usually in front of the television. Some families will dress up nicely every day, and some families are nudists.

This is again reflected in the business world. Some companies are known for being professionally styled businesses where everyone needs to wear a suit and must present themselves in a smart fashion, and in other companies, employees are allowed to wear whatever they want, be it jeans and a hoodie or otherwise.

Norms change all the time, depending on what we're used to and subject too.

So, bearing this in mind and pulling it back to taking control of this psychology, when it comes to influencing people, a powerful way to do so, thus changing and influencing someone's behavior, is to make your message consistent, normal, and habitual.

Meet Mark. Hi, Mark. Mark works for a software company and wears a suit to the office. He plays golf on the weekends and goes to bars with friends. He's not very cultured but likes to live for the weekend. One night in his favorite bar, he meets Melissa. Mark thinks Melissa is a "bit hippie," since she wears colorful dresses and scarves, and isn't really his type.

She likes yoga and spending her weekends in museums and art galleries. While very different, they hit it off and swap phone numbers and go on several dates. They get on well, and one day, Melissa invites Mark to join her at a yoga class. Now, ask Mark that question months ago, he would have said "absolutely not," and still does.

Melissa talks about the benefits of going and what she likes about it. It does her good and makes her feel good. When she gets in from her yoga class, she talks about how much better she feels and how the people there are always so nice. Over time, and by consistently sending a positive message, Mark agrees to join Melissa for a class, and he loves it. Now Mark loves yoga.

This is a very common example of how people can change their attitudes, beliefs, and behaviors when a message is made normal and is habitually sent. Mark would never have been around anybody who even spoke about yoga in the office and would have just a brief understanding of what it would have been like from the advertisements and shows he sees on TV.

However, over time, Melissa sends messages that make the practice of yoga become normal in Mark's life until it gets to a point where his behavior and attitude finally changes. In this example, this happens very naturally and probably without Melissa doing anything, so now imagine what you'll be able to achieve if you're consciously implementing this technique in your interactions.

So, how do you do it?

## Implement Repetitive Messages

When you want to form a new habit in your life, like running or eating properly, how do you do it? Well, you start doing it, and you try to be as consistent as you can. You do that thing over and over again, repeating it over and over until it finally becomes a normal part of your daily routine, and therefore a generated and nurtured habit. This mentality needs to be applied to the message you're sending.

Whether you're a lover or a hater of Donald Trump, there's no denying that his message stating "Make America Great Again" is an incredibly powerful form of persuasion. The message was repeated everywhere, across all his branding, television shows, hats, online content, banners, and more. It's this repetition that fixates in the minds of America that drives his campaign forward.

The brain loves to be comfortable. As a survival tool, if the brain recognizes something repeatedly, and it knows it to be a safe situation, then it's happy, and it will make you feel happy because your brain wants you to be safe. If you're put in a room with twelve scary looking bodyguards, you'll feel on edge. However, if you're familiar with these bodyguards, say they're your friends, you'll feel completely at ease.

This is known as the mere exposure effect, or the familiarity principle, a term coined by Robert Zajonc. When you're subject to something repeatedly, you begin to develop a positive mindset towards it as it becomes your comfort zone. This is why people go to bars and order the same drinks, the same item off the menu of their favorite restaurant, or become attached to the people in their lives.

There are plenty of examples where science has proven this to be the case. Researchers Mita, Dermer, and Knight, 1977, carried out a survey where they showed people and their friends two pictures: one of a person and one of their reflected selves. The results showed that individuals much preferred the photo of their reflected selves, whereas their friends preferred the actual unreflected photo of themselves.

When you consider that most of us walk around the house all day and only ever see the reflected version of ourselves, it's easy to see why the outcome was this. If you take a photo of yourself on your phone and then flip it using the editing features (available in the Photos app on most smartphones), you'll see what you'll actually look like to others, and it's probably going to make you feel really uncomfortable because you're not used to it. On the other hand, if you saw this image of yourself every day, you'd become used to it and even happy with it. This is the power of the repeated message.

The science behind this is also very simple. Imagine your mind is a jungle, and every time you do something, anything, a little version of you makes it way through the jungle. For example, you're learning how to play tennis. Every time you play, the little mental version of you is cutting through the jungle from one side to the other. This path represents the neural pathways in your brain. The more you practice tennis, the stronger these pathways become and the easier and more fluent at the task you become.

In the jungle metaphor, this is like starting something new for the first time, and you have to cut your way through the neural jungle with a machete. There are thick vines and undergrowth in your way. However, the more you walk that path, over time, it starts to clear. A small track is formed, and that turns into a big open tunnel through the jungle.

Over the years, you lay a concrete path through that jungle until eventually, you end up with a twelve-lane superhighway where you can travel down that same path at super speed. That's when you become incredibly familiar with doing something, which can only ever be achieved through repetition.

Now relate this concept to how you send your message to others.

In the beginning, if you're proposing something completely new and radical, people are going to take this message and, in their minds, it will be like cutting through the thick jungle of the brain. However, through repetition, you can start to clear the trees and undergrowth until a clear path is formed and the message becomes their norm.

There are several ways you can do this when it comes to persuading and influencing people.

## How to Influence and Persuade People Through Repetition

Through the rest of this chapter, I'm going to talk you through the process of introducing a concept to someone and then making that message habitual enough through repetition that it becomes their norm.

## Make the Message Simple

First things first, you need to send your message in the clearest and easiest way you possibly can. This is a process known as conceptual fluency. It states that the faster you can comprehend information coming into your brain, the higher the chance is that you will have a positive relationship with it.

If you've never played a game of chess and I tell you a Ka3+ would have been a great move to counter their Rb4, you'll have no idea what I'm talking about, and you'll probably be rather put off by the information. You mentally shove it away from you and want nothing to do with it. This is because you won't understand the complex chess language, and the idea feels too complicated.

Of course, through repetition and positive reinforcement, this could change over time, but you can't lead with that. Instead, if I said, "You can move your knight diagonally on a chessboard," this information is very easy to understand, and you'll be much more likely to have a positive relationship with it.

Think about this from a business perspective. If I said go out and buy some new trainers to start running with, you're probably going to buy from the brand you know the most because this is what is familiar to you and you understand it. There's no learning process that needs to take place. This is why marketing companies spend billions every year trying to make their brand the most recognizable to you in the simplest way possible.

Let's look at a real-life example.

You're trying to persuade your friend to come and see a new movie with you. This movie is not really your friend's taste, and they're indifferent to the idea, but you really want someone to go with you, and it would be nice to spend some time with them. How do you approach it?

Instead of going straight in by asking them to see the movie with you, talk about going to the movies with them, but not about anything specifically. Say things like "Ah, we haven't been to the cinema in such a long time. We should think about going," or "When was the last time you went to the cinema and saw something good?" You may want to be more specific, saying something like, "I love the sound quality of a cinema viewing. There's just no experience like it. It's the best way to enjoy movies."

When you do this for a couple of days, you're priming your friend with positive repetition. After a few days, your friend will have a positive mindset towards going to the cinema, in which they're much more likely to say yes to your request. It's all about building them up first before diving into requesting something from someone.

## Use Repetitions in Every Possible Sense

You can get creative with the way you repeat something to someone, and the more creative you can be, and the more ways you can repeat something, the more you're going to drive home your message. When it comes to writing a book like this, the layout is always the same in every chapter. I use the same fonts and the same size headers and chapter indicators.

Every chapter is laid out in the same way and written in the same format. This is a form of repetition. Imagine if each chapter was written differently with a different font. You'd be uncomfortable and have no idea what's going on and why, and you wouldn't end up reading the book, let alone absorbing the message that's being shared.

The human brain loves consistency and repetition, so do it in every possible way. If you're asking your colleague to the Christmas party as we spoke about in the last chapter, always ask in the same way. This means asking the same question and talking in the same volume and using the same tone of voice.

Really imagine if something asked you something three times in three different ways. The first time they whispered it to you, and the next, they shouted. Not only would you think they're crazy, but you're also definitely not going to agree with what they're saying.

# Chapter Nine – Incentivise! Rewarding for Results

*"An incentive is a bullet, a key: An often tiny object with astonishing power to change a situation."* – Steven Levitt

The title of this chapter says it all and really needs no introduction. If you want your kid to behave while shopping in the grocery store, you promise them sweets in return for good behavior. You get what you want on the promise that the other party will get something in return. It happens with dogs very clearly. You want them to behave or learn a new trick, you give them treats. It's an exchange that takes place, and it works exceptionally well within human beings.

The thing is, offering a dog or a child a reward for good behavior seems and feels like pretty standard stuff, but how far could you take it? How could you incentivize others as a means of persuading them to do something, and does it actually work similarly to the other ways we've already spoken about in this book?

Is there science and principle behind the concept?

Back in 1938, B.F Skinner, one of the best-known behavioral psychologists in the world, decided to find out. He ran an experiment that gave pigeons treats at set times. While completely unrelated to the pigeon's behaviors, the birds started to mimic the exact behavior they did before the treat was dispensed. For example, if a pigeon bobbed their head or made a sound and a treat came out, they would then repeat this action in the hopes of receiving more food.

In the experiment, one bird made a habit of turning counterclockwise, two or three turns between receiving a treat.

This may sound simple at best, and humans are, of course, very different from pigeons, but then again, are we really? How many people do you know who have a ritual or a "lucky thing" they do before they do something major? Many motivational speakers of the world jump on trampolines or physically move around to get their heart rates up before going out on stage to boost their energy levels. Yes, they can bring more energy into the event on a physical level, but it's really a behavioral ritual that gets the motivational speaker into a performing mindset.

Let's say that every time you got into the car, you touched wood as a good luck sign that nothing bad was going to happen. You get in the car, drive to work, and everything's fine. You do this again and again, and before you know it, touching wood is something you need to do every time you get in a car. Some people will actually be fearful something bad is going to happen if they break this ritual.

This is a prime example of incentivizing to modify your behavior. You do something, and something good comes from it. You know what I'm talking about, so I don't think there's any need to go much further into it, but in line with the purpose of this book, how can you utilize this as a behavioral strategy?

Let's find out.

## A Persuasion Strategy Through Incentives

Right off the bat, you need to understand that providing any kind of incentive isn't going to just work and persuade people to do things for you, change their behavior, nor make them act a certain way. For example, I'll give you a bag of sweets if you tidy my entire house top to bottom, dust everything, and do a really professional job.

The incentive isn't enough for the action, highlighting the two variables you need to be thinking about: A) what you're using as an incentive and B) what the behavioral change or action is. This leads us to the two types of motivation you need to be thinking about.

## Intrinsic Motivation and Extrinsic Motivation.

Intrinsic motivation is a motivation that comes from the heart and is something that someone is personally interested in. For example, there could be a task that someone finds enjoyable, so they're happy to do it. This is intrinsic. This could mean going clothes shopping, ordering food, or writing a book. People are intrinsically doing something because it brings them personal value.

On the other hand, extrinsic value is all about getting something external. You may ask someone to help you move to a new house. They don't necessarily want to do it, and it's not a truly enjoyable task, but you promised them pizza and beer afterward, so that makes it worthwhile. Of course, some actions can be both intrinsic and extrinsic, but here's where you can start persuading people.

First, understand that intrinsic motivation is almost always the main approach to influence you're going to want to focus on because it's far more effective. It's like asking what you would do for a million dollars. Everything has a limit, and some people would do some stuff for free, and some people would need more than a million dollars. This is the power of intrinsic motivation.

So, let's get into the meat of this.

## Defining the Quantity of the Incentive

In the situation where you're persuading someone, size really does matter. When you ask a favor from someone, you may think that giving them $10,000 is a great incentive, for example. Most people would think that's a great incentive, especially in comparison to a $1,000 incentive. After all, you're getting ten times more as a reward.

While this may seem like the case in your head, it can actually have the opposite effect in reality. When the incentive is too big, this can cause people to feel pressured to perform, and it can put people off going through with whatever they've agreed to do. A chess lover could go to a tournament with a $100 prize and do really well. The $100 is great if they win, but not too problematic if they lose. Alternatively, a $100,000 prize fund is a lot of money, a lot of pressure, which can put people off.

So, big incentives are bad and small incentives are good? Not entirely. It's a little more complicated than that. It's about finding the balance per situation, but it's also so much more than that. Back in 2009, Uri Gneezy conducted an experiment where students were told to go and collect money as donations.

There were three groups of students who went out. The first would receive 10% of the donations they made. The second would receive 1%, and the last would receive nothing. They would collect the donations, and all the money would go elsewhere. Who do you think made the most?

Common sense would suggest that students receiving the 10% donations would make the most because they would have the largest incentive to make more, but the reality turned out to be quite different. The student group who made nothing on the donations actually made the most, but why? Science shows, in particular Harmon-Jones, 2000, that when people are seeking rewards, they tend not to focus on the task at hand but are more focused on what they are getting out of it.

In this example, the people who were making 10% were focused on making as much money as possible, maybe even seeming desperate, because they wanted to make the most. The group earning 0% was only focused on collecting donations for the causes. This means less pressure on the money collecting aspect, and a more relaxed approach, thus generating more donations.

This relates back to intrinsic and extrinsic. If the incentive is too big, then it may become more extrinsic. This can work in some cases, but for long-term behavioral change, an intrinsic incentive is always going to be better. If the person you're persuading thinks that they're doing something because it will benefit them in the long term, this is a much more effective way of sending your message.

For example, if you're an employer and trying to make your staff work harder, you could do two things—pay them more, or offer incentives to move up the ranks into your management team. You could say, "If we hit targets this year, then everyone gets a bonus." This works in many amazing ways, and people will tend to work harder to hit targets, but this remains extrinsic. Once targets have been hit and the bonus paid out, you'll need to offer another bonus next year to achieve the same results.

On a more individual level, however, if you were to offer someone the chance to progress up the ranks of your company, you could do so by claiming that they'll earn more money long term and will have authority within your business, and it will look good on their resume, opening a whole new range of opportunities for them in their future.

This idea of a promotion then appeals to the intrinsic nature of the employee, because they'll be working hard to benefit themselves and grow themselves, as well as benefiting the business. When it comes to work targets, this person working their way up is much more likely to strive to hit targets year after year after year. See the difference?

What can you learn from all this?

Sometimes, incentives can be big. If you want someone to do something for you as a one-off, then the bigger your incentive is, the better. However, if you want long-lasting behavioral changes, a smaller, more intrinsic incentive could be the better option.

## Define What the Incentive Is

Of course, you need to think about what you're giving someone as an incentive. I've already spoken a lot about money and financial incentive being a great way to influence someone, but it's not always possible nor suitable to use money. This could be seen as bribing, and that's not a great way to be seen.

Take a look at this list of incentives you could use and try and see what kind of scope you can develop in your mind:

- Buying someone takeout
- Offering to take someone out
- Buying someone flowers
- Giving someone a hug
- Giving someone the opportunity to explore their creative passions
- Having the experience of a lifetime
- Praise and positive feedback

- Recognition
- Status
- A position of power

This is just a handful of ways you can incentivize people. A lot of people won't need money or anything physical but would rather be recognized for the work they do. Remember the story I was telling you a few chapters back when I worked in a supermarket under two team leaders? The female team leader was so talkative when it came to singing praises for the work that people had done.

I remember one Christmas, the store had a huge delivery, and we knew the work list wasn't going to be completed by the end of our shift when it should have been. However, the team leader motivated us to work hard, stating how we were all in this together, and everything was going well.

When I had finished my first job, I remembered her coming up to me and saying something along the lines of, "Well done, it's really appreciated how hard you worked to get that done. Thank you." Her words warmed something inside of me, and although I knew I only worked at a supermarket and was stacking shelves, I felt immense pride for the work I had done. I was recognized and appreciated. I was a valued member of the team.

Incentives can come in the form of anything; it's simply about tapping into the most intrinsic form of motivation you can think of in any situation. This will vary from person to person and will depend on the relationship you develop with them. If you need a recap, flick back to chapter four on nurturing a good relationship with people.

The more you know about another person and understand them, the more accurately you'll be able to incentivize them using intrinsic motivation. In some cases, you may even be able to give people their own choice, literally enabling them to tell you what incentive they would like. In some businesses, you may ask whether someone wants lieu days in payment for their overtime shifts or flat-out payment.

This can actually be a much more satisfying approach for the other person because they feel in control and as though you're giving something they want, something they are choosing to have. In reality, this is a false sense of control because you're clearly willing to incentivize with either to persuade them to do what it is you want them to do.

There's no denying that incentivizing someone when persuading or attempting to influence them is one of the most tried-and-tested approaches that deliver consistent results. When all else fails, you can pretty much guarantee that this is an approach that can work, but it's all about getting creative.

If you're a manager of a company and you're looking to fill overtime shifts desperately, you could ask and hope for the best, you could offer time and a half, or you could simply approach the situation in a way that makes the person want to work for you for nothing. This can only be achieved from positive interactions, a consideration that applies to every single persuasion method I've spoken about already.

This is the power of positivity.

# Chapter Ten – The Power of Positivity

*"Once you replace negative thoughts with positive ones, you'll start having positive results."*
– Willie Nelson

When I raised my idea for writing this book with my friends and family, some aired some concerns I hadn't thought about.

*"Is it possible to persuade someone to take drugs, or commit a crime?"*

*"Could you manipulate someone into sleeping with you or going on a date? That's illegal. That's blackmail. That's immoral."*

I thought about this for some time. While I like to look at the world positively and optimistically, there's no denying that there are people out there who are manipulative and immoral. Some people use the techniques in this book for their own personal gain and wish to harm others. I am not advocating this in any way, but it's an important topic to touch upon.

I've tried to write this chapter about a dozen times now, and I've never been sure how to approach it until I was sitting in a cafe one Saturday afternoon watching the world go by, and I saw a mother talking with her child. The kid must have been no older than four or five, and he was captivated by the dog laying on the floor, sleeping at the feet of his owner at another table. The mother was talking with a friend, and the kid kept walking over, smiling at the owner and then eagerly waiting to stroke the dog. The dog opened an eye and shut it again, indifference to the child's presence.

I watched for several minutes as the mother called her child back, told him to sit down next to her, and then carried on her conversation. The child would wait, never once taking his eyes off the dog, and would slowly get up and make his way back over. This happened three or four times before the mother snapped. Everyone jumped and looked in her direction, including the dog who had now sat bolt upright and stared with those absolute black eyes.

"GET OVER HERE THIS INSTANT AND DO NOT MOVE A MUSCLE AGAIN."

Her voice was terrifying. If I were the four-year-old, I probably would have cried my eyes out. Poor kid is probably going to have some kind of later life trauma related to his childhood. He didn't cry. He just solemnly walked back to the seat and sat. All the spark of happiness had gone from his eyes, and I couldn't help but feel bad for him. This was obviously something the kid had gone through before. You could see it in his face.

And then it hit me.

As human beings, we always have a choice on how we act and address certain situations. In this story, the mother lost her rag and went full-blown nuclear in a matter of minutes because she didn't have the time or patience to explain to the child what she wanted to do. Her persuasion and interpersonal skills were clearly non-existent, and I'm not to judge another's parenting skills, but I would do things so differently.

Sure, kids can be annoying at times, but it was clear that this explosive and ballistic approach doesn't work. It never does. Sure enough, a few minutes later, the color had returned to the kid's face, and he was back on the cafe floor, making his way over to the dog. The mother looked over, muttered something under her breath, and gave up.

While being forceful and aggressive with people can seem like a surefire way to make things happen, feeding off the fear of others and basically forcing them into a corner, this doesn't come without consequence and it doesn't ever have a lasting effect.

Imagine you're in a board meeting, and you're pitching an idea. There are two ideas, and the votes are evenly split. One person is left to vote, so you grab him by the cuff of the neck, throw him against a wall, and demand he votes for your idea, or else. He may well indeed vote for your idea out of fear, but your reputation is ruined, and people are never going to look at you the same way.

On the other hand, taking this guy to dinner and talking over your idea in a bit more detail, giving him some insight and giving him your full, undivided attention to make him feel like the center of your universe is a much more effective approach that is going to deliver much better results both short and long term.

Long story short, positivity works, and here's how.

## Positive Interactions Deliver Positive Results

Think about the last chapter and how if I asked you to help me move to a new house, I would treat you to pizza and beer at the end of the day. This is a very positive experience because I've created the image that we're going to work hard together in moving all my stuff, and then we can sit back and relax and enjoy the fruits of our labor with some good food and drink. It's a positive image that makes you want to be involved.

This positive reinforcement in my message (which in this case is asking you to help me move to a new house) starts from the moment I start talking about moving to a new house. If I was to say, "Oh, I have to move because I've been kicked out of my apartment. I've broken up with my partner, and I'm so sad."

This creates a very negative association with the idea of moving to a new house right off the bat. Then when it comes to your request, the other person is going to want to be as far as possible from this negative experience and will probably do all they can to get out of it, whether that's making excuses or flat out saying no.

Take the same people in the same situation, but instead, I say, "I'm moving to a new house next week. It's been a rough few weeks, having broken up with my girlfriend, but I'm ready to start moving forward and begin the next chapter of my life. I just need some help moving some stuff, and I'm all set to go."

This is the exact same request in the exact same circumstances, but the positive spin reframes the message in an entirely new way. It's far more positive, and far more likely, the person will want to be involved. When you add the incentive of pizza and beer afterward, the offer becomes a no-brainer.

Whenever you're heading into a situation when you're persuading or influencing someone, always craft and frame your message in the most positive way possible. That doesn't mean you need to lie and make everything seem like all sunshine and rainbows when it isn't but add a positive spin.

Note any animal welfare charity advertisements you may see on TV. They always show animals in heart-wrenching conditions that can make you squirm in your seat. The pain in their eyes. The horrible conditions. The blood or tattered fur. It's horrible to watch, and the very essence of a negative message, but the ads don't stop there.

They always move on, saying how you can help, and how your money can help turn this rescue dog into this, and then they show the same dog but a much happier and healthier version which is about to be rehomed to a loving family, and it's a very heartwarming story.

This is how effective you can be at reframing a negative message and turning it into something positive. It doesn't matter what message you're sending, whether it's inherently positive or negative, you can always make it positive with the right spin. There are plenty of ways you can do this, including:

- Reframing your message with a positive attitude
- Using positive language
- Create a positive situation when discussing the matter
- Using positive reinforcement
- Using positive associations

Now, there are variations on this, and the subject of being "positive" is not so black and white. For example, if you're trying to persuade a group of people to vote for a certain political party, you may not want to be positive in the traditional sense, but you may want to get people angry.

You could do this by highlighting all the negatives that are currently a problem in the current government, and then detail how your political party will make positive changes. You could rile up your audience to get them angry at the current government. You could make them livid and want to protest and riot (although I'm not recommending this at all). The point is that at the foundation of everything, the message you're sending is that you want positive change, and you're encouraging others to see your view in the same way.

Let's look into some more practical persuasion strategies along this line.

## Turning Negative Message Positive Through Slow Repetition

Let's say that you have a child who refuses to brush their teeth at night. They hate it, and it's always a hassle trying to get them into the bathroom to the sink, and it's a fuss and stress you don't want to deal with anymore. What do you do?

Well, you could shout at your kid and force them to get on with it, or you could change what is already associated as being a negative experience as being a positive one. You can do this by slowly changing the situation a little bit at a time. Another common example of this, again children-related, is getting them to eat vegetables at dinner they don't want to eat.

You start at the beginning. When it's time for your kid to brush their teeth, you start with positive language. If it's a problem so far, then you've probably shown your kid through your body language and verbal language that it's a stressful time, and problems are to be expected, so don't bring that back into the situation. Instead, remain fun, positive, and engaging.

This will certainly surprise your child, but they're probably still going to resist. No matter. If you keep implementing this positivity night after night without fail, a little bit at a time, slowly but surely, your kid will start to get used to it and will start seeing the time to brush their teeth as a positive time. This is a process known as **systematic desensitization**.

You can apply this in any situation. Say you're at work, and everyone goes into the morning meeting but always sighs and groans when it's time to go in, so you decide to switch things up and make a change. You become more engaging, and you make your body language and verbal language more charismatic and confident.

People in the meeting enjoy this new meeting, but they will still mumble and groan because it's probably a one-off. However, over time you keep implementing this energy into your meetings, and slowly the mentality of people starts to change. A once-negative experience becomes positive. Once people have had a positive experience for long enough, they'll suddenly notice that what they once hated they now love, and because they love it, they're going to keep doing it.

The moral of this story: Work hard at desensitizing any negative messages by turning them positive. Be patient and watch the results unfold before your very eyes.

## Persuading Through Repeated Positive Exposure

Let's say it's getting close to the yearly family vacation and you're looking for somewhere to go. The wife wants to go to Paris because it's romantic and beautiful, and it's always near the top of her bucket list. Her husband wants to do a road trip across Germany because he saw a car documentary and thought the route would be something he'd love to see from himself. Already we find ourselves at a bit of a stalemate.

What can the wife do to persuade her husband?

In this case, positive repeated exposure would be a great way to go forward. The husband may have his own thoughts about Paris. Maybe he thinks it's too full of tourists, or there's nothing that will take his fancy, so even without going, he's already created this idea in his head that he doesn't want to go. A negative situation, in this case, a negative thought against going to Paris. He's already created this thought association through repetition. Now it's up to his wife to reverse the thinking.

By subtly watching shows featuring Paris that will appeal to her husband's interest, leaving open websites on the shared computer, dropping in Paris in positive conversations, and maybe not so subtly leaving travel guides open about Paris, suddenly her husband starts to see Paris everywhere. As long as it's in a positive light, he'll start developing positive associations with the city.

Over time, just like the child brushing his teeth, lots of little positive reinforcements will slowly change his mind to see the subject in a positive light. When that next "where do you want to go on vacation" conversation comes around again, he's in a much more likely position to say yes.

When you think about it, it goes without saying that the more positively we think about something, the more we're going to resonate with it, but you can have more control over what people think is positive just through subtle cues and repetitions.

As you've probably guessed from reading chapter to chapter, the best way to persuade and influence people is by combining a lot of the various methods and meshing them all together. For example, you may want to incentivize someone, but you're going to borrow elements of positive persuasion to make it work.

With the kid brushing his teeth (last time I'm mentioning this kid, I swear), if he can brush his teeth and have a positive experience, with the incentive of having a bedtime story afterward, he's far more likely to brush his teeth without any hassle.

Of course, how you approach a certain situation, a certain person or group of people can vary dramatically depending on the individual circumstances you're in, which you're only going to figure out with practice and mastering these methods over time. This is exactly what we're going to focus on in our final chapter.

# Chapter Eleven – Getting Better with Practice (Tips & Tricks)

*"Knowledge is of no value unless you put it into practice."* – Anton Chekhov

As you near the end of your journey into mastering the art of persuasion and influence, an art that has never been more important in a world where communication is everything, sending a powerful and direct message has become harder than ever. There's just one more point you need to look at, bringing everything you've learned together.

Throughout this book's chapters, we've dived into all kinds of persuasion methods and approaches, from reading someone's body language to using NLP and more. It's a lot of information there to process, and you're probably left wondering, *How the hell am I supposed to bring all of this together?*

For starters, you've probably noticed that I keep referring to this process as "the art of persuasion." You may have just overlooked that as fancy wording, or you might see some truth to it, but it's crucial to your success that you start seeing your acts of influence and persuasion as indeed an art form.

Why?

What is art?

It's the ability to share strong emotions. It challenges the beliefs of the mind and expands understanding. It's complicated at times, and you can be sharing both simple and complex methods simultaneously. It's about sending a message and sharing a point of view, usually an original idea, and all of these factors are present in all forms of art.

From songs and paintings to drawings and books, persuasion is, at its very core, a form of art. It's part of the art of communication. And, just like an artist of any medium, you need to practice getting better. Nobody, or very rarely, can someone pick up a paintbrush and create a magnificent work of art that's adored by millions.

You need to pick up the paintbrush and try it out for yourself. You then need to explore how different brushstrokes work on various canvases and materials. You need to experiment with different colors and blend them to see what happens. You then need to fine-tune your technique and inventory by using better paintbrushes and upgrading the tools you use once you're ready to move on and know what you're doing.

This is exactly what you need to be doing when it comes to mastering the art of persuasion.

Using the information in this book, you'll need to figure out what works for you and each individual situation you're in. This can admittedly feel overwhelming at times, but with time and practice, you'll get better and better until it becomes second nature. You've just got to take those first steps and try.

It doesn't matter what walk of life you're from. Whether you're using persuasion in an obvious sense, perhaps if you're in business and working with clients, or in sales and communicating with customers, or you're trying to teach your kids new and healthy habits and life skills, or convincing your partner to go on a road trip you've always wanted to go on, persuasion is not manipulative or evil. It's merely a term used to describe the process of better communication.

It's interesting because now that you know and understand the factors that go into the art of persuasion, you'll start seeing people who do it to you, conversations and approaches you may never have noticed before. Many people do things unconsciously, such as using certain kinds of body language, but you'll soon be able to tell who's been practicing for themselves, and this a great way to learn for yourself.

Okay, okay, so how do you practice this fine art?

First, you're going to want to start small.

You can start with whatever you want and feel comfortable with, but I recommend starting with body language. This is where I started, and it was incredibly helpful when it came to mastering my body language and reading it in other people. You can then move onto more complex approaches, such as priming and finding incentives.

You can practice aspects of persuasion, like bringing a more positive tone into your language, at any time. Try writing or speaking and recording what you say and then listening to it back and seeing how you can make things better. The key is to be conscious and aware of your interactions with other people. Many people simply go through their lives unconsciously, just repeating their old habits and reactionary patterns and never expanding their horizons nor trying anything new. Once you understand this and can bring awareness to this, you start to grow and nurture real change in many areas throughout your life.

For the most part, much of your learning experience will come with trial and error, figuring out what works and what doesn't. You'll start seeing what works and what doesn't, what you feel comfortable with, and what techniques you enjoy using. This, like with any other skill a human being can learn these days, will help you get better and more skilled over time.

You'll also need to make sure you're focusing on the core foundations of what it means to influence and persuade someone. This means focusing on building a connection—a genuine connection—with the people you're speaking too. You're creating a relationship based on trust and honesty because nobody will be persuaded by someone who is neither of these things.

And so, with all this in mind and to summarize everything we've spoken about and to help you move forward in this new journey, here's the lowdown on this book, and the core points you're going to want to remember:

- Nurture trust
- Create a genuine connection
- Focus on powerful and effective communication
- Be positive
- Listen and understand the other person
- Mirror the other person
- Always appeal to wants over needs
- Be confident and assured in yourself
- Be focused and present in your interactions and conversations
- Practice at every opportunity

If you can bear these core points in mind, and then couple these with the techniques, approaches, and persuasive methods you've learned through this book, you'll be a master persuader in no time at all. Now it's over to you.

## Chapter Twelve – Final Thoughts

And we have officially reached the end of your journey into the art of persuasion. How do you feel? Have you already tried using some of these techniques in your own life, or are you getting ready to start practicing them? It can be a very exciting time when you start using them for the first time, and then after a short time, you'll start to see fantastic results.

You'll also see these techniques come in handy in other parts of your life. The chapter on being able to read people's body language brought so many benefits into my life, especially into my romantic relationships where I was able to better understand the people I love and see what they were trying to say to me, as well as being able to communicate more effectively. It's a lot of fun and bringing it all together, there's no doubt in my mind you're about to embark on a new chapter of your life in a direction you've never seen before!

***Good luck!***

# Book #5
# How to Make People Like You

*19 Science-Based Methods to Increase Your Charisma, Spark Attraction, Win Friends, and Connect Effortlessly*

*James W. Williams*

# **Introduction**

*"Confidence is the most beautiful thing you can possess." – Sabrina Carpenter*

Imagine being back in your school days. Take a moment to remember what it was like. I'm talking around the age of 13 or 14, just heading into your teenage years.

You come and go from school. You sit in lessons and play games during break time. You work on group projects with classmates and study for your essays and exams. You meet your first love, your first girlfriend or boyfriend, and run around on weekends with your friends.

As you grew up, you started to settle into your friend groups. You may have stayed friends with the people from your childhood, or as you moved into higher education, college, and university, you started mixing with new groups of friends. People came, and people went. As you learned more about yourself and what you liked and didn't like, you started meeting new people who liked the same things.

Whether you loved going out and partying, reading, hanging out, watching movies, playing video games, or loved sports, there were always people around you who you would call your friends. Maybe you're still friends with some of those people now, or perhaps you've gone off in different directions in life.

Over the last few years, I've been thinking about this journey of friendships that we all go through. I know some childhoods aren't great. Kids can be mean, and there are things like bullying that can leave some of them feeling a bit like an outcast. But even then, I remember kids in my school who were picked on by some of the other kids, but they still had a group of friends to call their own.

My ailment was my social anxiety. It wasn't too bad in school, but it started to kick in when I headed into my teenage years and then college. I just found that I couldn't speak to anyone and make new relationships. I had a few friends that I went to school with and stayed in touch with them now and then, but it was so difficult to meet and connect with new people.

I just couldn't seem to do it.

My self-esteem was through the floor, and this battered my confidence in myself. It felt like I was stuck in this vicious cycle of not being able to talk to people, feeling anxious about it, and then that further propelling the feelings of not being able to talk to others. It was holding my life back.

It got to a point during my 20s when I landed my first "real" job in sales and marketing when I started to realize that this was a problem that was holding me back. The fact you're reading this book right now means you probably already know what I'm talking about.

That feeling of looking back to your childhood years and wondering how you made friends so easily and how it was possible to talk to people without being shy or overthinking every interaction. That feeling of wonderment of how you could have so many friends and acquaintances when you were younger, but now you have a handful of friends, some of which you only speak to once in a blue moon.

Don't worry; you're not alone in this way of thinking.

**The New Age of Connection**

We all live in the new, unprecedented hyper-connected world that is the modern human era. Things like social media have taken over and become an absolute cornerstone in our everyday lives. Human connection is going through a shift that has never happened before in the history of the human race.

Statistics from 2019 found that 61% of Americans admit to having regular feelings of loneliness, up 7% on the year before, and that 52% feel lonely "most of the time" or "always." A similar YouGov poll in 2019 found that 21% of Americans have "no close friends," and 58% sometimes or always feel as though nobody knows them that well. As you can probably guess from these stats, it comes as no surprise that 53% of people find it difficult to make friends.

These statistics are mirrored globally in nearly all Western countries, including most of the EU, the United Kingdom, Mexico, Japan, Greece, Israel, and many more. This isn't just something happening in small pockets of the world; it's happening all over it.

These are many revelationary statistics, some of which probably surprise you, but they paint a clear picture. We are all becoming more disconnected from one another, and the more this disconnect continues, the harder it seems to become to reconnect again. When you chuck in the isolating nature of society, politics, gender, and race discussions, and not forgetting the massive impact of the 2020 COVID-19 pandemic, these are issues that are going to be causing more and more problems on a large scale.

But I don't want to talk about the large scale impact of this loneliness pandemic. It makes everything feel like there's too much doom and gloom, which is not the case. It may sound simple, but you've got to scale everything down and look at your relationships and ability to connect in your own life. You've got to focus on the small, personal scale.

Once you're here, you can start learning about how your mind works and what's happening within you to make you disconnect from others or discover why you're finding it hard to connect with new people. You can then take this information as a foundation to learn new techniques on how to nurture vibrant and exciting relationships and new skills on how to meet and talk to new people, even total strangers.

You give yourself the chance to build new friendships and then build them into friendships that can last for years to come. You learn how to reconnect, and this is exactly what we're going to be focusing on throughout this book.

**A New Day. A New Beginning.**

Riddled with social anxiety, I spent most of my early and mid-twenties in a rut. I was an outcast and felt lonely pretty much every day. I was that guy in the background at work that you probably knew my name or saw at the Christmas party once or twice, but you can't even remember having a conversation with. My cheeks are going red and hot just thinking about it.

It got to the point when I was about 28 when I thought, *Enough is enough. There must be a better way of living. I must be able to learn how to talk to people.* I remember one day there was a promotion coming up for a manager job in my sales firm. I was the lead project manager for a new client we were taking on, and it was one of those opportunities that fitted me perfectly. I knew that if I got the job, I would be so good at it. It would be my chance to shine. Unfortunately, I never dared to speak up, and even in my interview, my boss said I was good, but I just wasn't the people person they were looking for.

Do you know who did get the job?

The confident, charismatic guy that everyone loved, greeted when he walked into the office, and even the postman who came in would stop to chat with him. God, I used to be so envious of the way he was. It wasn't even arrogant or egotistic. It was natural charm and charisma that drew you in. He was genuine, and even if you had nothing in common interest-wise, you still wanted to chat with him and hear what he had to say.

I'm not a massive believer in auras and spiritual connection, but there's no doubt that he was one of those guys who walked into a room, and everyone felt his presence. I'm sure you know people in your life who are the same.

It took a few years and still a lot of practice to this day, and I found out that you can become like this person, but not exactly this person. You can become your *own* person. You can become the true, unadulterated, unfiltered, genuine, connection-worthy you. As with everything in life, all it takes is a little know-how, practice, and willingness to open your mind to what is possible.

Permit yourself right here and now to open your mind to this new way of being.

If you can't, then take that last sentence as me giving you permission to open your mind. Throughout the following pages of this book, I'm going to detail everything I've learned on my journey so you can increase your charisma, spark attraction among the people in your life, win friends, nurture and build relationships, attract romantic partners, and connect with other human beings in a way you've never connected with them before.

After a lot of work on myself, I've narrowed everything down to just 19 easy-to-follow methods, backed up by scientific research, and complete with everything you need to know about how to make friends in the modern age. Every single method here is actionable right here, right now, and by the time you're done reading this book, you're going to feel good about yourself in a way you wouldn't even believe.

And with that, I'm sure you've heard enough from me, and you're excited to get into it, so follow me down the rabbit hole, keep hands and feet inside the carriage at all times, and let's get learning.

*Communication Skills Training Series*

# Part One – The Start of Something New

*"Strangers are just friends waiting to happen." – Rod Mckuen*

Every single relationship that has, does, or will ever exist always starts the same, and that same way is one person talking to another person. In order to create a relationship, you need to meet people and start that initial connection.

It doesn't matter what kind of relationships you want in your life, or the kinds of relationships you're reading this book to try and attract. First impressions are always the most important impressions, and you need to have the ability to talk to new people, make them like you from the word go, and even have the confidence to make this all happen in the first place.

This is why I'm going to start here. Throughout the following chapters (which I'm going to be titling as methods), we're going to explore some of the best ways you have the confidence to meet and talk to new people, get the conversations flowing, and basically get your foot in the door when it comes to connecting with other people.

# Method 1 – It's About the Smile

*"When you're smiling, the whole world smiles with you."* – Louis Armstrong

When Louis Armstrong, one of the most popular jazz artists in history, sang these words for the first time, he probably never imagined that scientific studies would someday back up his claim. You probably know this already and have experienced it countless times throughout your life, which is why this is my first and foremost method for nurturing beautiful relationships with other people. It literally revolves around one action.

Smiling.

Simply smiling is such a powerful action, both on a physical and subconscious level. Smiling is a known human trait throughout the world, meaning it doesn't matter what culture you're in or what people you're talking to; smiling makes us feel the same. It's human instinct that we react the way we do when we see someone smiling. Best of all, this has been proven repeatedly, both by personal experiences and scientific studies.

In 2002, a Swedish study researching body language, mimicry, and emotional empathy found that people who were subject to pictures of other people smiling found it "incredibly difficult" to frown or display traditionally negative emotions. They actually went further than this and found that doing anything other than smiling when you see somebody else smiling needs to have a conscious effort to do. That's how natural smiling is.

Of course, smiling is a very positive emotion and makes you feel positive feelings. When it comes to building relationships and friendships with other people, you want people to see you in a positive way, which is why smiling is such a powerful method for attracting other people. Think about when you see someone at work crying, looking sad, or looking extremely angry. What do you do?

Well, if you're like most people, or at least like me, you'll feel very uncertain about how you're going to proceed. Do you talk to them? Help them? Try and make them laugh? Leave them on their own for a bit? There's so much uncertainty with these kinds of emotions, and everyone who experiences them is left feeling very unsure.

On the other hand, if you go into work and someone smiles towards, nods their head, or is even just smiling at their computer, the situation feels stable and secure. You can talk to that person, and if anything, you feel like you want to speak to that person more, just because they're smiling. As you're reading this, I'm sure you're imagining situations in your life where this has happened, or at least you are now!

Think about a restaurant you went to where the waitress greeted you with a massive smile before showing you to your table and how welcomed that made you feel. Now compare that with the grunt the other restaurant waiter gave you who was clearly having a bad day and made you feel uncomfortable. I'm sure you understand what I'm saying.

**Your Smile Changes How You See the World**

And how others perceive the world.

A study published in "Social Cognitive and Affective Neuroscience" in 2015 had researchers who did some very interesting research on this topic. In their study, they found that the very act of smiling or seeing somebody else smile physically changes our emotions and feelings. They found this out by actively monitoring the electrical activity in the brains of their volunteers. The results?

When people smiled at the volunteers, this instantly made them feel more positive. They ran many tests, and as a benchmark to this research, they discovered that when human beings see what you would call a "neutral" face, you would automatically assume that person to be feeling neutral. I mean, are there any surprises there?

But, when you see someone smiling, you automatically take that as the person feeling "happy." When it comes to making new friends and connecting with people, this is such an important consideration to take on board. By smiling, you're sharing positive energy with the people around you. This makes them want to approach you, connect with you, and simply be around you more. Just walking into a room and smiling is a great way to initially start a conversation and get people interested in what you have to say.

Likewise, when you smile yourself, your brain releases feel-good chemicals, known as serotonin, that make you feel good. Don't believe me? Try it right now. Look away from the book and out of a window, towards someone you love, a pet, a stranger, a tree, or anything that happens to be around you. Now simply smile. Even if you don't feel like smiling, just try it.

I'll give you a second.

Even when I did this right now, as I write this, I can't help but push air out of my nose and have a little laugh to myself. That's the power that smiling can have. Even if you're having the worst day you can imagine, taking some time to smile and just be present is enough to invoke a positive mindset. And, as research has proven time and time again, this positive effect reaches out to the people around you.

Never underestimate the power of a smile.

**Action Time: Smile More!**

Since this is the first chapter, I will make the takeaway easy and something you can start working on right now. Consider this your homework, but you don't get a grade at the end of it. You instead get the opportunity to create more meaningful relationships and connect much more easily with people who come and go in your life.

Here's what you need to do.

Ready?

You just need to smile more!

Yes, that is it. I know it sounds simple, and you probably guessed that's what I was going to say anyway, but, and I'll say this one last time to drive home this message, you can never underestimate the power a smile can have.

Try it. When you next go into a shop, talk to the cashier, pass someone in the street, talk to someone at work, or see your partner when you get into the house. Smile at them. Say hi and beam your best smile in their direction. If you're introducing yourself to a new customer, make the conscious effort to smile at them, and make yourself as appealing as possible.

The results of doing this speak for themselves, so try it and become your own proof. Now, I know this method is really simple, and you've probably heard something like this before, but you'll be amazed by how few people know how powerful this is. If you really can't bring yourself to smile, then you could always think about getting a dog.

Dogs always make people smile.

Anyway, all jokes aside, smiling more isn't the only approach to winning friends and becoming more approachable. This is just the tip of the iceberg. Let's get into some other approaches that can help you achieve your connection goals.

## Method 2 – Always Make the First Move

*"You can't stay in your corner of the Forest waiting for others to come to you. You have to go to them sometimes."* – A. Milne, Winnie-the-Pooh

Imagine this.

You could get onto a bus or a train, and the person sitting next to you may be someone you were destined to be best friends with. You may have so much in common: the same interests, the same music tastes, and the same love of classic movies. It's effortless that you two would share many great experiences and could spend an entire lifetime having fun, making memories, and enjoying life in so many amazing ways.

However, there's a catch. One of you has to speak to the other first.

It's heartbreaking to me that we live in such a closed-off and secluded world, isolating ourselves from one another. Hey, I've been on both sides. I've been the closed-off person who sits on the train and does everything I can to avoid acknowledging existence from everyone else around me. I've also been the guy who's sat and watched everyone else around me be that person.

We live in a world where we're afraid to talk to each other. Heck, we're afraid to look each other in the eye, even for just a split second. Instead, we stay in our comfort zones, scroll endlessly down the social media feeds we don't genuinely care about, stick our headphones in, and hide away from the world and any potential interaction. After all, imagine talking to someone and them rejecting your advances or conversation efforts!

Could you deal with that kind of rejection?

Well, I always thought the answer was no. I couldn't deal with it. I remember being in college, and there was a girl in the same course, but in a different class, and she was beautiful. I loved everything about her. Her voice. Her way with words. I was smitten in a way that was like nothing I had felt before. But did I speak to her once? No, of course not.

I wasn't confident enough to make the first move. And who knows, maybe she wasn't confident enough to make the first move with me but felt the same way. In a situation like this, you've got two people who want to have a deep and meaningful connection with each other. Yet neither of them has the confidence to say hi. When you think about that from a bird's-eye view, doesn't that seem ridiculous?

A friend of mine was the opposite. A few years back, he was really into the computer game *League of Legends*. You play with five other people on your team and can play with friends, or you can play with strangers on the internet. He played with someone, and they did well, winning a few games back to back.

They would talk over voice chat while playing, and it turns out the player was a girl. They eventually shared phone numbers, added each other on social media, and ended up dating for over a year. How crazy is that? The chances that they would be paired together, logging onto the computer game at exactly the right time to get paired up, out of 160 million other worldwide players, is practically impossible.

But then they managed to enjoy each other's company and have such a beautiful relationship with one another. They're not together now because of difficult mental health issues that were getting in the way, but they're still very close friends who chat every week and still play together from time to time. Isn't that beautiful?

These two human beings enjoyed each other's company because one of them made the first move, which allowed the relationship to blossom into something amazing that they both share. This brings me nicely to method numero two: always make the first move.

## The Science for Taking the First Step

As human beings, we're conditioned to fear rejection. We're social animals, and it's in our million-year-old instinct to stay a part of the pack. Human beings couldn't survive on their own. If you're wandering around the wildernesses of 1000 BC and you get sick or injure yourself, then chances are you're going to die. On the other hand, if you have your tribe around you, they can look after you, and you can look after them (more on this reciprocation nature later, by the way!). You're more likely to survive.

However, as time has progressed and we no longer live in tribes of 50 people or so, but instead have the ability to connect with literally millions of people across the internet, all judging and criticizing everything all the time, we're trained ourselves to hate rejection. In fact, we do everything we can to not risk being rejected at all, and that means we stop ourselves from taking that first, potentially embarrassing, and painful step.

If I had spoken to the girl I fancied at college and said, "Hey, want to get to know each other? I think you're cute," and she went "Urgh, get away from me, loser!" then yeah, I'm probably going to feel a little crushed. But, time being the best medicine, I would eventually get over it. Sure, the experience would then tell me not to do it again because 100% of the time I had been crushed, but think about how many friends you have had in your life.

You've spoken to them all for the first time at one point, so it's safe to say rejection doesn't happen all the time. As human beings are once more conditioned, we always remember the negative things that happen far more than we do the positives, which is why you need to consciously spend effort in thinking positively. This is another great reason why you should practice smiling to yourself more; to think more positively!

So, going back to taking the first step. Everyone is afraid of taking the first step, but in almost all situations, if you can do it, then you've taken the risk off of that other person, put them at ease, and now that first barrier is out of the way, you can start building your relationship with them.

Psychologists Steven Asher and Sherri Oden carried out a study that proves this to be the case. They studied elementary school children to see how they made friends with other children and how they were accepted, thus overcoming the fear of rejection.

They discovered one of the most important and essential skills a child needs to have when trying to make new friends and form new relationships is the ability to initiate an engagement—aka, taking that first step in communicating with another human being.

In this study, sure, the kids were inviting other kids to come and play in the fort castle or wanted to see if the other girl wanted to come and play with the same doll. If you have kids or have been around children, then you know that they'll do this. They'll bring over a toy to someone and see if you want to play together, and this is the foundation for the new relationship.

Of course, I'm not saying you need to invite your work colleagues over to play in a pillow fort together (some workplaces have rules against that kind of behavior), but there are more adult ways of taking that first step.

### Action Time – Take the First Step

I know what you're thinking, and I understand. It's hard to take the first step because you need a certain degree of confidence, and the pressures of being rejected can leave you feeling absolutely crushed, sometimes even paralyzed. I know. I've been there myself, and you may truly believe there's no other way to be.

I'm going to talk more about being confident and ways to boost this way of thinking in future chapters, but I want you to start small for now. By starting small, you can build up your confidence over time with little wins, and then this kind of personal development will really start to snowball. This is how it worked for me, as I'm sure it can work for you too.

When I say starting small, I mean to make the first move in small situations. This could be talking to the cashier in the shop. It only has to be small talk, but use the opportunity to practice. You can speak to the people around you in a queue, people at work, and even the people you live with. Keep building up your confidence and having these small interactions, and soon you'll be able to talk to anyone about anything, right from the time you meet them.

Over time, you'll get better and better at doing this, which will lead to the confidence you need to make deep, meaningful relationships and come across as the most confident, charismatic version of yourself possible. However, this isn't the only way to start a relationship. There's one more I want to talk about before moving on.

# Method 3 – Excuse Me. Can You Help Me?

*"The power of asking is the key to abundance living." – Lailah Gifty Akita*

There are a few things to think about when it comes to connecting with other people. You need trust on both sides. You need confidence. You need the ability to speak, make the first move, and create some kind of connection that will lead to friendship and beyond. While it may sound a little against the fray, one of the best ways to do this, psychologically speaking, is to ask someone for a favor.

Now, obviously, I'm not saying you'll sit next to someone on the train, start speaking to them, and then ask them to stay in your house to look after your dog. There are clearly big favors and small favors, but asking for a favor can be a great way to start and develop a relationship with someone.

Allow me to explain.

When you ask someone for a favor, you're not just asking for help from someone, but it's more the fact you're specifically asking the person you're asking. Let's say you're at work, and you're starting on a project for a new client. You have some ideas, but you're not sure which direction you want to take. What do you do?

Well, one thing you could do is ask for advice or a suggestion from a coworker. This is not only a sign of intimacy, but more importantly, it's a sign of trust. You're saying to that other person, hey, I respect you and your opinion, and I trust your judgment on this topic. Can you impart some of your wisdom to me? Obviously, you're not saying this out loud, but the fact you're asking for it implies that this is how you feel. After all, you're not going to ask someone for their opinion if you don't care for it, nor have any interest in that other person and their thoughts.

This means you've already suggested the foundations of a friendship, and if people think you like them (because you're not going to ask for a favor if you don't), then they'll already feel positively towards you. This then leads to a connection, and so on.

A Harvard study titled "Very Happy People" found there was a 0.7 correlation between people giving social support and their happiness. This means that the more people help other people, giving rather than taking, the happier they are. Just as a gauge, a 0.7 correlation is a higher correlation than the one between smoking and cancer.

This is why people get married. Because you're living your life together, you're supporting each other, through thick and thin. You help each other out with daily tasks, inspiring each other to live your best lives, and generally being there for each other when you need them.

## Making People Feel Good

The benefits of asking someone for help are endless when it comes to relationships. A study in human relations by Jon Decker found that asking for a favor helps boost the other person's self-esteem, and, in turn, they will like you more.

As human beings, we're wired to want to belong to a group of other people. We are social creatures. No human being wants to be an outcast from the group, and all humans want to be accepted. This includes acceptance for what they're able to bring to the table, both in terms of actions and ideas. It's like you're tapping into this area of the mind by asking for favors because you're ticking all the boxes. People you ask favors to feel secure and as though they belong. You're accepting them.

It also makes people feel capable because you're asking them since you believe they're capable of doing whatever it is you're asking them to do. This is a huge boost to their self-esteem and self-confidence, which comes from you, increasing how much of a positive light they see you in.

All of these are essential when it comes to making friends and making people feel good about themselves.

**Action Time – Asking for Small, Suitable Favors**

So, now we've gone through why asking for favors can be a great method for connecting with other people, it's time to put it all into action. As I said in the introduction of this chapter, you're not going to ask a complete stranger to look after your house for you, so start with small favors suitable for the people you're talking to.

For example, if you need help moving house or looking for a lift to the airport, you could ask a coworker. Thank them, maybe get them something to thank them from your vacation, and the favor is sorted. However, while this is, in essence, a quick favor, this interaction can do so much for building up your relationship with that person. Another example we've already spoken about is asking people for their ideas.

Whether you're working on a project at work, looking for vacation ideas, in need of a package to be picked up, or need a lift somewhere, these are all ideas you can use that are deemed acceptable for asking someone you may not know too well.

As your relationships start to get more trustworthy and meaningful, you can ask for more favors, such as babysitting your child, looking after a pet for the weekend, and things like this. Don't confuse this with having to always ask for favors if you don't need them. If you're just asking for favors just because you can, this isn't genuine, and it's not the best way to build a new relationship.

If you need help with something or are looking to open the doors to someone new in your life, making them feel welcomed, accepted, and appreciated, this is the best method to use every time. And with that, we come to the end of part one! What do you think so far? Have you learned some great ways to start speaking to people? This is, of course, the first step to being the charismatic and confident version of yourself, so make sure you get creative with how you use these methods and keep practicing them!

Moreover, and more excitingly, we're now moving into part two, where we're going to focus on a few of the methods you can use to deepen this connection to someone once you've started to get to know them. It's all about how you can take a relationship of any level, and turn it into a deep and meaningful one.

# Part Two – Sowing the Seeds for Something Beautiful

I love the phrasing of this chapter: *Sowing the seeds for something beautiful.* I know I wrote it, but when you think about it in the way that it relates to a relationship, it creates these beautiful images in your head of what a relationship in your own life can look like. It can be a friendship, a romantic relationship, a relationship with your parents, or even a professional relationship.

All relationships can be beautiful in their own way.

However, you need to get there first. When I first started dating, as I was working on tackling my social anxiety, I spent a lot of time tackling the things we spoke about in Part One. I was building up my confidence and making the first move when I met people. This was particularly evident in my dating life. I was working on being able to talk to girls and could ask them on a date, and that was fine. It took practice, but I got there.

Then it came to the date itself, and this was an entirely new ball game.

There's so much of a difference between talking to someone for the first time and talking to them again, getting to know them, and moving forward with this. I've dedicated the next five chapters to this part. We're going to explore five powerful methods that can help you build relationships, improve your charisma, win friends, and deepen your connections with other people.

Communication Skills Training Series

# Method 4 – Mastering the Art of Listening

*"When people talk, listen completely. Most people never listen." – Ernest Hemingway*

You've probably heard about this point before, but being able to listen to someone is one of the most important skills you can have when it comes to building a connection with someone. I'm sure you have been in a situation where you've been talking to someone about something you're interested in and excited about, but it doesn't feel like that other person is listening.

Maybe they're playing on their phone, looking out a window, or just everything about them, and their body language, says they don't care. I'm sure you remember times like this now, or someone you know who does this. Take a moment to think about how this feels.

How do you feel? Do you feel sad? Pushed away? Ignored? Unaccepted? As though what you have to say is not good enough or worth their time? However you feel, the feelings aren't good, and not listening to people and making them feel this way is not going to win you any friends whatsoever.

That being said, the opposite is true.

If you give someone your full attention and make them feel as though they're being listened to and that you genuinely care about what they're saying, you're going to make them feel happy, accepted, belonging, and as though you have a connection with them. This is why listening is so important when it comes to making friends.

Carl Rogers, a renowned American psychologist, famously stated that active and deep listening is at the very core of a healthy relationship. Through the art of listening, you'll be able to encourage strength and growth in any relationship, and people who are heard are less likely to be defensive and will be more open to new ideas themselves.

This means that not only will people be happier and more connected to you if you listen to them, but it will also increase the chances that they'll be listening to you. This is how a happy, two-way relationship is formed.

**The Two Types of Listening**

A study carried out in 2003 by Faye Doell discovered two main types of listening a person can do, three if you count not actually listening, but pretending to. If you're actively listening to someone speak, you're doing one of two things. You're either A, listening to understand the other person, or B, listening to respond to the other person.

How many times have you been in a conversation, and you already know what you're going to say before the other person has even finished talking? Yeah, I'm sure we all have at some point. This usually happens in arguments or heated discussions where you may not agree with what someone is saying, and they say their point, and you'll respond with something like "Yeah, but...", and then you'll go straight into your point.

This is listening to respond because you're not really listening; you're more waiting for the other person to finish, so you can have your say. This will not make the other person feel heard, and this is where your relationship will fall apart.

On the other hand, if you listen to understand, you're really taking the opportunity to listen to what the other person is saying and how they feel. Based on what they say, you then form a response that pushes the conversation further, whether you're asking a question for a greater understanding of what they're saying, or you're accepting what they're saying and then bringing up a counterpoint.

The same studies show that people who tend to listen to understand experience much greater and more satisfying relationships. Suppose you're the sort of person who wants to "fix" other people, while your intentions are good. In that case, you are perhaps most of the time listening to respond because you're flexing your desire to influence others, and this leads to you not actually listening to the other, but again listening to respond.

To cut a long story short, if you want better, more satisfying relationships where you're listened to properly, and you're happier with the people you're connected with, you need to learn how to listen to understand.

### Action Time – How to Become a Better Listener

While many of us, you included, may have some bad habits when it comes to listening to others, everyone can become a better listener by practicing a few key points. The more you practice these points, the better you'll become, and therefore the better the relationships you'll have. Let's get into them.

### Empathizing with the Speaker

First, and always a great way to become a better listener instantly, is to put yourself inside the mind of the person you're listening to. Become the person who is talking. This can bring so much more compassion and empathy into your conversations because you can resonate and understand what is being said.

For example, let's say someone comes to talk to you, and they've had a bad day at work. They made a mistake on a project, and they're worried about getting fired. You could listen to respond and have all these ideas on how things will get better, or they could redeem their mistake or advice on how to accept the situation they're in.

On the other hand, you can listen to understand and feel that yes, they are worried, and while they believe they may be getting fired, you can ask further questions to see whether that's likely, or what they think they can do to make things better. This is listening to understand, and it's far more helpful to approach a situation in this way.

Coupled with this point, you'll want to think about the meaning behind what the person is saying. This can be obvious, and other times it may be subtle, but listening for the meaning behind why someone is saying something will help you understand them tenfold.

When you take note of the tone of voice someone is saying something and the inflection they have on their words, you'll be able to further identify what they're saying to you. If I say, "Yeah, I hope you have a good day," this could mean anything, whether I'm nice or super passive-aggressive, depending on my tone of voice.

### Be Accepting and Non-Judgmental

Alan Watts famously speaks about how no human being knows anything in many of his talks, and it's true. At the end of the day, none of us know what's going on in the universe, and when it comes to the happenings of somebody's life, there's never a right or wrong answer. We are not the authorities of what is happening.

That being said, it's so important to make sure you're not judgmental when people are talking to you, or you at least try to be as non-judgmental as you can be, and I know that's easier said than done. However, if you can master this, you'll become an amazing listener because you're concentrating on what the person is saying rather than focusing on your preconceived judgments.

This can be difficult. When someone is talking about something you're passionate about or have strong feelings towards, then you may already have ideas that the other person is stupid or has no idea what they're talking about, which means you'll find yourself wrapped up in these thoughts, rather than listening to the person who's speaking. In essence, you're listening to respond, rather than listening to understand.

Of course, you're allowed to have opinions on things, and you're allowed to disagree with people, but in many cases, there's a lot of context that you may not know or understand as to why someone is saying what they're saying. If you can pay attention to this, rather than forming your own opinions in your head and making judgments, then your listening skills, and therefore your relationships with people, will skyrocket.

**A Note on Body Language**

There's no denying that body language is important when it comes to listening, and any kind of guide to communication you read or listen to will talk about body language. When listening, a great way to improve how much attention you're paying to the other person is to make eye contact with them. We seem to be living in a time where this is much harder than it first seems, and when I was in the depths of suffering from social anxiety, I literally couldn't do it.

However, it was a skill I was able to implement into my life with practice, and it made my relationships so much stronger. Regarding your body language, nodding is a great way to keep someone engaged with you while they're talking to you, and it non-verbally confirms that you want them to carry on and that you're interested in what they have to say.

You'll also want to pay attention to the speaker's body language. What are they doing, and where are they looking? Are they making eye contact with you, or are they looking everywhere else? Do they look fidgety and unsure of what they're saying, or are they confident and holding their own? Body language says so much about us all, and reading it will bring such a deeper dimension to your interactions.

And with that, our trip into the world of listening concludes. Like every other aspect and method of this book, this is all the information you need to know. It's just a case of sticking with it and putting it into practice. Start small and work on some of these tips over time, and you'll start to see some big changes in your life.

In case you were wondering, no, a relationship doesn't just mean you need to sit and listen to what someone has to say in silence. You get lots of chances to speak too, which is what we're going to explore now!

# Method 5 – Improving the Flow of Conversion

*"Nothing trumps good conversation." – Rich Eisen*

In the previous chapters, we've spoken a lot about introducing yourself to someone and how to start a conversation. The last chapter was about how you can listen to what another person says to give them your full attention. But there's one crucial piece of the puzzle missing.

What do you actually talk about?

It's all well and good having the courage to speak up and shake hands with another person, but if you can't take a conversation from there, and you end up stalling, sitting in awkward silences, and just being very distant in general, both you and the person you're speaking to are not going to have a nice or memorable conversation, at least not in a positive way. The chances are if they remember you for being awkward, or perhaps even boring, then you're not going to come across as charismatic, and they're not going to want to be your friend. Yeah, those are some hard truths.

First up, however, this isn't something you should worry about. While going through my self-improvement journey, at least at the beginning, there were at least a dozen times where I would fall into this situation. I remember when I was trying to speak to girls (I know, that classic chestnut, don't judge me!), and I was so confident and charismatic at the beginning.

We really hit it off and laughed and chatted about something that was happening across the road, but then something shifted, and neither of us knew what to say or how to carry the conversation on. It basically ended up with us having some awkward goodbyes and never seeing each other again. There's no denying I felt a little dumb initially, but hey, I'm still here, and that was years ago. If it happens to you, you may feel a little embarrassed for the rest of the day, but you'll get over it, and life will always go on.

Always try and remember this when you can. Practice makes perfect, so the more you put yourself in these situations, firstly the hardier you'll become to them going wrong, but secondly, and most importantly, the better you'll be at holding your own in a conversation with anyone. This is what I'm going to be focusing on in this chapter.

We're going to be talking about the art of conversational flow, which means the grace and lucidity in which you can traverse different topics, how effortlessly and confidently you can keep talking, and how to have conversations where when you both walk away, you're left with a smile on your face thinking, *Wow, that was a really good conversation!*

We've already spoken about the importance of listening, but don't forget that that is a massive part of having a conversation. These are some of the other points you'll need to be thinking about.

## Be Open and Honest

First things first: ALWAYS be open and honest in your conversations. Within us all, there is sometimes a bit of ego that wants to be validated, and we may feel the need to emphasize certain facts about our lives or make something sound much better than it actually was to make ourselves seem better or lucky or whatever to the person we're speaking to.

This never works. When someone is talking to you and starts boasting or exaggerating things, I think you'll agree that it's really easy to spot. You might not think about it at the time, but you'll get the feeling that something is not right or the person is putting on airs. Validating your ego to someone else is not the best way to connect and try to make friends with someone. In fact, some people would probably agree it's the worst, so avoid it at all costs.

The science behind this has been written about in a book titled *The (Honest) Truth About Dishonesty* by Dan Ariely. Here, he writes about how human beings can believe themselves to be honest, all while telling little lies or dishonest truths. Think about yourself right now and who you are. The chances are you think of yourself as an honest person, even though you almost definitely lie about little things in your life.

However, since you will mainly tell lies over little things you believe don't matter, you'll see yourself as an honest person. Don't worry, I'm not calling you a dishonest person since this is the way that most people go through life. If you're not feeling okay, but you don't want to talk about it, you may say everything's fine when it's not. You may say you don't know something when you do, or you may lie about something you do know when in reality, you're not sure.

So why do we do it?

Well, no matter which way you look at it, we're all telling lies, no matter how small they are, for one main reason: to protect ourselves.

You protect yourself from embarrassment, to protect your interests and to get what you want, to protect your self-image and the way others see you, to protect your assets and the things you have, including your energy levels and the time you don't want to waste on doing something else, or to protect the emotions and feelings of others.

Lying is just a way to manipulate reality so you can protect the way you see "good and right" in the world. You have an image of what you believe to be the right way of doing things, so you lie to maintain that reality. Interesting when you see it like that, isn't it?

Let's say you're at the gym, and people are talking about the polarizing topic of politics. However, while you're a firm supporter of the blue side, it seems everyone in the room supports red. What do you do? Do you lie and say you support the red side because you want to fit in and out of fear of being judged? Or do you say you support the blue side because it's truly who you are?

What about lying and not saying your truth to protect others' feelings, perhaps if you're afraid of hurting their feelings or making them not like you because they won't agree with what you have to say?

In the book *Nutureshock*, by Po Bronson and Ashley Merryman, they write about how parents will lie to their children about the most trivial things and that children will lie to their parents far more often than their parents will realize. This is because children believe they are telling their parents what they want to hear, and this will make them happier, like whether you've stolen some extra chocolate biscuits out of the cupboard or not.

This continues throughout many stages of your life, all stemming from when we were children. Children believe that their parents have these massive, unfulfillable expectations of them and that if they're not fulfilling them, it's going to make them sad, so they lie about what's going on. The research also found that if parents forcefully confront the lying to their younger children, this only convinces them to try to get better at lying.

If you want to make friends, you need to work on being yourself, which means stopping all the little lies and just being honest. This means standing up for what you believe in and being true to yourself and your beliefs. If you're able to do this, then eventually, you'll connect with people who share the same beliefs as you, and this is where true relationships are formed.

## Speak for Longer Than Normal

When you're talking, how long are the answers you give? When I was starting out with talking to people, I remember when someone would ask me a question, I always believed that people didn't really care about what I had to say and were more interested in themselves. I felt as though that most of the time, people were just asking because it was the polite thing to do, but then if you think that people are thinking this way, are you going to want friendships with them? Probably not.

When you're answering questions that people have for you, and this point leans into the just be yourself point above, answer the question with detail, giving the other person time to relate and keep the flow of conversation going. For example, saying your favorite movie is *The Matrix* and that's it doesn't open the floor to more conversation. In many cases, people will probably think you're just being blunt.

"Hey man, what's your favorite sport?" says the guy at the gym you're making small talk with in the changing room. "Treadmill," you reply. Great conversation. Everyone loves to be a part of it. Instead, how about trying something like this:

"Hey man, what's your favorite sport?"

"It's running on the treadmill at the moment, which is actually quite surprising because I used to hate running. I loved it as a kid but haven't done it for ages and for some reason just really find it enjoyable. Is that weird?"

See how much more personality this approach has, rather than just giving blunt, unfollowable answers? You're showcasing so much more of yourself, are being so much more confident, and bringing so much to the table. The person you're speaking to also has so much more conversational points to work with. Are they going to agree? Say they've also loved and hated it? Do they hate it? Do they understand your newfound love for it? And so on.

The Art of Charm website states that when talking to someone, always aim for two-sentence answers, as a rule of thumb, and one of the best tips to remember is to answer the question directly and then add the "why" to your answer. It's an easy way to have a proper conversation and give the other person something to respond to.

This is such a great tip to remember because not only will you be having a charismatic, confident conversation, but you'll also be learning lots about yourself and why you think the way you do, which will give you even more confidence in yourself!

## Asking the Right Questions

The final point to think about when it comes to keeping the flow of conversation, well, flowing, is to make sure that you're not just talking about yourself the whole time, but you're asking questions to dive deeper into the other person's life, and showing a genuine interest in what they have to say and the person that they are as an individual.

I remember when I started going to the gym, and there was a guy in there who was always in the swimming pool at the same time as me. He used to swim professionally when he was younger, many years ago, and all he would do was always talk about himself. Now, I didn't mind so much at the time because I didn't like talking about myself, but he was so boring. He would go on and on about swimming and the best way to breaststroke and how to train and what to eat and what he did for his job and his wife and kids and how politics is crazy and so on. It was so boring because not once did he ever ask a question about me or my life. Come to think of it, I don't think he knew a single thing about me over the few months we spoke.

I'm sure you don't need me to point out that there are people like this everywhere in life, and the chances are very high that you know someone who fits this description. What do you think about that person? Sure, they're not bad people, but there's no connection or friendship there. It's just you and whoever is sitting around listening to this other person talk. If you don't want to be that person, then you've got to start asking questions.

I wrote the heading for this section as asking the right questions, and hopefully, that got you thinking about what sort of questions you could be asking. The truth is, there are no right or wrong questions, but when it comes to making friends and helping people to connect with you, there's a type of question that knocks every other question out of the ballpark, and that's opinion questions.

How good does it make you feel when someone asked for your opinion on something that matters to them? It feels very good. Just like when you're asking someone for a favor, and this shows that you trust that other person, asking for someone's opinion works along the same lines. You're saying, "I value your opinion and your thoughts, and I want to hear them." It's this view that the other person has that you're interested in what they have to say that's going to bring you together.

Try it yourself. If you're trying to think of a movie to watch, a restaurant to go to, a way to approach a project, or which TV series or book you want to binge next, get someone else's opinion and see the conversation start to flow.

As with all the points we've spoken about throughout this chapter, the best way to keep a conversation flowing is to focus on the other person and put them at the center of the conversation. Whether you're asking them questions about themselves, asking for their opinion, or just hearing what they have to say, this is a method where you can't go wrong.

However, this isn't a method that's going to work with everyone. In fact, none of the methods you could ever learn about and try will work with everyone because you simply can't be friends with everyone. You need to find people who have similar interests to you and are, in essence, a reflection of yourself.

# Method 6 – Discovering the Reflection of Yourself

*"Friendship is born at that moment when one person says to another, 'What! You too? I thought I was the only one.'"* – C.S. Lewis

This is absolutely, 100%, certainly, beyond a doubt, one of the most important aspects of having a relationship with any human being on the planet. Whether that's with a friend, partner, parent, coworker, and so on, this is where you must have some kind of common ground.

There are nearly ten billion people on the planet, and that's a ton of diversity out there, and not everyone will be on the same page as you.

Think back to tribal times when humans were all living off the land, hunting, and gathering, and trying to survive day in and day out. At these times, we all share the common interest of surviving, whether that's hunting for food or looking after the children, so it's easy to work together and towards a common goal. This progresses further as civilization develops.

Some people want to sail boats, and some people want to conquer other lands. Some people want to be farmers and raise families, and some want to be explorers or artists. In the modern day, some people like certain genres of music and movies and not others. Some people love money and fast cars, and others like to walk down more spiritual paths and practice minimalism and so on.

What I'm saying is that it's hardwired into us to seek out people who have similar interests and beliefs as us. Thus, with every new interaction you have, your brain is trying to find a reflection of itself in the other people that you're speaking to. One study published in the *Social Cognitive and Affective Neuroscience Journal* confirmed that common ground is the first thing we look for on a psychological and neurological level when looking to make a connection.

In their studies, they took a group of people and gave them small electrical shocks. Some of the people were friends, and some people were strangers, and the whole time their brain activity was being monitored. As it turns out, when someone else is being shocked, the brain responds in different ways depending on who that person is.

If the person being shocked is a stranger, the brain barely reacts. However, if the person being shocked is a friend, the brain responds in basically an identical way to if *you* were being shocked. Coan, one of the leaders of the project, said:

*"The correlation between self and friend was remarkably similar. The findings show the brain's remarkable capacity to model self to others; that people close to us become a part of ourselves, and that isn't just a metaphor or poetry. It's a very real, physical change that occurs."*

What this means is that you are, or at least will be, part of the people you surround yourself with. Gary Vaynerchuck famously quotes that "you are the average of the five people you surround yourself with," and so having common ground with all these people is how you develop a friend group. Of course, even among your friend group, you're not going to have the exact same interests as everyone, but having some will be a foundation you need to have.

When it comes to making friends and connecting with new people, it's all about finding this common ground from which to build a relationship. Going back to my example of the guy who wouldn't shut up talking about himself when swimming, he clearly had a passionate interest in swimming, or himself. I'm not sure, but my interest was that I just enjoyed being in the water after working out. This is a slight common ground, but not enough to build a connection.

On the other hand, if we both loved the idea of competitive swimming, I'm sure we would have got on well. Think about the friends you've had throughout your life. In every relationship you've had, you've shared something in common, whether you love partying, reading, the same kind of music, and so on. It's all about finding that common ground.

## Action Time – How to Find Common Ground

So, how do you find these shared interests without interviewing the people you're talking to and making your interaction feel like an interrogation? Nobody likes to be interrogated. Well, you can take a few approaches, and which one you choose will all depend on the situation you're in. Allow me to explain.

We already spoke about this first method in the last chapter, but asking questions is the best way to find common ground. However, if you're asking forward, abrupt questions, this may seem a little unnatural, so try to tone it down and make things feel as natural as possible.

For example, asking someone what their dream holiday would be is a great way to gauge what kind of person they are. Do they want to book a hotel in the mountains and go hiking, or would they rather go to a beach party in Ibiza? Sure, you're playing off stereotypes here, but the chances are if they fit the stereotype, then you can see what kind of person they are and whether you have common ground.

What people say is a reflection about themselves, so you need to make sure you're as present as possible when listening to what people have to say, their body language, and the way they talk. If you're talking about a certain subject or something like politics comes up, and the person quickly dismisses it and changes the subject, then this is an obvious sign that they either don't care about politics or don't want to talk about it.

On the other hand, say you start talking about fishing; you may see the other person's eyes light up, and they'll start talking about all these different aspects of fishing with real excitement. If this happens, then you know you've found something the other person is interested in.

We've already talked a bit about making your conversations about the other person, and the same applies here. You don't want to jump straight in and say you caught the biggest fish ever and everyone loved you, and it was amazing because you're just making the conversation about yourself. You need to edge information out of the other person.

That doesn't mean you can't talk about yourself, but instead lead with the other person. So, combining all this together, here's the kind of method you'll want to take. First, listen to what the other person is saying to get hints about what kind of interests they have. Keep chatting until there's a topic that interests you both, and then dive into, asking them questions to explain more. Add in your own stories and experiences, but not in a boasting light, but in a way that progresses the conversation.

This method is the best way to find common ground, and once established, you should see a new friendship or relationship starting to bloom right before your eyes.

Now, it should go without saying that while this is an effective technique for building and nurturing relationships, you've probably heard the saying that you can't please everyone, nor can you be friends with absolutely everyone you meet. If you tried to, then at some point, you're going to end up faking and lying about who you are in order to fit in, and that's not what we're trying to achieve here.

As you go about your life and build your confidence and begin to interact with more and more people, you're going to find people you don't like, and there are going to be people who don't like you. There's nothing wrong with this at all because you literally cannot be everyone's cup of tea, which is a British saying that means the same thing.

This means that you'll need to know how to choose your friends, and how to choose who you're spending your energy on, and who you'll engage with for a little while before deciding if you actually want some kind of relationship with them, which is what we're going to be focusing on in the next chapter!

Communication Skills Training Series

# Method 7 – Choosing the Right Friends

*"Young people, choose your friends wisely. There's an old saying, show me your friends and I'll tell you who you are." – Unknown*

Choosing the right friends is never easy. While I was in school, I ended up hanging around with some kids that used to smoke drugs on the weekend, stolen from one of the boys' older brothers. I only tried it once myself, but I don't understand why I chose to hang around with them. We had nothing in common, and we didn't like each other that much, and the only time I did try it, we ended up getting a warning from the police, meaning I got in a lot of trouble when I got home.

Not every person out there will be, nor needs to, be your friend. As an individual interested in making strong relationships with people, you need to be selective with who you're creating these relationships with. You want to befriend people who are good for you and will raise you up to be the best version of yourself, especially since this is what you'll hopefully want to be doing for them.

Think about some of the people in your life now or who have been in your life in the past. We've all had toxic friends at some point; you know, the people who gossip behind everyone's back and say mean things, or perhaps even bully other friends because they think it's funny, even when no one else is laughing. Sure, everyone goes through stages, and some people will pretend to be someone they're not because they want to fit in, but as you grow up, you should start to see people for who they are.

It's strange when you think about it. In my sales company back in 2015, I worked with a guy who used to talk dirt behind everyone's back. We'd have a meeting, and someone would be nervous about giving their presentation, and afterward, he would moan and berate the person for being nervous and not being confident like he thought "all men should be." He did this with everyone about everything, and it never occurred to me that he would do the same about me.

Because he used to "open up" with all these little statements about everyone else to me, I thought we were friends, but of course, I overhear him talking about me and how annoying I am with the people he was just berating minutes beforehand, and I suddenly realized the kind of person he was. Aka, not the type of person I wanted to waste my time and energy on.

**The Science Behind Choosing Friends**

There's a saying I love, and while there are many different ways of wording it, it basically comes down to this one statement. Read it and read it again:

You are the people you surround yourself with.

Let's say you have a group of people around you, and there are six of you in total. Since you'll have a relationship based on things like proximity (meaning you see each other a lot, whether you're in school, at a club, or work) and common interests, you're people who know each other quite well.

However, that doesn't mean these are nice people, just because you have common interests. Look at the way these people think and how they look at the world, and you'll find that you "borrow" a bit of all of them. Some people might even say you're the average of those five people. If you haven't chosen your friendships but rather just associate with these people because they're physically close to you, they may not be the best people for you, nor may they be offering you the best kind of relationship you deserve.

This is such an important consideration you need to be thinking about because the people in this group of friends, whether obvious or not, will dictate so many aspects of your life.

A 2013 study published in *Psychological Science* found that if you're the sort of person who suffers from lack of discipline or low self-esteem, your best chances of improving these areas of your life are hanging out and interacting with people who are strong-willed and disciplined.

Likewise, the friends you keep will influence your choices massively, even if you think you're individually in control. A 2014 survey published in the *Journal of Consumer Research* discovered that friends are a key factor in making financially sound decisions and not making impulse purchases. However, this also works the other way around.

If you love to give in to temptations and you can easily spend money, your friends can amplify this since you're more likely to indulge together. Whether you look at this from a financial, health, or social standpoint, just being around certain people can leave you in a bad position you don't want to be in. This is what it means to be partners in crime.

To cut a long story short, if you hang out and become friends with people who make bad choices and put people down, then the chances are you're going to make bad choices and put people down. If you want to lift yourself up with others and make good choices, then you'll want to hang out with people who do all these things. Science says so.

When you're looking for friends, or want any kind of relationship, whether that's professional or romantic, you need to make sure you're choosing the right person; this may seem easier said than done unless you know what you're looking for. Below, we're going to explore some ways to do just this!

**Taking Things to the Next Level**

Ask yourself this: Where do you want to be in five years' time? Do you want a promotion? Do you want to be fitter and healthier? Do you want to be traveling, owning your own house, or starting your own business? Whatever it is you want to achieve, the people you surround yourself with will be the people who will get you there and will help you make the right decisions.

When you're going into a new relationship, ask yourself: Is this person going to help me be the best version of myself, or will they hold me back? When I started writing these books, I had a friend who was self-employed at the same time as a personal trainer. We would hang out every Friday, having a few drinks with each other, and then just chat about all these plans and ideas for new projects we had. We were both working on different things, but having the opportunity to be open and to get excited about what we were doing only propelled us going forward, and here we are today.

Before, when I was hanging out with the stoner people for a year or two, nobody wanted to do anything and was very content staying in the same place they had always been in and had no aspirations to do anything. That's fine if that's what they wanted to do, but it wasn't for me. It was making me miserable.

Be selective with who you want to be and get people who can help you get there. Naturally, you'll also be having the same effect on their life. That's not to say you can't talk to anyone outside of your friendships. It's all well and good to have acquaintance friends and people you just have small talk with and just relax, maybe have a drink with every once in a while. There's nothing wrong with that. You need to be thinking about who your close friends are and who you're going to give the time and energy to while allowing them into your inner circle.

### Finding Yourself in Others

Hand in hand with the last point and the last chapter (so don't worry, I'm not going to go on about it too much more!), finding out what your friend's goals and aspirations are is a great way to see if you could and should be friends. This is why it's so important to find common ground. If you're both able to aim towards the same aspiring goals, then you're going to be able to lift each other up, and you'll have a lot more in common, even if your goals are two different things.

Choose friends with big goals that are on a similar or higher level to your own. These don't even have to be things like starting a business, writing a book, or traveling the world. If you're just coming out of depression, for example, you may just have the goal of getting a social life with people you see regularly, or you may want to form the habits of exercising and looking after your health properly. Choosing friends with similar values will help you achieve your goals, no matter what they are.

### Choose Friends That Give and Take

A friendship, or any relationship for that matter, is all about give and take. It's a balancing act. You can't have a relationship where one person does everything for the other person, whether that's in the form of money, time, or emotional support, but gets nothing back. That's not to say you should be giving with the idea that you're going to get something back at some point, but your relationship won't be balanced, and you'll be left feeling unfulfilled. Eventually, you'll be filled with resentment for yourself and them.

This means you need to give what you expect to get and treat others how you would want to be treated yourself. This is the golden rule of friendships. If you can manage this and reduce the number of people who aren't treating you like you deserve, you'll find the relationships you have to be far more rewarding.

### Action Time – Get the Relationships You Deserve

The action times I've shared so far have all been about finding new friends and building the confidence to talk to people, but this one will be a bit different. This time I want you to take a look at the relationships you already have and start thinking about whether they are the relationships you want or deserve. Don't worry, I'm not saying you should say, "Oh, my girlfriend is pretty toxic, so I'm out." You don't need to be so reckless with your decisions, but take a moment to evaluate how you feel with the people you're spending time with.

You may find you're still friends with people you went to school or college with, but you've grown apart and don't have a lot in common anymore. You just hang out because it's your comfort zone to be together. Like I said earlier in the chapter, it's fine to have these friends. You're not trying to cut people out and say you're done with them, but you're considering how much of your time you're giving them.

If you're giving them all your time and you're hanging out multiple times per week, but you're not happy and want to instead spend your time with people who are more like you, then you'll need to cut back and find these new relationships that are more suited to who you are in your life right now.

However, if you find that you're friends with someone who's pretty toxic, you may want to start moving away from them completely. Don't worry; you're not alone in this. There are plenty of people out there, me included, who end up being friends with people who are pretty toxic, but you don't even see it until you think about it and open your eyes.

The truth is, most "toxic" people aren't toxic for the sake of being toxic, but rather they are hurt and dealing with a lot of emotional pain or baggage, perhaps stuff they have to deal with from past relationships or even from their relationships with their parents. However, these traumas are up to them to sort out, and it's no excuse for being a bad person.

This is where the decision-making process comes into play. Are you going to be friends with these people and support them on their journey, even if it gets worse before it gets better, or are you going to cut back the amount of time you're spending with them to focus on other relationships? The choice is up to you.

These can feel like big decisions to make. If you take some time to think about your partner and think, "Actually, this person isn't right for me," this can be a hard state of mind to come to terms with. In this situation, give it time and let things play out on their own accord. Everything will happen the way it's meant to. Just give it some thinking time, talk to the other person about how you feel in the relationship, and allow yourself to see what is really going on.

This way, you'll be opening the door to beautiful, balanced, and fulfilling relationships, where you're investing your time on the right people that are best suited for you while still allowing yourself to be civil with everybody else!

And with that, we come to the end of this chapter. As promised, this part of the book is all about sowing the seeds to beautiful relationships, whether that's becoming more confident in yourself or creating opportunities for these relationships to manifest in the first place. However, I've spoken a lot about talking and ways you can approach conversations.

There's one key part of any relationship that we haven't spoken about yet, and you may want to strap yourself in for this one because it's perhaps the most important one yet.

# Method 8 – Share Experiences. Make Memories.

*"We do not remember days, we remember moments." – Cesare Pavese*

Think of all the best relationships in your life. Scratch that, think of one relationship you've had in your life that meant something to you and was the most beautiful relationship you can think of. It can be about anyone at any time in your life. Have you got one? Nice.

Now think about what kind of relationship you had with that person. Did you go for coffee once a week, but this was the only time you saw them? Did you only ever see that person at work? Did you just see them now and then and have a phone catch up? No, the answer is probably not for all of the above. In reality, the chances are that when you think of the most beautiful relationship possible, you're thinking of relationships where you shared experiences and made memories together.

Remember the concerts you went to, the parties, the sleepovers, the all-night gaming sessions, the dates, the trips to the zoo, and the restaurants, and the vacations abroad, and crying with fits of laughter with each other, and so on? It's all well and good talking the talk and knowing *how* to talk to people, but so much of a connection will come from the experiences you share with each other.

As someone who wants to win friends and become more charismatic, it's up to you to create opportunities for these kinds of experiences to happen, which means training yourself to become a little more outgoing, confident in asking, and becoming a little more creative with the ideas you can come up with to do things. Ready for this one? Let's do it.

**The Science of Making Memories and, Therefore, Great Relationships**

What I love most about this concept is just how easy it is to grasp. The human brain may be infinitely complex, and we may not even understand half of how it works, but how it works on the surface is extremely simple. According to *Psychology Today,* friendships exist when pleasure is taken in the company of other people.

Whenever you do something in your life, your brain actively responds to it by releasing chemicals that make you feel good or bad about whatever situation you're in. If your body is hungry, it gives you hungry feelings. You then eat, and your body gives you feel-good chemicals like dopamine that reward you for taking action. Your brain wants you to survive, so it makes you feel good for carrying out essential tasks. With me so far?

These processes far exceed just basic survival tasks. Humans are social creatures who rely on the closeness and community of others around them. Just like feeling hungry, your mind rewards you for spending time with people because being social is hardwired into the survival part of our brain.

Now, we've come a long way from living in caves and needing each other to survive. It is very possible nowadays to live by yourself and thrive completely alone, but your brain will still make you feel lonely and release chemicals and hormones like cortisol, the stress chemical, because it wants you to interact with other people and be social. That's just human instinct.

Zeroing in on this subject a little more, if you have bad experiences with someone, like a bully or someone who beats you up or calls you names, your brain will record these experiences as being bad and will want to do everything it can to keep you away from them. This is why when you painfully break up with an ex, seeing them can bring up all those old, sad feelings that can make you feel quite strange, especially if you're not over them.

You may have agreed that you wanted to stay friends, but your brain still feels abandoned or betrayed by your ex, and will send signals to the rest of you that make you sad and, therefore, want to stay away from them. Of course, like everything we've spoken about in this book so far, and what we're going to focus on for the rest of this chapter, is that it works the other way too.

If you have a positive, fulfilling, and rewarding experience with someone, then your brain will release a ton of feel-good chemicals that record the experience as being good and the people involved as being people you want to spend more time with. It's funny because when you look at human beings in this way, it's easy to see we haven't gone very far from the kinds of people we used to be living in tribes and living off the land.

This is why typical activities you do with friends include going out to eat food or getting a takeaway delivered and then having a movie night. You could do something a bit more exhilarating, like going to a music concert, going on an assault course, or going on vacation to a beautiful place. Your mind loves all these new experiences and thrives off doing new things, expanding your comfort zone, and having a stress-free and pleasurable time, and it remembers the people you're doing these things with.

So, bringing all of this together, solid and fulfilling relationships require positive experiences. These could be anything from going somewhere or doing an activity together, or even being there for someone during a hard time. Being the person who turns negative experiences into positive experiences is another great way to build relationships, but you can't rely on this to happen. Focus on creating positive experiences from scratch.

From a science and psychology standpoint, positive experiences will relate to you as being a positive influence in the lives of the people you surround yourself with, and relationships can then grow over time.

## Action Time – Go Out and Have Fun

Perhaps my favorite action time of this book.

For this method, I want you to take someone you're friends with (it doesn't matter whether you're close or you're coworkers), and you want to get closer to them and take the plunge doing something together. If you're just starting out, then start off small. This could be asking someone to go for lunch or a coffee one afternoon. If you're more confident or closer to someone, you could go for a day out together, perhaps to the beach or the zoo. You could even go for a walk in a local park.

The essence of this part of the process is that it doesn't matter what you're doing. It's more the fact you're doing something with the other person. Of course, it's good to lose yourself in the activity you're doing, but take some time to be mindful, especially afterward, about how you felt towards that person during the activity and how your bond with them is now stronger.

When people say the proof is in the pudding, this is all you're going to need, and having a few experiences like this will be a huge boost in your confidence and will show you the power of positive experiences. As a quick note, hand in hand with the previous chapters, try to take some time to pick a good activity that will suit both of you and will be something you both enjoy (common interests), or allow them to choose something to do and know they're going to like (putting them first).

Enjoy yourself and have fun, but I can't stress enough how important it is to look back at the end of the day and see how you feel about the day and the person you spent it with. This is how you'll learn and truly understand what a difference it can make.

And with that, we come to the end of Part Two. Are you enjoying yourself so far? Are you learning lots? With everything we've discussed so far, you should have everything you need to meet new people, nurturing relationships with the people around you, and to start building up your confidence by knowing what to do around new people.

While we've covered the basics, as we head into Part Three, we're going to start looking more into the advanced strategies that go into taking existing relationships and then making them stronger than ever before.

# Part Three – The Advanced Teachings of Nurturing Stronger Relationships

Before I dive into the meat of this chapter, I want you to think about this question: What does a strong relationship mean to you?

To many, it means trusting each other, having respect for each other, having fun with each other, and being there for one another when you need each other. You want to feel safe and secure with this other person, and you'll want to understand each other. Perhaps it means inspiring each other or being committed to each other. Maybe it means sticking by each other no matter what.

No matter what a strong relationship means to you, the truth is that the foundations of a relationship don't come from the relationship and connection you have with someone else, but they instead come from within you. Take a moment to process that.

Suppose you're not comfortable, confident, and truly yourself with yourself. In that case, you can't expect you to be you when you're around other people, and a truly, meaningful relationship is never then going to form. Think of it this way. When you're out and about in your life, let's say you're at work, a parcel might get delivered. The person comes in, and you start chatting with them. You talk about the weather and stuff happening around you, and you put on a friendly voice, and it's a pleasant interaction.

This is what is known as "putting on airs" because it doesn't matter how you're feeling. Whether you're feeling super positive, super negative, or somewhere in between, you're going to act the same. While this is pretty understandable to act this way for someone you're probably never going to see again or will only see in passing, some of us do this to the people closest to us.

Hands up if you feel like you sometimes wear a metaphorical mask when you're hanging out with the people around you, and you don't feel like you're acting like your true self. Perhaps you act posher or politer than you are, or you talk in a certain way about particular subjects you wouldn't usually talk about because you think that's what the other person cares about, even if you don't. Maybe you filter yourself and the way you usually act because it may seem inappropriate.

Sure, there are times when this is acceptable, and you're going to need to do it, but if you want proper relationships with people, then you need to be yourself and not have to hide behind masks or filters. This can be hard, I know from experience, but it's not impossible to "find yourself" and be true to yourself. When you're allowing yourself to open up and be yourself, you'll see such a huge shift in yourself, how you view yourself, and your connection with the people around you.

This is what I'm going to be focusing on throughout this section of the book. We're going to cover topics like becoming vulnerable, how to be yourself, learning about the art of giving and taking, and mastering how your words make such a big difference in other people's lives. Anyway, enough talking about—let's jump into it.

## Method 9 – How to Open Up and Become Vulnerable

*"When we were children, we used to think that when we were grown-up we would no longer be vulnerable. But to grow up is to accept vulnerability… To be alive is to be vulnerable." – Madeleine L'Engle*

Brene Brown, a famous psychology researcher, author, and motivational speaker, speaks about how the most crucial aspect to think about when it comes to being happy and forming positive, meaningful, and fulfilling relationships with others comes down to being vulnerable. Being vulnerable, you may ask? Surely not.

When most people think of being vulnerable, they think it means to be weak or damaged. If I ask you to think about a "vulnerable animal," you'll probably think of a rescue animal before it's been rescued, or one that's been hurt and is being hunted by a predator on a nature documentary. Either way, it's not somewhere you consciously want to be.

But that's not entirely true.

When I, Brene Brown, or anybody else interested in happiness and social well-being talk about vulnerability, we're talking about the art of opening yourself up and being your true self, both with yourself and when you're around other people. Here's an example.

Let's say you're in a relationship with someone, and you have some trust issues. Your last partner cheated on you, and now you have these niggly little thoughts, doubts, and insecurities that come up now and then. They play on your mind and make you miserable, but you don't want to talk about them with your partner out of fear of being rejected. They might think you're silly or weak-minded, or even stupid for having these thoughts, so you keep them to yourself.

Anything that happens that triggers these feelings, you put up walls and push down insecurities, always trying not to think about them and never opening up and talking to other people, especially your partner, about them.

A situation like this never ends well. These insecurities build up and up over time, and eventually, they'll spill over the edge. You'll resent your partner because they keep triggering you, even though you won't know this at the time. Your paranoid attitude will cause you to do things like checking your partner's social media over and over or even reading through their text messages to see who they're talking to. We all do weird things in our relationships like this from time to time, but is it a healthy relationship? Of course not.

A healthy relationship would require you to be vulnerable and open up about your insecurities. This means being vulnerable and talking to your partner about how you feel and the stuff you're going through. Sure, they may try and help, or they may not know what to say, but that's not the point. The point is that you're opening up and allowing yourself to be out there and open to the world. You're saying this is me and what I'm going through, both good and bad, and I don't need to be ashamed of any of it.

Once you can get to this stage—and it's a journey, believe me—you'll find it's quite a liberating and refreshing experience. However, getting there is a whole other story, and it can definitely feel like a frightening one.

I know what you're thinking: *Uh, I don't want to open up about the things that are wrong with me and the things that scare me. I don't want to be open. I just want to push all the bad stuff down, never think about it, and put all those walls up to protect myself. If I don't think about it, it will go away eventually, right?*

Not so much. If you genuinely want to progress on your self-improvement journey and discover true happiness, even if this is just with yourself and not even concerning your relationships with other people, this is a process you're going to need to go through.

There's no denying that researchers like Brene Brown have pioneered this research field and put together all the science behind this over the last few decades. If you want to know more, I highly recommend checking out her book *Daring Greatly* or watching her TED talk, which is where it all started and remains one of the most-watched TED talks to this day. For now, though, I'll take some of the key lessons and takeaways that I learned from her speeches and books and share them with you here.

## The First Step is Courage

It would be amazing if you could just snap your fingers, be vulnerable and open with everyone, and just truly focus on being yourself as naturally as possible, but that would be too simple. Instead, there are some steps to take.

However, the first point to think about is that being vulnerable, in the words of Brown herself, takes a certain amount of courage. You need to be brave, and there will come the point where you need to step out of your comfort zone and take the plunge. You could read every book and listen to every podcast on the subject, but there will always come a time where you open up to someone else and lay who you are out on the table for everyone else to see.

And this takes courage. You may not feel like you're ready now, but that's okay. You can build up to that over time. This is why it's wrong to see being vulnerable as a sign of weakness because, in fact, it's one of the strongest and most powerful things you can do. By going down this path and going for it, you'll be able to be your true and authentic self.

This will come in time, and you can start with little things to build up your courage like we've spoken about in previous chapters. I'm also not saying that you need to lay everything out on the table to one person straight away. You wouldn't go on a date and lay out all your baggage on the first night. That's the best way to scare people away because you're oversharing to someone you have no relationship with. It's all about building up your vulnerability and how open you can be with someone as your relationship with them grows.

The best thing to do is to take one thing at a time. Let's say you feel bad because you have a weight insecurity about yourself. You're talking to someone you're getting to know, and what they're saying is triggering you. Instead of pushing down your feelings and not speaking about it, you'll need to find the courage to open up and talk about how you feel. If someone is saying something like, "Oh, weight issues are just rubbish. It's just people trying to justify eating badly," you may want to share your beliefs on the subject.

You don't need to put someone down or take offense, but instead, just share your point of view. A lot of things happen here. Firstly, whether the person disagrees or not, they'll respect you for voicing your beliefs and not just going along with what they said. Then, they'll either listen to you, or they'll ignore you. If they listen and they're open to what you're saying and go along with something like "Oh yeah, I suppose I've never looked at it from this angle before," then this says a lot about that person, and they could be a good person to be friends with.

If, on the other hand, they say something like "Ppftt, what do you know?" and are pretty closed off about it, then do you want to have some kind of relationship with that person anyway? Probably not. Either way, it all starts with having the courage to open up and be yourself unapologetically.

**Start Learning About Your True Self**

I've spoken a lot about being your "true" self, or your authentic self, and you may be wondering who that is, and this in itself is an essential part of becoming vulnerable. But how can you be your true self if you don't know who that is?

For a lot of my life, I suffered from social anxiety, and as the years went by, I started to believe that this was who I was. I was the guy who worked in sales who went to work, went home, perhaps forced myself to see a friend every other now and then but couldn't wait to get home and just wrap myself up in my own world. I was single, a background guy, and just getting by. I used to write things like "I'm surviving, not thriving," quite regularly in my journal.

As I continued being this way, I started to believe that this was my identity. *How is there anything I can do about my social anxiety? It's just who I am at my very core.* It wasn't. Sure, you may be reading this and thinking, "Yeah, I am a shy, introverted person, and I get exhausted speaking to a lot of people." That's fine. What I'm saying is that so many have all these ideas in our heads about who we are, and the more often they're repeated, the more firmly we start to believe them. What we forget is that we're so much more than these identities that we accept for ourselves.

One of the most important aspects of becoming vulnerable is to become self-aware. This means understanding what beliefs you hold about yourself, how you identify with yourself, and therefore who you are. I could write a whole book in itself about this topic, so I'll leave you with the main takeaway.

**Action Time – Become Vulnerable with Yourself**

Start paying attention to your thoughts and emotions.

When anything happens in your life, whether you're watching the news, a movie, or chatting with someone, pay attention to how you feel and what emotions are coming up. When you get a moment, explore those emotions, discover how you feel, and then question why you feel this way. The answers you get may surprise you.

I remember I started doing this by beginning my own meditation practice and keeping a journal. I understand this is not for everyone, so figure out what works for you. Either way, I listened to my thoughts and feelings and realized that I wasn't a shy person who loved being alone. I was just lonely and justifying this loneliness. Understanding this opened the door for my self-care journey and gave me great insight into where I was in my life and who I am.

When you piece together all these points, you'll start learning about who you are, and you'll start being able to be yourself around other people. Yes, it takes a tremendous amount of courage to open up, but once you do, you'll be opening the door to some amazing relationships that you wouldn't even believe could exist.

# Method 10 – Opening Your Door to the World

*"Your real self may be hiding somewhere, look for it within, when you find yourself, you can freely be what you want to be." – Michael Bassey Johnson*

Hand in hand with the last chapter, it's all well and good taking time to learn about yourself and who you are on the inside, but do you know who you are on the outside? One of the biggest problems for me while overcoming my social anxiety was that I had locked myself away in my apartment doing the bare minimum for so many years, it got to a point where I didn't know who I was.

What music and movies did I like? What food did I like? What kind of places did I want to travel to, and what types of books did I want to read? What activities, or exercises, or sports did I like doing? I indeed didn't have answers for these, and if asked, I would just go off the answers I would have given if I was still a teenager. Then, when I think about it, would those answers be the same? No, probably not.

As we change, our choices, tastes, likes, and dislikes change, and if you're looking to get to know someone and have a relationship with them, which is based on the foundations of common ground, then you need to know what you're interested in. This may sound like fundamental stuff, but I want you to take a moment to think about it.

Remember the music you used to like and how that's changed since you were a kid. And movies. Think about your guilty pleasures. All of these things become who you are, and they're not static things. You may hate musicals, and the very idea of them makes you cringe. Then, one day, you take the time to see one, perhaps not out of choice, and you enjoy yourself. Throughout an evening, something you had no interest in doesn't seem too bad. Your true self is continuously changing and evolving as you go through your life, but only if you let it.

I'm sure everyone would agree that it's easy to get stuck in your ways, especially as you get older and more experienced. Unless you're able to open your door to the world and embrace new experiences, even if you're giving them a try to see whether they're for you or not, this is how you grow as a person and understand yourself better. And of course, the better you understand yourself, the better your relationships will be because you won't be settling! See how it's all tying together?

It's true; there are going to be experiences out there that you don't like. That new sushi restaurant down the road? Yuck. I can't think of eating anything worse than raw fish, but then one day, you give it a go with a new friend, and lo and behold, you don't think it's too bad. You even agree that you might consider going again. How about that?

Not only are you trying new experiences (which is a chance to connect with people in your life), but you're diving in and seeing who you are as a person, giving new things a go, and then making up your mind. What's more, science says that trying new things can be incredible for your brain and mindset.

Dr. Papp of Harvard University wrote:

*"Until the mid-1990s, we thought that people were born with however many brain cells they would die with. We now know that the growth of new cells—a process called neurogenesis—occurs throughout life, even in older age,"*

This means your brain is always growing new cells and is changing all the time. If you don't do new things and have new experiences, your brain doesn't tend to grow much because it's familiar with everything around it. Of course, not every day can be a new and wondrous adventure where you try new things, but you don't need to. Doing new things when you can is great for providing yourself with these benefits.

By stimulating your brain in different ways by doing new things and trying new activities, you're allowing your brain to grow in new and exciting ways. This will make you want to do more new things, and this is what it means to be outgoing. Remember how outgoing you were as a kid? It's entirely possible to get that back if you open your mind and say yes to new opportunities.

**Action Time – Do Something New!**

I bet you saw this one coming.

When I say do something new, you don't need to go for the most outlandish and crazy thing you can think of. I'm not saying go skydiving or take up wakeboarding, but if an opportunity presents itself, such as going to a new restaurant or seeing a play, joining a book club, or taking dance lessons, then this action time is to say yes.

Go into the activity with an open mind and give it your best shot. If you don't enjoy yourself, then that's fine. You're not going to enjoy everything, and you've still taken another step on your journey when it comes to understanding yourself. However, if you try something new and absolutely love it, you've opened a brand new door, of which there are plenty of beautiful new experiences for you to try.

Don't deny yourself of what could be something amazing!

You can try these new experiences with other people to improve your relationships, or you can take your experiences, and you'll have far more to talk about with everybody in your life. It all starts with you opening your mind to what could be.

Now that the last two chapters have included a bit of time working on yourself and your mindset, we're going to take a little trip back into the art of relationships themselves, this time taking a look at the art of giving and taking, or in this case, not taking.

# Method 11 – Unconditionally Giving and Not Taking

*"Blessed are those who can give without remembering, and take without forgetting" – Unknown*

Method 3 was all about asking for favors and getting people to help you out as a way to spark a connection and implement trust, but one of the most fantastic ways to form and build on a friendship is by giving. And by giving, I mean giving and not just giving because you're expecting something back at a later date. In fact, I'm not even talking about the act of giving someone a gift or a physical item, but rather the art of reciprocating.

In 2009, a study was carried out by Peter DeSciolo and Robert Kurzban titled "The Alliance Hypothesis of Human Friendship." Within the study, the researchers discovered that if you want to have a "true friendship" with somebody, the age-old saying "I'll scratch your back and you scratch mine" might not cut the mustard. You need to go deeper than this.

When you think about it, the act of helping out someone else and them helping you out—aka, having each other's backs—makes sense. We've spoken a lot about the survival aspect of human nature, and how as social creatures, we're instinctively hardwired to come together to look out for one another. This, for many people, is the basis of most relationships, or at least a fundamental part. However, to take your relationship one step further, you'll need to learn to give without taking, which means to give without expecting anything in return.

Now, I know what you're thinking because I thought the same thing. If you give and give and give in relationships, then, of course, people are going to like you. You could always cover the bills for coffee, be a shoulder to cry on, organize everything, and always be the one carrying the conversations, but if you get nothing back ever, then this is just someone taking advantage of you, and that's true. Relationships are a balance between giving and taking, and there is a line that can be crossed. Don't worry; if you feel like this is the case in any of your relationships, you will have some deep-rooted feeling telling you that this is the case.

It will be very hard to miss.

The trick is to give in your relationships without losing sight of who you are, and without, as the Tiny Buddha website writes, sacrificing your needs. Doing this properly is a balancing act between being yourself and managing your own life, and then making a life with someone else. Of course, I'm not just talking about romantic and dating partners. This is evident in all kinds of relationships.

## What I Mean By Giving

I'm writing this short section just so we're on the same page. When I say you're giving without taking, this can refer to anything. You may get home early from work and decide to deep clean the entire house before your partner gets home. You may get takeout to eat that night after someone in your life has had a stressful day. You may rub their feet in the evening or make them breakfast in bed off the cuff and for no real reason.

You may help them out by buying something when they're short on money or take them out just because you care about them. If they're going through a hard time, you might have them stay over, or you stay over at their house, you might do an activity to take their mind off things, or you may sit and talk about their situation with them.

It doesn't matter what you're giving; the point is that you're doing it because you want to make the other person happy, not because you want something in return. I had a friend in college who moved in with his girlfriend during his final year, and while an average guy, he had some weird ways of being in a relationship.

I remember once, while his girlfriend was doing her finals, that he tidied up the entire apartment, made dinner, and set up the lounge all nice for a movie night so his girlfriend could have a night off and destress. On the surface, this is a nice, selfless thing to do, and it's easy to see when you're doing things like this that relationships are strengthened by the minute.

However, the two ended up arguing, and the night was ruined. When my friend told me about this the next day, he explained how they got to bed after the movie, and he wanted to be intimate with his girlfriend. She said she was tired and wanted to go to sleep, but was grateful for the evening. He then got upset because he had put so much effort in and thought his girlfriend wasn't giving anything back. He thought her selfish.

Now, I agree with you if you think this is a very toxic way to look at things, but there's no doubt this is a trap that we all fall into every now and then. Just because we're doing something nice for someone, that doesn't mean that they have to do anything back. When you give without asking, it's unconditional. If the guy I went to college with had understood this, he would have gone to sleep with his girlfriend, finished a lovely evening, and the argument may never have happened.

Fast forward to the future. If he was having a stressful time, she might think to do something nice for him. Even if she doesn't, the relationship is still strong because you know that even if you're in a bad, stressful place, your friend or partner or whoever it is will be there to make you feel okay again.

In this situation, him acting up because he didn't get anything back taints the act of giving. Anything he does in the future, his girlfriend will think, *Oh well, he's only being nice because he wants something in return later,* and this way of thinking will help cause relationships to fall apart. The relationship becomes about a power balance, with people counting who owes who what, rather than just enjoying being in each other's company.

## The Importance of Boundaries

I've said already that it's a fine line between giving to build a relationship and making someone happy and being used, but this is something you'll have to figure out for yourself. Say the guy is a decent guy who likes doing things to make his girlfriend happy. He organizes dates, cooks dinner, and sets up romantic evenings, which goes for months, perhaps even years.

However, while expecting nothing back, the relationship feels empty. She goes out with her friends all the time, and they spend very little time together outside of the things he organized. They lack a connection and don't do activities together, and the whole relationship feels very one-sided.

This can be a danger zone. In some cases, the guy may try extra hard to be nice in an attempt to make his girlfriend notice and appreciate him more, but then we're back at square one of him doing these things because he wants something in return. In this example, he wants her love and affection.

Unfortunately, there are no hard and fast guidelines to what you should do here, and it's up to you to decide where you put your boundaries. This is why it's essential to know and understand yourself.

A healthy relationship is like a dance. You step left, and you step right together. Sometimes one of you leads, and then you switch. You take it in turns to spin. Sure, there will be times when you stand on each other's toes, and you need to find your footing and rhythm again, and that's okay. However, if you're always trying to sync up or feel as though you're carrying all the weight, this isn't a healthy relationship.

Again, where you set your boundaries is up to you. If you feel like you're giving loads, but the relationships you're in are very one-sided, then talk to the person involved about how you feel. Have a conversation with yourself about how you feel and why you feel the way you do.

This can become a very complicated area when you dive into giving and taking. If you're giving because you want something back, whether it's a physical or emotional "thing," then this may be a sign you feel lonely or invalidated, and you're craving validation from someone else. This can be a form of attachment or a display of insecurity, which you'll want to work through by reading or getting counseling. This affects both professional and personal relationships of all kinds. Find the balance between giving because you care about the person and giving because you want something back.

If you're able to find the balance that works for you, and you've discovered your own boundaries, your relationships will begin to flourish. This is because you'll be taking care of your own needs for security and validation within yourself, and then everything you give to the people in your life comes from a place of love.

**Action Time – Learn to Validate Yourself**

A lot of giving happens in today's world because people want something back. As a kid, I would tidy the house and put all my toys away before my parents got home from work, not because I wanted to live in a tidy house and loved having space, but because I wanted my parents to tell me I did a good job. This is clearly not a healthy mindset to have because it leads to unhealthy giving.

For this action time, I want you to think about things you do in your life for other people and then ask yourself why you do them.

Sure, there are things in life that we just have to do, like washing the dishes or sweeping the floors, but pay attention to your thoughts when you do certain things. Are you buying your partner a coffee because you want them to forgive you for a mistaken comment, or because you just want a pleasant experience with them? Are you working hard on your project at work because you want to do well in your job or because you want to make your boss happy?

During my time in sales, a lot of my work was focused on making my boss happy, and it made me resent what I did. Sure, the aim of the game is to make the customer happy and get good results, but I wasn't working to my standards (you could say my boundaries), but I was seeking out the validation of my boss.

When I switched my mindset to working as hard as I could to get a project done to the best of my ability, and I looked at it and thought, *Yes, this is exactly what I'm aiming for,* success came to me in ways I could never have imagined beforehand. When you're going throughout your life, start doing things for yourself, and validating yourself. Tell yourself you've done a job well, and treat yourself with the kindness you'd want from others.

From here, you'll find your boundaries naturally. You'll be able to give unconditionally to the people around you, especially to the ones you love, which can strengthen your relationship beyond belief. It takes practice, but it's a lifelong skill that will change everything.

# Method 12 – Words: The Power of Light and Dark Magic

*"Speak with integrity. Say only what you mean. Avoid using the word to speak against yourself or to gossip about others. Use your power of your word in the direction of truth and love." – Don Miguel Ruiz*

One of the best books I've ever read is a book called *The Four Agreements* by Don Miguel Quiz. The book outlines four Toltec beliefs on how we live our lives and how our mind works. By understanding these beliefs, we can then choose how we want to show up in the world, all while choosing the kind of person we want to be and removing any self-limiting beliefs we may have.

One of the most powerful chapters in this book is about the words we use, which Don refers to as light and dark magic. Don writes amazingly, so I'm going to paraphrase the example he uses in the book about how the way we talk to people affects not only those individuals on a personal level but also our relationships with them. Using only words, you can pick someone up and place them on top of a mountain, or you can crush them. It's up to you.

## The Story of the Singing Girl

In the chapter "The First Agreement," Don writes about a woman, a fairly normal, intelligent, kindhearted woman, and her daughter, who she loved a great deal. The mother gets home from work one day and, after a stressful day in the office through no fault of her own, she's in a bad mood.

When she arrives home, her daughter, who may be five or six, is singing. Her daughter loves to sing because it makes her feel free and beautiful, and it is her favorite thing to do. Stressed from the day and suffering from a giant headache, her mother gets home and says, "Can you please shut up? Your voice is doing my head in," or words to this effect.

Now, the mother didn't mean to be so aggressive. She was just acting out in the moment because she was suffering, and the daughter didn't mean to antagonize the mother; she didn't even know the mother was suffering. But, the mother's words cut into the daughter, and she then believed that her voice was horrible and was "doing her mother's head in." She believed her mother's words and never sang again, depriving herself of all those lovely, beautiful feelings and robbing the world of the beautiful gift she held.

Your words have power. Your words affect your relationships with others, and by understanding the power that your words have, you can choose how you can affect people with them. As Don eloquently puts it, will you use your words (magic) to cast spells of light or to create darkness in others? I think it goes without saying that relationships will thrive if you use your words to create light.

## The Psychology of Words and the Mind

There is an absolute ton of research that's been done into the way words affect the brain that could easily fill several books, so I'll give you the lowdown.

First, the way you use your words affects how they are taken. Obviously. The tone, pitch, and intonation of the way you say something can mean you're happy, sad, passive-aggressive, sarcastic, etc. It all depends on how you present what you say. One study researching the impact of intelligible speech through the left temporal lobe found that the way we speak affects everyone on an incredibly deep, emotional level.

The example Learning Mind gives is if an everyday person said: "I have a dream" and compared that to how Martin Luther King said those famous four words, you have a very different emotional reaction because of how he said it and the emotion in his voice was sending such a powerful message through the words.

What's more, other researchers discovered that the type of language you use is incredibly reflective of how you see yourself and others around you. Dr. James Pennebaker from the University of Texas said:

*"The way that people refer to themselves and others is highly diagnostic of their mental state."*

This means that the language you use creates an image of you and the situation you're in. If you use negative or depressive language, this reflects how you feel, the same as if you use positive, energetic language.

Here are some statements you could say when someone asks how your day has been:

"It's been really good, thank you."

"It's been steady."

"It was okay."

"It was a day."

"Man, it was so good!"

Even through writing, you can tell what kind of day it was, even though from a linguistic point of view, they're all pretty close to each other on the "good day" scale, if that's even a thing.

Putting both these points together—what you say and how you say things—greatly impacts how people look at you and acknowledge you as an individual. If you want to be more charismatic, work on what you say and how you say it. If you want more in-depth relationships, work on what you say and how you say it. Let's put it into action.

### Action Time – Using Words for Better Relationships

In any future conversion you have, I want you to slow down your responses and take a moment to think before you speak. Ah yes, that old chestnut of a saying. Do this both in the way you talk to others and, more importantly, the way you speak to yourself.

For example, when you go to work and you "have to" work on that latest project, you say this to a colleague, and it gives the impression you're forced to do something, you're complaining, or resisting reality. It's a bit of a moan, and doing this too often isn't going to win you any friends.

Instead, you could say something like, "I get to work on that new project." This portrays excitement in what you're doing, and even though you're only working, it creates a whole new impression of how you're looking at work and how others see you doing work. Everyone wants to have the kind of excitement you have for what they do, so in a sense, you're going to be inspiring them to do so.

The proof is in the pudding, so give it a try and see the results for yourself.

And that brings us nicely to the end of Part Three, or if I'm choosing my words carefully, it brings us to the start of Part Four. Part Four is my favorite part of this book because we're going to dive into the mechanics of what this book is about. Still focusing on you, I'm going to cover real actionable tips on being more charismatic, more confident, and more outgoing.

If you take anything away from this book and plan to use any methods, these are the methods you're going to want to focus on, but combining them with the other techniques in this book will work wonders. Well, what are you waiting for? Let's not hang around.

# Part Four – It's Time to Work on You

While life would be fantastic if it worked this way, you can't snap your fingers and just decide to be more charismatic and confident. You can from a mental and psychological standpoint, but taking action to be more confident takes time and practice, just like anything else in life.

What I would recommend for this part of the book is to read through it and let the information settle, and then start practicing a bit at a time. Some aspects will resonate more with you than others. Some bits you might do already, and some bits you may never have thought of, so take the bits you want and work with them. If you're feeling spicy, then sure, try a bit you may not have thought about trying.

My point is, try things out and find what works for you. This way, you'll be discovering yourself and your style of charisma along the way. Let's go!

# Method 13 – Becoming More Charismatic

*"Charisma is the fragrance of soul." – Toba Beta*

One of this book's main focuses was to help you understand what it takes to be more charismatic within yourself and your relationships. While you already know a lot of methods, this chapter is all about the hard and fast things you can do to actively become a more charismatic person. So firstly, what do I mean by "charisma?"

To be charismatic means to have the charm and attractiveness about you, both physically and intellectually, that makes other people want to be around you and want to know more about you. You may draw people in with how you talk and the way you are, you may have people hanging off your every word, or you may inspire something in people that make them want to be better.

I'm sure you know some charismatic people in your life, the kinds of people who make you feel like you want to be them, but not in an egotistical way—more in a natural way that just gives you a certain sense of peace around them. Fortunately, anyone can be this kind of person. It's something you learn and practice, although it does come more naturally to some people. Here's how. By the way, these are all action times in their own right!

## Awareness of Your Values

It's impossible to be confident and charismatic in yourself if you're unsure of what you stand for. This means you need to understand your values and what your abilities are. What do you stand for, what do you believe in, and what potential do you have to do amazing things in your life?

The answer to the last one is an unbelievably huge amount.

If you put your mind to something, you can achieve great things, but unless you truly believe you're capable of doing these things, then you're never going to be able to do them. Without this belief, it's impossible to be charismatic because you will believe that what you can do has limitations. Of course, you do have limitations, but being aware of what these are is essential because you can be confident and still have the ability to admit that there are things you can't do.

## Own Integrity

Integrity is the ability to stick to your values and do the things you say you're going to do. This is essential when it comes to trusting relationships and with others around you and believing in yourself. For example, if you say you're going vegan and continue to eat meat, what you said is your values don't align with your actions. Therefore, you lose integrity in other people's eyes.

The bottom line of this point is to not do things that oppose your values. Of course, your values are allowed to change over time, especially as you gain a greater understanding of the world through others and your experiences, but you don't want to be corrupted by others.

Say you have the values of keeping your head clear and not smoking because it's unhealthy, but you go to a bar, and someone offers you a cigarette, and you give in to temptation or peer pressure. This means you lack integrity because you're not standing up for what you believe in, and this isn't a very charismatic way to be.

### Think for Yourself

You've probably heard the phrase "to be a sheep," which means to follow everyone else around and just believe what you're told. This isn't a very charismatic way to be because you're not thinking for yourself and making up your own mind. The most charismatic people think for themselves, regardless of what the status quo thinks, which makes them such inspiring people to be around.

The best way to do this is not to take everything at face value but instead, dig a bit deeper. I had a conversation not too long ago with a man who worked in a factory his whole life and complained about how health and safety requirements have gotten out of control. I said I could see his point, but if he had lost a family member because of poor health and safety standards in a workplace, he would probably see things differently.

The sheep way to think is to go along with everything, perhaps the common opinion of the people around you. In contrast, a charismatic person will take the time to look at things from different angles before making up their minds and perspectives. What's more, a charismatic person can change their mind fluidly and won't be stuck in a singular way of thinking. This, in itself, is a very attractive quality to have.

### Have a Flame Inside You

There is nothing more attractive than having a flame or a spark inside you that makes you go out and get what you want in the world. When I first decided I wanted to start writing books, it took me so long to get off the ground. I would toss and turn, write up drafts and then abandon them for months on end, thinking that I wasn't good enough and it wasn't going to work.

Is this an attractive and inspiring way to be? Obviously not.

Over time, after I had been working on my charisma and confidence, this began to light a fire in me, a burning passion for writing, and once I acknowledged that fire inside me, I knew there was nothing that was going to stop me from doing the things I wanted to do. The most charismatic people find this fire within themselves and stop at nothing to keep going. It's this energy that people are attracted to.

When it comes to your own life, ask yourself questions about what makes you feel good and passionate about life. What things in life make you feel alive? These aren't answers you're going to get overnight, or you may already have some idea, so find these things and pursue them. There's nothing more attractive or charismatic than a person with ambition and drive to make the most out of life.

### Step Out of Your Comfort Zone

Charismatic people are comfortable with getting uncomfortable. There will always be times and situations throughout your life where you're uncomfortable and not feeling yourself, but how you respond and act in these situations will define you as an individual. Do you shy away from these situations and avoid them at all costs, or do you courageously face them and do everything you can to make the most out of them?

The choice is up to you.

Putting yourself in or simply accepting uncomfortable situations, rather than running from them, basically forces you to expand your comfort zone. This will help you grow as an individual, rather than remaining stagnant and where you are. This means you'll be open to new opportunities, thus becoming more outgoing and then being more naturally charismatic.

I still suffer from social anxiety from time to time, and there are definitely days where I'd love to stay in and watch Netflix. When I get invited to go out somewhere with a friend, it would be so easy to say no and just carry on with doing nothing. However, I recognize this mindset and will instead say yes, forcing myself to go to the event.

I always find this is the right decision and will buzz off the connection I receive from other people, meaning I can become more energetic and more confident in myself and have the opportunity to create new relationships. To cut a long story short, push your boundaries and limits, do things you don't want to do, and make the most out of any situation.

**Be in Control of Your Emotions**

Being an emotional person is not a great place to be. Now, I don't say this because emotions are bad. Emotions are useful because they're a clear indication of who we are as individuals and what we care about. However, if you allow your emotions to consume you and take over, this is where things can get problematic.

It's like when you're driving, and someone cuts you off or messes up, and you get this momentary rage ripple through you. You have a choice whether you let that emotion take control of you and ruin your day, or you choose to let it go and not bother you. This requires you to be mindful of your emotions and how you're feeling, and then choosing to react in the way you want to react, rather than just reacting and acting through the emotion itself.

If you're a slave to your emotions and let them control you, then you're not in control of your life. If you feel sad and act and talk to people through this filter of sadness, you're not yourself, and this is where problems occur. If you have an emotional conversation with a partner, say during an argument, this can lead you to say things you don't mean, leading to more problems and many regrets.

To be charismatic is to be more stable and in control of your emotions. Instead of letting them use you like a puppet, you are mindful of them and act with awareness of how you feel. This allows you to become a lot more grounded and rational with everything that happens in your life, and it's is an admirable trait to have.

If you follow these points and work on them where you can, you'll notice a considerable change in your sense of self, as you'll become far more charismatic and confident in yourself. You'll also notice that people will become drawn to you, attracted to you, and want to form relationships with you. You'll also feel far more fulfilled in yourself, which will do wonders for your satisfaction in life.

While many people use charisma and confidence interchangeably, and they are relatively similar, I'm going to dedicate the next chapter to solely improving your confidence and understanding the key differences between the two.

# Method 14 – Everything You Need to Know about Confidence

*"It is confidence in our bodies, minds, and spirits that allows us to keep looking for new adventures."* – Oprah Winfrey

Just like the previous chapter, and so we're on the same page as we make our way through this one, the official definition of being confident is having the willingness to act accordingly when meeting life's challenges and having the drive to succeed. This goes hand in hand with stepping outside of your comfort zone, settling into uncomfortable situations, and even going on a journey to becoming more charismatic while believing in yourself.

If you don't have confidence, you're not going to have what it takes to be the best version of yourself. You need that passion and inner motivation to step forward into your true self and be yourself. Your relationship with yourself requires this, and this ripples out to every other relationship you'll have in your life, like all the ones we've spoken about in previous chapters.

Just like before, all of the following sections of this chapter are actionable, so there's no action time here. Just go through each point, see what resonates with you, and find what works for you. Take these points and guidelines that will help you to become the most confident version of yourself.

**Find Your Limiting Beliefs**

There will be times in your life where you are naturally confident already, so a great place to start when trying to expand this confidence "zone" is to take some time to think about where you are not so confident. Are you not so outspoken around strangers? Do you shy into yourself when you're around your parents? Do you feel overshadowed at work? Whenever you're trying to get better at anything in life, you need to know where you're starting from, and that's precisely what you're doing here.

Literally, sit down and make a list of when you get shy and unconfident in your life—making this list alone should be enough to highlight what areas of yourself you'll want to work on. From your list, make another, more condensed list of what areas of your life you want to be more confident in, and then start working on them!

**Define Your Confidence Style**

Everybody is confident in their own individual and personal way, and while being loud and outspoken may be ideal for some people, others take a quieter, more humble approach. For you, you may sit at either end of the scale or somewhere in the middle, so figure it out, and then you'll know what to aim for.

The best way to do this is to think about the times in your life when you felt the most confidence. Where were you, and what were you doing? Who were you with? When you can figure out why you felt so empowered during those moments, you'll have the opportunity to bring these ideas into other areas of your life.

### Minimize Comparison With Others

Elon Musk once quoted that "comparison is the thief of joy," which is so true it hurts. Everybody is different and is walking their own path in life. Comparing yourself to someone else and what position they're in is only going to make you feel bad about yourself and diminish your achievements. The only person you should be comparing yourself with is yourself.

Let's say you're about to give a presentation at work, but you're comparing yourself with some of the best TED talk speakers in the world. Of course, your presentation will pale compared to these experienced speakers, but that doesn't mean you're bad or not worthy. Always aim to do the best you can and understand that you'll always get better through experience. Compare yourself to yourself rather than outwards to anyone else, and you'll find yourself growing in confidence with everything you do.

### Keep on Learning

If you close your mind off to new ways of learning, you'll become stagnant, like a flowing river that ceases to flow and turns into a murky pool of water. When you take time to learn something new, whether it's a fact about the world or specifically a new skill, you'll give yourself a little boost in confidence because you're proving to yourself that you're enough and you're fully capable.

Always be open to learning new things, and you'll be amazed at what this can do for your mindset and how much of a boost it will give to your self-esteem.

### Be True to Yourself

Yes, we're back to this point again, but I can't help but want to drive home how important this point is. Suppose you're masking yourself and pretending to be someone you're not for the supposed benefits of others. In that case, you're not going to be confident in yourself because you're spending all your energy focusing on hiding this person.

When you can freely be yourself and truly embrace who you are, there's no reason to spend energy on hiding yourself. A great way to do this is to think about who you are, then write down who you are and what makes you who you are. This relates to the previous chapter, where we spoke about understanding yourself and your values and then having the integrity to stick with these.

When you're true to yourself and reflect this to the people around you, you'll be able to be your genuine, confident self where you'll have nothing to hide from anyone. This naturally invites new opportunities for relationships because people know who you are and genuinely relate to you.

And with that, we come to the end of this method. Becoming confident using the methods above will take some time and practice, much like the rest of this book, but if you start implementing a few things at first, you'll start to see significant changes right off the bat. Just take the time to snowball these results and keep up the momentum of progress!

While we're on the subject of confidence, I did want to take a chapter to talk about outside appearances. We've spoken a lot about working on your inner self and discovering who you are so you can share this individual with other people and form amazing relationships, but what's on the outside does count for a lot as well. Allow me to explain.

*Communication Skills Training Series*

# Method 15 – Your Outside Reflects Your Inside

*"To love oneself is the beginning of a lifelong romance."* – Oscar Wilde

Back in 2019, a study published in the *International Journal of Environmental Research and Public Health* discovered two things. One, poor hygiene habits are a prominent risk factor when it comes to preventable diseases. And secondly, poor hygiene is a risk factor when it comes to social rejection. And this makes sense.

I remember working a summer job in a factory during my second college year, and there was a guy there. He must have been 30-odd, and his breath was awful. And I'm not talking about the kind of breath where he may have eaten something, and it's stuck in his teeth that morning. I'm talking about consistent bad breath that seemed to get worse every day. He was a nightmare to work with at the time, but his poor hygiene habits only made things worse.

Put yourself in this situation. If you're at work or in a bar—any social situation—and you're talking to someone with nasty body odor, are you going to be focusing on what the person is saying, or are you going to be trying to get away from them? Probably the latter.

Likewise, if you see someone walking down the street and they're wearing dirty clothes and don't look like they look after themselves, do you want to associate yourself with this person? Turning the tables, if you're the person who looks like they don't look after themselves, do you think people will want to associate with you?

It's all well and good being a good, genuine person, but if you don't look after yourself, you're going to be pushing people away. More realistically, if you're not looking after yourself, you're probably not going to be confident in yourself, which will lead to you being even more socially anxious than you already are, which will ultimately make relationships harder to form and maintain.

To cut a long story short, it pays to look after yourself and to treat your body with respect, both for the attraction of others and for boosting the confidence you have in yourself. If you look and feel the part of the person you want to be, everything else will fall into place naturally. In this chapter, we're going to look at some of the things you can do to properly look after yourself.

**Find Your Style**

Everybody has their own style, so it's important for your confidence and self-esteem to find yours. What kind of clothes do you like to wear, and what clothes do you feel best in? It's good to try different clothes to see what you like and don't like, and don't just stick with what you know because it's what you've always liked.

During the peak years of my social anxiety, I would only wear tracksuit bottoms and hoodies, always black, and pretty much nothing else. However, I pulled some old button-up shirts and started wearing them after reading up on how we should dress to be comfortable, not just for other people. The positive effects were instant. I felt so much better about myself, and even just choosing nice clothes for me to wear was boosting my self-confidence and making it feel as though I was putting effort into myself. This then started to ripple out into other areas of my life.

Even if you're not someone who's into fashion, taking the time to pick out and wear clothes that make you feel good can have such a positive effect on your confidence and self-esteem. If you're looking for a way to empower yourself, this is one of the best approaches to take.

## Develop a Daily Routine

Proper hygiene is vital if you want to be confident in yourself, and if you want others to be attracted to you. I'm sure you've had examples in your own life where you've met someone with poor hygiene who made you want to be anywhere but next to them. Don't be that person!

The best way to stay on top of your hygiene efforts is to get yourself a daily and weekly routine. Your daily routine should consist of all the essentials like brushing your teeth twice a day for two minutes at a time, washing your skin thoroughly, both in the morning and at night, and making sure you wear fresh socks and underwear every day.

You can also develop a skincare routine if you're interested in using products to counter certain conditions, such as dry skin or acne. You should do other essential hygiene tips now and then, such as flossing, using mouthwash, and shaving or plucking eyebrows. It's really up to you what you do. It's just a case of actually putting effort into seeing what you can do and then sticking with it until it becomes a habit.

Even taking the time to learn how to brush your teeth properly can make a world of difference. I had an awful wisdom tooth experience that opened my eyes to how important dental care is. I bought an electric toothbrush that connects to an app that monitors where you're brushing your teeth and how much pressure you're putting on the brush. It works like a treat.

All of this combined means you're taking the time to look after yourself, thus helping you love yourself more and making yourself incredibly attractive to the people around you.

## Exercise Regularly

I know you probably saw this one coming, but again, it's an essential part of looking after yourself. If you can get it down to a routine where you don't even need to think about it, exercising regularly will give you so much more energy as you go through your day; you'll be fitter, healthier, happier, more satisfied with your life, and all of this is going to make you feel good about yourself and will attract other people if you're working out and looking your best.

Again, you don't need a vigorous exercise plan but rather need to take time to figure out what you want to do and how you can make exercising enjoyable. Do you like running, swimming, or jogging? Do you want to join a team? Would you rather go to a gym or exercise outside? Try all the options available to you to see which activity you resonate with, therefore narrowing down the activities you're more likely to stick with for more extended periods of time.

Endless studies prove that exercise is important for maintaining a balanced state of mental health, reducing stress levels, and building up your confidence. You'll also improve your social relationships when you exercise with a partner, friend, join a team, and improve your abilities to successfully create powerful and beneficial habits.

## Eat a Healthy Diet

Eating a proper, healthy diet goes hand in hand with exercising properly and making sure you're looking after yourself in the best possible way, therefore allowing all the positive benefits to come into your life. Now, this isn't a traditional diet point, and I'm not going to harp on about how you should cut out a load of foods and be strict via creating meal plans and punishing yourself if you get takeout. Sure, you can be strict if that's what works for you, but if you're an average person, then here are some tips that take minimal effort.

First, increase the amount of fruit and veggies you eat. You should typically be aiming for five full portions a day, which roughly translates into 80-gram portions. That's 80 grams of grapes, or an apple, or a large banana, for example. You can eat veggies any way you want, whether that's frozen, fresh, dried, or even juiced, which is great when you don't want to spend a fortune on food. You can simply shop in the best way to suit you.

Secondly, try to avoid snacking. Eat three set meals per day, making sure not to skip breakfast, and minimize eating between these meals. Obviously, you can if you're hungry, but having three meals per day at set times helps to set your body up in a rhythm and natural pattern, which will do it a world of good when it comes to digestion and giving your body the energy it needs to get through the day.

You could also try intermittent fasting. I would research this yourself because there are many options out there, but the best option that worked for me was only eating between the hours of 12 pm and 8 pm. This gives the body 16 hours to digest food and allows you to rest and digest properly.

On top of this, make sure you're not overeating sugar, fatty foods, and salt. The final consideration to think about is drinking enough water, of which you should be aiming for around two liters per day. Getting a one-liter bottle was one of the best purchases I made because you just need to fill it up twice a day, and you know you've drunk enough. The benefits from this water point alone will bring so much positive change into your life.

Now, I could go on and on about all the health tips you could follow, and I really could write a whole other book just about that topic, but fortunately, there is a ton of information online. Remember, before you make any drastic changes to your lifestyle, make sure you're taking things slow and speaking to a healthcare professional, especially if you're living with any kind of physical condition.

Bringing everything full circle, if you can look after yourself health-wise, then your confidence and self-esteem will go through the roof. You'll feel better about yourself, which will have a massive effect on your relationships, both new and old. You'll want to spend time with people, and they'll want to spend time with you. By following these tips, changes in your life will happen, so naturally, you'll be able to look back in a few months and find yourself amazed and everything that has happened.

Now, ready for the final characteristic you need to have to form healthy relationships?

# Method 16 – Trust is Everything

*"Trust takes years to build, seconds to break, and forever to repair." – Unknown*

If you've ever been lied to or betrayed by someone, then you know how much it hurts to have trust in a relationship broken. Having trust is fundamental to any relationship. Even though you might see yourself as a trustworthy person, it's vital that you think about how you can be more trustworthy and prove this to the people around you consistently and naturally.

Take a moment to think about how often you tell little white lies. The lies that don't mean anything, but you tell them anyway. In sales, I used to say all the time that work on a project was done, and I'll send it over Monday because my internet was acting up. The work wasn't done. I was just sitting at home feeling sorry for myself and was making up excuses to give myself more time. Now, you might think these lies are harmless, but when people can see through them, they create an impression of you, and they damage your relationships.

From the other person's perspective, they see that you're going through a rough time but don't want to approach you. Obviously, you're lying because you don't want to talk about it. However, that person will feel negatively towards you because you lied to them, and while it may seem little, they're not going to trust you on much bigger, more important topics.

Imagine if, taking this example, you were to say to your boss, "I haven't been able to do the work because I've been struggling this week. I'm going to get it done by Monday for sure. I just need a little time to get myself back on track." Sure, there's probably a voice in your head telling you that wouldn't go down so well, but at least you were honest, and your boss is far more likely to respect you for saying this, thus improving your relationship with them. It's an incredibly respectful thing to do.

A 2016 global study on some of the top CEOs in the world found that 55% of CEOs in the world's biggest companies said that a "lack of trust" was among the biggest threats to a company's stability and success. Just like in my example above, if you don't trust the people you're working with, this creates a huge shift in the team's dynamic because nobody knows who is telling the truth. Problems are guaranteed to arise at some point.

The same applies to your relationships. If you break trust in a relationship, both romantic relationships or friendships, depending on the person involved, they may never fully trust you again, and there's no stability. It doesn't matter what you say to that other person; they can just say, "I don't believe you," and there's nothing you can do to make things better.

As a rule of thumb, always be honest with people from the moment you meet them. Never give them a reason to think you're untrustworthy. If people can trust you with their lives, your relationships will be stronger than you can imagine. So, how do you do it?

## How to Be More Trustworthy in Your Relationships

Of course, I could just say for this point that you shouldn't tell lies, and this can be enough, but it's not. People all have different life experiences, and if you meet someone who's been lied to by the people in their lives for as long as they can remember, they may not trust you, even if you're a trustworthy person. You need to have the integrity to prove that you are, and you can do this by following the points below.

**Start Off Slow and Build Up Trust**

We already spoke about how important it is to be vulnerable, which comes up again here. To build trust, you need to be vulnerable. If you're openly and honestly telling people about how you think and feel, you're telling people that you're an open book and you can be trusted since you're trusting them with what you're telling them.

However, it's important to remember when you're getting to know someone that you don't just jump in the deep end and share all your baggage. This is known as being "too vulnerable," as we discussed before. Start slowly when you're getting to know someone and build up to the more intimate and vulnerable details of your thinking as you go. Remember, while you want the other person to trust you, you always want to be able to trust them, so find the right balance between giving and taking.

**Putting in the Time**

Imagine two people are working in an office together. They have worked in the same office for 30 years and only really talk in passing. They talk about the weather and exchange short statements about changes in the company. You wouldn't call them close or even friends, despite knowing each other for so long.

Now compare that to two people who work on projects together in the same office. They have been working together for two months, but work very close to each other, are interacting every single day about work and share their social lives, and have to experience both the good and the bad together where they work.

The relationship, while in similar circumstances physically, produces two very different relationships. Trust doesn't happen overnight, but it doesn't come without effort. If you want someone's trust, you need to put in the time and have experiences with this person. The more positive time you put in the relationship, the more you'll be trusted.

**Avoid Emotionally Harming Someone**

When someone tells you something that they're trusting you with, you must pay them respect and avoid damaging them and hurting them, even if you do it unintentionally. This is one of the quickest ways to break your trust with someone.

Let's say someone is telling you something about their private life that they've been a bit unsure about telling anyone else. Perhaps it's private, or maybe they think that nobody else cares. The worst thing you can do is belittle that person, make them feel less than normal, or even view them with contempt, disgust, or condescend to them. The more intimate your relationship is with someone, the more important it is not to cross a line because your words will be more powerful, the closer you are to someone.

Remember, your words have the ability to create magic, and it's up to you what spells you cast.

This doesn't mean you can't be honest about how you feel with the people in your life and that you have to effectively shut up and listen. It means you need to be mindful of the way you're reacting to something. If someone tells you about their partner, remember that you're only hearing one side of the story, an emotionally tainted side at that, and therefore you shouldn't judge or jump to conclusions.

In many cases, unless someone asks for advice, you don't need to give it, and the person is instead speaking to you because they just want to get something off of their chest. A great way to deal with this point is simply, no matter what the situation is, to respect them and give them the benefit of the doubt until proven otherwise. This way, you can maintain your connection and your trust no matter what.

**Be Honest with Your Feelings**

Just like the example at the beginning of this chapter when you could be talking to your boss when you're not feeling yourself, you must remain true to yourself and others around you, especially when it's hard and tough to do so. Sometimes, telling the truth can seem like a hard thing to do, and you may be afraid of hurting others, letting them down, or even putting yourself in a bad light.

However, the best relationships are formed between people who can be open and honest, even if it would be easier not to. This will create a huge amount of respect for you among the people in your relationships, and the trust will only help strengthen these connections.

With all these points in the chapters we've covered throughout this part of the book, you should have more than enough information to work with. When it comes to working on yourself, I want to remind you not to try and change everything at once, nor should you try and believe that you need changing.

You are perfectly enough for the world just the way you are right now, and this is a mantra you should repeat for a considerable boost in your self-confidence! However, no matter how you look at it, everything in life is a skill, and skills can be practiced. All the points we've covered are backed by science to deliver positive results into your life. These will help make you happier, more fulfilled, and healthier in general, and all of these effects will be seen throughout your relationships.

# Part Five – Maintaining Your Relationships & Looking to the Future

And here we are, Part Five. Throughout this book, we've covered everything you'll want to know when it comes to increasing your charisma, building your confidence, winning friends, making people attracted to you, and developing all your relationships from your professional connections to your romantic partners and everyone in between and on either side.

Within this final chapter, I'm going to be leaving you with three methods you'll want to bear in mind for the future of your self-development journey. These are how you spend your time with people and develop patience with yourself, others, and your entire journey through life, and how to forgive.

# Method 17 – Time: Quality Over Quantity

*"Relationships are built on small, consistent deposits of time. You can't cram for what's most important. If you want to connect with your kids, you've got to be available consistently, not randomly." – Andy Stanley*

When I was a teenager, I found myself in some very clingy relationships. I had maybe two people I would call best friends and would jump from one romantic relationship to another and would spend all my time with these people. Now, I had a large group of friends but rarely spent time with them. For some crazy reason, I believed that I would spend all my time with the same people, and that's how life worked.

It doesn't work this way, and in fact, it's a very unhealthy way to live life.

Just because you love someone and have a connection with them doesn't mean you should spend all your time with them. The time you spend with people—anybody for that matter, not just the people who are close to you—should be quality time. Quality time could be a couple of hours once a week, or even every now and then. It all depends on the individual relationship.

It can be counterproductive to your relationship if you spend too much time with someone because you're not allowing each other to see other people, thus getting a fresh perspective on the work, and you do not have alone time to be by yourself, process emotions, and think your own thoughts free from distraction. We all need alone time now and then, even if we don't want to admit it.

A study published back in 1999 by Zimmer and Gembeck found that women who jump into new relationships and spend a lot of time with their partners will rapidly spend less time with their friends, and this creates problems in both the romantic relationship and the friendship.

If you're spending all your time with just a handful of people all the time, then any goals or aspirations you'll want to work on will be impossible because where are you going to find the time? You'll also be hindering the achievements of the people you're spending time with, and this can lead to both attachment and resentment. If you're resenting each other, even if you're not thinking it directly, this will again cause problems within the relationship.

So, the best thing to do here is to take a step back and find balance. Hand in hand with creating memories and having positive experiences with people, don't spend all your time with other people you're close to but remember to be an individual and live your own life. The other people in your relationships shouldn't be your entire life, but rather people that complement it and are a part of it.

### Action Time – Have Some You Time

You're going to appreciate this action time because it feels so good and energizing when you've done it properly. Once a week, I want you to disconnect from the world for an hour or so. This means turning off your phone or at least blocking your social media apps. Watch a movie from start to finish, read a book, learn a language, meditate, have a bath, or do whatever you want to do, but do whatever it is as quality time with yourself.

Give yourself the same amount of attention and love you would give when spending time with someone you love. By doing this regularly, you'll be able to connect and stay connected with who you are as a person, and then you'll be able to bring this truly-loved self into your relationships.

# Method 18 – Developing Patience for the Journey

*"To lose patience is to lose the battle."* – Mahatma Gandhi

Whether you're developing yourself, getting to know someone, dealing with a difficult time in your relationship, or basically dealing with any kind of situation in life, you're going to need patience. Focusing on the relationship side of things, if you don't have patience, you'll find that stressful situations start to snowball.

When something happens, or we take something personally, or the other person struggles to find the right words to say, you may find yourself becoming irritable, defensive, or even lashing out and saying something you don't mean. This will only make matters worse and cause more stress, and therefore more problems, and the vicious cycle continues.

Developing patience is all about feeling those initially stressful emotions, taking a deep breath, and then allowing yourself to remain grounded and calm. Let's say someone at work is freaking out because some part of the project hasn't been done, and the client is breathing down the boss's neck. Now everyone is getting stressed.

Instead of freaking out alongside everyone else and watching the team fall apart (some people getting thrown under the bus and people starting to point fingers), you remain patient and let everyone have their turn. When it comes to you, you instead speak from a calm place, highlight the work that needs to be done, and then what solutions are available. This will generate a huge amount of respect from the people around you.

If you go through life with an impatient attitude, then the only person who will suffer is you. Always take time to see things, even the worst situations, from a peaceful state of mind. This can, admittedly, feel impossible to do sometimes, especially when the people you're interacting with are showing no patience whatsoever. Still, it's always a good idea for your mental well-being to remain cool, calm, and collected.

## Action Time – How to Develop Patience

There are endless ways to be more patient. You could meditate, journal, and even write affirmations on your hands to remind yourself to be more patient throughout the day. I tried setting alarms on my phone tagged with "be more patient" texts to remind me at random times.

However, the one key way to become more patient, and the act that worked for me was simply to breathe. I suppose this is a kind of meditation, but it didn't matter what I was doing or who I was with. I started working on the habit of taking a deep breath before doing or saying anything. I didn't make it super obvious, but it was more of a mindful breath. Even in favorable situations, like hanging out with friends, this was something I did.

This breath was a reminder to be patient. Eventually, when I found myself in a less-than-desirable situation, which I didn't have to wait long for, I would breathe and stay patient, meaning I was much more grounded when it came to answering other people and thinking with a sound state of mind. This process helped me to develop a much more positive mindset towards life and made my relationships stronger.

*Communication Skills Training Series*

# Method 19 – The Power of Forgiveness

*"There is no love without forgiveness, and there is no forgiveness without love."* – Bryant H. McGill

I've saved this point 'til now because I wanted to end with a bang. Before sitting down to write this book, I read about the story of Immaculee Llibagiza. In fact, it was her story that partly inspired me to write this book, simply because her story is so powerful and it shows how so many of us are missing out on such an important aspect of our relationships.

Every person on the planet is a human being and only a human being. It seems obvious, but so many of us forget that being human means we can make mistakes, and we're guaranteed to make many throughout our lives. We're going to hurt other people at some point, even when we try not to, and other people are going to hurt us. However, no matter what, learning about the power behind forgiveness can change everything.

I spoke briefly about being cheated on by my ex-girlfriend a few years ago and being so angry, I punched a windscreen, and this was hate and anger I held on to for years. I blamed my sadness and pain on my ex, and when I found myself getting involved in new relationships, I still held that resentment, and it affected me in so many ways. I had trust issues and was paranoid, and simply believed I was going to be hurt again. The problem wasn't with my new partners or friends; it was with me. I hadn't learned to let go of the past.

**The Story of Immaculee Llibagiza**

Immaculee Llibagiza was born in Uganda, and as a young girl, she was subject to the Ugandan genocide and traumatic event that ravaged the country. Being a girl, barely a teenager, Immaculee was hidden in a Catholic priest's bathroom in his house with a group of other girls while the militia came through to kill anyone who wasn't of the superior religion.

The bathroom was three feet by four feet. While the priest thought hiding the girls would be something he did for a few days until the militia moved on, the genocide lasted several months. Immaculee remained in that bathroom, cramped and surrounded by other girls for several months, never speaking a word to anyone the entire time out of fear of being discovered. The bathroom door was hidden behind a bookshelf to hide it while the house was raided multiple times.

Eventually, the government was overthrown and a new party elected. The men involved in the genocide were arrested, and the country taken back under control, but not before over one million people had been killed by the rampage. When Immaculee emerged from the bathroom, she discovered she had lost everyone. Her mother, her brothers, and friends. Everyone had been killed. Her small town had been destroyed.

Immaculee had spent her time in the bathroom, reading the Bible over and over again, praying to God that everyone was going to be okay, and it was here she learned about forgiveness. Years passed, and she was given the opportunity to see the man who killed her family, who was locked in prison.

When she arrived, the guard offered to hold the man so she could hit him and spit on him, and do whatever she wanted to take revenge on the man for killing all those people, just like other people had been doing when they visited for years. The man looked broken.

Instead, Immaculee did the unthinkable. She sat opposite the man, took his hand, and said, "I forgive you." Such an incredibly powerful moment.

## The Power of Forgiving

Many of us will never be in a situation like Immaculee was, and reading her story, you may think about how much rage and hurt you would hold towards the man who killed everyone you know and brought such pain and suffering into your life. However, Immaculee knew that forgiving was healing, and holding so much pain and resentment towards the man would only bring more pain and suffering into her life.

She wanted to heal and let the pain go and find peace with the situation, which meant forgiving him for what he had done. It takes a certain kind of strength to do this, but I truly believe that Immaculee is on to something. By holding in everything that anyone has ever done to hurt you, you're only ever hurting yourself. Holding any pain or hurt will affect all your relationships, including your relationship with yourself.

## Action Time – Forgive Someone

I'm not saying you need to reach out and actively forgive someone for something they've done in the past. It might be a little weird contacting someone you haven't spoken to for many years. What you can do, however, is write down some past resentment or hurt that you feel like you're still holding on to.

Write it down on a piece of paper with a message to the person who's involved. Write as much or as little as you want, vent out all your anger and feelings, and put all your thoughts down in a letter format. In the end, simply write, *I forgive you*. Read the letter through, then rip it up and throw it away or burn it; a statement that will help you let go and truly forgive.

Be mindful of how you feel the following days after doing this, and you'll see just how powerful it can be.

# Final Thoughts

And with that, we come to the end of our journey!

I hope more than anything you were able to find value in these pages and that you enjoyed reading this book as much as I enjoyed writing it. Self-discovery and development of any kind can be scary and daunting, and very isolating if you're not sure where you're going or what you're doing, but I hope this book can act as a guide to help you find your way and make the improvements you want to make in your life.

Relationships are such an essential part of living, and so using the methods and information you've just read, it would be amazing to see how much of a difference they make. There's no end to the benefits that boosting your charisma and confidence can bring, and, as the saying goes, it's not what you know in life, but who you know, and know you've got the skills to bring these amazing relationships to life. Who knows what opportunities now await you.

# Book #6
# How to Talk to Anyone About Anything

*Improve Your Social Skills, Master Small Talk, Connect Effortlessly, and Make Real Friends*

*James W. Williams*

# Introduction

Not too long ago, my friend Kyle came to me and told me a story of the weekend past when he had recently attended his sister's wedding. Kyle himself had been married for nearly twenty years before his divorce a few months prior, and this wedding was one of the first "outings" he attended by himself.

Over a beer, he told me about the big day. At ten, he was surrounded by friends and family, people he saw nearly every week, or at least sent a text message to every now and then. The ceremony was beautiful. Everyone was happy. They took taxis from the church to the reception held in this big fancy downtown hotel. Upon arriving, Kyle was busy making sure everything was running smoothly behind the scenes.

In true wedding fashion, people ate food, had some drinks, started dancing, and overall just let their hair down for a good time. Relatives from both sides of the new family came together to celebrate this wonderful occasion.

But for Kyle, it wasn't all smiles, booze, and confetti.

Plunged into the vast depths outside of his comfort zone, he told me that as soon as he started interacting with strangers, friends of friends, and distant relatives, he soon realized he had absolutely no idea how to talk to any of them.

He recalled a particularly embarrassing moment where his sister's new husband's cousin came over and said, "Hey," and he froze up, literally not saying a single word. Awkward was an understatement.

After the compulsory "How are you?" and "It's a beautiful service, right?" Kyle was stuck. His mind started to fill with anxiety. Endless thoughts bombarded him like, *What do I say? How can I make this person laugh? Do they even care about what I have to say? Who is this person? What are their interests?* and so on.

Outside his mind and back in reality, this all emerged as generic small talk, awkward silences, and uncertain looks towards the floor.

"God, it was terrible. Kathy (Kyle's ex-wife) was such a charismatic person, but I didn't realize how much she carried our conversations while we were married. I feel like I don't have the ability to talk to anyone. What do you talk about? Do people care about what I have to say? Even if they did, I don't think I have the confidence to even try. Lord knows how I'm ever going to start dating again, if ever."

As we finished our drinks and paid the tab, I told him that becoming confident, or even just speaking to other human beings, isn't some far-off idea reserved for only the most extroverted humans who ooze natural charisma. Oh no.

You see, over a decade ago, and then for most of my entire life, I was like Kyle. I went through school, college, university, and a scattering of first and part-time jobs and eventually on to the beginning of my career being awkward, shy, and withdrawn.

I was the guy who sat in the middle of the class, not cool enough for the back or smart enough for the front. I was the invisible one.

I had some friends I'd known all my life, but the older I became, the more social anxiety I felt, and the more isolated I found myself. It was crippling. I hadn't pushed myself to talk to anyone or had taken risks when meeting new people since I was a child. After all the passing years, it was like I'd forgotten how to do it at all.

It was hard to meet new people. I found it impossible to date. Speaking with the customers in my part-time jobs was messy, and selling to clients in my career was unreliable at best. I could only sometimes talk to someone without breaking a sweat or feeling like I was on the verge of having a panic attack. I had good days and bad days, but as years went by, I had two main realizations that ultimately led to me changing my life.

**First, your connection to other people is everything.**

Your relationships with others, your job, yourself, and your levels of overall happiness and life satisfaction are all determined by your ability to communicate and connect. You could have millions of dollars in the bank, have everything that someone can be deemed successful for having, but if you're lonely, you're not happy.

You can be poor and materially have nothing, but if you're surrounded by caring people with whom you share a meaningful connection, and you can feel like the wealthiest person on the planet.

My second realization was just as life-changing.

Being confident, charismatic, and open to connecting with others is *not* a trait you're born with. I used to believe that the confident people, those who could hold an entire audience or keep you hooked intimately on their every word, were gifted with a natural talent for confidence. I was wrong.

Confidence and charisma are skills that can be learned, honed, and practiced. They can even be mastered.

Have you ever gone into a room and saw that one person who dominates the conversation, maybe in a group of friends or in a meeting at work? Perhaps you had a friend who can seemingly speak to anyone about anything, and no matter the situation, they carry the flow of the conversation seemingly without effort? Ever found yourself envious of that person?

That's not the first time that person is doing that. You're seeing years of practice. Years of trial and error. Years of making mistakes, practicing new techniques, and learning from each experience along the way. They would have had awkward moments in school, embarrassing meetings, and conversations, where nothing seemed to work.

And this all raises more questions.

How can you do things differently? How do you become confident? How can you talk to anyone about anything?

I've been the shy guy. I spent most of my life as him. I was afraid of sharing my thoughts, and now I'm writing books you're reading (which still blows my mind to this day!). I can date people and hold my own. I can present meetings and engage everyone in the room. I can share stories with groups of friends and have them hang off my every word. I gave a talk in a public speaking group not too long ago, and a member of the audience came up and told me it was one of the best talks they had seen in years.

I'm not saying that to brag. I know my public speaking skills have a long way to go compared with the greats, but seeing my own journey of being the awkward kid to then being capable of speaking to a group of 30 people warmed my heart. If it's possible for me, it's possible for anybody.

Final questions.

How do you get better at swimming? You spend time in the pool.

How do you get better at writing? You write.

How do you get better at connecting with people? You connect with people.

Like all life skills, confidence is an act that's practiced and honed over time, but like an athlete needs a coach, I'm writing this book to help guide you along the path of your own journey. First, we're going to cover your mindset and get that in check, so you're actually ready for meeting new people.

Then we're going on to the real meat of this book. This is where I will cover subjects like how to start a conversation with someone, find similar interests, and guide the conversation with questions. You'll also find out how to be more charismatic and confident and how to act and present yourself in any situation you may find yourself in.

This book aims to be the key that will unlock so many doors in your life through connection and opportunities, so let's hang around no longer.

## The Beginning

When it comes to making a change in your life, these are the three essential elements you're going to need to focus on:

Education. Awareness. Practice.

You need knowledge and information, so you know what decisions you're going to make. You need awareness to apply everything you've learned, to recognize where you go wrong, what you do right, and to be aware of where you need to get better.

Finally, you need to keep practicing and just keep getting better and better.

I've been on this journey.

During my mid-20s, I was unfulfilled and unsatisfied with my life. I lived in a big city with nobody around me that I could really call a close friend. No partner. It should have been an exciting time, starting my new career with high prospects, but I held myself back. I was ticking the boxes creatively, but I wasn't a people person, and people are the ones who give the opportunities.

I decided I needed to make a change.

I got educated. I read studies, scientific data, articles, and research reports. I read books and listened to podcasts. I took all this information and applied it in my own life, being aware of what I was doing so I could judge for myself what was right and what was wrong. I figured out what works for me, practiced it, and used these experiences to give myself the momentum to get where I am today.

The best thing about it all?

It works like an absolute treat.

Using my own experiences, scientific studies, and a ton of research, I've compiled this book to basically be everything you're going to need to know when learning how to speak with other people.

So, as we move into the true grit of this book, I want you to open your mind. Be willing to learn and take on board what you read. I highly recommend getting a pen and notebook to jot down ideas, techniques, and communication strategies that resonate with you, which will improve your ability to take them on board.

It's time.

# Chapter One – Everything Starts with You

*"No matter who you are, no matter what you did, no matter where you've come from, you can always change, become a better version of yourself."* – **Madonna**

When you first picked this book up, you probably read the title and created this image in your head of what it would actually be like to have the ability to speak with anyone. Maybe you have a fantasy of telling stories around the water cooler, everyone wide-eyed at how good your stories are.

Maybe it's the same with your dating life, and you crave to be the charismatic boy or girl that charms all who listen to you. Perhaps you want to communicate better with your colleagues, managers, bosses, or clients.

Yikes! I'm sure you're starting to see how vastly communicating with others literally affects every part of your life! However, I want you to put these fantasies aside for now (I promise we'll make them become a reality later) because we need to start with you.

Yup. It's time to take a long, hard look at ourselves in the mirror because guess what? There's a reason why people say, "You can't love other people properly until you learn to love yourself first." It sounds philosophical and perhaps something you've heard before, but hear me out.

We're going to make this actionable.

Let's start with the foundations of who you are, right here, right now. Your sense of self has to be defined because it will literally dictate how you act in every single situation from here on out, and you can either unconsciously let this happen, or you can be aware and in control of it. Don't worry; this will all make sense as we move forward.

A question to get the juices flowing:

**Who are you?**

Just consider and be aware of whatever thoughts come to mind. Now take those thoughts and drop the basic identity stuff, like your name, age, or your job. Now how do you see yourself? What kind of person do you associate yourself with? What beliefs and values do you have? Yup, we're jumping straight into the deep end here.

When I was 23 years old, and my self-development was beginning to take shape, I remember journaling one night for what must have been for one of the first times in my life (I had just watched a YouTube video on how *life-changing* it can be), and I asked myself these very questions.

Shockingly, I had no answers. What did I believe in? What did I value? Who was I? Well, I believe it's wrong to murder people. I believe that gravity exists. I believe that fast food should be eaten in moderation. As you can see, I was really scraping the barrel for ideas and didn't really have an answer with depth. I realized I didn't have a sense of self.

Your sense of self is everything. It defines you.

In the study of psychology, the sense of self is an all-encompassing view you have on yourself, your beliefs, your purpose in this world, and who you are. Guess what? If you don't know your own sense of self, how can you expect to *be* yourself when you're around others?

Having a sense of self motivates you to get up in the morning because you're fully aware of your mission in life and what causes you're fighting for. You know where you stand and what matters to you. Now, that's not to say your sense of self can't and won't change over time. In fact, if it didn't change, this can also be unhealthy, commonly known as being stuck in your ways. However, having some idea of your sense of self is vital. You cannot be confident without it.

Erika Myers, a professional counselor based in Oregon, sums it up perfectly.

*"Having a well-developed sense of self is hugely beneficial in helping us make choices in life. From something as small as favorite foods to larger concerns like personal values, knowing what comes from our own self versus what comes from others allows us to live authentically."*

Authentic living. Isn't that the dream? No, it's not a dream. It's a **necessity**.

When you can learn to authentically be yourself *with* yourself, you can then begin to authentically be yourself with other people. You know how people say you can only really love others when you learn to love yourself? Well, we're playing on the same board as that ideology.

Being authentically you means you know you're not perfect (and that nobody is), but you're willing to accept your flaws and simultaneously embrace your strengths because they define you more than anything.

A lack of a sense of self is a problem.

Without any ideas of who you are or what you stand for, you'll find yourself drifting through life. You'll be uncertain and indecisive. Your life will lack momentum and drive. You'll feel anxious and unsatisfied, but you won't be able to put your finger on why because you don't understand what you want and don't want.

Remember my friend Kyle at his sister's wedding? In many ways, his whole sense of self had been derived from his marriage, and he didn't know who he was without it. When speaking with others at the wedding, he was drifting.

Was he there to have a good time? To simply show his face and support his sister? Was he there to meet new people? Was he looking to date someone new or even to hook up with someone? None of these things are good or bad because it depends on the individual and their wants or needs. However, without understanding what these wants or needs are, nothing can be done about them, and so the perpetual loop of anxiety continues.

## Developing Your Sense of Self

To stress once again, you can't have relationships with others until you learn to have a relationship with yourself, which brings us nicely to your first exercise in this book. Don't worry. While it may sound a bit overwhelming, we're going to break it down and do this together. I got you.

Take a pen and paper and title it, *Checking in with Myself*. As it suggests, we're going to check in and explore who you are right now. Make sure you're in a quiet place where you can be with yourself and hear your own thoughts.

As defined by Healthline.com, your sense of self will fall somewhere on a spectrum. Either you have a solid, complete sense of self, none at all, or you fall somewhere in the middle. So let's figure out where you are.

Ask yourself some of these questions and write down whatever comes to mind. Also, I know what it's like reading books like this, and it's easy just to skim over these action points and try to do them in your head. If you want real change in your life (which is why I'm assuming you picked up this book in the first place), then actually take the time to do this activity, and see what happens.

If you're not proactive in actually doing something new, how can you expect anything to change? Anyway, that's something I wish someone had told me years ago. On to the questions!

- *What kind of person do you want to be?*
- *What kind of person are you right now?*
- *How would you describe yourself?*
- *Do you believe you've changed a lot over the years?*
- *What things in life are you good at?*
- *What things in life are you not so good at?*
- *What are you passionate about loving?*
- *What are you passionate about hating?*
- *What kinds of relationships do you have in your life?*
- *What kinds of relationships do you want in your life?*
- *How in control of your life do you feel?*

You don't need to answer all these questions, but if you look at one of them and think it's a bit difficult, then I recommend spending a bit *more* time answering it because that's where you'll find the interesting answers. Try to be as honest as possible.

Be aware that many of your answers will be influenced by how you see yourself as an individual and how others have told you they see you. For example, if your partner sees you as being lazy and always calls you that, you might start to believe you are actually lazy, even when you think, deep down, you're not. This is one of the ways you can acquire a *false* sense of self. This process is all about discovering your *true* sense of self, not just what other people and their views they've forced onto you.

The same applies in social groups, whether you're at school, in a friend group, with family, or in the workplace. You may act a certain way in order to fit in, but not actually be the person you're acting like. Try to cut through these false beliefs and write down who you actually think you are, for better or for worse.

When you're done, take some time to read back your answers.

Did you surprise yourself with what you wrote? Did things come up you hadn't thought about in a long time? Did you expect some of the answers? Did you tap briefly into a part of a "past you" you had forgotten about or thought was lost? Good. No matter what came up, clarity is on its way.

From here, take some time, maybe a couple of days or a week, to process what you wrote down. New ideas may come to you the more you think about this whole idea (so add them to your existing answers), and you may change your mind or have more certainty with other points you put down.

At the end of the week, read through everything once more, and move on to the next step.

## Your Sense of Self is Born

With this information, like a phoenix from the ashes, it's time to be reborn as the true you.

This isn't something that will happen overnight, but a continuous process that evolves into a lifelong journey. As you have new experiences and learn new things, your sense of self will change and adapt, and that's a beautiful thing. What we're doing now is creating that initial foundation on which to build on.

I remember going through this process and being shocked by just how passive I was in my life. With family, friends, and coworkers, I adopted a different persona of trying to be who I thought these other people wanted me to be, rather than just being myself. I was living in anxiety, scared of judgment and rejections, and suppressing my true self the entire time. I craved freedom, and this is how I got it.

### *Set Your Values*

Did you write down about how much you love animals or your passion for saving the planet? If so, it's time to start choosing cruelty-free brands and spending time getting more educated about the food you eat and the clothes you wear.

Did you write down how you value your health and looking after yourself? It's time to start working out and eating well.

Do you value relationships and experiences with others? It's time to call your mother and start organizing plans with friends.

Do you value genuine people and honest relationships? It's time to start thinking about what you're going to do about that toxic friend you've been trying to ignore.

Using the information you discovered about yourself in the previous section, you should be able to set at least some values that you believe in, all of which will then allow you to make choices in your life that you actually want to make. Life satisfaction and a sense of self will be derived from you making these choices.

What's more, you can learn to cut out the things that don't matter to you and don't serve your beliefs and values. I value connected relationships but felt lonely and didn't address my needs, so I plugged the gaps with video games.

Now, while I enjoyed computer games from time to time, I didn't enjoy playing them for six hours a day to stop myself feeling lonely, so I took action to only play for two hours on weekends and spent the regained time on my relationships. By making these proper choices, I naturally started to find balance in my life.

Set your values. Discover what matters to you. Make the right choices. Your sense of self will come from this action.

### *Having Proper You Time*

The only way you can figure out what matters to you is by having proper quiet time with yourself, allowing yourself to listen to your thoughts and process how you're feeling. It's so easy to have a bad day and just numb it all out with TV, Netflix, and social media, but how are you going to learn about yourself if you don't think about it?

There are plenty of ways you can do this, whether you're a fan of reading or listening to music, or you can use some more hands-on self-help techniques, like journaling and meditation. It's entirely up to you, and if you're not sure, try a whole bunch of different approaches to see what works for you as an individual.

### *Get Help if Needed*

The final point I want you to remember is that your self-help journey doesn't have to be one you go through alone. If someone you loved was going through this journey themselves, then it's pretty safe to say that if they needed help or support, you would help if you could. The same applies to you. People will always be willing to help you, especially if they're a loved one, but they need to know that you want the help first.

Suppose you're dealing with anything you can't seem to face, perhaps a mental health condition like depression or anxiety (both of which are very common with those who have a lack of a sense of self). In that case, professional guidance is always an option.

### The Summary

And with that, we come to the end of the first chapter. Is the journey what you expected so far? Went a little deep, didn't we? It's okay. It's all essential, and what's amazing is that by focusing on just developing your sense of self, you'll instantly see real changes in your life and within your relationships with others.

Because you know yourself, you'll naturally be more confident in yourself. Since you know what you believe in, you can share your opinions with others and start to have more in-depth, meaningful conversations.

As a lightning-fast recap, you first need to focus on developing your sense of self by:

- **Defining your values and beliefs**
- **Spending time getting to know yourself**
- **Understanding what makes you, you**

As I said above, this is just the groundwork for becoming better at small talk, and if you want to go into this further, you're welcome to do some more research. However, in our journey together, we're going to pull back around to how to talk to anyone, starting off with one of the most essential skills you need to know.

# Chapter Two – It All Begins with Listening

*"When you talk, you are only repeating what you already know. But if you listen, you may learn something new."* — **Dalai Lama**

Chances are, you saw this coming. Every relationship you have, have had, and will have throughout your entire life is based and founded on effective communication. The most significant part of that is being able to listen to others communicating with you.

Listening is essential because you're giving someone attention that grants you clarity on what they're saying, and this is the best basis for a real relationship. Every human being wants to be heard and understood by others.

A 2015 study carried out by the Michigan State University backed this up and found that active listening (listening with intent) will enable you to talk more clearly and concisely with others and better understand the world.

Listening, therefore, not only improves your own speaking skills but also helps you connect with those around you. Imagine talking to someone who you can tell is not really listening to you. You've been there, right? It's horrible, and you don't want to be around that person for long. Let's explore how you can be a better listener.

## The Two Types of Listening

Listening. You have a conversation, hear the other person, and respond to what they said, right? That's a conversation. Relationships are founded from this. Right? Simple stuff. Not entirely.

Research shows there are actually 18 different types of listening, including states of listening like biased listening, inactive listening, deep listening, empathetic listening, comprehensive listening, and so on. Still, for simplistic sake, I want to break it down into just two types.

> - ***Listening to understand***
> - ***Listening to respond***

When you speak to the vast majority of people, they will instinctively be listening to respond. This basically means that instead of *listening* to someone, this person already knows what point they want to share next, so they are, in essence, just waiting for the other person to finish speaking so they can have their turn.

A great example of this came up when I first dated my partner, and we went to visit her parents for the weekend. My partner had decided she would try a vegan diet after reading all the health benefits and didn't sit comfortably with the idea of eating an animal. Upon telling her dad, he replied,

"Why do you want to do that? Meat is so good. You know you'll never be able to eat burgers again?"

"Or delicious steak!" her mother chimed in.

My partner tried to explain, "Well, the impact of the meat industry on the rest of the planet is just not something I want on my conscience, and don't even get me started on how poorly the living creatures are treated."

To which he replied, "I couldn't do it. I just love steak too much."

Had my partner been listened to? No. As much as her dad is a nice guy, he has the thought process that meat is good and nothing can get in the way of that. It doesn't matter what my partner said; he would have stuck to his guns about how meat is amazing and the best thing ever.

They are listening to respond. To have a progressive conversation, he could have said something like, "Why? What are the health benefits? What impact does animal agriculture have on the planet?" and if he heard her out and still didn't mind eating meat, then at least he would have listened and given it a chance. They missed an opportunity to understand their daughter on an individual level simply by listening to her response.

The best, most meaningful conversations are based on everyone's aim within the conversation to understand each other, sharing what the facts are, and why people think and feel what they do. By taking this approach, you begin to understand others as individuals rather than force your own narrative.

## How to Listen to Understand

This is logically the next question. So how do you listen to understand?

The same MSU study found, like most confidence and communication techniques, that listening to understand is a skill that can be learned and practiced, and to quote the report directly:

*"Active listening takes time and practice. However, every time you use active listening, it gets a little easier. It can help you to navigate through difficult conversations. More than that, it helps improve overall communication, builds a better understanding, and ultimately leads to better relationships with family, friends, and coworkers."*

Practice really does make perfect, so here are the skills on how to actionably listen to understand.

> ➢ ***Give Your Full Attention***

This may sound obvious, but be honest with yourself; how many times are you listening to someone and you clock out, perhaps thinking about what you should be doing next, what's on TV later, or how you're going to respond? This isn't giving someone your full attention.

You can do this by:

- *Minimizing distractions, such as not playing with your phone or watching TV*
- *Make eye contact with someone*
- *Face the person you're speaking to*
- *Don't multi-task*
- *Bring yourself back to the present when you find yourself drifting*

A great trick I learned to help you keep focus is to concentrate on the center of your palm. You can do it now, and you'll notice how your attention travels there to the center of your hand. See how it makes your thinking stop and how much more focused you are? Try it in your conversations and see how effective it is.

I know this all sounds like simple stuff, but it's because it's so simple that it's easy to forget and get stuck in bad habits. A Harvard study as far back as 1957 even carried out courses to help people listen using these same techniques, which resulted in a 40% increase of people's listening capabilities, so try it for yourself!

> ### *Hear the Other Person Out*

When someone is talking to you, it's incredibly easy to fall into the habit of interrupting, which is a very bad habit. It also means you're not listening to understand the person, you're listening so you can now talk your own points, and that's not the foundation for a meaningful conversation. To help not interrupt people, you can:

- *Minimize distractions, so you're not answering a phone, for example*
- *You don't hold on to your point, but let it go and respond to what the other person is saying*
- *Wait until they have finished speaking*
- *Ask a question if you need more clarity on what they said, rather than just going back to your original point*

This is an important technique to think about because interrupting is a missed opportunity to understand the other person, but it also sends the message that you don't respect the other person enough or feel like their opinions are not worth listening to, and however you're interrupting them is more important than them.

This won't paint you in a favorable light.

> ### *Use Your Body to Listen*

Hand in hand with improving your listening skills, being conscious of your body and how you're controlling it can be a great way to improve how attentive you are. While I already mentioned making eye contact, you can do other things like:

- *Turning your body to face the person who's talking*
- *Nod occasionally*
- *Smiling, but not excessively (don't want them to think you're weird)*
- *Saying "uh-huh" to show you're engaged in the conversation and want them to keep going*
- *Adopt an open posture*

> ### *Repeat back their points for clarity*

One of the most popular ways to improve a conversation is always cited as being the repetition of a point. If someone says, "I like chocolate because it's sweet," you show you understand by starting your next sentence with "Because it's sweet? But which brand is your favorite?" Other ways you can do this include:

- *Paraphrasing what has been said by saying things like, "What I'm hearing is…" or "It sounds like you're saying…"*

- *Ask questions like "What do you mean by..." or "Do you mean..."*
- *Repeat key words back to the person every now and then*

That repetition of what the other person has said shows that you're taking on board and listening to what they have to say, meaning they'll feel like they can be a lot more open and connected with you.

> **Then Respond**

Since you've been actively listening to the other person, and they've finished speaking, now you can respond. You don't want to fall into the trap here of just going back to what you wanted to say originally, but instead, reply to what they're actually saying. You can do this by:

- *Addressing the key point of what they said, again for clarity*
- *Pause for several seconds that shows that you're thinking about what they said*
- *Convey your points in the best way possible*

Don't worry about this last section so much since the rest of the book is going to be dedicated to helping you know what to say in any situation, so we'll be covering this all in a lot more depth.

## The Summary

By using these techniques alone, you'll notice such a huge difference in how connected you are to other people within your conversations and how you're being listened to yourself. When you listen to others and respect what they have to say, most people will unconsciously do the same back to you.

It's only when the other person doesn't feel listened to or respected that tempers start to rise, and things get out of hand. Remember, practice makes perfect, and even incorporating these points into your next conversation will make such an amazing difference. Try it for yourself!

For a quick reference, when listening to people, you're going to want to focus on:

- Understanding the two types of listening
- Practice listening to understand
- Avoid listening to respond
- Give someone your full attention
- Never interrupt someone
- Listen with your body, not just your ears
- Repeat back key points the other person said
- Respond to the point after everything else

And with that, we move on to the next chapter.

In one chapter's time, we're going to be focusing on the core mechanics of actually speaking to someone and starting a conversation, so if you want to skip ahead, that's no problem, but for clarity, the next chapter is going to explore some of the more advanced techniques you can use to actively listen more effectively.

# Chapter Three – Further Listening Skills

*"No one is as deaf as the man who will not listen."* — Proverb

A chapter that needs no introduction, since I did that a minute ago, so let's jump straight into it.

There are basically endless ways you can advance your listening skills, and since everyone is different, and we all have our own bad habits, some of these may apply to you, and some may not, but I like to think of this section as a great reminder of how to listen, as well as to help you set the overall intention of becoming a better listener.

## *Minimize Distractions*

A study back in 2012 carried out by Larry D. Rosen Ph.D. researched 300 middle school, high school, and university students to see how distracted they became, depending on their environment. The students were supposed to be studying, although they were surrounded by phones, computers, and televisions.

The results were shocking, showing that when surrounded by technology, the students could only study for around **three minutes** at a time—laptops and phones providing the most distraction. Only three minutes. That's such a low attention span.

I understand life is busy, and things need to get done. Sometimes, multi-tasking is the only viable solution to make things happen since it feels as though there aren't enough hours in the day. However, if you want to have meaningful conversations and connect with people, there are going to need to be times when you sit down and talk to each other, without the distractions we're typically surrounded by. When someone is speaking to you, you can minimize distractions by:

- *Putting down and locking your phone*
- *Switching off the TV*
- *Turning off your computer monitor*
- *Not eating or drinking while talking with someone*

No matter where you are or what you're doing, whether you're at home or at work, these tips will make your conversations and your relationships far better.

## *Be Free from Judgments*

It's crucial to think about how your judgments affect your ability to listen. If you're stuck in your ways and feeling rather close-minded or defensive on a subject, you can end up not actually listening to someone but instead zoning out or getting ready to tell them why they are wrong.

If you're able to step outside of that and open your mind, you may hear something and learn a new perspective. You may even sway your opinion or can give you more information to help solidify how you feel. Either way, you're going to grow as an individual by listening, so don't let the judgments stop you from doing just that!

To be less judgemental, focus on:

- Being more open-minded
- Notice judgments when they arise
- Become more accepting of other people's ideas
- Accept imperfections in people

### *Ask the Right Questions*

Active listening to someone is all about understanding that other person, which is really all communication, in general, is about. Whether you're sharing thoughts or ideas or trying to solve a problem or even just entertaining, you need to be understanding, and people need to understand you.

Sometimes, people aren't going to be the best communicators, and you're going to require a little more information to understand them, and that's okay.

However, this is such an important element to think about that we're going to cover it in a lot more detail over the next chapter, so stay tuned!

### **The Summary**

For now, these should be enough techniques and strategies to help you become the best listener possible. Some may seem basic to you, and some things you may never have thought of, so take your pick to see what you want to work on, and the chances are you should see positive results even with your first interactions from reading this chapter, so good luck, and see it all in action for yourself.

Let's continue our journey into the art of talking to anyone.

# Chapter Four - It's All About Questions

*"At the end of the day, the questions we ask of ourselves determine the type of people that we will become."*

— **Leo Babauta**

We ended the last chapter talking about the importance of asking the right questions, and it's a topic that deserves a lot of love. That's because when it comes to talking to anyone about anything, the best strategy you can ever have by your side is being able to ask the right questions at the right time.

It's pretty self-explanatory. Asking questions enables you to guide the conversation in whichever direction you want, helps you acquire clarity on what the other person is saying, and helps you find common ground and similar interests. Questions are everything!

Now, don't forget that you don't want to interrogate someone by bombarding them with questions. Instead, find a balance of asking questions and talking, just as it's important to get the topic of your questions right. When you bring together your newfound listening skills and mix them with your new ability to ask questions, you've got yourself a great conversation in the works!

## The Power of Questions

You need to be direct with your questions and use this powerful conversational tool to make the other person feel like they can talk to you, to guide the conversation, and to make the other person feel understood.

We'll refer to each of these elements as:

- **Direction**
- **Clarity**
- **Understanding**

All of these are important when you want to engage in a proper, meaningful conversation.

Let's say you're talking to a colleague at work. It's Monday morning, and everyone is settling in for the day.

"Hey! How are you? How was your weekend?"

"It was okay. Just watched Netflix, really. What about you?"

"Yeah, it was good. Had a barbeque Saturday and just puttered about the house on Sunday."

Not the most enthralling conversation of all time, but a pretty common one nonetheless. Now, you can use questions in a variety of ways here.

If you want direction, you could ask something like:

*Communication Skills Training Series*

> *"What did you watch on Netflix? I'm looking for something action-packed myself. I just finished Breaking Bad, and I've got to say, it's pretty good."*

Now, through your questioning, you're guiding the conversation towards Netflix and TV series, which is a perfectly valid small-talk topic, especially if action-packed shows are something you share an interest in. You've taken control of the flow of conversation.

Other times, you're going to want some clarity, and this is useful for making sure you understood the other person correctly. You also make the other person feel like you really want to know more about what they have to say, thus making them feel more connected to you and more open with the topic at hand. Taking the same introduction as the last example, you get the reply:

> *"I got a new dog this weekend."*

How would you respond? Would you ask for its name? Its age? The breed? If you don't really know dog breeds very well yourself, then asking for the dog's breed isn't really a genuine question because as soon as they answer, you're going to be stumped with what to say next.

**Never** just go for the question you think is right, just because you're going through the motions. Really apply yourself to thinking of better, more progressive questions. This is what it means to ask the right questions.

Instead, what about asking something like:

> *"Oh yeah? How's he or she settling in?"*

Interesting. Not a typical question. Requires a bit of thought. The person you're speaking with begins to engage more with the conversation.

> *"Yeah, not too bad, actually. He's starting to chew the edges of the sofa, though. He's quite young, so I don't know if he's teething or not."*

What's your answer? Another question? What would you go for? It's really up to you. Just remember you've got three main options: Direction, Clarity, and Understanding.

If you want direction, you could say anything, depending on which aspect of the conversation you want to go into. Let's say you're not enjoying the dog conversation and want to move on. You could say something like:

> *"Might be a good excuse to get a new sofa. Or renovate completely. Would you if you could?"*

You're redirecting the dog conversation to something a bit funnier or hypothetical. A bit lighthearted, if you will. If you instead wanted clarity—for example, you knew about dogs and their capability to bite through the corners of sofas—you might ask something like:

> *"Oh really? Is the dog chewing it all the time or just certain hours of the day?"*

Now you're seeking clarity and diving into the topic deeper. If, however, you want the other person to feel understood, you can repeat back what they are saying to make them feel heard.

> *"It could be an age thing if it's a puppy. Have you looked it up or spoken to a vet?"*

Of course, there are infinite ways you can guide the conversation based on the questions you ask, but this should give you a clear idea of how questions are so powerful when it comes to communicating and a massive part of talking to anyone.

Think of it this way. If you're asking questions and the other person is talking, you don't even need to be speaking most of the time, meaning there's little effort or chances to get anxious on your behalf!

## Starting Conversations with Questions

Of course, one of the most powerful ways to use questions is by using them to *initiate* conversations in the first place. However, you don't want to be boring. There's no denying the tried and tested questions like "How are you?" and "Where are you from?" are boring and too generic. These aren't the best ways to start a conversation. There are definitely better options to choose from.

So, let's break it down.

First, you need to get the conversation going. I'm going to assume you're not just talking to a random stranger on the street, but perhaps talking to a colleague at work, or a new client, as part of a networking event while on a date with someone, or so on.

As a side note, however, If you did want to talk to a stranger on the street, then always start with a conversation about something in the immediate environment, such as asking for directions, a good place to eat, the time, or commenting on something that is going on around you.

For example, if there's a carnival happening, you could ask something like, "When was the last time you went to one of these?"

For brevity, let's say you're talking to someone you know in a familiar place. It's time to get involved with some decent conversations. Here are some questions you could ask that can open a great conversation in various situations.

## Meeting Someone New (Networking, social event, etc.)

### *Tell me something about yourself?*

This is a great question because you let the other person take control and tell them what they want you to know, because of course, no one is going to tell you something they don't want you to know, allowing you to have a real insight into who this person is and what they're all about.

### *What was your highlight of this week?*

This is one of my favorite questions because it allows the conversation to take a positive tone and allows the other person to really think about what matters to them. When they're thinking about positive things, they're going to be feeling positive emotions. It's far better than "How are you?"

### *Are you working on anything exciting at the moment?*

Another chance for someone to get excited about talking to you, this question is ideal for when you want someone to be passionate with. Of course, they'll talk about the most important thing in their life, another great way to get to know someone and see what matters to them.

### Have you been here before?

An open-ended question you can use to gauge someone's familiar with a place or person. If you're in a meeting or at an event, such as a business meeting, social event, birthday party (did you come last year?) and so on, you'll get a nice idea of how connected this person is.

Other questions you can ask when getting to know someone, especially on a professional level, include questions like:

- *Where did you go to school?*
- *What was your favorite part of school?*
- *How did you join this industry?*
- *Do you think your career path is similar to people like you?*
- *What's the biggest obstacle in your career?*
- *What's your favorite part of your job?*
- *Is your day quite varied?*
- *What does your typical workweek look like?*
- *What are your plans or aspirations for the future?*
- *What's it like working in your office?*

Of course, once you've asked these questions, these nicely lead to other questions you can ask that dive deeper into the topic you choose, depending on what answers they give you.

## Questions to Ask While on a Date

- *What do you do in your free time?*
- *Are you a morning or night person?*
- *What would be your dream job?*
- *Who is the most interesting person you've met?*
- *How would your friends describe you?*
- *What song or artist do you never get tired of?*
- *What animal do you find the cutest?*
- *What animal do you find most ugly?*
- *What city would you love to live in?*
- *What is your greatest accomplishment?*
- *When was the last time you sang to yourself, and what song?*
- *What trends have you never been able to understand?*
- *What "thing" says the most about a person?*
- *What was the strangest turning point in your life?*

## Fun, Personal Small-Talk Questions for Anywhere

Whether you're talking to your coworkers, friends, on a date, or just passing the time in a line somewhere, these are fun little questions you can ask anywhere.

There are a ton of fun questions you can ask people, and while they may sound a little out there, you'll usually find that people love answering them because they can have so many interesting answers, especially when you're with a group of people, allowing you to compare and casually critique each other's answers.

Basically, these are fun conversation starters that everyone can get involved in. Great for one-on-one or group chats!

- *What do you hope never changes in this world?*
- *What is your dream car?*
- *What's your guilty pleasure song?*
- *If you could learn any skill, what would it be?*
- *What do you wish you knew more about?*
- *How different was your life a year ago?*
- *What's the furthest you've been from home?*
- *If you could go to any fictional place, where would you go?*

## Tips for Asking the Right Questions

### Find the Line

Just a quick note, which acts as more of a disclaimer than anything else: Don't jump straight in and start asking really personal questions, or those on sensitive subjects, like race, sex, politics, religion, and so on. These can be hot topics, and while it would be nice to live in an ideal world where we can all talk about things openly without judgments, we're not quite there yet.

Instead, save these conversations for when there's a right time and place to speak about them, or you're with people you trust and are comfortable enough with to have these conversations.

### Remember Social Hierarchy

Personally, I think it kind of sucks that we can't just be ourselves around everyone (and I know, a lot of what I've said already is about being yourself), but for many other people, you won't be able to connect with them unless you speak to them in a way they're going to understand.

For example, if you're talking to a peer or colleague, you're going to use different language and come across differently than if you were talking to your boss. Similarly, you would talk to the president or the Queen of England differently.

When speaking to others, try to adapt the way you talk and the questions you ask in a way that will be most effective to the listener. If you're talking to a client and they're quite a fancy person, then talking in a genuinely "fancy" way is going to make them connect with you far more than if you fill your sentences with slang.

*"Ah, yes, we're very excited about the project here. What are your thoughts on it so far?"*

*"Yeah, the project's lookin' good. You excited to get going?"*

The question is the same in both instances; it's just how it's framed that makes all the difference.

**Keep Your Questions Open-Ended**

Finally, always try to keep your questions as open-ended as possible because you're inviting someone to give you a comprehensive answer.

*"How are you?"*

*"Good."*

That is not a great conversation.

*"What was the highlight of your week?"*

*"Nice question. Let me think. Probably getting a panini for free in my favorite cafe because they know me and were being nice."*

*"Wow, that's cool they did that. How long have you been going there?"*

Far more interesting. While on this note, you can make questions more open-ended by changing them to include words like what, who, and how. You can also say, "Tell me more," allowing someone the opportunity to elaborate on what they're saying.

With that, you should now understand how important it is to ask questions in your conversations and the benefits you can enjoy by doing so.

**The Summary**

Just to recap this chapter, you're going to want to remember to:

- **Ask lots of questions to get to know someone**
- **Keep the questions open-ended using words like what and how**
- **Use questions for conversational direction, clarity, or for further understanding**
- **Have a backlog of go-to questions to remember depending on the situation**
- **Don't get too personal or head into sensitive subjects**

Armed with this new information, I'm now going to take you down a different rabbit hole, and that's being able to talk to someone in the first place, no matter what situation you're in.

*James W. Williams*

# Chapter Five - How to Have a Conversation with Anyone

*"Good conversation can leave you more exhilarated than alcohol; more refreshed than the theater or a concert. It can bring you entertainment and pleasure; it can help you get ahead, solve problems, spark the imagination of others. It can increase your knowledge and education. It can erase misunderstandings, and bring you closer to those you love."*

**— Dorothy Sarnoff**

This next chapter is pretty much the crux of this book.

Within the next few pages, I'm going to share with you and explore a literal step-by-step way you can have a conversation with anybody about anything. We'll talk more about what you can talk about and how to carry these conversations to be even better in the following chapters, but for now, we're going to cover the absolute fundamentals, building the foundations for your next conversations to stand on.

Ready? Let's go.

## Step One - First Impressions

First impressions always count, so how do you want yours to be perceived in the eyes of others?

After all, you have complete control over it, even if it may not seem like it at times.

*As a quick note, this section could also cover topics like dressing well, dressing for the occasion, making sure your personal hygiene is up to scratch, and so forth because these are all very important points to remember if you're looking to connect with someone and make a positive first impression.*

However, sticking with the interpersonal conversational skills side of things, whenever you meet someone new, you're going to want to create a first impression that helps them connect with you. After all, while we're taught to never judge a book by its cover, let's be honest: We all do this all the time. If you head into a meeting with a new client or go on a first date, you judge that person to see if they're someone you want to work with or spend more time with.

Moreover, while you're giving your first impression to them, they also give one to you. So what does theirs say? Lots to think about, but let's cover both sides of this first impressions coin.

### *Reading the Room*

Remember when you were in school, and your teacher would call in sick, and you'd have a substitute teacher in to cover for them?

I remember having one in my French class, and for the first few lessons, everybody would behave and stay reasonably quiet. While this was quite unconscious, it's clear in hindsight that we were trying to suss out whether the teacher was incredibly strict or a bit of a pushover. As we became more comfortable and pushed the limits, we started to misbehave, which most children do, more and more.

As soon as it was clear the teacher was trying to be a "cool" teacher and wasn't going to crack a whip in our direction for the slightest problem, the class slowly began a descent into chaos.

This same logic applies in your own conversations and interactions.

Whenever you go into a new interaction, start by reading the other person and seeing what type of person they are. Test the waters and see what kind of feedback you're getting. Some questions to ask and things to focus on include:

- *What kind of tone of voice are they using?*
- *What clothes are they wearing?*
- *Are they busy?*
- *Are they at work or relaxing?*
- *Do they look stressed out?*
- *Are they smiling?*
- *How firm is their handshake?*
- *How on time to meet you are they?*
- *What is their body language telling you?*
- *How polite are they?*
- *What manners do they have?*
- *What does your gut instinct say about them?*

Some people are a lot easier to read than others, and you may instantly know the kind of person you're talking to, especially if they're very forthcoming. Alternatively, you may need to gauge a little and start the conversation flowing to really get a feel for who this person is, and therefore, how you're going to effectively communicate with them.

For example, if someone is withdrawn, are they shy, or are they trying to hide something?

The situation you're in will provide a lot of context. The trick here is to look past what the person is saying and instead read their body language and all the other factors we just spoke about. However, someone's body language is very important.

Research shows that around 55% of all communication happens through body language, and 30% happens through tone of voice, so be conscious of it!

Some tricks to remember when reading body language include;

- *Posture. Is someone's head up and confident, or unsure and looking at the ground, avoiding eye contact?*
- *Appearance. What clothes are they wearing? Casual? Smart? Relaxed? Doesn't care?*
- *Crossed arms and legs tend to portray defensive feelings*
- *Hands in pockets (or hidden hands) suggest the person is hiding something*
- *Lip biting or nail picking can be a sign of feeling under pressure*
- *Facial expressions*

By observing these traits, you should be able to read the other person you're speaking with quite well, and then you can use this information to respond in the way that seems appropriate. Remember, people will respond to you how they perceive you are speaking to them, so adapt how you talk for the best results. Once you start getting to know someone and go deeper with them, you can start showing more of yourself.

An example of this initial conversation may be speaking to someone who is looking shy, stressed, or sad. If you read these kinds of signals, you may want to approach them in a nicer, more compassionate way than you would normally speak to someone.

Even if you're finding it hard to read someone, remember: Your gut instinct is usually right when it picks up on cues, so trust it.

Research shows that people who are more tuned into sensing their body sensations in high-pressure situations (in the case of the study, they were looking at people who worked in high-stress London trading floors) were making better, more successful decisions than those who were out of sync with their gut instinct.

In other words, if you have a feeling and your body makes you feel a certain way, it's trying to tell you something, so let it guide you!

### *Writing the Room*

Hand in hand with the point above, it's important to use the information you've learned to take control of your own first impressions and adjust how people are perceiving you. If you walk abruptly into a room and you're crashing around and stumble and then hide in the corner, this creates a very different impression to one who walks in and sits down gracefully and with confidence.

You have control of this!

Some quick-fire points to think about include:

- *How you are dressed*
- *Your tone of voice when speaking*
- *What does your body language say about you?*
- *The firmness of your handshake*
- *Are you making eye contact with the other person?*
- *Are you staring too much?*
- *Are you giving someone your full attention, or are you distracted?*

Be mindful of how you're portraying yourself in the eyes of others, and you'll get a reaction based on what you do. This gives you full control of a situation when talking to anyone, which is going to make you feel far more confident in your abilities to talk to someone.

Another great example of this comes from Patrick King's *Better Small Talk*. In his book, he talks about children and how they haven't developed the social filters many of us develop as we grow older. We have insecurities, anxieties, and traits that children don't yet possess. This is why when we talk to children, we talk to them in a certain way based on how they are talking to us.

In most cases, younger children will just act like themselves. This is why kids happily cry in public or act the same in front of elderly relatives as they do with younger family members. Kids are themselves, usually to funny or embarrassing ends.

However, the confidence that children have with just being themselves means that they are confidently writing the room around them, in which adults will follow suit and will respond a certain way. This is why it's so easy to talk to children, because they can speak with such confidence, without censorship, while being so forthcoming.

## Step 2 - Making the First Move

There's no denying that so many of us put so much pressure on "breaking the ice" and making the first move, almost certainly to the extent that so many of us are so afraid to speak first that we end up not speaking at all. Over time, we've ended up where we are now and having to retrain ourselves to be more confident. There's such a huge fear that we'll be rejected by the other person, judged, or hurt in some way, even if it's just asking a stranger on the street for directions.

Really let that sink in and realize how true that is for many people! However, making the first move is essential if you want success in your conversation, and that's not just success in making them happen in the first place. A study found that making the first move results in so much success in so many areas of your life. In business, making the first offer puts you more in control and more likely to get a better deal. In dating, making the first move is more likely for you to get what you want.

But how do you build the confidence to do it?

The reality of the situation is that breaking the ice and making the first move isn't really that hard. All you need to do is "cut the fluff" and go straight for what you want. I could say just be confident, don't put too much pressure on yourself and the end result, but instead, be in the moment, but I'm guessing that doesn't really help, so let's break it down.

Take dating as an example (I like using this example a lot, but that's because we tend to add so much pressure to ourselves in these situations, most of the time so unnecessarily).

There's a whole taboo subject that you need to have "game" when trying to ask someone out. You need to be slick and have "tactics" to make it work, but this isn't real life, and it's not going to get you to where you want to be.

For some reason, we've forgotten that just going up to someone and being our genuine, authentic selves is easily the best way to get someone's attention and will develop a much stronger connection over the long term. This, of course, applies to all situations, not just dating.

Still, that doesn't help you make the first move. You may feel like you're inconveniencing someone by talking to them, holding them up, or interrupting them. You may not want to speak to a stranger in case you disturb them or they find you annoying. This is social anxiety in full swing.

The actionable step here?

Indirectly approach someone for something, for some reason, and have this reason clear in your head at all times, but don't make it a long-term reason. Don't think, *Wow, I want to talk to this person because I want to date them and marry them* and so on.

Thinking this way means you're putting far too much pressure on yourself because if you're rejected, it's going to hurt. There's too much focus on the outcome, and it's going to make you buckle when the conversations feel too much.

Start small. Think, *Hey, this person seems nice. I'll ask if they want to FaceTime or go for dinner.* Asking someone to go to dinner is way smaller a commitment than thinking long term, and you don't even need to have the pressure of this kind of event if it's too much.

Create a reason to speak to someone, even if there isn't one. Again, this is a fantastic thing to practice because it gives you the chance to try something new, boost your confidence, and get better at speaking with people. Most interactions will not be the most important ones you'll ever have, so relax and try to have fun with them!

Some of the things you can say or ask include:
- *Do you have the time?*
- *Where is the closest bank?*
- *Is the food good here?*
- *What time is the show starting?*
- *Have you seen this movie before?*
- *I love the music here. Do you?*
- *Do you know anyone here?*

These are all small statements you can ask to break the ice, opening the doorways for engaging small talk and conversation, and ultimately deeper connection, should you want to continue speaking with them.

## Step Three - Find the Connection

Now you're talking with someone you've approached the right way, the ice has broken, and the conversation is starting to pick up and find its pace. What do you do now?

The best approach for finding a connection is to find similarities you have with that other person. This means finding common ground on things you're interested in, whether that's a hobby, passion, or music taste, or even just commenting and sharing opinions of what is happening in the immediate environment or situation you're in. An example of the latter would be commenting on the music at a concert you're at.

This is where your listening skills come into play because you're focusing on what someone is saying (and what their body language is saying) and then picking out the bits they seem most connected to, then running with it. Let me give you an example.

Let's say you're at a concert and you're engaging in small talk with someone at the bar. Your first impression is that they are not really having a good time. They just look into their drink, not really focusing on the music, and seem to be mentally somewhere else.

Everything about them suggests they're having a rough time, so you choose to act compassionately and ask if everything's okay, perhaps saying something like, "Is the music too loud for you?" This is lighthearted, not too personal, but also suggesting that you know that something isn't right, and you're willing to talk to them about it.

Depending on their answer, you can then figure out what's wrong and how you can deal with the situation, and you could be on the road to making a close friend.

In any given situation, depending on the context, you can find things in common by asking things like:
- *Where did you go to school?*
- *Where do you work?*
- *What sports team do you support?*
- *What music do you like?*
- *What food is your favorite?*
- *Where do you like to eat?*
- *What kind of movies do you like?*

It's also important to make sure you're vocal about what you agree on. It's all well and good thinking ("Hey, me too!"), but you're not going to connect with the other person unless you tell them that you're on the same page. Vocalizing this is a great way to build rapport and to make someone want to connect with you, which leads us nicely to the next point.

### *The Mastery of Mirroring*

Mirroring is such an important part of any conversation because it makes you more relatable to the person you're speaking to. Mirroring is basically a practice where you're consciously copying (but not too obviously) the tone of voice, posture, body language, speed of speech, and overall physical appearance of the person you're speaking to, which dramatically improves how connected people feel to you.

You can also mirror based on the language and visual style that someone is speaking to you in, such as the amount of slang they're using, but sticking with physical mirroring is enough for most conversations.

A study (Anderson, 1998) also found that people felt more positive towards strangers when mirroring occurs.

Taking the bar example above, if someone is leaning at the bar slouched, and you pull up next to them and do the same, this is mirroring. If they speak slowly and without enthusiasm, mirroring this will help them take on board what you're saying more effectively because you've already created common ground through physical acts alone.

Some things to remember to mirror someone properly include:
- *Mimicking voice speed and tone*
- *Copying volume of gestures*
- *Copying body language, such as posture and leaning*
- *The inflection on certain words*
- *Usage of slang*
- *The energy and excitement for a topic*

You know when you meet someone, and you discover that you share a love for the same band, movie franchise, or sports team, and there's that moment when you look at each other like, "Oh my god, you love them too? That's amazing!" and your energy levels spike, and it's like you both build momentum with each other? That's the magic of mirroring in full effect.

## Step Four - Addressing Obstacles You May Face

If you follow the three steps above, you'll be able to converse with anyone about anything, so that's where we'll end the book. Thanks for reading. Enjoy your day.

I'm joking, of course. In an ideal situation, you'll follow these points, and people will respond to you positively, and the conversations will be able to flow naturally from here on out. However, not everybody is relatable in such a way, and talking to some people can be less enthralling than chatting with a brick wall.

This can happen for many reasons: whether the person is having a bad day, is surprised by you talking to them in the first place, is stressed out, is shy and anxious, or just isn't in the mood for talking. When you talk to people like this, and the conversation feels like it's scraping by with friction, it can be hard to know what to do next. Do you force the conversation to go further, or do you cut and run?

First, remember you can always leave a conversation if you don't want to continue. Just say something along the lines of "Oh, I've got to dash to make the train/get some food/meet someone else," and so on, and you can just leave.

However, there may be times when you need to talk to someone, such as conversing with someone at work, trying to get a job done, interviewing someone, networking, or trying to get information from them. Don't worry; that's not as malicious as it sounds. Imagine you're trying to organize a surprise party for someone and need to know their schedule without actually telling them what's going on. How can you press the conversation forward?

Perhaps the most common technique to use here is elicitation, a communication technique developed by the FBI for interrogation purposes. Now, I'm not advocating that you go out and interrogate people for information—far from it. Teachers use this technique in the classroom all the time, although perhaps without realizing its origins.

Elicitation is the process of getting people to share information that they are holding on to by using statements that guide the person into speaking, even if they don't really want to.

An example of this would be to recognize and compliment someone. Human beings, while complex, are really rather simple when it comes to how we work. We are social creatures who are instinctively wired to receive praise and recognition from others because it shows we're being accepted into a larger group, which back in the day would have been essential for our survival in tribes and larger groups.

Giving someone a compliment about how they are or their physical appearance can be a great way to get them talking. Some statements you can use include:

- *I really like your coat. It suits you.*
- *Damn, I love how hardworking you are.*
- *Your attention to detail is incredible.*

- *The way you express yourself is great.*

Another way to engage in elicitation is to complain, and as I'm sure you know, human beings love to mutually dislike someone, whether it's an opposing sports team, the grey weather, or just a mutually shared situation, like having to stay late after work to get a project completed.

People love to complain. Studies even show that the average person complains between 15–30 times a day, and ActofLibraries.com rates "starting a conversation" as their number one reason for complaining in the first place.

A quick complaint into something can be a very powerful way to open people up and get them speaking, especially if they're looking to vent about a situation they're dealing with.

With all this in mind, next time you watch a crime thriller or detective series when a police interview is taking place, you may start to notice these tactics in full effect. I recently sat down to watch *Breaking Bad* again and (mild spoiler alert) saw the episode where Brock is poisoned, and Jesse has to go into the police station to say why he believes Brock was poisoned by a super-rare substance.

The detectives say things like:

- *We don't need to get the lawyers involved. It's all pen-pushing and a lot of hassle.*
- *We know these situations can be stressful. Just relax. We're just chatting.*
- *You're a smart guy, Jesse.*
- *You're a kind, caring guy. We know you only want to do what's right.*

Even in a situation like where someone is being interrogated for a supposed crime, the detectives use compliments to encourage them to talk, even if they don't want to.

And with that, we come to the end of this chapter. As an actionable recap, when it comes to starting a conversation, you'll want to:

- **Read the other person**
- **Aim to create the first impression you want to give**
- **Break the ice with a question**
- **Have a goal in mind for the conversation**
- **Find similar interests**
- **Find the connection you share**
- **Mirror the person you're speaking to**
- **Practice talking to unresponsive people**

# Chapter Six – Mastering the Art of Small Talk

*"Small talk is the biggest talk we do."* — **Susan RoAne**

The main problem my friend Kyle had while attending his sister's wedding was not being able to get the conversation off the ground in the first place, and I know from personal experience that that's one of the hardest parts of meeting and getting to know new people.

A few years ago, I spent a lot of time on dating apps like Tinder and Bumble before I met my current partner, and I always struggled with what the hell I was going to say after the initial "hey" (which was usually followed by a cringey waving emoji, but I won't go further into that). But then again, what are you supposed to say to be interesting, charismatic, and genuinely be someone that someone else wants to speak to?

Throughout other times in my life, like lining up at the gym to go into a spinning class, I'm surrounded by strangers, and you say the generic small talk stuff about the weather and the problems and politics of the gym, poor management, and so on, but where do you go from there? You're not exactly going to make best friends with someone with that kind of talk.

That's what I'm dedicating this chapter to—mastering small talk.

Every single relationship you've ever had (except that with your parents, maybe your siblings) would have started with small talk of some kind. A test of the water to see whether the person is someone you connect with or not, someone you want to be friends with or not, a client or business is one you want to work with or not, and so on.

Mastering this art, like listening, will take a bit of practice, but with the knowledge we're going to explore in this chapter, you'll have everything you need for success. So, let's get into it.

## The Core Strategies of Small Talk

To start with, it's worth noting that much like listening, the art of small talk has seemingly infinite depth, and it's a lifelong skill you can always work on improving. With over nine billion people on the planet, there's always going to be a new way to get through to someone and a new way of talking to learn.

That being said, we can actually boil the art of small talk down to just four core foundations that everything else is built on. Fortunately, the first three steps are points you already know: to ask questions (especially open-ended ones), be proactive with your listening, and minimize distractions.

So, what's the fourth, mysterious foundation? Any guesses?

It is, in fact, showing enthusiasm. Bringing energy into your conversations. Showing you're passionate. Resonating vibrancy into your interactions. You can talk about anything, and it can be engaging as long as you have enthusiasm.

### The Power of Enthusiasm

Small talk may not be the most interesting thing in the world, but that's only the generic small talk we've all become so painfully used to. Showing energy and enthusiasm for connection can be such a powerful gateway into having a deeper relationship, no matter what you're talking about, and helps the person you're speaking with open up and be themselves, thus nurturing a meaningful relationship even further.

Even if you just act enthusiastic about even the most mundane conversations, you'll see a turnaround in how you connect with people. Try it now in your head. Imagine a standard conversation with someone in your life, and now imagine that same conversation with three times the enthusiasm and imagine how they'd react. I'm not saying you need to be like this all the time, nor do you need to give it ten times the energy when you're talking about traffic. You pick your times and places to go all in.

Adding this degree of energy to your conversations is all about your attitude and your intentions. When you go into any conversation, professional or personal, friends or family, lovers or children, if you have the mindset that you want to know more about this person, or you just want to have fun or learn something new, suddenly you'll start viewing human interaction in a completely different way, and subsequently, life changes.

You'll soon realize that there are endless people out there to meet, infinite views and perspectives to learn from, and fun stories and experiences to share, and isn't it these kinds of values that you wanted when you picked up this book in the first place?

So, how do you do it?

It can be hard to bring enthusiasm to a conversation, especially if you're not a particularly energetic person by nature, and going above and beyond how you would usually be may make you feel fake or as though you're not really being yourself, but this isn't a direction you want to head down. You want your energy levels to be genuine.

Fortunately, there are plenty of ways you can do this.

> ### Act More Energetic

Even adjusting tiny details in the way you converse can make such a big difference. You can talk a little louder in terms of volume (I'm not saying shout, but you know what I mean), and you can change your tone of voice to make it more diverse. You can also emphasize certain words and adjust your inflection to make what you're saying more interesting to listen to.

For example, take the two sentences below:

> *I got a new cat over the weekend.*
>
> *Oh my, I got my NEW cat over the weekend, and she's so CUTE!*

The emphasis is on the large words, and you can see how just slightly adjusting what you're saying can bring so much more power to your words.

You can, of course, amplify your body language to enhance what you're saying as well. For example, instead of saying, "Well, you have two choices. A or B?" you can use your hands to highlight the options, indicating them right for A and left for B. You're not really pointing at anything, but you're amplifying the fact there's a choice to be made and two options to choose from.

Overall, this kind of action makes the conversation seem more interactive.

> ### Highlight How You Feel

You don't need to agree with everything everyone ever says to you for them to like you. In fact, it's better if you surround yourself with people of opposing views because it helps you stop being stuck in your own ways.

There will be things you disagree with, just like they'll be statements that resonate with you, but whichever you feel, highlight that this is how you're feeling. This is one of the best ways to bring energy into a conversation because it's a great way to simply be yourself.

For example, if someone says something you resonate with or says something that you couldn't have said better yourself, then tell that person that that's how you feel. Check out these statements:

*Yes! I completely agree. You worded that way better than I ever could!*

*I'm so glad you brought that up. I feel the same!*

*Wait, you're interested in that too?*

*I see what you're saying, but I'm the opposite. I love XYZ.*

*I really don't agree with you. I really feel like...*

See how much energy statements like these can bring to a conversation and how validating it will feel for the other person?

Be genuine and say how you feel. When you're being open and honest, the conversation becomes less placid and passive and is instead more direct and assertive.

### ➢ *Exert Natural Energy*

A really quick note here. I'm not here to tell you how to live your life on a healthy level, but it's common knowledge that if you look after your body, you naturally have a ton of untapped energy that will naturally rise up in the way you live your life.

By this, I mean exercising regularly, eating well, drinking lots of water, getting enough sleep each night, and so on. If you look after yourself, you'll naturally have more energy. This may all sound a little basic, but hey, I know for a fact that I used to not really look after myself properly, and taking control of that brought about a lot of positive changes.

### ➢ *Surround Yourself with the Right People*

Granted, you're not going to be around positive, happy people at every waking moment of your life, nor would that be a healthy thing. Sounds like some weird cult thing happening in that world. However, you do need some stable positive people in your life that you spend regular time with if you want to adopt these personality traits yourself.

Negativity is physically and mentally draining, and you're not going to feel energetic or on the ball in any sense if you feel depressed and drained. It just won't happen unless you're incredibly passionate about faking how you feel.

Seek out to spend time with people who fill you up with energy, make you feel good, and consistently don't bring toxicity and negativity into your life.

## Discovering Engaging Small-Talk Topics

Okay, so you're following the tips above, and you're starting to bring your own brand of energy into your conversations.

It doesn't matter where you are or who you're speaking with—you're attractive to listen to. You're also listening to the other person, you're asking questions, and everything seems to be running smoothly. I'm sure you're able to see how everything we've spoken about already is coming together to ensure your conversations are perhaps like no other conversations you've had before.

Notice how at the beginning, I said being charismatic and confident is something that can be learned? Take a moment to think about everything you've learned so far and how applying this information will evolve your relationships and interactions. Perhaps you've already tried it yourself, and you're starting to experience the results? Fortunately, there's more to discover.

A question we've already run into time and time again is what actual topics you can talk about. While there are practically infinite topics to talk about, it can be hard to remember the best ones, and while someone may care a lot about one topic, another person could have no interest whatsoever, leaving you stuck with no ideas on how to move forward. This section is here to help.

Jumping straight into it, here are some great topics to have in your back pocket that you can pull out in any conversation.

- Talking about the location you're in (immediate environment)
- Food, restaurants, and cooking
- Travel, vacations, holidays, dream destinations
- Sports
- Hobbies and passions
- Art
- Favorite local places

When you head into a conversation with someone, if you're listening carefully (which is why we covered this skill in the first chapters), you can pick up clues that can help you identify which topics are best to engage in. Here's an example conversation of two people waiting quietly at a bus stop on a grey rainy day.

*A: Hey. You okay? You're looking a bit down.*

*B: Yeah, I'm fine. I've never much been a fan of waiting or the rain.*

See how they start talking about the weather? It's a typical small talk conversation commenting on the immediate environment, which makes it easy to talk about, but what's interesting is the fact person B used it as an excuse for not feeling okay right now. All this is picked up on by listening to one sentence.

*A: Oh yeah, more of a sun worshipper?*

*B: Yup. Any day of the week.*

*A: Where would you go if the bus could take you anywhere in the world?*

A beautiful transition away from traditional small talk and into a more interesting topic of conversation that's open-ended enough for them to answer however they want. If they reply creatively, you know the person is down for actually talking. If they're pretty blunt and answer with something like, "Hm, I don't know," then you know they're probably not in the mood.

> B: Probably south of France. I love it down there. The sun is beautiful on the coast.

> A: Oh, right. Have you been before? I'd love to go there myself.

And so on.

More than you probably realize, people will give you topics to talk about in everything they say because they're already thinking about themselves and how they perceive the world at all times. In this example, Person B loves going abroad and being in the sun, and this is a fact that shines through in the very first thing they say.

Notice how person A ends with "I'd love to go there myself," bringing that energy and passion into the conversation that invites person B to open up more and start sharing the energy they have for something they love—in this case, warm countries. They don't seem very engaged in the conversation at first, but they can start to be themselves in just a few sentences. The conversation begins to find a rhythm.

## You Will Need to Carry the Conversation... At First

You may feel this kind of conversation feels very one-sided, with you doing all the talking and the other person not really asking you questions but unfortunately, that's just the way things are these days for many people. That's not to say that everyone is like that, but there are multiple reasons why.

Either people love talking about themselves or, especially if they're talking with a stranger, won't think to ask them about their life, or are too afraid to ask because they feel like they're being intrusive. Other people may not be used to talking to other people so openly, so it can take a little while for them to open up and come out of their shells.

There are endless reasons how we've reached this point. Studies and research suggest that we're drifting apart from each other, or we're so reliant on social media that we're losing our social communication skills. There are many studies out there, like the 2018 study on "Social Media Use and Perceived Social Isolation Among Young Adults in the U.S," that social media use is a massive contributing factor to ever-growing feelings of isolation and loneliness, suggesting that we're disconnecting from one another in a way like never before.

However, everyone is different, and whatever the reason for someone being too withdrawn to talk to you and step out of their own shell, you have the tools to help the people you speak with to come out of the other side and realize we don't have to be so closed off with each other.

## Meaningful Relationships Take Time

Going back to my line in the gym for a spinning class example, there are plenty of things to talk about with others around me. I could talk about the quality of the class, the music choice, how easy it was to park outside this evening, gym announcements that have been made, and so on.

These might not initially sound like interesting subjects at first, but that doesn't make them any less essential. Remember, you should try not to be judgmental since you never know what you're going to learn or what topics of conversation will arise as a result of the typical small-talk topics.

What's more, having small talk with easy topics first is essential for opening the door to deeper conversations down the line. If you're talking to someone, you need to build up your connection with them to lead to deeper, more meaningful subjects.

Trust and respect are key parts of any relationship, and they take time to build up.

A really beautiful example that illustrates this point comes from my mother and father trying pottery classes when they first retired. When catching up, they would tell me about the boring conversations they had at first, and perhaps these classes weren't for them. It was all small talk and no substance, gossip, and the sorts, which didn't really interest my parents. I told them to hang in there and give it time. It was only like this because they were new, and the relationships were forming.

Over time, they came to know that one of the other attendees, Maisie, was going through a battle with cancer, and while on a Sunday afternoon walk, they took flowers and chocolates to her house as a surprise and had an afternoon of tea. Their relationship kept going, and once Maisie had recovered from her therapy, my parents, Maisie, her husband, and a few others from the pottery class even went on vacation together.

All these opportunities started with small talk in a pottery class on those first few sessions. Every relationship needs to start somewhere.

This is why it's a good idea to have some key go-to small-talk topics up your sleeve that you can pull out at any time. I know we've covered a lot of topics you can talk about already, but just for clarity sake, some more topics include:

- ***The Weather***

It's easy. It's neutral. Everyone can talk about it. It's a great starting off point. When you're just starting out on your journey to becoming more confident with your small talk, this is a great topic to practice and to use to improve your skills.

> *I wonder who ordered this beautiful weather?*
>
> *It's like monsoon season today.*
>
> *I love days where the fog is like this. It's so eerie.*

- ***Entertainment***

Another firm favorite. People are bound to be interested in something during their free time, whether that's books, movies, TV shows, cinema, sports, restaurants, and basically any form of leisure activity. Jump in and find out what other people like.

> *Any great books you're reading at the moment? I need some good recommendations.*
>
> *Do you listen to podcasts? I'm trying to get into them.*
>
> *Do you have any fun apps on your phone?*

*What team do you support?*

*Been to the movies recently? I haven't been in so long!*

*Are you watching the tennis championship at the moment?*

- ***Personal Life***

You don't want to get too personal with people you've just met (this can be seen as being too forward or even intrusive), but a few personal questions that help you get to know someone better is fine.

*Where does your family come from originally?*

*Have you ever looked into your heritage?*

*How long have you and your partner been together?*

*Do you have brothers and sisters? (Pets is also a decent question)*

I'm sure you get the idea. Other great topics you can talk about include:

- *Hobbies*
- *Travel*
- *Food interests*
- *Celebrity gossip*
- *Information on hometown*
- *Work-life and career*

If you're really struggling for ideas, you can always talk about what is happening right here, right now in the location you're in. Listen carefully to find relatable topics that both you and the other person find interesting. If one of you isn't interested in sports at all, then it's not a good place to go unless you're talking about how uneducated you are in sports, which can be quite humorous when communicated in the right way).

Keep asking questions and let the topics of conversation involve naturally.

## Small-Talk Topics You MUST Avoid

I've spoken a lot about small-talk topics you can dive into, but very little on topics you should probably avoid talking about at all costs, which is what I'm going to dedicate this section to. It's very easy to get caught out and stuck in talking about these topics, and while they may be okay with some people, generally speaking, I would steer clear of them.

Quick note: That's not to say you can't ever talk about these things with other people in your life, but they're usually reserved for conversations with people you can trust, and you know you respect and can speak openly with.

- **Finances**

I mean, imagine if someone came up to you and asked you how much you earned. You probably wouldn't be very willing to share because it's a personal topic. What's more, how much we earn would only usually be asked as a way to judge someone on who they are, which nobody wants. Avoid at all costs (no pun intended).

- **Religion**

Always a controversial topic. You never know what other people believe, so you're going to want to save this topic until you know someone and have enough respect to listen to each other and actually talk about how you feel on the subject, rather than making snap judgments on someone you barely know.

- **Politics**

Hand in hand with religion, the topic of politics has the potential to get really emotionally charged and out of hand, especially when you're unaware of the views of the other person. There could be a time and a place where it's fine, but generally speaking, avoid this topic until you know someone really well.

- **Death**

This topic should probably be on this list without needing to mention it, but if you're trying to enjoy a positive conversation with someone you want to get to know, you should perhaps avoid such heavy topics like death and loss. These can be emotionally driven and upsetting, not feelings you want to be associated with in your initial meetings.

- **Sex**

Sex is personal. Making jokes, dropping innuendos, and talking openly about sex with strangers has the potential to make people feel really uncomfortable and will remember you in a bad light. Sure, there are times, perhaps if you're flirting, where it could be the perfect time to talk about it, but you're going to want to pick your moments wisely.

- **Health and well-being**

Have you ever been speaking to someone, and you've accidentally dropped that you're not feeling well, and suddenly they jump in with all these quick fixes and remedies? It's the most annoying thing, especially when the other person has no idea about the details of your condition or the complexity of it (nor are they usually a trained healthcare professional). Don't be that person.

- **Personal life gossip**

By all means, talk about celebrity gossip because these are people who put their lives out there in the public eye, but sharing gossip about people in your life is not a good idea. While people may be engaged and interested in what you're saying, this kind of topic paints you in a negative light, and people will consciously avoid you in case you end up sharing personal information about them.

- **Offensive jokes**

Sure, you can use your most sexist, racist, and most out-there offensive jokes when you're around people you love, whether that's friends or family. I'm not advocating hate, but I understand that comedy is comedy, no matter what form it takes. However, it's extremely dangerous ground to share these with people you don't know and could end up getting you in a lot of trouble. Imagine sharing one on your first day at work in a new office and pushing everyone away. It's a bad situation to be in.

- **Physical appearance**

Quite a traditional topic to avoid. It's best not to ask how old someone is or comment on their physical appearance, just because you don't know how sensitive someone may be. A common example of this is asking someone how far in their pregnancy they are when they're not even pregnant. Imagine being in that situation.

- **Ex-partners or friendships**

If you're on a first date with someone, it's pretty common knowledge that you're not going to want to start talking about your exes. It's a bitter place to take the conversation, and it's probably going to make the conversation turn negative, which is not something you want to be connected with when people are spending time with you. Avoid!

- **Any limited conversation topics**

Let's say you start talking about your hobbies—swimming, for example—but the other person has absolutely no interest in swimming and hasn't even swum in years. Why are you going to keep going on about swimming? It's as though you're trying to bore and push away the other person. If someone doesn't seem interested in the topic of conversation, switch it up.

## *Ending the Conversation*

In many ways, how you end your conversations is just as important as how you start them. While you've already created your first impression, how you end an interaction will determine your *lasting* impression and how people treat you the next time you see them. This is why it's a good idea to practice and rehearse some key exit lines you can always fall back on to leave a positive lasting impression. Here are some ideas to get you started.

*It has been really great meeting you. Do you have a number or social media?*

*I can't wait to hear how your project/meeting/event goes. See you next time?*

*Well, this has been great. I'm going to grab something to eat. See you around?*

*Wow. It's true you learn something new every day. Thank you for that. I've got to rush off now, but would it be okay to swap details and carry this on another time?*

You'll need to adapt what you say, the words you use, and the way you say what you say depending on the situation you're in, just like we've done in every aspect of conversation before. For example, you're going to speak differently to a professional-client than you would someone you're asking on a date, but you can get creative.

The best idea, however, is to have some ideas of how you can positively sign off on a conversation, make your exit, and leave the situation so that the person you were speaking with will remember you and this experience positively.

## Practicing the Art of Small Talk

All of these methods and topics we've covered in this chapter are great when it comes to being better at small talk, but as I keep saying, just reading about them now isn't going to make a difference to how good you are. It's only through practice that you'll get better.

I love the metaphor, so I'm going to say it again (probably the last time, though, I promise...maybe).

If you want to get good at swimming, you need to spend time in the pool.

If you're wondering how you're supposed to "get in the pool" when it comes to small talk, this section has got you covered as we explore some of the ways you can integrate small talk into your everyday life, thus becoming better at it.

### *Keep Your Eyes Open for Opportunities*

By speaking with lots of different people about lots of different topics, you'll start to develop your own opening and closing statements, and you'll start to get a real feel for how you can traverse various topics of conversation and what subjects you can talk about passionately. However, these are all social aspects that come with experience, so get the experience!

No matter what you're doing in your life and what situation you're in, keep your eye open for opportunities to practice small talk.

Talk to the cashier at the store. The person behind you in line. The man at the bar. The class teacher after the lesson. I can't stress enough how much practicing is going to benefit you. Of course, not everyone is going to be interested in talking for whatever reason, but that's okay. Just keep going and keep getting better. Step outside your comfort zone!

### *Pretend You are Friends*

When it came to my personal small-talk improvement journey, this was perhaps the biggest game-changer that opened so many doors. I worked in sales for a lot of years and found it difficult talking to new clients and project managers. I could present my projects and proposals because I had direction but was useless when it came to anything outside of that.

However, as soon as I switched my mindset into believing that anyone I was speaking to was already a friend, someone I knew, or someone I could trust and was close to, I unconsciously started treating them as friends, which meant I was more open, more confident, and more charismatic.

It's a quick mental shift—a trick, if you like—that can help alter your perspective into relaxing and being more comfortable in your own skin.

### *Be Patient with Yourself*

Throughout any self-improvement journey, you're going to make mistakes. While these can be embarrassing, especially when it comes to talking with new people you're trying to have a positive relationship with, it's all part of the journey and a part you're going to look back on in years to come and laugh at while reveling in how far you've come.

Messing up is not a big deal, and if you try to protect yourself in life so you never mess up, you're never going to get anywhere or learn the lessons that will change your life.

### *Set Objectives*

While small talk with someone is not a military operation, although it can sometimes feel like it, it can really help you have direction with what you say if you're setting goals and targets for your conversations. Take Kyle at his sister's wedding. Is he trying to have a good time? Get to know people? Have a laugh? Meet someone?

Having a clear objective helps you to determine what kind of energy you're bringing to the table, what kind of topics you want to cover, and what kind of people you're going to invest your time speaking to.

### The Summary

And that's it! That wasn't too bad, was it? When it comes to mastering small talk, the core points you're going to want to focus on practicing are:

- **Being energetic and enthusiastic**
- **Be genuinely yourself regarding your interests**
- **Become confident with a range of small-talk topics**
- **Practice ending conversations strongly**
- **Practice small talk when and where you can**
- **Act like close friends with strangers**
- **Have conversational goals with people**
- **Remember that practice makes perfect!**

Everything we've spoken about within this chapter should give you a deep enough insight into small talk that you can become a master of it. As I said before, take the points and strategies that resonate with you and apply them to your own life. Don't try and apply everything at once because that's just overwhelming and unsustainable. Take your journey to getting better one step at a time.

Now we can move on to my favorite chapter.

*Communication Skills Training Series*

# Chapter Seven – Intricate Ways to Be More Charismatic

*"Charisma is a sparkle in people that money can't buy. It's an invisible energy with visible effects."* —
*Marianne Williamson*

What does charisma mean to you?

Google defines charisma as being the quality of personal magnetism and charm that you've probably experienced several times in your life. Those are people who speak, and you listen to, and you just can't help but think, *Damn, this person is cool. I want to spend more time with this person and explore what they have to offer.*

I saw this "charm" in the sales industry all the time. I would go into meetings with clients and would listen to companies that would come pitch to us or us to them, and some of the people I saw would have you hanging on their every word from the moment they opened their mouths. They were just so good at public speaking. When they finished, it was like being snapped back into reality, and I was left questioning where I've been the last hour.

Being around a charismatic person is more like an experience than a conversation.

Maybe you've met a boy or girl in a bar and started chatting with them, only to find yourself lost in the experience of them just being, well, them. It doesn't matter how long that experience lasts; you're always left wanting more. They leave an imprint that you don't forget.

If you've watched television shows like *Mad Men, the Queen's Gambit,* and even *Friends,* you'll know that charisma doesn't just come in the standard big ego kind of way. It's not just men in suits who know their industry inside out or women in attractive dresses who act mysterious and subtle that hold people's attention. Very far from it. Perhaps these are traditional views on charisma, but nowadays, these are outdated and barely relevant.

Charisma comes in all different shapes and sizes, and even someone who you may consider a "book nerd," for example, could have so much charisma when it comes to talking about their favorite characters, plot lines, and endings. So, how do you tap into your own pool of charisma? How do you charm others and make them, essentially, attracted to you and the energy you have to offer the world?

Just like small talk and listening, this is a skill that can be learned by understanding a few core truths.

### You Own the Situation

What's the one thing that the charismatic people in your life have never been?

Well, they probably have at some points in their lives, but I mean, at the time they were charismatic, what were they not?

I'll give you a clue. It's that same feeling you get when you're about to get on a roller coaster, and you don't know what's going to happen. Is it going to be fun or scary? Are you going to shout or scream? Are you going to pee yourself or throw up? God forbid either hits the kid behind you if you do. Yeah, I'm not a massive fan of theme parks, if you can't tell.

The trait is, of course, nervousness.

Charismatic people have a way of managing their nerves, so they are confident and believe that they are supposed to be a part of the interactions they're in. If you don't feel as though you belong, you're going to feel nervous. If you're putting too much pressure on the outcome of the situation, you're going to feel nervous, and that's just ridiculous when you boil it down to the reality of the situation.

Let's say you're back in college and you see a boy or girl you like, and you want to ask them out.

If you feel nervous, this means you're placing all the importance of the conversation on what their answer is. When someone's answer (the outcome of the situation) becomes the most important part of the conversation, you're not in the moment. Remember how the motivational quotes say life isn't about the destination, but the journey? The same logic applies here.

Doing this means you're creating too much pressure on how the conversation goes. Hence, you're going to believe you need to "act" perfectly in order to get what you want, which is, of course, impossible. Instead, by being present, actively listening, and just having a conversation with this love interest with the goal to enjoy their company right here and now, then it really doesn't matter whether they say yes or no to asking them out, because that doesn't matter. The quality of the interaction you're having is, instead, the most important point.

Paradoxically, when you're not focused on the outcome, there's less pressure, you'll naturally be more charismatic and confident, so if you do ask the other person out, they're having a much more positive time than having to deal with the nervous version of you, and are therefore more likely to say yes.

To summarize, don't put too much pressure on yourself in any social situations. Don't focus on the outcome or the "end goal," but instead focus on enjoying the interaction itself. You'll be less nervous and naturally more charismatic.

## *Relatability is Key*

The subheading says it all. I remember I went to a blood doner's session a few years back, and after you've donated blood, you have to wait ten minutes to make sure you're not going to pass out and everything goes okay. You get a cup of tea and a biscuit, so it's not all bad.

Anyway, one time I was there waiting in the post-donation room, and a guy came and sat next to me. I have no idea how, but we ended up talking, and when I say we, I mean he, about his swimming history, and how to be better at gliding through the water and how to go faster and be more efficient, and then on to all the medals he won, and so on. I'm starting to think swimming is something I should start thinking about introducing to my life with the amount I'm talking about it.

What he was saying was all fine, and some of it was actually quite interesting. Being someone who consciously puts effort into listening, yeah, I may have learned a thing or two, but there was a problem. I couldn't help but not be disinterested in what he had to say because it wasn't relatable at all. I didn't swim, nor did I really care about it. It felt as though he was just using me as an opportunity to talk about himself and his achievements, and I was forced to just go along with everything he said.

That's not a two-way conversation, and it's very boring for me. It would be very boring for anyone.

Apply this in your own interactions and make what you're saying relatable to the person you're speaking with. The more you get to know someone, the easier this will be. However, until you get to that point, try focusing on asking the right questions that will help you understand the other person better, thus being able to choose topics you can both talk about.

Charismatic people include everyone and don't just use conversations to talk about themselves.

### *Remember People's Names*

One of my favorite quotes from Dale Carnegie, one of the most popular and influential authors in sales training and interpersonal skills, is:

*"A person's name is the sweetest sound in the world to that person."*

And it's true. We all like to be called by our own name, and you should already know how awkward it can be when speaking with someone and you can't remember their name for the life of you. Being like this isn't going to make someone feel special, nor positively relate to you. Taking the time to consciously and purposefully remember someone's name can make a world of difference in your relationships with them. It shows you care and respect that person enough to get to know them properly. These are powerful, charismatic traits. Here are some tips to help:

- Be present when talking to the other person, so you hear their name correctly
- Repeat the person's name back to them to make sure you heard it properly
- Create an association (i.e., Harry with the round glasses)
- Make a rhyme out of their name
- Ask someone else their name if you forgot

### *Be Funny*

I was debating whether I wanted to include this section because yes, if you want to connect with people, being funny and humorous is an extremely good way to go about it, but not everyone is funny in the same way, and we all find different things comical. This may make it hard to connect with others because if your sense of humor is not the same as someone else's, things might not go down too well.

Remember what we said about avoiding offensive jokes? Comedy is hard, especially around strangers.

That being said, a charismatic person will be able to read the room, select the right level of funny, and can make it work. If you have found in the past that you're a naturally funny person, even if you're funny in your own way, then embrace that when the time arises.

Charisma and humor go hand in hand with each other, and being able to put a smile on someone else's face is a priceless gift you should own within yourself. Here are some quick-fire tips to get funnier in your conversations, should you believe you have the potential to be:

- Watch comedy programs and live shows to get ideas of what is funny
- Find and follow comedians you like
- Learn three awesome jokes you like and learn how to tell them perfectly
- Practice not being offended by other forms of comedy

### *Give, Give, Give*

This is another interesting point to think about.

Eric Matthews from Start Co., in an interview with Success.com, said that giving more than you take is one of the most beneficial ways you can be charismatic in the business world, and this also applies to life in general. To be charismatic by nature is to lift up those around you and to make their lives better in some way.

You can do this in simple ways, like giving someone your full attention, or paying them a compliment. You can validate and reassure their thoughts by repeating back what they said.

There's no human on Earth who doesn't want this kind of attention. The real trick here is to first put the other person in the center of your attention. People love this and will be much more willing to converse with you further and deeper.

Second, you can't expect to get anything back. This does, to a degree, suck because a lot of conversations you have can feel very one-sided, but here's a little reminder that you don't always need to speak to that person ever again if they're not someone you want to spend time with and it doesn't become a two-way experience when you're with them. You don't need to be friends with everyone, but that doesn't mean you can't be a charismatic individual.

A few tips for clarity:
- Give genuine compliments if you mean them
- Give someone your full attention
- Don't expect anything in return
- Be polite with good manners
- Be open and honest with the other person (don't wear a mask)

## The Summary

Being charismatic is no easy feat, and it takes time and practice. Don't worry if you didn't feel like you got everything you came for in this chapter since this is just an introduction for things you can work on. Give these points some time, and you'll see instant improvements with how charismatic you are. We're going to go deeper in the next chapters.

For reference, the core values you're going to want to remember here are:
- **Remember you belong in any situation you're in**
- **Be relatable to people you're speaking too**
- **Remember the names of people you speak to**
- **Let humor come naturally**
- **Give to people without expecting anything in return**

For now, these should be enough little tricks and pointers to keep you going on your way to being a charismatic person who can speak to anyone. Granted, it's not easy stuff, and it's going to take a bit of practice, but it will all come together in time. Just be mindful of what you're doing, and actually step out of your comfort zone to try new things!

This is the only way you'll see the results for yourself!

# Chapter Eight – How to Be More Confident

*"The most beautiful thing you can wear is confidence."* — **Blake Lively**

Hand in hand with being charismatic, there's the ability to be confident. Be honest—you saw this coming, and believing you have a lack of confidence is probably one of the reasons you picked up this book in the first place. If so, this is the chapter that's going to help, but I'm hoping you can see how everything we've spoken about already ties into each other and will naturally help you become more confident, simply because you have more strategies to implement within your upcoming conversations.

Being charismatic and being confident are two different things, although they support each other wholeheartedly.

By dictionary definition, being charismatic is having a charm that makes people want to be around you and spend time with you; being confident is having the belief to know that the outcome of a situation will be favorable to you. In other words, you're able to go into a conversation knowing that everything is going to be alright and you're not going to be embarrassed or make a mistake, and even if you do, then you know everything is still going to be okay.

Remember what we were talking about in the last chapter about asking someone on a date? If you feel nervous and unconfident, then you're going to act nervous and unconfident, and the whole situation becomes a bit of a self-fulfilling prophecy. On the other hand, if you're confident and carry yourself well, the chances you'll get a date increase dramatically.

So, how do you do it? Let's find out.

**Fake It 'Til You Make It**

You've probably heard this saying from time to time, but the science exists that suggests that *acting* a certain way is one of the best ways to *become* a certain way. In other words, if you pretend to be confident, then you will actually become confident.

In psychology and neuroscience, this is known as the Hebbian Principle. How it works is that when a human being does something, which can literally be anything, the tiny neural circuits in their brain light up and start firing to make the "thing" happen. Say you want to lift your right arm up right now. You think about it, and those circuits start firing to make it happen, sending the signals for your body to lift your arm. Now, you can resist doing it if you really want, but how aware of your arm are you right now?

If you're to lift your arm, then the message sent becomes a "link," and the more you allow this link to happen, the easier it becomes. The human brain likes the easy life, and this is why so many of us have habits. We've done the same habit over and over again so often that we do it without thinking, so the brain saves energy and just "does," rather than spending all its time thinking.

Still with me?

Now, we've evolved so far up to this point that you can actually trick this system into developing new habits or, in this case, entirely new states of mind by purely thinking about doing something. Let's keep it related to confidence.

If you were to get up in the morning, go to the mirror, and act like your most confident self, portraying the level of confidence you want yourself to have, and actively act out how you would be (yes, this means talking to yourself out loud), then over time, you would naturally become more confident because you're firing up those circuits saying that you want to be more confident, and then carrying out that command.

You're actively hard-wiring your brain. It's such a clever technique.

This is why motivational speakers will jump up and down and build up their energy before going on stage. Popular speaker Tony Robbins actually has a mini-trampoline he jumps on just moments before heading in front of the crowd. It's to build up his energy and get his blood flowing, so when it comes to show time, he's already in the high-energy state of mind he needs to be in to deliver.

You can do the same!

Basically, define the type of person you want to be and what level of confidence you want to have, practice it in your free time, and then start to implement this level of confidence naturally in your interactions, and you'll notice an incredible difference! Here are some tips that helped me through this process:

- Watch movies and TV shows and see what kind of people you resonate with to define your style of confidence
- Do the same with people in your life
- Practice in front of the mirror for five minutes every single day
- Experiment with different styles of confidence
- Apply your practices to everyday situations you find yourself in

## Overcome Thoughts That Hold You Back

Thoughts that stop you from living the life you want to live and hold you back are known as limiting beliefs, and these are crushing your confidence.

Imagine you're going into a job interview, and you're feeling so nervous. You can't help but think you're going to mess everything up, and you keep playing through all the various negative ways the meeting could go. If you're focusing on the bad stuff, then how can you expect to be confident going forward? You're definitely not going to be your best self.

The way to get around this problem is to become aware of what your limiting beliefs are. You can do this long-term through journaling, meditation, counseling, and doing everything we talked about in the first chapter regarding developing your sense of self. However, there is something we can do right now, and it's a fun little exercise I love.

### *A Quick Little Exercise*

Grab a pen and paper and imagine you are going to meet with someone for the first time.

That could be a new client, a stranger in a cafe or on the street, or you're heading into an unfamiliar situation where you need to talk to people, but you don't really know them very well, if at all.

Take a moment to imagine it clearly, and now write down all the negative thoughts that come up. Do you think these people will think you're weird or annoying? Are you conscious of your physical appearance?

Are you worried that they won't like you or will talk down to you? Write down anything that comes to mind.

When you read them back, these are your limiting beliefs and things you're going to need to work on when it comes to becoming confident. These are the thoughts that will hold you back and stop you from reaching your full potential. Of course, there's an infinite number of thoughts that could come up here, and it will take time to work through them all, but fortunately, there are tons of articles, books, and websites that can help you address your issues.

For me, I thought people would believe I didn't know what I was talking about, and I wasn't qualified to share my experience because I was still young. However, after some research, I discovered this is a state of mind called Imposter Syndrome, and I was able to take steps to work on letting these limiting thoughts go.

While a little unrelated, I found this limiting beliefs discovery technique very fun when it comes to looking at your finances. Get your pen and paper again and write down your dream wage you'd like to earn in a year. Now add a zero to the end (the right-hand side end) and write down all the reasons why you can't earn that amount. These are your limiting beliefs, and it can be incredibly interesting to see what comes up!

**Adopt Confident Body Language**

A leading Harvard psychologist, Amy Cuddy, looked into body language and how the way we act physically affects our mindset, state of mind, and overall confidence. In her studies, she took 42 men and women and had them perform what is known as low and high power poses.

These are basically poses that show how confident someone is. In other words, the stereotypical view of a shy person is crouched over and small, hunched, as though trying to hide and not be noticed. On the other hand, a power pose beaming confidence would be something like the Superman pose, with hands on their hips and their head held high.

In the study, the participants were asked to hold certain poses for two minutes, and then saliva samples were taken.

The results were clear. Those people who had adopted high-power poses, similar to the Superman pose, showed lower cortisol levels (the stress hormone) and increased testosterone levels—both of which indicate the person was more relaxed, more confident, less stressed, and more willing to take rests. And this was all just for adopting a different pose.

Hand in hand with faking it until you're making it, you can feel the effects right now. Assuming you're reading this sitting down, straighten your back, and sit back with your hands behind your head, more commonly referred to as the "President's Pose." It looks like the classic office desk pose where you've completed a sale and cross your legs up on the desk because you're so happy with what you've just achieved, although having your legs on the desk is optional.

Have strength in your pose, widen your chest, and do a pose that reminds you of feeling proud. All the stereotypical poses that come to mind will do. Hold the pose for 30 seconds to a minute. How do you feel? How confident and ready to take on the world does it make you feel? This is just how powerful such a simple act can be. Practice these poses when going into tense situations to become far more confident than you would normally be!

### Get Hands-On

Hand in hand with the point above, using your hands as your main expressive form of body language can be a great way to feel, look, and become confident. Research by Carol Kinsey Gorman found that listeners will have a much more positive connection with public speakers who gesture with their hands to exaggerate and communicate their points.

The same works the other way around too. If you're playing with your hair, fiddling with your sleeves or your clothes, or keeping your hands still in between your legs while sitting, this can convey the image that you're nervous or anxious. Take control of your hands and channel your inner energy for whatever topic you're talking about!

### Implement Eye Contact

Being able to hold and maintain eye contact is pretty much the cornerstone of confidence. If you look away from someone when they're talking to you, look at the ground, or basically anywhere other than you, then it just oozes a lack of confidence. When someone is ashamed of something they've done, they look at the ground because they can't bring themselves to make eye contact. Even dogs do this!

A Texan study held back in 2013 found that people on average make eye contact between 30 and 60% of the time, but if you're looking to make an emotional connection with someone, then you're going to need to up this to about 60–70% of the time. And it's not easy.

If you're consciously thinking about making eye contact with someone for a longer-than-normal period of time, but it's not something you're used to, then chances are, you're going to feel uncomfortable and maybe even as though you're staring. This will make you nervous, and the whole confidence thing starts to fall apart.

However, there are some tips you can follow to make it easy, and also remember, practice makes perfect, so keep trying!

Firstly, you don't need to lock your eyes on both of the eyes of the other person, but instead, focus on one eye. This may sound a little strange, but it works. If you're still feeling uncomfortable, try looking at their eyebrows. Don't look higher than this or lower than their eye level because it will just feel weird, as though you're not paying full attention. Eyebrows are fine. Practice with yourself in the mirror for better results.

When you're coupling this tip with the others we've been speaking about throughout this book, then you should find yourself naturally being able to make eye contact more and more. Just keep practicing, and the results will come.

### Slow Down

It's a common trait that people will speak quickly when they are nervous, and this is especially prevalent with people who are new to public speaking. The idea is that someone speaks as fast as possible so they can finish what they're saying quickly, and then no longer have to talk. However, this is a clear sign you're both nervous and anxious, not only showing this to the other person but also validating your fears with yourself.

The simple solution is to slow down. Consciously slow down the speed at which you're talking.

I'm not saying go monotone and drag everything on, but find a nice pace you're comfortable with (which you can find practicing in the mirror!), and then when you're nervous and find yourself speeding up, you can mindfully slow yourself back down. Research shows that around 190 words per minute are the ideal speaking speed for being comfortable and sending across your message effectively.

**The Summary**

For now, this should be enough confidence content for you to sink your teeth into to have an idea on how to become more confident in your conversations. Remember, if you look good, you'll feel good, so go into every situation from here on out to have the intention to control your self-image and portray yourself as the person you want to be.

Naturally, you'll become this person, and that's who you'll be! I know it sounds simple, but it really is. We overcomplicate things so much and add so much pressure to being the best version of ourselves that we forget it's the power in the little choices we make that shape our reality.

I love the Matt D'avella way of looking at this. Usually, it's taking the smallest steps that will help you make the biggest leaps, so once you're able to knuckle down these small yet powerful tactics, the bigger benefits will fall into place.

For clarity, the key points we covered for you to remember when it comes to being a more confident version of yourself are:

- **Act confident to become confident!**
- **Work on letting go of your limiting beliefs**
- **Take control of your hand gestures**
- **Make eye contact**
- **Slow down your speaking process**
- **Practice!**

# Chapter Nine – How to Tell Stories That Land

*"Inside each of us is a natural-born storyteller, waiting to be released."* — **Robin Moore**

For as long as humans have been living in caves and painting on the walls, we've been storytellers. This is why thousands of new books are published every year and why the pictures drawn onto the walls of the pyramids recount days gone past. Humans love stories, and one of the best ways to connect with someone is to tell them a good one.

The small-talk topics we've already covered are amazing when it comes to breaking the ice, but the crux of the matter is that many people you'll meet in your life are people who want to engage and interact with interesting people. Traditional small talk will only get you so far before people start looking for real substance in what you're saying to them. There will come a time when people want real stories.

But how can you tell someone a story that's going to captivate them and have them hooked off your every word if you're living a pretty generic, typical, mundane life?

Well, to start with, stop believing that your life is any of those things because it's not. It only feels like it to you because you live it day in, day out, and get to see all those mundane aspects, like brushing your teeth and walking into town.

The actual substance of your life is incredibly interesting because you're the only person in the world who has ever done what you've done, made the decisions you've made, and the only human who will experience what you've experienced in all of humanity to come. I'm not going to get any more philosophical than that for now (I just love how mindblowing that whole thought experiment is), but my point is that we all have interesting lives.

**You included.**

The problem is that not all of us are born storytellers, but again, like all kinds of communication, it's a skill that can be learned and practiced. If you do this, and you're able to tell stories about your life that hook people off your every word and make them want to know more, you literally will be able to talk to anyone about anything, which, of course, is why we're here.

**Finding That Killer Plotline**

First things first.

You're not going to be able to tell stories if you don't know any. By this, I'm referring to the skill of being able to look into your own daily life and find stories that matter and that can be retold in a captivating way. I know, the first thought that comes to mind is that your life really isn't that interesting, at least not compared to other people's, surely? It is. You just might need to do some digging.

There are, of course, going to be key moments in your life that will naturally be great stories. The day you get married or go on that first date, and everything is new and exciting. Maybe you go away on vacation for your birthday and have an amazing time. Maybe you went to a protest or saw a global event happen. These are easy stories.

Yet, when it comes to pulling out the stories from your everyday life, you may at first need to dig a little deeper.

"So, what do you do for work?"

"I'm a manager in a supermarket."

Stop. Is that the best, most enthralling, and most exciting way you can present that information? It may not seem like it, but it's this kind of information that can be woven into the foundations of a beautiful story. Try again.

"So, what do you do for work?"

*"I'm a manager in a supermarket, although sometimes I feel like I'm a detective. Just the other day, I had to follow a shady-looking guy around the store* Mission Impossible-*style who looked like he was going to steal several cases of alcohol."*

Damn, now the creative juices are flowing, and the listener is thinking, *Hold up, a guy in the store stealing alcohol? What happened? Did you catch him? Did he attempt to steal anything?* As with all good stories, you've introduced conflict and a plot. Now the listener wants to know more.

See how you've managed to take the really typical and boring question of "What do you do?" that you could hear literally anywhere from a networking meeting to a BBQ with mutual friends, but your response has suddenly drawn in the attention of everyone around you? All it took was a few extras words and a few extra seconds of talking.

Right now, I want you to try it for yourself, right here, out loud. I've just met you and asked you what you do. Don't worry if this is your first time trying this. I'm only here in writing, and no one is here to judge, so get creative.

*So, what do you do?*

Layer your response with what you do and a little story that happened to you. Something that's happened in the last month. Whatever comes to mind. At this point, we're just practicing and getting those synapses working. The more you practice recalling, the better the stories that will come up. Here are some tips that can help you spot interesting stories in your life.

- Keep a diary or journal and write down everything that's interesting that stands out. You'll be amazed at how much you forget by the end of the day.
- Practice meditation and gratitude; a great way to improve your focus as you go about your day
- Put yourself in interesting situations. Take the long road to work. Speak to new people and see what comes up. You never know what experiences will come your way.
- Make notes on your phone of things that happen and practice dramatizing them.

**Writing Your Story Collection**

Okay, you don't actually need to write a memoir of short stories about your life, but having a few stories in the bank that you can use when replying to commonly asked questions can be a great idea because they'll be well-rehearsed (at least they will be over time) and you'll have experience in retelling them (even if at first that is just telling them back to yourself in the mirror).

Some topics you can gather up for some of these mini-stories include:

- Your job, career, or occupation
- Something that has happened in the last week
- Any plans you've got coming up in the future
- Stories about your local area
- Stories about the hobbies you do

Last weekend, I watched a pretty mediocre samurai movie, but the ninja guy main character would meditate while working on his bonsai trees. I felt so inspired by the whole scene that I bought myself a bonsai growing kit, the seeds of which I planted this week. I thought you just planted the seeds in the dirt and waited for them to grow, but oh no. The instructions said to soak them in water for 48 hours and then put them in the fridge, where they'll sit for two months. The crazy bit? The seeds turned the water a solid, swamp-water green. So green, in fact, I dropped it out of shock, and it stained my worktops. I'm still trying to scrub it out today.

In reality, I'm just living my life and trying a new little pastime, but this is just a brief example of how you can take an everyday situation of your life and share it in a way that makes people listen. However, this story in itself is not perfect, but I'll show you how and why in the following section.

For now, keep thinking of your own story ideas! Let's try again.

*"Hey! Welcome back to the grind time. How was your weekend?"*

*"Yeah, not bad. I watched Netflix."*

*"Fun."*

*"Yup."*

Woah. Great story. Not mundane in the slightest. Let's try that again, but this time, let's bring a story element into it.

*"Hey! Welcome back. How was your weekend?"*

*"My weekend was fine, but it was nothing compared to Friday night. My cat went crazy and started jumping on all the furniture and got stuck on a cabinet. We had to poke her down with a stick."*

*"Wait, what?!"*

As you can see, finding these little stories from your life makes for a much greater conversation. You're replying to the general small-talk questions people use, but you're not giving the boring answers that, let's face it, nobody really wants to hear. People want to talk. Yes. We're social creatures. But answering small-talk questions can be great up to a point, but in reality, people want more. After all, isn't that what you want from your conversations?

So, how do you find these interesting stories in your life? After all, poking your cat down from a cabinet with a stick is just something you need to do, but to other people, it could be comedy gold. How do you figure out the difference between the mundane and the interesting?

In all honesty, anything can be a good story. It's the way you tell it, which is what is going to attract people. The best way to figure this out is to think about what you find interesting in a story. These are the stories you'll be most passionate about.

Some questions to help you figure this out are:

- Do you like silly stories about pets?
- Do you like exciting, unbelievable, reality-is-stranger-than-fiction type stories?
- Do you like wholesome stories?
- Do you like serious stories?
- Do you like informative stories?
- Do you like stories on current affairs?
- Do you like cute, loving stories?

Whatever kind of story you like, this is the kind of tale you're going to be able to tell with the most energy and passion, so start taking note of what happens. On top of this, you'll need to remember that a good story will always have something relatable in it, which is the element that we'll resonate with the most.

This is why people like gossip, happy endings, and embarrassing moments. We've all been there, and we know what it feels like, for better or for worse, all feelings that make these stories a little more impactful. We all love stories that make us *feel*.

## How to Tell a Good Story

There are, of course, infinite ways you can tell a story. You could tell a micro-story, like the ones in the examples we've spoken about above, or you could share a full-on tale. Think sitting around the campfire telling longer tales to one another. Either way, how do you tell a story that people are actually going to want to listen to?

## Consider the Length

The length of your story will depend on the context of the situation you're in. If you're chatting with someone in a line, you don't want to go on and on, potentially holding them up and irritating them. If you're an anxious kind of person, then telling a longer story may mean there's more time for you to worry about the delivery of what you're saying. In this case, it would always be better to stick to shorter stories until you're feeling more confident.

Always judge the length of your story based on the situation you're in. You can adapt the length of your story by changing how much detail you give. If you've been engaging in small talk with the listener already and you've already established some common ground, then try to include details that are going to specifically resonate with them.

## Choosing the Right Details

Personally, I found that using the 1:1:1 method is the best way to tell people short stories. Each '1' stands for:

- One action
- One sentence summary
- One emotion

For the sake of brevity, a short story should include every one of these in some way. It's not as overwhelming as it may first appear. See if you can spot each element in the following stories.

> *I went on a date last week and immediately dropped my plate of food onto my lap. I didn't know what to do, so I just got up and left without saying anything—such an embarrassing situation.*

> *I was crossing the road the other day, and a taxi swung around the corner and almost hit me. I was so scared I nearly pooped myself!*

> *We accidentally deleted the client project and had to start from scratch. We worked 16 hours a day for two weeks, but when it was finished, man, there's no better feeling.*

As you can see, in just two sentences, there's an action that the story is based around, the story itself is short and sweet, and there's an emotion that makes the story relatable. Now you can expand on these stories as much as you wish, adding in details, jokes, more emotions, and so on, but that's all up to you and your personal style when it comes to storytelling.

The trick to using the 1:1:1 method is to be able to summarize your story in just one sentence and to start close to the end of the clinch of your story. Start close to the "grit" so you give as much information as possible in the least amount of time.

A great way to remember this strategy is to imagine a story about a jailbreak taking place. It doesn't matter if you describe what happens in one sentence or write an entire book on the event. The endpoint of the story is that the jailbreak happened.

## Building on Your Stories

Using the 1:1:1 method is perhaps the easiest way out there to tell a good short story that people are going to want to listen to. Those three factors always make a great foundation to build your story on (and works as a standalone) since you can add as much or as little detail as you want or need.

Some people will make do with little details, but some people are going to want to hear more of what you have to say, so how do you keep your conversational momentum flowing? You use structure.

I'm going to list out the points that make up a story structure, but you can add and adjust them however you see fit. This is the same process that the cartoon studio Pixar uses when creating and writing their stories. This is literally the step-by-step guide they use when making their movies, so take note!

- ***Setting the foundations***

Setting the stage of the story. Here you introduce characters and build the world. Only use this section if it affects the rest of the story. Otherwise, you can easily skip this part most of the time.

- ***Introduction***

Usually, in the first section, you'll introduce a character and their life, what their routine is, and build up tension for the rest of the story. Make this bit quick so you can get to the exciting part.

- ***Introduce conflict***

A big event happens, something that disrupts the normal flow of life and throws a spanner in the works. Make sure you include the emotion of what happens here. This is the moment everything flips upside down.

- ***The consequences of conflict***

*How has the conflict and change affected everything? What are the consequences of the event taking place?*

- ***Further consequences***

*If necessary, add more consequences to really drive home what is going on and how big the event was. You can skip this bit, but usually, two conflicts are ideal.*

- **MORE CONSEQUENCES**

*You can really drive home your points with even more conflict. (I'll show you in the example below how this works well.) The more emotional resonance you have in the last three stages, the more emotionally attached to your story your listener will be!*

- ***Conclusion***

*What does the main character do in the story to deal with or resolve the conflict? What action needs to be taken? What problem needs to be solved, and how does this happen? Conclude how the story is wrapped up.*

- ***Aftermath***

*What happened after the conflict was resolved and everyone has moved on? More emotion here. Is it a better or worse ending? How have the characters been affected by the event?*

Of course, this is a lot to take in, but don't let it overwhelm you. If something happens to you in your life that you want to remember, and you think it's going to make a great story, take some time to remember the details.

Later, you can then adjust your story and build on it, so it fits this structure. If you want to keep things simple, you can just remember the general structure of what happened and tell it in order.

I know all of this might seem like a lot, to begin with, and you may even be thinking that surely this is not how people tell great stories? It's so much behind-the-scenes work, but then when you think about the performances of motivational speakers and stand-up comedies, this is exactly the level of effort they put into their stories, which is what makes them so successful.

Sure, you might not want to go all the way with the structuring and so on, but at least you have this knowledge to work with, and you know how it all works. Let's say something happens, and you know this is a good story to tell other people. You might want to work on how you're adding emotions into your tale, or highlighting the conflict of what happened, and so on. With practice and experience, your stories will just get better and better.

Ultimately, this is all with the aim of allowing you to share your stories more naturally while still understanding where to apply details in the right places.

**Here's an example story to show you exactly how this structure works.**

*I was heading to work driving along the main road; you know the ones with the trees and fields along the side? I was behind this lorry, and there was a car up front with hazard lights on, parked at the side of the road. I slowed down, and suddenly this dog ran out into the road.*

*The truck swerved to miss it, which it did by such a tiny amount, and it jumped the ditch and ran into the woods. The truck carried on, and I pulled over to the side. The woman in the front of the car was crying her eyes out, having a panic attack as her dog had jumped out the window while she was driving, and she couldn't get it to come back. It kept coming back, running across the road, and then back again, thinking it was a game.*

*I stayed with her for half an hour while another car pulled over, and the man inside helped. We walked through the woods and eventually managed to get hold of the dog and bring it back to the owner, who started crying in happiness. It was such a heartfelt moment. She vowed never to drive with her windows all the way down again.*

True story, by the way.

This is a casual story written in the way you would say it out loud, maybe in response to "Why are you late for work?" and while it contains all the elements you'd look for in a story, it's a little long and can be refined to become more comprehensive. Here's an edited version with the structure highlighted.

**(Introduction)** *I was driving down a country road and saw a car parked up ahead, the hazard lights blinking.* **(Conflict)** *As I slowed down to see if I could help, a dog suddenly ran out into the road, right in front of an oncoming truck* **(Consequence)**. *Thank God it missed it, but it was only by just enough.*

*The truck swerved, and the dog jumped the ditch and ran back into the woods.* **(Consequence)** *I pulled over and saw the woman in the parked car. Through tears, she told me she was having a panic attack* **(consequence)** *since her dog jumped out the window while she was driving, and she couldn't get it to come back. It kept running across the road and then back into the woods, thinking it was a game.*

*I stayed for half an hour while another driver and I came to help. We walked through the woods and finally managed to get hold of the dog and bring it back to the owner.* **(Resolution/Conclusion)** *It was so beautiful seeing her face light up. She vowed never to drive with her windows all the way down again.* **(Aftermath)**

Now, you're probably not going to have enough time to think and edit your story as you say it when you're in a real-life conversation, which is why I say you should take some time to get familiar with this structure in your own time. You don't need to do this for every story that matters, just the ones that count.

The point is to get to grips with these skills and this structure of storytelling that all comes with practice and awareness that this is how it all works. I've lost count of how many hours I've spent in front of the mirror or tidying up my house, just talking to myself and experimenting with the best way to tell a story like this to someone.

However, the benefits of this practice and this behind-the-scenes work have always paid off when I'm around the water cooler, and everyone is hooked on my every word.

## The Summary

In your life, be mindful of events and situations you find yourself in and be aware of them. They can be the most mundane of experiences, but how you tell the story (and how much energy you put into it) is everything and is what will make you a great, charismatic, and confident storyteller.

Whenever you find a story in your life you want to hold on to, set to work on organizing the structure, identify the various elements that make the story great, and you'll be able to bring them all together to tell a story about your everyday life that will captivate and wow anybody you're speaking to.

And so, bringing all this together, you should now have the ability to come up with compelling stories of events that happen in your life, not only picking good story ideas but also telling your stories in creative, captivating ways that will blow your listeners away.

# Chapter Ten - Becoming an Interesting Person

*"Your life is your canvas, and you are the masterpiece. There are a million ways to be kind, amazing, fabulous, creative, bold, and interesting."* — **Kerli**

When my social anxiety was at its peak, I was roughly 22 years old, and it seemed as though my life consisted of nothing more than going to work, going home, playing video games, and that's about it. I wasn't going out and doing anything, I wasn't having new experiences, and I certainly wasn't making memories that were going to last a lifetime.

While in the last chapter we spoke about the fact you can make stories sound interesting, regardless of what is actually happening in your life, there's no doubt that you can be proactive in making your life more interesting by changing a few simple things. The thing is, not only will doing more with your life make you more interesting to talk to since you'll have more to talk about, but you're also going to be happier with yourself and your life. Thus, you're going to be more confident, more charismatic, and more yourself.

Come on, be honest. Raise your hand if you've found yourself stuck in some bad habits that don't bring value into your life? Maybe you binge entertainment, haven't created anything for a long time, or you have dreams of doing something, starting something, or going somewhere, but you're always putting it off, even though you don't really have a reason why.

This was my relationship with writing for many years.

For as long as I can remember, I wanted to write books. I loved the idea of writing, and throughout my early twenties, I would write here and there, but I never put effort into making it a proper habit. I would go weeks and then months without writing anything, and it never really progressed anywhere. I can't tell people I'm writing or want to be a writer if I'm not writing, so something had to change.

I want to dedicate this chapter to sharing some tips and advice that I found helpful when it came to becoming a more interesting person and ultimately lead a more fulfilling life. In the very real sense, this isn't for anybody else but yourself, but there's no doubt that doing more interesting things, or at least becoming aware and educated about more things in life, will help you connect more effortlessly with other people.

As a quick note, notice how I'm not saying you need to do *more* with your life. This chapter is more focused on helping you realize what's important to you, what fuels your sense of self (see chapter one), and then giving you the intention to cut out everything else that doesn't actually serve you nor brings value to your existence.

Okay, I'm sure you get the point. Let's jump into the tips.

## Read More Books

A really simple tip to get us started. How many books do you have at home that you've been excited to read but just haven't got around to doing it yet, nor do you really have any solid plans to start? That's me all over. My hobby is just buying new books that I never actually read.

Reading is such an amazing pastime because it can not only be entertaining and an absolute joy to read and get lost in other worlds and the lives of fictional characters, but it opens the doorway to more opportunities than you can ever imagine.

For example, I just finished reading *Dark Matter* by Blake Crouch (which I highly recommend), which talks about Multiverse theory and quantum mechanics.

The story is incredible and one of my favorite books in a long time (I read the whole thing in one sitting), but I also was interested in learning more about quantum mechanics. Now, I definitely don't understand how it all works, but I went down the rabbit hole and ended up discussing it all with someone at work who shared a love for the same thing.

This opportunity came from reading. If I didn't read the books, I wouldn't be connecting with my colleague in a new, interesting, and meaningful way. You never know what opportunities are right around the corner. Some tips to help you read include:

- Find some books you love. Fiction or non-fiction. Get a stack of them and make your way through the list.
- Try books you would never normally try, just to see what they're like.
- Find books you're interested in that inspire you, educate you, and make you want to try and explore new things in life.

If you need any further convincing to start a reading habit, there's endless research that found that the activity of reading trains your brain to be better at processing information. It can also reduce your risk of age-related cognitive decline, lowers your risk of conditions like dementia (proven with a large 14-year study and another 2018 study in China carried out on 16,000 people), reduces stress, and helps you live longer.

**Switch Up Your Routine**

One of the best and most simple changes I have made over the last two years is occasionally setting my alarm much earlier than normal, so I get up at silly o'clock in the morning (usually around 5 a.m.) and then walk to the highest point in my city and watch the sunrise. It's a strange little ritual I do perhaps once a month, and it really does bring so much joy into my life.

Switching up your routine and doing things "just because" is a great way to keep you on your toes and keep things in your life interesting. When it comes to conversations, I can share my experiences (I sometimes even take the people I'm talking to next time I go, and we enjoy it together). It makes for interesting experiences that break up the monotony of everyday life that we all fall victim to every now and then.

What's more, you never know what other experiences you're going to have when you go on an unplanned whim. The last time I did the hike, I saw a group of baby foxes rummaging through bins, and it was such a beautiful sight. I would have missed it all had I stayed in bed.

**Volunteer Your Time**

Volunteering your time is a win-win for everyone involved.

Not only are you dedicating some time of your life to help others and actually benefit the communities or causes you're working for, but you also become more interesting because of the experiences you're getting involved in.

My partner and I spent a few months in 2020 helping out at a cat shelter. It wasn't the best experience since I spent most of the time cleaning out cages and washing some of the cats, but it was so interesting to see how the cats come in, what the process is for dealing and rehoming cats, and just seeing how difficult and tough it can be for both the humans and animals.

It's all a learning experience, and it can all bring so much into your life if you're willing to let it in.

## Embrace Fear

An actionable tip you can try right now. Whenever you go to do something new, or you're entering an experience that you aren't sure about, do you get that little pang in your stomach? That fear that you don't really know how to move forward? Notice that feeling and try to step through it. Embrace the fear, and don't let it hold you back.

Will Smith famously said in an interview that "Everything that's good in life can be found on the other side of fear." You just need to take the leap of faith in yourself. Remember, the fear of being uninteresting makes you uninteresting. These emotions shut you down and hold you in place, rather than allowing you to live free.

## Invest Your Time Wisely

It's common knowledge that the only real resource you ever have to invest in your life is the time you're alive. Even when you're working, you're basically exchanging your time for money. While there are things that we have to do to survive, it can change so much when you really start to see where your time is going.

Are you watching TV all the time? Binging your social media feeds? Going to the same vacation spots every year? Drinking and partying every weekend? Sure, if you're doing what you love, then keep spending your time in that way. That's fine.

However, this is definitely not the case for all of us, and so many of us face the very real realizations that we're probably wasting our lives. If you want to be interesting and feel as though you can get more out of life, start treating your time as a currency, and look at where you're spending it.

## Have Interesting Conversations

If you're asking someone how they are, but you don't really care about the answer, this is going to show up like a house on fire.

Lazy, uninteresting people stick to small-talk topics like the weather and ask if they're watching any good TV series (remember that watching most TV is just a passive activity that won't really bring you any gain), or ask what you do for a career. BORING! It's fine every now and then, and when you're starting out, but after everything you've read so far, you're definitely beyond this point now.

Instead of boring topics, open the doorway to new, interesting conversations, like asking what personal projects someone is working on, what the weirdest thing they have ever eaten is, what items you could find on their bucket list, or if they're learning any new skills.

Getting answers to these questions can introduce you to whole new worlds that you didn't even know existed. You never know—you might be introduced to something new that you love, or you may learn something new that changes your life.

**Try New Hobbies**

This doesn't really need a lot of explaining, so I'll be brief.

At the beginning of 2020, I sat down and wrote down all the things I actually care about. I enjoyed writing. I liked to explore spiritual concepts, like meditating and lucid dreaming. I wanted to learn to speak French. I wanted to learn how to play chess properly. I wanted to read more books. I wanted to learn how to play the Blues guitar. This was simply me sitting down to write a list of all the hobbies I wanted to get involved in.

Take a pen and paper right now and write down all the things you're interested in and would love to get involved in. Even if you've never really given the activity or hobby much thought before, but it's more of a fleeting idea, still write it down.

These are all the things you care about, and you know you did because you took the time to write them down! Now figure out which hobbies you love the most and which ones you want to get involved in. Make time for them and enjoy the experience you have doing them! Not only will you meet new people, but you'll also have interesting things to talk about with others!

**The Summary**

There are endless ways you can be proactive and become a more interesting person, thus having more to talk about and just being more satisfied with the way you're spending your life. Everybody has what it takes to be more interesting. It's just a matter of taking action into your own hands.

Sure, you might just need to work on breaking out of some old habits, replacing them with good ones, and overcoming the fear that's holding you back, but this is where you need to exercise patience and believe in the long term. Remember, little steps help you make giant leaps.

# Chapter Eleven – Developing Meaningful Relationships

*"Each friend represents a world in us, a world possibly not born until they arrive, and it is only by this meeting that a new world is born." — **Anais Nin***

And here we are. We've arrived at the final part of this book. As you can see, the final title of this book reads "Developing Meaningful Relationships," but so far, we've spent all our time on conversations and being able to talk to anyone about anything, which you should be able to do by now. However, the last question that remains is simple.

How can you go from knowing someone and wowing them with your charm, confidence, and small talk, and then actually develop a proper relationship with them? How can you meet people and become true friends with them?

It's a weird thought that so many of us are becoming more and more disconnected in a world that's more hyper-connected than ever before. I can't remember entirely, but when I was a kid back in school, it seemed like making friends was so easy. Sure, you wouldn't get along or like the company of everyone (it would be weird if you did), but there were no inhibitions in talking to new people. You would just chat about whatever was going on, and if you got along, you became friends.

It feels like there's an underlying level of pressure and anxiety that stops things today from being that easy. It's a cringey thought to imagine walking up to someone and just talking to them and then becoming lifelong friends. Maybe in an ideal world, right? Maybe you believe that logic only works in the movies? It's not. It just takes some time and effort to see what life can alternatively be like.

Taking everything you know so far, how can you go from meeting someone for the first time, small talking with them, telling them stories, charming them with your charisma and confidence, and then ultimately becoming friends with them, or at least developing a meaningful relationship of some kind?

This chapter is all about showing you how.

## The Benefits are Unparalleled

While having strong connections with people in your life and talking to lots of people is definitely going to make you feel less lonely and more charismatic and confident, having a million acquaintances is no substitute for having five friends that you have a deep and meaningful connection with.

Research shows that having proper connections with people can bring so many benefits into your life; it's hard to know where to begin. A 2014 study carried out by the Society for Personality, and Social Psychology, found that meaningful relationships will:

- Help you live longer
- Improves many aspects of your mental health
- Improves your ability to judge your own well-being
- Increases your self-confidence
- Provides you with wide perspectives
- Provides you with increased resilience in most aspects of your life

There are even sources that claim that having meaningful relationships is "the healthiest thing you can do for yourself" (Medical Daily, 2014). In other words, focus on developing meaningful relationships. This will bring so much goodness into your life.

**Understanding the Barriers**

To fully understand how to make close friends, you need to know the things that are holding you back. The two main culprits of this are:

- Technology ruining our attention span, make it harder to concentrate, and emulates the feeling of being connected to those we love and care about
- Having busy lives, such as working full-time jobs, working on side projects, and trying to keep up with the fast-paced life that feels common, as promoted by the "mainstream" way of living.

In other words, just because you see your best friend's name on your Facebook feed, that doesn't mean you're actually connecting with them. You need to put your phone down and reach out to them properly and make time to have actual experiences with them, but more on that in a bit.

Now we're going to explore how to take these initial relationships in your life and move forward, forming stronger bonds than ever before and being able to connect with these people that you might one day say you love.

**You Can't Be Friends with Everyone**

Before we really get into the tips, make sure you're aware of the fact that you're not going to be friends with everyone, and nor should you try to be.

I'm not saying you should outwardly be blunt and forceful to people you don't like. Stay civil. Instead, if you really feel a natural draw to someone, and you feel a connection is there, then it's definitely something you should pursue. If not, that doesn't matter. You're just a step closer to finding the people who are right in your life.

**Spend Time with Your New Friends**

As I write this book, the world has been gripped by the COVID-19 pandemic, and it's mixed up the world in ways that we could have never predicted. This has made many of us become more disconnected due to lockdown rules, but the happiest people were the ones who still found a way to connect and spend time together.

If you want to connect with someone and deepen your relationship with them, you need to spend time with them, create memories together, and be in each other's presence, not just online. It's clear that times like the COVID-19 pandemic means that connecting in such an intimate way isn't always possible, but that doesn't mean dedicating time to each other is any less essential.

Whether you're going for a socially distanced walk, hosting online activities like Zoom quiz nights or group Netflix streams, or even just chatting via a video call, spending time with people is a must. Dedicating time to each other (and making sure it's fair both ways) is how relationships grow.

## Support Each Other

The latest research shows that friends become closer than ever when they help each other through hard times. This doesn't just mean dealing with a tragedy or trauma, but instead could just be offering support on a friend's self-improvement journey. It's always easier and more effective to go through change with someone by your side.

In a 2008 study, researchers placed some participants at the top of a hill either alone, alongside a stranger, or standing next to a friend. When asked to grade how steep the hill was, the participants who were next to a friend thought the hill to be far less steep than those who were standing alone. In other words, when you're standing with someone you're connected to, the hard times aren't so bad.

## Be Yourself

Finally, and perhaps most importantly, be yourself around those you love.

It can be hard sometimes to even acknowledge we're wearing masks around those we love, let alone trying to take them off, but it's never been more important to embrace who you are and just be you.

If you're pretending to be someone you're not with your friends, then eventually, it's going to backfire. Either you won't be happy or your friends won't, so save yourself the drama and just be unapologetically you. Even if you change over time (which everyone does), real friends will be accepting of exactly who you are.

And that's it! If you can follow these simple tricks and tips, you'll be able to take the people you know and like in your life and turn them into friends that you share a deep, meaningful connection with, and the world becomes your oyster.

## The Summary

Relationships are important. If you take everything you've learned in this book but just jump around from person to person, attracting them with your charm, hooking them with your stories and become such a memorable person in their lives, but then move on without creating deeper relationships with people along the way, you're going to feel lonely and unsatisfied with your life.

Take time to invest yourself into your relationships. Sure, you can pick and choose who you're friends with, but it's important to give people a shot. Having lived with social anxiety for many years, I know it can be hard and scary to open up to other people, but trust me when I say it will be one of the best things you ever do.

To recap, some of the elements you'll want to focus on include:

- **Understanding what holds you back**
- **Remember, you can't be friends with everyone**
- **Spend time with one another**
- **Always be yourself!**

Now it's time to say farewell!

# Final Thoughts

And so, we come to the end of our journey, and it's all over to you!

I hope you've enjoyed reading this more than anything, and you've learned a lot. I know I said I was going to say it one last time chapters ago, but here's another for good measure: Don't give up on your learning path! The path to better communication, like all self-improvement journeys, is a continuous learning curve with an infinite skill cap. You can always just keep getting better and better.

However, the only way you're going to do this is by practicing over and over again, being willing to embrace any fears or anxieties you may have in order to overcome them. Just keep at it, take everything we've spoken about with baby steps, and you'll see big improvements in no time at all!

I'm only a human being doing what I love, but I'm always striving to be better and to give you the best experience I can! I also love hearing all the amazing ways these books help you see life in a different way, so let me know and inspire me to keep going!

# Book #7
# Listening Skills Training

*How to Truly Listen, Understand, and Validate for Better and Deeper Connections*

*James W. Williams*

# Introduction

*"Listening is an art that requires attention over talent, spirit over ego, others over self." Dean Jackson*

Are you listening?

More and more, I, like many others all over the world, am coming to a very real and somewhat saddening realization. I apologize in advance if it's something you haven't noticed before, but now that I say it, you're never going to be able to unsee it.

There are so few people out there who are good listeners. In fact, I'd go as far as to say most people are actually terrible.

Just last night, I sat down after work and started to watch the news. There was some debate being aired about LGBT movements, which is, of course, an important topic of conversation that needs to be spoken about. Except, despite being live and on-air to potentially hundreds of thousands of people, every person at the desk was shouting over one another. These so-called experts and professional broadcasters, the supposed top of their fields, were shouting over one another, not allowing anyone to be acknowledged, heard, or understood.

There was no conversation or discourse taking place here. Just shouting, ego-boosting, and playing "gotcha!" with one another. Honestly, it was pretty disgraceful and made me fairly sad that this is where we have gotten to as a society, especially with important issues like that.

I turned the television off and sat in the silence of my apartment, a thought started to form in my mind. Poor listening is everywhere. Literally everywhere. It's an epidemic.

It occurs in politics, on reality television shows, across the internet in comment sections across every platform. Few people are listening at work, in the street, and, most importantly, in your own personal relationships.

After a bit of research, it turns out that even when it comes to communicating and understanding the people we love the most, many of us fail to listen properly and actually hear the person talking to us. The chances are you've felt this yourself. You've experienced your partner listening to you firsthand, and although they are listening to the words you're saying, they do not actually hear you and your message. On the flip side, the chances are you've been the individual who's not been listening to others. I know without a doubt I'm guilty of being that guy.

Looking back with hindsight, it feels as though I've been living my life on autopilot, especially when it comes to my relationships with partners. I couldn't seem to keep a relationship for more than a year for much of my early life. They almost always seemed to conclude with a dramatic and explosive end. I told myself I hadn't perhaps met the one yet and that when I did, everything was going to come together perfectly, and I'd find my happily-ever-after. Of course, that was never going to happen. Still, it wasn't until years later that I can look back and say with a strange cocktail of confidence and embarrassment that the problem was me and, predominantly, my lack of ability to listen.

I'll share an example, and you can see whether you can figure out for yourself what the problem is. I'll set the scene. I'm sitting at the table in my apartment. My girlfriend gets in from work and sits down at the table like we do every night. I've cooked dinner, we start eating, and after a bit of small talk, my girlfriend, who we'll call Nicole for this example, says this:

> **Nicole:** "Work is just so stressful. I think I'm going to start looking for another job because I seriously have no idea how much longer I can take this," she said, swirling her glass in her hand.
>
> **Me:** "Do you think you'll find one that pays as well, though?"
>
> **Nicole:** "I don't know."
>
> **Me:** "What kind of job would you like to do if you could do any?"
>
> **Nicole:** "I don't know."
>
> **Me:** "Well, I wouldn't give up the one you have until you find something else to replace it."

It makes my body feel tense whenever I replay that conversation in my head, especially with the knowledge and skills I have now. It's one of those memories that burn vividly in the back of my mind.

Besides the point, did you see what went wrong in that conversation?

Quite clearly, I wasn't listening to my partner properly, if at all.

For brevity, I'm going to jump straight to the point. There's no reason to dress this up because being able to listen to someone is one of the most important skills you'll ever learn. You know when you Google *How to have a better relationship,* or you watch a movie featuring a scene with couples counselling, and they always talk about how the best thing a relationship can do to be better is get better at communicating? Surprise, they're not wrong. I just wish I'd known it earlier.

Mastering the art of listening brings so many benefits to your life and the lives of those around you.

In the conversation with my partner, you can clearly tell that I'm not listening because I'm injecting my own thoughts into the conversation, piggybacking what my partner is talking about and making the conversation all about me than taking the opportunity to connect with her. I'm failing to dive any deeper into how she is feeling or thinking. This is the girl I was supposed to love, and I didn't even let her explain how she felt.

Now imagine how often this happens to you. And how many times do you do that to other people? As I said before, poor listening is truly an epidemic.

Here's a rewrite of how the conversation should have gone had I been a skilled listener.

> **Nicole:** "Work is just so stressful. I think I'm going to start looking for another job because I seriously have no idea how much longer I can take this."
>
> **Me:** "Hey. Talk to me about it. What's going on?"
>
> **Nicole:** "Where do I start? The managers treat me awfully. My coworkers are horrible. The work is tedious and unrewarding. The hours suck. I never get to spend time with you anymore. God, listen to me moaning. I should be grateful to even have a job in the current climate."
>
> **Me:** "No, it's okay. Anyone would feel like that in your situation. Do you think you're holding onto the job because you feel you should be grateful for it?"
>
> **Nicole:** "I guess that's part of it."

**Me:** "Well, is there anything you do like about your current job?"

And so on. Can you see how much of a difference there is in both conversations?

I'm not forcing my narrative or my own ideas into the conversation, hijacking the talk with the forced desire to communicate my own needs. Instead, I'm stepping up and allowing Nicole to express herself, to go into detail about how she feels, asking questions so I can gain much more clarity and understanding about how she feels, and, most importantly, I'm enabling her through validating her experience.

Validation. The absolute key to any successful conversation or interaction. In the first version of the conversation, you'll fail to find any sign of validation, and I'm sure you've felt this way in your own life. Those moments where you've opened up to someone, and they respond in such a way that it feels as though they took nothing of what you said on board and are instead pursuing their own agendas, using the opportunity to share how they feel, rather than listening to you.

Validation is such a powerful element of conversation. Granted, it's a pretty basic concept to understand at first, but it goes deep. I say I'm scared of the dark, and you say it's okay to feel that way. Let's do something to make your experience better. Validation can literally be that easy, but when you start adding in the complexities of the real world, it can become a lot more difficult to understand.

**Person A:** "I can't sleep. I'm scared of the dark."

**Person B:** "Why? It's only dark. I thought that's something you would have grown out of by now?"

See the effect that your words can have? See how invalidating that last statement is? How's that going to make the scared person feel? How would you feel in that situation? Do you feel that way often? Do you make people feel like that in your own conversations?

These are all questions you're going to be working on throughout this book.

## How to Use This Book to Master Listening

This book is designed to help you to become the best listener you can be. It's a process, and it's not something that's going to miraculously happen overnight, although we will be covering tips that deliver instant results. To make things easy, the following chapters have broken down the art of listening into all the different components that will come together to introduce the skills you need to know and the knowledge you can work with day-to-day. I'm basically saying that everything you'll read from this point on is fully actionable.

We're going to start with the basics, exploring the current state of listening in your life and highlighting some of the problems so many of us face, preventing us from actually hearing people when they are talking to us. Of course, these are the same problems that stop people from hearing us. We'll then dive into the core tips that will enable you to actively become a better listener by the end of the chapter with tips you can put into action instantly, all backed by science and psychology, of course.

Once the basics of listening have been mastered, we're then going to get into the crux of this book, exploring the essential and psychological aspects of listening, including the important, powerful methods behind validating someone, how to mindread people in order to understand and identify the true meanings in what they're saying, and then overcoming the more advanced listening problems you're going to face along the way.

You can consume the information in this book however you like. It's best to read through from front to back as special care has been taken to order the chapters that will enable you to lay a solid foundation to build your skills and understanding before moving on to the more advanced teachings. However, I understand that sometimes you may want a little teaser of the good stuff and see where this book is heading, so feel free to dive in and see what's in store.

That being said, when you're ready, let's dive into the art of listening. Use this book as the key to open a new door in your life to a world of better relationships, deeper understanding, and ultimately more meaningful connections with the people in your life.

# Chapter One - Never Has the World Been Louder, Yet No One Is Listening

*"When people talk, listen completely. Most people never listen." Ernest Hemingway*

I've always been a firm believer that very few people out there in the world are bad people, but instead, the world is full of people simply trying to do the best they can. Before starting this chapter, I went for a mindful walk, but while waiting for the kettle to boil to make my first coffee of the day, I ended up diving into the rabbit hole they call Twitter. Of course, whether you're a user or not, you'll have heard the complaints that Twitter is a platform notorious for people all over the world shouting into the ether, slamming down their points of view in the most aggressive fashions, and becoming keyboard warriors to further their causes.

Look at any highly-viewed post (especially the posts that news websites share), and you'll see examples of this everywhere. Yet, while there are so many people talking and sharing their opinions and perspectives, it's blatantly obvious that nobody is listening to anyone else. And this is just one place. Throughout the modern world, it feels as though everyone is talking all the time. The air is always filled with chatter, but nobody is listening to it.

Even in your own life, there are plenty of good people who have your best interests at heart, from your parents and romantic partners to your friends and coworkers. All of these groups of people would want to help you during a time of need. This is what I mean by the good intentions are there, and there are few bad people, but that doesn't mean that they have the skills and know-how to actually give you what you need, and few can resolve problems properly.

**Here's an example.**

Let's say you're feeling low for whatever reason, say you've lost your job, and you need a little support to get you back on your feet. Are you going to turn to someone? What do they say? Do they listen to how you're feeling, or do they feed you the generic "Don't worry, it will get better in time" line? Does this kind of advice make you feel listened to, or are they going through the motions?

Perhaps you've tried speaking out in the past, but because you don't feel listened to or understood, you've convinced yourself that it's easier to stay quiet. I'm not saying your friends or partners are bad people. I am saying that they, like the vast majority of society, lack the essential communication skills they need to listen properly. For many people, it's not that they don't want to help. It's that they don't really know how.

If people aren't listening to you in such a way, then the chances are that you're not listening to them either. Switch the roles of the example and think about what you would say. Personally, all of this is a heartbreaking realization.

I want to be the person that someone else I care about a lot can come to for help whenever they need it. I want to be reliable. I want to do what I can to help others. I want to understand and connect with other people and enjoy the meaningful relationships that stem from these experiences.

So, all of this begs a very important question: Why do we all suck at listening?

## Why We Suck at Listening

Well, there are several ways to look at this, but the first question to ask that will take you to the root of the cause is to ask: When have you ever been taught how to listen properly?

Maybe in school? Not really. When I was in school, I was told to just sit in my chair and remain quiet. If anyone in the class made a noise or spoke to someone else, the teacher would just tell us off and reaffirm that we needed to remain quiet while she spoke. This means that even from a young age, we're being told that the act of listening isn't to actually listen and hear what the other person is saying with the intent to understand them and their message, but it's simply to remain quiet while someone else is speaking and await our chance to speak to share our perspectives or answers.

*These aren't good habits for later in life.*

These kinds of teachings we learn from a young age build momentum through our lives. As Mark Shrayber, a lifestyle blogger, writes,

"When we are taught about listening, it's often presented as a passive skill, something you have to do while you allow your eyes to glaze over, your mind to drift, all as you simply wait for your opportunity to speak again."

Waiting for the opportunity to speak again. When written like this, does this really sound like the definition of listening? Of course it doesn't, yet this is what so many of us do. Don't worry if that resonated because it defines the large majority of people and the extent of our listening skills. Fortunately, active listening is a skill that can be learned, practiced, and mastered, which is what this book is about!

That's how this book works. We're going to highlight the issues with listening, becoming aware of bad communication habits so we can undo them, and then replace them with better, more productive listening habits that help you make stronger connections with the people in your life.

Here are some of the main reasons why you may find it so hard to listen and the obstacles you may be facing unconsciously.

- You are too lost in your thoughts.
- You are not actively paying attention to the other person.
- You are distracted by someone or something else.
- You are held back by your preconceived judgments on the person or conversation topic.
- A lack of comprehensive understanding (i.e., not understanding context or language used within a conversation).
- You have a short attention span.

Reading through this list, many of these points sound bad, but many of them simply come down to the way of the world that we have been born into.

For example, over 48.1% of people have a smartphone. In the Western world, that translates to pretty much everyone being distracted by pings and notifications all the time. From the moment we wake up to the moment we go to sleep. Just constant pinging and being connected. This degree of distraction is a huge obstacle to active listening.

On top of this, statistics show that attention spans have shrunk by over 50% over the last ten years (2007–2017). Whereas a child could have an average attention span of twelve minutes back in 1998, this has shrunk to just five minutes in 2008. Guess what? As of 2017, the average for people under eighteen is now just a measly eight seconds. This is why TV and online advertisements, social media videos, and so on are all so short in duration. Snapchats and TikToks are seven seconds long because app developers know this is all we have the attention span for.

What I'm saying is that a lot of the problems you're dealing with are problems that everyone is dealing with, and it's a bit of a self-perpetuating cycle. We scroll down our social media feeds, spending less than a second on each image, which shrinks our attention spans, which affects our listening, and it's just getting worse. Casey Neistat, the YouTuber and filmmaker, summed it up perfectly.

He asked his viewers to imagine sitting in front of a television screen and scrolling through the channels but spending less than a second on each channel. Could you find what you're looking for in that time? No? That's exactly what we're doing when we fast-scroll down our Facebook timelines. You see my point?

Depressing? Perhaps. Inspirational? Definitely. With this information, I'm hoping you'll be inspired and motivated enough to become aware of your own habits and ultimately do something about them.

Furthermore, Listen.org also has a ton of helpful statistics that show why we're such terrible listeners, coupling it with what I listed out above. There are statistics like:

- The average person can listen to around 175 words per minute but can think at 2,000 words per minute, so of course, it's easy to get lost in and distracted by our thoughts while listening.
- Most people will only remember 50% of what has just been said to them.
- Over the long term, the average person will only remember around 20% of what has been spoken to them.
- Around 70% of our time at work is spent communicating with other people, and this is broken down into 45% of the time listening, 30% talking, 16% reading, and 9% writing things down.

To cut a long story short, all of this combined clearly shows we're all suffering from sensory overload, and we're all exhausted from it. We spend so much time listening and consuming information from so many sources, all while forgetting more than half of it in the long term anyway. Then, top that with our overactive minds, it's no wonder that proper listening is so difficult.

But, as I've said, it's possible to develop new listening skills and break yourself free from the cycle that so many of us are stuck in, and with so many great reasons to do so.

## The Benefits of Proper Active Listening

There's a reason you picked up this book, but if it all seems like doom and gloom so far, don't worry, it's really not. I remember reading those statistics for the first time and being like, *Wow, this is where we've got to?* but I soon switched my mindset to remember that with this knowledge, you're able to move forward. It's like a journey. You're marking on the map where you are now (not a great listener), highlighting where you want to go (to becoming a better listener), and now we're plotting the route of how you're going to get there.

But before we leave, what are you going to find at the other end? What are the benefits of listening? Fortunately, there is a lot to consider.

- You'll be able to make better decisions because you'll have more information to work with in any given situation because you've listened to all sides of a story or learned new data from other people.
- You'll be able to see the hidden messages and agendas behind what someone is saying, potentially uncovering underlying issues in people's lives, and can tell when people are lying to you.
- You'll have better, deeper, more connected relationships with the people in your life, meaning you'll be happier, more fulfilled, and more satisfied with your life and can provide proper support when needed.
- You have more substantial and more fulfilling conversations, even when engaged in small talk.
- You'll become a far more compassionate, empathetic, and grateful person because you'll be appreciating the contributions other people have made far more often.

As you can see, the benefits can tap into every area of your life. Psychologist Carl Rogers writes about how active and deep listening is at the heart of every healthy relationship, and for so many reasons. You read any article or book on how to have better relationships, and the number one tip always refers to learning how to communicate better.

Studies show that listening and showing someone you understand what they're saying makes them more open and more democratic in their future conversations with you. Listening also naturally makes people less defensive. Listening and making attempts to understand someone also strengthens relationships because it shows you care about them and what they have to say. This, in turn, makes them more inclined to listen to you back.

All of this is backed by science. In a 2001 study, Willard Harley, a psychologist, discovered the top ten most important elements that people want when focusing on intimate relationships. Among the top ten results was the need for *intimate conversation,* which boiled down to people wanting their partners to give and receive undivided attention while communicating.

Take a moment to think about your current relationships with people who mean the most to you. Remember times when you've been arguing and how uncompassionate and unconnected you feel from your partner at the heat of the interaction? Now reimagine those times turning out the way you would want them to turn out. Conversations that are typically arguments but instead are conversations with little to no judgments, more democracy, openness, and less defensive attitudes. How much stronger would your relationships be if that's how your conversations went? How much more productive and beneficial would your conversations be?

It's all possible through the practice of listening and mindfully trying to understand other people. By now, I think it's safe to say that we get where we're at as listeners now and what is possible by actively listening, so I'm going to cut myself short and start moving into the meat of this book. Just like all the top blogs and books say, listening is so important, so now I think it's about time to dive into how to do it better.

Once you're ready to start making big positive changes in your life, it's time to turn the page and take that first step on your new journey.

# Chapter Two - The Psychology of Listening

*"The most basic of all human needs is to understand and be understood. The best way to understand people is to listen to them." Ralph Nichols*

What is listening?

Is it to hear the words that someone else is saying? Is it to nod politely and await your turn for speaking? The dictionary definition of listening is perhaps a surprising one, which reads:

*To give attention with the ear closely for the purpose of hearing.*

A more modern definition would include being able to listen with the intent to understand what is being said. We can all hear words sent our way, but the real skill of listening comes from being able to understand the message of what's being said. This chapter is all about understanding the basic skills needed to listen and understand, so by the end of this chapter, you're already going to be well on your way to becoming a better listener.

## Selective Hearing: The Downfall of Listening

The science behind the psychology of listening is one of the most interesting fields of science I've ever looked into, which is where we're going to start, and the first stop is to the station of selective hearing. Chances are, you've been in a situation where you've said something to someone, but it feels as though they're only picking out the certain bits that they want to hear. This is commonly referred to as "selective hearing."

Here's an example. You might have had a conversation with your partner that goes along the lines of:

**Person A:** "Hey, there's a show happening next week with that actor I like. Do you think you'd be interested in getting some tickets?"

Let's imagine the partner is sitting in a chair playing on their phone. They might grunt, or half-respond, or could perhaps ignore the statement completely. This isn't done specifically to be malicious, but rather they are listening, but their selective hearing has decided that because they're not interested in going to the show, they just don't want to respond.

However, in the same sentence, Person A could say:

**Person A:** "Hey, there's a show happening next week with that actor I like. Do you think you'd be interested in getting some tickets? We could get some for the football game while we're there."

Suddenly, Person B puts their phone down and engages in conversation because they picked up on a subject that they're interested in. I can't tell you how many times I've been there.

Of course, this isn't a healthy way to converse with your loved ones, but you'll be amazed at how often this kind of listening occurs in day-to-day conversations. If you're having an in-depth conversation with someone, you'll start to notice that many people only respond to the topics of conversation they care about.

This makes sense, to a degree. The problem is that if you say something important, and they selectively hear but a little of what you said, you're going to unconsciously feel misunderstood and not listened to, and you'll end up becoming defensive. Ultimately, from here, the conversation is doomed.

To be a well-rounded listener, you need the ability to focus and understand everything that's being said, not just picking out the bits you care about. Remember the example conversation I shared in the introduction about my partner wanting to leave her job? By only responding with concerns of money and bill paying, I'm selectively hearing the part of the conversation that I care about and ignoring everything else, including what matters to my partner.

To overcome issues and conflicts like this happening, you need to branch out to switch up your style of listening. Fortunately, according to science and psychology, there are 27 unique types of listening that you can dive into and try for yourself (sometimes 33, depending on the research you're referring to).

Let's cover them below for clarity's sake, but don't feel like you need to remember them all right away. We'll break it down further afterward.

## The 27 Types of Listening

| Type of Listening | Description |
| --- | --- |
| **Active Listening** | Listening to someone with your full attention while actively moving to encourage further speaking (such as nodding your head) and physically showing you're interested. |
| **Appreciative Listening** | Actively listening to someone while looking for opportunities to praise and share an appreciation for what is being said. For example, listening to an athlete talking about running and then giving them praise for their skill. |
| **Attentive Listening** | Showing active attention to someone, making sure to listen to all words and inflections. |
| **Biased Listening** | Listening to someone, but only through your own personal bias and preconceived judgments you already have. |
| **Casual Listening** | Listening without displaying true interest, but actual levels of attention can vary a lot. |
| **Comprehension Listening** | Listening with a solid intent to understand and learn more from the person speaking. |
| **Content Listening** | Listening with a solid intent to understand and learn more from the person speaking (same as above). |

| Critical Listening | Listening with the intent to criticize, evaluate, or judge what someone is saying. |
|---|---|
| Deep Listening | Listening to someone very intently to understand them, their words, personality, motives, goals, and motivations. |
| Dialogic Listening | Listening with the intent to ask questions to seek a deeper understanding of what someone is saying. |
| Discriminative Listening | Listening for something specific while dismissing and ignoring everything else you can hear, such as trying to listen out for a car or someone crying. |
| Empathetic Listening | Listening with the intent of understanding the feelings behind what someone is saying. |
| Evaluative Listening | Listening with the intent to criticize, evaluate, or judge what someone is saying (same as Critical Listening). |
| False Listening | Pretending to listen to someone, but more often than not just caught up in your own thoughts. |
| Full Listening | Listening with the full and honest intent to listen and understand what someone is saying. This means being active in seeking meaning in their words. |
| High-Integrity Listening | Listening with a concern for what the other person is saying. |
| Inactive Listening | Similar to false listening, pretending to listen and give attention. |
| Informative Listening | Listening to understand and get meaning from what is being said. |
| Initial Listening | Listening to the first points shared and then having the intention to interrupt. |
| Judgmental Listening | Same as critical and evaluative listening, but usually with negative intent. Typically have preconceived biases that affect the listening ability. |
| Partial Listening | Listening some of the time, but more engaged with thinking or daydreaming. |
| Reflective Listening | Listening to a conversation and then actively repeating back what the other person said. |

| **Relationship Listening** | Listening with the intent to emotionally support or build a relationship with the other person. |
|---|---|
| **Sympathetic Listening** | Listening with the intent to focus on the other person's feelings plus concern for their overall well-being. |
| **Therapeutic Listening** | Listening with the intent to understand the emotions of someone and to act empathetically towards them. |
| **Total Listening** | Listening with the maximum amount of attention it is possible to give someone, all with the intent to seek actual meaning through what is being said. |
| **Whole-Person Listening** | Listening with the intent to not only understand what is being said but also to understand the person, personality, and feelings of who is speaking on an individual level. |

Phew! That's a lot to take in.

Remember, you don't need to remember all these different listening types, especially since you'll see that many tie in with each other or mean the same thing. However, you should have a deeper understanding of how many different layers to listening there are and how going into any conversation with different intentions will dramatically affect the outcome of the interaction.

The art of getting better at listening is literally about that. It's about being mindful as you go into your conversations and thinking, *What kind of listener do I want to be going into this conversation?* and then proceeding with control, rather than acting mindlessly while on unconscious autopilot.

Let's say, for example, you're talking with a Trump supporter, but you don't support Trump yourself.

It can be so easy to engage in judgemental and critical listening because you already have your beliefs about Trump and how you see Trump supporters act. Instead of hearing the other person, you're just waiting for the opportunity to tear apart what they're saying. Imagine you went into such a conversation with the intent to sympathetically listen or deep listen. Imagine trying to understand the person on an individual and personal level. Imagine how differently the conversation can go and what relationships and progress can form from this.

I'm not saying you need to listen and become friends with everyone you meet. Far from it. Active listening is all about achieving a beneficial outcome where you can actually learn and become a better, more rounded, more compassionate, and more educated person who can make deep and meaningful decisions, connections, and relationships with people when you want to.

Again, there's a lot of listening types to understand there, so we're going to break it all down a little further into just four of the most important types of listening, and these are the ones you're going to want to remember moving forward.

### Appreciative Listening

When you listen to something to enjoy what you can hear. You could be listening to a TED Talk for fun while getting educated. You could be listening to someone talk passionately about something they're interested in, such as your friend talking about their vacation or their new business ideas. You could be listening to music. You could be watching a movie or listening to stand-up comedy. You could be listening to someone you're on a video call with.

All in all, appreciative listening means you're listening because you enjoy listening.

### Comprehensive Listening

This is all about listening to understand. When you watch the news or listen to a teacher, you are comprehensively listening. You actively listen to absorb as much topical information as you can, but this is considered more difficult than most other kinds of listening because it becomes a conscious effort to listen and understand information that you don't already know.

### Critical Listening

This form of listening is all about taking on new information to find out more and evaluate what is being said to you. This ranges from someone in a shop trying to sell you a new smartphone to your friend sharing their medical test results with you, and then you want to find out more about what happens next. This listening type is all about evaluating the content and making judgments to form your own opinion.

### Empathetic Listening

This kind of listening is all about listening with concern and empathy for the other person and their well-being. If someone is going through a hard time and needs support, this is the kind of listening you'll try to give. You'll try putting yourself in the other person's shoes, and you'll give them your full attention, rather than trying to speak yourself. This kind of listening is all about understanding others.

These are the main types of listening, and you're definitely going to want to put effort into remembering these because they will come up the most. Go back to my first example conversation from the introduction and apply it to yourself.

Your partner has just told you they hate their job and they're looking for an out. What kind of listening are you going to apply here?

You could be critical, but it's clear they're not really looking for judgment. You could be appreciative, but the conversation won't move forward unless you're a bit sadistic and enjoy listening to others talking about how much they hate parts of their lives. These listening types are not really what you're looking for. Instead, if you apply comprehensive and empathetic listening, you're much more likely to make your partner feel understood, and you'll actually understand how they're feeling and why.

Once the conversation progresses and starts to move through the initial emotional stage, you can implement critical listening as you explore new ideas of what your partner can do next and how they can resolve the situation.

Should they stay where they are or look for something else? What are the issues you'll need to work through financially? What is your partner looking for? Those are all evolved conversations that require some degree of judgment, but it stems from you starting with the comprehensive listening type first.

Finally, it's worth mentioning that all four of the listening types we've listed above are forms of *Active Listening*. This means to show the person you're speaking with that you're intently listening and giving them your full attention, rather than just half-heartedly listening.

## The Two Final Approaches to Listening

Just to make things even more complicated (only joking!), there are two other listening types you'll need to be aware of before we move forward. I bet you didn't think there were this many kinds of listening, right? If you find it easier to remember these two listening techniques instead of remembering all the others, then feel free to make these types your primary focus in future conversations until you get the hang of them.

### *Listening to Respond*

This is the typical approach to listening that most people take.

You've done it to others, and others will have done it to you. Listening to respond is the type of listening when you're in a conversation with someone, and instead of listening to what they are saying, you already have what you want to say in mind, and you're simply waiting for them to finish. This is so you can jump in and have your say, or you may even interrupt to share your point. We spoke about this listening type earlier.

There are obvious downsides to this approach. You won't understand the person you're listening to, but more importantly, it's incredibly obvious to the other person. Once they notice, they become defensive and won't listen to you. Then, the whole conversation ends up going nowhere.

### *Listening to Understand*

The polar opposite of listening to respond, this kind of listening involves letting go of everything you want to say and truly listening to the other person using the approaches and methods we've explored above. This is the most productive form of listening since it provides all the benefits we've described.

In the following chapters, I'm going to show you how to combine everything you've just learned into one powerful learning strategy, but hopefully, you've got a clear understanding as to just how deep the psychology of listening goes from a scientific standpoint.

However, you don't need to know all the ins and outs yourself. Of course, you can if you want to, but having a basic understanding, for now, is enough to move forward. As a recap for the most important aspects:

- Always make sure you're listening to understand others, not just waiting to force your point of view.
- Active listening is the best kind of listening.
- You can be mindful of different styles of listening in different situations by asking yourself what the best outcome of the conversation will be and deciding what the other person needs.

# Chapter Three - How to Be a Better Active Listener 101

*"The first duty of love is to listen." Paul Tillich*

Ready for the crux for this book? Good, because we're here, and we're heading in fast.

By now, you should know everything about the science and psychology of listening. In other words, what it is, what true listening requires, and a *ton* of different listening types. But while you have the information on what listening is, the methods themselves don't explain *how* to do it, which is what we're going to explore in this chapter.

We'll start with basic listening skills that you need to know as your foundation for becoming a better listener, and then we'll move on to some more advanced tactics. This will be an intense chapter that includes everything you need to know, so feel free to take it a section at a time!

## Bringing Awareness to Yourself (It All Starts with You!)

First things first, you need to be aware of yourself and how you show up in conversations.

When it comes to self-improvement of any kind, it all starts with, well, yourself, and the same applies when you're mastering the art of listening.

Here are some powerful tips you can start with that will immediately improve your ability to listen. This is going to be a tip-heavy chapter, so feel free to take it in stages or even bookmark this page, so you can come back at any time to refresh your memory on existing skills you've learned, or to learn new ones!

### *Realizing Your Judgements and Biases*

What do you think about the current state of politics? How do you feel about Hollywood? What are your thoughts on the Royal Family? What are your concepts of Wall Street, the health of the environment, and Nikki Minaj?

The first thoughts that come to your mind on these topics are your judgments and biases towards them, and they can hold you back from listening properly. Here's an example:

> *Marie and Kyle have been married for a few years. One day, they are driving to the zoo. Kyle believes himself to be a great driver, and as Marie drives, she hesitates at a roundabout, whereas Kyle would have claimed the free space. Kyle comments with the aim of advising Marie to be a more confident driver, but Marie says it was fine and smiles at him.*
>
> *Later, the couple is talking about what happened, and the conversation gets heated, and Kyle ends up getting angry and making an aggressive comment that he later regrets.*

The problem with this kind of common conversation is that Kyle doesn't know (or maybe he does and doesn't apply the knowledge) the fact that her past ex-partners have demeaned Marie for not doing things right in her life, whether that's driving, cooking, cleaning, or just living her life.

At the same time, Kyle was bullied in school and made to feel powerless, and now unconsciously seeks validation for the topics he does know about—in this case, his ability and knowledge when it comes to driving.

Both Kyle and Marie have preconceived biases and ideals that affect the direction of the conversation. Marie's past experiences and bias make Kyle's friendly advice feel like piercing criticism. Marie's reluctance to learn from the criticism makes Kyle feel like his knowledge of driving is invalid and puts him on the defensive.

Now, you're certainly not able to control other people's biases, but you *can* control your own by being mindful of your own automatic and unconscious thoughts and feelings whenever they arise. If Kyle gives advice and Marie shuts it down, he needs to develop the ability to recognize the defensive feelings that come up from him being triggered. Suppose he can recognize them as being triggering rather than being consumed emotionally. In that case, he can voice these concerns with Marie and have a much more therapeutic conversation, rather than the aggressive outburst it later leads to.

These automatic responses that we feel towards everything are known as thought patterns, and you don't need to feel bad about having them because we all do. The trick is to become aware of what they are, perhaps through journaling, meditation, or even counseling if your thoughts are based on past traumas (like Kyle's bullying and Marie's ex-boyfriend problem), and then working through them, ensuring your negative patterns can turn positive.

Some considerations to remember here include:
- Learning to recognize a judgment, bias, or negative thought pattern when it arises.
- Write preexisting thought patterns down to remember them and bring more focus to them later.
- Including someone on your self-discovery journey to help you identify your less obvious patterns.
- Recording your reactions to conversations or events (writing or video).
- Try new positive reactions the next time you're in a similar conversation or situation where you want to let go of an old thought pattern.

Piece all this together, and you'll be able to go into any conversation with an open mind with the very real ability to learn and listen to others. Here's one more example to bring it home.

Let's say you hate social media. You dislike everything about it and think the world is better off without it. Someone starts talking to you about a fundraising campaign that happened on Instagram. However, as soon as they mention Instagram, you shut down and think, *I don't want to hear this because Instagram is an awful platform,* and it's a horrible conversation where everyone gets invalidated.

On the flip side, you may first have the thought that Instagram is a horrible platform, but you instead notice the judgment through awareness, and you let it go. You listen to the other person tell you about an amazing fundraising project and instead say something like, "Well, I don't use Instagram, but that sounds like an amazing project. If I give you the money, can you donate for me?"

See how different the conversation can be by dropping your judgments and listening?

### *Acknowledging Your Expectations*

Whenever you have a conversation, you're going to be affected by your conditioning and will have expectations that dictate how you listen, just like you do with your judgments. Think about situations like going into a job interview, and you're so nervous because you simply believe it's going to go terribly. It's these expectations that will hold you back from listening properly. In this case, this will certainly ruin the job interview and turn your thoughts into a self-fulfilling prophecy.

I use the Trump supporter and anti-Trump example a lot, but that's because it was so relevant over the last few years.

Whenever these two types of people go "against" each other (especially in examples captured on video), these people will not listen to each other because their preconceived expectations prevent them from being open to what the other person has to say. It's these expectations that prevent any real, productive conversations from taking place with the potential for a positive outcome.

It's important to be aware and mindful of your own expectations and preconceptions that could be stopping you from being a proper listener in your own life. Perhaps someone at work did something stupid once, and you've always seen them as a bit of an idiot because of it. This stops you from talking to them and prevents you from accessing any of the opportunities they could bring into your life.

The same goes for your parents, partners, children, coworkers, and basically anyone you know or could meet. Some top tips to remember here to overcome your expectations include:

- Keeping a journal and writing down the thoughts whenever you have an expectation pop up.
- Making a list of all the expectations you have with different people in your life. This works because writing down your thoughts helps you focus on them more, thus making it easier to identify when they come up. When you notice them pop up, you can let them go and focus properly.
- Be active in discovering your conditioning by giving yourself keywords like money, language, immigrants, politics, religion, and the names of people in your life. Write down whatever comes to mind, and you'll soon discover how you feel and what you can learn to let go of.
- Whenever you feel an expectation or bias come into your mind when talking to someone, take a moment to breathe and let it go.

I was speaking to a friend of mine a few years back, and he started talking about his spiritual journey and how he was getting into ideas like chakras and astral projection. As we walked, he asked me what I thought, and the first thing that came to mind was how it's all spiritual rubbish and wasn't real. I believed it was false hope and that kind of thing.

However, instead of just jumping to my conditioned way of thinking and responding mindlessly, I said something along the lines of:

"You know, the first thing that came to mind was how that sounds like nonsense, but I'm not sure whether that's just because I have no experience in it. Tell me more about it, and I'll try and see through that train of thought."

This is all that needs to be said in a situation like this. Let's say your partner wants to go and try a new diet. You can say that you agree or disagree with the diet they're choosing to try, but this is just your preconceived expectation since the chances are you know nothing about it. Let your partner know this and say you're going to work on being open-minded and seeing how it goes.

The truth is, as a human being, you know practically nothing. What you don't know is almost always more important than what you do know. To quote a famous motivational speaker, you don't know enough. If you did, then your life and the lives of everyone around you would be where you want them to be.

Accept this notion, and you open up a whole new way of living in the world.

### *Practice Your Mindfulness Skills*

A lot of everything we've spoken about so far, and easily one of the most actionable pieces of advice any listening guide or expert can give you is to be present in your conversations. This means to give the other person your full attention, and you can do this by actively improving your mindfulness skills. To be mindful is to be aware of your thoughts and in control of your attention.

With human attention spans now averaging less than that of a goldfish, you're going to need to engage in a process. It's going to be hard work. Even writing this chapter, I'm constantly feeling the pull of social media and wanting to go on my phone. As I wrote the word phone, I immediately wanted to jump on Instagram or check to see if someone has texted or emailed me.

How often do you find your mind wandering in the same way, especially when you're talking to others?

I've lost count of the number of times that someone has been talking to me, and I just zone out. It could be seconds or minutes before I think, *Damn it, I have no idea what was just said or what's going on. I've been daydreaming*. Then you have to struggle to pick up where you left off.

The act of mindfulness means having the skill to notice when your mind wanders off or isn't focused fully on the conversation you're having and then gently pulling it back.

The more you practice mindfulness, the better at it you'll become, and the shorter the time frame will be that your mind allows itself to wander. Here are some tips to help you develop your mindfulness skills:

- Bring your whole heart into a moment by using your senses to stay connected to the present. What can you see, hear, smell, and touch? Your senses help you stay grounded.
- Focus on your breathing. This is a classic meditation technique, but you'll notice how even while you read this, you can focus on your breathing and the words, and all other thoughts cease to bother you. This is a great technique to use in conversations.
- Focus on the center of your hand. This works the same as the method above, but I found it much easier to put into practice. Look at your hand and place a finger in the center of your palm. Now focus on that point, as though your awareness is inside your hand.

You can remove your finger and still focus on that bit. Keep your attention there while you read or converse with someone to maintain your focus.

- Practice meditation. Sure, meditation isn't for everyone, but there's really no better way to improve your ability to stay present and focused in everything you do in life.
- Be grateful for the moment you're living in. Gratitude is such a big part of being present. If you can appreciate that your partner, someone who loves you very much, is in front of you, this is a great way to stay focused, all because you don't want to miss another moment with them.

## *Controlling Your Emotions (Developing Emotional Intelligence)*

If someone says something and you're offended by it, stirred by it, or even motivated by it, it's so easy to lose focus in a conversation and then to start projecting those expectations and preconceptions we spoke about earlier. If you're offended, your defenses go up, and it becomes incredibly difficult to actually hear what the other person is saying.

It takes a bit of self-development to increase your emotional intelligence, which refers to your ability to notice when your emotions arise, yet still being able to control yourself to have the outcome you want. Remember, emotions are always your body's first unconscious response, and it's so easy just to let your mind wander away with them without thinking.

A great example of this is to imagine you're in a bar and you've bought your first drink after a hard week at work. A group of people walks past you, and due to lack of space, someone accidentally knocks your drink out of your hand before you even get to enjoy the first sip.

How do you respond?

There are two ways you can go. You may feel a flood of anger and irritation towards that other person. You could feel the urge to start fighting with them, projecting your anger and irritation onto them. You react solely through emotion, completely on autopilot, as you throw your weight around and try to put that other person in their place.

This is clearly not a very emotionally intelligent way to respond.

On the other hand, the other approach doesn't mean you won't still feel that same rush of irritation and anger towards the other person. How could you not? You were so looking forward to the drink, and now you can't help but feel disappointed. However, being an emotionally intelligent person, you recognize your rising emotions, take a deep breath, and wait calmly for them to settle down before continuing with your evening. You know full well that knocking your drink over was an accident.

This is the same logic you need to apply in your own conversations if you want to be an emotionally intelligent listener. Listen, watch your emotions, and then respond in the best possible way. Unfortunately, you can't just become emotionally intelligent overnight but instead, have to keep working on it. It's a lifelong journey that you'll just need to keep working at, especially as you grow and evolve as a person.

However, there are four characteristics that come together to make an emotionally intelligent person that you'll need to master. These are:

- **Being Self-Aware:** This means having the skill to recognize your own emotions as they arise and how to express them to others honestly and effectively.
- **Capable of Self-Management:** Having the skills to control your emotions and not mindlessly get carried away with them, resulting in you acting unconsciously and without control.
- **Being Socially Aware:** Being able to recognize others' emotions and pick up their non-verbal communications.
- **Capable of Having Stable Relationships:** Having the skills to communicate effectively with others, having empathy and compassion, and knowing how to interact with different people based on their own emotional intelligence.

With that in mind, these are the actionable tips you'll need to know on how to become more emotionally intelligent, thus developing these traits. Note, we're not carrying on with our list of how to be a better listener just now (although it obviously all ties together). The following points are all about how to increase your emotional intelligence.

- **Assess Where You Are Now**

Start with self-reflecting to see where you are now, basically gauging how emotionally intelligent you are. However, this first step is definitely the most challenging since it involves taking a real hard look at yourself. It's best to do this with a pen and paper, maybe a diary or journal, and just write about how you handle situations in your life.

Ask yourself these questions to help you figure out where you are:

- Do I react differently around different people?
- Do I get anxious when talking with other people?
- What feelings do I have?
- Do I get angry quickly?
- Do I have triggers with certain topics?
- Do events in my life, such as stressful events, control how I act in situations?

The whole idea here is to highlight your strengths and weaknesses so you know what to focus on and improve.

- **Learn to See Emotions in Others**

While it's important to acknowledge your own emotions in any given situation, you need to be proactive in paying attention to others and acknowledging theirs. This is predominately and initially done using your gut instinct (which we'll talk more about later).

Whenever you're speaking with someone, take a time-out to judge how the other person is feeling. You can literally use the "How are you?" small-talk question as a reminder. Listen to their answer, and then take a second or two to feel how you feel the other person is feeling. If they say they're fine, but your gut instinct says that they feel stressed, this could be an indication to dive a bit deeper.

You can always say, "I'm glad you're okay. You do look a bit stressed, though. Is everything alright?" effectively making sure you gauged their emotions correctly. This is another skill that you'll get better with as long as you're practicing it often.

- **Be Responsible for Your Actions and Decisions**

As with the spilled drink at the bar example above, a person controlled by their emotions is acting unconsciously and without control. They are careless and will make decisions they'll regret.

I know I say this as though all lack of control is negative, but it works both ways. Imagine someone who is having so much fun at a music festival and is so overwhelmed with happiness. They then decide (without control) to let go of all their inhibitions and carelessly take random narcotics offered to them because they're lost having a good time.

The chances are a situation like that won't end well, so responsibility needs to be taken for their actions. This trait is quite simple, but it takes confidence to apply it to your life.

- If you make a mistake, own it.

- If something goes wrong in your life, learn from the experience and do the best you can next time.
- Adjust your reactions when you need to.
- If you hurt someone, apologize to them.
- Let go of your ego and aim to grow and be a better version of yourself.

*Only you can make it happen.*

- **Be Self Disciplined and Have Self Control**

Every human being experiences a whole spectrum of emotions throughout different times in their life, and there are going to be times where you feel so emotional it feels as though you could lose control. It's during these times you'll be tested to see how far you've come on your emotional intelligence journey.

If you find yourself in a tense, heated, or stressful situation, you must learn how to take a step back and take a few deep breaths. When you feel the emotions rising inside you, the rage or the anxiousness or whatever you're feeling, these are the moments where you start to control your breathing in an attempt to settle these feelings.

Taking this time-out allows you to think properly and make the decisions you want to make, rather than acting unconsciously.

Some good practices and habits to bring into your life include doing things like taking the time to think before you speak since this gives you time to breathe and consider what you're going to say next. You can also meditate daily, as this will help you bring presence and attention to your emotions.

There are endless strategies out there that can help you be more disciplined, and all of them will affect every area of your life, not just when it comes to your listening skills. If you've ever had hopes, dreams, and aspirations you want to turn into a reality, you're going to need the discipline to get there.

I could give you the basic advice. Even if you get 1% better than you were yesterday, you're still making progress on your journey. But I'm sure you're thinking that's slow and you want more instant results. I know I sure did when I was in the same position.

Unfortunately, it doesn't happen overnight, and you will need to get better over time. There's no other way it can happen. However, you can increase your chances of succeeding by doing the following:

- Have no excuses for your behavior
- Take ownership of your decisions and your mistakes
- Forgive yourself when you mess up (and you will mess up) and try again
- Never give up
- Set yourself rewards you can only have once you've mindfully practiced this skill
- Meditate and write down what you excel at and what you can improve on daily

- **Assert Yourself**

Since following these tips and steps will enable you to become gradually more emotionally intelligent, you'll be far more in tune with your emotions and how you're feeling, which will allow you to very clearly know your wants, needs, desires, and feelings.

This means you can be assertive with people around you, which is essential if you want to be an effective communicator. You can learn how to tell people what you want and what you need from them directly, without having to beat around the bush. You can also tell people where you stand on certain topics.

Did someone say something that really angered you? Instead of flying off the handle, you'll be able to tell them how that made them feel and help them see your side of the story. Being assertive is about finding the perfect balance between being passive and being aggressive. For example:

**A:** "Hey. Did you see the new girl at the reception this morning? I'd love to take her home and go wild with her!"

**B:** "That's incredibly inappropriate and disrespectful."

**A:** "Oh, lighten up. I'm just trash-talking."

**B:** "I'm just saying you crossed a line. Think what you want, but you should have respect for others."

**A:** "She's not here. It doesn't matter."

**B:** "How would you like it if other people spoke about your daughter in the same way? Have a bit of empathy."

**A:** "Yeah. Okay. I see what you mean. Sorry, I wasn't thinking."

**B:** "It's okay. I'm glad we didn't have to fight about it."

A tense conversation. It would be very easy for people to join into a conversation like this to try and fight in with 'office banter,' although thankful it's been addressed increasingly, or to not say anything at all, despite person A clearly crossing a line.

It's actions and conversations like this that create a far more productive conversation where people are open to learning from each other rather than fighting. Some other tips you can follow for being more assertive include doing things like:

- Believing that embarking on this journey is helping you become a better version of yourself
- Saying no to things in life that don't serve or resonate with you
- Asserting yourself in small-scale conversations
- Always remaining positive towards the outcome of a situation
- Being aware of other people's feelings and their points of view

## A Summary of Becoming Emotionally Intelligent

By harnessing the power of each point we've discussed, you'll be able to ultimately become a far better listener than you could imagine since you'll be so grounded and in control of yourself, no matter who you're speaking with.

There are so many benefits to developing your emotional intelligence in this way. It will truly affect every aspect of your life, from your personal relationships and career to your confidence and levels of charisma. Anyway, that was a bit of a detour. Let's return to our list of ways to become a better active listener.

- **Awareness of Your Physical Self**

Body language is a huge part of communication (research shows that it makes up around 55% of all communication, whereas verbal communication makes up just 7%), so it pays to be in control of your own body language and creating the image you want to give to other people.

I'm going to talk a whole lot more about body language in a later chapter. Still, for now, I'll cover some actionable tips you can start introducing into your conversations right now to automatically become a better listener.

- Maintain a balanced degree of eye contact. Don't just stare at people, but don't avoid eye contact altogether. Show you're listening with the amount of eye contact that feels comfortable.
- Keep your back straight and sit upright. You don't want to overdo this to seem as though you're trying to overpower the other person with confidence, but you don't want to slouch to seem bored or disconnected. Give the impression you're engaged in the conversation.
- Don't fiddle with anything or play with your hands. This sends the message you're either nervous or distracted, neither of which you want other people to think since they'll start talking to you differently.
- Use expressions. When you're talking, talk with your whole body as this will make you seem far more engaged and a part of the conversation. Use hand gestures to emphasize your points.
- Nod and smile as a sign of acknowledgment that you want the other person to keep speaking and encourage them to keep going while you're listening.

- **Awareness of Your Vocal Self**

Finally, you want to pay attention to how you're coming across while you're talking back, answering questions, and sharing your points of view. It's all well and good showing good body language, but many people will react to how you're saying what you're saying and how you're presenting yourself.

The main considerations you need to be thinking about are things like:

- The volume of your voice (are you whispering or shouting?)
- The tone of voice you have (whether you're stern, sarcastic, happy, energetic, and so on)
- What kind of inflection you place on certain words

It's always best to speak in a cool, calm, and collected fashion to portray your message if you want to be listened to.

However, there will be times when you need to speak sternly, such as if you're disciplining a child or times when you want to be hyper and excited, like when you're going to a concert with friends. It's all about the context of the conversation you're in, so be active in choosing the right kind of voice for the situation.

As you can see, for a lot of these points, it's all about taking your mind and body off autopilot and taking back control of how you communicate and how you listen to others. It's applying control in this way that you'll get the outcome you want from the conversation.

## The Key Active Listening Skills You Need to Know

These are the first skills that come into play when you want to listen to someone more effectively and deeply. You can apply the following tips literally right now and see an instant improvement in your ability to communicate and listen.

### Let Someone Speak without Interruption

When I started work on bettering my skills as a listener, it became shockingly apparent how much I interrupted people and how much they interrupted me. Interrupting seems to be commonplace nowadays, and reading this right now will make you so much more aware of it in your own conversations. Sorry about that. Another thing you won't be able to unsee.

You can counter this by being mindful and aware enough to let others finish everything they're saying. This way, you'll be able to get the full context out of their message, and it will make the person speaking feel as though you care about what they're saying, rather than just trying to shoehorn your perspective into the conversation.

### Minimize Distractions

You can't give someone your full attention if you're distracted by other things that are going on around you. When someone starts speaking to you, put your phone down so you can't see the screen, close your book, and turn off your computer monitor. If you're talking in a loud place where you can't hear thanks to external noises, you can suggest moving to a quieter location.

It's actions like this that show you care.

### Show How Much You're Paying Attention

There are plenty of ways you can use your body to not only show you're giving someone your full attention but also trick your body into actually giving someone your full attention. You can easily do this by:

- Making eye contact
- Leaning forward towards the speaker when they say something that interests you
- Nodding in agreement to points
- Saying "yes" and "uh-huh" to encourage the speaker to keep going at the appropriate points in the conversation
- Smiling to show shared humor within the conversation

### Avoid Making Judgments

As soon as you're aware that you're making judgments on what someone is saying, you're taking yourself out of listening and are instead distracted by thoughts, which means you're not listening. Through practice, you'll be able to become aware of distracting, judgmental thoughts, which you can nip in the bud by reapplying your focus to listening. When you're judging, you're not listening.

This applies to your preconceived judgments and biases, as we spoke about in the last section, and if someone uses the wrong word to describe something or speaks out of context. Simple mistakes can happen, and not everyone is a brilliant communicator. If someone makes a mistake and it stops you from listening, you need to let your judgments go if you want the conversation to continue being productive.

### Repeat Back What You Heard

I will speak about this point a lot more in the following chapters, but a great way to improve your listening skills is to repeat back the key points of what you just heard.

Imagine someone says something along the lines of:

> "I really love running because I feel so free and peaceful."

You can reply with something like:

> "It makes you feel free? In what way?"

It's the act of repeating the information back that not only clarifies what's being said in your own head, meaning there's much less of a chance you're going to forget it, but you're showing the other person you're genuinely taking on board what they're saying and hearing their message.

## The Key Active Listening Habits You Need to Avoid

Just like there are plenty of habits and skills you can use to improve your abilities as an active listener, you should avoid the mistakes and bad habits that will make you seem like a passive listener or someone who isn't paying attention. However, by learning what they are, you'll be able to avoid them.

### Rushing Someone to Finish

I've seen people who have been quite abrupt with rushing someone to finish speaking literally by saying things like "Come on, get to the point," and so on.

However, there are other more subtle ways this can happen, such as checking a watch or phone for the time or looking anywhere other than at the person who's speaking. This unconsciously makes it look like you're looking for a way out.

Rushing someone to finish will not make the other person feel listened to but will rather distract them from saying what they want to say.

Sure, there can be times when people will talk too much and won't be speaking concisely, but if you want a relationship with someone, you've got to have the respect to let them express themselves how they want to.

### Changing the Subject Abruptly

Another common trait I see among people all the time.

We've all been in situations where someone is speaking about something that matters to them, and the conversation changes suddenly. This is another way of rushing the person to finish and making them believe that what they were talking about isn't relevant or cared about.

Changing the subject will shut the other person down, makes them defensive, and ultimately makes them less likely to listen to you. This is only going to cause conflict in your conversations. Here's an example that happened a week or so ago when I was visiting my parents.

I, my mother, and my father were doing the dishes after dinner. Dad's talking about how he follows the shares his bank gave him but doesn't know why he spends time doing that since he hasn't done anything with the stocks in over a decade.

**Dad:** "But yeah, I guess it's just a habit to check them."

**Me:** "Do you think it's something you would be interested in spending more time on now that you're retired?"

**Mom:** "Oh, what is that smell?"

From here, my dad became extremely defensive and asked my mother to repeat what he had just said, to which she couldn't answer, and an argument proceeded about not being listened to, and quite rightly too. The blatant change in subject only said my mother didn't care at all about what my father was saying, which made him defensive, and the conversation derailed.

In short, just avoid changing the subject abruptly and let people get to the end of what they're saying, simply out of the same respect you would want from other people.

### Using Humor at the Wrong Times

I'm massively guilty of this one.

For a long time, humor was a big coping mechanism for me, and even when the situation wasn't funny or the topic was negative, I would still laugh or make a joke because it helped me process the information and deal with the potential awkwardness of talking about it. It wasn't even laughing in a "haha, that's funny" kind of way, but it was more of a nervous laugh.

Still, not everyone I spoke to knew that.

This was a completely unconscious response I had, and if someone didn't know me very well, the laugh could so easily be taken out of context and made to feel as though I was making a joke out of the situation. This, again, makes people feel as though I'm not listening, nor taking the situation seriously, therefore not respecting what the other person has to say.

### Focusing on Small Details Rather Than Bigger Picture

It's so easy to fall into the trap of focusing on the small point of what someone is saying rather than seeing the big picture of the ideas they're sharing. I saw this all the time during my career in sales and marketing when we were brainstorming client ideas, and someone would always get hung up on the details.

An example of this could be two people discussing ideas for redecorating a living room.

**A:** "I'm thinking we go with a nice blue wall with maybe a mirror at the back. You see this photo? I really like the lighting the mirror helps create. It makes the color nicer."

**B:** "I don't really like the mirror, though. The frame isn't that nice and doesn't fit what we're going for."

In this situation, person B wasn't listening to person A. The point wasn't about the mirror being nice or something they would have, but instead, they were talking about the effect the mirror had on the room. Comments like what person B made are only going to make A feel as though they're not being listened to nor understood.

If you're able to bear all these points in mind and start applying them to your own conversations, you're going to instantly see such a big improvement in the quality of your conversations and ultimately how people talk to you, listen to you, and connect with you.

Maybe you have some bad habits when it comes to conversing. Mine included such an absence of eye contact, laughing at the wrong time, interrupting people, and it was hard to start incorporating the advice.

For example, it felt unnatural and weird to make eye contact at all, let alone for a suitable amount of time, but being aware of the changes I wanted to make and knowing that doing so would improve my relationships tenfold, I was able to introduce the positive habit into my life.

I became my own proof that the methods work.

Keep practicing and incorporating them. Like any life skill, it will take time for them to become conversational traits that you don't even need to think about, but you can only get there through experience, so don't give up! Now we're going to dive into more advanced listening strategies that will take your conversations to a whole other level.

*Communication Skills Training Series*

# Chapter Four - Validation: The Key to Extraordinary Listening

*"Just like children, emotions heal when they are heard and validated."- Jill Bolte Taylor*

From the introduction of this book, I've spoken here and there about the aspect of validation, of course promising that we're going to dive into it in more detail. I've called it such an important aspect of conversation and effective communication that it demands its own dedicated chapter, so here we are!

Let's start with the basics.

What is validation?

There are many myths out there, the biggest one being that validation means that you just agree with someone with anything they say. That's not validation at all. That's just being agreeable.

Genuine validation is a little different. If someone says you're baking a cake the wrong way or that the Kardashians are the best thing to happen to the US since sliced bread, validating that person and their opinion doesn't mean you're agreeing with those ideas and taking them as facts. *That's validating someone's ego.*

True communicative validation is all about accepting the person you're speaking with as the *person* they are, which means listening to them and accepting that what they're saying is their belief. This is how you make someone heard and feel listened to, and this is how true relationships are formed.

You can disagree with absolutely everything someone is saying, but you can still validate them.

Here's an example for clarity.

My father was a very conservative man.

He worked every day of his life, ran his own business with ten or so employees, and made a good, stable income to support his family. My father despised paying taxes. He lived in Canada and paid taxes there. Canada also has a welfare system, but he hated that his taxes were paying the welfare of people he thought "simply couldn't be bothered to work" and were leeching off the system.

Now, as most of us know, the welfare system is incredibly complicated. While there are certainly people who take from the system when they don't need to, statistics show that the vast majority of people on the system are on it because they need the support it offers.

If you have a mother who's newly single and has two children, of course, the state is going to help her get back on her feet. When she can work, she'll earn, support her children, pay her taxes back in, and once her children grow up, having been supported by the state, they'll be able to make their own contributions, and so the system continues to cycle.

The subject is infinitely complex, but whenever my father had his yearly tax bill notification come through the post, we would have the same conversation. He was adamant he was being ripped off, and there was nothing he could do about it. I don't necessarily agree with his point of view that the welfare system is a con for the reasons above—far from it. But, I can see why my father would hate to pay 30% tax on everything he earned. That's a pretty decent chunk of income, especially when he was only slightly over the higher tax bracket.

Because I validated my father whenever we spoke about this situation, we still maintained a positive, nurturing, and deep relationship through the time he was alive. We were also close and always got along, even if we had differing opinions on certain subjects, such as paying taxes.

We still listened to each other and accepted each other for who we were.

Think about this on the flip side.

How many people do you know who are so stuck in their ways of thinking, they don't want to hear anyone else's opinion? It's impossible to have a meaningful, satisfying relationship if you can't listen to the people in them and hear what they're saying. The most powerful way you can prove that you are doing these things is through validation.

If you're looking for a powerful visual example, head over to YouTube and type in *Jordan Peterson calmly dismantles feminism* (Jordan Peterson, *Daily Politics Show*, 2018).

This isn't about whether or not you agree with the video's content, but it's a fantastic example of how terrible communication is in the modern age, especially when it comes to controversial conversations like race discrimination and politics. Watch the video and see how the two presenters aren't listening to Jordan speak whatsoever, nor validating anything he says, but how he does.

It's mind-blowing to me how poor their listening skills are, and these are people who are supposed to be interviewing someone but instead take the opportunity to shoehorn in their own points of view and try to catch him out.

This may be an extreme case, but this is exactly what so many of us do in our own relationships with the people we love. We hear what we want to hear. We make assumptions based on certain parts of what someone is saying so that their words fit our own narratives, and we drive home our perspectives rather than developing a proper conversation.

By learning how to validate the people you're speaking to, you'll improve your own listening skills and make the other person feel heard, making them less defensive and more open and honest with you, creating a meaningful relationship in the process.

So, how do you do it? Fortunately, there's a six-step guide that details everything you need to know.

## The Six-Step Guide to Validating Someone

The following actionable process I'm going to share has been highlighted over the years by psychologists and researchers like Dr. Marsha Linehan, the creator of dialectical behavior therapy (known as DBT). Top life coaches also recommend this process, and authors like Patrick King in his book *How to Listen, Hear, and Validate*.

You don't need to memorize every step of this process, but instead, work on one step at a time, apply the teachings to your conversations, and build up your conversational capabilities. With experience, you'll become far better at validating others, and you'll see the results almost instantly.

When I first came across these techniques, I read about them on the train to work, and with the information fresh in mind, I applied the methods when I arrived and found the changes were immediate. That's how powerful these subtle changes in your behaviors can be. So, let's get into the steps.

## Step One - Be Present

First and foremost, you have to be present in your conversations. We've spoken about this already, but it's just as important as the rest of these steps. As a quick recap, you need to:

- Give someone your full attention
- Listen to what they're saying
- Be mindful of the words and tone someone is using

If you're playing on your phone or working on a computer, you're distracted and not present, and you won't be able to fully engage with any of the following steps.

Imagine how much better your conversations with your loved ones would be if you gave them your full attention with this step alone. This is especially important during tough conversations. If someone is sharing a problem or negative emotions with you, and you're not sure how to deal with what you're being told, perhaps they're even shouting at you aggressively, this can make you uncomfortable, and you'll want to distract yourself.

This means you'll begin to lack presence, thus invalidating the person you're speaking with, and the conversation will begin to spiral downwards.

Here's an example.

**A:** "I'm so mad at you right now. You had no right to go and spend money on that account without asking me. I feel like you're betraying me or don't believe we're a team, and you can approach me to talk about big decisions like this."

**B:** "But I wanted to surprise you. I know it's a lot of money, but I just wanted to make things nicer."

**A:** Can you see how betrayed this would make me feel? Imagine if I did the same to you. How would you feel?"

B feels ashamed and starts to look at the ground, playing with their hair, fiddling with things on the table, and not looking at person A. Person A becomes more infuriated.

**A:** "What do you have to say then? Are you even listening?"

It's a hard conversation for both A and B. When B gets distracted and loses presence in the conversation, person A immediately gets defensive, and the conversation escalates to unproductive levels of aggression. Sure, it may not be right for person A to be so aggressive, but you can't control other people. You can only ever control your own actions and responses.

Let's say person B was practicing being present.

**A:** "I'm so mad at you right now. You had no right to go and spend money on that account without asking me. I feel like you're betraying me or don't believe we're a team, and you can approach me to talk about big decisions like this."

**B:** "But I wanted to surprise you. I know it's a lot of money, but I just wanted to make things nicer."

**A:** "Can you see how betrayed this would make me feel? Imagine if I did the same to you. How would you feel?"

Person B maintains eye contact and remains present in the conversation, even though they're mindful that they want to look away and disconnect from the conversation.

**B:** "Yes. I can see what you're saying, and I'm putting myself in your shoes. I would feel the same."

Person A takes a deep breath, understanding that they have been listened to and understood.

**A:** "I'm glad you can see how I'm feeling. I'm sorry I shouted. I just felt really intense about it all."

As you can see, from one change in the conversation, just by remaining present, the entire direction and outcome of the conversation changed to be far more positive than it would be before. To remain present in a conversation, here are some actionable tips to remember.

- Maintain eye contact.
- Listen with your body.
- If you feel yourself wanting to do something else, become aware of that thought and choose an alternative action.
- Keep a diary where you make notes on conversations you had throughout the day and highlight times where you weren't present and times you were. This will help you focus on being more present in future conversations.
- Meditate to increase your mindfulness abilities and sense of presence in conversations.
- Start the conversation off positively using your tone and language. If you're not going into a conversation positively, you're going to want to get out as quickly as possible and thus will end up looking for a way out and are, therefore, no longer present.

### Step Two - It's All About Reflection

Taking step one into account, you're present, and you're listening to the people you're speaking with. You're taking on their ideas and hearing what they say. From here, the next step is to be reflective of what you've just heard. This is the part of the process where you need to be able to hear what someone is saying and look past your own personal beliefs, judgments, and biases.

There are plenty of ways you can do this, such as repeating back what someone has said to ensure what you've heard is correct, and you've taken on board what the other person has said and, most importantly, have understood the message the way it was intended.

That's not always easy. Sometimes people you'll speak with will have very valid points, but due to poor communication skills, there can be a lot of rambling that you need to sift through, which is why it's important to reflect on what the person has said, provide them with a summary (in your own words), and get to the point of what's being spoken about before formulating your own response.

Take the spending money example from the last step.

**A:** "I'm so mad at you right now. You had no right to go and spend money on that account without asking me. I feel like you're betraying me or don't believe we're a team, and you can approach me to talk about big decisions like this."

**B:** "But I wanted to surprise you. I know it's a lot of money, but I just wanted to make things nicer."

**A:** "Can you see how betrayed this would make me feel? Imagine if I did the same to you. How would you feel?"

**B:** "Yes. I understand you feel betrayed because I went behind your back and made a big decision without discussing it with you. If you did that to me, I would feel the same."

See how person B reflects back on what person A said, puts the message into their own words, and repeats it back, accurately reflecting the message and therefore validating what's been said? There is no doubt in person A's mind that they haven't been listened to nor understood, which will allow the conversation to progress productively.

However, understandably, this is person B agreeing with what person A said and is understood. If greater clarity was needed, the conversation could look something like:

**A:** "I'm so mad at you right now. You had no right to go and spend money on that account without asking me. I feel like you're betraying me or don't believe we're a team, and you can approach me to talk about big decisions like this."

**B:** "But I wanted to surprise you. I know it's a lot of money, but I just wanted to make things nicer."

**A:** "Can you see how betrayed this would make me feel? Imagine if I did the same to you. How would you feel?"

**B:** "I understand you're upset because it's a lot of money, but it was spent on both of us, more as a present for you that we can both enjoy. Can you tell me more about how you feel betrayed? If I spent the money on myself and not you, and didn't tell you, then I would understand the feelings of being betrayed. Explain just so I can understand where you're coming from properly."

With this kind of response, person B is validating the feelings of person A by basically saying, "Okay, I understand how you're feeling, and I'm not disputing you're wrong in feeling the way you do. I accept you feel the way you feel, but I still need clarity when it comes to understanding why you're thinking the way you're thinking."

Some of the best ways to be accurately reflective include:

- Repeating back a summary of what the person said in *your own* words. You're not a parrot!
- Asking thoughtful questions when you need more information on what someone has said and need more understanding.
- Matching the person's tone and inflection, positively or negatively.

### Step Three - Implement Feeling Words

The next step that works hand in hand with the step above is using "feeling" words in your conversations to help you connect and understand even further.

If someone feels as though you're not really listening, understanding, nor empathizing with what they have said, this is the step that will help you overcome this conversational obstacle.

It's a shame that people living in the modern age are so disconnected from their feelings. Usually, through no fault of their own, people may have been invalidated by their parents, teachers, or peers from a young age, leading to them being emotionally disconnected from themselves as adults.

An example of this would be a child who enjoys drawing and painting. They draw and paint pictures like other children do, and naturally needing validation from their parents, the child shows them. This is a perfectly natural chain of events.

However, imagine a situation where a child paints a snail or a cat and shows their mother who is on the phone at the time. The child shows the painting and the mother, who's occupied, simply dismisses the painting, telling the child to go away because she's busy or gives a simple "Oh yes, that's great, honey."

This may seem like nothing to you or me, but from a child's perspective, when a parent is the king or queen of their world and is so dismissive, such dismissals and acts of invalidation can be devastating, especially when it happens consistently and frequently. This invalidates the child and their feelings over a long-term period.

Another example would be where a child falls over and hurts themselves. In a bid to calm the child down, the parents will say something like, "Oh, you're okay. It doesn't hurt."

See how there's such a lack of validation for how the child feels in a statement such as that? The child is thinking, *I hurt. It hurts. I want someone to make it better.*

We know as adults that falling over and hurting yourself is not so much of a big deal. Heartbreak or breaking a bone is much more painful, which is why we can dismiss the child's pain as a minor injury, yet to a child, this could be the biggest pain they're faced in their entire lives, so relatively speaking, it really does hurt.

For a parent to dismiss and actively invalidate their child in such a way will only lead to the child doubting that how they feel at any given time is valid. They believe they feel feelings that they shouldn't be feeling, as this way of thinking is how many people are as adults.

By using feeling words in your conversations, you're helping the person you're speaking with to open up about how they feel. Not only are you helping and encouraging them to express themselves because you're saying, "It's okay to talk about this because it's how you're feeling," but you're also validating how they feel because, as with step two, you're repeating back their message.

Let's head back to our example. I've highlighted the feeling words that help to validate person A's message.

    **A:** "I'm so mad at you right now. You had no right to go and spend money on that account without asking me. I feel like you're betraying me or don't believe we're a team, and you can approach me to talk about big decisions like this."

    **B:** "But I wanted to surprise you. I know it's a lot of money, but I just wanted to make things nicer."

    **A:** "Can you see how betrayed this would make me feel? Imagine if I did the same to you. How would you feel?"

    **B:** "I understand you're angry and upset because it's a lot of money, but it was spent on both of us, more as a present for you that we can both enjoy. Can you tell me more about how you feel betrayed? If I spent the money on myself and not you, and didn't tell you, then I would understand the feelings of being betrayed. Explain a little more, just so I can understand where you're coming from properly."

Person B is repeating back the exact feeling words that person A used ("betrayed" and "angry"), which validates them and then adds their own words like "upset." While person A never used the word upset, person B uses it to show they're listening and understanding how person A feels.

Of course, there's always the chance that the person you're speaking with may correct you. They may say, "No, I'm not nervous, I'm excited," or "No, that's not right. I'm not confused. I'm curious," and that's perfectly fine to be corrected as well. This is all part of having a proper conversation that will lead to productive outcomes and more meaningful relationships.

The trick here is just to use feelings words, so here are some example sentences to give you an idea of how this is possible.

- I can see that you're angry.

- I'm so happy for you! You must feel amazing right now.
- I imagine that comment from your boss was pretty hurtful.
- God, that text must have made you feel so angry.
- That's really sad.
- Wow, you must have been so happy to hear that news.
- I'm so jealous. You must have found that meal so delicious.

Some powerful invalidating feeling responses that you should avoid include statements like:

- It will be fine in the end.
- It probably could be worse, though.
- Just smile, and it will be fine.
- It will probably work out.
- I don't know why you're sad. It's not that much of a big deal.

**Step Four - Discover the Context, Based on the Individual You're Talking To**

Step four is the most important in your validation process because it's all about connecting with the person you're speaking with on an individual level.

It can be difficult to validate someone who you don't know because you're validating on the whim of how they are acting at that moment in time. For example, someone might be having a really bad day and have reached their breaking point, resulting in them being loud and outspoken when they are just stressed and are usually quite quiet and reserved.

On the flip side, the more you know someone and the closer you get to them, the better you'll be able to validate them because you can base your responses on their behaviors that you instinctively know. There are two key areas you'll want to think about here:

- The person's history
- The person's biology

Don't worry, when I first started learning about this process, I read those and thought, *What? This is getting way too complicated now!* but it's not as complex as you may first believe.

A really simple example of this would be someone who was scratched, bitten, or chased by a dog, even just one time, but now they really don't like being around dogs and feel really uncomfortable with them. In a situation like this, you would validate how they're feeling by saying something like, "Given your history, I can see why you don't want to come into the garden when the dog's here."

Since you've validating how they feel, you can then move on by saying something like:

"Given that the experience was ten or so years ago, you could always try and let it go. Perhaps not now, but my dog is really friendly and won't bite. Here, do you want to try to meet him slowly?"

They might say yes or no, but it doesn't matter. The point is that you're communicating effectively, showing you understand the person's concerns, but you're still progressing productively.

Back to the example.

**A:** "I'm so mad at you right now. You had no right to go and spend money on that account without asking me. I feel like you're betraying me or don't believe we're a team, and you can approach me to talk about big decisions like this."

Taking everything we've known now, you can really start to change up your responses by removing the first comment and jumping straight into the validation part of the conversation.

**B:** "I understand you're angry and upset. It's a lot of money. I justified the spending in my mind because it was spent on something we can both enjoy."

**A:** "I can see that."

**B:** "I can see why you feel this way. I remember you saying your ex-boyfriend was very controlling when it came to how you spent money and that me doing this could be very triggering. I'm sorry. I wasn't thinking about that at the time, but I can see it now."

In this example, person A and person B could be husband and wife, and since they know each other very well, they will know each other's history and why they are responding in the way they are. Person A could be very worried about money because they've had poor money management experiences in the past, or in this case, had an ex-partner who was very controlling when it came to finances. This is why they are responding in such a negative way.

The context to which someone will respond or feel in a conversation and in any given situation will obviously vary dramatically depending on the individual you're talking to, which is why you can validate them far more effectively if you know someone. If you don't know someone, then you'll just need to do the best you can.

You can do this by asking questions. If someone seems apprehensive about going into a garden with your dog, you can ask, "Are you okay? Have you had a bad experience with dogs before?"

Some tips to remember when centering someone while validating them include:

- Remembering past experiences, memories, and topics the person you're speaking with has told you about their life and how it relates to the current situation.
- Remembering that everybody has prejudices, judgments, and preconceptions on ideas and topics that can fog what they actually believe.
- Past experiences will affect people's judgments in any given situation.
- Judgments can be overcome by acknowledging them, validating them, and then offering a different alternative way forward.
- If you don't know enough about someone to know their experiences, you can ask them for clarity, but always be careful and make sure you're not crossing any typical social boundaries. You don't want to go too personal with someone you don't know. You need to build trust first.

### Step Five - Create an Accepting Environment, Dismiss Judgments

When someone opens up about a situation in their life or shares their point of view, it's hard not to feel alone in how they feel. If you've ever been through a breakup and you've been telling your friends what happened, you could be so upset to the point where you're balling your eyes out, but your friends can still look fairly neutral. Even though they're supporting you, you're still going to feel as though you're the only one feeling the way you do, which is going to make you feel isolated and potentially judged.

Switch the roles around and imagine you're comforting a friend who's been through a breakup. As a listener who's supporting your friend, you want to create an environment that validates their grief and shows that you're not judging what's being said or how they're feeling.

This is known as "normalizing" and is the core element that goes into step five.

In this situation, you would say something like, "Of course you're going to feel upset. Anybody who goes through a breakup is going to feel exactly the same."

This normalizes how the person feels, but it's essential to make sure you're not following this through with something like, "You're going to be fine." It's statements like this that then invalidate how the person feels because it claims that how they are feeling now is not fine when in reality, it's perfectly acceptable. See the step above for a recap on that.

Sure, it's not nice to feel sad and upset, nor to be in a position where you're mourning a relationship, but it's perfectly normal to feel that way, and while we all know it gets better in time, that will happen when it's meant to. There's no need to rush this process. This is another example of how you can communicate in a non-accepting environment using just your words, even when you're attempting, in this case, to make someone feel better.

The best way to remember this step is by thinking about the fact you're validating someone through human experiences that everyone has. Simply put, if someone is crying because they are sad, you can validate their emotions by saying that's fine. Most people will cry when they're sad. Here are some other examples of ways you can implement step five in various situations.

- Don't worry; everyone gets stressed out and loses their cool from time to time.
- It's quite natural to be scared of bees. Lots of people are.
- Oh yes, loads of people love U2. They have millions of hits on YouTube.
- Lots of people enjoy Rick Astley.
- It's okay to feel sad. Anyone would if they were in your position.
- I would definitely be angry as well if I were in your shoes.

**Step Six - Show Genuine Care and Validation**

Finally, we get to step six, which is an interesting one. When I first came across the DBT process, I believed that all the steps up until here were about showing genuine care and validation for those we were listening to. What else could be said?

Well, the keyword here to remember is "genuine."

If you pretend to do any of the steps above but aren't really engaged in the conversations, and you're just following the steps because you feel like it's the right thing to do, this will come across as disingenuous, and that will cause problems in itself. Even if you know all the verbal and body language tips, you're human and can't fake them all, and it takes a lot of effort to know how to trick another person's human instinct, even if they can't put their finger on why they feel you're disingenuous.

Whenever you communicate with someone, and you're in the process of validating them, always make sure you're coming from a place where you're honest and truthful, but also authentic. If you don't really care about the person you're speaking with, that's also okay, but you need to make this known because if you just hang around and let the person open up, you're going to hurt them even more in the long term, but more on that in a moment.

Take Step Two, for example. You could so easily go into a conversation and just mimic everything they are saying to you in an emotionless way and believe that's normalizing and validating for them, but it's not. You'll create a power vacuum where the person will start striving for your validation, and this is the crux of most negative relationships.

When you don't genuinely validate your partner, but you're allowing them to open up, they end up trying harder to get your validation. Over many weeks, months, or even years, this can create such an unbalanced power dynamic. The needy partner is constantly harassing the partner for attention and acceptance or will shut down completely, perhaps opening up to other people outside the relationship, which risks a whole new set of problems.

For some people, they may get a kick out of someone constantly craving validation from them. It's a temporary fix that someone wants them and their connectivity so badly, but again, long term, there are no winners. Whenever you create a power imbalance in a relationship, you have a "winner" and a "loser," but the winner has to live with the loser, making both people losers. The real winning comes from genuinely caring about each other and wanting to support each other's growth, healing, and development.

Sure, there are going to be times when you have a stressful day, you're tired, you're sick, or you're dealing with a load of other things, and your partner wants to open up to you. This is the make-or-break moment where you either genuinely tell them that you can talk about it later, or you move forward disingenuously. It can be a hard decision to make, especially if you want to be there for your partner, but if you need a rest first, then say, "Can we talk about this a bit later? Perhaps this evening, where I'll be able to give you my full attention?"

This is much more respectful than just going forward with the conversation, going through the motions, not giving your partner your full attention, and then having to deal with all the negative consequences that come from that approach.

To summarize:
- Be genuine in your conversations and interactions
- If you're not interested, tell the other person respectfully
- If you want to support someone but need to take care of yourself first, let the other person know respectfully

And with that, we come to the end of this chapter.

Agreeably, that was a bit of a chunky chapter with a lot to take in, but that is the main component of proper listening, and mastering these steps will take you so incredibly far. As I said above, like any skill, it will take practice to wrap your head around, but you'll get there.

Just take the process one step at a time, taking small steps by applying a bit of the technique here and there, and you'll see such big progress as time moves on.

However, we're not done yet. There are still plenty of listening concepts we need to cover, like overcoming the common and not-so-common obstacles you may come across when conversing with different people and, most importantly, how to see if people are actually saying what they want to say and are telling you an honest message, which is exactly what I'm going to be talking about in the next chapter.

# Chapter Five - The Art of Mindreading Through Awareness

*"It is understanding that gives us an ability to have peace. When we understand the other fellow's viewpoint, and he understands ours, then we can sit down and work out our differences."* Harry S. Truman

There have been countless times in my life where I'm speaking to someone, and I'm hearing what they're saying. However, the message of the actual words they're using doesn't make any sense in the conversation context.

In the light of our global listening problem, it should go without saying that misunderstanding is a huge part of the problem. We live in a world of emojis, texting, and digital messaging, and we've become lazy with how we speak to one another.

I'm sure you've had a text, and you've been unsure of whether the person who sent it is happy, sad, sarcastic, passive-aggressive, or a mixture of all of them, which only leaves you scratching your head, unsure of the best way to respond. Whether you're talking online or face-to-face, a massive part of listening is having the skills to decipher what someone is saying and tunneling your way down to the true message they're trying to give you.

Let's start with the basics. Say someone comes up to you and says something along the lines of:

"I really loved our date tonight. It was perfect."

I know. It sounds simple, but there's very little room here to misinterpret what someone is saying. Every word here conveys positive emotions and makes you feel good about what's being said. Easy peasy. Try this one:

"My god. It was absolutely brutal!"

Again, going off words alone, you imagine something like a breakup or a fight has just happened, and someone's ended up getting really hurt. It was "brutal." This implies negative connotations, but, what happens if someone is actually talking about the horror movie they've just seen, and when they say it was brutal, this is actually a really positive thing?

As you can see, the first step in understanding what someone is saying is to understand the context of what they're talking about.

Take a moment to think about what someone is saying and the topic they are on, and it will give you a much greater understanding of what is being said. This goes back to what we were saying about being present in your conversations.

Even if you zone out for a sentence or two, you can completely lose what is going on. This is guaranteed to make the person feel as though they're not being listened to.

Of course, this is all basic stuff. Understand the context of a conversation, and you'll be able to understand the message that's being told to you. Still, humans and the way they converse with each other are typically more complicated than the simple examples above. The act of "mindreading" someone to find out the deeper messages also goes a lot deeper than this.

## Learning to Engage with Your Gut Instinct

I've teased this point throughout this book, and that's because gut instinct is such a massive part of human psychology. It can teach you so much as long as you're willing to tune in and listen to it. Your brain is an amazing thing in this way if you can put it to good use.

The chances are you've been with someone, and they've said that everything is fine, but you have that deep-rooted inner feeling that it's really not. Perhaps you've got home from work, and your partner is aggressively tidying the house.

"Hey, is everything okay? You seem stressed."

"Yup. Everything is fine."

"Are you sure? You can talk to me."

"Yup."

As your partner darts about the room cleaning up, they're not making eye contact with you, they're speaking in short, abrupt sentences, and not engaging with you in the way they normally do. Going off verbal cues alone, perhaps if these sentences were sent over text messages, you would feel you're right in thinking everything is okay, but in reality, this doesn't seem to be the case.

There are so many factors here that your body is picking up on and your mind is processing. Their lack of engagement, eye contact, and connectedness with you. Their tone of voice. Their bluntness. You're a human being who has been around for decades. You've got a memory bank full of experiences that gives your brain enough information to know when someone who says they're okay really isn't. Your natural, intuitive mind is programmed to recognize these signs, also known as your gut instinct.

The concept of "gut instinct" has been around for a very long time and is a very well-researched area of human behavior and psychology.

Psychologist Daniel Kahneman, who was awarded the Nobel Memorial Prize back in 2002, called this bodily function "System 1." Gary Klein, Ph.D., the author of *Sources of Power*, talks about how emergency services staff, such as firefighters and medical staff, rely on gut instincts to make literal life-or-death decisions, based on the information their brains can process in a matter of seconds, without having to step back and overthink and analyze a situation.

Malcolm Gladwell, the Canadian author, journalist, and public speaker, wrote *Blink*, a book where he talks about how our gut instinct is always active and always working. He uses examples like how our brain can press the brakes on our cars while traveling at high speeds on a highway when approaching stand-still traffic or grabbing your young child if they look like they're going to fall off the sofa.

You've probably experienced gut instinct in full effect yourself when you feel as though you're going to drop your phone, and you instantly do a little dance with your arms to stop it from falling to the ground. You didn't think about doing that action. Your brain just does it.

I could go on and on about all the advocates for the power of instinct, but I'm sure you get the idea. Bringing it back to conversations, your brain uses these gut instinct systems to judge the experience you're having when talking to someone else. If you get an impulse that someone is feeling a certain way or something isn't quite right, the chances are the impulse is correct.

But, not all the time. Yeah, I'm going to make things confusing now.

If human beings solely relied on gut instinct decisions, our relationships would fail. Our businesses would crumble because gut instinct is all about living in the moment and making decisions that benefit us now, rather than planning for the long term. The decision-making process doesn't take into account things like logic and analytical behaviors.

The takeaway here is to use your gut instinct in conversations as a first step to gauge how someone is feeling and what kind of message they're giving you. Noticing this impulse message, you can then bring in your analytical brain to make logical decisions on how you're going to proceed in your conversation.

Let's go back to the first example with your partner frantically cleaning up and see how it plays out.

"Hey, is everything okay? You seem stressed."

"Yup. Everything is fine."

Your gut instinct is triggered. You know from your partner's body language and tone of voice that your partner isn't fine. Your gut instinct has done part of its job. Now bring in your analytical thinking mind. What's the best way to respond? Here are some options.

- "Yeah, everything is fine? Are you sure about that?"
- "I can tell something is wrong. Talk to me."
- Just accept they are feeling okay and take what they're saying as the truth.
- "You don't seem okay. If you want to talk about it, I'm here."
- "Well, okay then."
- "Hey. Come here. Talk to me. What's up?"

There are multiple approaches here that could lead to positive and negative outcomes. You might say, "Well, okay then," and that just upsets your partner even more because they were unconsciously testing whether you cared enough to talk about what was wrong with them. The last option is probably the best for most situations because it shows you're stopping what you're doing and putting them at the center of the conversation. It shows you're ready to provide support.

However, the best approach for you will depend on the person you're speaking to and the relationship you have with them. In other words, use your logical, thinking mind to consider the person you're speaking with and their past behaviors, and how they are currently in effect.

If your partner is the type of person to say that everything is okay when it's not, and this has been a common past experience, then you know there's a high chance something is wrong, but perhaps they don't want to burden you with their problems. In a situation like this, using everything you know, you can validate how your partner feels, say it's okay to talk about their problems, and they can vent if they want to, and then the conversation can proceed.

Using psychology skills, you've just listened to the real meaning behind what someone is saying and moved the conversation on in the best possible way.

## Considerations and Thinks to Look Out For

While these figures can vary depending on individuals, cultures, and prior conditioning, most communication can be broken down into:

- 55% body language

- 38% tone of voice
- 7% verbal words and chosen language

When you really want to listen to what someone is saying, you're going to need to look at their body language first, then their tone of voice, then the words they're saying, and this way, you'll get a very accurate idea of the message someone is giving you. So, let's start at the top.

## How to Read Body Language

This section will be a bit of a crash course where I'll show you the basics of reading body language, which will be more than enough to help you read the vast majority of people you meet and interact with within your day-to-day life. However, bear in mind this isn't the complete guide. If you want to know more as you're developing your skills, there are plenty of books and courses out there dedicated to the art of body language and explaining the nuances of this skill.

### *Start with the eyes*

Many believe the eyes are the gateway to the soul, which is true when it comes to the truth of a conversation. If someone has a real lack of eye contact, it means they could be trying to avoid the truth and can't look you in the eyes because they know what they're saying isn't true, or they're ashamed of something. They could also be nervous or intimidated, which makes them not want to make eye contact.

Think about children who will instinctively look down at the ground when they're embarrassed or are getting told off after they've been caught doing something red-handed. The same applies to adults. Likewise, however, if someone is making too much eye contact, this could be a sign that they're forcing eye contact, or it could mean anger and hate. Think about times you've been so angry with someone, and you're just trying to stare them down.

Alternatively, there are positive emotions linked with intense eye contact, such as affection, longing, flirting, interest, and desire. This means you need to judge the context of the conversation (as we discussed earlier) since this will also affect the message you're receiving.

Ideally, in any situation, you want a balanced amount of eye contact that lasts a few seconds, then you can look away, perhaps to think, and then go back to making eye contact. This indicates an honest and forthcoming person.

### *Recognize posture*

Someone's posture is a massive indication of how they're feeling and what message they are sending. If someone is sitting or standing with a straight, upright back, with their head held high, this means they are comfortable and confident in the situation, but it can also portray feelings of authority and power. Either way, a confident posture indicates they are engaged in the conversation.

On the other hand, someone who is depressed, sad, or intimidated will shrink away. On a physical level, this is someone's physical attempt to make themselves smaller as though hiding from the interaction and making themselves less noticeable. Hunched or raised shoulders also indicate stress.

If someone has their arms and hands open with their chest exposed, this is a very vulnerable position to be in and usually means they trust you. Any kind of body language that exposes the chest means this because, in the wild and before civilized times, having an exposed chest meant something would be able to hurt you quite easily.

On the flip side, if someone is closed off, has their arms crossed in front of their chest, or covers parts of themselves more than usual, this is a sign they are uncomfortable, anxious, or defensive.

### *Handshakes or hugs*

Whenever someone shakes your hand, the level of grip you feel indicates how the other person is feeling within the situation. A firm or intensely firm handshake is a sign of confidence and power, but a weak handshake is a sign of nervousness and shyness. An overly strong handshake can be taken as a sign of aggression.

### *Watch their smile*

It's very easy for someone to fake a smile to hide when they're feeling negative or trying to hide their emotions. We all know the classic fake smile actors do in movies when they've gone through a breakup or lost their job, and they're trying to let everyone know they're feeling okay.

However, while smiles can be faked, you can easily see the giveaways if you're paying attention. If someone is giving you a real, genuine smile, you will see a crinkle appear in the corner of both of their eyes, creating what is typically referred to as "crow's feet." See this pattern during a smile, and you know the person is genuinely comfortable and happy in this situation.

### *Note physical proximity*

While a traditional body language trait, it will be interesting to see what happens now we're hopefully coming to the end of the COVID-19 pandemic. With social distancing happening for over a year now, many people will find it strange to be standing close to others, especially if they're strangers or people at work.

That being said, physical proximity is a massive part of non-verbal communication. Simply put, if someone is standing or sitting close to you, this means they're comfortable in your personal space and enjoy having you close. If someone is standing a distance apart from you, then they are keeping a distance between you to feel safe.

### *A note on the tone of voice and inflection*

A very important part of reading someone, the tone of voice and inflection someone is using makes up, on average, around 38% of their total communication, which shows it's such a huge consideration to think about. Fortunately, it's relatively easy to judge the tone of voice of someone. You just need to keep an ear open for the volume they're talking at and the kind of tone they have.

This sounds like simple stuff. If someone is shouting at you and sounds irritated, the chances are that they're angry and irritated. You might be reading this like, *Well, dur. Obviously!* but there's a fair few people in my own life that don't seem to grasp this simple concept.

A woman I used to work with used to never get a hint that she talked way too much. During lunch breaks, we'd go into the city to get something to eat, and she would talk about everything that's going on in her life. It was fine. It wasn't horrible or anything like that, but everyone would let her get on with it. But as time went on, people would reply with less enthusiasm and would make it very clear with their tones of voice that they were bored.

"Yes, Hannah. Cool." (Read in the most boring voice you can muster.) But still, she never got the hint because she was never listening to what others had to say. My mother was the same. She would get so stuck trying to prove her point when arguing with my father that she never seemed to notice his tone of voice change from diplomatic to annoyed.

In short, keep an ear open for the tone of voice someone is using since it will tell you so much.

And finally, I want to talk about inflection. Inflection is the term given to emphasis placed on certain words that completely change the meaning of the sentence. Take a look at the following sentences and see if you can figure out the meanings behind them.

| Statement |
| --- |
| "I didn't tell him you took the last piece of cake." |

Any ideas? The words are the same, but how the sentence is said completely redefines the message behind it.

| Statement | Meaning |
| --- | --- |
| "I didn't tell him you took the last piece of cake." | "I told someone, but not him, that you took the piece of cake." |
| "I didn't tell him you took the last piece of cake." | "I told him you took something else instead of the piece of cake." |
| "I didn't tell him you took the last piece of cake." | "I didn't tell him you took the piece of cake." |
| "I didn't tell him you took the last piece of cake." | "I'm lying that I didn't tell him you took the piece of cake." |

It's essential for effective communication that you take the time to listen to the nuances of how things are said to you because it can mean so much.

A lot of the skill for doing this ties back in with what we said earlier about going with your gut instinct because it's this part of you that will notice it first. If you feel the impulse of your gut, take a note of what's been said and how it makes you feel, then replay what's been said to get to the true meaning.

## Summary on Body Language

Reading all of these cues can take skill and practice, but it's so interesting once you start noticing the traits because the vast majority of people will follow these rules unconsciously and without thinking. Speaking unconsciously without any control or mindfulness is basically a habit for most people, meaning it's a great way to read the situation and what people say to you.

Combining everything you've learned already, if someone is really personal and open, but they're keeping their distance from you and have their arms crossed, while their words say they're comfortable, their body language suggests otherwise.

Using this information, you can then decide whether the person is being genuine to you or identify what their motives could be.

## How to Tell When Someone is Lying

There's a big difference between someone saying they're okay when they're not because they don't want to burden you with their troubles or don't have the energy to go into what they're going through—and someone flat-out, maliciously lying to you, or perhaps even gaslighting you.

The truth is that everybody lies. In an interview with British QC, Jordan Peterson stated that "Everybody lies, but the trick is to be incredibly careful about how you do it, to whom, and your motives behind masking the truth."

Put it this way. If you're lying about stealing something from someone and you're claiming someone else did it, even though it was you, that makes you a fairly malicious person. However, if you're lying to someone because you're taking them to their surprise birthday party, this is one of the more acceptable lies.

That being said, modern-day humans seem to lie far more often than you may believe.

According to 2017 statistics, 90% of children will have grasped the concept of lying by the age of four, and some estimates suggest that around 60% of adults can't talk for more than ten minutes without lying or distorting the truth more than once. The average was lying three times within that time frame.

Here are some other "fun" statistics:

- 12% of adults lie often
- 13% of patients will lie to their doctors
- 30% of adults lie about their diet and exercise habits
- Women lie three times a day to their partners, coworkers, and bosses
- Men tell six lies a day to the same people
- Lying is more common in phone calls than face-to-face conversation
- 10% of lies are exaggerations
- 60% are blatant deceptions of the truth

As you can see, averaging speaking, lying is quite commonplace (unless people lied in the surveys!), and having the ability to see through these lies to get the truth out of people, or being able to confirm when someone is directly telling you the truth, can be an incredibly useful skill to have.

Whether you lie (even if it's now and then) or your coworkers and partners are lying to you, it's something you need to be aware of. Truth and honesty are the best foundations possible for any kind of relationship. These statistics on how often people lie clearly indicate why so many modern relationships fail.

Estimates suggest over 50% of relationships will fail. The main reasons why from couples surveyed?? This is the order from Darcy Sterling, Ph.D. writing for *Psychology Today*:

- Trust issues
- Communication issues
- Different life priorities
- Different values
- And so on

Notice how the two first items she lists are trust issues and communication issues? If you can sort out the quality of communication in your relationship and base your connection on trust and honesty, your relationships will improve infinitely.

So, how do you do it? How do you figure out when someone is lying to you? The best way is to keep an eye open for the signs.

## The Signs of Lying

These are signs of lying inspired from Pamela Meyer's *Liespotting* book, as well as her sixteen-million-view TED Talk (which is available on YouTube by searching her name), and are the key signs you'll want to look out for in your conversations.

### *Inconsistency in the message*

The majority of people will lie off the cuff because they're hiding a certain fact, don't want to own up to something, or don't want to admit the truth, and are making up a story to cover themselves and something they've done.

However, people put way less thought into these lies than you would first believe, meaning it's very easy to catch people out when you ask them to repeat the details.

This is known as "'getting your story straight."

If you ask someone who's telling the truth to repeat their story, the details will always remain the same. Stories that are actually lies tend to change every retelling, which is why this is deemed the most consistent way to catch someone lying to you. Here's how you can implement this technique to find out.

> "And then the dog ran out into the road and was nearly hit by this truck. It was so scary!"

> "The dog nearly got hit? Wow. How fast was the motorbike going?"

> "Pretty fast."

In this example, you weren't corrected by intentionally repeating with an incorrect detail, which can be seen as a tell-tale sign the person is lying. Sometimes, you won't notice someone is lying because they'll tell you a story, and you won't recognize the change in details until you hear it again, which could be weeks or months later. Again, if your gut instinct picks up on something, then the chances are you've just cottoned onto a lie.

### Body language and expressions

We spoke a lot about body language in the last section, so I'll make this quick. There are some tell-tale expressions and physical signs someone is lying, and if you spot them, then it may be time to pay closer attention to what is being said so you're able to find out the truth.

Some of these psychological signs that typically happen unconsciously include things like:

- Fake smiles
- Rapid blinking
- Flaring nostrils
- Excessive hand movements. A study back in 2015 carried out by the University of Michigan found that people who lie use their hands far more in conversation than those who tell the truth.
- Fidgeting or Itching. If someone is lying, they will typically be restless, pick at their nails, or play with their hair, and try to fidget around as though trying to get comfortable.
- A lack of eye contact. People who are lying tend to avoid making eye contact with you.
- Lip movements. If someone is rolling their lips or can't keep them still, this can be a sign they are lying to you. It's as though the body is unconsciously trying to hold back the truth.

The important thing to remember here is that these aren't confirmations that someone is lying, but more subconscious indications that they could be. If you notice them, focus harder on what is being said to make your own decision, mixing this sign with the others on this list.

### Stalling in conversation

If you're calling someone up on a lie or asking for more detail on a story, you may notice a pause in the conversation that could be the other person stalling for time as they think of an answer, especially if they've been asked a very unexpected question.

**A:** "Yeah, I can't believe how amazing it was that I bumped into Michael Jackson in New York. I was so starstruck!"

**B:** "Sounds amazing. What's he like in person?"

**A:** "Just like you would expect. Quiet. A bit reserved. I can't believe nobody else around us noticed him."

**B:** "Whereabouts did you see him?"

**A:** "Oh, what? Where did I see him? Like where in New York?"

**B:** "Yeah."

**A:** "Oh, just in Times Square. Not sure where exactly. Just out on the street."

Again, repeating the question is not a confirmation that someone is lying, but if this sign appears alongside other points we've spoken about, and it happens frequently, then the chances are that you could be being fed lies.

### A suddenness to stop or move on the conversation

Another important sign you should look out for is someone telling you something and then wanting to drastically change the conversation. If someone is abruptly hurrying a conversation onto a new subject out of the blue, is trying to take the focus off of themselves, and ultimately doesn't want to hang around on the point they've just made, then it could have been a lie.

> **A:** "Yeah, I can't believe I won $10 on a scratch-off. It's the first time I've won anything."
>
> **B:** "I won $100 on a scratch-off once."
>
> **A:** "Oh, cool. What did you spend it on?"
>
> **B:** "Oh. Not much. Which card did you buy?"
>
> **A:** "Just the $2 one. Come on, $100? You must have been so happy."
>
> **B:** "Yeah. Wasn't bad. Hey, listen. What are you doing for the rest of the day?"
>
> **A:** "Probably going to treat myself to a nice lunch. What about you?"

And so on. You can imagine the readiness to move on in conversation if A was lying about their win because they had nothing really to add to the conversation, nor was being very happy for B.

### *The choice of language*

While not a tell-tale way to prove someone is lying, the language someone chooses to use can be another indication when paired with the other points in this section. If someone has to remind you or convince you they're not lying, they will use language to help their cause. You may hear statements like:

- Honestly, it did happen.
- I swear on so-and-so's life.
- I swear on the Bible that...
- If I'm being completely honest...

And so on. Other signs here can include someone giving you way too much detail in a story. It's as though they're trying to make the story as believable as possible or going back on what they've already said to change the details they've told you in an attempt to make it more realistic.

As with most of these points, don't notice just one and convince yourself the person is lying. Instead, if you notice a sign, look for the other signs and then piece what they are saying together. If it happens frequently and lots of signs are met, then the person could be lying.

Identifying a lie allows you to choose how you proceed. You can call them up on it, let it slide, or be extra mindful of seeing if they lie anymore. Whatever approach you take is up to you and depends on what you want out of the relationship you're referring to.

## Understanding the Power of Motives

Every human being in the world is motivated by something. Every single decision you make is a motivation in action, whether you're aware that you're doing it or not. On a basic level, you eat because you're motivated by hunger, and drink because you're motivated by thirst. Your body motivates you to do these things because otherwise, well, you'll die.

Things can get a little more complicated when it comes to your goals, relationships, and day-to-day habits. You might be dieting, motivated by an Instagram post you saw, or a pair of jeans you want to fit into by the time summer comes around. But you might eat a huge bit of cake because you're motivated to feel better after a bad day. Our motivations overlap all the time. Our priorities are constantly changing depending on what's happening in our lives.

When it comes to conversations, it's important to think about what people are motivated by when they're talking to you, so you're able to find out the truth of what they're saying and whether there are any hidden agendas you need to be aware of.

You can get all this from listening and taking time to understand what's being said to you, but mindfully highlighting someone's motive can really open up the truth about the situation you're in. Take this conversation as an example.

**A:** "Hey. Do you mind going to get me a coffee?"

**B:** "Er, sure. I'll do it after I've booked the meeting room. Just waiting for the computer."

**A:** "Ah, I would really appreciate having one now. I need to go to see a client soon."

**B:** "Okay. Be right back."

What's happening here? You may think it's a conversation happening between a businessman and their assistant, and he needs his coffee before his meeting. If this is the case, then he may really need some help because he's so busy.

However, depending on the context of the situation, it could be two employees talking, and both want to book the meeting room, and person A is trying to get person B to get a coffee, so he gets the first pick of the available meeting room slots.

This kind of thing is what we call a "hidden agenda," and to be the best listener possible, you need to know how you can identify when someone is genuine with you and when someone is trying to get something out of you (or someone else you're close to) without you realizing.

Fortunately, the psychology of human behavior and communication research has the answers to help you dive deeper and highlight the truth in what someone is up to and is trying to manipulate you with their own secret missions.

### The conversation is always about them

If someone is trying to manipulate you, then the chances are they will always have the subject of conversation revolve around them. However, while in the conversation, this can be very difficult to notice. This is why you must be able to take a step back and see the reality of a situation.

Again, a lot of this is going to rely on your gut instinct.

This is typical behavior from people with hidden agendas since they are typically narcissistic people who are out to get what they want. This can't happen if people aren't talking about them and their wants or desires. If there's an impatience around someone and they want to get back to talking about them, then make sure you pay special attention to this conversation trend.

### You are continually talking about a certain subject

Hand in hand with the consideration above, if someone has a hidden agenda, you may not notice at first. Still, if the person you're speaking with keeps coming back to the same subject over and over again, then this can be a clear sign that they haven't yet received the outcome they want and are once again trying to force it.

### *The standard lack of body language*

Just like when people are lying to you, if someone is trying to force a narrative or has a secret agenda they're trying to push through, the body physically matches this deception with the classic tell-tale signs like a lack of eye contact or stiffness of the body.

If someone is a true narcissist, they may have picked up on this trait and learned how to force body language to make themselves more believable. However, since you also know the tricks of the trade, you'll easily be able to tell the difference between someone genuinely being themselves and someone who's being fake.

### *They explore different approaches with the same goal*

Another approach that couples with the signs I've mentioned above is someone trying to force the same outcome, but they're using different conversational approaches, usually within the same conversation. While they may not directly be suggesting something, they are trying to get the outcome they want through force.

For example, let's say someone is manipulating their group of friends to go to a Chinese-styled takeaway while everyone is deciding where to go out for food. Perhaps a relatively harmless example, but the same principles can apply in any conversation.

They may say things like:

- Why don't we go to Golden House?
- Last time we went to Golden House, you said you really liked it.
- It's a really nice atmosphere there.
- Didn't you go there for a birthday a few years ago? What did you think?
- Well, if you guys can't decide, we should just go to Golden House.
- You don't want to walk far? It's only two blocks away.

### *They show manipulative tendencies*

This point may seem a little obvious, but if you're not on the lookout for it nor aware that someone has manipulative tendencies, then it's easy to forget yourself and just take what they're saying at face value.

If someone has proven to be a manipulative person in the past, whether they have acted that way directly to you, or you know they have acted that way to other people, always take what they're saying with a pinch of salt and keep your eyes open for hidden agendas.

### *You feel used*

Again, this is your gut instinct being the very powerful force of nature that it is. If you've just finished interacting with someone and you *feel,* deep down, like you're being used and manipulated, then take a step back and evaluate the situation. Why do you feel that way? What was it that the person you said or did that made you feel used?

Perhaps the answer is obvious, or maybe you can't put your finger on it. The most important thing is that you become aware of the feeling itself and apply caution when heading into any future interactions with that person.

## How to Deal With Gaslighting

The final point I want to discuss within this chapter is the act of gaslighting.

Gaslighting has been a massive talking point over the last few years, a term made popular back in 1944 in the movie *Gaslight*. *Gaslight* was a movie about a young couple where the man manipulated his wife into thinking she was crazy by distorting her reality. Over time, this made her doubt whether she was sane, ultimately not being able to trust herself and putting all her will and control into the hands of her husband, who basically dictated her life.

The movie got the name from the fact he would dim the gaslight lamps in the room whenever she was out. Whenever she returned to the room, she would question that the room became darker, to which he would deny that ever happened. When this happens all the time, the wife began to doubt her thoughts, leading to her thinking she was crazy.

This kind of manipulation and hidden agenda happens so often in modern-day society that it's actually crazy. There are stories of it happening in the media all the time, especially with the rise of movements like #MeToo. Domestic abuse cases at home are still so high—about 20% of children in UK households live with some degree of domestic violence—there's no doubt that gaslighting is happening since it's a core part of victim control.

So, what can you do about it, and how can you use listening to know whether you're being gaslighted? First, you need to start listening to what's being said to you.

Have you ever shared a point of view, only for it to be shot down?

In a bleak example, let's say you saw a message from a coworker pop up on your partner's phone.

You only catch the preview, but it looks pretty flirty. You're a bit concerned and bring it up to your partner, who dismisses you and says the text doesn't exist. You're sure it did. After all, you saw it with your own eyes, but your partner saying it doesn't make you doubt that you ever saw it all. Thus, you've been gaslit and made to doubt yourself and your sanity. This is a dangerous path to be on.

Some really easy statements to look out for that can gaslight you include lines like:
- It was only a joke. Don't be so sensitive.
- You're crazy. That's not how things happened at all.
- Do you really think you know what you're talking about?
- You're definitely imagining that.

Now, just because you may have heard these statements before, that doesn't mean you're definitely being gaslighted.

Let's say your partner says that they are happy to go and visit your parents over the weekend in two weeks. Then the two weeks come around, and they say something like:

"No, you definitely said we're visiting your parents next week, not this week. I have a lot of work I have to do this weekend and can't go."

Maybe gaslighting, but it could be an honest mistake from either side. Perhaps you did say three weeks instead of two, or perhaps your partner misheard you (this is why it's so important to practice effective communication in your relationships because then situations like this will never happen!), and that's fine.

However, if you're experiencing situations like this repeatedly, then gaslighting is certainly something you're going to want to be aware of and on the lookout for. Some of the key ways you can be gaslighted include techniques like:

| **Countering You** | If something happens, the gaslighter may switch around the event, so you are in the wrong, even if you're not. They may fabricate new details of the event or deny certain things have happened. |
|---|---|
| **Trivializing What You Say** | Whatever feelings you share, they invalidate quickly. They say that how you feel and your emotions don't matter. They may also suggest that you're overreacting. |
| **Withholding Information** | Whenever you try to discuss a situation, they dismiss your arguments. They may claim that you're trying to confuse them with what you're saying. |
| **Forgetting or Denying Statements and Events** | If you share details of an event, they may completely forget or deny that certain things have or haven't happened to prove their point. |
| **Discrediting Your Thoughts** | Will state that you're unable to recall details properly will give examples of the past (true or not) where you proved what you say can't be trusted, thus invalidating what you're saying now. |
| **Diverting Your Conversations** | If you bring a conversation up and it's quickly dismissed as though it's not important, and the conversation is forced to be moved on without you being listened to. |

If you're noticing traits like these on a regular and consistent basis, then it's time to start thinking about what you can do to stop yourself from being gaslighted.

Remember, you may be gaslighted by your partner, coworkers, boss, customers, and so on. It isn't just restricted to your personal life.

# The Five Steps to Identifying and Dealing with Gaslighting

### Step One - Identify the Gaslighting

We've covered this in the previous section, so I'll be quick. Suppose you notice any of the signs we spoke about above. In that case, you feel regularly invalidated in your conversations, you doubt yourself, constantly ask yourself whether you're too much of a sensitive person, frequently apologize for your actions or sharing your thoughts, and generally feel unhappy when around a certain person, then you could be being gaslighted.

### Step Two - Step Back

As you can tell from Step One, if you're being gaslighted, then there will be many confusing and contrasting emotions spinning around in your head. Although you've practiced emotional intelligence to deal with this, it can be a good idea to step back and take a breather from the situation.

It's always important to remain calm in any given situation. Otherwise, you're not going to have the best outcomes when you address the issues. Practice taking a time out, whether that means going for a walk, meditating, reading, or however you're able to take a break.

### Step Three - Build Your Case

Next, you need evidence to secure your side of the story. You may want to start doing things like screenshotting emails and text messages, noting the times and dates of conversations you're having, and even writing down quotes from conversations.

With this solid proof that you're recording after a conversation has taken place, then you know your version of events is real. If the person you're involved with denies that something happened, then you know with absolute certainty that you're being gaslighted.

### Step Four - Address the Behavior

Once you're certain you're being gaslighted, it's time to speak up. In the best-case scenario, the person you address will realize what they're doing and vow to be better. In which case, you can watch the journey and move forward. If the behavior comes back, you'll need to start again.

However, if you're dealing with a true narcissist, then they may agree to defuse the situation, or they may dismiss what you're saying completely. For example, a coworker may say something like, "You've done no work this week and definitely aren't pulling your weight."

You can then address the behavior by saying, "That isn't true. I've completed these tasks for the week. Would you like to go through them with me now?" This is where your evidence comes in. Remember, when addressing this behavior, remain calm, neutral, and polite.

### Step Five - Moving Forward

Depending on the last few steps' outcomes, you've got some decisions to make on how you want to move forward. If the person denies that anything wrong is happening, it could be time to get other people involved. If they are your partner, you may want to go to counseling.

If they don't want help or still deny anything is wrong, then you may want to start thinking about leaving the relationship and moving on. This can be a hard decision to make, but if you're unhappy with your life, then going into a new chapter is certainly going to be better for you in the long run.

The most important thing to remember throughout this process is to focus on yourself and your own self-care. It's important to keep an eye on how you're looking after yourself, your habits, and your levels of peace. This could sound a little spiritual, but you'll be amazed at how much more capable you'll be at dealing with the situation when you're at peak physical and mental health.

As you can see, there's a lot of power that comes with listening, especially when it comes to more complicated relationships like one when someone in your life is gaslighting you. If you're worried about being gaslighted and you want more information, then there's a ton of advice out there that can help you with your own personal journey. Remember, you never have to go through that process alone.

There are always support networks out there for you to help you move away from toxic relationships and to deal with the effects of gaslighting.

Phew. That was a chunky chapter, but one that's so important when you're trying to understand other people and use your listening skills to develop the best, most satisfying relationship possible with the right people in your life.

As we come to the end of this book, we have but two chapters to go. Next, we'll discuss some of the potential problems you may encounter while listening to other people, basically highlighting things to look out for to make your skills even better. Then we'll talk about how you can do everything you've learned to become the best conversationalist you can be.

Let's go!

# Chapter Six - Addressing the Obstacles of Listening

*"No one is as deaf as the man who will not listen."* Proverb

This chapter is going to be short and sweet. We've spoken a lot about some of the potential problems you'll encounter when trying to listen to someone else. As a quick recap, these tips included things like:

- Minimizing distractions
- Removing conversational expectations
- Not judging the other person
- Acknowledging your biases towards people or conversation subjects

And so on. Check back to chapter three if you need to refresh your memory. However, these aren't the only barriers you may come across, so this is what we're going to dive into here in a quick-fire guide that will clear up any loose ends that are left to clear up.

### Avoid Having Multiple Conversations at Once

Perhaps a no-brainer to some, but it's easy to get caught into the trap of having multiple conversations at once, whether that means literally having conversations with the people around you or listening to talks on the TV or radio.

I remember working in my last firm and having the annual Christmas meal. Three conversations were going on around me: one on each side of me and the other on the opposite side of the table. It was so hard to focus or give my attention to any of them.

Instead, pick a conversation and stick to it, politely declining other conversational opportunities until you're ready to move on.

### Not Making Judgments Based on Physical Appearance

Just because you don't find the person you're speaking with physically attractive or sexy doesn't mean you can't listen to what they have to say.

Likewise, if you find the person attractive, you may be distracted by their looks and not listening to what they say. Pay attention to your thoughts, acknowledge your wandering mind, and gently bring your focus back to the conversation at hand. This is another reason why it pays to be mindful.

### Not Being Interested

Granted, you're not going to find every single conversation you have the most exciting conversation in the world, and there are topics you simply won't be interested in.

However, instead of just letting the other person talk and you end up drifting away, you can literally just say, "I'm not interested in this kind of conversation," or "I'm just not as passionate about this subject as you." Here's an example where you won't come across as being rude nor risk offending the person you're talking to. It depends on how much confidence you can say it with.

**A:** "So I got these new fish, and one is a Korean Koi, and I have to keep the outdoor pond heated to 60 degrees, but then I got this isolation tube to put in the end to stop it losing temperature as it goes through the filter."

**B:** "Ah, I'm sorry. I'm naive about this kind of thing. I'm glad you're so passionate about it, though. It's nice to see that people are still passionate about things these days."

**A:** "Oh yes. I'm very passionate. I love my fish."

**B:** "That's really nice. I can see it in your eyes you mean it as well. Anyway, I must bounce. My lunch break is over. Catch up soon?"

As long as you're saying these statements in a calm, polite, and friendly way, there shouldn't be a problem. I know we spoke about not interrupting someone earlier, and we just did in this situation, but you're not doing it in a rude way where you're trying to force your point of view down someone's throat.

Instead, you're not interested in the conversation, and you're still able to break free from it in a way that isn't offensive. If you remain in the conversation and get bored, you're much more likely to leave in an abusive way. Of course, you'll have emotional intelligence training to stop that from happening, but some people can really test you from time to time.

### Not Empathizing with the Other Person

We've touched on this briefly, but empathizing with someone is not the same as sympathizing with them. To have sympathy is to pity the person you're speaking with for their situation, but to have empathy is to proactively put yourself in their shoes to feel and understand how they're feeling.

Both ways of connecting to the other person will help you listen in different ways because you'll be able to feel the emotions of the speaker, therefore having more insight into the message behind what they're saying. For example:

**A:** "I just don't know what to do with my relationship. I love him a lot, but there's so many little things I can't stand about him. I don't know if I'm just kidding myself."

**B:** "I get that it's hard when you have so many feelings. How long have you been together?"

**A:** "About six years now."

**B:** "That's a long time with someone. It's no wonder it's hard. Anybody would feel the same. Have you spoken to him about how you feel?"

Notice in this example how there are plenty of opportunities to put yourself in the shoes of person A. You can imagine how hard it can be to be in a relationship for so long but not be happy. Become the person you're speaking with and really try to show as much compassion as you can.

For clarity, it would be incredibly unempathetic and soulless to say things like:

- Just dump him and move.
- Oh, just be grateful you're in a relationship
- There are plenty more fish in the sea
- Just fight it out with him

### Being Affected by Physical or Mental Health

If you're not feeling well, you're sick, hungry, thirsty, tired, exhausted, or mentally drained, then these are all reasons why you may not be capable of listening to someone properly. It's okay to feel like this, and if you feel like it's affecting your ability to listen, then you can politely say to the person talking that you're not feeling as though you're giving them the attention they deserve, and you would be happy to carry on this conversation at a later date.

And there we have it, some of the key barriers you'll come up against in your journey to becoming a better listener. By combining everything from all the chapters in this book, you'll be able to rapidly become an incredible listener who can take on board new ideas, connect and empathize with other people, and have all the required foundations for building the most meaningful relationships with the people in your life.

Of course, there is one more stop on your journey, which is to now, after listening to the other person talk, to respond in a productive and meaningful way. Our last chapter is all about continuing the conversation.

*Communication Skills Training Series*

# Chapter Seven - Continuing the Conversation

*"Conversation should touch everything, but should concentrate itself on nothing."* Oscar Wilde

First, you may be thinking, *Hey, we already covered validation, so surely that's what I'll say next and how I respond?* and you'd be right. However, this chapter is all about sharing a few points to help you focus on the conversation at hand and give you a solid foundation to generate a response to anything you've been told that will help you effectively convey your ideas, thoughts, feelings, and emotions.

There's no time to mess around now!

## How to Respond in a Conversation

Let's start with an example. Your boss comes into your office, and he's not happy. He's stressed. The project you and the team are working on doesn't look like it's going to be done by the deadline, and the client is not going to be happy. He comes over to you to try and get things moving and says something along the lines of:

"Right, this isn't looking good. The deadline for the project is on Friday, and we're nowhere close. We're over budget and so behind. What can we do?"

How do you respond?

Taking from everything we've learned, you'll go through the following process.

First, don't take what is being said personally. Your boss is talking to you but not blaming you for the problem, even if they say something that makes it feel that way. If you do feel that way, notice the emotion and don't take it personally.

Using empathy, put yourself in your boss's shoes and notice that they are probably taking heat from both the customer and their bosses, and now they're trying to get the situation resolved. So, your boss is stressed, under pressure, and looking for answers. Let's start with validating their feelings with something like:

Understandably, everyone is stressed. I dread to think how your bosses are coming down on you. I agree. Let's get this sorted. We start by tidying up the loose ends and listing out everything that needs to be done. Then we can delegate. Get half the team on the big projects, get the other half on clearing the small tasks, and then we can all bundle in at the end. Have you got an overtime budget, just in case?"

Amazing answer.

You started by validating your boss and connecting with them, normalizing how they feel by saying that anybody would understandably feel stressed in their position. You made your boss feel understood. Because you identified that your boss is looking for answers, you jumped straight into providing an actionable answer concisely and ended with a question, allowing them to give their input and progress the conversation forward productively.

What's more, you used your emotional intelligence to not minimize your boss's stress or anxiety, didn't take their comments personally, and didn't let emotion dictate your response. You could so easily have gotten angry or defensive with your boss coming to you but instead chose to stay neutral and diplomatic.

See the idea? Let's try another one.

You're having dinner with your partner, and the dreaded "Hey, can we talk about something?" comes up. I'll give you a rundown of the conversation, see what you would change and improve, and then we can go through it together. We'll use Mark and Sarah as an example.

**Mark:** "Hey, can we talk about something?"

**Sarah:** "Sure, what's up?"

**Mark:** "I've been thinking about how intimate we are, or in my eyes, how much we lack it. I want to be closer with you."

**Sarah:** "You want more sex?"

**Mark:** "Yeah. A bit more often, at least. I feel really disconnected from you."

**Sarah:** "I just don't want to. I get so stressed at work, and I'm so tired when I get home. I just don't have it in me. We've spoken about this before."

**Mark:** "Yup. I know."

**Sarah:** "So you're going to start sulking with me again?"

**Mark:** "Nope. You said you don't want to. I hear you."

**Sarah:** "No. I didn't mean that. I meant—"

**Mark:** "It's fine. It's whatever."

**Sarah:** "Can we talk about this?"

**Mark:** "Nope. You made yourself perfectly clear."

*Mark gets up and walks off.

Wow. Well, it feels like that conversation went well, yet it's almost certain we've all had a conversation like this, perhaps about a different subject, but along the same lines. There are so many issues with this conversation, and taking on board everything you've learned, you should be able to highlight the problems.

We'll go into a reformed example after this breakdown of the conversation.

| | |
|---|---|
| **Mark:** "Hey, can we talk about something?" | A suitable introduction to a conversation. Not the best, but fairly casual. |
| **Sarah:** "Sure, what's up?" | Fine response, but since they were eating dinner, Sarah could put her knife and fork down, turn off any background music, show that she is preparing for the conversation, minimize all distractions, and give Mark her full attention. |
| **Mark:** "I've been thinking about how intimate we are, or in my eyes, how much we lack it. I want to be closer with you." | Not a very concise way of conveying his point, and it would perhaps be better if he had taken the time to think about his thoughts to present them more comprehensively. |

## Communication Skills Training Series

| | |
|---|---|
| **Sarah:** "You want more sex?" | No validation of Mark's feelings whatsoever. This is a very defensive response that Sarah is saying she can't be bothered to have the conversation. She just makes it seem like Mark is only interested in having sex, not addressing his point's emotional side. It's a very generic and hurtful response. |
| **Mark:** "Yeah. A bit more often, at least. I feel really disconnected from you." | Mark does well in not taking the blunt response personally and tries to portray the emotional side of how he feels, although his points could be made, again, more comprehensively. |
| **Sarah:** "I just don't want to. I get so stressed at work, and I'm so tired when I get home. I just don't have it in me. We've spoken about this before." | Sarah, again, doesn't validate anything Mark says and instead gives a sharp reply that offers no productive progress. She then tries to cut the conversation short by saying this talk has already been spoken about before, basically saying that she hasn't changed her point of view, doesn't want to revisit the subject, and won't change how she feels. |
| **Mark:** "Yup. I know." | Mark, feeling hurt by the conversation's bluntness, the lack of validation, and the unwillingness to communicate, shuts down and puts up his defensive barriers. |
| **Sarah:** "So you're going to start sulking with me again?" | Another hurtful comment. You can see where Sarah is coming from, especially if she is bored of the conversation and it has happened before, but there is zero empathy coming from her. Mark's feelings are only negatively validated. |
| **Mark:** "Nope. You said you don't want to. I hear you." | Mark is clearly done, and the conversation has fallen apart. Mark now resents Sarah for invalidating him and has disconnected completely. There are basically no chances at this point for the conversation to be redeemed. |
| **Sarah:** "No. I didn't mean that. I meant—" | Sarah notices the defensiveness, which triggers her own insecurities of her partner now pushing her away. She wants to be close with him and starts to try and pull him back into the conversation, now saying she'll listen. |
| **Mark:** "It's fine. It's whatever." | He's gone. |
| **Sarah:** "Can we talk about this?" | Sarah seeks validation and connection after being pushed away. |
| **Mark:** "Nope. You made yourself perfectly clear." | Still unresponsive. |

Breaking this conversation down in such a way can show that so much of what we say and do has such a dramatic impact on the direction of which way the conversation will go. And this doesn't even take into account the body language that was going on!

Taking everything we've learned, let's go back to the beginning and try a much more productive way of having this conversation.

>**Mark:** "Hey, Sarah. I've been thinking about something important to me. Are you okay to chat?"
>
>**Sarah:** "Is it serious? Work was pretty intense today, but I can try my best."
>
>**Mark:** "That's fine. We don't have to really go into it. It's more just something to think about."
>
>**Sarah:** "Sure. Talk to me."

*At this point, Sarah turns off the background music in the kitchen and puts down her knife and fork, giving Mark her full attention*

>**Mark:** "I was thinking about us and sex. I know we've spoken about this before, but I feel really disconnected from you lately, how with us both working so much. I feel like we lack intimacy."
>
>**Sarah:** "Yeah. We don't spend as much time together as we used to. I feel disconnected from you as well. I just feel so tired all the time. I don't have the energy to do anything for myself, let alone both together. But I do see where you're coming from."
>
>**Mark:** "That's understandable. Maybe it's not about sex, but actually about doing something, well, anything together. Maybe bringing date nights back, or something like that?"
>
>**Sarah:** "Yeah, I do miss our date nights. Remember when we tried to make a cake and forgot about it?"
>
>**Mark:** "The oven still has burn marks!"
>
>**Sarah:** "Well, how about this Friday, we get some ingredients and cook dinner together as we used to?"
>
>**Mark:** "You focus on work. I'll grab some surprise ingredients when I'm done, so it's all ready when you get home, and we can get straight into it. Don't worry. It won't be a three-course meal. Just nice and fast so we can eat and cuddle. Want me to find a movie as well?"
>
>**Sarah:** "That sounds perfect. Then, we can see what happens."
>
>**Mark:** "It's a date."

See how different that conversation is? Both Mark and Sarah are acknowledging, empathizing, and validating each other and how they feel. They are both giving each other their full attention, staying calm and respectful to each other, and keeping the conversation moving forward productively.

Again, this doesn't even consider body language, apart from them both minimizing distractions, like eye contact and vulnerable posturing. Towards the end of the conversation, you can imagine them both laughing, making lots of eye contact at each other, and even winking in a flirty way, which is pulling them together.

To add to the conversation, if Mark or Sarah were unsure about how they were feeling, they would be able to ask each other questions for clarity. Instead, they did understand each other and were able to normalize how they felt (in this case, the feelings of disconnect or being tired due to overworking).

Apply this kind of logic in your own interactions. Whether you're at work, at home, with friends, or with family, taking what you've learned and applying it to your conversations isn't too difficult. Sure, it can feel like there's a lot to remember, but over time and by working on bettering yourself just one step at a time, you'll be amazed at how much of a difference it all makes.

Listening and having conversations in such a way can literally change your life.

# Final Thoughts

Wow. What a journey that was, and what a conclusion. I'm hoping that now that you've read this book, you are already starting to apply these tips into your own life, and you're already seeing how much of a difference it can make. Remember, as with any self-improvement journey, your journey and results are unique to you, which is amazing since you get to be your own proof and see how quickly things can get better.

Being a good listener isn't just about hearing what people say. It's about being proactive in being an effective communicator that aims to make every relationship better and more fulfilling by using skills, experience, and knowledge in both human behaviors and psychology, all of which you now have a foundation of and will continue to expand on throughout your lifetime.

*James W. Williams*

# Thank you!

Before you go, I just wanted to say thank you for purchasing my book.

You could have picked from dozens of other books on the same topic but you took a chance and chose this one.

So, a HUGE thanks to you for getting this book and for reading all the way to the end.

Now I wanted to ask you for a small favor. **Could you please consider posting a review on the platform? Reviews are one of the easiest ways to support the work of independent authors.**

This feedback will help me continue to write the type of books that will help you get the results you want. So if you enjoyed it, please let me know.